I0804162

HIKING

JOSHUA TREE

THE LAND OF SCULPTED STONE

Michel Digonnet

Copyright © 2025 by Michel Digonnet
All rights reserved

Maps, illustrations, and book design by the author
Photographs by the author, unless otherwise specified

Publisher: Michel Digonnet
Copy Editor: Susan Cole
Cover Designer: Karen Frankel

Published in Palo Alto, California
Printed and bound in the United States of America

Front cover: Super Dome and pinnacles from Willow Hole, Wonderland of Rocks

Back cover:

Joshua trees at sunset, Wonderland of Rocks (courtesy of Alice Fermigier)

Summit Springs, Munsen Canyon, Coxcomb Mountains

Desert lily, Pinto Mountains

Winch, Lost Horse Mine, Little San Bernardino Mountains

Collared lizard

Library of Congress Control Number: 2024926644

ISBN: 978-0-9659178-7-2

To Alice

Wandering alone in that infinite, ancient wilderness, planting feet on land that likely had not been touched by human presence, seeing things no other human eye had seen, existing in a world beyond imagination, always discovering something that could not have been anticipated—that, to me, was heaven.

William E. Glassley
A Wilder Time

By the same author:

Hiking Death Valley (two editions)
Hiking Western Death Valley National Park (two editions)
Hiking the Mojave Desert (two editions)
Mojave Desert Peaks
Mojave Trails National Monument (in preparation)

ACKNOWLEDGMENTS

As always, I want to thank family and friends for joining me on some of the trips to Joshua Tree National Park I took over the past ten years to research this book—Fran and Sheldon Cole, Noli Cole, David Goldstein, Nikki Cole, Sarah Lewis, Marc Fermigier, and Caroline Manowicz. I want to include Greg Kipp, who trudged with me on my very first backpacking trip into the Wonderland of Rocks long ago, before trailhead signs and wilderness permits.

A very special thank you goes again to Alice Fermigier and Pierre-Baptiste Vigneron, who always pushed harder to hike deeper into the wilderness, and to my wife Susan for the many instances when she waited patiently in the middle of the desert while I went exploring further, and endured returns late at night in the dim beams of our headlamps. I would like to thank Susan also for letting me take the time to escape to the desert several times a year, to write about it on countless evenings, and for the meticulous job she did editing this book.

I am indebted to former Park Superintendent David Smith for always answering emails and providing valuable information about the park. I also thank park employees Cynthia Anderson, Christian Delich, Nathan Rhyne, Lynn Robinson, Jane Rodgers, and Kevin Turner for their kind assistance with reviewing sections of this book, directions to more remote areas of the park, reporting acts of vandalism, registering the names of unreported arches, and clarifying the park's complex campground regulations.

Finally, I extend a warm thank you once again to Karen Frankel for sifting through hundreds of photographs and designing the book cover with her usual keen eye for details, and for her assistance in formatting the book layout.

Table of Contents

WARNING

Many of the hikes suggested in this book are potentially dangerous. They involve hours of strenuous physical activity across often rugged terrain, with no water, little to no shade, in a hot desert. They should be attempted only by hikers in excellent physical condition, with prior experience in desert hiking and good route-finding skills. Although many of the dangers of specific routes are mentioned in the text, all of them cannot possibly be covered. The information contained in this book should not be considered a substitute for common sense. The author declines all responsibilities for any injuries, physical or otherwise, anyone might sustain while hiking any of the routes suggested herein.

FOREWORD

In California's vast mosaic of desert parks, Joshua Tree National Park is best known for being home to some of the most surreal landscapes in North America. Throughout the park's mountainous highland, the region's granitic heart has been splintered by tectonic forces, then deeply eroded into waves upon waves of fantastic boulders and rock formations that rival for boldness in shape. Because the park straddles the boundary between two deserts, the Mojave Desert on the west side and the Sonora Desert on the east side, it also holds one of the greatest plant diversities in the North American deserts. The land is bristling with a motley crew of cacti and yuccas best represented by the park's namesake, the Joshua tree. The frazzled silhouettes of millions of these eerie residents—hairy trunks and limbs tipped with orbs of olive-green spikes—haunt the Mojave section. The Sonora Desert has its own cohort of odd plants—the fluorescent teddy-bear cholla, the scarlet-flowered ocotillo, the disheveled ironwoods, the palo verde so radiant in the spring that they seem to have been transplanted. Wildlife adds another layer of weirdness. Both deserts are inhabited by antediluvian tortoises, wacky jackrabbits and roadrunners, elusive bighorn sheep, a whole menagerie of lizards, and admirably adaptable coyotes as much at home in this strange land as anywhere else.

Hiking in these improbable landscapes that combine spectacular stone sculptures and extravagant biology takes on a peculiar dimension. Immersed in a world at the limit of reality, you expect the unexpected—and your wish occasionally comes true. Hundreds of square miles of deeply dissected topography are sprinkled with countless unique geological oddities. There are house-size monoliths, hoodoos in every imaginable familiar shape, monuments of vertical fins, erect spires so tall and slender that they should fall, stacks of homomorphic boulders posing like artwork, and many times more arches, albeit smaller, than in Arches National Park. When exploring on foot, the destination becomes secondary. The motivation is the journey itself, the sum total of these random encounters with thrilling anomalies.

Not so long ago, before deserts became popular, and before countless bloggers advertized them to the whole world for free, Joshua Tree was a secret paradise. Almost any day of the year, you could walk the primitive track that looped around Hidden Valley and be alone the whole time. You could duck into a small alcove at night and sleep under the stars. You could drive to Keys Ranch and visit the extensive remains of this historic homestead on your own. You could stop in the middle of a dirt road anywhere and go out for a long walk without concern that your car was blocking the way, because no one was going to drive by, sometime for days.

Today, the US population is approximately only 50% larger, but visitation has increased six fold, to 3 million annually. On a typical spring day, hundreds of people walk the Hidden Valley loop. In the Wonderland of Rocks, one of the most scenic and heavily visited ranges, except on the hottest summer days the most popular trails are busy. As much as Joshua Tree is a tale of two botanical deserts, it is also a tale of two radically different human environments, one tamed and one wild. The west side, closer to civilization and more easily accessible, receives most of the visitation. To accommodate a majority of visitors with little to no knowledge of the desert, hundred of miles of trails have been built and signed. There are parking lots, toilets, interpretive boards, warning signs, gates, mile markers, trail signs, stairs, and countless arrows and rock alignments telling you where to go. As important as these developed areas are to novices, they foreshadow a not-so-distant future when deserts will no longer be desert, every square foot will have been cataloged, and a lottery will be required to enter the park.

The park's eastern section—more than half in area—is the opposite: it is *wild*. With few exceptions, there the desert is the same as it has been for eons. It is still vibrant with unknown, with exhilarating freedom, and with this essential undertone of danger without which there cannot be adventure. While the west side gives a premonition of a likely unavoidable future, the east side is a time capsule, a heartening expression of an enduring past. Seasoned hikers will find there unexplored territory, canyons free of footprints, open bajadas to walk freely for miles, mountains so convoluted that they border on impenetrable, and the same dreamy rock spaces of alternate reality as the west side—minus the crowds.

This is the unsung beauty of Joshua Tree—it offers a glimpse into both worlds. Hikers unfamiliar with the desert can enjoy signed trails where they can sample this beautiful land in the comforting company of others. And adventurous souls can still wander across large virgin tracts on their own, and possibly discover natural wonders no one has ever seen.

This book was designed to capture and celebrate the spirit of both.

Palo Alto, California
August 31, 2024

About This Book

This volume is divided into eight parts. The first three parts provide general information about the park. Part 4 covers safety tips, park regulations, and ethics of hiking in nature. The remaining six parts describe individual hikes in six of the park's seven mountain ranges, arranged from west to east starting on the north side (Wonderland of Rocks, Pinto Mountains, and Coxcomb Mountains) and continuing on the south side (Little San Bernardino, Hexie, and Eagle mountains).

If you are new to the area, check out first the summary of hikes near the end of the book. It summarizes in a table the ~160 destinations, categorized into points of interest and types (trails, loops, etc.).

The difficulty ratings take into account distance and elevation gain, roughness and steepness of the terrain, whether there is trail, and the number and seriousness of obstacles. They assume that the hike is done *in one day, in cool to warm weather*. In hot weather, the difficulty worsens considerably, and these ratings underestimate the difficulty.

- Very easy: a short hike on open terrain and/or trail.
- Easy: a moderately long hike (3–4 miles each way) on obstacle-free ground or trail with modest grades; accessible to most people.
- Moderate: a longer hike (4–6 miles one way) with moderate grades and obstacles; accessible to anyone in reasonably good shape.
- Difficult: steep grades (1,000 feet/mile) over 4–5 miles one way, substantial elevation change (2,000 feet or more), rough terrain, uneasy footing, usually no trail; good physical condition is imperative.
- Very difficult: much the same but with steeper grades, larger elevation changes (3,000 feet or more) and distances (5–7 miles one way), and/or very rough terrain; good physical condition is imperative.
- Strenuous: one or more of the following: very steep grades (1,500 feet per mile or more), long distances (7 miles or more one way), large

TOPOGRAPHIC MAPS LEGEND

Symbol	Meaning	Symbol	Meaning
62	Highway/Paved road		Contour line
	Unpaved road (2WD)		Contour line (every fifth line)
	4WD-HC road	8400	Elevation, in feet
	Hiking trail		Wash
	Cross-country route		Broad gravel or sand wash
	Pass		Wash distributary
	Gate		Fall/Boulder jam/Chockstone
	Manmade structure		Sand dunes
	Ruin		Natural bridge/Arch
	Grave		Summit
	Campground		Pond/Lake
	Visitor center/Ranger station		Spring
	Picnic area		Well
	Guzzler		Water tank
	Corral		Adit/tunnel
	Windmill		Collapsed adit
•S	Starting point of hike		Mine shaft
			Open pit/Surface mine
-N-	North Star	x	Prospect
		To Indio (25 mi)	Mileage from edge of map

elevation changes (4,000 feet or more), and very challenging terrain; requires excellent physical condition, training, and practice.

This scale is obviously subjective. I did my best to be consistent throughout this book, and my other books. If you disagree with it, you can still use it as a relative scale. For example, you may decide that hikes rated moderate are usually easy for you.

The classes of climbing difficulty used in this book are defined as:

- Class 1: Walking with no need for hands.
- Class 2: Use of hands for scrambling or balance, or on short easy walls or dry falls with little exposure.
- Class 3: Use of hands to climb on steep and somewhat exposed rock surfaces; beginners may find a rope helpful. A fall could be fatal.
- Class 4: Simple climbing moves with high exposure; natural protection can be found, although a rope may be required.
- Class 5: Technical climbing on sheer rock surfaces with small footholds and handholds; requires skill, training, and protection.

In the tables provided in each description, distances are accurate to at least 5%. An entry in parenthesis indicates the distance to a locale away from the main line of travel, measured from the previous entry.

■

— 1 —

Introduction To Joshua Tree

A Tale of Two Deserts

The topography of much of southern California is the brainchild of the San Andreas Fault. From Santa Barbara to Palm Springs, the world-famous fault has uplifted a 300-mile cordillera that slashes east to west, perpendicular to most ranges in the state. The Santa Ynez Mountains, San Gabriel Mountains, and San Bernardino Mountains are all part of these renegade uplands collectively known as the Transverse Ranges. Joshua Tree National Park is at the eastern terminus of this topographic anomaly. Covering 794,000 acres, it protects a spectacular highland of rugged mountains and desert valleys, and some of North America's most outlandish landscapes. Its main claim to fame is sculpted stones. The park's extensive granitic core has been shattered by tectonic stresses and fashioned by erosion into stacks of giant boulders and fantastically shaped formations. It is a land of awe-inspiring contrasts. To the west, the San Bernardino Mountains—the Swiss Alps of southern California—tower more than 2 miles above the sea. Along the park's southern boundary, mountains plunge thousands of feet into below-sea-level Coachella Valley. On Coachella Valley's far side, the San Jacinto Mountains rise nearly 11,000 feet up what is the sheerest mountain face in the conterminous United States.

This outrageous geology is matched by equally spectacular botanical treasures. The park straddles the boundary between two deserts, the Mojave Desert on the west side and the Sonoran Desert on the east side. This conjunction is responsible for the park's exceptional plant diversity, which is one of the greatest in North American deserts. The Mojave Desert's high valleys are green with oaks, junipers, and pinyon pine. Vast tracks are covered with forests of emblematic Joshua trees. The Sonoran Desert portion is home to intriguing representatives of this lower, hotter, and starker desert—shaggy ironwood, spidery ocotillo, and smoke trees that rise from open washes like ghosts. Both deserts are interspersed, sometimes profusely, with a fascinating assortment of cacti that beguile visitors with exuberant flowers in the warm season. Together, rocks and plants have spawned an enchanted landscape filled with eeriness, grandeur, and sensuality, a spellbinding playground that enthralls millions of visitors from all over the world every year.

Creation of Joshua Tree National Park

In the 1920s, as a leading US oil-producing region southern California was growing in leaps and bounds, and city sprawl crept east into the desert. The swift adoption of the automobile and air conditioning made the desert easily accessible and increasingly popular. This sudden influx had both positive and negative consequences. The desert was assaulted by plant collectors and vandals, who uprooted cacti for home gardens, cut down conifers for firewood, or torched live Joshua trees at night as beacons for visitors. The world's largest Joshua Tree, an 80-foot giant in Antelope Valley, was set on fire in 1930 and died. Fortunately, an equally important ethical shift also started to take place. A greater fraction of the public stopped seeing the desert as a wasteland and gained growing admiration for it.

The desert's most fervent advocate was a visionary activist from South Pasadena named Minerva Hoyt. Raised on a Mississippi plantation, she moved to California in 1897, where she developed a passion for gardening on her five-acre property, and a fascination for desert plants. After the loss of her boy at a very young age, then of her husband in 1918, she took frequent trips to the Joshua Tree area for peace and comfort. Over time, she became alarmed by the destruction of the desert. To sensitize the public to the urgency of preserving the desert, she organized an exhibit of California and Arizona cacti for the Garden Club of America's show in New York City in 1928. Hoyt presented it at other venues in the country, and as far as London. In 1930, she took her fight one step further and began lobbying to the National Park Service for the creation of a park that would set aside over one million acres of southern California's high desert. She was an empassioned, tireless, and persuasive crusader, and key officials came to endorse her bold proposal. Supporters, which included preeminent botanists Edmund Jaeger and Philip Munz, saw in it the preservation of the fragile desert biota and recreation for southern California's fast-growing population.

The park's creation unfortunately faced serious difficulties. The area was then a checkerboard of federal and state lands, homesteads, and mining claims. A Southern Pacific land grant covering thousands of acres ran through it. The Colorado River Aqueduct, then under construction, prevented extension south to the Salton Sea, as Hoyt had originally envisioned. The project had to be scaled down, but Hoyt's persistence paid off. In 1932, president Franklin Roosevelt launched a series of conservation programs. After years of negotiations between state and federal agencies, on August 10, 1936 Roosevelt signed a proclamation that established Joshua Tree National Monument.

Since then, thanks to its remarkable scenery and location in environmentally conscious California, much more of the region has been preserved. In 1994, as a mitigation against development, Congress expanded the monument and upgraded it to national park status. To the west the San Bernardino Mountains' lofty summits are now protected in Sand to Snow National Monument. To the northeast the park is contiguous with 1.6-million-acre Mojave Trails National Monument. To the east and south the Palen, Chuckwalla, and Orocopia mountains are preserved in 410,00 acres of wilderness. To the southwest, Santa Rosa San Jacinto Mountains National Monument protects Coachella Valley's imposing backdrop. Even the vast Bullion Mountains north of the park are a *de facto* wilderness. Home of the Marine Corps Air Ground Combat Center, they are as wild as a park, and actively managed for the conservation of wildlife corridors and critical habitats.

The Lay of the Land

Topography. The park has seven mountain ranges, from west to east: the Wonderland of Rocks and the Pinto Mountains along the north side, the Hexie Mountains in the middle, and the Little San Bernardino, Cottonwood, and Eagle mountains on the south side. The Coxcomb Mountains bookend the park at its east end. The high points range from 4,372 feet in the Cottonwood Mountains to 5,813 feet in the Little San Bernardino Mountains. In the western section, the mountains are interspersed with small high-desert valleys, comparatively cool and filled with botanical gardens. In the eastern section, the mountains encircle Pinto Basin, a hot, vast, and desolate creosote plain more than 30 miles long.

Two main paved roads cross these two very different environments. Park Boulevard gives an eye-filling sample of the Mojave Desert as it circles around the Wonderland of Rocks. It is the park's uncontested crown jewel, coming within snapshot of countless outrageously scenic rock formations and cactus gardens, and the starting point of many short trails that wander into the park's most iconic landscapes. The other main paved road, the Pinto Basin Road, dips into the Sonoran Desert as it crosses Pinto Basin, then squeezes down through Cottonwood Canyon to exit the park in Chuckwalla Valley. These two roads illustrate the striking contrast between the two deserts. One road is a treasure chest of nooks and crannies loaded with hidden secrets, the other a grand celebration of the vastness of the American West.

Gateway towns. In spite of the resounding success of land conservation, the western half of the park's perimeter is hemmed in by suburban sprawl. Morongo Basin, the long valley along the park's northern boundary, is lined with towns—Yucca Valley, Joshua Tree, and Twentynine Palms. Coachella Valley on the southwest side is even more developed, overtaken by a 35-mile string of cities from Palm Springs to Thermal. For most visitors, the proximity of gateway cities is a blessing: you don't have to rough it. Between the endless choice of amenities outside the park and the excess of signed trails and interpreted sites in the park, that area of the park has lost its wildness.

Each community has its own cultural character. Coachella Valley's desert cities are a typical sunbelt urban grid of golf courses and impeccable gated communities. The business districts are famous for their fine restaurants and luxury hotels, spas, casinos, boutiques, resorts, and the glitz that comes with it. On the north side, other than busy Yucca Valley, the towns are more rural and better matched to the laid-back mood of a desert park. Joshua Tree is a small community. Over the last two decades, artists, photographers, and intellects have been drawn by its tranquility and low-cost real estate. The small downtown of Old West rustic buildings houses unassuming shops and restaurants. The desert is often just a few blocks away—you may well spot a roadrunner dashing through someone's yard. Twentynine Palms is a notch funkier, its long main drag bordered with decrepit cabins, metal sculptures, and junky fenced yards. The frontier spirit of the miners and homesteaders who helped establish this town is still very much alive, and its connection to the park's history is tangible.

Entrances. The park has three main entrances. The busy west entrance, the closest to the popular Wonderland of Rocks, is on Park Boulevard in Joshua Tree on Highway 62. The north entrance is on Utah Trail, 16 miles east in Twentynine Palms. The quieter south entrance is a few miles north from the Cottonwood Springs Road exit on Interstate 10, 25 miles east of Indio. The park can also be entered on paved roads at Black Rock Canyon 4.2 miles west of Park Boulevard, at

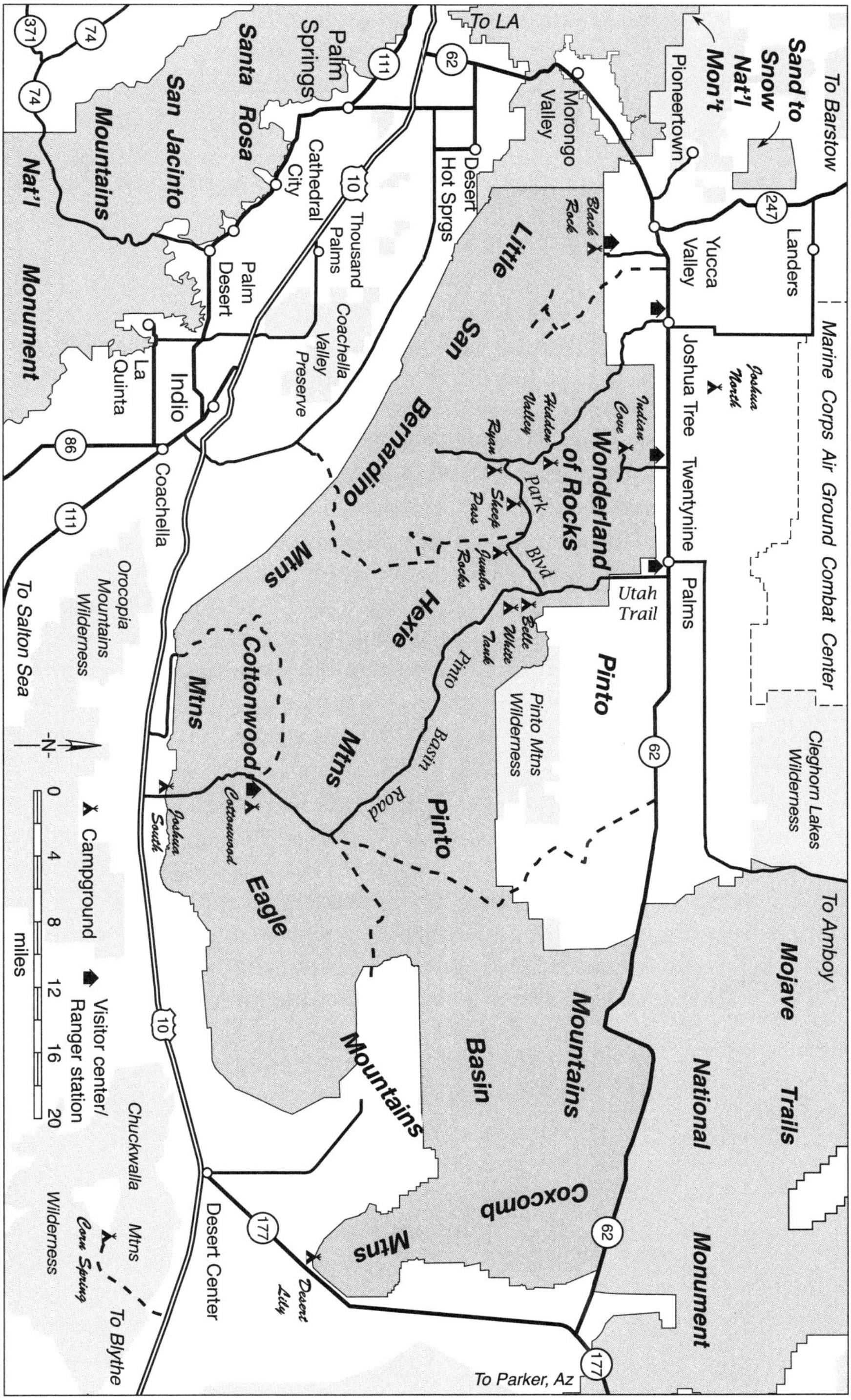
To Barstow
Sand to Snow Nat'l Mon't
Pioneertown
To LA
Morongo Valley
Desert Hot Sprgs
Palm Springs
Cathedral City
Thousand Palms
Palm Desert
Coachella Valley Preserve
La Quinta
Indio
Coachella
Santa Rosa
San Jacinto
Mountains
Nat'l
Monument
Landers
Yucca Valley
Joshua Tree
Twentynine
Palms
Marine Corps Air Ground Combat Center
Joshua North
Black Rock
Indian Cove
Hidden Valley
Ryan
Sheep Pass
Jumbo Rocks
Belle
White Tank
Little San Bernardino Mtns
Wonderland of Rocks
Park Blvd
Utah Trail
Pinto
Pinto Mtns Wilderness
Pinto Basin Road
Hexie Mtns
Pinto
Cottonwood Mtns
Cottonwood
Joshua South
Eagle
Mountains
Basin
Mountains
Coxcomb
Mtns
Cleghorn Lakes Wilderness
To Amboy
Mojave Trails National Monument
Orocopia Mountains Wilderness
To Salton Sea
Chuckwalla Mtns Wilderness
Cow Spring
Desert Center
Desert Lily
To Blythe
To Parker, Az
Campground
Visitor center/ Ranger station
0 4 8 12 16 20 miles
N
10
62
111
74
371
247
86
177

Indian Cove about halfway between the west and north entrances, and at Canyon Road 1.8 miles east of Indian Cove.

A few primitive roads also cross into the park, Upper Covington Flat Road near Black Rock, the Gold Crown Road 14.3 miles east of Utah Trail, the Pinkham Canyon Road and Thermal Canyon Road off Interstate 10 east of Indio, and the Berdoo Canyon Road north of Indio.

Climate

Joshua Tree is a land of climatic extremes. Summers are stifling hot. The sky will stay heartbreakingly clear for days on end. The temperature in the park's high valleys often reaches the mid-90s and sometimes over 100°F. In the lower areas surrounding the park, especially in Coachella Valley and Chuckwalla Valley, it is not uncommon for the temperature to exceed 110°F. Any time of year, weeks can go by without rain. But then during the winter or in the summer monsoon, thunderstorms with devastating powers can turn dry arroyos into raging torrents. Winters are surprisingly cold, especially on windy days. For many weeks into the spring, snow caps San Gorgonio Mountain and San Jacinto Peak. Occasionally a freak snow storm will blanket the western part of the park, down to 4,000 feet or lower. Late winter and early spring are the seasons that are the most temperate and comfortable to most visitors.

Services

Visitor centers. The park has two ranger stations, along the Indian Cove Road and near the Black Rock Campground, and three visitor centers. The smaller Cottonwood Visitor Center is near Cottonwood Spring north of the south entrance; besides the campgrounds, it is the only public facility in the park. The Joshua Tree Visitor Center is in Joshua Tree at the west end of Park Boulevard. The Oasis Visitor Center and park headquarters are in Twentynine Palms on Utah Trail.

Park campgrounds. The park has nine campgrounds offering a total of 500 sites. Black Rock (and equestrian camp), Cottonwood (and group camp), Indian Cove (and group camp), Jumbo Rocks, Ryan, and Sheep Pass require reservation year round. Any site that has not been reserved is available on a first-come, first-served basis for one night at a time. In the future, some loops at Indian cove, Black Rock, and Jumbo Rocks may be set aside as first-come, first-served only sites for the summer season (from about June to September). Belle, White Tank, and Hidden Valley are first-come first-served campgrounds year round. All campgrounds may be subject to partial and full closures,

Average temperatures (°F) in the southern Mojave Desert								
	Yucca Valley (3,200 feet)		Old Dale (1,270 feet)		Palm Springs (520 feet)		Coachella (-70 feet)	
	Low	High	Low	High	Low	High	Low	High
January	38	61	37	65	46	69	37	69
February	39	61	42	68	48	73	42	73
March	40	69	46	75	53	79	46	78
April	44	74	54	83	57	85	53	86
May	54	86	64	92	65	93	60	93
June	60	92	72	103	71	102	68	100
July	72	102	78	107	77	107	75	105
August	68	99	75	107	78	106	73	104
September	64	96	67	99	73	100	68	100
October	53	80	55	86	62	89	55	89
November	44	70	43	73	52	77	44	78
December	36	58	38	63	44	67	37	69

especially in summer when visitation is low. Reservations can be booked on-line at recreation.gov, up to six months in advance.

All campgrounds usually fill up on weekends. In the spring, and on all holidays, they are usually full the whole week. Advance booking helps guarantee a spot, as does on-site registration early in the day. Check on-line for the latest rules and campground status.

BLM and private campgrounds. The BLM has a few campgrounds near the park (see map). Joshua Tree South Campground is just outside the boundary on Cottonwood Springs Road. There is a campground at the Desert Lily Sanctuary, along Highway 177 at the southern tip of the Coxcomb Mountains. Southeast of Desert Center in the Chuckwalla Mountains is the more remote Corn Spring Campground. The northeast shore of the Salton Sea also has a few BLM campgrounds. On the north side, the Joshua North Campground is in Joshua Tree, 2 miles north of Highway 62 on Cascade Road to 2 Mile Road, then two blocks east. There is a dispersed campground 2.5 miles further north, near Coyote Lake. Many towns have private campgrounds or RV parks.

Car camping on surrounding public lands. Because the park has no services and car camping is prohibited, unless you stay in a campground or backpack, every evening you must leave the park. This imposed discontinuity, as justified as it may be, is a major difference with other large desert parks, where you can spend days driving and exploring on foot without having to return to civilization and break the spell. There is fortunately ample space outside the park to make up for it and car camp under the stars. The best areas are the Pinto Mountains south of Highway 62 between Twentynine Palms and Dale Lake, the New Dixie Mine Road corridor west of Landers, and around Desert Center. Some of these areas are prized among locals, who often drive in bright and early or linger until late at night for target shooting, four wheeling, or dirt biking. These are not always the desert's quietest spots, but they are usually quieter than public campgrounds.

Local amenities. The neighboring towns offer a full range of services. As far as food is concerned, the popular north side has a few gems. In Twentynine Palms, John's Place is a casual café for a hearty American breakfast. The Rib Co. serves great barbecued steaks, ribs, chicken, and seafood dinners. Unless it is 100° or freezing cold, the front patio is a fun place for outdoor dining, in the fragrant smoke of the barbecue. The Restaurant at the 29 Palms Inn, tucked away in a lush setting, offers what may be the most refined menu on the north side. In Joshua Tree, Pie For The People dishes out popular New-York-style pizzas, hand-tossed and baked in stone-deck ovens, well worth the wait. All three towns also have a few good dives, places you might not try at home, but after a long day in the wild most foods taste great.

Pioneertown, a few miles northwest of Yucca Valley, is a local icon. The tiny town center looks like a Hollywood set for a Western production—and it is. It was built for a 1980s movie set and doubled as residences for the actors. The former cantina was converted to Pappy & Harriet's, a lively hamburger and BBQ joint with live music and shows.

Finding a place to stay indoors is not a problem: the park is so hugely popular that there is a glut of accommodations for all budgets and tastes, including no fewer than 1,800 airbnbs. Their wide range of styles reflects the inherently eclectic architectural spirit of the desert towns along Highway 62. You can choose from a historic manor set in a large palm grove, off-the-grid glamping sites, luxury modernist rentals, retro trailers, an invisible house, a floating box, renovated shacks, hacienda-style homes, or your favorite brand of hotel. Some are right in town; many are scattered in the quieter, sparsely populated valley north of the main drag. And in the morning you can be right back in the park in 20 minutes.

■

— 2 —

Natural History

Geology

In most of the California desert, the oldest rocks, the metamorphosed Proterozoic formations over one billion years old that form the deep basement, are exposed over limited areas. In Joshua Tree National Park, the oldest rocks cover close to 50% of the mountains. In the Proterozoic, the area was at the approximate center of a supercontinent pointing northeast called Rodinia, in which Antarctica was welded to Australia, North America, Greenland, and northern Europe. The 1.7-billion-year gneisses found in Joshua Tree today were part of the chain of mountains that formed Rodinia's long spine. Similar gneisses exist near Adelaide in southern Australia, then a day's drive away.

When Rodinia broke up around 800 million years ago, it opened up a planet-size rift between North America and Australia that became the Pacific Ocean. For the next 550 million years, Joshua Tree and eastern California were part of an equatorial continental shelf that received considerable amounts of sand and mud washed down from the coast. The exoskeletons of bivalves, ammonites, trilobites, fusilinids, cephalopods, and many other early marine species composed a major portion of these slow but in the end formidable deposits. Elsewhere in the California desert, these miles-thick strata of sandstone, limestone, and dolomite form entire mountains. In Joshua Tree they are almost entirely missing, perhaps because this area was further away from the coast and did not receive as many sediments, or because they were later eroded. They survive only on a few square miles in the Pinto, Eagle, and Coxcomb mountains, not in their original form but metamorphosed by later intrusions into schists, marble, and quartzite.

We owe Joshua Tree's striking geology to plutonic rocks emplaced much later, in the Mesozoic. The engine behind these massive intrusions was plate tectonics. At the dawn of that disruptive era, 250 million years ago, North America started drifting west, and the Pacific Ocean plate subducted under it. As the subducting plate ground against the continent's underbelly, it was shoved deep into the mantle and melted into large reservoirs of magma. The phenomenal friction launched compression waves through the continental margin that folded and faulted the mantle. The magma found pathways up through the faults and erupted in a chain of volcanoes along the continent's edge. Volcanism eased up through the Middle Jurassic and Early Cretaceous periods. Concurrently and during the rest of the Cretaceous, magma crystallized in enormous granitic chambers. The largest one was a 400-mile-long batholith that was later uplifted into the Sierra Nevada. Dozens of smaller plutons were implanted all over Joshua Tree. Large-scale blending of the rising magma with mantle and crust material created a suite of igneous rocks with a nearly continuous spectrum of compositions and grain sizes, including the handsome White Tank and Queen Mountain monzogranites that now make up most of superbly scenic Wonderland of Rocks. The diversity is so extreme that even on a short walk you will run into several types of rocks that are obviously different even to the untrained eye. The infiltrating magma also metamorphosed pre-existing ancient gneisses a second time, which created striking twice-cooked formations. The most famous one is Pinto Gneiss. These delightfully complex rocks, spotted or foliated, layered with garnet and pegmatite, or imprinted with tight folds, are a prized hallmark of the Joshua Tree highlands.

Around 70 million years later, near the end of the Cretaceous, disruptions in magmatic currents caused the ocean plate to subduct at a shallower angle. It no longer reached deep enough to melt, and plutonism stopped. The angle of subduction steepened again 35 million years later, likely triggered by the collision of India and Asia. It launched another wave of volcanism that lasted 20 million years. Although volcanic ranges from that era dominate large portions of the Mojave, in Joshua Tree these rocks were stripped by erosion, and exposures are very limited. Another radical disruption, about 25 million years ago, put an end to subduction. The two plates began sliding parallel to each other instead, grinding each other's edge along a shifting boundary that evolved over time into the San Andreas Fault.

The San Andreas Fault is responsible for both Joshua Tree's desert climate and turbulent topography. From north of San Francisco the fault follows a fairly straight southeasterly course. Where it enters

ERA	Epoch	AGE (Million years)	MAIN EVENTS	LITHOLOGY
Cenozoic	Holocene	0.01	**Faulting, erosion**	Sand, dunes, lake playa, boulders, and alluvial fans
	Pleistocene	2.6	**Major faulting, minor volcanism, erosion, ice age**	Lake playa and alluvial fans
	Tertiary	15	**Erosion**	Alluvial fans
		30	**Major volcanism**	Basalt
		50	**Erosion**	Alluvial fans
		66	**Subduction and plutonism**	Dikes
Mesozoic	Cretaceous	145		Coxcomb Granodiorite Oasis Monzogranite White Tank Monzogranite Granodiorite of Pinto Basin Queen Mountain Monzogranite Monzogranite of Cottonwood Pass
	Jurassic	201		Virginia Dale Quartz Monzonite Gold Park Gabbrodiorite Granodiorite of Music Valley
	Triassic	252		29 Palms Megacrystic Q. Monzo. Monzodiorite of Munsen Canyon
Paleozoic	Permian ⋮ Cambrian	541	**Sedimentation**	All formations eroded since
Precambrian	Neo-proterozoic	1000	**Sedimentation and continental drift**	
	Meso-proterozoic	1600		Dolomite of Iron Chief Mine
	Paleo-proterozoic		**Plutonism and metamorphism**	Quartzite of Pinto Mountain Pinto Gneiss: - *Augen Gneiss of Monument Mtn* - *Metasedimentary suite of Placer Cyn* - *Metasedimentary suite of Pinkham Cyn* - *Joshua Tree Augen Gneiss*
		1870	**Orogeny**	

Fins of White Tank Monzogranite near Arch Rock in the Pinto Mountains

southern California at the coastal bend, it angles nearly east to the Salton Sea, then veers southeast again to the Gulf of Mexico. Along this east–west segment, the fault is transverse to the Pacific Plate's northwesterly motion. When the crust gives way, the two plates move along each other, but along this segment the oceanic plate pushes into the continental plate. For the last 25 million years, the compressive forces have fractured the edges of the plates and shoved up the pieces into a rogue cordillera that slashes east to west, perpendicular to most ranges in the state. Known as the Transverse Ranges, it extends 300 miles from near Santa Barbara to Joshua Tree. The Santa Ynez and the San Gabriel mountains were pushed up first, then the San Bernardino Mountains, and finally the mountains of Joshua Tree. In the early part of that era, the climate was subtropical. Lions, camels, llamas, deer, and wolves roamed what was then a subdued grassland. By about five million years ago, the Transverse Ranges were high enough that they blocked a good portion of the moisture from the Pacific Ocean. Joshua Tree slowly turned into a desert, and much of this fauna vanished.

The massive jumbles of sculpted rocks emblematic of Joshua Tree are a more recent addition also created by plate tectonics, combined with the handiwork of erosion. Compressive stresses on the crust broke up underground granitic stock along conjugate joints, two sets of parallel cracks at a 60-degree angle, like the diamond pattern on a jester's suit. Horizontal fractures also developed as erosion removed

Face Rock, Wonderland of Rocks

Checkerboard, Willow Hole

Boulders, Rattlesnake Canyon

surface rock and the underlying granite floated back up, like a ship unloading its cargo. In the last few million years, percolating water has been decomposing bedrock preferentially along these joints, breaking it into piles of giant boulders. These buried structures were eventually uplifted, exposed by top-soil erosion, and further carved by rain and wind. They occur only where the rock is strong and homogeneous enough to break into large chunks over large areas. Their visual appeal lies in the uncommon symmetry they inherited from conjugate joints—rows of look-alike pinnacles, cliffs slashed by repetitive patterns of cracks, or heaps of boulders with similar shapes.

Although not officially included in the Great Basin, Joshua Tree is definitely a part of it: none of the park's valleys have an outlet to the sea. Off and on during wet periods between 186,000 and 11,000 years ago, every valley was flooded under a pluvial lake. The drying climate eventually desiccated all lakes, leaving behind playas of cracked mud or evaporites. The only one within the park boundary is the shallow playa in Pleasant Valley. All surrounding valleys had then miles of beaches—Lake Dale, Lake Cadiz, Lake Palen, and the Salton Sea, large enough to qualify as a small inland sea.

Today, water still plays a major role in reshaping the Joshua Tree landscape, usually more slowly, yet sometimes in cataclysmic events. On the night of October 12, 2018, a violent thunderstorm swept across the greater Joshua Tree area. From Coachella Valley to as far east as Arizona, several billion gallons of rain crashed down onto the desert. For hours, the night sky was unzipped by bolts of lightning and deafening crashes of thunder. The soil was too dry to absorb all this water fast enough, and too barren to slow it down. With little to stop it, running water acquired destructive momentum. Freeways were flooded 12 feet deep, and cars buried in storm debris. Hail broke through skylights and mudflows ripped through homes. That night, many canyons were redesigned by devastating torrents. Even though the desert has been eons in the making, a single day can still change it dramatically.

Botany

As lame as it was, the name originally proposed for Joshua Tree—Desert Plants National Park—underscores the early recognition, nearly a century ago, of this land's exceptional botanical wealth: the park is home to at least 750 species of vascular plants. This surprising diversity is due to a large degree to the park's location at the boundary between two deserts, the Mojave Desert to the northwest, and the Sonoran Desert to the southeast. Although it is hard to learn to identify so many plants, most of the biomass is composed of only two or three dozen plants. In the western part of the park, for example, creosote, desert almond, juniper, Joshua trees, Mojave yucca, oak, pinyon pine, and saltbush rank among the most conspicuous common plants. In many places, they all grow within a short distance of each other. Learning to identify just this small subset gives a satisfying sense of familiarity with the desert, and a greater appreciation of its diversity.

Botanists divide the flora of a biogeographic region into communities, plant associations that are relatively uniform and traditionally named after the one or two dominant plants. This classification is visually intuitive: when contemplating a landscape, we notice first the species that occupy the greatest space. To a layperson, distinguishing between communities can be difficult, because they all contain many of the same species, only in different proportions. Communities tend to grade into each other, forming a quasi-continuous tapestry that evolves slowly with elevation. This evolution is best apparent when climbing a mountain and witnessing the gradual transformation of the assemblage of plants, typically from a dominance of yucca and creosote in the lower desert, to a woodland of conifers at the summit.

Escapers, avoiders, and endurers. The desert flora has devised admirably efficient strategies to cope with the scarcity of water. Plants must acquire what little soil moisture is available, then minimize water loss. Different species deal with the first problem by using water stored at different levels underground. Fast-growing plants like annuals have shallow roots that mine moisture from the first few inches of soil. Some root systems cover a large area to capture as much water as possible during light rains. Most larger shrubs get their water from deeper down, usually below a foot. Mesquite and willows send roots tens of feet underground to reach the water table, often in washes, and they are less dependent on the fickle rains. The dominant shrubs that draw water from comparable depths are often evenly spaced to better share the water. The dominant plants in the creosote community, creosote and burrobush, are evenly spaced for another reason: they both secrete a poison that inhibit the growth of their neighbors' roots. Cacti have a different tactic: when it rains they load up on water through their shallow roots and store it in fleshy tissues. After a heavy rain, a barrel cactus can be noticeably more plump than after a long dry spell.

Multiple adaptations have also evolved to minimize water loss. They fall into three categories. Drought escapers are plants that lie dormant as seeds for extended dry periods, waiting for a good rain to quickly germinate, grow, flower, seed, and die. Most annuals are drought escapers: they are around only around springtime, and some seeds do not grow for years, sometimes decades. Following the El Niño of 1996, which inundated the desert with 500-year rainfalls, some species were identified where they had never been seen before.

Drought avoiders reduce water loss by minimizing evaporation, which is the largest source of loss. Transpiration occurs through tiny holes (stomates) in the leaves, whose role is also to absorb carbon dioxide through photosynthesis. The plant must therefore strike a compromise between photosynthesis efficiency (stomates open) and water conservation (stomates closed). Desert plants have developed an impressive number of stratagems to meet this delicate balance. Most plants have evolved small or curled leaves, leaves with hair or thick cuticle, or sunken stomates. Some species drop their leaves during extremely dry periods. The ocotillo leaves may grow and fall up to six times a year depending on rainfall. Cacti have done away with leaves altogether, and replaced them with spines. They often have cylindrical stems to minimize transpiration. Cacti extract carbon dioxide at night, so that their stomates are closed during the day to reduce evaporation.

The last category, drought endurers, is in a way the most amazing. They have evolved cells that are resistant to the stress associated with expansion during extreme water loss, and they can perform photosynthesis while continuing to grow. They are green year-round, although often some branches die to direct the limited moisture and nutrients to the rest of the plant so that it can survive. Many common shrubs large and small are drought endurers, including juniper, pinyon pine, cliffrose, and the ubiquitous creosote bush.

Mojave Desert flora: the Joshua-tree empire. In a land replete with strange plants right out of a fairy tale, the Joshua tree is the oddest of the odd, so iconic of the Mojave Desert that a whole park was named after it. Its hairy trunk holds forked branches tipped with orbs of green spikes, decorated with a bayonet of luscious creamy flowers in the spring. They come in an infinite range of shapes, each individual radiating a distinctive aura. Their presence is so palpable that in a Joshua tree forest you may well be compelled to stop in mid-stride and stare.

Joshua trees do not grow everywhere in the Mojave, but if you see one you are probably in the Mojave. The subspecies found in the park, *brevifolia,* has a taller trunk, larger leaves, and a thinner crown than the *jaegeriana* species of the northern and eastern Mojave. Joshua trees are particular about their habitat. They need well-drained loamy soil, at least 3 but no more than 12 inches of rain a year, and temperatures neither too high (the summer is too hot for them below about 3,500 feet) nor too low (winter is too cold above about 6,000 feet). Their domain is so vast and some of it so little known that exceptionally large specimens are still periodically discovered. The latest is a 24-foot giant spotted in 2020 near Spirit Mountain in Nevada. In the park, their best strongholds are Lost Horse Valley and Queen Valley, where their open woodlands go on for miles. They are also found in extensive groves mixed with evergreen on Covington Flat, on the steppes of Juniper Flat, and among boulders throughout the park's western mountains.

Joshua-tree woodlands include many mid-elevation species—lycium, squawbush, catclaw, brittlebush, paperbag bush, buckwheat, and succulents, of which Mojave yucca is the most common. Its unmistakable rosette gathers numerous stiff daggers 2–3 feet long edged by curly fibers, often at the top of a spine-covered trunk. Chollas have multiple branches composed of jointed cylindrical segments covered with needles. The silver cholla, a compact bush with a thick crown of shorter stem-joints, is the most widespread. The diamond cholla is recognized by much narrower stems with a purplish tinge, and longer spines at geometric angles that make it look like a toy model of a molecule. Four species of prickly-pear live in Joshua-tree woodlands. The beavertail cactus has low spineless pads dotted with clumps of short

Cacti, Yuccas, and Agaves of Joshua Tree National Park		
COMMON NAME	**SPECIES**	**RANGE**
CACTACEAE		
Barrel cactus	*Ferocactus cylindraceus*	Widespread and abundant, up to 5,200′
Beavertail cactus	*Opuntia basilaris* var. *basilaris*	Widespread but usually solitary, 1,000′–6,000′
Cushion foxtail cact.	*Coryphantha alversonii*	Uncommon but locally abundant, 2,000′–5,000′
Calico cactus	*Echinocereus engelmannii*	Widespread, up to ~7,000′
Chollas	*Cylindropuntia*	
Diamond cholla	*C. ramosissima*	Widespread, up to 4,000′
Silver cholla	*C. echinocarpa*	Widespread, up to ~6,000′
Teddy-bear cholla	*C. bigelovii*	South- and west-facing fans & rocky slopes, 1,000′–3,000′
Common fishhook	*Mammillaria tetrancistra*	Widespread, uncommon, 450′–5,400′
Cottontop cactus	*E. polycephalus* var. *polyceph.*	Widespread, up to 4,800′
Mound cactus	*Echinocereus triglochidiatus*	Widespread, above ~3,000′
Parish club-cholla	*Grusonia parishii*	Uncommon, 3,000′–5,000′
Prickly-pear	*Opuntia*	
Brown-spined	*O. phaeacantha*	Widespread distribution but uncommon, above 300′
Grizzly bear cactus	*O. polyacantha* var. *erinacea*	Widespread, above ~3,500′
Pancake	*O. chlorotica*	Widespread, above ~2,000′
AGAVACEAE		
Desert agave	*Agave deserti* var. *deserti*	Uncommon–rare, 300′–5,000′
Joshua tree	*Yucca brevifolia* var. *jaegeriana*	Widespread and abundant, ~3,500′–6,000′
Mojave yucca	*Yucca schidigera*	Widespread and abundant, low lands up to woodlands
NOLINAS		
Bigelow nolina	*Nolina bigelovii*	Widespread, rocky slopes, 2,000′–4,100′
Parry nolina	*Nolina parryi*	Less common, granitic soils and boulders, 4,000′–6,900′
OCOTILLO		
Ocotillo	*Fouquieria splendens*	Uncommon, locally abundant, lower desert

bristles. Mature pancake prickly-pear look like a squat tree with Ping-Pong pads for branches. The brown-spined prickly-pear, less common, grows in prone carpets, especially in the Wonderland of Rocks.

Sonoran Desert flora. The main factor that explains the floristic differences between the Sonoran and the Mojave deserts is elevation. The Sonoran Desert is much lower and therefore hotter. Combined with the irregularity and low frequency of rainfalls, it reduces the abundance and diversity of the vegetation. Much of it is also a patchwork of basins with no outlets to the sea surrounded by lower, highly eroded mountains. All of the park's eastern half drains into either the Salton Sea, Chuckwalla Valley, Palen Valley, or Cadiz Valley, all closed basins. Inflowing water picks up evaporites from the rocks and leaves a salty residue when it evaporates. Over time the soil has become alkaline, which further limits the number of plants.

There is no better place in the park to witness the drastic differences between the two deserts than the Pinto Basin Road where it crosses from one to the other at Wilson Canyon. At the top of the canyon you are in the Mojave Desert, in a relatively lush and pleasing Joshua-tree woodland. At the bottom of the canyon you have just entered the Sonoran Desert. The vegetation is scarcer, more stunted, subdued. With a thinner plant cover, the surrounding hills are darker; they have lost the visual appeal of the bright high plateau you just left.

In spite of local differences, in the two deserts the plant communities are similar. If you can identify the dozen most common plants in the Mojave Desert, you will spot them in the Sonoran Desert too. The differences lie mostly in the relative abundance of plants in like communities. Several plants are much more common in the Sonoran Desert, at least within the park boundary. This is true of nolinas, bladderpod, desert lavender, desert almond, manzanita, and pancake prickly-pear. The most unusual denizens may well be the ocotillo and teddy-bear cholla. Ocotillo is an attractive plant that looks from a distance like an odd bouquet of tall bare rods, each one tipped in the spring by a bright vermillion flame-like blossom. It is relatively common in the upper reaches of bajadas, and it extends high into some ranges, like the Eagle Mountains. The teddy-bear cholla is a beautiful cholla with short stems so completely covered with spines that it has the fuzzy appearance of a felt bear. The whole plant radiates a supernatural glow when sunlight passes through it. It is a handsome plant, yet by no means cuddly. At the slightest contact its barbed spines will impale a careless boot or body part, a segment will detach itself and come along for the ride—hence the other nickname of jumping cholla.

The Sonoran Desert has no Joshua trees, but it does have trees of its own—ironwood, palo verde, and smoke tree. Like Joshua trees, they each have their own oddities, they dominate the plant

Grizzly bear cactus

Nolina in bloom

Ocotillo

cover, and they impose their mood on the landscape. Ironwood is an imposing tree up to 30 feet tall with a tousled crown and a profuse crop of purple flowers in springtime. It hardly ever loses all of its leaves, and provides cool shade year-round. It grows extremely slowly—its wood is so dense that it does not float. Considered the old growth of the desert—some trees are 800 years old—it is rare in California. In Joshua Tree it is confined to the southern edge of the Eagle and Cottonwood mountains.

The palo verde is a spiny tree that derives its name from its green bark. It can photosynthesize through its bark, an important adaptation for a tree that drops its leaves in summer and fall. At full maturity, it is a bushy tree that can reach 40 feet. When in bloom, its crown is consumed by masses of canary-yellow flowers that brighten broad expanses of the landscape. The smoke tree is an attractive smaller tree with tiny leaves on multiple small branches tipped with a sharp spine. Most of the year, its diffuse crown has the diaphanous appearance of puffs of smoke. In the spring, it comes alive with a multitude of indigo flowers. Both palo verde and smoke trees often grace the lower washes and bajadas throughout the Sonoran Desert section of the park.

Oaks. Oaks are often the first tree one runs into when hiking up a mountain canyon. A genus not usually adapted to drought conditions, oaks live in the park's cooler and wetter mountains, usually in rocky terrains where water can percolate to their roots. The most common one is Muller's oak, also known as scrub oak. It is a handsome small deciduous tree that does not get much taller than 10 feet. It resembles the live oaks of California's coastal and inland regions, with curled leaves about an inch long protected by spiny margins. The park's other three species of oak differ visually mostly by the shape and size of their leaves. In hot weather, an encounter with an oak is a blessing, as it provides deep shade and a good excuse to rest.

Conifer woodlands. Like in all deserts, the ranges of Joshua Tree enjoy a cooler and slightly wetter microclimate, and they are home to a greater variety of flora and fauna. Unable to make the journey across the much hotter and drier surrounding valleys, much of this richer life is prisoner of its gilded cage. Over time, these sky islands have become isolated refuges for species not found for tens of miles around. The most widespread manifestation of this insularity is the juniper-pinyon pine community. The two dominant species are California juniper, which occurs at lower elevations, and pinyon pine, which grow at higher elevations and overlap with juniper at mid elevations. With the exception of the lower and drier Hexie Mountains, all the park's ranges support pockets of pine and juniper. The dominant species is the single-leaved pinyon pine, an aromatic tree with a dense crown of short needles arranged, unlike all other pine trees, in single needles. Slow-growing, they can reach a height of 40 feet and live two centuries. California juniper is a handsome shrubby tree with multiple trunks and peeling bark often concealed by an emerald-green head of scale-like leaves. When conditions are favorable, it can reach a height of 25 or 30 feet; in more stressed environments, it is the size of a shrub. It bears pale-blue berry-like cones that taste, for a good reason, very

Smoke trees at sunset, eastern Pinto Mountains

much like gin. In their lower reaches, conifer forests grade into Joshua-tree and oak-tree communities. This conjunction of ecosystems make montane forests home to the most contrasted landscapes in the desert. Desert almond and yucca rub elbows with ephedra, nolina, saltbush, grizzly bear cactus, and big sagebrush, creating an infinite spectrum of greens sharply offset against the land's endless shades of ochre. Canyons offer slightly different plant associations, with a higher representation of rabbitbrush, mesquite, catclaw, as well as willows and baccharis near groundwater. These unique woodlands offer human visitors a welcome change of scenery, crisper, brighter, more lush and hospitable than the lower desert.

Palm oases. We often associate palm trees with deserts. Yet contrary to popular belief, except for a few species of conifers that have miraculously survived since the Ice Age, palm trees are the rarest of large native plants in the California desert. The species found in the park, California fan palms, might total no more than 300. They grow only where aquifer water rises to the surface along the faults. So in addition to being rare, they are also confined to a few locations: the Wonderland of Rocks area, and Cottonwood, Lost Palms, and Munsen canyons in the Eagle Mountains.

California fan palms are an odd plant, as if their design had gone awry. Their trunks are ridiculously tall and slender, even though there is no shortage of sunlight, and no competition for it. Their small crop of frazzled greenery perched high above the ground is equally comical. Yet like all palm trees their groves exude a distinctly magical aura. Perhaps it is because in their native state they occur often in exotic places, the beaches of remote tropical islands or the forsaken expanses of the Sahara, in isolated groves that offer shade, sometimes water, and a shelter from the elements. We identify palm oases with nurturing sanctuaries to seek refuge from harsh environments, a harbor of peace generously gifted by nature when we need it the most. There is still truth to these feelings, an experience that can be earned the hard way, by hiking to the least accessible of the park's palm oases.

Wildflowers. The desert seems an unlikely place for such delicate things as flowers. Yet on a good year, it produces more wildflowers per unit area than almost any other environment on Earth. When the season starts in early March, even after low rainfalls Joshua Tree is decorated with many annuals and perennials in bloom. There may be only small patches of flowers here and there, but they are always there, on time to cheer the coming of spring—blue bell and phacelia, desertgold, evening primrose, sand verbena, and many others. For a few weeks, the hills and grasslands boast a cheery five-o'clock shadow of green shoots. If the winter rains have been plentiful and evenly spaced, and the temperatures not too low, the wildflower show can be so unbelievably abundant that it alone warrants a trip to the desert. In the spring of 2023, following the wettest winter in years, from Covington Flat to the Coxcomb Mountains gravel normally lifeless was spiked with millions of yellow dandelion, red nama, white primrose, golden little daisy, orange desert gold poppy, and blue lupine. Even tiptoeing, it was impossible not to step on them. In one outing you could run into more specimens of rare species, like the desert lily, than in a lifetime.

The flower displays slowly migrate to higher elevations, reaching the highest summits in summer. Fall brings a second, smaller crop, a farewell to season's end. The summer flowers—globemallow, Indian paintbrush, penstemon, lupine, and Mojave aster—are equally attractive. Many classic beauties will stop you dead in your tracks: the masses of canary blossoms of bladderpod, the indigo bush so deep purple that it borders our range of vision, and the arresting white trumpets of sacred datura. The most dazzling are unquestionably the cacti. They put forth a profusion of large flowers in shades of vermillion, magenta, yellow, and shocking pink so intense that they seem unnatural.

Wildlife

When visiting natural places, wildlife is often high on our list of anticipated attractions. Thanks to its large size and wide range of elevations, Joshua Tree encompasses a variety of habitats that support many animal species. It is home to 250 species of birds, 57 mammals, and 44 reptiles. In comparison, Yosemite National Park, which covers a similar area but has a temperate climate, has about as many birds (although a much greater percentage is residents), about twice as many mammals (which fare better in wetter regions), and about half as many reptiles (which fare better in hotter climates). Although the total number of species is comparable, in Joshua Tree the density of wildlife is lower, which reduces the probability of an encounter, but the terrain is much more open, which makes it easier to spot wildlife. In a temperate forest you may unknowingly walk within 20 feet of a large mammal. In Joshua Tree you will spot a coyote a quarter of a mile away.

To survive in this harsh land offering little food, even less water, and excessive heat half of the year, wildlife have developed a remarkable array of adaptation. Over time scales of millions to hundreds of millions of years, their diet, home, sleeping schedule, defense strategies, food and water procurement, reproduction, and countless other physical and behavioral features have been shaped and tweaked by natural selection to maximize their chance of survival.

Many mammals in Joshua Tree are paler in color than their relatives in more temperature climates, an evolutionary trait that helps reduce absorption of sunlight and elude predators against the dominantly light-colored rocks. Snakes have developed patterns and colors that blend with their habitat, enabling them to hide from predators. Some lizards, like the zebra-tailed and desert horned lizards, have in fact become masters of camouflage. Their skin mimics gravel so perfectly well that they virtually disappear as soon as they stop moving. Most desert mammals are also smaller, in part to minimize the amount of food needed to survive. For rodents, a smaller size also makes it easier to burrow into the ground or hide in crevices in the rocks.

Numerous strategies for water economy have been conceived. Most animals have developed metabolisms that require little drinking. The kangaroo rat can survive without drinking a drop of water its entire life. It gets its moisture from its seed diet. To minimize water loss, it excretes uric acid as a solid instead of urinating. Its nostrils also have complex passages that condense moisture. Although desert tortoises and most other reptiles will drink from pools of rainwater, they also rarely drink, and they too pass a solid urine. Snakes and lizards are well adapted to the scarcity of water in other ways: their scales reduce water loss through evaporation. Wood rats and pack rats can synthesize water from the molecules in the food they eat. The kit fox, which inhabits desert flats, a particularly dry environment, also does not drink often. To increase its water intake, it consumes much more prey than needed for energy. In contrast, most birds require drinking daily. Their main adaptation is their ability to fly to springs inside and outside the park, or to escape to the mountains. Unlike most mammals, few desert mammals use perspiration or panting to keep cool, methods that result in a substantial loss of water. In the winter, bighorn sheep do not drink, but they get their water needs from plants too. In the summer they drink every few days if water is available, otherwise they rest during the day and feed at night.

While most birds, lizards, and ground squirrels are active during the day, other wildlife avoids the daytime heat by being active at night. This is true of coyote, snakes, bighorn sheep, jackrabbits, desert banded geckos, kangaroo rats, and other rodents. The best times of day to view wildlife are then dawn and dusk, when diurnal and nocturnal wildlife overlap. The best season is spring, when most animals are out there enjoying greener plants and looking for a mate. Winter is a good time for birding, when many species migrate through the park. Palm oases and other springs are all around good places to spy on wildlife—and the more isolated, the least frequented by humans, the better.

Many smaller mammals and most snakes take refuge in burrows to avoid heat and cold. On a cross-country hike in sandy terrain, you may walk by hundreds of burrows—and sink into a few. The burrows' entrances are often plugged to keep out the outside air and increase the relative humidity. In the winter, when food is generally scarcer, most lizards go on a self-imposed diet by hibernating. Desert tortoises take this avoidance technique to the extreme: they come out of their burrows only for a few weeks in the spring and fall to build up their fat reserve and reproduce. Their burrows are unmistakable oval openings that they dig in sandy soil with their flattened front legs. Some areas have a couple of dozen per mile—yet encountering their occupants is a lifetime event. Snakes also crawl into holes or in cracks in rocks during the day. Some lizards prefer living among the branches of desert plants. Some adaptations are truly remarkable. Desert wood rats and cactus wrens build their nests among the spiky crowns of cholla to deter predators—how they do not get skewered is a mystery. For additional protection, the wren builds a bulky nest with a narrow entrance that restricts access. The yucca night lizard has carved out yet another habitat for itself: it may live its entire life under the protective bark of a decaying Joshua tree, where it feasts on ants and termites.

Tarantulas are the world's largest spider. The females are larger, and thus dominant, and the romantic life of male tarantulas does not always go smoothly. They live most of the time alone in their burrows, which they enlarge as they grow. They hunt close to home at night, mostly large insects and other arthropods. The most likely time to see a tarantula is fall, when males wander in search of a mate. When a male finds a female, if all goes well he gets lucky, then quickly leaves the scene before she devours him; sometimes the male gets eaten *during* copulation.

Of this motley crew of wildlife fine-tuned to the tough conditions of desert living, the most commonly sighted species in the daytime are lizards. Being cold-blooded, they get their heat mostly from the environment and very little from food. Most lizards do so by basking in the sun, which is one reason why they are more visible. The other reason is that because they do not need much water or food, they sustain larger populations. Lizards are often spotted running when spooked, or catching some sun on boulders, like California side-blotched lizards, Great Basin fence lizards, or chuckwallas, the park's largest.

Desert wildlife has also developed an arsenal of ingenious defense mechanisms. In response to a threat, some animals play dead, like horned lizards, or they freeze in a head stand like some species of beetle, hoping that a predator will lose interest in their corpse. Most lizards will dash into a close-by hiding place, or sprint madly in a straight line, like the zebra-tailed lizard, which can cover 20 feet in a second. When stressed, the collared lizard and others will flip abruptly 180 degrees in mid-air and hiss like a would-be T-Rex. Some species rupture capillaries around their eyes and squirt an irritating fluid at their predator. Rattlesnakes do not need to inject their venom in self-defense: they can squirt it too. I once ran into a gopher snake that tried to pass for a rattlesnake and shook its erect rattle-less tail up to try to scare me away. When confronted by a snake, a horned lizard will move around to present the widest part of its flat, spiked body to discourage the attacker. In many lizard species, the tail is designed to break off when grasped by a predator. The broken-off tail continues to wriggle, distracting the predator and giving the lizard a head start to escape. A new, smaller tail will grow back, and it can be broken off again. Poorwills and a few resident birds will feign injury to lure attackers away from their nest by appearing to be an easy meal. Kangaroo rats escape yet another way: they use their disproportionately long rear legs to leap up to 9 feet off the ground. The fringe-toed lizard has evolved fringes of pointed scales on the edges of its toes to race across loose sand. It also uses them to swim into sand and to escape a predator or avoid extreme temperatures. It even has special valves, lids, and flaps to keep sand out of its nose, eyes, and ears. The variety and ingenuity of survival tricks is almost limitless.

In a park that straddles two deserts, it is hardly surprising that there would be several species of rattlesnakes. All seven species are common, and venomous. Western diamond-back rattlesnakes (*Crotalus atrox*) prefer the more thickly vegetated southern section of the park. The Mojave Desert and Colorado sidewinders (*C. cerastes*) have a predilection for sandy areas. They are noted for their method of locomotion: they move while maintaining an S shape and touching the ground at only a few points, which helps them on loose sand and minimizes contact with hot ground. Southwestern speckled rattlesnake (*C. mitchellii*) are found mostly on rocky slopes and in canyons. Southern Pacific rattlesnakes (*C. oreganus*) inhabit conifer woodlands in the northwestern section. Red diamond rattlesnake (*C. ruber*) are more common in areas with brush, boulders, and cactus patches in the western section. The Mojave rattlesnake (C. *Scutulatus*) is restricted to valley floors at the northwestern edge of the park, which is a good thing: it is by far the most venomous, and it tends to have a temper.

Chuckwalla

Arguably, the desert's most famous bird is the roadrunner. Although it certainly does not run around pestering coyotes, unlike fictionalized in Walt Disney cartoons, and despite its zany demeanor, it is a skilled raptor. It will shove its body into a burrow to yank out a live rodent, and relishes fresh rattlesnake. Sometimes the birds work in pairs, one bird distracting the snake while the other attacks it from behind. When hunting alone, a roadrunner will flap its wings and puff its crest while making quick frontal dashes at the snake, until it finds the right opening and pinches the snake's head with its long beak. The coup de grâce is administered by repeatedly bashing the snake's head against the ground. Unlike bobcats, who tear their prey apart and enjoy a taste of it, a roadrunner with swallow its kill whole.

Bighorn sheep are iconic to North American deserts. They live in small herds, mostly in the mountains where they can spot approaching predators from afar and use their remarkable agility in rough terrain to escape.. They come down to lower elevations mainly to access water at springs, often at dawn. Most herds are declining. There might be 40 or 50 individuals in the Wonderland of Rocks, their best historic stronghold, and fewer in other ranges; some ranges have no permanent herd. An encounter is a rare thrill, usually all too brief as sheep will flee surprisingly fast, even on the rockiest terrain, as soon as they see a human. In a few areas, like in the Little San Bernardino Mountains north of Desert Hot Springs, they have become habituated to humans and can often be observed leisurely at relatively close range.

Mule deer are the largest native mammal in the park. They are a little more common, but still seldom seen. They live mostly in sagebrush and forested habitats in the high country. They roam over fairly small areas, often in small herds for protection. In hot weather, they huddle in the shade during the day, browse in the evening and at night, and thrive to drink every day.

The top predators in the park are mountain lions, coyotes, foxes, and bobcats. Mountain lions are extremely rare: there might be a handful in the Little San Bernardino Mountains. They are solitary animals, and among the world's stealthiest predators. If you get near one, chances are that it will see you, but you will likely not see it. Coyotes are far more numerous, mostly because they are supreme opportunists and not too picky about what they eat and where they hang out. They have adapted superbly well to almost every desert environment, from open valleys to rocky mountains and quiet suburbs. They can hunt by day or by night, in packs or alone, feast on a fresh kill or carrion, and enjoy wild berries, insects, lizards, birds, rabbits, or cholesterol-rich leftovers. Combined with their wise inclination to be stealth, this versatility has enabled coyotes to pull through centuries of persecution. All too often, all we see of a coyote is a flash of pale blond fur vanishing behind a bush. Even if they are invisible during the day, they serenade us at dusk with their playful howling as they start hunting, and wake us with their chilling calls when they regroup at dawn.

A whole menagerie of mice, rats, squirrels, and gophers live in the park, in general more numerous as their size decreases. One of the commonly sighted and most charming is the kangaroo rat, a silky critter with a head almost as big as his body and a tail nearly twice as long, who bounces in comical leaps like kangaroos. Black-tailed hare and desert cottontail are common. During the predator low in the predator-prey population cycle, there might be dozens per square mile. In the low desert, you might be lucky to spot a kit fox, a badger, or a bobcat. Many species of bats come out of caves and mines at dusk and hunt for insects in frenetic zigzags against the darkening sky.

Birds need a fair amount of food, which is why only a third of the species identified in the park are residents—the rest migrate or move in and out. Yet birds are among the most common sightings. Every so often a lone raven will fly by on some important business, carefully ignoring you yet fully aware of your presence. A black-throated sparrow may be singing her heart out from the top of a Joshua tree. It is not uncommon to run across a covey of quail crisscrossing each other's paths hurriedly between bushes, nodding their heads at each step; to be awoken a little before sunrise by their melodious call; or to get startled deep in a deserted canyon by a dozen quail bursting into low flight all at once in a noisy blast of whirring wings. A Costa's hummingbird may buzz by to check out the red trim on your pack. The sight of a roadrunner dashing off at breakneck speed, body fully extended and hell-bent on not flying, is always a source of enjoyment. They are not common in the park, but strangely enough they are often seen buzzing in neighborhoods. On many occasions, canyon wrens have surprised me in the middle of nowhere with their crisp descending chirping songs, as if they were dropping into a deep well. Only a very few resident birds of prey are common—the colorful American kestrel, the loggerhead shrike, and the red-tailed hawk, designed, it seems, for effortless soaring. Turkey vultures are uncommon, although they do migrate through the park. Even when driving back late at night you may spot birds, perhaps a dove sitting in the middle of the road, or a barn owl flying ponderously, like a portent shadow.

■

To keep park wildlife wild...

- *Hunting is prohibited*
- *Pets must be leashed at all times, and are not allowed on trails*
- *Do not camp within 200 yards of springs*
- *Do not feed wildlife*
- *Do not approach wild animals*
- *Do not view wildlife with artificial light*
- *Do not annoy, bother, disturb, exasperate, hassle, hound, irk, infuriate, irritate, madden, nag, pester, torment, or otherwise vex wild animals*

— 3 —

CULTURAL HISTORY

Native American History

In pre-contact days, the region of high plateaus and mountains that now forms Joshua Tree National Park was part of the homelands of three Native American desert cultures, the Serrano, Cahuilla, and Chemehuevi. The Cahuilla land covered approximately 2,400 square miles centered on today's Palm Springs area. It extended along the park's southern border—the Eagle, Cottonwood, and Little San Bernardino mountains—west to the southern foothills of the San Bernardino Mountains, and south into the Anza-Borrego Desert. The Serrano territory was slightly larger and stretched north across the park and the Bullion Mountains, and from there west to Antelope Valley. The park's northeastern corner—the eastern Pinto Mountains, Pinto Basin, and the Coxcomb Mountains—was part of the vast Chemehuevi homeland, which reached far east over the driest portions of the Mojave Desert to the Colorado River. These territories were generally not bound by hard frontiers but by porous, overlapping boundaries that were periodically freely crossed to access resources or sacred grounds, and to maintain trade relationships with far-away tribes.

The Cahuilla population, which may have numbered as high as 6,000, was divided into six or more independent groups. Each one comprised between four and about a dozen exogamous lineages that included several extended families and totaled about 70 to 120 individuals. Each lineage lived in spread-out permanent villages located near a reliable water source. Each village owned its land, which included areas with abundant plant and animal resources a good part of the year. Typical houses had either a dome shape or a pitched roof often made of a combination of willow and palm fronds, with a ramada for outdoor living. At different times of the year, families moved to smaller camps to harvest specific seasonal foods.

To survive in one of the most forbidding North American deserts, the Cahuilla and the Serrano had adopted a hunter-gatherer lifestyle. Both were highly skilled at exploiting the wide spectrum of resources available from the desert's diverse climate and biological life zones. They each had access to desert valleys, which provided about 40% of the plants they exploited, and high mountains reaching over 10,000 feet, the San Bernardino Mountains for the Serrano and the San Jacinto Mountains for the Cahuilla. The fortunate groups who inhabited these privileged areas enjoyed higher rainfall and cooler average temperatures, more abundant water and a different kind of vegetation. The desert groups still benefited from the wealth of plants available in these regions. Except during severe droughts, they always managed to handle the lack of water. They relied on springs, dug wells, and built earthen dams in canyon washes to catch storm waters.

Both cultures had acquired a sophisticated knowledge of desert plants. The Cahuilla used more than 200 plant species for food, medicine, construction, religious practices, and as recreational drugs. Willows and yucca roots were used for basketry. Arrowweed and ocotillo went into the construction of dwellings, windbreaks, and sweat houses. Hunting bows were made of juniper and the arrows of willow. Through what must have taken centuries of cautious experiments on countless patients, a task that was usually reserved for shamans and women doctors, they developed an extensive medicine cabinet. They found out that creosote could heal many ailments or induce vomiting; that boiled cottonwood bark relieved headaches; that brittlebush was good for toothaches, desert senna as a laxative, and sacred datura to get stoned. They had remedies for colds, pleurisy, ulcers, colic, wounds, headaches, muscle strain, rheumatism, menstrual pain, and baldness (the formula has unfortunately been lost).

Their diet was equally impressive. The most important staples were agave, oaks, mesquite, pinyon pine, palms, cacti, and yuccas, for which they had many recipes accompanied by dozens of other plants. They made a refreshing beverage with ephedra, porridge with wild oats, dessert with the palm's sweet fruit, cakes from a formidable variety of flour, and a coffee substitute with manzanita. Yucca had so many usages that life may not have been the same without it. Every part of the plant—roots, leaves, stalks, flowers, pods, and seeds—was put to good use, to make strings, ropes, nets, brushes, baskets, mats, sandals, blankets, shirts, hats, soap, toys, necklaces, and ingenuous dishes. For protein they hunted rabbits, quails, squirrels, and grasshoppers—all still delicacies in many parts of the world. Food procurement and preparation took a good fraction of their time. Women often took care of shopping, and (surprise!) men handled the artillery and hunting. They also engaged in small-scale agriculture, even in precontact times, raising in particular corn and melon. They knew how to increase the land productivity with small prescribed burns, and how to cultivate coyote tobacco as a mild narcotic.

Maria Los Angeles, Cahuilla woman, circa 1900. Photo: James, George Wharton. Source: USC Digital Library. California Historical Society Collection.

There were many parallels between the Serrano and the Cahuilla. They shared a common language. The Serrano too led a semi-sedentary life in villages of up to about 80 people, with thatched-roof shelters and sweat houses. They engaged in ceremonial face-painting, and they valued mesquite beans, acorn, and pinyon nuts. They were also broadly divided into two groups, one living in the highlands of the San Bernardino Mountains, and the other in the lower desert, primarily along the Mojave River. When Francisco Garcés visited the area in 1776, he found the desert Serrano more destitute. A quiet and inoffensive people, they wore coats made of rabbit pelt, and subsisted on a diverse diet harvested from the desert and small game that they trapped in snares made of wild hemp. In both cultures, women took great pride in being fine basket makers. They used personal, creative designs often depicting spirit animals like the eagle, and an eye-pleasing combination of black and red dyes against the natural color of the fiber material. Baskets were used for anything from collecting plants to preparing, storing, and even cooking food. The weave was so tight that they could hold water.

The Chemehuevi were in a very different predicament. Contrary to the Cahuilla and the Serrano, their lands ranked among the poorest in the state. They likely numbered fewer than 1,000—on average, only one inhabitant per 10 square miles. They survived by living a nomadic existence, migrating annually in a great circle around their territory. They were famous for "visiting," which meant constantly being away. They traveled in small groups, probably centered around a family nucleus. Chemehuevi men had the caricatural profile of weightlifters, with broad shoulders and slender waists. They walked very fast, covering up to 20 miles a day for days without a break, arduous journeys they completed wearing moccasins and deer-skin shirts. They carried a hook to pull small animals like gophers and rabbits out of their holes. They hunted pronghorn antelope and bighorn sheep with bows and arrows tipped with a stone point. They had also mastered the fine art of weaving baskets, light and resistant vessels well adapted to migratory life. Their settlements ranged from temporary campsites to permanent villages. They occasionally farmed on small lots at well-watered springs, with limited success.

Only a small fraction of these three cultures spent time in what is today Joshua Tree National Park, and mostly during seasonal rounds. The most populated place was probably the Oasis of Mara, the birthplace of Twentynine Palms behind today's visitor center. Mara was a major source of water that supported a lush grove of palms with valuable plants and wildlife. It was used by the Serrano for centuries, and shared with the Cahuilla. A group of Chemehuevi also lived at the oasis starting in 1867, after they were defeated by the Mohave and forced to move out of the Colorado River area. They also frequented the other three palm oases in the park, for their shade, water, large game like mule deer and bighorn sheep, and specific plants. Archaeological studies have uncovered dozens of other sites throughout the park that bear witness to widespread occupation going back at least 8,000 years. Among these were more than a dozen residential areas, many temporary camps and milling stations where plants were ground in holes in boulders or bedrock, several quarries, and many areas with scattered artifacts, stone rings, storage pits, manos, pestles, and rock shelters. Centuries later, their refuse piles revealed invaluable information about their diet, their lifestyle, and the remarkable variety of specialized stone and wooden tools they had developed.

After the arrival of the Spanish in the 1770s, these small bands suffered great losses from massacres by settlers and smallpox outbreaks.

There was still a community of Serrano living at Mara in the 1820s. By 1834 most of them had been, sometimes forcibly, relocated to missions. The small remaining population of Cahuilla and Serrano now lives in the vicinity of the Santa Rosa Mountains on Cahuilla reservations. The two tribes have intermarried for so long that they are now difficult to distinguish—the Serrano have been assimilated by both culture and nature. All that you are likely to find as you wander through the park are—if you are lucky—the ghostly images they painted on the rocks.

Ranching and Homesteading

The first immigrants to settle in present-day Joshua Tree National Park were cattlemen. Back then, around 1870, the weather was much wetter than it is today. In late fall and winter the low desert received more regular rains, the snow pack in the mountains was thicker, and it lingered later into the spring. Stockmen ran cattle and sheep in the low desert to take advantage of the green spring grass. The park's highland was also a valuable source of browse, especially abundant plants like saltbush, mesquite, big sagebrush, and many species of grass. Most of the grazing took place in Lost Horse Valley, Queen Valley, and Pleasant Valley, all located in the higher and wetter western section. Stockraising was initially centered around the few main springs—Quail Springs, Stubbe Spring, Pinyon Well, and Cottonwood Spring. Over time, stockmen supplemented these small natural watering holes with tanks and wells. Tanks were created by impounding the seasonal flow of washes in the mountains at the edges of the valleys. The local topography was particularly suitable, especially in the Wonderland of Rocks, where washes often squeeze between tight rock walls, ideal spots where a very small dam can hold back a sizeable pond. Many tanks are still there—at Keys Ranch, Cow Camp, Barker Dam, White Tank, and Squaw Tank. When the winter rains have been generous, they still collect up to an acre or more of water, and their smooth surface reflects the most perfect inverted image of the fantastically shaped surroundings. Small valleys enclosed in impassable walls like Hidden Valley provided convenient natural corrals.

The first known cattleman in the park was Oliver Smith. Between 1870 and 1876 he ran Texas longhorns around Quail Springs, perhaps also using the springs in the nearby canyon that now bears his name. In the late 1880s, Johnny Lang and his father George ran a cattle operation out of the Indio area, and their animals grazed near a well in Lost Horse Valley. Following the serendipitous discovery of a gold seam, they switched to developing the rich Lost Horse Mine. The area was then under the control of the infamous McHaney gang, half a dozen rustlers led by the two McHaney brothers. Starting in 1879, they used the Wonderland of Rocks' convoluted terrain to hide and rebrand stolen cattle before selling them locally. Their headquarters was a small ranch named Cow Camp hidden in a remote finger canyon. They also eventually converted to mining at the Desert Queen Mine, which they took over their way, by murdering the mine's discoverer.

The McHaneys remained a main presence until around 1895, when rustling stopped, discouraged by the growing number of legitimate stockmen. Over the next five decades, several businesses competed for the desert's limited browse and water. The Swarthout Cattle Company, headquartered at the Oasis of Mara, ran its cattle into the Lucerne Valley. The three Talmadge brothers operated out of Warren's Well, around which Yucca Valley eventually grew, and they moved their cattle as far as Big Bear and Palm Springs. C. O. Barker, a well-known local who had been raising cattle and horses around the Oasis of Mara since at least the 1890s, made a smart move around 1905 when he formed a partnership with county sheriff Bill Shay. In those troubled days of heated conflicts over land and water rights, having the law on his side gave him a much-needed edge over the competition. Over time, at least a dozen outfits operated in the region. Most of them owned between 200 and 800 heads and used the park's high valleys seasonally for a portion of their stock.

Others raised small herds—homesteaders as part of their livelihood, and miners to supplement their trade's sporadic income. The Ryan Ranch was a prime example. Started by brothers Jepp and Tom Ryan and their families in the mid-1890s near Witch Springs in Lost Horse Valley, it was engaged in stockraising first, then in mining after they acquired the Lost Horse Mine, which they turned into a profitable operation. The Ryan Ranch grew into a sizable property, with a main adobe house, several cabins for the miners and ranch hands, a barn, assaying office, corrals, and a two-stamp mill. It supported a small community of over 60 people at its peak into the early 1940s, including Matt Ryan, one of the monument's first rangers.

Not all settlers were this successful. In the late 1920s and through the 1930s, John Samuelson and his wife ran a small homestead below Quail Springs. In the difficult Great Depression years, they made a meager living raising a few cows and working a local mine. A little before they left, Worth Bagley and his wife started a cattle ranch on the edge of the Wonderland of Rocks. Strangely enough, both ventures were doomed for the same reason—insanity. John Samuelson ended up in an asylum after killing someone in a brawl, and half-crazed Bagley was killed in a gunfight over trespassing.

Painted concrete bunker at the Sunset Mine

Of the many characters who shaped the park' homesteading and mining history, the most famous and successful was unquestionably Bill Keys. Keys came to this area in 1910, at the age of 31. A miner and ranch hand by training, a jack of all trades with remarkable self-reliance by nature, he quickly found his place in this rough frontier environment. He first worked at local mines in the Twentynine Palms area, including at the Desert Queen Mine, where he was employed as watchman, assayer, conveyor, and repairman. When the owner died, Keys inherited the mine in payment for past services. In 1916, he acquired the McHaneys property in the Wonderland of Rocks, and developed it into what became his home for the rest of his life. After he married in 1918, he and his wife Frances lived and raised four children on Keys Ranch. The couple survived through a combination of hard work and impressive resourcefulness. He built a reservoir above the ranch house and stocked it with catfish, and piped the water to his orchard and garden. They raised up to 100 heads of cattle, as well as burros as pack animals, and goats, rabbits, and chickens for food. The ranch was expanded to include houses for relatives and tourists. Over time Keys acquired many abandoned mines all over, which he either worked, leased to make a little extra money, or scavenged for parts that he used at the ranch or traded for supplies or services. Although he got in trouble for resorting to firearms—in his youth at the infamous Battle of Wingate Pass where his brother was wounded, and in 1943 when he shot Worth Bagley dead in self-defense—he was a kind man, generous with his time, attentive to other settlers. The creation of the monument in 1936, which Keys vehemently opposed, spelled the end of his way of life. Pre-existing homesteads were allowed to continue, but they died one by one. Keys Ranch was the last large one to close down, in 1964. By then, Bill Keys left his mark in more places than any other single individual. Over the course of his 50-year tenure, he had witnessed so many historic events and interacted with so many locals that he had become a legend, and the desert's living memory.

Mining History

Like in the rest of the California desert, mining played a key role in shaping the landscape and history of the Joshua Tree area. For more than a century, countless hopefuls combed the rugged landscape in search of gold, silver, and heavy metals. They built trails and bladed roads, sweat blood and tears blasting tunnels and shafts, lugging back-breaking equipment, and crushing rocks in deafening mills. They rested at night in squalid camps deprived of the most basic commodities. In the end, almost all of them came out empty handed, sometimes poorer than when they started. Although most of Joshua Tree is composed of granitic formations, which tend to be prime hosts for precious metals, it had even less gold than the rest of the desert.

The first wave of mining started in the wake of the California Gold Rush. As the rush declined through the second half of the 1850s, thousands of fortune seekers drifted into the desert looking for new gold fields. The rich strikes at the Comstock mines in western Nevada in 1859, then at Cerro Gordo in the Inyo Mountains in 1865, confirmed the presence of large and profitable silver lodes in the desert. The Panamint City frenzy of 1872, even though it was not exactly a success, also prolonged the belief that the desert had more wealth in store. By the time gold seekers fanned out into the Joshua Tree area in the mid-1880s, they had good reasons to hope and dream.

Back then prospectors did not have the benefit of satellite images, geology maps, and the wide array of precise instruments available today, yet they were exceedingly good at locating precious and base metals. Most of the very few valuable deposits within the park boundaries were identified, exploited, and essentially exhausted in a matter of years. The Lost Horse Mine in the Little San Bernardino Mountains was among the first ones to be developed, and it was the most productive. Discovered in 1893, it was worked off and on until the 1930s, but most of its gold was removed in the first two and a half years. The Desert Queen Mine in the Wonderland of Rocks, which started around the same time, was the richest silver property, and it had also ran out

Activity and production of main mines in Joshua Tree National Park and vicinity

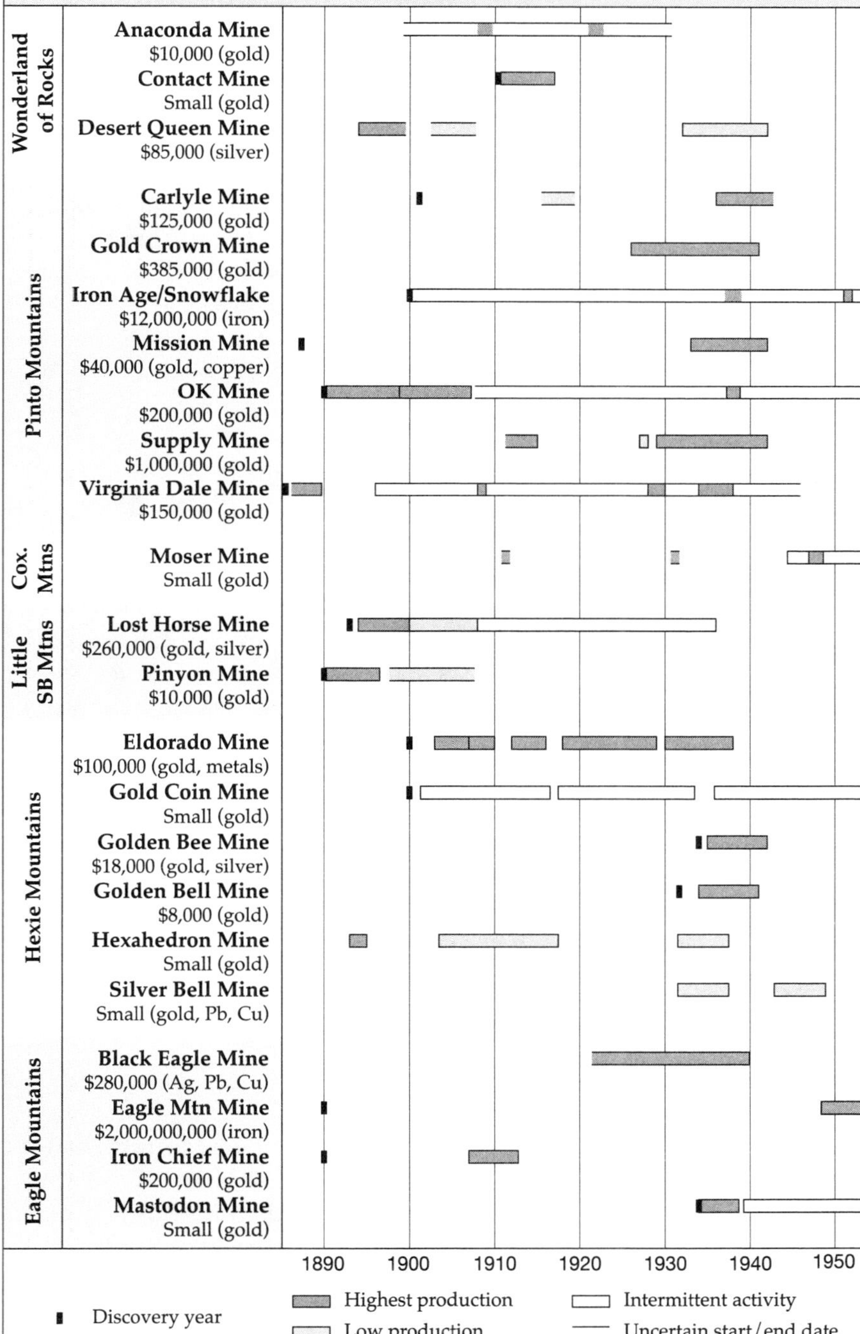

of most of its good ore by 1896. The Pinyon Mine, a few miles south of the Lost Horse Mine, had opened a few years earlier. Although it was not rich, its road provided the main access over the mountains to the district, and its camp was a valued social center in what was then an isolated desert. The last of the earliest mines that made a name for itself, the Hexahedron in the Hexie Mountains, is the only one that did not have much to show.

The second wave took place in the years preceding the first world war and during the war, and it was driven in part by the need for strategic base metals. This global resurgence was further stimulated by the appearance of automobiles, which made desert travel cheaper, faster, and safer, and gave access to more remote areas. Improved transportation by rail and advances in mining and ore-processing technologies also helped revive desert mining. Old tailings were explored again for lead, zinc, tungsten, and manganese, and new mines were opened. Joshua Tree lacked these commodities in economic quantities, and this effort produced very little. The exception is the Eldorado Mine in the Hexie Mountains, the second richest historic property. It had plenty of silver, and a forfeit of metals, and for close to 40 years it remained active at a high level longer than any other mine in the park. Its mill was also instrumental in helping neighboring mines that could not afford a mill treat their ore locally and reduce transportation costs.

The third wave took place during the Great Depression, and it was the busiest in the park's history. The financial and industrial slump of 1929 and subsequent years triggered a large influx of jobless people disgruntled with city life who moved to the desert and resorted to mining to try to make a better living. Lower operating costs and the nearly two-fold increase in the price of gold in 1934 were other significant incentives. Throughout the area, old tailings were reexamined for left-over gold and silver. The Black Eagle Mine in the Eagle Mountains continued to churn out rich silver-lead ore and copper. It is also the era when the Mastodon Mine, a typical mom-and-pop Great Depression venture, went into business in the same range. The Hexie Mountains were the busiest. Older mines like the Eldorado and the Hexahedron were put back to work, and new properties like the Golden Bell and the Golden Bee started producing a little gold.

After 1936, while mining in the newly created monument was restricted to existing claims and fizzled, the portion of the Pinto Mountains outside of the monument remained open for business. That part of the range had a large gold reserve, and it was excluded from the monument specifically so that mining would continue to thrive. And it did. The Dale Mining District, which had been active since the

1880s, witnessed the area's greatest revival. Since its inception, it had at least 40 mines with a recorded name. Most of them were looking for gold. Every other mine had its own mill, ranging from simple crushers to 10-stamp behemoths like at the OK Mine. The richest properties produced their best ore then. The Supply Mine was the richest: it put out around a million dollars in gold. The Gold Crown Mine and several others had outputs in the low six-digit figures. Many smaller mines had no known production, although some openings indicate that fair quantities of ore were extracted. The district's total production, including earlier years, has been estimated at over 5 tons of gold, or more than $4 million. As far as gold went, it was by far the area's richest.

In 1942, a government order closed down nearly all non-essential mines to encourage mining of base metals crucial to the second-world-war effort. Almost all gold mines in and around the park shut down overnight, and many never reopened.

The final wave was the post-war years leading into the 1980s, when fortune seekers prompted by the skyrocketing price of gold explored old shafts and tunnels again in search of the yellow metal, especially in the Pinto Mountains. These were sometimes city people who took up mining more as a hobby than as a source of income. This last effort produced insignificant returns—with the blatant exception of iron mining. Huge iron deposits had been known to exist in the eastern part of the park since at least 1890, but the incentive to exploit them did not arise until the 1950s. But when it did, iron mining broke all records. The Iron Age Mine and its neighbor the Snowflake Mine, in the eastern Pinto Mountains, had a joint production of 1.3 million tons worth more than all of the park's gold. The Eagle Mountain Mine, in the Eagle Mountains outside the park, was active for 25 years, and it produced nearly 100 times as much, becoming the region's richest.

In retrospect, as far as mining is concerned the land protected by the national park today was a dead loss. Joshua Tree has approximately 300 abandoned mines totalling about 800 openings. Most mines had no production record. Mojave National Preserve, twice as large in area, has over 10,000 workings. The Lost Horse Mine produced an estimated $250,000. In comparison, the Yellow Aster Mine near Ridgecrest made over $12 million in gold, Cerro Gordo $17 million in silver, and many mines in the Mojave Desert exceeded the one-million mark.

In spite of this dismal production, Joshua Tree's mining history did have its cast of interesting characters. It was shaped in part by a few visionary prospectors. The earliest days of the Dale Mining District are indebted to John Burt, a miner and prospector with a flair for gold and business. In 1890 he located in the Pinto Mountains what would become the rich OK Mine and Brooklyn Mine. A few years later he dug a well at the edge of Dale Lake that soon became the lifeline of Virginia Dale, a booming mining town of 1,000 that supported miners working the new district, including the lodes he had discovered. The early mining history would also not have been the same without Ed Holland and Alfred Tingman, the successful Indio merchants who discovered and/or first developed three of the most prominent early mines, the Pinyon, Lost Horse, and Hexahedron. For many years their Pinyon Mine provided valuable services to the local community—their mill by processing the ore of neighboring mines, and their well by providing much-needed water to miners and homesteaders.

Joshua Tree had its crooks and criminals too. At the Lost Horse Mine, co-owner Johnny Lang was caught stealing gold in the 1890s, was forced by his partners to sell his shares, and went on to live off the stolen gold. In the earliest days of the Desert Queen Mine, a ruthless gang of exiled cowboys headed by infamous Jim McHaney killed the mine discoverer, took control of the mine, and made a small fortune digging up its rich silver pockets.

On the other hand, there was also a line-up of hard-working individuals and families. The Ryan family developed the Desert Queen in style following its dark beginnings, while also keeping a ranch. Eloge Auclair, a Frenchman with a passion for gold mining, did the same at his Golden Bee Mine for nearly a decade. The Hulsey family ran the Mastodon Mine and a couple of mills off and on for nearly 40 years.

The region was not rich enough to attract well-known investors, except for one, Henry Kaiser, a wealthy entrepreneur famous, among other achievements, for constructing the Hoover Dam and Grand Coulee Dam. He financed the developments of the region's three iron mines to supply his steel plant in southern California, and from there his shipyards and automobile factories.

Joshua Tree also had its share of dreamers and romantics, people like Chester Moorten, aka Cactus Jim, who worked for Hollywood on the Keystone Cops series and kept a worthless mine and tiny mill near Cottonwood Spring to be surrounded by his beloved succulents. There was also Barry Storm, a small-time novelist and chronic schmoozer who claimed to have discovered the secret source of the Maya jade up in the Eagle Mountains. The list ended with no other than veteran homesteader Bill Keys. Long after the mining dust had settled, he continued to acquire rights to many of the monument's abandoned mines. By then most of them had played out, yet his hopes never waned, even though he reigned over a gutted empire.

■

— 4 —

SAFETY TIPS, REGULATIONS, AND ETHICS

The desert can be unforgiving. An emergency situation that would be taken care of with a simple phone call elsewhere can become life-threatening, as help may not arrive for days. This section provides a brief summary of what to do and not do to minimize both your chances of running into trouble and your impact on the desert. This is *not* a survival guide. Refer to one if you need more substantial advice.

Backcountry Driving

Road conditions and vehicle requirements. Most of the mining roads that once reached into the park's furthest recesses were closed to driving decades ago to preserve the park's peace and integrity. Today, most of the hikes start from a paved road or a graded road, which tend to be superbly maintained. Compared to other desert parks, there is often no need for a high-clearance vehicle; an ordinary car will do. The only exceptions are the nine rougher primitive roads that are still open to the public—the Lower and Upper Covington Flat Roads, Berdoo Canyon Road, Pinkham Canyon Road, and the lower end of the Thermal Canyon Road, all in the Little San Bernardino Mountains; the Geology Tour Road in Pleasant Valley; the Black Eagle Mine Road in the Eagle Mountains; and the Old Dale Road and Brooklyn Mine Road in Pinto Basin. Many miles of primitive roads also crisscross the BLM portion of the Pinto Mountains, including the Gold Crown Road and the Gold Park Road. Although a standard vehicle will get you part way up some of these rougher roads, all these roads are unmaintained and require high clearance, sometimes four-wheel drive as well, especially up in the mountains. A more rugged vehicle will also make such longer trips safer, and greatly increase your chances of reaching your destination. Clearance is generally more critical than power. Four-wheel-drive sedans often do not fair much better than a normal vehicle because they lack clearance. The higher clearance and greater power of a larger four-wheel-drive vehicle will also make it easier to drive over rough spots. Four-wheel drive and power combined are particularly critical to tackle roads with deep sand (as is commonplace in the Pinto Mountains) or steep and rocky grades (in the mountain canyons).

The most common breakdown on dirt roads is a flat tire. The cause is often nothing bigger than a tiny sharp pebble that gets rammed into the treads. SUVs and rental four-wheel-drive vehicles are particularly at risk because they are generally equipped with thinner city tires more prone to flats. If possible, rent a vehicle with heavy-duty tires—they are available from several places, in particular Yucca Valley.

The road conditions mentioned in this book assume dry weather. After a heavy rain, a primitive road can very quickly become muddy, flooded, or washed out, and be at least temporarily impracticable. If you are several miles out on a primitive road with a passenger car and it starts raining seriously, it is safest to drive back right away.

Inquire about road conditions before heading out. Some of the park's backcountry roads may be closed for a couple of days after a snow storm. A road may remain closed for several months if it gets washed out by heavy rains. Up-to-date information on road conditions is available on the park's website and from the local BLM offices.

Driving. The park's graded roads are generally wide, straight, and smooth, and they encourage a higher speed than is safe to travel. Sudden braking or swerving on a gravelly surface can result in hydroplaning, loss of control, overturning, and dangerously long braking distances. Respect the posted speed limit, or the common-sense safe speed of 30–35 mph if none is posted.

The incidence of a flat tire increases rapidly with speed. To minimize the risk, do not exceed 15 mph on primitive roads. Take a flat tire kit with you; it may fix the leak long enough to get you back to asphalt. Inspect your spare tire before each trip.

Whether your vehicle makes it over a poor road depends in part on your determination and willingness to push it. It may require plucking out rocks, filling in dips, trying different angles, and changing tires in high heat. If you are new at this, take enough short drives to get exposed to, and learn how to handle, large stones, sharp rocks, washboards, sand, crowns, tight spots, washouts, lopsided bedrock, encroaching vegetation, mud, water, and more. It may take dozens of trips to be ready for longer distances. Sand may be the most treacherous trap. A common scenario goes something like this: the car stops going forward, the wheels spin into soft ground, and bury themselves part way to the axles. As soon as the spinning starts, stop feeding gas. If you are on a slope, it is usually easy to get out of the soft spot by reversing the direction of travel or pushing your vehicle. On level ground, driving the car forward and backward repeatedly to acquire momentum can be effective. Otherwise, try to dig the wheels out. To this end, always keep in your trunk a shovel, a few sturdy boards or strips of carpet, and a jack. Dig a trench in front of the buried tires deep enough to jam a board underneath them for better traction, or jack up the car to slip a board, rocks, or a carpet underneath the tires, and slowly drive out of the ruts.

If your vehicle gets stuck or breaks down, either call 911 or a towing company, or wait for help to come to you if you have no cell phone or no reception. Unless you are certain that you can walk to help safely, stay with your vehicle: it is much easier for rescuers to spot a vehicle than a person. Weather permitting, open all doors to make your vehicle more visible (and to provide shade if need be). Use the horn and headlights for signals. Always keep in your vehicle plenty of water and food, flashlights, matches, a rope, jumper cables, a toolbox, flares, and a good book. Have proper sleeping gear as well in the winter: you must be able to survive overnight if it comes to that.

There are no gas stations in the park and in the areas surrounding its western half. Always top off your tank at the last gas station—even a gallon can later save the day. Monitor your gas gauge frequently. Drive back to a gas station well before it is too late.

Hiking Tips

Physical preparedness. The difficulties inherent to hiking in Joshua Tree National Park cover a very broad range, from very easy and level trails a fraction of a mile long to long scrambles up bouldery canyons and grueling treks up steep, trailless, rocky mountain slopes. While many hikes require no particular preparedness, just as many are much more strenuous than most people care to put up with, and being in excellent physical shape is essential. It even helps on easy hikes when the weather is very hot.

The message is: get in shape if you are not; make sure to stay in shape if you are. Hike near where you live once a week or more, covering occasionally the same distance and elevation change (if possible) as you plan to do in the desert. Cross train. Occasionally push yourself to assess your limits; it is safer to do this near home than in unfamiliar terrain. Make a habit of stretching before and after a hike. If you are pre-middle age it may well make no noticeable difference, but in the long run it reduces wear and tear on joints, tendons, and ligaments. It increases the chance that you will be able to hike at a higher level of difficulty later in your life. Use lightweight hiking boots, especially if you have weak ankles. Try shoes padded with air or a gel. Though not as sturdy, they are lighter and on long hikes they reduce joint pain.

If you are new to desert hiking, test yourself on short, easy walks. If possible, hike with a friend who knows the desert. Keep track of your water and food needs, tolerance to sun and heat, hiking speed and fatigue. If possible, hike along old roads rather than cross-country; even if it means a slightly longer route, it will likely be easier and possibly faster. Do not take risks that far exceed your abilities. Build up your endurance and slowly work up to more substantial hikes. It may take a few dozen outings to graduate to a challenging full-day hike.

Orienteering. The widespread use of GPS to navigate vehicles and humans has created a new breed of drivers who cannot get around town without a GPS, and hikers who cannot navigate in nature unaided. If their GPS gives out in the wild, because of poor reception, dead battery, or failure, they may not find their way back.

My humble advice to hikers who have not yet succumbed to the GPS addiction is to develop and use their own orienteering skills; and to those who have, to kick the habit once in a while to keep their sense of direction honed. Fortunately, vast portions of the desert are so wide open that orienteering is considerably easier than in regions with limited long-distance visibility. It is not uncommon to see your destination or its general vicinity from the start of a hike. All you have to do is locate your destination using a topographic map. If you do not know how to read topo maps and use a compass, take a crash course from a book or on-line, and practice on easy hikes. Always take a topo map with you, or a copy of the map supplied in this book (which often shows features not shown on the USGS topo, as well as the route). All USGS 7.5′ topographic maps are available on-line from store.usgs.org and other sources. Unless you intend to cover a good fraction of a map, you may want to take with you only photocopies of the targeted areas, or download what you need on your cell phone.

When out on a desert hike, look back early on and identify at least one landmark that will help you locate your vehicle when you return. A peak or a notch on the skyline is preferable because they can be seen until well after sunset. During the hike, memorize features you pass by—an unusual plant or outcrop—to give you the extra confidence that you are on the right path on your way back. Canyons can be troublesome because they limit your line of sight. When traveling uphill in a canyon, chances of wandering off into the wrong fork are surprisingly good. It can be a serious error if you are trying to get back to your car. Frequently keep good track of your location on your map.

Partly protected shaft at the Golden Bell Mine

Water needs. Surface water is rare in Joshua Tree. You need to carry your own water. How much depends on several factors, starting with the season and elevation. During the cooler months (approximately November through February), you need about as much water as in temperate regions. For any reasonable hiking distance, two quarts a day should be sufficient. The rest of the year, you will need more, possibly much more. Your water needs will depend on humidity, the amount of shade and wind, the length and difficulty of the outing, your clothing, and your metabolism. As a rule of thumb, when hiking on level ground in 100°F heat, allow a minimum of one quart per hour. You will need less while resting, about one or two cups per hour. On steep uphill slopes, you may need as much as two quarts per hour. This may seem like a lot of liquid to ingest, but do not underestimate this most vital body need. A common mistake is to think that you can personally get by with drinking less, and become dehydrated. If you have not done this before, monitor your water consumption safely, on short, easy walks. Slowly work up to longer hikes, increasing the water you take with you accordingly.

Water is dense. To complete a 10-hour hike in the summer you may need to start with 10 to 20 pounds of it on your back. The only redeeming feature is that your load will lighten up as you drink it and sweat it off, so that on the average you will be carrying only half what you start with. But this is still heavy, and it may adversely affect both your enjoyment and the distance you can cover. Being in excellent physical shape is again essential.

In hot weather, you lose minerals and salts through perspiration. To offset this loss, take multi-vitamin/mineral tablets, or drink a mineralized drink instead of straight water. The salts and minerals prevent your muscles from cramping, in particular your stomach, and after a tiring hike they help keep the water down.

Most surface water in the park is used by wildlife and likely biologically contaminated, in particular with giardia. If you must drink it, always purify it chemically or by boiling or filtering it. Always carry with you a vial of iodine pills, and make sure to know how to use them properly. These treatments do not get rid of minerals. Heavily mineralized water may upset your stomach (which may be preferable to heat exhaustion).

A good way to handle the water weight problem on multiple-day desert treks is to cache water ahead of time along your anticipated route. It is also useful on an out-and-back day hike: stash one third of your water after traveling one third of the total distance, and pick it up on your way back. Keep your water in appropriately sized containers. Make sure to retrieve all containers. Follow park rules by writing down on each container the drop-off and expected pick-up dates. Always keep a few gallons of water in your car for both human and vehicle emergency needs.

Food. While out on a long and/or demanding hike, eat small amounts of food often to keep your energy up. If you wait too long you might get too exhausted to feel like food. Bring a variety of foods—protein, carbs, nuts, cheese, bread, energy bars, dried fruit, banana, chocolate—and either listen to what your body is craving or experiment to determine what keeps you going the best. Keep in your car a good supply of food in a good cooler with plenty of ice. In summer, a 20-pound bag of ice will last about two days.

Hiking time. On fairly level cross-country terrain, count on hiking at about 80% of your normal speed on established trails, from a typical

3 mph to 2.5 mph. With a light daypack you can expect to cover 12 to 14 miles in an eight-hour day, including breaks. Allow additional time when climbing, about 15 minutes per 1,000 feet depending on the grade and obstructions. If you are carrying a heavier pack like a backpack, count on 1.5 to 2 mph, including breaks, less in hot weather, when you might need to rest 10 minutes or so every hour.

Scrambling and rock climbing. Some canyon routes require scrambling or technical climbing on dry falls or steep boulders. Rock climbing in remote areas can be dangerous. The best advice for novices is not to climb alone. In case of an accident, having a partner can save your life. Where one person finds it impossible to climb, two people can sometimes make it by helping each other. To this end, bring a short rope or webbing, and climbing shoes. Before climbing up, make sure that you can come back down, which is often more difficult. If a climb looks too difficult, look for a safer way around it. If none is available, turn around. Train closer to home under more controlled conditions to learn basic moves. Build up or maintain upper body strength.

Best seasons to visit. The best times to visit are dictated almost entirely by temperature. For most people the comfort zone in and around the park extends approximately from mid-October to mid-April, depending on elevation and personal tolerance for heat and cold. Consult the temperature charts in the first chapter to assess the times that suit you best. February through April is ideal. The blooming season is then in full swing, and wildlife is more active and abundant. The days are longer and more action-packed. Snow graces the higher summits. Early fall is a good second best. It offers fairly balanced diurnal and nocturnal temperatures, and the days are still relatively long. The fall often has a small pulse of wildflowers, mostly at higher elevations. Fall days also tend to be clear and not as windy. Both seasons are also best for photography because the sun is not so high in the sky.

Between these two best periods, from mid-November to mid-February it may not be very warm during the day, and it may freeze at night above a few thousand feet. The days are short, which reduces hiking and sightseeing time. To take best advantage of winter days, at such times consider hiking in the lower eastern areas of the park, and out of Coachella Valley. Conversely, between April and September the high desert is noticeably cooler than the low desert. When the temperature peaks above 100°F in Twentynine Palms, in the park above about 4,500 feet it is often "only" in the low 90s. The air is generally hazy, which is not ideal for photography. The best times are after a rainstorm has scrubbed the atmosphere; and on partly cloudy days or in evenings, when clouds and shadows add depth to the landscape.

As expected, two of the three peak tourist seasons coincide with this comfort zone: Easter and Thanksgiving, the third being the Christmas season. Increased visitation is quite noticeable then, especially in the western part of the park and in adjoining BLM lands.

Avoiding the crowds. Joshua Tree is a busy place. It is the backyard of half a million people, and relatively close to southern California's coastal megapolis. It is also a world-class rock-climbing destination, and the main attractions are confined to a fairly small area. In 2018 it received 2.94 million visitors. On a typical spring weekend, the line of cars at the busiest west entrance can be 45 minutes long. There is even a wait in the evening to exit the park. On the most popular trails, on just about any weekend it is rare not to see another hiker.

If you are looking for solitude or quiet time away from people and oversigned trails, seclusion is fortunately not very far. On busy days, try using the quieter north or south entrances. Avoid the Wonderland of Rocks. Take longer and/or trailless hikes. Select a hike in the far less visited eastern part of the park, which is permeated with a satisfying sense of remoteness. There the desert is still free of trails and signs, and you can have the pleasure of finding your own way.

Summer hiking tips. Of the few serious perils that await a hiker in the desert, three are more likely to occur than others: physical exhaustion, dehydration, and heat exhaustion. When hiking in challenging terrain in a hot and physically stressful environment, these three conditions tend to occur in unison, and it helps to think of them as one combined issue. The first manifestation of dehydration is thirst, a signal that your body has lost too much water (between 0.5 to 1 quart, depending on your weight) and needs to be hydrated. A subsequent signal is dark urine. Prolonged exposure to heat without sufficient drinking produces further water loss and may lead to heat exhaustion. Blood is then directed away from the brain to irrigate and cool the skin, resulting in excessive sweating, dizziness, tiredness, and vomiting. If water loss and exertion persist, a heat stroke may occur. Blood becomes too thick to be pumped fast enough through the body and glands stop producing sweat. The body's main cooling mechanisms essentially shut down. The symptoms are red, dry skin, headache, fever, dizziness, delirium, and nausea.

These warnings foreshadow trouble. Learn to recognize them, and take timely measures. Always take plenty of water with you. Do not wander into the desert without water, even for an intended short walk. Thirst lags behind your body's need for water, so do not wait until you are thirsty to drink. Drink every 15 minutes, even if you think you do not need to. At the first signs of dehydration, start drinking more right away. If you feel you are getting into the second stage of dehydration, rest in a place sheltered from the sun and wind. Drink plenty of mineralized water, at least a couple of quarts. Often this will restore sufficient strength to return to your vehicle. The third stage is a serious condition that requires prompt medical attention. In the meantime, keep your body cool in the shade, covered with wet clothes, if possible.

Other simple preventative measures help deal with the heat. Wear a wide-brimmed hat to reduce evaporation through your head and exposure to harmful ultraviolet radiation. Dress lightly, but do wear a light-colored long-sleeve shirt and long pants to insulate your body from the sun and wind and reduce water loss. Use high-strength sunblock and lip balm, liberally and often. Avoid hiking around midday. When it is windy, your rate of dehydration can be significantly higher. Drink more, and stay out of the wind during the hottest hours.

If you run out of water, and you are too far from potable water to reach it without getting in more trouble, check your map for springs, creeks, wells, guzzlers, and windmills. Use questionable spring water to soak your clothes and a headband to cool you down.

Winter hiking tips. In the winter in the mountains the mercury often dips into the low 30s or even 20s, and the wind chill can make it feel a lot colder. In the morning, there can be frost on the ground and the water in your bottle may not be entirely liquid. There can be snow and ice on the park's highest summits. Come as well prepared as for winter hiking in temperate regions. Take with you warm clothes, a warm sleeping bag and a tent even if you are not planning to camp, in case you get stranded overnight. Keep plenty of water and food in your vehicle, enough for a couple of days longer than your intended stay. While hiking, avoid protracted exposure to wet or cold without proper gear, which could lead to hypothermia. Be prepared for possible large daily temperature variations. Wear several layers, including a toasty jacket, gloves, a warm hat, and proper footwear. Symptoms of hypothermia include chills, shaking, upset stomach, and vomiting. If it happens not far from your vehicle, get back to it, turn the heater on high, change to warm dry clothes, drink hot liquids, and go take a long hot shower if possible. If out in the wild, get into your sleeping bag and tent, preferably with another warm body in it with you. Stay dry.

Winter days are deceptively short. In December the sun rises around 7 a.m. and sets around 4:30–5:00 p.m. For long hikes, get an early start. Bring a flashlight in case you return at dark.

Desert Hazards

Snakes. Of the park's many species of snakes, nine are venomous. The desert night snake and California lyre snake are mildly toxic and not considered dangerous to humans. The rattlesnakes are dangerous, and the ones to watch for. The red diamondback is mild tempered, rarely strikes unless pestered, and its venom is the least toxic. The Mojave rattlesnake is likely the most dangerous snake in the country. It is edgy and defensive, and its venom is highly toxic because it contains both hemotoxins and neurotoxins. Hemotoxins attack muscles and the circulatory system, and may cause loss of motor skills. Neurotoxins impair the nervous system and may result in breathing difficulties or heart failure. A Mojave bite is a severe injury, often fatal if not treated. Even the red diamondback's bite is serious. A bite can be painful, often at least temporarily disabling to the point of not being able to walk very far, and requires prompt medical attention.

Given all this, it is prudent to assume that they are all Mojave rattlesnakes. Learn to identify rattlesnakes in general, by the distinctive and obvious triangular head, narrow neck, rattles, and skin pattern. To reduce the chance of getting bitten, stay alert. Be even more alert when hiking into the wind: if there is a rattlesnake ahead of you, it may not smell you, and if it cannot smell you it cannot warn you. If you hear rattling (the sound of a loud cricket) but do not see the snake, stop, locate it by sound or sight, then move away from it. If you cannot spot it, take a small step on open ground and listen. If you are getting closer to it, the snake will crank up the volume. If you are moving away, it will soon reduce the rattling intensity. Above about 90°F rattlers do not survive long in full sun, and they hole up. It is then relatively safe to walk in full sun. But do not jump into an area, or reach up with your hands onto a rock surface, that you cannot see. That said, snakes are not numerous. Most snakes will move out of the way when approached. Unless provoked or cornered, even a rattler is more likely to warn you than strike. They are largely nocturnal; daytime encounters are rare. I see on average one every 300 miles or so of walking.

Mines. The park is pockmarked with literally hundreds of mine shafts, tunnels, and prospect holes. Although many of them have been capped with grates or meshing, on BLM land most of them have not. Many shafts lie wide open. Most tunnels are unsupported, and occasionally a tunnel will lead to a hidden shaft. Tunnels may be infected with hantavirus by rodents. The chance of getting in trouble is slight, but an accident could be fatal. To be safe, do not enter mine openings.

Wind. Persistent winds can cause irritability, anxiety, insomnia, and allergic reactions. They can also make hiking tedious and nights sleepless. If you are susceptible to these symptoms and high winds are forecast (which is relatively frequent), you might want to postpone your trip. If the wind keeps you awake at night, try driving to a higher elevation, a sheltered spot, or sleeping in your vehicle. During the day, use a scarf to protect your eyes and nose from wind-blown dust.

Flashfloods. Flashfloods can occur in narrow canyons, especially in summer. If you are planning to hike in one, consult the weather forecast. If a major storm is predicted, postpone your trip, use another route, or be very careful. Periodically inspect the sky up canyon, and stay alert for advance warnings such as rumbling sounds. If a storm catches you in a canyon, climb to higher ground. Keep an eye open for escape routes to places at least 10 feet above the wash. In narrow drainages always camp at least 20 feet above a main wash.

Insects and arachnids. Mosquitoes are not typically a problem. There is just not enough standing water for them to breed in numbers. However, in the spring or a few weeks after heavy rains, areas near valleys can be wet enough for gnats to be a nuisance. Black flies can also be a pest. Bring repellents if this is going to bother you.

Arachnids are seldom a problem either. Tarantulas tend to be harmless. I have spotted only three scorpions in my life, and no black widow or brown recluse. Ticks are more common and troublesome. Encounters occur almost exclusively in the warm season. They crawl on you slowly in search of the best spot, sometimes for a long time. When a tick starts digging, it feels like a prick. A tick must stay in you at least 24 hours to infect you with Lyme disease. Only a small percentage of ticks carry it. Learn to identify ticks; check your body and clothes carefully and often. Wearing long sleeves and pants helps. If you find a tick in you, do not pinch it to pull it out, which would flush its fluids into your body. Use a tick-removal tool, or cover it with oil to force it to come out. Save the tick's body to have it tested for disease.

Mountain lions. Mountain lions are rare in the park. They generally avoid contact with humans, but elsewhere they have occasionally attacked humans, so be watchful. Should you encounter a lion displaying hostility, do not approach it. Do not run away either, which might trigger a chase. Do all you can to appear as large as possible, by spreading out your arms or opening your jacket. Do not crouch or bend over. Speak firmly in a low voice. If attacked, fight back. On occasion, throwing stones has been effective.

Regulations

Because the park is heavily visited, regulations tighter than in other desert parks have been put in place both for the safety of visitors and to minimize impact on the park's fragile resources. This section summarizes the main rules and restrictions. Consult the park's website for additional information.

Park passes. To visit JTNP, a park pass is required. Passes can be purchased at the west and north entrance stations, at one of the park's three visitor centers, or on-line to skip the lines. A single-entry pass is valid seven consecutive days. An annual pass gives access to all NPS units for one year starting from the month of purchase, and a senior pass for a lifetime.

Off-road driving. To spare the land and wildlife, driving off roads is strictly prohibited in the park. On adjacent BLM lands, driving is allowed only on designated open roads. A road is open when a number is posted on a flexible stake at its start. A road *without* a sign is closed. Some open roads are unfortunately *not* signed, usually because someone removed the sign. To be on the safe side, keep track of your location using this book's descriptions and maps, or consult the BLM's sub-region maps, available on-line and posted at main access points.

Camping and campfires. Car camping is prohibited anywhere in the park, including in parking areas and along roadsides. To sleep overnight in the park, the only options are staying in a designated campground or backpacking. Backpacking is restricted to trails that start from one of the park's 13 backcountry boards. A permit is required. It is free, and easy to pick up and fill out at the trailhead. Do not camp within 1 mile of any road, 500 feet of a trail, in washes (to avoid flashfloods), and in day-use areas. On surrounding BLM lands, there is no camping permit or registration system.

Backcountry campfires are prohibited. To conserve the scant desert wood, the gathering of native wood, dead or alive, including kindling, is unlawful. So is burning lumber from historical structures. Camp stoves are allowed.

Garbage. Carry plastic bags and pack out all garbage; do not bury any of it, biodegradable or not. For human waste, dig a six-inch-deep hole, at least 300 feet from water, camp, and trails, and cover it after use. Pack out all toilet paper and hygiene products.

Day-use areas. Some popular areas, including the heart of the Wonderland of Rocks, are day-use only. These areas are clearly indicated on maps at trailheads and backcountry boards, and on the six general maps in this book.

Pets. Pets must be leashed at all times. They are prohibited on trails and beyond 100 feet of any road, campground, and picnic area.

Weapons. In the park the discharge of weapons is prohibited. This applies to firearms, air guns, bows and arrows, slingshots, and similar weapons. Traps are also not allowed.

Wildlife. Do not pester or harm wildlife. Feeding any wildlife is prohibited. Wild animals fed by humans tend to become dependent on this easy food source. They lose their ability to be self-sufficient and function properly in the wild, which puts their survival at risk. Some wild animals also carry communicable diseases, like rabies. Store all food and garbage in a manner that will prevent access by wildlife. If an animal comes begging for food, scare it away gently. For their own survival, they must learn that humans are their worst enemy.

Natural resources. Disturbing natural areas, and the removal of rocks, plants, or animals, are strictly prohibited in the park. Do not write on rocks or plants; this is punishable by law. In JTNP, building cairns, whether as "ornaments" or a marker, is prohibited.

Cultural resources. All cultural resources in the desert, under all jurisdictions, including historical structures (mines, mining camps, ghost towns, and railways) and archaeological sites, are protected by federal law. At historical sites, do not disturb, damage, burn, or remove anything, even the seemingly worthless bits of metal and wood lying around. The sea of broken artifacts littering many historic sites as a result of decades of vandalism is a sad reminder of the high cost of ignorance. Leave everything where you find it so others have the pleasure of discovering it too. Sanctions for breaking this law include jail time and/or hefty fines.

It is illegal and punishable by law to disturb, damage, or remove anything from archaeological sites. This applies to rock art (which tarnishes and wears under repeated contact and should never be touched), rock alignments (which lose their significance when disturbed), artifacts, and camps. These sites are part of the heritage of contemporary Native American tribes. They are important to their traditions, and many of them are sacred. Treat them with respect.

Wilderness Ethics

- Be considerate to others.
- When other hikers are nearby, speak quietly, or not at all. Do not play music out of a speaker; use earphones instead, leaving one ear free to listen for rattlesnakes and other possible imminent dangers.
- Avoid hiking in large groups. It violates the wilderness spirit, and it is hard on the fragile desert environment. Large groups are also more noisy and visible, which is unfair to other visitors.
- Do not beep your car when locking or unlocking it in campgrounds or at trailheads. Close each car door and the trunk only once while getting ready in the morning or at night. Respect quiet hours.
- Minimize the traces you leave behind. Most perennial desert plants are slow growers and slow healers, and important fodder or habitat for wildlife. Avoid stepping on or near them. To limit damage to the desert crust, walk in washes, on rocks, or on trails. Practice low-impact camping. Pack out what you pack in.
- Do not litter, even biodegradable material, which still can take a long time to decompose. It will be perceived as an intrusion by others, possibly for months to come.
- To minimize impact when car camping outside the park, select a campsite that has been previously used. Set up your tent off the road but leave your vehicle on the road if it does not block access.
- Use rocks as markers only when absolutely necessary and for *your* benefit only, and destroy them on your way back. They may otherwise mislead other hikers, and they take away from other hikers the pleasure of finding their own route.
- Do not build rock sculptures, or place rocks on top of rock formations or outcrops; they are visually intrusive.
- Do not write on rocks or plants.
- Drones are prohibited in the park and wilderness areas.
- Summit registers may be an endearing tradition, but they are also an intrusion into the wilderness. Like litter and graffiti, they violate the old adage—leave only footprints. Do not put up new registers.

■

— 5 —

WONDERLANDS OF ROCKS

The Wonderland of Rocks generally designates the park's most scenic region, roughly between Indian Cove to the north and Hidden Valley to the south. Because of the similarity in terrain and geology, by extension it refers here to the much larger mountainous mass encircled by Park Boulevard and Highway 62. It is bounded to the north by Morongo Basin, to the east by the Pinto Mountains, to the south by Queen Valley and Lost Horse Valley, and to the west by the Little San Bernardino Mountains. By conventional standards, it does not look like a mountain. Once a taller range, it has been reduced by erosion to what is today much closer to a fragmented sloping plateau. But the same erosional forces that wore it down have also sculpted what remains into a vast playground of fantastically shaped hoodoos, tens of square miles packed with smooth domes, slickrock, spires, buttes, and boulder piles immersed in green desert gardens. It is one of the most fascinating landscapes in the American West. No other area in the Mojave Desert holds bare-rock moonscapes so diverse, so extensive, and so spectacular. This unique wonderland defines Joshua Tree National Park more vividly than its emblematic Joshua trees.

Geology

The majority of the Wonderland of Rocks is made of White Tank Monzogranite, the priceless Late-Cretaceous formation without which the park would just not be the same. The rest of it, occupying a square block at the northeastern corner of the range north from Queen Mountain, is mostly Queen Mountain Monzogranite (Early Cretaceous), with an island of Oasis Monzogranite (Late Cretaceous) west of Joshua Mountain, and a fringe of Twentynine Palms Megacrystic Quartz Monzonite (Jurassic) overlooking Twentynine Palms. Small outcrops of Proterozoic gneiss are scattered throughout the range. The park's most photogenic spots—Indian Cove, Hidden Valley, Jumbo Rocks, White Tank, among others—are underlain by the smooth, light-colored, fine-grained White Tank pluton. The Queen Mountain Monzogranite is a close second: this hard, fractured, slightly darker stock is responsible for the extensive region of bald domes and cliffs on and north of Queen Mountain.

Slashed by deep parallel trenches, the Wonderland of Rocks is a giant labyrinth of interlaced canyons. One set of trenches is oriented approximately northwest, the other at about 60 degrees, roughly east-northeast. Like in Canyonlands' Maze or Zion National Park's Virgin River canyon system, this symmetric topography probably developed from internal stresses that built up in the rock. Later uplifting applied tensions that caused the range to snap preferentially along these weaker stress planes. When you hike on Wonderland Plateau or in Indian Cove's orthogonal canyons, you trace these ancient fault lines.

The proliferation of equally symmetric arrangements of jointed boulders and fractured walls has the same origin, on a smaller physical scale. Compressive stresses broke the rock along conjugate joints, two sets of parallel cracks at a 60-degree angle. Horizontal fractures also develop as erosion removes surface rock and the underlying granite stock floats back up, like a ship when unloading its cargo. The Wonderland of Rocks' deeply carved landscape results from differential chemical and mechanical weathering along these countless fractures. It took place mostly between the Miocene and Quaternary, when the climate was wetter and cooler. Percolating surface water decomposed bedrock preferentially along these joints, breaking it into piles of giant boulders. These buried structures were eventually uplifted, exposed by top-soil erosion, and further sculpted by rain, wind, and frost-heat cycles. Erosion progresses considerably faster on exposed corners and edges, the reason for countless spheroidal boulders. The Wonderland of Rocks' stunning visual appeal lies in the pleasing symmetry it inherited from conjugate joints—rows of look-alike pinnacles, cliffs slashed by repetitive patterns of cracks, or towers of boulders with similar shapes.

As erosion proceeded, the range's southern front, along Queen Mountain, receded northward, gradually shedding off the pediment surfaces that became Lost Horse Valley and Queen Valley immediately south of it. Both valleys are prime examples of the vestigial planed bedrock ground down during the removal of a mountain. The other-

Carved inselberg and juniper along Split Rock Loop

worldly inselbergs strewn across them are the harder core stones that have, so far, survived erosion.

Botany

This contorted geography gave us another gift, somewhat difficult to reconcile with a desert—a remarkable vegetation. Big vertical rocks create small spaces with shade, greater moisture, and relative protection from the wind. As a result of this serendipitous combination and of the relatively high elevation, the vegetation in the Wonderland of Rocks is among the densest, greenest, and most diverse at this altitude in the Mojave Desert. Very different plant zones co-exist in the same area in some free-for-all botanical nirvana. Low-desert creosote, catclaw, and silver cholla grow next to mid-elevation species like yucca, nolina, oak, and Joshua trees, and plants found normally at higher elevations, like conifers. Nearby mountains hundreds of feet taller do not support a single evergreen.

Almost every type of cactus that lives in the park can be found in the Wonderland of Rocks, even the less common cushion foxtail cactus. Even plants that tend to prefer the Sonoran Desert are comparatively common. The two worlds, mineral and vegetal, compliment each other

Old pickup truck near Wall Street Mill

in stunning visual harmony, the green vegetation enhanced by the pale monuments of sculpted granites, the bareness of the stones softened by the extravagant vegetation.

Rock Climbing and Natural Resources Protection

With such a profusion of smooth, cohesive, high-quality vertical surfaces laced with crevasses, pits, knobs, holes, pimples, and indentations for powerful fingers and nimble toes to cling to, the Wonderland of Rocks has been for decades a world-class climbing site. Any serious climber has skinned knuckles on White Tank Monzogranite. This popularity stems not only from the incredible selection of climbing routes (in excess of 8,000), but also from the broad spectrum of difficulties, and from the setting at the heart of superb scenery. The park's proximity to two enormous urban centers also contributes greatly to the heavy use. In 2010, in 29% of polled parties of visitors at least one person participated in rock climbing activities in either the current visit or past visits. In a subset of these respondents, nearly all climbed in the Wonderland of Rocks. Scaled to the 2024 visitation level, these figures suggest that at least 300,000 people climb in this range every year. At many places, especially around Hidden Valley, Indian Cove, and Jumbo Rocks, you are very likely to run into climbers.

To protect wildlife and other natural resources from this heavy visitation, in particular bighorn sheep, who are easily displaced by prolonged human activity, most of this range is day use only. The only portions that are not are the extreme southeastern tip (roughly south from Pine City), and the west end (west from the Boy Scout Trail).

Mining and Ranching History

In historic times, the Wonderland of Rocks had about a dozen mines, almost all in the southern range, almost all seeking gold with a lining of silver. None of them made it big, except for one, the Desert Queen, and it did so well that it became one of the park's most productive mines. Over its 60-year lifespan following its discovery in 1894, it made a small mint in gold in the late 1890s, then was run intermittently by a long list of owners, lessees, and scavengers. Ore was mined from at least eight tunnels, six shafts, and more than 1,800 feet of galleries. It produced a total of around $80,000, most of it prior to 1900.

The only other mine with a known production, albeit approximate, is the Anaconda, at the range's eastern rim. First opened prior to 1900, it was owned during most of its active life by Twentynine Palms early homesteader Phil Sullivan. It was operated off and on until at least 1930, and had enough ore to warrant an on-site two-stamp mill, then in 1908 a larger mill in town. In 1922 a permit was even issued to sell company stock. In its life, the Anaconda Mine's two shafts produced at least $10,000 worth of gold and far outperformed most local mines.

In the mid 1890s, the McHaney brothers operated a ranch in a secluded canyon at the southwestern edge of the range. It was for many years the headquarters of their cattle ranging business and mining operations at the Desert Queen Mine. After they left in 1916, Bill Keys acquired the property and developed a homestead on an 80-acre parcel. After he married Frances Lawton in 1918, the couple lived and raised a family on what became known as Keys Ranch. They survived in what was then an isolated wilderness by ranching, farming, mining, securing reliable water sources, and leasing reclaimed mines. Through patience, hard work, and self-reliance, they built a unique self-sustained desert empire that perdured until the 1960s.

Hiking

The Wonderland of Rocks offers a seemingly endless selection of outdoor pursuits, countless canyons splitting into side canyons that radiate into more side canyons, water-carved narrows, sharp hills of gargantuan boulders, scenic coves wrapped in sculpted cliffs, and the most breathtaking collection of hoodoos on this side of southern Utah. There are also a few scattered springs, small artificial lakes left over from the ranching days, and palm groves, two at Fortynine Palms Oasis, and one at the Oasis of Mara behind the park headquarters. This

Suggested Hikes in the Wonderland of Rocks					
Route/Destination	Dist. (mi)	Elev. gain	Mean elev.	Difficulty	Page
Short hikes (under 5 miles round trip)					
Arrastra Canyon (1)	2.8	320'	3,570'	Class 2	165
Bagley's Ranch (1)	0.7	40'	4,290'	Very easy	119
Barker Dam (1)	1.4	60'	4,260'	Very easy	115
Contact Mine	2.0	770'	3,200'	Easy-mod.	91
Desert Queen Mine (1)	1.8	350'	4,410'	Easy	147
Eagle Cliff Mine	1.8	860'	4,440'	Easy-mod.	153
East Queen Mountain	2.0	1,260'	4,810'	Difficult	133
Face Rock	0.9	330'	4,320'	Very easy	157
Fortynine Palms Canyon	1.6	630'	2,480'	Easy-mod.	83
Fortynine Palms Oasis (trail)	1.6	720'	2,900'	Easy-mod.	83
Garrett's Arch	1.9	290'	2,330'	Easy	126
Gunsight Canyon	0.75	560'	3,520'	Class 2	67
Hidden Valley Nature Tr. (1)	1.1	130'	4,220'	Very easy	111
Hidden Valley (lower) (1)	2.5	230'	4,150'	Easy	112
Indian Cove Nature Trail (1)	0.65	70'	3,300'	Very easy	75
Johns Camp	1.2	160'	3,890'	Very easy	161
Joshua Mountain	1.4	1,190'	2,950'	Mod.-diff.	87
North Canyon (fall)	1.2	410'	3,790'	Easy	95
Pine City	1.6	200'	4,500'	Very easy	137
Pine City Viewpoint	2.0	290'	4,520'	Very easy	137
Pine Spring	2.1	400'	4,490'	Easy	137
Pinto Wye Arrastra	1.0	230'	3,640'	Easy	165
Queen Mountain	2.0	1,230'	4,810'	Difficult	133
Rattlesnake Canyon				Class 2	
to top of 100-foot slot	0.6	210'	3,070'	Moderate	77
to caves	1.3	560'	3,230'	Difficult	77
to Willow Hole	2.4	1,060'	3,520'	Strenuous	82
Sneakeye Spring Canyon				Class 2	
Foot of upper ravine	0.6	400'	3,450'	Difficult	71
Summit cove	1.0	780'	3,570'	Strenuous	71
South Astro Dome	1.1	160'	4,310'	Easy	123
Split Rock Loop (1)	2.4	330'	4,300'	Very easy	157
Wall Street Mill	0.8	70'	4,300'	Very easy	129

Key: (1) Loop; (2) HC or 4WD access road
Distances: one way for out-and-back hikes, round-trip for loops
Elev. gain: sum of all elevation gains on the round-trip/loop

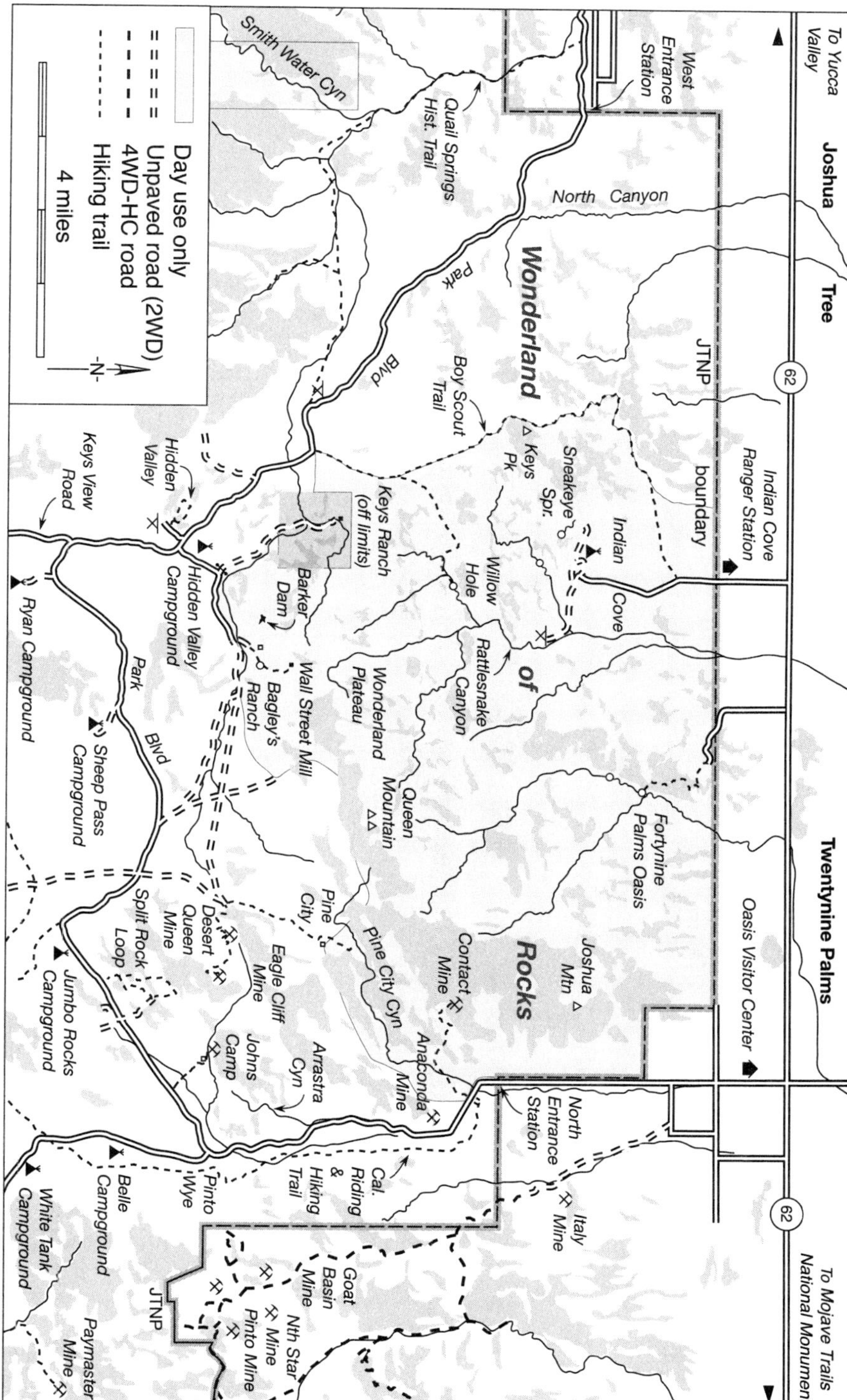
To Yucca Valley
Joshua Tree
Twentynine Palms
To Mojave Trails National Monument
62
West Entrance Station
Indian Cove Ranger Station
Oasis Visitor Center
North Entrance Station
Quail Springs Hist. Trail
Smith Water Cyn
North Canyon
JTNP
JTNP boundary
Park Blvd
Wonderland of Rocks
Boy Scout Trail
Keys Pk
Sneakeye Spr.
Indian Cove
Willow Hole
Keys Ranch (off limits)
Barker Dam
Rattlesnake Canyon
Wonderland Plateau
Wall Street Mill
Bagley's Ranch
Hidden Valley
Hidden Valley Campground
Keys View Road
Ryan Campground
Sheep Pass Campground
Queen Mountain
Fortynine Palms Oasis
Joshua Mtn
Contact Mine
Pine City
Pine City Cyn
Desert Queen Mine
Split Rock Loop
Eagle Cliff Mine
Jumbo Rocks Campground
Johns Camp
Arrastra Cyn
Anaconda Mine
Cal. Riding & Hiking Trail
Pinto Wye
Belle Campground
White Tank Campground
Italy Mine
Goat Basin Mine
Nth Star Mine
Pinto Mine
Paymaster Mine
Day use only
Unpaved road (2WD)
4WD-HC road
Hiking trail
4 miles
N

Suggested Hikes in the Wonderland of Rocks (Ctn'd)					
Route/Destination	Dist. (mi)	Elev. gain	Mean elev.	Difficulty	Page
Intermediate hikes (5–12 miles round trip)					
Keys Peak	3.6	640'	4,120'	Class 2	105
North Canyon	2.5	900'	3,520'	Class 5	95
Pine City Canyon	5.6	1,840'	3,860'	Class 3	141
Willow Hole	3.7	340'	4,100'	Easy-mod.	107
Long hikes (over 12 miles round trip)					
Boy Scout Trail					
Park Blvd to Indian Cove	8.1	1,900'	3,770'	Very diff.	99
Indian Cove to overlook	3.5	1,290'	3,340'	Moderate	99
Park Blvd to overlook	4.6	610'	4,090'	Moderate	99
Key: (1) Loop; (2) HC or 4WD access road Distances: one way for out-and-back hikes, round-trip for loops Elev. gain: sum of all elevation gains on round-trips and on loops					

relatively small corner of the park is filled with so many wonders that it is where most visitors spend most of their time. There are, as a result, more foot trails in this range than any other area of the park. A downside of this popularity is that many trails have been grossly oversigned, even in wilderness areas, which has greatly diminished their natural character. Some of the less impacted trails are described in the following pages. Many others, like the Maze-Window Loop, were left out, although they will likely appeal to novices not yet ready to face unmarked desert trails on their own.

This range also has many interesting historic sites. A well-preserved mill can be found at the Wall Street Mill, mill foundations at the Anaconda Mine and Gold Hill Mine, obsolete mining equipment at the Desert Queen Mine and Contact Mine, and a delightful miner's cave at the Eagle Cliff Mine. The pièce de resistance is undeniably Keys Ranch's well-preserved homestead. Off limits to visitors except on regular ranger-led hikes, it offers a fascinating glimpse at the lifestyle of early settlers, and at the skills, ingenuity, and tenacity that it took to survive the hardships of the desert a century ago.

■

GUNSIGHT CANYON

Most of the popular destinations in the Wonderland of Rocks are reached by either a convenient open wash or a manmade trail. Yet in the majority of this range, the only way to get around is scrambling along ravines of giant boulders. Gunsight Canyon is a good example of this extreme topography. A 2-mile canyon draining from the high plateau west of the Wonderland of Rocks into Indian Cove, it is in its upper reaches an easy-going sand river, until it comes to the cove's precipitous brink and plummets down a boulder-clogged gorge. Scaling this challenging trench up from Indian Cove is a lot of fun, and it gives access to wild and awe-inspiring scenery.

General Information
Road status: Cross-country hiking; graded access road
The Slit: 0.35 mi, 180 ft up, 40 ft down one way / moderate (Class 2)
Upper wash: 0.75 mi, 520 ft up, 40 ft down one way / moderate (Class 2)
Main attractions: A canyon of giant boulders, boulder caves, conifers
USGS 7.5' topo map: Indian Cove
Maps: pp. 69

Location and Access

Gunsight Canyon and the next three destinations are accessed from Indian Cove, on the north side of the Wonderland of Rocks, which is reached via its own dead-end paved road. From Adobe Road in the center of Twentynine Palms, drive Highway 62 west 5.8 miles to the signed Indian Cove Road. Coming from the town of Joshua Tree, this intersection is 9.2 miles east of Park Boulevard. Turn south on Indian Cove Road (right turn coming from Joshua Tree) and drive 3.0 miles to a T junction. Turn right, and work your way (slowly to minimize dust and noise) through the Indian Cove Campground. Park where the graded road loops back at the campground's west end.

In the summer, the road through the campground is closed; from the highway go only 2.7 miles to the graded group-campground road on the right, which is open. Drive it west 0.6 mile to its end, and park. If you start from the group campground, look for a use trail between sites 11 and 12. Follow it 0.15 mile to the Indian Cove Nature Trail, and make a left. The nature trail will take you in 0.2 mile to a junction. Turn left and in 30 yards you will reach the loop at the end of the campground road.

The Gunsight (left of center) seen from the lower canyon

Route Description

From the loop, Gunsight Canyon is the V-shaped notch in the skyline straight ahead, to the southwest. To get to its mouth, walk the dirt road past the boulders that block the end of the parking loop. After 0.1 mile, take one of the use trails down the hillside to the right, to the wash visible at the bottom of the hill. Use the main trail to minimize damage. This should put you right at the mouth of Gunsight Canyon. On the way there the Gunsight pops into view, a tall obelisk that points skyward in the V of the canyon—the canyon's namesake.

Right away Gunsight Canyon revs up into high gear. You find yourself at the foot of a wash so steep that it has been subsumed under a staircase of giant boulders. They overwhelm the narrow bottom of a superb trench of granite framed on one side by a long sculpted wall, on the other by a chaotic slope crowded with hoodoos. Every surface is rounded into silky, pale beige monzonite, the seductive signature of Joshua Tree. In this stone monopoly, oaks and pinyon pines managed to find purchase and thrive, as if to heighten the smoothness and paleness of the rocks with their shaggy emerald-green heads.

From its mouth, the canyon first goes up its steepest section for 0.2 mile; then it makes a lazy zigzag and continues 0.55 mile to the upper end of the boulder run. The wash is exposed only a few times, and very briefly. The boulders are often a few layers deep. Much of the

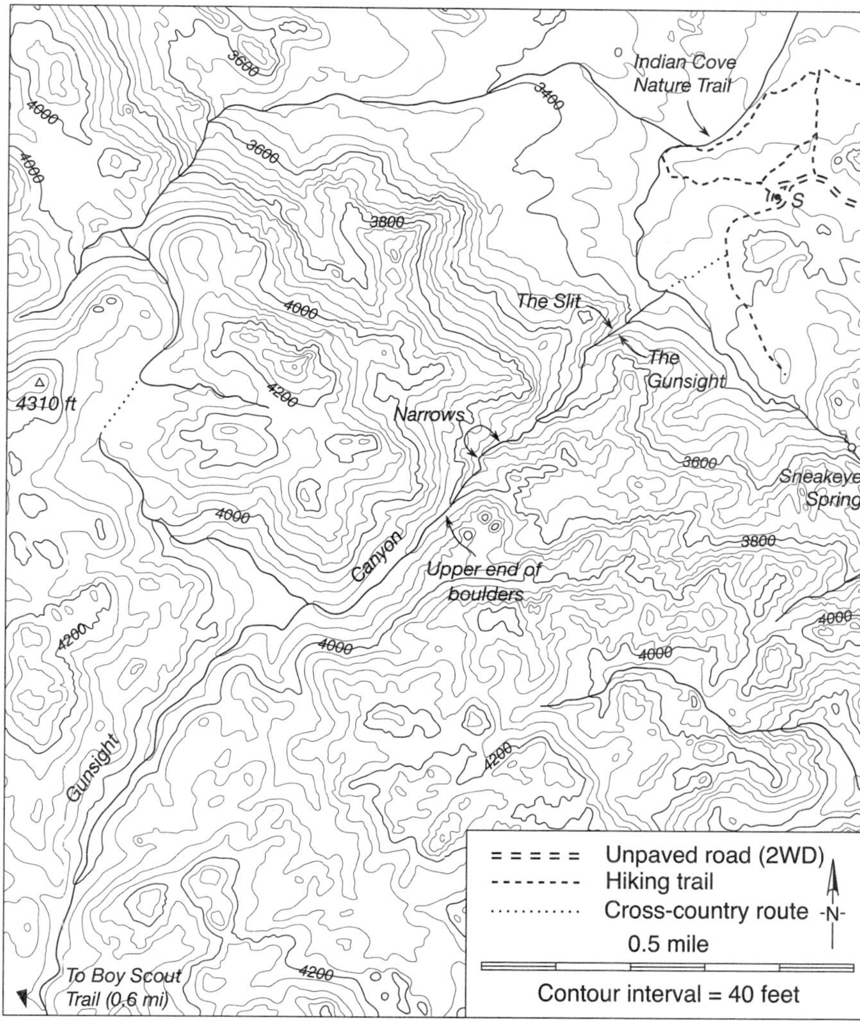

Gunsight Canyon		
	Dist.(mi)	Elev.(ft)
Loop at end of campground	0.0	3,334
Leave road	0.1	3,380
Wash at mouth of canyon	0.2	3,340
The Gunsight / The Slit	0.35	3,470
Top of steep section	0.4	3,510
Narrows (start)	0.55	3,670
End of boulders	0.75	3,810

The Slit

time you do not get to walk: you hop. When you can't hop, you scramble; when scrambling is not an option either, you climb. If you all fails, you try another route, which is half the fun!

Even in this place of superlatives, nature has managed to sprinkle a few extra gems. In the steepest first section, the river that once tumbled through the canyon polished in bedrock a narrow slide of potholes. Further up, just past the Gunsight, it opened up a small fault into the Slit, a tall crack trapped between wavy walls. Boulders wedged in its high ceiling cast a restful penumbra. Above this section, the grade lessens a bit but the boulders are occasionally in collusion with shrubs to challenge progress. The high-rising east slope is bristling with eerie clusters of fins all slanted at gravity-defying angles. The facing wall is a towering dome splintered by swarms of vertical fractures. Twice you duck and squeeze under gargantuan overhanging boulders. Not far before the end of the boulder run, water has carved narrows with scooped bedrock and pools of sand.

Yet the best might be the caves. Some boulder piles are so huge that they form cavities tall enough to stand. Sometimes a cave will go through and taper to a tight opening where you wiggle, stem, and mantle your way back out into sunlight. Oddly enough, in this dazzling outdoors it is this secret underworld that holds the strongest appeal—the caves, the slits, the overhangs, the tight spaces where the land has folded upon itself and you are surrounded by more rock than sky.

It easily takes a few hours to explore this breathtaking place. You may not be on the move the whole time. Sitting on a monolith or under a shady pine, you may find yourself spellbound by yet another irresistible scenery and linger long moments while staring in a daze.

■

SNEAKEYE SPRING CANYON

The main reason for coming here is not the spring—it is now almost inexistent—but the challenge of conquering the cascade of giant boulders that clog the steep ravine where it is located, and the pleasure of discovering the little valley filled with cacti that is tucked above it. Scrambling up through the boulder-choked upper canyon will take you to a secluded cove surrounded by weathered domes on the high rim. Nearby Gunsight Canyon is a little less intense; if unsure, try it first.

General Information
Road status: Hiking on trails and cross-country; graded access road
Sneakeye Spring: 0.5 mi, 260 ft up, 60 ft down one way / diff. (Class 2)
Summit cove: 1.0 mi, 720 ft up, 60 ft down one way / strenuous (Class 2)
Main attractions: A short canyon filled with giant boulders, botany
USGS 7.5' topo map: Indian Cove
Maps: pp. 73*, 65

Location and Access

Sneakeye Spring Canyon cuts into the southwest corner of Indian Cove just east of Gunsight Canyon. Where they exit the mountain, the washes of the two canyons merge and become the main drainage on the west side of the cove. Refer to *Gunsight Canyon* for directions.

Route Description

At the parking at the southwestern tip of the loop, a rutted and bumpy track climbs south by southwest up a ridge of hard-packed dirt. It ends in 0.3 mile at an overlook with an intimidating view ahead of a steep mountain slope drained by a shallow ravine, all of it smothered under a tumble of gigantic boulders. The ravine is the lower end of Sneakeye Spring Canyon. Although its exact location is no longer certain, the spring itself is part way up it, among the pockets of oak and pinyon pine scattered on its west flank. To get to it, there is no option but to scramble up across this tsunami of megastones.

From the viewpoint, a use trail on the left curves down to the thick oasis of catclaw and oak at the mouth of the ravine. From there to the top of the ravine, it is a short 0.3 mile with an elevation gain of just 210 feet, or a decent 16% slope, but it is hard work. Many of the boulders are 8 feet across or bigger. Boulders small enough to hop on are a minority. You touch gravel at only half a dozen places, and not for long. The rest of the time, you levitate on solid rock an unknown distance above ground. It requires agility and upper-body strength. Some boulders are broad and smooth, and friction is the only means of getting over them. Others have sub-angular top edges that make good handholds. There is exposure at a few places; it can be minimal if you choose your route well. Plants are fortunately few, although you may have to negotiate with a couple of catclaw and oak. In the summer, the rocks are too hot to touch for long, especially when pressing hard on them to mantle. At one point, my best option other than losing hard-earned elevation was to crawl under a boulder that would not fit in my living room. I moved cautiously, acutely aware that if I were a rattlesnake, this shelter a good 15 degrees cooler than the surface is exactly where I would want to hang out.

Sculpted cliffs

Like a rite of passage, this rigorous traverse ushers you into a hidden world permeated with isolation and a strange kind of beauty. The boulders are shaped by simple, well-rounded curves, and displayed with a harmony that suggests art more than the randomness of nature. The low-ceilinged caves deep beneath them are lit in pale shades of blue and gold by strips of sunlight funneled between slender gaps. Halfway up, the ravine levels off briefly at a striking wall sliced in a textbook grid of 60-degree conjugate joints. As you gain elevation, Indian Cove's outrageous stony crags gradually come into view, backed in the distance by Twentynine Palms. The cove's abrupt slopes and peaks bristle with tight ranks of pinnacles, all oddly stretched skyward at the same canted angle as if drawn by the light, a landscape more surreal than augmented reality.

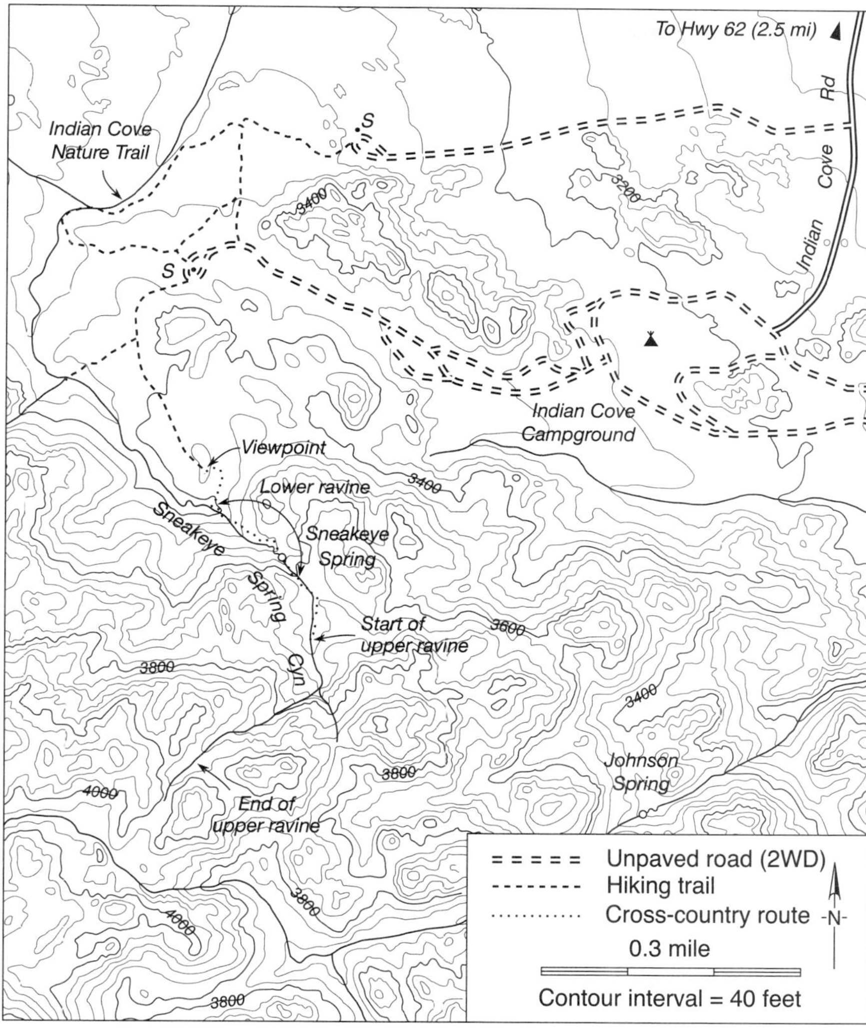

Sneakeye Spring Canyon

	Dist.(mi)	Elev.(ft)
West end of campground road	0.0	3,334
Viewpoint at end of dirt track	0.3	3,440
Canyon mouth	0.35	3,395
Sneakeye Spring	~0.5	~3,540
Top of lower ravine	0.55	3,600
Foot of upper ravine	0.6	3,620
Head	~1.0	3,990

Diced wall just below Sneakeye Spring

At the top of the lower ravine the boulders let up and you emerge into a nearly level, more open canyon. The sandy wash hosts a brilliant flora of catclaw and yucca, barrel and calico cacti, and large patches of prickly-pear. It wanders a short distance among scenic steep-sided hills of boulders festooned with oak, to the base of the upper ravine. This is a peaceful spot, shielded from the rest of the world, and a good turning point if you have had your fill of scrambling.

Twice as long as the lower ravine, and nearly twice as tall, the upper ravine crosses even more challenging terrain. It is chock-full of boulders all the way to the crest, without a single break. The boulders are imposingly large, several over 20 feet long, especially in the narrower gully near the top. It is a fun scramble, but it is hard work, with some exposure depending on your route. Patience helps too: you try a passage that looks promising, come to an impassable spot, and retrace your steps to try another way. It may take over an hour to cross this ridiculously short space. At the very top, the canyon opens up suddenly onto a beautiful cove of sand and trees cocooned in a ring of low granitic domes. Compared to the terrain you just crossed, this idyllic enclave seems abnormally serene. Like the upper ravine, it commands dramatic vistas, an inspiring spectacle that epitomizes both the vastness and the magnificence of this very special range.

■

INDIAN COVE NATURE TRAIL

The Indian Cove Nature Trail is a popular short loop that samples a scenic embayment encircled by spectacular mountains near the Indian Cove Campground. Vegetated with a wide variety of cacti, grasses, perennial shrubs, small trees, and spring flowers, this is a good place to learn to identify the local plants with the help of interpretive signs while admiring the ragged Wonderland of Rocks.

General Information

Road status: Hiking on trail; graded access road
Indian Cove Nature Trail: 0.65 mi, 70 ft up loop/very easy
Main attractions: Short trail, botany, scenic ring of sculpted mountains
USGS 7.5′ topo map: Indian Cove
Maps: pp. 73*, 65

Location and Access

The Indian Cove Nature Trail starts at the west end of the Indian Cove Campground. Refer to *Gunsight Canyon* for directions.

Route Description

The Indian Cove area is the most convoluted of the park's most convoluted range. When you drive up to it on the park's access road, its tightly chiseled, miles-wide skyline rears up as if it had just boiled out of the Earth. On the map, the contour lines look like the doodlings of a lunatic. On the ground, the mountains are a labyrinth carved out of a cubic mile of plutonic rock, an entanglement of sheer buttes, fallen blocks, and trenches oriented in all directions, all conspiring to cut you off. The right of passage is hard to earn. You may come out of there without understanding exactly how you got through.

Indian Cove Nature Trail		
	Dist.(mi)	Elev.(ft)
Trailhead	0.0	3,334
Wash	0.15	3,300
Trail leaves wash	0.35	3,280
Trail junction (right)	0.55	3,320
Back to trailhead	0.65	3,334

Indian Cove skyline at sunset from the nature trail

When walking the Indian Cove Nature Trail, you get to enjoy this sumptuous spectacle from a distance, without sweating the hard work. The trail is nearly level, well marked by interpretive signs, free of obstacles. It first goes gently down a creased bench to a wide shallow wash, follows it downstream, then exits it and circles back across the bench. Even in this landscape of minimal relief, plants express surprisingly strong geographical preferences. The bench vegetation is mostly dry and prickly—creosote, chollas, ephedra, Mojave yucca, and stiff grasses. In the wash, the ground humidity is only slightly higher, yet the dominant plants are almost entirely different. The sand is flushed with disconcertingly green thickets of manzanita, oak, catclaw, desert almond, and desert willow. Wildlife likes this spot. We saw zebra-tailed lizards, jackrabbits, ground squirrels, a Le Conte's thrasher, and the den of a desert tortoise. As you circle the trail, different parts of the surrounding mountains come into closer view, jagged, fractured, lacerated, and capped with spires, all competing for extravagance.

Except during summer closure, most nights the campground is home to a transient population of a few hundred people. The best time to find peace on this walk is dawn, when everyone is still asleep, and the pale light of morning holds the sweet promise of new beginnings.

■

RATTLESNAKE CANYON

Rattlesnake Canyon crosses one of the roughest and most scenic regions of the already famously rough and scenic Wonderland of Rocks. The sedate lower canyon leads through great boulder stacks to a river-carved 100-foot slot where a creek occasionally flows in the cooler season. The upper canyon above it is more convoluted than a brain. Exploring it, including the spectacular Class-2 traverse to Willow Hole, requires serious scrambling, excellent orienteering skills, and a healthy dose of stamina. I have returned to Rattlesnake Canyon many times, and the magic has not worn thin.

General Information
Road status: Roadless; standard-clearance graded access road
Top of slot: 0.6 mi, 200 ft up, 10 ft down one way / moderate
The caves: 1.3 mi, 560 ft up, 20 ft down one way / strenuous
Willow Hole: 2.4 mi, 1,030 ft up, 30 ft down one way / strenuous
Main attractions: A water-carved canyon with boulders, creek, & caves
USGS 7.5' topo map: Indian Cove
Maps: pp. 81*, 65

Location and Access

Rattlesnake Canyon cuts through the heart of the Wonderland of Rocks and emerges in the southeastern corner of Indian Cove, the usual point of entry into it. From Adobe Road in the center of Twentynine Palms, drive Highway 62 5.8 miles west to the signed Indian Cove Road. Coming from Joshua Tree, this intersection is 9.2 miles east of Park Boulevard. Turn south (left coming from Twentynine Palms) on Indian Cove Road and drive 2.95 miles to the T junction just before the Indian Cove Campground. Turn left on a graded road and go 1.2 miles to the small loop at the end. Rattlesnake Canyon is the obvious break in the bouldery mountain front up ahead to the south.

Route Description

The lower canyon. Rattlesnake Canyon is popular, but most visitors do not go very far. You would not know it at first. Where it enters the mountain, just beyond the road, it is a peaceful avenue of sand. The scenery is pure Wonderland of Rocks, extreme in its audacity. The Earth has thrust itself upward and snapped into long, parallel, sheer-sided spines of bare granite hundreds of feet high. Hordes of cracks

Potholes at the base of the slot in lower Rattlesnake Canyon

have sliced them into staggered stacks of boulders, and gravity wreaked havoc rearranging the loose pieces. Boulders are suspended on inclines, balanced on shelves, crammed in ravines, and lying at their final resting place beside the wash. At a few places boulders have encroached on the wash. They were shed by a Triassic pluton perched on the canyon's east flank called Twentynine Palms and famous in geology circles for the size of its megacrystals. Some boulders are a solid mass of feldspar crystals up to 2 inches long. Soon after, the wash bends sharply left and passes by a green spring of mesquite and fragrant sumac. By then, less than half a mile out, the end of the easy part of Rattlesnake Canyon looms in full sight up ahead, a 100-foot-tall shield of steep slickrock that fiercely blocks the way.

This is a sight to remember. Bedrock swells abruptly out of the ground in a grand sweep of White Tank Monzogranite, the same elegant formation that makes up this bright and furious landscape. Eons ago, a raging river ran through the canyon. This massive monolith was in the river's way, but it could not hold back the water. Over time the river gouged out a vertical slot right down the middle of it. Water exploded down the slot in a ladder of waterfalls, choking through the

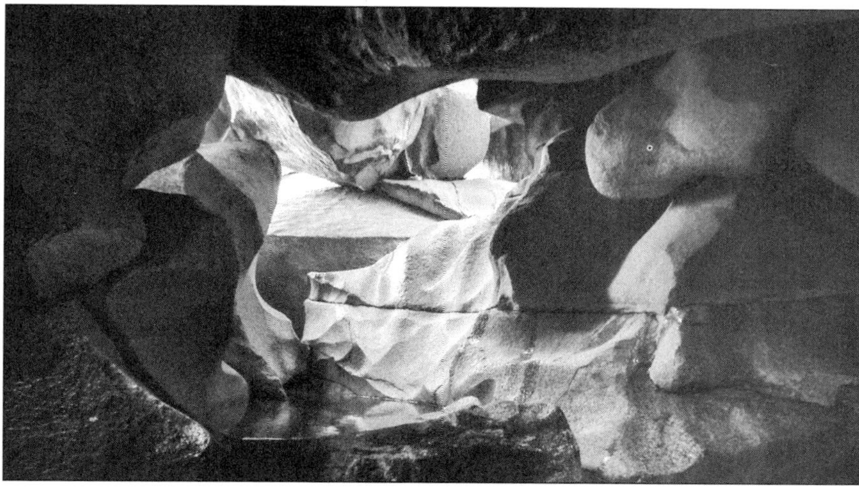

Flooded boulder cave in south fork of Rattlesnake Canyon
Photo by/credit to: Stav Basis (stavislost.com)

tight space and churning powerful eddies. The slot's floor was etched into a lacework of deep potholes so closely spaced that today there is no room to walk. Even on the slickrock benches below the slot, where the river had lost most of its momentum, the flow was strong enough to drill caldrons as big as jacuzzis.

After heavy rainstorms, rainwater rediscovers forgotten pathways and collects into a stream that livens up the canyon with calming gurgles. The slot funnels it into a foaming torrent that performs once again, for a few days, the ageless ritual of erosion. The stream may then run through most of the canyon. Long after it dries up, the potholes remain filled with stagnant water and sustain wildlife from all corners of the kingdom, from red spotted toads and California tree frogs to bighorn sheep, raptors, and the canyon's dreaded namesake.

Homo sapiens sapiens also like to linger here, to inspect the tinajas and try scaling the fall. The slickrock incline to the right of the slot is partly a steep friction walk. At its top there are two 8-foot angular boulders capped by a thick horizontal slab. The route goes through the slit between them, or around them, then over a field of boulders. The left side of the slot seems to be more popular. The hard part is avoiding or negotiating the large blocks near the top, which may take a few tries. Not everyone makes it. I have seen kids with barely two digits to their age scramble up effortlessly, and a dozen rescuers pulling out a climber stranded in the slot... A chance to explore this geological artwork, hollowed, dimpled, stepped, and fissured, is a reward in itself.

The upper canyon. Above the fall, the wash holds for some distance the memory of the ancient stream. At the top of the slot it incised a sensual miniature trench that snakes tightly between polished buttresses. Up canyon the stream bed is still fully exposed, a pavement of slickrock inscribed with potholes, flow channels, and the polished lips of cascades. There are two easy boulder jams, then a harder one where the canyon bends to the west, and finally a short patch of open sand, the canyon's last concession to easiness. On the dry sand, the most recent stream deposited strings of symbols, a sift of dessicated leaves, minerals, seeds, and shriveled berries. The high-water line is marked by vegetation debris caught on the upstream side of plants. In this strange crossroad blessed with more water than most, the vegetation is a rebellious mix of oak and pancake cactus, willow and yucca, nolinas and honey mesquite, and everywhere plump bunches of grasses—deer grass, rabbitfoot grass, red brome, and crimson fountain. Far above the wash, spires and fractured cliffs patrol around like indifferent sentries.

Past the sandy area is the start of Rattlesnake Canyon's epic boulders. There are still small pockets of open wash, but not for long. Soon the wash is cluttered with tall boulders and trees, and hiking becomes persistently strenuous. You walk on the tips of boulders, focusing on aim and balance, weighing compromises between rocks and thorns, slipping through caves when necessary, oblivious to the scenery. Progress is *very* slow. The head of the canyon is not even a mile away, but it may take two hours to get there. There are harder routes beyond, to Johnson Spring and Indian Cove, up and down boulder-choked gullies and Class-3 ridges. But in this sumptuous chaos of perplexing sculptures, a set goal is secondary—finding a way to connect one place to another provides ample fulfillment. A friend and I spent a whole

Rattlesnake Canyon

	Dist.(mi)	Elev.(ft)
End of road	0.0	3,017
Base of 100-ft fall	0.4	3,110
Top of fall	0.55	3,210
South fork (left)	1.2	3,375
Head of Rattlesnake Canyon	(0.9)	3,850
Boulder caves (spring)	~1.3	~3,560
Fork (right between domes)	1.5	3,740
Boulder-filled passage	1.6	3,780
Willow Hole	2.4	4,015

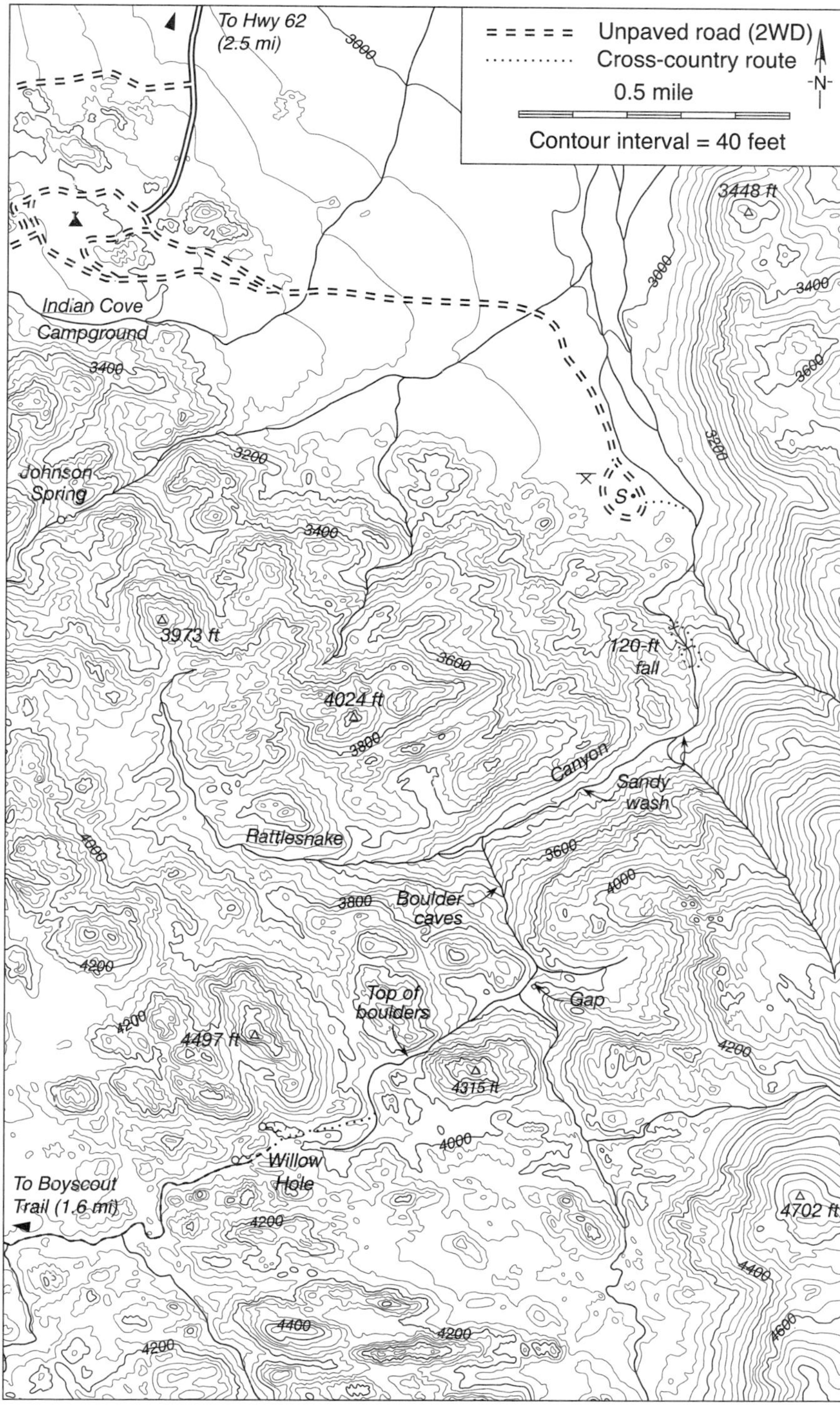
Unpaved road (2WD)
Cross-country route
0.5 mile
Contour interval = 40 feet
N
To Hwy 62 (2.5 mi)
Indian Cove Campground
Johnson Spring
3448 ft
3973 ft
4024 ft
120-ft fall
Rattlesnake Canyon
Sandy wash
Boulder caves
Top of boulders
Gap
4497 ft
4315 ft
Willow Hole
To Boyscout Trail (1.6 mi)
4702 ft
S

day climbing through just one boulder-choked crack. We were constantly calculating, searching for passages, studying how the topography was hinged together to minimize failed detours. It was a lesson in humility, yet in the end the land delivered a superb treat. At its very top, the canyon opened up onto a secret cove of pristine sand and sculpted pines bathed in the prized light of evening.

Willow Hole traverse. One of Joshua Tree's greatest hiking challenges and most awesome sceneries is the circuitous Class-2 traverse to Willow Hole through Rattlesnake Canyon's south fork. This fork starts 0.3 mile past the end of the sandy wash, on the left—a steep, narrow, rock-filled gulch that looks nothing like a canyon. Scramble up, generally south-southeast, to a short right-left jog, then as far again to a gap between two domes on the right. Cross the gap to a sandy wash at a fork. Go right (west) 100 yards to a second fork, then left (southwest) up a steep ravine burdened under layers of boulders. The heavy-duty scrambling ends at the top of it. From there the much more level wash curves left to the south-southeast. Just past a neck, angle right (west) into a nearly level corridor. It will take you through a cleft to a shallow depression with a spring, then to Willow Hole 250 yards further.

It is an exhilarating crossing. The whole way you are in a maze of articulated canyons. Every stone is a source of wonder, abrupt shields of granite, collapsing cliffs, staircases of shelves, loose slabs held by the whim of friction, and ranks of spherical boulders so similar that they seem to rhyme. This shattered landscape is pressed together so tightly that it seems impassable. Making progress demands constantly solving puzzles. You have to reconfigure your body to duck under chockstones, tiptoe around pools, slip through clefts, and crawl underground. You conquer one horizon of boulders, only to find yourself facing more boulders. It may take three or four hours to reach Willow Hole. Then you have to get back. Make sure you know what you are getting into. Leave early enough not to have to hike here at dark.

You do not have to go far up the south fork to enjoy its wild spirit. Two thirds of the way up to the jog there is a set of caves trapped under giant boulders, with just enough light filtering in to reveal a magical underworld. Curvaceous bedrock has been chiseled in facets like a jewel. Water from a seep drapes the rock in shiny sheets and collects in limpid pools. Out of sight, water drips into water, one drop every few seconds, day after day, like a timeless clock. In the silence of the desert, the sound is mesmerizing, rekindling the mystery of water hidden in utterly dry places.

■

FORTYNINE PALMS OASIS

The very word oasis is magical. It conjures pictures of towering palms and luxuriant gardens irrigated by providential water lost in the middle of a barren desert. Fortynine Palms Oasis does not disappoint. Sheltered in a rocky gorge, it is a restful haven of greenery, sensitive plants, and wildlife, shaded by a grove of majestic fan palms. As the park's most easily accessible backcountry palm oases, it is a very popular destination. If you prefer your oases peaceful, come here when it is super hot, super cold, or Super Bowl.

General Information
Road status: Hiking on trail; paved access road
49 Palms Oasis (trail): 1.6 mi, 400 ft up, 320 ft down one way / easy-mod.
49 Palms Oasis (cyn): 1.6 mi, 610 ft up, 20 ft down one way / easy-mod.
Main attractions: Trail to palm oasis in rugged canyon, botany, wildlife
USGS 7.5′ topo map: Queen Mountain
Maps: pp. 85*, *65*

Location and Access

From just below Queen Mountain north to the edge of the town of Twentynine Palms, a major drainage called Fortynine Palms Canyon slices a long swath down through the Wonderland of Rocks' northeastern quadrant and nearly severs it in half. Fortynine Palms Oasis is located in the middle of the canyon's stony lower gorge. It can be reached by hiking up the canyon from the south end of Encelia Avenue in town, a quiet hike up a bouldery wash. Most hikers take the easier but also often busy Fortynine Palms Oasis Trail instead, which approaches the oasis from the northwest over a more subdued ridge. The trailhead is reached by its own paved road. On Highway 62 in Twentynine Palms, look for the signed road to Fortynine Palms Oasis (Canyon Road). It is 1.8 miles east of the Indian Cove Road, and 5.0 miles west of Utah Trail. Drive this road south, then east, 1.7 miles to the large parking loop at its end.

Route Description

This is an easy trail, all of 3.2 miles round trip with 720 feet of total elevation gain, most of it gradual, with stone stairs and switchbacks where the grade gets a little steep. From the parking it climbs to the rim of Fortynine Palms Canyon, and to a high point just beyond. Then it descends south across the canyon's broad western slope, crossing a few minor tributaries along the way, to the oasis on the canyon floor.

The trail spans three Mesozoic plutons in a row: Twentynine Palms porphyritic quartz monzonite up to the rim, Pinto Gneiss around the rim, and Queen Mountain Monzogranite down to the oasis. They all have different compositions and weathering habits, which has produced outcrops with a variety of textures and shapes, from grainy to laminar, and from well-rounded to sub-angular and jagged. Being often on high ground, the trail commands panoramic views of this complex geology. On the way up to the rim, sharp hills and low boulder mounds protruding from the hillsides form an austere, alien landscape. To the north, low ridges covered with dense swarms of rounded outcrops descend a long way to Twentynine Palms. In late-afternoon sunlight, they take on a deep apricot glow. On the rim the gneiss is heavily varnished, which lends the area a somber mood, reinforced by the thin vegetation. The canyon side is different still, looking out over the Wonderland of Rocks' central summits and the rugged far side of Fortynine Palms Canyon, strewn with rusted boulders.

On these hard slopes seared by the valley's hot breath, the vegetation is disconcertingly scarce. There are no trees. The dominant plants—brittlebush, desert lavender, ephedra, and manzanita—are stunted and understated. The only exception is the sizable colonies of barrel cactus, their eye-catching bulbous heads shining a cheerful vermillion against the rocky ground. Yet in the springtime, when every single brittlebush is crowned with countless sunflowers, this area becomes its own antithesis, as brilliant as an alpine meadow in full bloom.

Fortynine Palms Oasis is one of these sites so unexpected that it will make you stop and take in some air. Although you can catch a glimpse of the tops of a few palms along the descent, it does not come into full view until the last moment, as you crest a small ridge overlooking the canyon wash. A few dozen fan palms are huddled along the steep wash, rising majestically against the sheer canyon walls. In this rockscape overwhelmed by browns and chaos, they seem impossibly green and symmetrical. The trail ends at a wooden platform inside the main grove. When not too many people are around, it is an idyllic spot, shaded by the high canopy of fronds swooshing in the breeze, a microcosm of peace and sanity in a sun-blasted desert. Among the low boulders that clog the narrow wash, water gathers in a tier of tiny pools edged by grasses and cattail. You may not see water—you are asked to stay on the platform not to damage the sensitive vegetation—but you will hear it gurgling under the bushes. Sunrays filtering

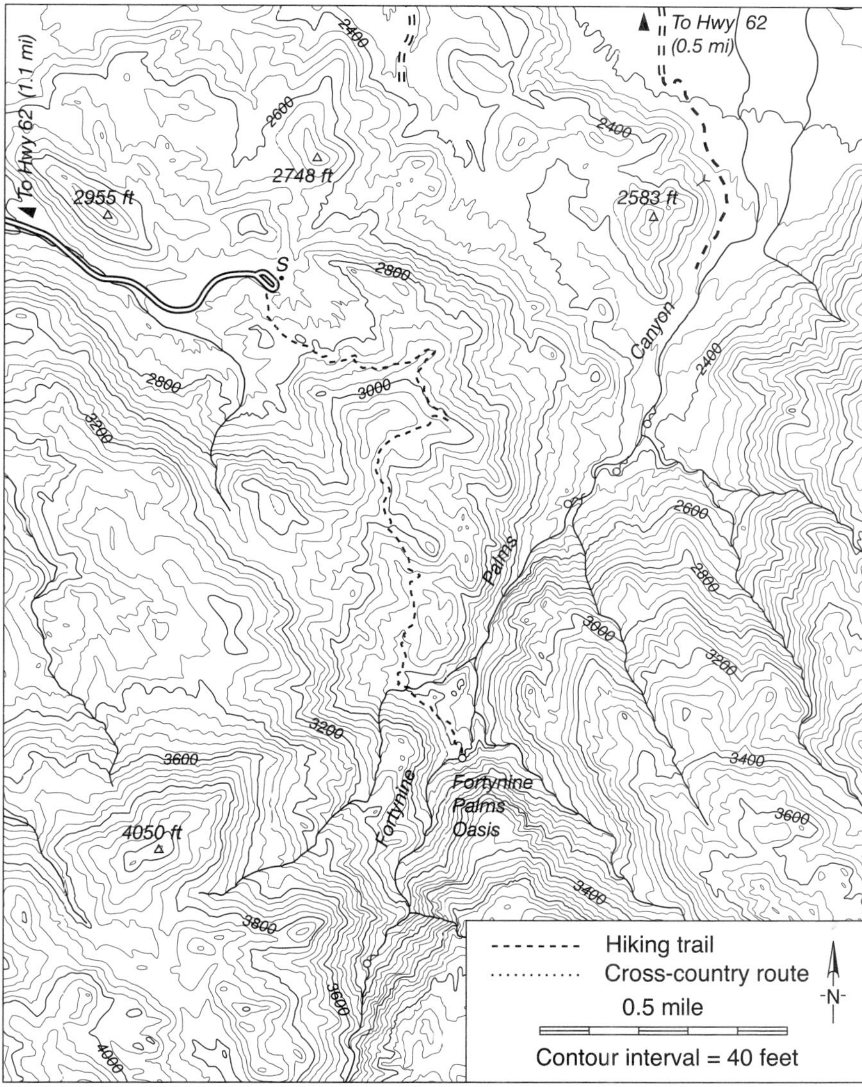

Fortynine Palms Oasis		
	Dist.(mi)	Elev.(ft)
Trailhead	0.0	2,790
Rim of Fortynine Palms Cyn	0.5	2,965
Fortynine Palms Oasis	1.6	2,800
End of road / park boundary	2.8	2,285
Encelia Rd at park boundary	3.2	2,190

Fortynine Palms Oasis from near the end of the trail

through the foliage cast mottled light on an understory of mesquite, willow, and arrowweed. Among them grows one of the desert's rarest residents, the stream orchid, a species adapted to tropical forests that has somehow managed to survive in this minuscule microclimate.

Reptiles, birds, mammals, amphibians, insects, and arachnids are drawn to this inviting enclave by its water, shade, coolness, and the prospect of a different menu. You might spot a finch or an oriole flashing their colorful plumage, quails scurrying under the bushes, a collared lizard pumping iron on a boulder, a coachwhip, a chuckwalla, a rattlesnake, or a California tree frog motionless at the edge of a pool. Coyotes and bighorn sheep regularly come out to quench their thirst.

One of the greatest attributes of a wild oasis is silence. There will very likely be other people around while you visit this place. Out of respect for them, perhaps for the short time you will be there make a vow of silence. If you must speak, whisper. To preserve the rare species that live at the spring, stay on the trail. To give shyer wildlife a chance to use this spring without disruption, this is a day-use-only area. Make sure to get back on time—the parking-lot gate closes at sundown.

■

JOSHUA MOUNTAIN

Joshua Mountain is an imposing cliff-bounded tower perched high on the chaotic eastern front of the Wonderland of Rocks. The climb is short, exhilarating, and a little demanding, first on a rough primitive trail up an abrupt ravine filled with boulders of beautiful megaporphyritic monzonite, then up the summit block on an exposed ramp of inclined slickrock. The peak offers a fine perspective of the small town of Twentynine Palms, eastern Morongo Basin, and the sand-encrusted Bullion Mountains in the background.

General Information

Road status: Hiking mostly on rough use trail; paved access road
Joshua Mountain: 1.35 mi, 1,150 ft up, 40 ft down one way / mod.–diff.
Main attractions: A short, vigorous climb to a tall sculpted monolith
USGS 7.5' topo map: Queen Mountain
Maps: pp. 89*, *65*

Location and Access

Joshua Mountain is at the very eastern edge of the Wonderland of Rocks, where the range drops precipitously into the small valley that separates it from Twentynine Palms Mountain to the east. Its stocky summit block protruding high above the range is a conspicuous landmark visible from the road to the park's north entrance. On Highway 62 in Twentynine Palms, about a mile east of the town center, turn south on Utah Trail. Drive 3.0 miles to the signed Wellock Road on the left. Coming from inside the park, this is 1.1 miles north of the north entrance station. Joshua Mountain soars about 1 air mile and 1,100 feet higher to the west, at the top of the ridge. The curb makes it hard to park on the paved road, so park on dirt at the start of Wellock Road.

Route Description

Joshua Mountain is a stately rock. Its monolithic summit block stands sentinel high above the desert like a fortress anchored on an invincible rock. Below it, the sheer mountain front is overflowing with enormous outcrops. The boulder-choked ravine that tumbles straight down from the summit's southern brow to the foot of the range is obviously the shortest route. It is also the least difficult, though by no means easy: it plunges about 950 feet in 0.6 air mile—a sustained 30% slope, most of it encumbered by large rocks.

From the road, first cross the short stretch of valley floor almost due west to the mouth of the ravine. This area is an interesting piece of desert real estate, dissected by a web of sandy washes small and large. Storm waters have churned not only the terrain but the plant community as well. A surprising number of plants not too common in this type of habitat live intermixed with more typical flora, an eclectic blend of desert lavender, manzanita, coyote melon, desert larkspur, Mojave linanthus, and even smoke trees—which do not normally grow at this high elevation.

The easiest way up the ravine is not the wash itself, where boulders are a major hindrance, but the slightly more open slope on the south side. There is now a use trail, never farther than about 100 feet from the wash. It starts at the foot of the low ridge of finer alluvia that frames the south side of the ravine at its mouth. Misguided people had marked the trail with cairns and reflectors. If you are thinking of putting up markers again, remember that others are resentful of signage in the wild, because it takes away their elemental pleasure of finding the way on their own. If you do not find the trail right away, you will likely run into it higher up, and once you have found it, it takes little effort to keep track of its whereabouts. Most of it is steep, gravelly, and slippery, meandering tightly between rocks. Even if you do not find the trail at all it is no big deal, as it makes the ascent only marginally easier. The ravine climbs in two steep pitches separated by a short, more level stretch about a third of the way up. Joshua Mountain first emerges above the mountain's heads of boulders at the top of the first pitch, its sculpted cliffs slowly rotating and getting more ominous as you climb. Not far below it the ravine splits. The trail continues on the same side of the wash a little longer, then crosses the boulder-filled wash to the north side. It then stays on that side the short remaining distance to the top of the ravine.

One of the pleasures of this climb is the rocks. All of Joshua Mountain is megaporphyritic monzonite, an unusual Mesozoic intrusive rock that contains huge feldspar crystals. Most of the exposures along the ravine are loaded with these eye-catching pink and white megacrysts, often perfect rectangles up to 4 inches in length. On flat surfaces they stand out sharply against the monzonite's darker groundmass, discordant tokens of order in the midst of chaos.

The head of the ravine is flush with the foot of the mountain block. Up ahead, a long sink of sand and creosote opens up, enclosed on the valley side by bouldery hills. From the head of the ravine it is a short stroll clockwise to the west side of the mountain block, where a long ramp climbs steadily the remaining 160 feet to the summit. This last

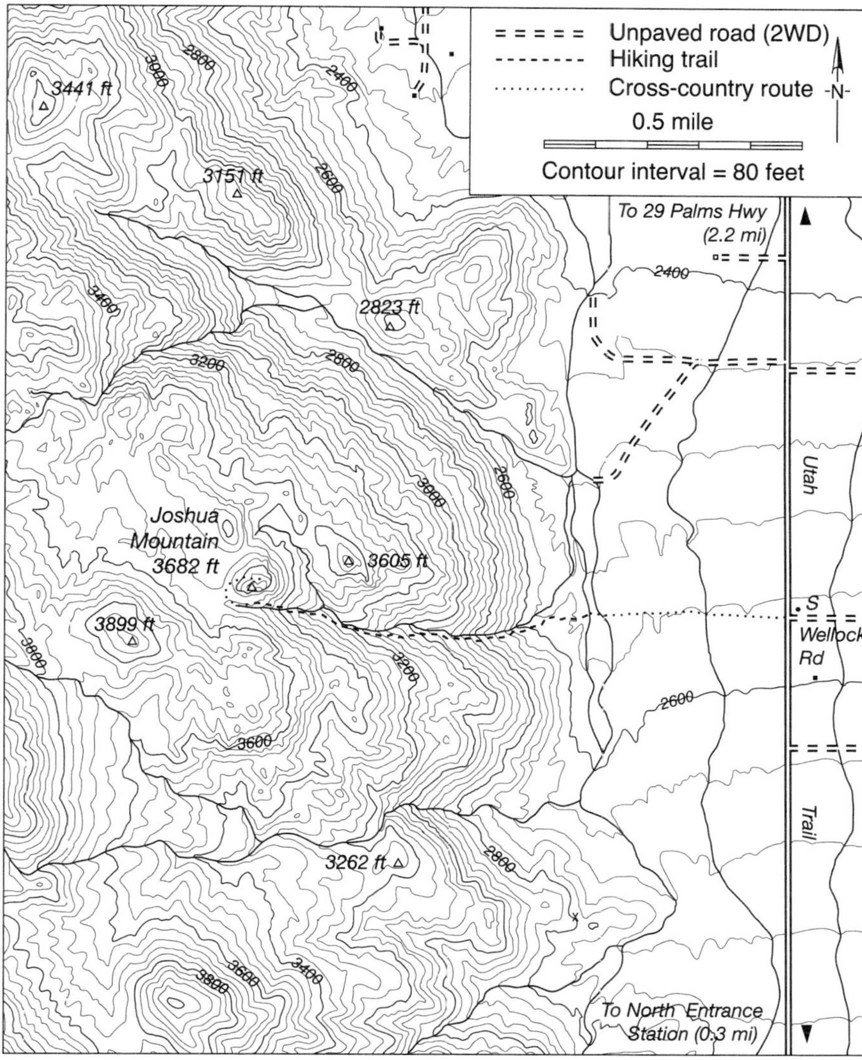

Joshua Mountain		
	Dist.(mi)	Elev.(ft)
Utah Trail at Wellock Road	0.0	2,570
Foot of mountain	0.4	2,540
Across from fork in ravine	1.0	~3,260
Top of ravine	1.15	3,520
Foot of summit block	1.25	3,530
Joshua Mountain	1.35	3,682

Joshua Mountain's summit block from the fork in the ravine

stretch is aerial, up bumpy, tiered slickrock overlooking the range's abrupt eastern flank. Just below and east of the summit there are two abrupt 5-foot steps in the slickrock. They can be avoided by going far enough south and winding around them, although it is very exposed.

The summit is a bald plug of exfoliating stone rising high above thin air. When the wind is blowing hard, it seems too small to safely stand. Bighorn sheep know of it. After a good rain, when the small tinaja etched into the summit is full of water, a ram will occasionally trot up here to take a sip, lay down, and fertilize the slickrock while contemplating the view. The summit does command an inspiring 180° panorama of Morongo Basin. The focus is Twentynine Palms, its compact grid of rectangular streets posed like a toy town on the edge of the basin's large reserve of undeveloped land. The proliferation of roads crossing the valley to single dwellings may inspire ruminations on whether there is still room to grow or still time to preserve. A consortium of government agencies and private organizations concluded the latter years ago, and have been saving this little jewel of a desert valley piece by piece ever since, before it turns into another desert city.

■

THE CONTACT MINE

Hidden in a curvy canyon, the Contact Mine is a little more fun to look for than most. It is a fairly easy, scenic hike up to it, first along a smooth wash lined with tall shrubs, then on an abandoned mining road that climbs into a relatively gentle canyon pierced with darkly stained outcrops. In spite of a probably unglamorous past, the mine still has interesting remains, including the vestiges of a cabin, a well-preserved winch, and several intriguing pieces of equipment.

General Information

Road access: Hiking cross-country and on trail; paved access road
Contact Mine: 2.0 mi, 750 ft up, 20 ft down one way / easy–moderate
Main attractions: Old road to gold mine, mining equipment, botany
USGS 7.5' topo map: Queen Mountain
Maps: pp. 93*, 65

Location and Access

The Contact Mine is located a little over a mile up a canyon that drains the eastern front of the Wonderland of Rocks. To get to the trailhead, drive Park Boulevard 0.45 mile south from the north entrance, or 4.1 miles north from Pinto Wye. Park at the dirt pullout with a backcountry board on the west (mountain) side.

Route Description

Starting in 1910, and for many years, the Contact Mine was owned by Phil Sullivan, a miner, assessor, and blacksmith who had been homesteading with his family in an adobe house near the Oasis of Mara since 1897. Sullivan had other nearby properties, including the Anaconda Mine to the east along Park Boulevard, and the Silver Bell Mine across the valley. The Contact ore was milled at a burro-powered arrastra that he and Bill McHaney built near the oasis. The property was active again in the early 1930s and in 1940. Hand-sorted ore was treated by amalgamation and produced gold and silver at the modest tune of $70 per ton. Like a surprisingly large number of mines in the park, the Contact Mine was developed fairly extensively, yet there is little record of its history, and no record of its production. Perhaps the lawlessness that ruled the West lingered a little longer in this corner of the desert. Had it not been for its fortuitous collection of mining paraphernalia, no one would be talking about the Contact Mine today...

The lower part of the old road to the Contact Mine was erased long ago by desert storms. From the pavement, only the first 250 yards are still there as a rock-lined trail, until it meets a wide wash, slips into it, and vanishes. For the next half a mile you walk in the wash's broad swath of loose sand. It would be challenging to get lost, even without the half a dozen bright red 4-foot signs posted in the wash. Just follow the widest wash, southwesterly, staying close to the edge of the mountain on the right. This is a pretty area, with periodic banks of boulders, bosques of creosote, thickets of manzanita, islands of desert lavender, and mixed borders of bladderpod, mesquite, and desert willow.

The upper part of the mining road, in the canyon where the Contact Mine is located, is still extant, and not too difficult to find. As you approach the canyon entrance—the first canyon since the trailhead—the wash narrows conspicuously. About 0.7 mile from the trailhead, and 200 feet before the wash angles sharply right into the canyon, the road becomes visible on the left side of the side canyon climbing a low bank in eight long stairs. It was a well-built road, and it is still continuous up to just below the mine. Supported on its downslope side by a crude stone wall, it snakes up along the canyon slope, paralleling the wash below. The terrain is a little stark at first, the surrounding hillsides a stubble of scrawny grasses, low outcrops, and small boulders. The scenery improves noticeably up canyon, where the hills are increasingly covered with rounded boulders. The final quarter-mile of straight road before the mine is the most scenic. The canyon's south side is smothered under close-packed knobs of beige monzonite stained with black varnish, as if they had been charred. Even without the mine, it would be worth coming here just to indulge in a bit of scrambling through this eerie fantasyland.

The mine tailings become visible up ahead along this straight stretch of road, where the roadway gradually pinches down to a single track. About 100 yards from the mine, the road reaches a cluttered talus and forks. Beyond this point, it shrivels to a much fainter track

The Contact Mine

	Dist.(mi)	Elev.(ft)
Pullout on Park Boulevard	0.0	2,915
End of foot trail	0.15	2,960
Lower end of mining road	0.70	3,050
Fork in mining road	1.85	3,545
Contact Mine	1.95	3,640

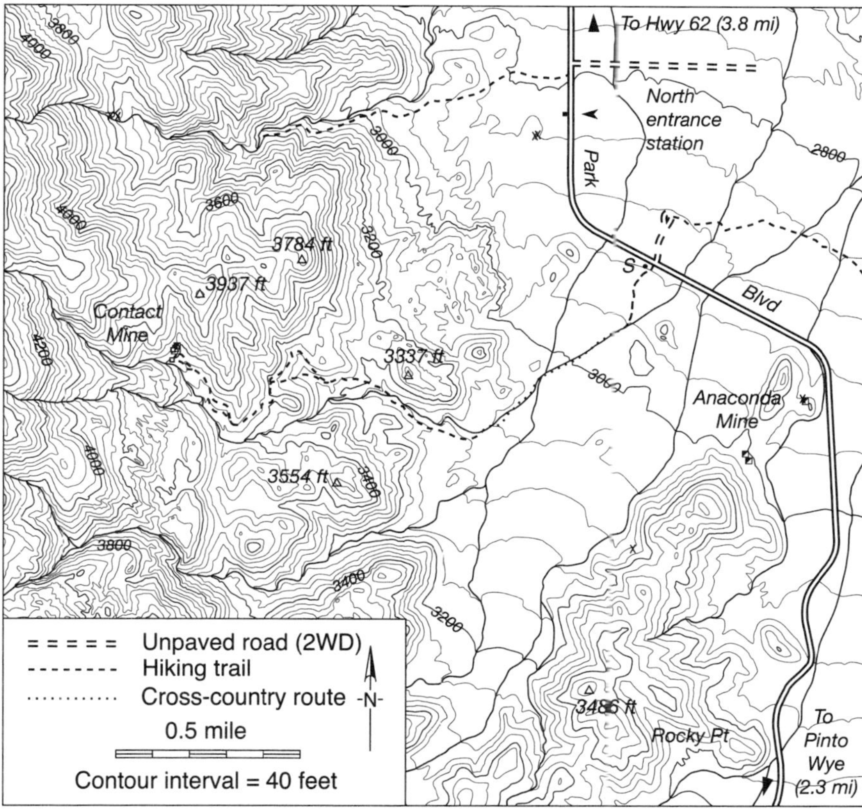

and makes a 300-yard loop below the tailings. The left branch soon reaches the southern base of the tailings, where a small miner's cabin once stood. Its remains are shattered as if it had exploded. The area is littered with square sheets of corrugated-metal roofing, the broken pieces of a cast-iron stove, a partly buried box spring, a stovepipe and a small water tank. The mine's three shafts, capped with metal grates, are on the tailings' broad flat top just above the cabin site. The forked rail track that serviced the main, 150-foot shaft still crosses the tailings, brightened in the springtime by brittlebush in bloom and the green gourds of coyote melons. The winch that hoisted the ore out of the main shaft presides on a narrow pad above it. In its own way, it is a mechanical beauty. It still has its spool and cable, cogs, flywheel, and even its handbrake. Few hoisting machinery this fine have survived in their original setting in the California desert.

Other pieces of mining equipment lie around. One of them is a curious gasoline-powered piston near the rail track. The other ones are along the northern branch of the loop trail, which starts below the

Winch and rail track at the Contact Mine

middle of the tailings. There is a truck chassis with leaf-spring suspension, a large contraption combining cogs, pulleys, and flywheels—perhaps part of the engine that powered the winch—and other wreckages with uncertain functions. A good part of the fun is figuring out what these scattered bits of equipment did, how they fit together in space and over time, and peering a little into the foggy past of a little-known mine. If nothing else, the experience is a vivid reminder of the power of gold fever. The delusion is so powerful that it will drive men to move to this harsh environment, build roads, drag in, operate, and maintain heavy machinery, and live in sub-standard conditions, for the main purpose, against formidable odds, of getting rich.

■

NORTH CANYON

The name itself is not exactly inviting. Surely there cannot be anything remarkable about a place that landed a name as glamorous as "North." Whoever named this canyon had either never set foot in it or suffered from a serious deficiency in romanticism. North Canyon has it all—narrows lined with stunning sliced walls, crystal-coated boulders, an interesting fall to negotiate, wildlife, solitude, and a healthy collection of chimneys and other hoodoos that should have inspired plenty of more befitting names.

General Information
Road status: Hiking in sandy washes; paved access road
North Canyon fall: 1.2 mi, 0 ft up, 410 ft down one way / easy
Full canyon: 2.5 mi, 0 ft up, 900 ft down one way / moderate
Main attractions: Scenic canyon with narrows and hoodoos, wildlife
USGS 7.5' topo map: Indian Cove
Maps: pp. 97, 65*

Location and Access

North Canyon is a 3-mile drainage that cuts west, then due north across the very western end of the Wonderland of Rocks. The starting point is the four-car dirt parking area on the left side of Park Boulevard 1.8 miles from the west entrance, in a right bend. Coming from the other direction, it is 7 miles from the Hidden Valley Junction.

Route Description

North Canyon starts slowly. The trail named after it follows an open wash dusted with oaks, juniper, and Joshua trees that wanders down among low hills of loose rubble pinpricked with yucca. But then bend by bend, the rubble grow into tumbled boulders, the boulders become angular outcrops, until the hills have solidified into massive granite. The trail climbs out of the wash on the left and leaves it right where the fun begins, 0.7 mile in. Continue down the wash instead. The walking is easy, over sand sprinkled with low boulders and a fine assortment of catclaw, desert almond, and manzanita. The canyon gradually deepens, the slopes become more deeply sculpted, and soon you are immersed in the typical indescribable chaos that is the hall-mark of Joshua Tree. Giant shelves rise in staggered steps, lacerated by cracks, fissures, and clefts, capped by slabs that lie precariously in improbable arrangements. Wildlife easily outnumbers humans. I flushed countless quails and lizards. Ravens bickering in flight landed on a spire to watch me go by. A pair of doves perched on a tall outcrop let me approach them within 15 feet while they shamelessly courted. The bark of woody shrubs had been recently stripped by hungry bighorn, and their dainty prints stitched the sand. Well-fed coyotes with a flair for an easy meal had generously fertilized the wash.

About 1.2 miles down, past the largest boulder pile yet, the wash is clipped abruptly by a 12-foot fall. It will stop most hikers, but climbers will enjoy the challenge of this low-5 descent. The top is a shallow incised scoop, easy to get into. The rest is too steep to see—a camera on a selfie stick comes in handy to scope the holds, and a rope for safety. There is a deep, wide pocket two feet down, a broad ledge four feet below it, and sand two feet down. The alternative is to return to the trail, hike it to the Burro Loop, and follow this trail to where it crosses North Canyon—a long route. It is worth looking for a shorter bypass.

The best part of this canyon is, as Murphy's Law would have it, below the fall. Over the next mile, it squeezes through two narrows. The upper narrows start shortly below the fall, at a tall dam of four-foot boulders that subsumes the wash. It is a cramped passage encased in low broken walls, littered with small boulders. At its lower end, it opens onto a secluded valley a quarter of a mile long, terminated by a wide boulder dam where the Burro Loop crosses the canyon.

The lower narrows, deeper, tighter, start about there, and they are the most impressive. Most of this corridor is hemmed in by broken bulwarks of stone. Long ago, compressive forces weakened bedrock into thin parallel slabs that now stand on end, like books on a shelf. On the rims 60 feet above the wash, the tips of the slices protrude like the

North Canyon

	Dist.(mi)	Elev.(ft)
Trailhead	0.0	3,960
North Canyon Trail in wash	0.1	3,930
Trail leaves wash/stay in wash	0.7	3,780
12-foot fall	1.15	3,550
Upper narrows	1.3	3,500
Lower narrows/Burro Loop	1.7	3,380
Back to wash via trails	(1.5)	3,780
End of lower narrows	2.1	3,170
Canyon mouth	2.5	3,060

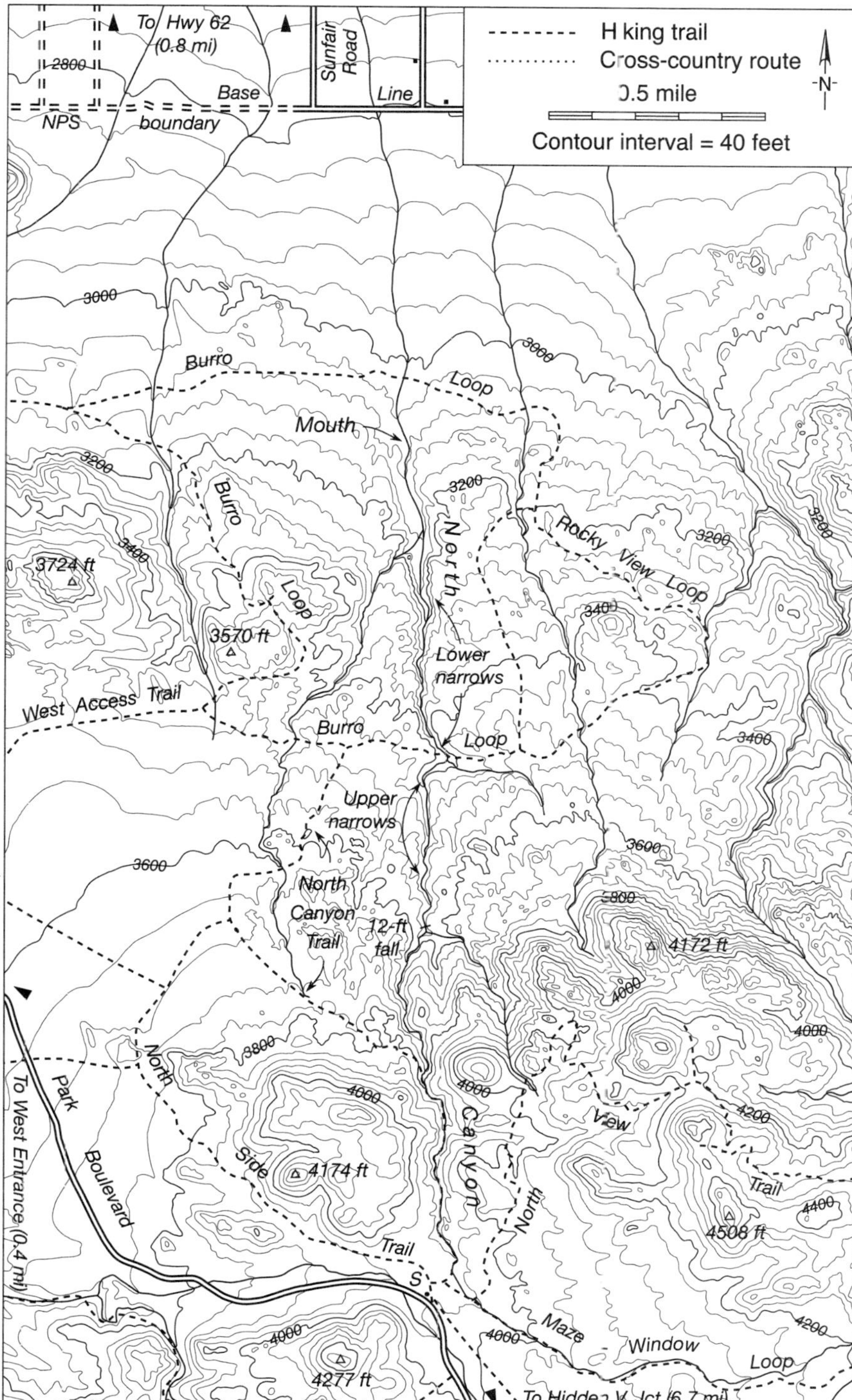

H king trail
Cross-country route
0.5 mile
N
Contour interval = 40 feet
To Hwy 62 (0.8 mi)
Sunfair Road
Base Line
NPS boundary
2800
3000
Burro Loop
Mouth
3200
Burro Loop
3724 ft
3570 ft
3400
North
Rocky View Loop
Lower narrows
West Access Trail
Burro Loop
Upper narrows
3600
North Canyon Trail
12-ft fall
4172 ft
4000
3800
North Side Trail
Park Boulevard
To West Entrance (0.4 mi)
4174 ft
North Canyon
North View Trail
4200
4400
4508 ft
Maze Window Loop
4277 ft
To Hidden V. Jct (6.7 mi)

North Canyon's diced walls in the lower narrows

turrets of a castle, abraded into armies of rounded hoodoos. The most fragile turrets have split into blocks, some the size of cobbles, some ten feet across, which now rest at sharp angles. The wash is partly filled with the blocks that lost their fight against gravity and crashed from the rims. You hop from one to the next, weave along crooked strips of sand, and climb on little slants of water-carved bedrock. Plants have trouble getting purchase. You occasionally brush by a desert almond or a dwarf juniper, or gingerly move aside the thorny branch of a catclaw to get by unscathed. The landscape is all White Tank Monzogranite, salt and pepper or washed with apricot streaks, shimmering in the sunlight. Boulders have shattered along veins of pink and gray pegmatite forged in the deep earth eons ago, now exposed in exquisite carpets of interlocked crystals. Whenever you look up, you stare at more turrets, towers, and boulders balanced high overhead.

North Canyon ends as quietly as it started. The walls morph back to rubbly hills spiked with random outcrops, and the wash widens to a channel of tidy sand. Islands of greenery grow in the middle of it, each one a monoculture of desert willows, saltbush, or creosote lined with bladderpods. In summer the willows are shockingly lush, skirted by last season's dead leaves. In early spring the bladderpods are in full regalia, each one an explosion of bright yellow blossoms. By now you have covered the full spectrum, from the wild high desert down through a dry canyon to an unlikely green desert on the edge of town.

■

BOY SCOUT TRAIL

Connecting the park's most popular area near Hidden Valley to Indian Cove, the Boy Scout Trail cuts a long tortuous path across the scenic western edge of the Wonderland of Rocks. In the process it traverses a Joshua-tree forest, switchbacks down an imposing canyon coated with sculpted rocks, squeezes through narrows, and emerges in the low desert on a vast creosote-covered fan. Whether you hike parts or all of it, in a day or overnight, it is a great way to sample the natural wonders and diversity of this exceptional range.

General Information
Road status: Hiking on trail; paved access roads
Boy Scout Trail: 8.1 mi, 1,430 ft up, 470 ft down one way / very diff.
Indian Cove to overlook: 3.5 mi, 1,170 ft up, 120 ft down one way / mod.
Park Blvd to overlook: 4.6 mi, 260 ft up, 350 ft down one way / moderate
Main attractions: A long trail across a deep canyon and valleys, views
USGS 7.5' topo map: Indian Cove
Maps: pp. 101*, 103*, *65*

Location and Access

To hike the Boy Scout Trail northbound, drive Park Boulevard to the large, well-signed dirt parking area for the Boy Scout Trail, 6.5 miles southeast from the west entrance, on the left side. Coming from the other direction, it is 2.4 miles from the Barker Dam turnoff. To hike the trail southbound, from Highway 62 on the west side of Twentynine Palms drive the signed Indian Cove Road 1.5 miles south to the signed trailhead, on the right a short distance inside the park.

Route Description

Logistics. The Boy Scout Trail is comparatively long, 8.1 miles one way with a total elevation change of 1,900 feet. To hike it in a day, it is best to arrange a shuttle and to do it one way, preferably northbound, which is the direction described below. The sun will be mostly at your back, the views are better, and the only steep portion of trail is then hiked downhill and easier. This is a popular trail for backpacking. Land adjoining the trail to the east is a day-use-only area, so you must set up camp on the west side of the trail. If you decide to hike only a portion of the trail, the overlook in the mountains is about the optimum turning point, from either trailhead.

The narrows in the lower canyon

The southern plateau. For the first 3 miles the Boy Scout Trail traverses a spacious plateau generously covered with high-desert vegetation. Platoons of Joshua trees stand guard all around, their spiked bodies competing for oddness, in ranks tight enough to paint the horizon solid green. Desolate stands of rounded boulders rise nearby, backed on the horizon by 2-mile-high San Gorgonio Mountain. Along the first mile, the horizon is closed off up ahead by the Wonderland of Rocks' imposing crest, dissected in countless turrets and battlements. It is the kind of scenery between reality and fiction that makes you wonder whether you just got spontaneously stoned. Stoned or not, it would be hard to wander astray. Most of the southern Boy Scout Trail is to trails what freeways are to roads—broad, straight, mostly level, hard-packed, free of rocks, and oversigned. This area hosts many typical Mojave Desert plants—desert almond, saltbush, clusters of tall diamond cholla, thornbush, calico and mound cactus, and less common plants like rock pea and live-forever in the rocky swales. On a wet year the wildflowers are unbelievably prolific. Vast tracks are blanketed in chia, pincushion, globemallow, blue bell, and wooly daisy.

At the junction 1.2 miles in, the Boy Scout Trail continues to the left. Most of the foot traffic heads right, to Willow Hole; the rest of the way is generally much less traveled. Over the next 2 miles, the trail

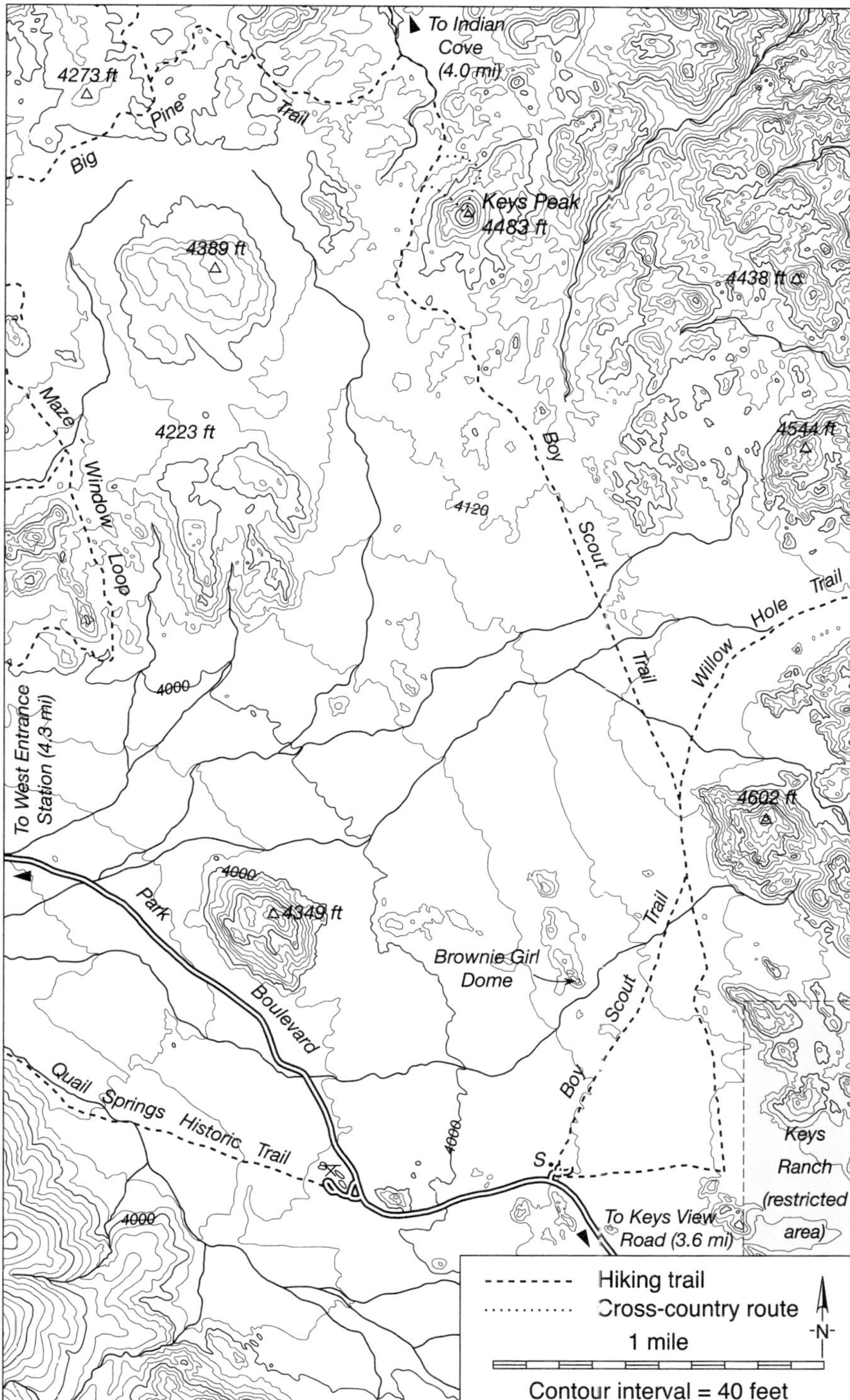
To Indian Cove (4.0 mi)
4273 ft
Big Pine Trail
Keys Peak 4483 ft
4389 ft
4438 ft
Maze
4223 ft
Window Loop
Boy Scout Trail
4120
4544 ft
Willow Hole Trail
4000
To West Entrance Station (4.3 mi)
4602 ft
Park Boulevard
4349 ft
Brownie Girl Dome
Boy Scout Trail
Quail Springs Historic Trail
S
To Keys View Road (3.6 mi)
Keys Ranch (restricted area)
Hiking trail
Cross-country route
1 mile
N
Contour interval = 40 feet

roughly parallels the front of the Wonderland of Rocks, offering good views of its jumbled flanks. The most spectacular areas are where it comes close to the range, especially at the majestic cliffs near the junction, and at the smaller outcrop about half a mile further. Rock climbers can often be seen scaling these popular areas. In the hot months, the small bosques of juniper and pine below the cliffs offer welcome shade. As the trail approaches the southwestern base of Keys Peak a little over 3.0 miles in, it narrows and wiggles over a very low and broad rolling pass. Shortly after, it angles north-northeast and enters the very shallow upper drainage of the canyon system that takes it across the mountains on its long descent to Indian Cove.

The canyon. The descent into the canyon is the most scenic part of this hike. In the upper drainage, just north of Keys Peak, a little wash of sand first snakes lazily between short walls of cracked granite, a closer, more intimate landscape where you brush by oak, juniper, and pine. Shortly after the Big Pine Trail junction, the canyon is much rougher. To avoid it, the trail leaves the wash on the left, cuts over to a side canyon to the west, and reaches its high rim at an impressive overlook. Down below, the land opens into the deep V-shaped valley of the central canyon. Immense, unbroken slopes of fractured granite drop several hundred feet to the hidden canyon floor. Above them, the horizon is filled with the long disjointed ridges of the Bullion Mountains. For nearly half a mile, the trail picks its way down over this sea of naked stone, often folding onto itself in tight switchbacks. It first passes by sculpted pinnacles and pointed summits, then drops along boulder-strewn slopes peppered with low bushes. This is prime

Boy Scout Trail

	Dist.(mi)	Elev.(ft)
Trailhead at Park Boulevard	0.0	4,040
Willow Hole junction	1.2	4,142
Pass (SW shoulder of Keys Pk)	3.05	~4,160
Big Pine Trail junction	3.9	4,055
Trail leaves canyon wash	4.25	3,930
Overlook	4.55	3,950
Trail joins canyon wash	5.1	3,550
Narrows	5.9	~3,340
Canyon mouth (leave wash)	6.55	3,320
Trailhead at Indian Cove Road	8.1	3,045

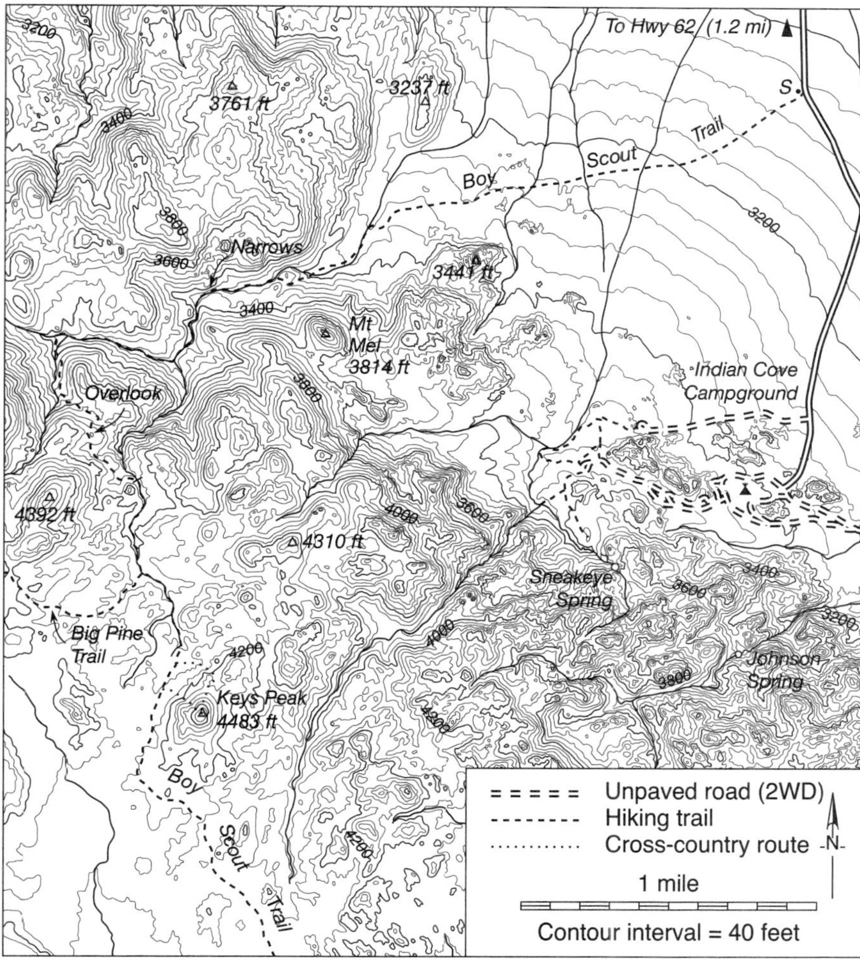

bighorn territory. As I was walking down the trail, a ewe and her two lambs clambered effortlessly straight up a hillside of boulders.

At the bottom of the slope, the trail joins the canyon wash again. The rest of the canyon crossing is mostly over sand and very gradual. The wash meanders between granitic walls, three-dimensional puzzles of rounded boulders and fractured outcrops, some patterned vertically, others horizontally, many randomly. Part way down, it traverses a scenic 200-yard set of narrows with near-vertical walls that taper handsomely upward into sharp pinnacles. From that point, it is a pleasant canyon walk, down a narrow serpentine wash lined with fanciful formations. By then you are in the low desert, surrounded by a very different vegetation. The larger plants are mostly manzanita, desert

Pinnacles and pointed summits looking north from near the viewpoint

almond, and rabbitbrush; barrel cactus and Mojave yucca cling to the rocky flanks. After a short trail on the south side to avoid a bouldery section, the trail reaches the mouth of the canyon.

Indian Cove. At the canyon mouth the wash swells to a 100-yard-wide tangle of sand channels woven around low islands of vegetation. It soon veers northeast, while the trail continues east, climbs 20 feet out of the wash, and descends the remaining 1.5 miles across Indian Cove to the paved road. It is an easy stroll, on a trail 7 feet wide and very slightly downhill. It traverses a plain dominated by large creosote, catclaw, and Mojave yucca, and small burrobush, chollas, and grasses. To the north it leads the eyes to a quiet suburb of Twentynine Palms. To the south, steep-sided inselbergs tower at close range, and behind them the wildly sculpted crest of the Wonderland of Rocks backing the cove. Besides the spectacle and the satisfaction of crossing a whole mountain range, this may be the greatest value of this hike—experiencing the region's remarkable diversity, from a Joshua-tree woodland to a forest of oak and conifers, a complex canyon ecosystem, and finally this spacious creosote plain so emblematic of the North American deserts.

■

KEYS PEAK

> *This scenery-charged climb comes in two stages, first a nearly level trail hike across a vast plain with a limitless supply of cacti and Joshua trees, then a rigorous scramble up a steep, 360-foot hillside smothered in boulders to the summit of Keys Peak. Even a partial climb will deliver inspiring views of the Wonderland of Rocks' otherworldly jumble of standing stones.*

General Information
Road status: Hiking on trail and cross-country; paved access road
Keys Peak: 3.6 mi, 540 ft up, 100 ft down one way / moderate–difficult
Main attractions: Steep bouldery peak, views of Wonderland of Rocks
USGS 7.5' topo map: Indian Cove
Maps: pp. 101*, 103, *65*

Location and Access

Keys Peak is a free-standing conical inselberg at the southwestern margin of the Wonderland of Rocks. The most direct route to its summit is via the Boy Scout Trail from Park Boulevard. Refer to *Boy Scout Trail* for directions. From the trailhead, Keys Peak is visible between the Joshua trees about 3 miles a little west of north.

Route Description

The first part of this hike, up to where the trail bends to the north-northeast 3.1 miles in, is the same as described under *Boy Scout Trail.* At that point Keys Peak is the sharp hill rising a short distance to the northwest. The easiest route to its summit is about 0.3 mile past the bend, up the gully in the peak's northwestern face. It is a hearty Class-2 scramble, up a slowly steepening slide overrun by boulders. What

Keys Peak		
	Dist.(mi)	Elev.(ft)
Boy Scout Trail at Park Blvd	0.0	4,040
Willow Hole junction	1.2	4,142
Pass (Keys Peak's SW shoulder)	3.05	~4,160
Northwestern foot of Keys Pk	3.4	4,125
Keys Peak	3.6	4,483

The route up Keys Peak from the Boy Scout Trail

little room is not occupied by rocks has been annexed by Mojave yucca, juniper, young Joshua trees, and a few pinyon pine near the top. Most of the way you never touch ground but hop from stone to stone. It is a demanding little mountain; you have to make concessions, and accept having to give up on a route to try another one. It is generally best to favor the left side of the gully, where the rocks are smaller and the trees fewer. Near the top it is easiest to drift back to the gully to avoid the larger boulders that frame it on both sides.

The summit is a remnant of the original mountain range, a flattish surface broken into 90-degree jointed boulders colonized by a few yucca and dwarf pine. The rocks make perfect front-row benches to sit down and take in the Wonderland of Rocks, its fantastic crest a miniature range of knolls, domes, nipples, and hoodoos unfurling from the foot of Keys Peak for several miles. In the late afternoon, every cliff, boulder, and spindle takes on a pale apricot glow as long bolts of lavender shadows fill in the notches and hollows between them. Beyond lie the wind-swept vastness of Morongo Basin, a haze of further ranges, and mountains high enough to hold deep snow. Even if this scenery were the only reward, it would be well worth the climb.

■

WILLOW HOLE

Near the center of the Wonderland of Rocks' sculpted western section, tectonic movements have opened up a small depression just deep enough to collect rainwater and support a lush spring of stately trees known as Willow Hole. This is a particularly impressive place, a long sandy trench framed by majestic walls carved with an astonishing level of detail. It is fortuitously reached by an easy walk with barely any elevation change, on a sandy trail that wanders first through a classic Joshua tree woodland, then among wild formations that rival Wonderland Plateau for magnificence. Even in Joshua Tree, few hikes pack in so many wonders over a handful of miles.

General Information

Road status: Hiking on trails; paved access road
Willow Hole: 3.7 mi, 150 ft up, 190 ft down one way / easy-moderate
Main attractions: A lush spring among spectacular cliffs, Joshua trees
USGS 7.5' topo map: Indian Cove
Maps: pp. 109*, *65*

Location and Access

The easiest access to Willow Hole is on the Boy Scout Trail, starting from the south trailhead. To get there, drive Park Boulevard to the signed parking area for the Boy Scout Trail, which is 6.5 miles from the west entrance, on the left side. Coming from the other direction, it is 2.4 miles from the Barker Dam turnoff.

Route Description

There are two parts to this hike, on two different trails, both scenic for different reasons. From the trailhead you first go north on the Boy Scout Trail, across a beautiful valley generously covered with an emblematic Joshua-tree woodland (see *The southern plateau* under *Boy Scout Trail*). After 1.2 miles and all of about 130 feet of elevation gain, the trail reaches a signed fork. Turn right on the Willow Hole Trail, which is heavily traveled and generally easy to follow because its often loose sand is churned by the passage of countless boots. The trail ends in 2.3 miles at Willow Hole.

Willow Hole Trail ranks very high on the long list of Joshua Tree's gorgeous trails. The imminence of awesome rockscapes becomes obvious three quarters of a mile up the trail, at a low pass overlooking the

Super Dome above Willow Hole

Wonderland of Rocks. Up ahead, half a mile away, the horizon is crowded with a continuum of huge boulder piles and imposing white domes, the tallest a swollen sugarloaf appropriately called Super Dome. The trail first descends gently to this packed maze along a tapering bay sprinkled with isolated monuments. When it reaches the maze, it merges with a small wash that meanders its way between formations. It squeezes through narrow gateways, skirts vertical waves of rock, passes by walls of smooth jointed boulders, lacerated cliffs, and petrified antediluvian beasts. Trees grow all over, juniper and Joshua trees at first on the open banks, then mature oak and pinyon pine along the wash, thick enough at places to feel like a small forest. Closer to the spring, the sand is fringed with water-loving baccharis, mesquite, and elegant bunches of tall grass. The deeper in, the bigger and the more closely spaced the formations get, in some impeccably choreographed crescendo. In the final quarter of a mile you are in the tectonic trench, a straight corridor of sand flanked by the most awesome formations yet. The south wall is a battery of pointed columns, each one clipped into tiered terraces decorated with balanced boulders. The north wall has nothing short of monumental proportions. It leaps up nearly 500 feet in a quarter of a mile, first a sheer auburn stack of canted pinnacles, then a bulging white dome called Super Slab, with Super Dome towering behind it.

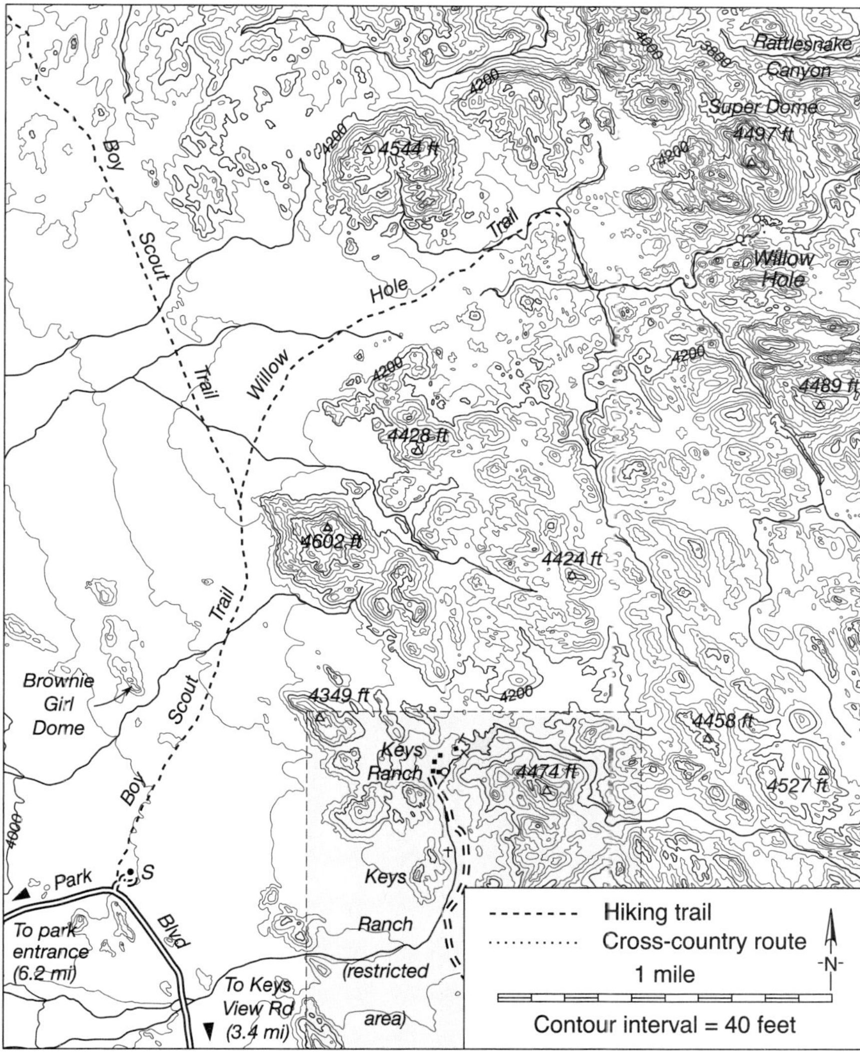

Willow Hole		
	Dist.(mi)	Elev.(ft)
Boy South Trail (south end)	0.0	4,040
Willow Hole Trail	1.2	4,142
Pass	2.0	4,170
Enter wash/Wonderl. of Rocks	2.4	4,120
Willow Hole/end of trail	3.5	4,015
Lower spring (depression)	3.65	4,000

Willow Hole looking west from the choke point in the wash

Willow Hole is at the foot of all this, just before a bookcase of fins that blocks the wash almost completely. Its dense grove of desert willow and oak boil right out of the sand, incongruously green and organic in this pale mineral extravagance. Although it lacks the stature of palm oases, it glows with the aura of rare and exceptional places. In rainy winters, a shallow pond floods its understory. In the spring, the willows are festooned with countless orchid-like white flowers. In the summer it is flushed with grass, Mojave thistle, and sacred datura in bloom. In the fall it turns into a romantic carpet of curled fallen leaves.

At the east end of the main grove, a narrow passage leads across the block of fins to the bottom of the depression beyond them. It has a pleasant pocket of greenery too, dwarfed by Super Slab's striated wall soaring right behind it. For most visitors, this is the end of the line—beyond lies relentlessly rough country ruled by merciless rocks. Even without this barrier, it would be hard to leave this intriguing landscape. Mesmerized by its singular beauty, you are compelled to linger, to scramble up high ledges and stare at new perspectives, humbled to a reverent silence by a land more surreal than virtual reality.

■

HIDDEN VALLEY

At the juncture between the Little San Bernardino Mountains and the Wonderland of Rocks, overlooking Lost Horse Valley's scenic Joshua-tree woodland, stands an isolated block of golden granite a mile long by half a mile wide fantastically sculpted by erosion. Ancient waters have gouged its core into a beautiful pasture lined with high cliffs and boulder stacks known as Hidden Valley. The trail that loops leisurely around it is one of the three or four most emblematic in Joshua Tree. At its lower end, the valley tightens into a beautiful canyon with high walls, boulders, and large trees, a secluded alternative ingress into this popular classic.

General Information

Road access: Hiking on trails and cross-country; paved access road
Hidden Valley Nature Trail: 1.1 mi, 130 ft up loop/very easy
Loop via lower Hidden Valley: 2.5 mi, 230 ft up loop/easy
Main attractions: Impressive granitic cliffs, botany, nature trail
USGS 7.5' topo map: Indian Cove
Maps: pp. 113*, *65*

Location and Access

For the most direct and popular access to the Hidden Valley Nature Trail, from the west entrance drive Park Boulevard 8.8 miles to the signed turnoff for the Hidden Valley picnic area, and turn right. Coming the other way, this junction is 1.7 miles from the Keys View Road. Continue 0.3 mile, past the split in the road, to the trailhead on the right, marked by an interpretive board, and park. The nature trail is heavily used. To minimize damage to plants and soil, stay on the main trail. To explore the boulders, use existing climbers' trails.

To hike into Hidden Valley via its lower end, drive only 7.4 miles from the west entrance (3.0 miles from the Keys View Road), and turn right on the good graded road to the old Lost Horse Ranger Station (which has been closed for many years). Drive this road 0.5 mile to a small pullout on the left, and park. The lower end of Hidden Valley is the wall-framed canyon on the left side of the road (southeast).

Route Description

Hidden Valley is aptly named. From the outside it is undetectable. Walk the tenth of a mile of trail up through a gateway of boulders and you are in it, shielded from the outside by a ring of massive stone sculptures. The trail splits right away. Turn left and hike it clockwise, as suggested by the trail sign, to minimize encounters with fellow hikers. The trail makes a 0.9-mile, nearly level loop along the valley's perimeter back to this junction.

Every place in this range is different, sometimes in subtle ways. What is remarkable about Hidden Valley is the diversity and intricacy of the formations. The most impressive are the walls. The largest and tallest is the Sentinel, a giant, domed flexure of shattered granite on the left a short distance in. The Thin Wall, on the left 0.15 mile further, is an imposing vertical slab that long orthogonal grooves have diced into a striking checkerboard. Across the valley rises the Great Burrito, similar but bigger still. The wall fronting it is chiseled into a tight stand of organ pipes that grade into chaos on the right side, like an unfinished masterpiece. Between these giants lie dozens of other landforms, boulder piles, stacks of slender vertical fins, skylines of jagged spires, and everywhere the inevitable dregs of erosion—boulders. The valley floor is heightened by an equally exuberant plant community—the flamboyant spikes of yucca and nolina, the ragged crowns of catclaw, and the lush heads of scrub oak, juniper, and pinyon pine.

In the late 1800s, the McHaney brothers were running a lucrative rustling operation in this general area. They stole cattle in southern Arizona and drove them back to sell them in the Joshua Tree area, then returned with stolen horses that they sold in Arizona. The Wonderland of Rocks' complex topography offered plenty of natural corrals enclosed by rock walls to conceal and rebrand stolen cattle. Hidden Valley was likely one of them. It was used some years later by lawful cowboys to hold cattle, and still later by Bill Keys to corral his horses (he blasted the gateway near the trailhead in 1936, presumably for easier access). It must have been a hell of a place to lose a cow...

The best way to approach Hidden Valley is the other direction, up the canyon that drains out of it. This route is considerably less crowded, quite scenic, gently sloped, and it provides both a more intimate contact with the land and a means to start and end this hike in serenity. From the graded road, walk up the wash that crosses the road 50 yards beyond the pullout. The sandy wash quickly enters the lower end of Hidden Valley, at this point a canyon funneled between a towering, finely structured wall on the left side known as Lost Horse Wall, and tall involute outcrops on the right. This is a beautiful passage, flushed with the same plants as the upper valley, its low screes of exquisitely rounded boulders peppered with the perennial greens of oaks and pines. Soon the canyon bunches tighter, and the boulders and trees

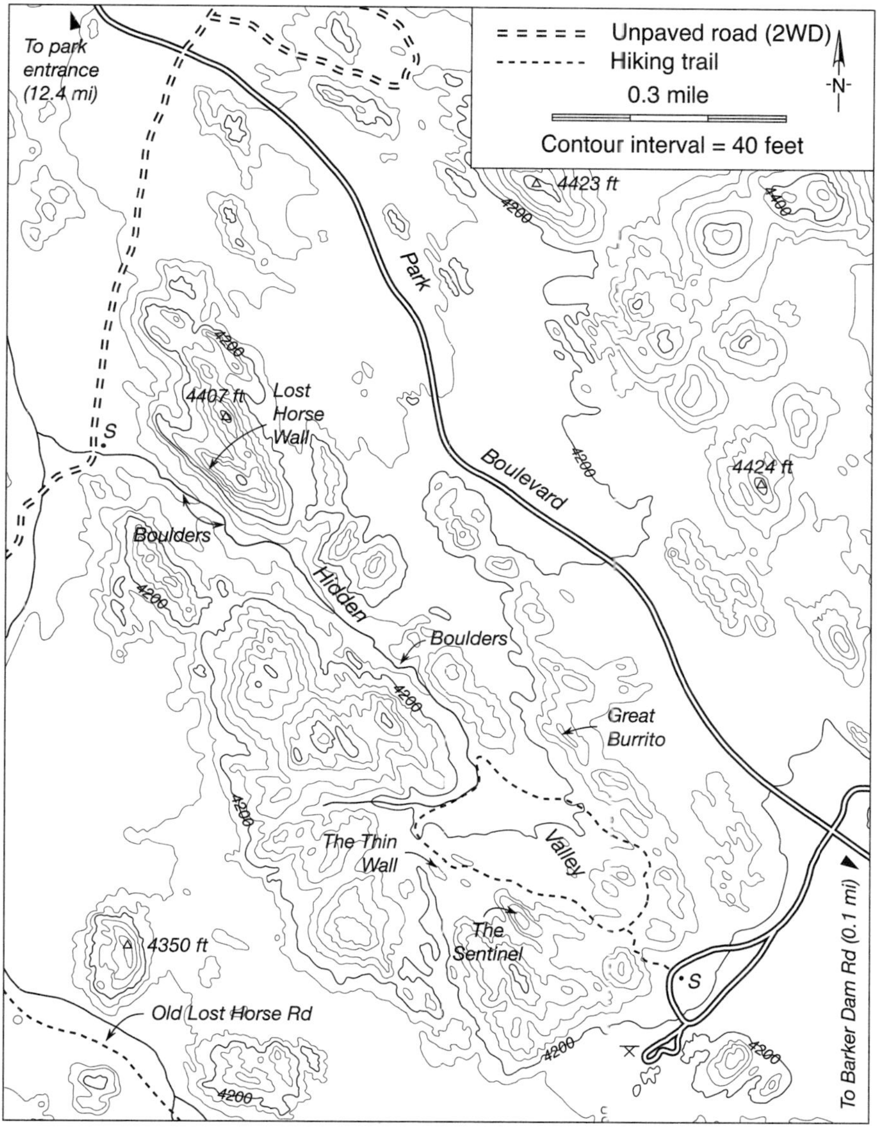

Hidden Valley		
	Dist.(mi)	Elev.(ft)
Parking	0.0	4,210
Far end of loop (wash/stairs)	0.55	4,180
Graded rd via lower Hidden V.	(0.8)	4,065
Back to parking	1.1	4,210

Late-afternoon skyline and storm clouds in upper Hidden Valley

invade the wash. This is a fun area for easy scrambles; use trails bypass this first set of boulders on either side. The rest of the way is mostly up a gradual sandy wash, interrupted by a few minor boulder jams or trees, circumvented too by use trails, mostly on the right side. After 0.8 mile the wash reaches the nature trail near its northwesternmost point. Coming from the trail, this junction is where the trail exits the wash and curves right up a flight of stairs.

Hidden Valley is, understandably, one of the park's most popular climbing spots. One of the attractions is watching climbers as they wriggle up its cracked crags, on routes with provocative names like *Loose Lady* and *Chocolate Is Better Than Sex*. We climb for the thrill of braving verticality, for the physical and mental challenges, and for the elation of success. The view from the top is secondary, the icing on the cake. Here the paradigm is reversed, at least for laypeople. Scrambling up any set of boulders, even just 30 feet, is likely to deliver vistas even more breathtaking than from the ground. The best time is early morning and evening, when every nook and cranny is highlighted by its own shadow, and row upon row of monuments stretch out into the golden light.

■

BARKER DAM

Barker Dam is a sizable reservoir built by cattlemen over a century ago for their livestock, and later associated with local legend Bill Keys. Rimmed by scenic granitic domes, it is reached by a very easy and popular trail that loops through a fantasyland of sculpted rocks. If possible, visit after a wet winter to enjoy the visual delight of this rare desert lake and the wildlife and riparian plants that it supports.

General Information
Road status: Hiking on maintained trail; paved access road
Barker Dam: 1.4 mi, 60 ft up loop / very easy
Main attractions: A desert lake, wildlife, ranching history, botany
USGS 7.5' topo map: Indian Cove
Maps: pp. 117*, 65

Location and Access

Barker Dam is at the southern periphery of the Wonderland of Rocks, northeast of Hidden Valley. The signed road to it branches off on the north side of Park Boulevard, 8.9 miles from the west entrance, or 1.6 miles west from Keys View Road. Drive the paved Barker Dam Road 1.6 miles to the large parking lot at the trailhead.

History: Bitter Fights Over Desert Water

From 1870 until the 1940s, many outfits large and small ran up to hundreds of cattle in what is today Joshua Tree National Park, especially in Queen Valley and Lost Horse Valley. Of the many reservoirs that cattlemen developed to supply water to their animals, Barker Dam is one of three largest. C. O. Barker, a Banning resident who ran horses and cattle in Twentynine Palms since at least the 1890s, built the original 9-foot dam around 1902. He ramped up his business in 1905 with the acquisition of the cattle interests of George Meyers, a member of McHaney's gang, which Meyers had acquired from Bill McHaney himself a decade earlier. Shortly after, Barker formed a merger with county sheriff Bill Shay. The Barker and Shay Cattle Company remained a key local player until it sold its business in 1923. Conflicts among cattlemen and homesteaders over water rights were common. Because of its large size and proximity to prime grazing ground, Barker Dam caused its share of trouble, even after it was set aside as a Public Water Reserve in 1914. Bill Keys filed homesteads around the

Reflections in Barker Dam reservoir after a rainy winter

dam so that Shay and others could not gain access to it. Cattlemen took revenge on his fences. Over time, cattle were stolen or shot, watering holes appropriated, boundaries violated, and at least one person killed. After Joshua Tree National Monument was created in 1936, grazing was prohibited except on existing homesteads, including Keys Ranch. In 1949 and 1950, with most competitors gone, the Keys family raised Barker Dam a few feet, perhaps to compensate for decreasing rainfalls. But by then the days of homesteads in Joshua Tree were numbered. Keys Ranch closed down in 1964. Since then, Barker Dam has been a silent reminder of the hardships of life in the Old West, dutifully fulfilling its mission, providing water for wildlife and enchantment for sightseers.

Route Description

The trail enters the Wonderland of Rocks almost right away, at a north-south defile typical of this range. Where it forks soon after, go straight to minimize encounters with fellow hikers. The sandy path continues along the scenic defile, past sculpted monoliths and cracked walls lined with dark oaks and pinyon pine, before veering off between tall rock piles and emerging at the historic dam.

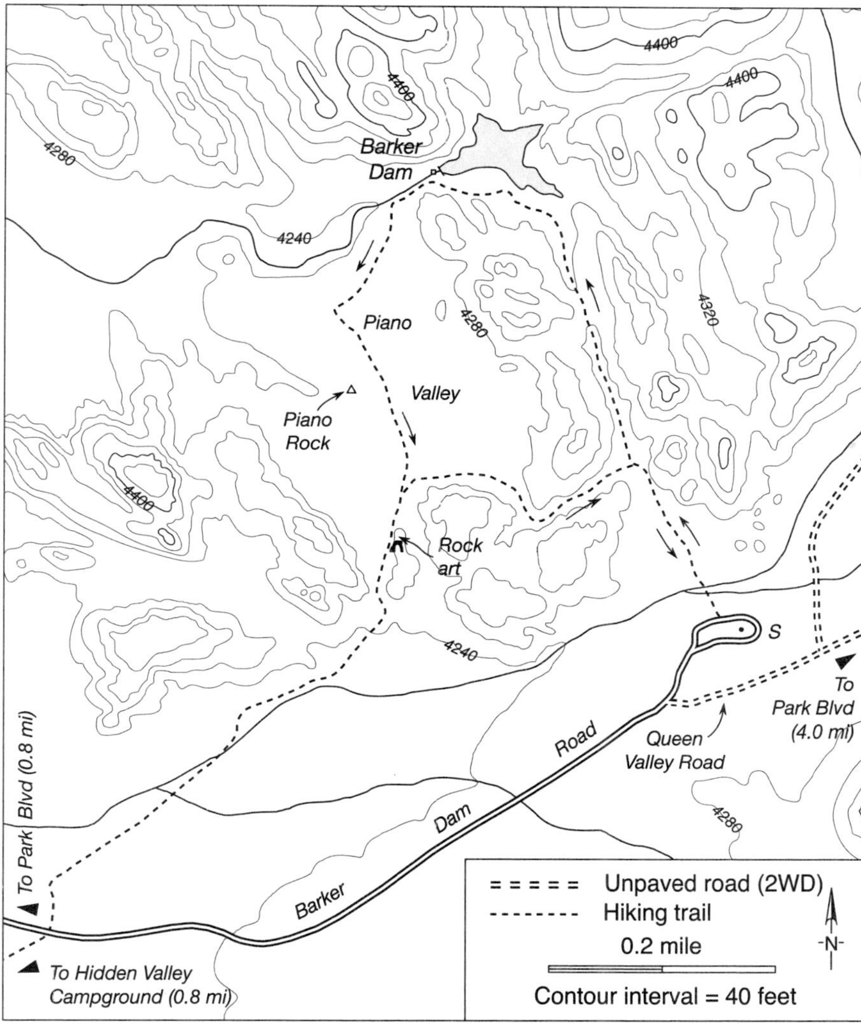

Barker Dam

	Dist.(mi)	Elev.(ft)
Barker Dam parking	0.0	4,260
Trail junction (right)	0.15	4,270
Barker Dam	0.5	4,275
Trail junction to Hidden Valley	0.85	4,250
Pictograph panel	(0.05)	4,260
Trail junction (left)	1.1	4,270
Barker Dam parking	1.3	4,260

Barker Dam is cupped in a charming little valley ringed with giant domes of granite exfoliating into interlocked slabs. The dam's lower level is the original wall of cobble-faced concrete built by Barker. At its south end, a historic inscription commemorates the completion of the concrete upper level by the Keys family. When the reservoir is near capacity, the landscape seems out of balance, reflected in a deep-blue lake bordered by tender-green willows. It is a pleasant walk east along the south shore, a fractal stitchery of tiny beaches and bumpy slickrock, then around to the north shore for different perspectives.

As always, water transforms the desert in astonishing ways. Below the dam, seepage irrigates a wetland of cattail and willow surrounded by large oaks and pines. A low concrete wall built by Keys still impounds the water. Two watering troughs remain, a wooden wagon box and a curious double-wall oval tub. The overflow collects in a lazy creek a couple of inches deep that flows a few hundred feet along banks of baccharis and catclaw laden with mistletoe. Long strands of bright-green algae wave in the slow current. Red-spotted toads celebrate the end of their protracted dormancy. Waterbugs and small armies of jade-black tadpoles patrol the water's edge. This is expectedly one of the park's best places to view wildlife. In summer, bighorn sheep are sighted almost daily; perhaps it is why the dam is also known as Big Horn Dam. Over time I saw ground squirrels, lizards, jackrabbits, kangaroo rats, many bird species, and a ram munching on young grass in the dry reservoir, alert to every sound.

From the dam the trail goes down rock stairs to Piano Valley, crosses it south, then loops back to the junction in the defile. Named for a piano that was brought here in the 1950s to entertain visitors, it is a scenic meadow dotted with Joshua trees and enclosed by piles of staggered boulders. Near its south end, a side trail leads 100 yards to a petroglyph site in a photogenic overhang with a small arch. The rock art's vivid colors are not original. They were added by a movie crew filming here in the 1960s so that the figures would stand out more prominently—a deplorable act that destroyed priceless cultural heritage.

Even when the lake is dry, this area is delightful for its particularly eye-pleasing botany of conifers, oaks, shrubs, herbs, and cacti. There is striking synergy between plants and rocks, often arranged as if to enhance each other's visual appeal. Handsome nolinas grow up on cliffs, and prickly-pear pose against artful boulders. Trail signs showcase the tricks that plants and wildlife have developed to survive, from creosote poisoning their neighbors to pack rats nesting in cacti. Like the ranchers of long ago, they fight endlessly for their water rights.

▪

BAGLEY'S RANCH

To settle a simple matter of right-of-way, in 1943 local ranch owner Worth Bagley, a mentally unstable ex-police officer, ambushed his neighbor Bill Keys, who shot him dead in self-defense. This very easy hike wanders through Bagley's ranch, from the ruins of his house to the contested road, the windmill of the Desert Queen Well, and the spot where he met his demise. Bagley's vicious personality, and Keys' homicide, highly publicized trial, and eventual pardon, may well exert a compelling grip as you walk around the doomed site.

General Information
Road status: Hiking on trails; graded access road
Bagley's Ranch: 0.7 mi, 40 ft up loop / very easy
Main attractions: History, homestead ruins, archaeology
USGS 7.5' topo map: Indian Cove
Maps: pp. 131*, 127, *65*

Location and Access

Variously known as the Ohlson House, the Pink House, Wonderland Ranch, or Uncle Willie's Health Food Store, the colorful ruins of this homestead are on the edge of the range just east of Barker Dam. From the west entrance, drive Park Boulevard 8.9 miles to the signed Barker Dam Road, on the left. Go 1.5 miles on the Barker Dam Road to a fork, and turn right on the graded Queen Valley Road. At the next fork (0.15 mile), turn left, and park after 0.25 mile at the end of the road. The trail to the Ohlson House is to the left of the outhouse.

Route Description

The wide sandy trail that leads from the parking to Bagley's Ranch is the old road that Bill Keys used for many years to access the Desert Queen Well and the Wall Street Mill. It passes through a small enclosed valley that has not seen a wildfire in decades. The ground is green with healthy desert shrubs. Joshua trees hang over the roadway. In 100 yards there is a junction. The well and the mill are straight ahead. Make a left instead. The ruins of Bagley's house are 200 yards further, tucked in a scenic cove framed by oak, pine, and low rocky bluffs.

In 1936 Worth Bagley and his wife Isabelle purchased 80 acres of land here and started a ranch. Their property stretched from this house, which may have pre-existed the acquisition, east to the Desert

Queen Well and north to the county line. The land adjacent to it across the county line, the site of the Wall Street Mill, was owned by Bill and Frances Keys. Bagley had served in the Navy and as a deputy sheriff in Los Angeles County. He was a mentally unstable man, subject to fits of anger, vicious, armed, and dangerous. The police department had recently let him go because he was cruel to prisoners, and feared and disliked by his coworkers. It is no surprise that he was a troublesome neighbor too, and that he went after Bill Keys with a vengeance.

The main source of dispute was the road that led to Keys' mill. For years the road was public and the Keys used it often, but now it happened to cross Bagley's private property. Bill Keys was friendly with his neighbors, but he was also determined and not easily intimidated. He stopped using the Desert Queen Well with good grace, but he continued using the road, which was the only driving access to his mill. Bagley overtly threatened Bill Keys and his family if he continued. He also resented Keys' cattle coming close to his ranch. To appease Bagley, Keys agreed to pay for and install a fence around Bagley's land. Bagley would still occasionally shoot one of Keys' cows, or block the road with logs or broken glass. His desire to kill Keys became obsessive.

On May 11, 1943, Bill Keys was driving back from his Wall Street Mill when he came upon a sign posted across Bagley's road. It said: "Keys, this is my last warning. Stay off of my property." Part way down the road, he saw Bagley walking toward him with a gun in his hand. Keys grabbed his rifle and stepped out of his car. Bagley fired and missed. Bill Keys had resorted to firearms to settle disputes before. In 1929 he had shot and wounded a cowboy over the use of a well, and was tried and acquitted. That fateful day of 1943, Keys used a weapon again and fired once, aiming for Bagley's gun hand. Bagley started running in zigzags, as he had learned to do in his police training. Keys fired two more shots, and Worth Bagley dropped dead.

Bagley's Ranch

	Dist.(mi)	Elev.(ft)
Parking	0.0	4,270
First trail junction (go left)	0.05	4,275
Ohlson House/Caves	0.2	4,280
Back to first trail jct (go left)	0.35	4,275
Second trail junction (go left)	0.45	4,285
Old car body	(0.05)	4,285
Desert Queen Well	0.6	4,307

The Ohlson House (2016)

Bill Keys turned himself in that evening for shooting a man in self-defense. During his two-week trial in July, the prosecution argued that Keys was trespassing, that he made no attempt to retreat when he saw Bagley with a gun, and that he shot Bagley in the back while Bagley was seeking cover. Bill Keys was found guilty of manslaughter and sentenced to up to ten years in San Quentin.

While Keys was serving his sentence, his family and friends fought tirelessly to reverse the decision. One of his strongest advocates was his long-time friend Erle Stanley Gardner, famous author of the Perry Mason mysteries that would later be featured in popular TV series. Upon hearing about Keys' imprisonment, Gardner, a few volunteer experts, and a state assemblyman put in long hours studying the court proceedings. They reviewed Bagley's medical record and deposed his ex-wife Isabelle Clark, evidence that had been denied during the trial. They discovered that Bagley had spent much time planning Keys' execution. It was not in his character to escape: when he was shot, he was most likely trying to beat Keys to the draw. As Keys had asserted, he had not shot Bagley in the back. The new evidence quickly convinced a governor's advisory board that the defendant had been wrongly convicted. Soon after, in October 1948, Bill Keys was released on parole.

He returned to his beloved desert ranch, where he lived the rest of his life. He was pardoned in 1956, at the age of 76.

Once a large one-story building of hand-made concrete blocks, Bagley's house is now a puzzle of broken walls, vacant doorways and windows, its wooden lintels charred by a late 1970s fire, its stucco still psychedelic pink. Yet enough is left to identify some rooms in its odd layout. The fireplace and chimney probably point to the living room, the front room with a door and a picture window to the kitchen, and the steel pipes to the washroom (the toilet was an outhouse). In the oak thickets west of the house, three shallow tafoni caves with faint rock art and a bedrock mortar attest to much earlier occupation. One of them, partly walled in, may be the cave that Bagley used to store dynamite. Smaller ruins are scattered around. After Bagley's death, the house was acquired by Signe Ohlson, the owner of a health food store in Yucca Valley. It must have been peaceful to live here then, before interstates, sprawling desert towns, and extensive tourism.

Go back to the trail junction, turn left, and you will be walking on the road where Bagley bet his life in a gun duel and lost. A short distance up, where Bagley dropped dead, Bill Keys had erected a stone marker that read: "Here is where Worth Bagley bit the dust at the hand of W. F. Keys May 11 1943." After people vandalized it, the NPS replaced it with a sign. A little further, a rusty pickup with a Rolls-Royce engine is forever parked 100 yards to the left of the trail. Was it the cistern truck that Bagley used to haul water from the Desert Queen Well the day he died? A few more minutes and you will reach the well. Dug in 1908, it was for decades a critical water supply for ranchers, miners, and homesteaders. Before Bagley acquired the property, Bill Keys was given permission by the railroad company to take the well's windmill. Being who he was, Bagley requested that Keys bring it back. The tall windmill, now bladeless, still caps the well, one of the last of its kind in the park.

Pump at the Desert Queen Well

■

WONDERLAND PLATEAU

On one of my visits to Wonderland Plateau, a woman just coming out of it said to me with infectious enthusiasm: "It is absolutely beautiful back in there." I did not have the heart to temper her thunder, so I just nodded and replied: "I can't wait!" And I truly could not. This is vintage Joshua Tree landscape, the heart of the Wonderland of Rocks, the archetypical sensual chaos of mega boulders and outlandish formations that instantly enthralls countless park visitors every year. Wonderland Plateau has dozens of inspiring destinations, many uncommonly easy to reach, be it the roaring pinnacle known as the Creature, the massive Astro Domes, nameless box canyons leading to secluded amphitheaters, or Garrett's Arch, the park's largest. To introduce a friend to the stone wonders of Joshua Tree, there may be no better place.

General Information
Road access: Hiking on use trail and cross-country; graded access road
South Astro Dome: 1.1 mi, 130 ft up, 30 ft down one way/easy
Garrett's Arch: 1.9 mi, 240 ft up, 50 ft down one way/easy
Main attractions: Awesome rock formations, Garrett's Arch, flora
USGS 7.5' topo map: Indian Cove
Maps: pp. 127*, *65*

Location and Access

Located just east of Barker Dam, Wonderland Wash is one of multiple parallel fault-bounded drainages that slice north-northwest across the Wonderland of Rocks' western section. It ascends gently in less than a mile to Wonderland Plateau, a broad highland of beautifully sculpted White Tank Monzogranite. The starting point is the same dirt parking area as for the hike to the Ohlson House (see *Bagley's Ranch*).

Route Description

From the trailhead walk the trail to the first junction 100 yards out, make a left, and go 0.1 mile to Wonderland Ranch. To the left of the main ruin, go through a short screen of trees to a wash, and follow it as it curves almost immediately to the right (north), just past an old dam.

Wonderland Wash is a twisted river of sand, mostly narrow, barely inclined, funneled between alignments of giant monuments. Steep piles of oddly shaped boulders come right down to its banks. Behind them rise tall bluffs, beautifully misshapen, cracked and sliced by slanted dikes. For climbers from all over the world, this is a revered mecca. Even for non-climbers, almost every direction is an invitation to scramble, on slabs, slants, and slickrock, for the challenge, a glimpse from higher ground, or a closer look at a stone sculpture. The most distinctive one is an eye-catching monument on the right known as either the Creature or the Walrus. Viewed from downhill, it resembles the upper body of a marine mammal. From uphill it looks like a horrific chimera, its head disproportionally enormous, its mouth frozen in a gaping roar wide enough to crunch a T rex.

Here too, a good part of the seduction comes from the sharp contrast between naked ivory stone and a vegetation so intensely green that it seems out of place. In the confines of this relatively narrow passage, the trees, cacti, and shrubs have an even stronger presence. Oaks, pinyon pine, juniper, and manzanita grow everywhere—along the wash, high up on ridges, out of clefts in the walls. Somehow, the wash manages to squeeze through this entanglement of rocks and plants. Only at a few places, where trees or fallen boulders or a low rock dam from the pioneer days block the way, climbers have worn short bypass paths on the low banks. You brush against soft nolina and scratchy foliage, duck under low branches, tiptoe around prickly-pear, sidestep the frazzled daggers of Mojave yucca. The prickly-pear are particularly impressive. Generally less common, here they grow with abandon, in sprawling mats that often hug the trail and demand vigilance. In May and June, every single one bears impossibly bright canary flowers, as alluring as a rose.

Half a mile up, shortly past the Creature, Wonderland Wash widens as it reaches the southern edge of Wonderland Plateau, a fairly level, square-mile highland covered with a surfeit of outstanding formations. Most of them are domes, massive monoliths bounded by sheer faces and cliffs, all carved in complex shapes. They are aligned in orderly tectonic ranks on both sides of a wide sandy trench, the northern extension of Wonderland Wash. The first one that comes into view, on the left, is South Astro Dome. It is the tallest, an immense, 260-foot hump faced from summit to base with a vertical cliff. The narrow sugarloaf rising against its right flank is North Astro Dome. Both are imposing structures, streaked by tall curtains of brown desert varnish that accentuate their heights. For their superb high-quality routes, they are popular among climbers. It is a short walk west to their base, across waves of swollen bedrock, past stray boulders and gnarled trees. Experienced climbers are impressive to watch, slipping up these immense walls on invisible holds with surprising grace.

The Creature, aka the Walrus

Garrett's Arch, named after the ranger who discovered it, is slowly becoming a main off-beat destination in this area. It is fairly easy to find, thanks to a fortuitous set of easily identifiable landmarks. Across from South Astro Dome, continue 0.1 mile north, where a main wash veers off to the left (northwest). Go straight on a sandy wash instead, in the same direction as Wonderland Wash, aiming to the right of a 100-foot dome with three isolated boulders resting on it precariously. Just 0.25 mile further you will walk by a curious formation on the right aptly named Freak Brothers Dome, a triplet of adjacent, oddly similar pointed towers, each one neatly clipped by a square overhang. Ninety steps past the middle tower, a fat pinnacle called the Weenie towers on the right. In 50 more steps, a sliver of a sandy wash squeezes between two low outcrops on the right. Follow it east along a nearly level corridor flushed with oak and pine, and framed by sumptuous cliffs carved into vertical ribs and pillars. The Red Obelisk stands by the wash halfway through, a stand-alone 25-foot tower. Its west face is a cleaved wall of rusty desert varnish, its east face a wavy flank of tafoni. This passage ends in 0.25 mile at a valley enclosed by stone monuments. Straight ahead, there is a broad saddle in the mountain on the horizon. In front of it and slightly to the left, spot the 140-foot spheroidal outcrop with a capital A eroded across its face. Garrett's Arch is hidden inside this outcrop. About 50 steps into the valley, look for a foot trail on the low bench on the left. It wanders across the valley roughly east-northeast 0.25 mile to Garrett's Arch. If you cannot find the trail, cut a beeline to it, following washes as much as possible to avoid damaging plants and cryptobiotic soil.

Garrett's Arch keeps you guessing until the last moment, when you skirt the capital-A outcrop still wondering where it is and it finally appears, high up on the outcrop's rim. It is a magnificent stonework. Its elliptical opening, about 20 feet tall, is punched in the recess of a shallow, high-vaulted cave perched at the top of steep slickrock

It is tempting to climb to it. The most direct way, up the exfoliating slickrock, is slippery and exposed. There is a more strenuous but safer way, up the long straight groove that slashes sideways across the slick-rock up to the base of the cave. Below the groove's lower end, at ground level, a stack of large boulders forms a cave just tall enough to stand. From the cave a slender person can slither up through a narrow chimney to the groove, then walk up alongside the groove.

Life always seems to find a way. On the cave's floor, in shallow sand that hardly ever receives rain or direct sunlight, there is a hanging nursery of very old plants. A lanky Mojave yucca presides over a scraggly oak and a pine, an enormous sacred datura, and a few mound cactus, the largest one a cluster of 200 heads. Undisturbed by most large wildlife their entire lives, these recluse plants thrive. The view from their elevated balcony is amazing, encompassing the green, tree-dotted valley and its ring of broken domes and fallen boulders. Tread lightly on this lost Ark; stay away from the loamy sand, step on rock surfaces only, give them a chance to live another century.

Wonderland Plateau

	Dist.(mi)	Elev.(ft)
Parking area	0.0	4,270
Trail junction (go left)	0.1	4,275
Wonderland Ranch	0.2	4,280
Dam/Wonderland Wash	0.22	4,280
The Creature/the Walrus	0.65	~4,320
Across from South Astro Dome	0.9	~4,340
South Astro Dome (base)	(0.2)	4,370
Freak Brothers Dome (base)	1.3	~4,325
Garrett's Arch	1.9	~4,460

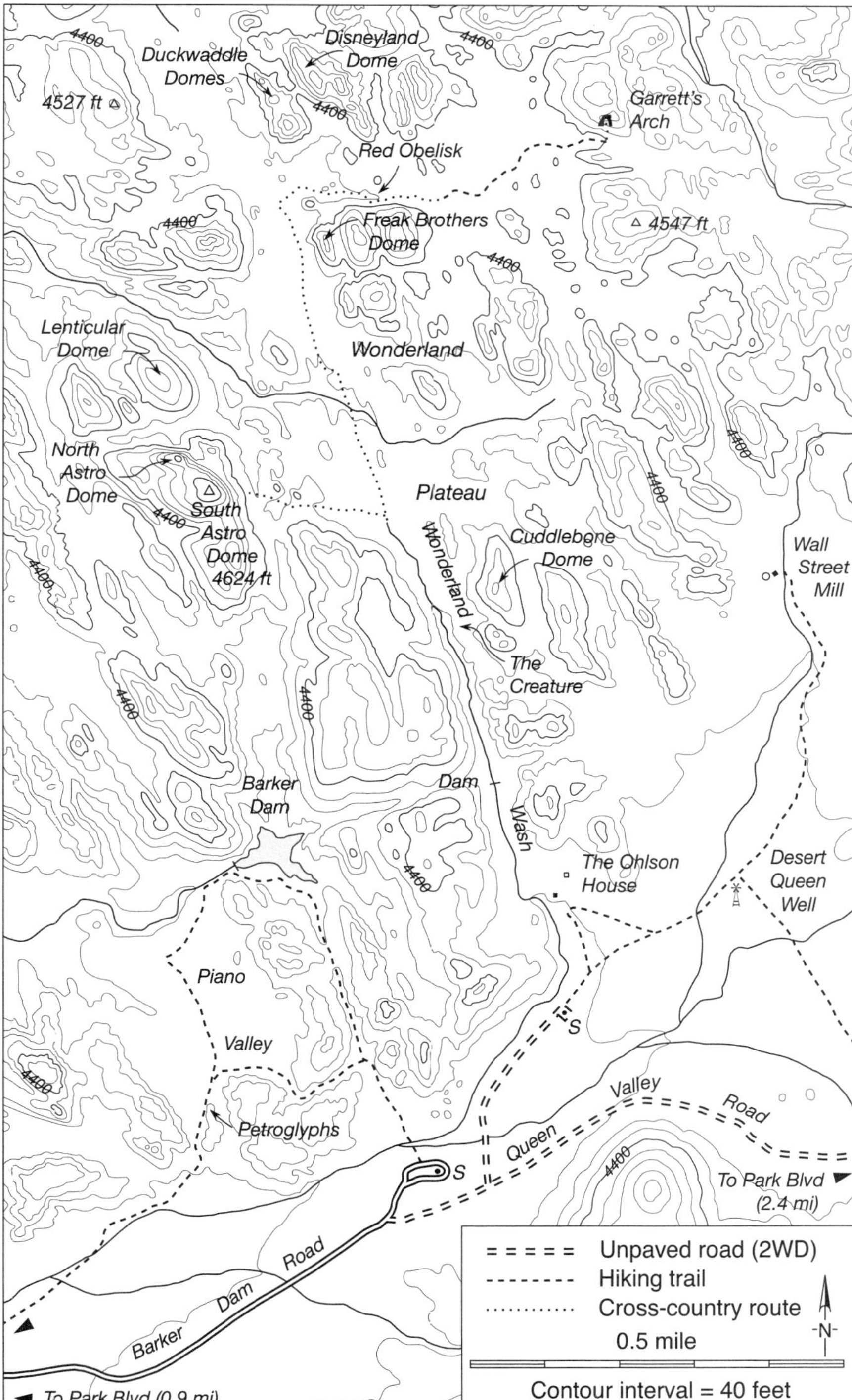
Duckwaddle Domes
Disneyland Dome
4527 ft
Garrett's Arch
Red Obelisk
Freak Brothers Dome
4547 ft
Lenticular Dome
Wonderland
North Astro Dome
South Astro Dome 4624 ft
Plateau
Wonderland
Cuddlebone Dome
Wall Street Mill
The Creature
Barker Dam
Dam
Wash
The Ohlson House
Desert Queen Well
Piano
Valley
Petroglyphs
S
Queen
Valley
Road
To Park Blvd (2.4 mi)
Barker
Dam
Road
To Park Blvd (0.9 mi)
4400
Unpaved road (2WD)
Hiking trail
Cross-country route
0.5 mile
N
Contour interval = 40 feet

Garrett's Arch (photo by Susan Cole)

In this generous topography where every direction is enormously attractive, it is easy to feel overwhelmed. There is only enough time in a day to visit a fraction of it. You could spend a whole day just in the exquisite canyon past the Astro Domes and Lenticular Dome, where you must slide down chutes and crawl through tunnels to make it through. You could spend another day beyond Freak Brothers Dome and Duckwaddle Domes' spectacular walls, exploring side canyons and secluded coves. This is a perfect place to be a vagabond. No matter where you go, like the woman I met, you will come back euphoric, your mind reeling with surreal images, elated to have discovered a special spot on Earth, and hoping that, one day, you will return.

■

THE WALL STREET MILL

Hidden in the jungle of oak and pinyon pine that borders the Wonderland of Rocks, the Wall Street Mill is the most complete of its kind in the park. It is a touching symbol of a bygone era, surrounded by the carcasses of vintage cars and the well that provided the water vital to its operation. Reached by a short and easy trail through a green desert valley, this exquisite repository of historic technology is a must to anyone interested in the mining and ranching history of the park.

General Information

Road status: Hiking on trail; graded access road
Wall Street Mill: 0.8 mi, 70 ft up, 0 ft down one way / very easy
Main attractions: Well-preserved historic mill, vintage cars, history
USGS 7.5' topo map: Indian Cove
Maps: pp. 131*, *65*

Location and Access

The Wall Street Mill is in a deep cove at the west end of Queen Valley, between Barker Dam and Queen Mountain. To get to the trailhead, follow the directions to the Ohlson House (see *Bagley's Ranch*).

Route Description

When the weather is clement, it is a gentle stroll to the Wall Street Mill on the dirt road that gave access to it in historic times. In the first third of a mile the road passes by the two short side trails on the left to the Ohlson House, visible through a screen of Joshua trees, then it crosses a wash and reaches the Desert Queen Well (see *Bagley's Ranch*). The mill is another half a mile up the trail. This whole area is a delightful transition zone between mountain and valley, so lush that you may not think you are in a desert. The naked outcrops of the Wonderland of Rocks to the left are fringed with healthy pinyon pine. Queen Valley spreads out across from them, a botanical garden crowded with mid-elevation plant species. The Wall Street Mill comes into view suddenly, concealed in a dense woodland of ancient scrub oak.

The tale of the Wall Street Mill started long ago, with a simple well. It is said that it was Bill McHaney who sunk it in 1896, during the golden era of the Desert Queen Mine, to provide water for his cattle. In the desert, water is a coveted resource. After McHaney abandoned the well two years later, several ranchers took it over. In 1900, a preacher built an arrastra near it, and for five years milled gold-bearing quartz from the Louise Mine a half hour's walk away. In 1929, after the well had fallen into disuse for years, a miner named Oran Booth and two partners filed a mill site on the property to treat ore from their Wall Street Mine across Queen Valley. They built a bunkhouse and refurbished the well, but following a dispute their venture fell through. The well changed hands one last time in 1930 when local landlord Bill Keys, always eager to expand his estate, bought the mill site.

That summer, Keys leased his new property to miners working the nearby Gold Tiger Mine. Thinking that they needed a mill, the ambitious lessees hauled the idle two-stamp mill at Pinyon Well in the Little San Bernardino Mountains 12 rough miles to the wash below the well, where the arrastra once stood. They did not find much ore, and after all this labor they quit. In 1933, Keys dismantled the mill and reassembled it piece by piece at its present location, right next to the well. The name of Booth's failed mine stuck, and it became known as the Wall Street Mill.

Keys already had a five-stamp mill at his ranch. He might have acquired this smaller mill because it was closer to his Desert Queen Mine, and more efficient to handle small loads. He might have seen it as an investment too, to run custom jobs for local miners who could not afford a mill. He charged $5 a ton, including his time. Sometimes a friend, a family member, or a miner would take a shift at the mill and stay overnight at the bunkhouse. The Wall Street Mill probably did not make a killing. Between 1933 and 1941, the 41 tons of ore from the Desert Queen Mine that it processed averaged $25 a ton in gold. The handful of mines that used its services were likely poorer. The mill's last user may have been Bill Keys' son Willis. After his release from the Army in 1948, he worked the Desert Queen with a few former service buddies, but they too found little gold and quit in 1949. For old times' sake, in the summer of 1966 Bill Keys and a few friends repaired the aging mill and fired up its stamps one last time. It heralded the end of both a technology that had become obsolete, and of small-time mining.

The Wall Street Mill is an odd structure, low-slung and sprawled across a shallow incline like a marooned craft. Its machinery is mostly hidden inside a misshapen shell of corrugated iron. If you did not know what a mill looked like, you may not be entirely sure what it is. As a protection against malice and thievery, the mill is enclosed in a barbed-wire fence and off-limits. You peer into it with your imagination. The inclined tramway at the south end is where the half-ton ore car was winched up to a first pulley visible at the top of the mill. The

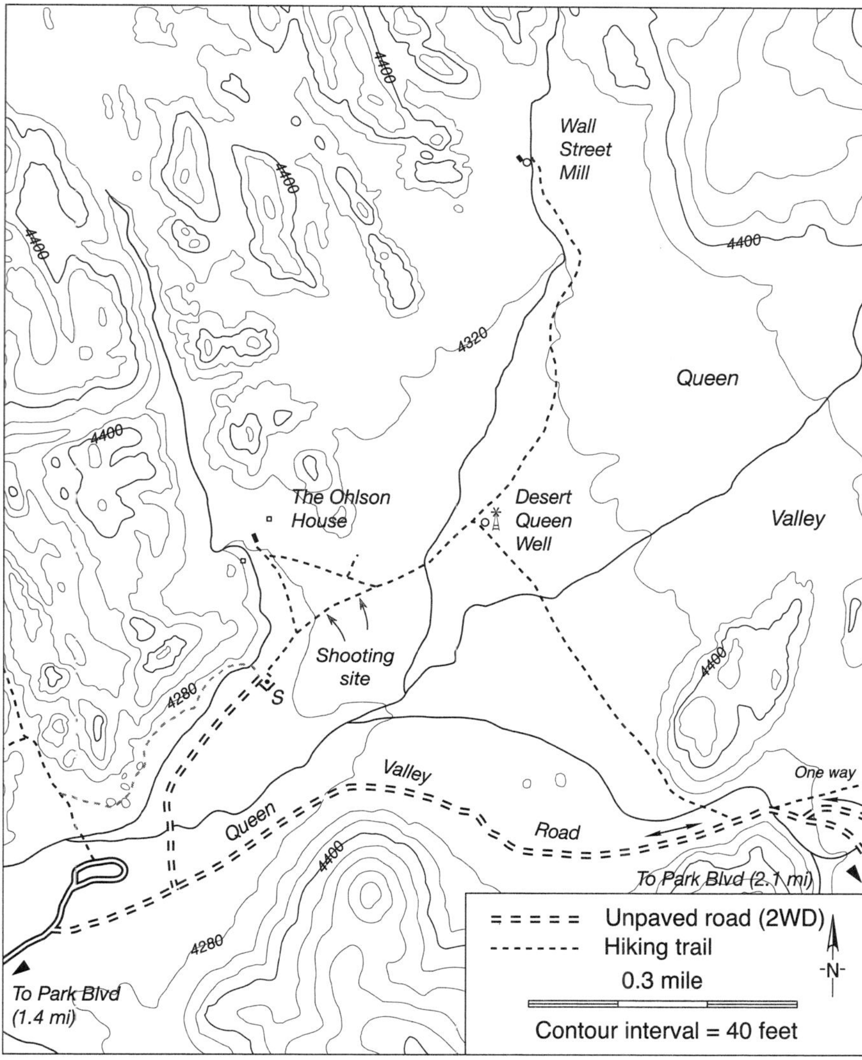

The Wall Street Mill		
	Dist.(mi)	Elev.(ft)
Parking area	0.0	4,270
Junction (go straight)	0.05	4,275
Ohlson House	(0.15)	4,280
Desert Queen Well	0.3	4,306
Wall Street Mill	0.75	4,337
Old pickup	0.8	4,340

Inclined tramway and water tanks at the Wall Street Mill

ore was conveyed to a second pulley, where a jaw crusher ground it into gravel. It was then fed into the stamps, just below the turret past the second pulley, where it was pulverized to a pulp. The pulp was treated on an amalgamation table, where the free gold particles chemically bonded to mercury. A concentration table was used to recover the last of the gold from the remaining pulp. Both tables were located under the sloped roof at the north end of the mill.

There are other remnants from that era outside the fenced area. A 1940s-era pickup with shredded tires and bug-eyed headlights is parked up the wash. Another vintage vehicle is buried axle-deep in the sand under a giant oak. Among the outcrops behind the mill is the small quarry where Bill Keys harvested the stone marker that he erected at the site of Worth Bagley's killing. The well that started it all is still there, near the eastern corner of the fence, over 130 years old and counting. A wooden platform caps its casing. The rusted machinery looking like a toilet on wheels that rests on top of it is the reciprocating pump. The pipes that carried water from the pump to the two tanks beside the mill stop in midair, waiting for water that will never come.

■

QUEEN MOUNTAIN

The highest summit in the Wonderland of Rocks, Queen Mountain is a lofty mesa of carved monzogranite that drops 1,000 feet from the southern edge of the range into Queen Valley's scenic arboretums. The climb from valley floor to rimrock is hard work, up a sheer rock-strewn ravine traced by a rough use trail. Even if you cannot make the final rock-climbing to the two neighboring summits, for much of this ascent the views of the colossal sculptures surrounding the mountain are breathtaking.

General Information

Road status: Roadless; graded access road (2WD)
East Queen Mtn: ~2.0 mi, 1,230 ft up, 30 ft down one way / difficult
Queen Mountain: ~2.0 mi, 1,220 ft up, 10 ft down one way / difficult
Main attractions: Scenic cactus gardens, views of Wonderland of Rocks
USGS 7.5′ topo map: Queen Mountain
Maps: pp. 135*, 65

Location and Access

Work your way to the signed Big Horn Pass Road, a graded road that starts off Park Boulevard 5.0 miles east from the junction with Keys View Road (or 5.8 miles west from Pinto Wye). The Big Horn Pass Road heads northwest across Queen Valley towards the Wonderland of Rocks. After 0.4 mile, turn right at a fork onto the unsigned O'Dell Road. At the four-road crossing 0.6 mile further, continue straight toward Queen Mountain's twin summits rising up ahead. Drive 0.9 mile to the small loop at the end of the road and park. These roads are passable with a standard-clearance vehicle.

Route Description

Queen Mountain is shaped like a mesa more than a desert mountain, a 1.5-mile long, 600-foot thick plateau of exceptionally hard monzogranite that drops from sky to valley like a pleated curtain. The rock is so resilient that the combined erosional powers of water, wind, heat, frost, and gravity have not cut a single canyon into it. But they have carved in the mountain's flank a spectacular mile-long parapet of hulking towers and sheared cliffs revered like a shrine by hard-core climbers for their remote, high-quality routes. The most striking outcrop is the Cirque of the Climbables, a rack of vertical ribs hanging above a sheer ravine. A couple of climbers will occasionally hike up the aging trail beyond the road and painstakingly trudge up the ravine to scale the Cirque. Queen Mountain stands above it, a bulb of naked stone surrounded by a capricious geography.

To those who lack the agility of a spider monkey the mountain offers an alternative, a ravine a little less rough that does not require levitating on footholds the size of bread crumbs. It is about a mile northeast of the end of the road, hidden by a fold in the mountain. If you walk due east from the end of the road about 400 yards, the second wash you will cross is the wash that drains out from the ravine. Walking up the wash's ribbon of fine sand across Queen Valley's serene countryside is a delight. It passes by a collage of desert gardens delineated by tiny washes, low swells, and erratic boulders. Monocultures of grizzly bear cactus alternate with stands of juvenile Joshua trees, hillsides of yucca and pancake prickly-pear, and scenic coves of juniper and silver cholla, all growing out of meager gravel. The wash soon crosses a line of low hills at a slanted fall of layered monzogranite, then wanders on to the ravine at the foot of the range.

The ravine is impressive. A shallow, 30-foot wide trench, it screams up the mountain on a high parabola, funneled between raised rims of pale boulders at its base, some the size of a Cadillac. Its wash is cluttered with large flat-topped boulders and angular falls, and it is *steep*. Where the boulders became too crowded I exited up a propitious side drainage onto the east rim, where the climbing was easier, though not for long. The rim soon ran into a cliff that forced me back down into the ravine. The wash uphill from that point is clogged with vertical boulders. I crossed it and found salvation—a dusty use trail that took me the rest of the way and most of the ascent—to the crest. It is crooked, rocky, slippery, and it occasionally flirts with eminently prickly plants, but it is better than nothing.

At the crest the trail enters a serene cove sheltered by sheer bluffs. Large pine and oak, tall yucca, and pancake cactus grow in this unexpected garden high above the valley. The taller bluff on the west side is Queen Mountain. The one on the east side is too—so says the 1937 USGS benchmark irreverently glued to it. Yes, Queen Mountain has not one but two summits—*noblesse oblige*. The true high point (west) is girdled on its north, west, and south sides with hard cliffs, climbing routes like G Spot and Cactus Slump that will burn through muscles faster than it takes to fall. Its more sedate east side, facing the cove, is the only spot left for ordinary humans to reach the top, up tilted slabs.

From the cove the 10-foot shorter eastern twin looks even more daunting, but here too there is an easier option. The trail cuts north

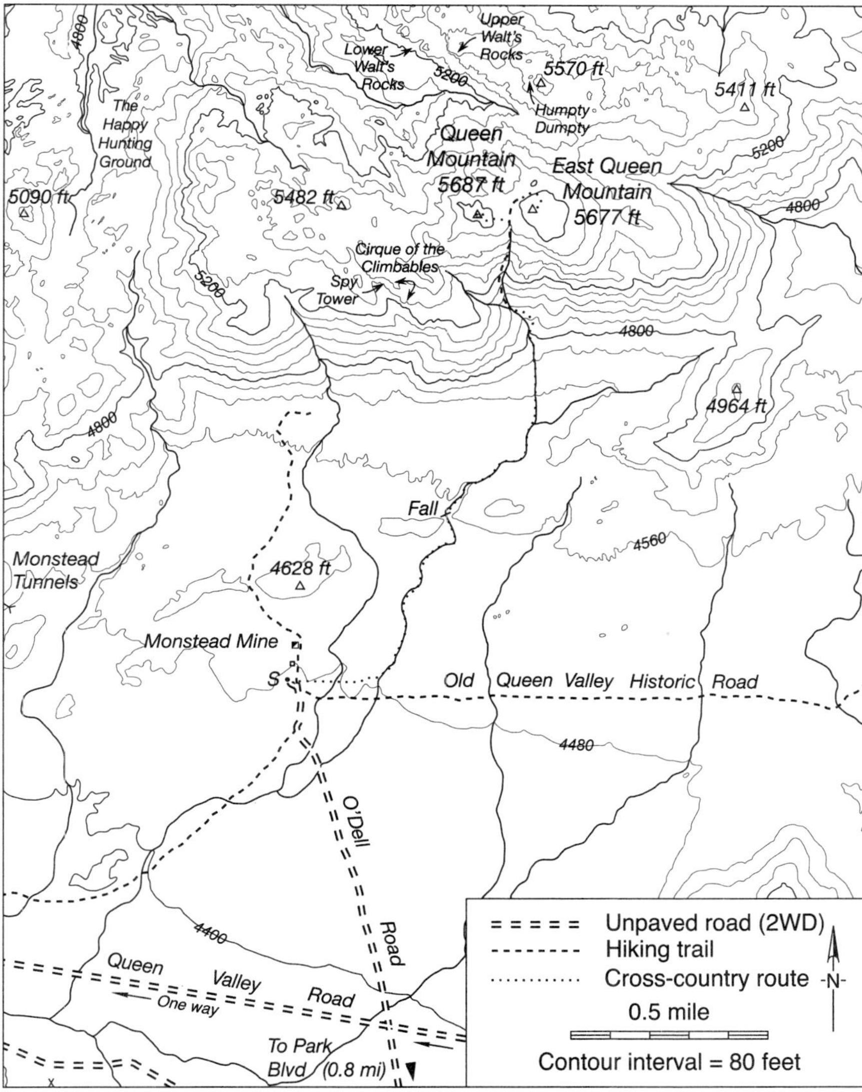

Queen Mountain	Dist.(mi)	Elev.(ft)
O'Dell Road	0.0	4,475
Foot of ravine	1.1	4,600
Cove at crest	1.8	~5,530
East Queen Mountain	(0.15)	5,677
Queen Mountain	1.95	5,687

The Wonderland of Rocks from below East Queen Mountain

across the cove, then descends a little as it circles clockwise to the northeast side of this second summit. From there it is an easy cross-country climb, first up a short talus spotted with pine, then through a small jungle of oak and giant nolinas to the eastern foot of the summit block, and finally up stepped slickrock to the top.

In every direction the view is beautiful. The true summit looks west over the G Spot at a maze of fins so dislocated that a ewe would have trouble finding her lamb. To the north a canyon with bulging cliffs flows gracefully down toward the Wonderland of Rocks' petrified waves of stone, past Walt's Rocks and other premier climbing sites, its wash a pigmy forest of oak and evergreen. To the south, the mountain plunges over its own rim and disappears. Queen Valley spreads out half a mile beyond, dotted with sharp hills and boulder islands, edged far away by a high cordillera of mountains. In the late afternoon every rock in the valley glows against its own shadow, a tableau so crisp one could reach out and touch it. An evening return down the precipitous ravine has the dreamy quality of a descent on a hot-air balloon, an intemporal suspension in space, Queen Valley a brilliant fantasy slowly turning to amber, then ash.

■

PINE CITY

Once the mining camp of a luckless mine, Pine City is reached by an easy and uncharacteristically uneventful trail in Queen Valley. There is nothing left of it except its empty streets lined with broken walls, and its tunnels are just as elusive. But being set among beautiful boulders, juniper, and pinyon pine in the cooler high desert, it is a pleasant area to explore, to ponder where its cabins once stood, and visit a nearby spring once used for bootlegging.

General Information

Road status: Hiking mostly on trails; graded access road
Pine City: 1.6 mi, 160 ft up, 40 ft down one way / very easy
Pine City Viewpoint: 2.0 mi, 230 ft up, 60 ft down one way / very easy
Pine Spring: 2.1 mi, 170 ft up, 230 ft down one way / easy
Main attractions: Easy trails to scenic boulders, spring, and viewpoint
USGS 7.5' topo map: Queen Mountain
Maps: pp. 139*, *65*

Location and Access

Pine City is located in the southeastern foothills of the Wonderland of Rocks, a mile and a half north of the Desert Queen Mine. A trail leads up to it starting from the same point as the hike to the Desert Queen Mine. Refer to *The Desert Queen Mine* for directions.

Route Description

Pine City. The Pine City Trail is a century-old mining road that crosses a short stretch of Queen Valley and ends just inside the Wonderland of Rocks. The walking is easy, over even, almost level terrain. At first the terrain and the vegetation is subdued. You have to be patient. As you approach the mountain, plants gradually increase in health, density, and diversity. Half a mile in, the dominant plants are noticeably larger and denser. In another half a mile the first oak and pinyon pine show up, then manzanita and nolina. Even cacti, so thrifty with water, find the habitat more desirable—at least nine species grow along the trail. By the time you reach Pine City, you are in prime Joshua Tree country, immersed in a crisp landscape of cool boulder piles, lush desert gardens, and the expected pine.

Like other grand-sounding names of historic desert mines, Pine City was a vast exaggeration. It was never a town, let alone a city. At its apex, it likely had at most a few cabins and the obligatory outhouse. The mine that justified its existence, the Pine Springs Lode, was minimal too. Its only claim to fame is that it was re-located in July 1923 by local homesteaders Bill and Frances Keys. It is unknown how much work the Keys performed on this property. Bill Keys reportedly stated that the two miners who worked it before him thought they had found silver when it was ordinary iron ore, and they did not produce anything of value. Neither Pine City nor the mine made history.

After 1.5 miles, the Pine City Trail reaches the first large outcrop, a wide 20-foot wall of stacked boulders. This is the south end of a square block 250 yards on the side crisscrossed by a grid of perpendicular trenches, like the layout of a city. Pine City was hidden in this maze of rock. Where the trail curves left in front of the outcrop, there is a large pine tree. Fifty yards before it, a broad path at 2 o'clock leads 75 yards to the main avenue. Its sandy path is lined with thick, closely spaced pine and oak, and decorated with nolina and cactuses. Cut off from its surroundings by its rocky cocoon, this forested enclave has the feel of a secret arboretum. Streets open up on the left and right. Between them, the city blocks are eroded fins of stone, anything from proud edifices to rubbles of fallen boulders. Pine City's name may have been inspired not by visions of grandeur but by this coincidental similarity to a city grid. Today, all that is left of Pine City are these vacant arteries. Some go through. Others are barely wide enough to get in, or dead end. The appeal of visiting this lost city is exploring these secret passages, and figuring out where its cabins might have stood a century ago.

The Pine City Viewpoint. From the large pine tree, the main trail circles around the outcrop's west side and continues north. The three shafts of the Pine Springs Lode were located along the next 0.3 mile on both sides, but most of them are now hard to spot. This general area is peppered with large boulders, and hikers linger without fail to admire the scenery. On each side, the land slips off into a shallow canyon lined with fantastic outcrops in various stages of composition, as if the sculptor had left before completing her job. The maintained trail ends at the divide with Pine City Canyon to the north. The rocky trail on the left climbs to the viewpoint, a low hilltop with fine views of the canyon, Pine City, Negro Hill, and Queen Mountain.

Pine Spring. Hidden in a forested canyon on the outskirts of Pine City, this small spring is a good excuse to explore the area's scenic bouldery landscape. Locate the primitive trail that skirts the southern edge of Pine City. Almost right away it descends east-northeast into a

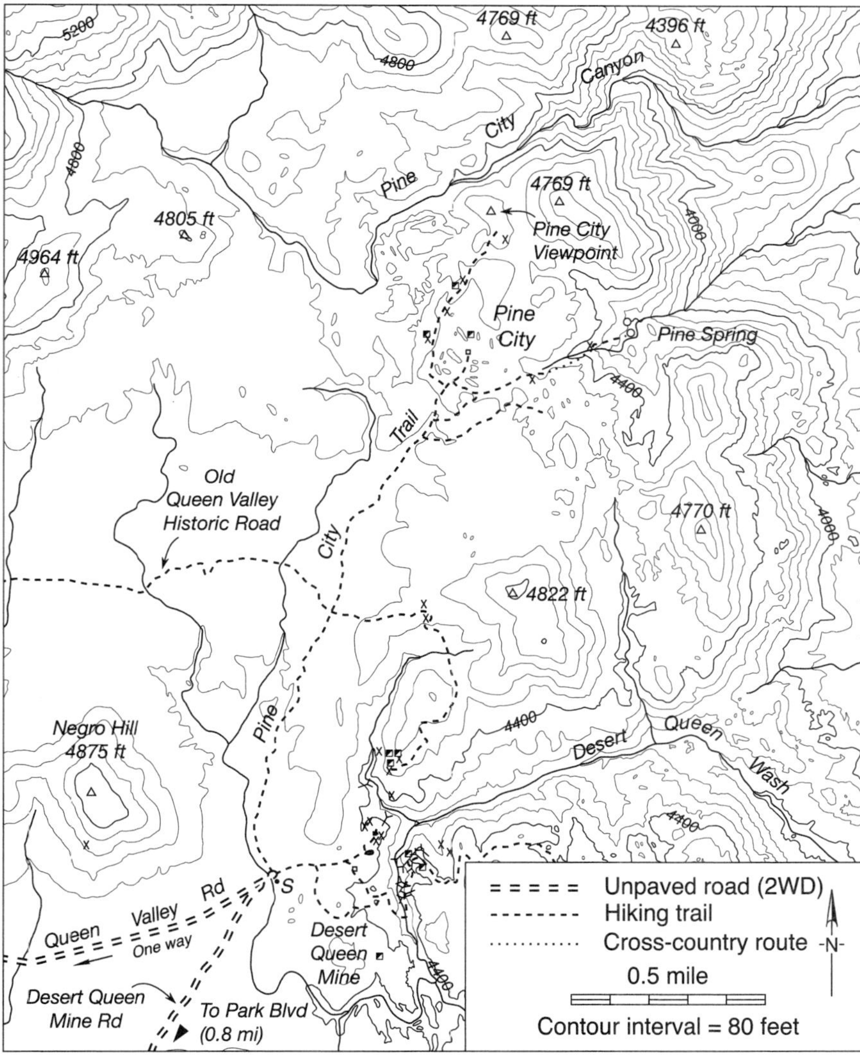

Pine City		
	Dist.(mi)	Elev.(ft)
Pine City trailhead	0.0	4,436
Pine City junction	1.45	~4,560
Pine City	(0.1)	~4,560
Pine City junction	1.45	~4,560
Pine Spring	(0.65)	~4,380
Pine City Viewpoint	2.0	~4,605

Entrance to the Pine City maze of rock

broad drainage. After just 0.2 mile the drainage has deepened to a ravine choked with boulders, and the trail vanishes. Over the next quarter of a mile you scramble down over and between boulders into a canyon framed with vertically sliced outcrops. Here too, pine trees are numerous. The trail resumes on the left side where the canyon opens up again. The spring is located at the more level confluence between three side canyons bristling with short outcrops.

Pine Spring has not had the best of luck in recent decades. When the Keys re-located the Pine Springs Lode, the spring was part of it, and a short tunnel was bored into bedrock, mostly to provide water for their cattle. Later, during the Prohibition, they made a little cash leasing it to a party who set up a small camp and operated a still. For some time now, the spring has been disfigured by a monster guzzler, an unsightly apple-green contraption that blends in like a bull in a penguin colony. But it may make you think about hydrology and plumbing, and reflect on the ethics of helping wildlife overcome anthropogenic difficulties, creating populations that are a little healthier but no longer function fully autonomously, like chipmunks fed by tourists. The original spring, in the bend just down the open wash, is an impenetrable patch of riparian plants, and a peaceful spot for a break.

■

PINE CITY CANYON

> *Of the few major canyons in the park, Pine City Canyon is possibly the nicest, a rugged gorge several hundred feet deep that slices down through a mosaic of plutonic formations. The canyon bottom is coursed by a wash that winds on and on, littered with boulders and interrupted by four high falls and scores of small boulder jams. The rapidly changing topography, the diversity and beauty of the rocks, and the challenge of the boulders make for a memorable little trek through the stony heart of a lightly visited canyon.*

General Information
Road status: Graded access road
Pine City Cyn: 5.6 mi, 160 ft up, 1,680 ft down one way / diff. (Class 3)
Main attractions: Awesome canyon with narrows, falls, and boulders
USGS 7.5' topo map: Queen Mountain
Maps: pp. 145*, 139, *65*

Location and Access

Pine City Canyon drains the east slope of the Wonderland of Rocks, starting on the east flank of Queen Mountain and cutting a roughly easterly, then northeasterly course to end near the park's north entrance. To hike it uphill, the starting point is the same as the signed trailhead for the Contact Mine. Park at the dirt pullout with a large interpretive display on the right (west), 0.5 mile after entering the park at the north entrance. To hike the canyon downhill, which is the direction described here, the starting point is the same as for Pine City (see *The Desert Queen Mine* for directions).

Route Description

To hike Pine City Canyon downhill, from the Desert Queen Mine trailhead walk the Pine City Trail 2 miles north to its end on the south rim of the canyon and a sign that reads "not a maintained trail beyond this point" (see *Pine City* for details). The trail splits into two fainter trails. Take the one on the right, a rocky path that leads down a steep draw into the canyon. It only goes part way down; the lower half of the descent is over a series of rock terraces and gravelly slopes. It is a little steep (230 feet in 0.2 mile) and brushy, but it is a small admission price to get into this great canyon.

Central gorge in Pine City Canyon

From just below the point of entry to its mouth, a distance of 2.1 miles, Pine City Canyon is a true canyon that cuts a deep V into the core of the mountains. The top 1.5 miles is a narrower gorge trapped between rocky walls, 500 feet at its deepest. In the upper part of the gorge, the inner walls come together to form a short stretch of narrows. The entire canyon is tortuous on a small scale, the wash winding tightly enough that you often cannot see very far. I felt removed from the rest of the world, dwarfed by the volume of stone rising all around, never exactly sure where I was.

Like other places in this range, Pine City Canyon might best be characterized by one word—boulders. From start to finish the wash is a river of well-rounded rocks, anything from boulders low enough to step on to 10-ton giants. There are stretches of open gravel, but none very long; most of the time, you walk on rocks. Although the slope is generally modest, at a few places the canyon floor up ahead drops out of sight as it plunges a few tens of feet. These sharp inclines have high boulder jams and hard-rock falls. Four of them are harder to negotiate than the rest, each one a little easier than the previous one. The first one is a 14-foot fall in solid monzogranite inside the narrows. Sub-vertical and dissected into square steps several inches across, it is relatively straightforward to climb down (or up), although it is an exposed

Central gorge looking down canyon in fall afternoon light

Class 2–3 and requires experience. The second one is a tall cataract of giant overhanging boulders. It can be bypassed on the south side, down a long shallow chute that descends more gradually. The third obstacle is a 10-foot fall with a convenient foot-wide ledge that slices down across it. The last one is Slickrock Fall, a very wide and long slant of water-worn bedrock exposing a beautiful mosaic of large inclusions, some blue gray, others beige tinged with bright red, slashed by long white dikes. It is so shallow that one can slide down its smooth surface seated. Besides these four falls, there are dozens of smaller boulder falls. It may take two or three hours to cover this uneven bit of ground. Fortunately, the plants are hardly ever in the way, although my friend, new to the perils of the desert, did draw blood on a spirited catclaw.

Besides the physical challenge, what makes this canyon so exciting is the diversity of rocks and landforms. The gorge happens to cut through four plutonic formations, all more than once, each with its own chemical composition, granularity, color, and erosional patterns. From the point of entry down to a little past the 14-foot fall, it is all Queen Mountain Monzogranite, a rock fractured into stacks of angular blocks, with so few dark minerals that it is almost white. Further down, in the big clockwise bend, Oasis Monzogranite looms in sheer walls sliced along parallel vertical breaks into clusters of standing rocks. The granite is bright, specked with garnet crystals. Soon after, there is a section of Gold Park Gabbrodiorite, as black as a god statue from ancient Egypt, then a long tract of White Tank Monzogranite, where huge rounded boulders rest precariously on interior rims. The lower gorge is a chaotic repository of the dregs left over from the creation of a canyon, a tumble of gneiss, porphyritic granite, bedrock tinted with rust, and mosaics of dark-gray inclusions. The gneiss exposures are the most visually appealing, as veined and knotted as petrified wood. The vegetation is a pleasant scattered mix of manzanita, desert almond, squawbush, nolina, oak, and pine. Their vibrant greens add to the cold pale stone a touch of warmth and life.

During the devastating thunderstorm that drenched the park in October 2018, several canyons in the Wonderland of Rocks became recipients of raging torrents and were redesigned by the power of flowing water. Pine City Canyon was one of them. Even though its watershed is less than two square miles, the equivalent water content of a couple of thousand Olympic swimming pools was funneled down to its wash. The water roiled over open sand bars, gushed between boulders, spilled over rock falls, and plunged into pools deep enough to drown. Pine City Canyon was transformed that night into a chain of white waterfalls and foaming pools linked by segments of a turbulent stream. It must have been a sight to behold.

When I hiked down the canyon six weeks later, it had completely dried, but the aftereffects were still conspicuous—and some of them will be visible for years. At the base of each and every fall and boulder jam, big and small, this and earlier floods had excavated a deep scoop

Pine City Canyon

	Dist.(mi)	Elev.(ft)
Pine City Trailhead	0.0	4,436
End of maintained trail/saddle	2.0	~4580
Pine City Canyon wash	2.15	4,350
Upper end of gorge	2.2	4,320
14-foot fall	2.4	4,170
Main boulder jam	2.75	~3,900
Slickrock Fall	~3.1	~3,665
Lower end of gorge	~3.7	~3,400
Mouth	4.2	3,240
Park Boulevard	5.6	2,915

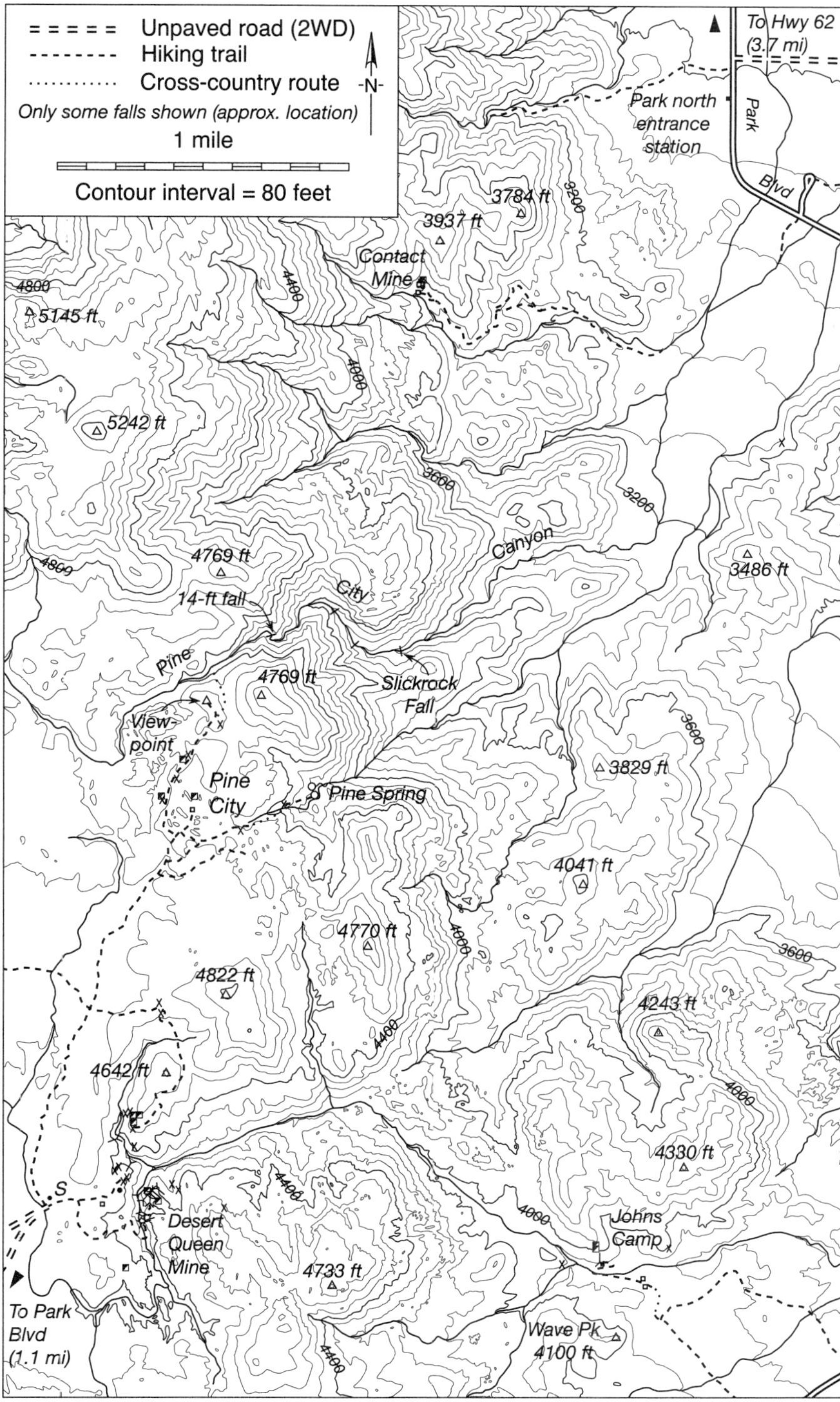

= = = = = Unpaved road (2WD)
- - - - - - - Hiking trail
.... Cross-country route
-N-
Only some falls shown (approx. location)
1 mile
Contour interval = 80 feet
To Hwy 62 (3.7 mi)
Park north entrance station
Park Blvd
3784 ft
3937 ft
3200
Contact Mine
4400
4800
5145 ft
5242 ft
4000
3600
3200
Canyon
4769 ft
4800
City
14-ft fall
Pine
4769 ft
Slickrock Fall
3486 ft
View-point
Pine City
Pine Spring
3600
3829 ft
4041 ft
4770 ft
4000
4822 ft
3600
4243 ft
4400
4642 ft
4000
4330 ft
S
4400
Desert Queen Mine
4000
Johns Camp
4733 ft
To Park Blvd (1.1 mi)
Wave Pk 4100 ft
4400

in the gravel. The largest pools were big enough to swallow a car. Some pools were lined with the bathtub rings of silt deposited by the turbid water as it slowly percolated into the porous soil. The wash was as smooth as dune sand, except for the footprints of a lone hiker. The vegetation, normally driest in late November, was fooled into full springtime regalia.

Narrow chute in central canyon

Below the gorge, the canyon widens, and the density and size of the boulders decrease gradually. By the time you reach the canyon mouth, the wash is mostly free of rocks. The rest of the hike to the trailhead, a distance of 1.4 miles, is as easy as the gorge is tedious. The wash crosses an open and gently sloped embayment peppered with mature shrubs and small trees. Even well after the monsoon, the fragrance of desert lavender in bloom drifts through the air like lavender sometimes does on summer nights in the south of France.

This hike is long enough and hard enough that if you are planning to hike the whole canyon, it is best to arrange a shuttle. Have a back up plan with the shuttle driver in case one of the falls stops you and you have to turn around. If climbing the falls is a concern, consider hiking up into the canyon from the lower trailhead. In this direction the difficulty steadily increases, and it is less likely to get stranded. If you must start from the top, hike down to the main fall and back, which gives a good sense of the geology and beauty of the canyon.

■

THE DESERT QUEEN MINE

One of the few relatively prolific historic mines in the park, the Desert Queen had a tormented history that started with a bang. In its first two years it witnessed a take-over by cold-blooded murder and a very good gold production, then it quickly played out and ended with an agonizing, 60-year-long whimper. Located on the scenic rim of a steep-walled gulch and reached by a short and easy trail, it is a fun place to visit, with interesting mining paraphernalia tucked all over and many workings and waste-rock piles to inspect.

General Information

Road status: Hiking on trails; excellent graded access road
Desert Queen Mine: 1.8 mi, 350 ft up loop/easy
Main attractions: A historic gold mine with good ruins, easy access trail
USGS 7.5' topo map: Queen Mountain
Maps: pp. 151*, 155, *65*

Location and Access

The Desert Queen Mine is on a low ridge near the southeastern tip of the Wonderland of Rocks. Drive Park Boulevard to the signed Desert Queen Mine Road, which is 5.1 miles west from Pinto Wye, or 5.7 miles east from Keys View Road. Follow the graded Desert Queen Mine Road 1.3 miles to the junction with the Queen Valley Road. Turn right, and park at the parking area 200 feet further.

History

The story of the Desert Queen Mine's discovery would make a perfect screenplay for a Western thriller, complete with a coveted gold mine, a prospector murdered by ruthless thugs, and a scandalous acquittal. The discoverer was Frank L. James, a miner employed at the nearby Lost Horse Mine who spent his spare time prospecting for gold. He spotted the rich gold seam at the future Desert Queen Mine in 1894, but did not get to enjoy it for very long. News of his discovery drew the attention of a notorious gang of cattle rustlers led by brothers Jim and Bill McHaney. Chased out of the San Bernardino Mountains a few years earlier by angry ranchers, they had since then set up shop at Cow Camp, in the western Wonderland of Rocks. James had barely started working his mine when gang member Charles Martin jumped his claim. In April 1894, the gang got into an argument with James, and Martin shot James dead. Martin was summarily acquitted on the pretense of self-defense, and the McHaneys took over the property.

Over the next two years, the McHaneys made a fortune from the Desert Queen Mine. Starting in the spring of 1895, the ore was hauled on a rough wagon road to the two-stamp mill at Pinyon Well. The first few mill runs returned over $10,000 in gold, and there was plenty of good ore in sight. In 1895 and 1896, the official recorded gold production was a remarkable 3,630 ounces, worth $75,000 at the time. The McHaneys, especially Jim, quickly squandered their earnings to lead lavish lives, until too little money was left to run the mine. The mine went through foreclosure, and they dropped out of sight. Ruined by his extravagant lifestyle, Jim turned to counterfeiting, for which he served seven years in a penitentiary.

In the wake of its early success, for half a century the Desert Queen went through a convoluted series of ownerships, bonds, acquisitions, leases, quitclaims, and the inevitable litigations. A banker named Zambro, who had run the mine in the McHaneys' era, returned in the 1900s, and claimed milling two million dollars in gold, a splendid exaggeration. Around 1911, local legend Bill Keys, then a young man, became the mine's watchman, then caretaker. After the mine owner died in 1917, Keys obtained title to the Desert Queen in payment for back wages. From 1932 to 1941 the mine produced nearly continuously, operated by either Keys or lessees. The ore was treated in a steam-powered stamp mill at Keys Ranch, then at the Wall Street Mill after around 1933. In 1935, an insurance agent named Charles Phelps, his wife Della, and a partner Robert Saunders installed leaching tanks below the mine and painstakingly processed crudely screened ore and waste rock for two years. In retrospect, all this hard labor—the drilling, blasting, mucking, crushing, milling, and cyaniding—was for naught. By 1896 the Desert Queen had already been gutted. All subsequent work brought only 217 ounces, a third of it in 1900. The figure for the final 20 years, from 1941 through 1961, was zero. Bill Keys made more money leasing his property than mining it...

Route Description

From the parking area the trail cuts east across the edge of Queen Valley. In 0.25 mile it passes a wide trail on the right, once the access road to the mine, then stone house ruins off to the right, before reaching the rim of a 170-foot-deep gulch at a beat-up metallic water tank. This overlook gives a good bird's-eye view of the mine. The gulch is known as Desert Queen Wash, or more romantically as Gold Dust Gulch. Across it, near its opposite rim, is the Desert Queen Mine, its many workings bleeding pale avalanches of waste rock all over the steep slope. The main tailing spills down 80 feet to the gulch's sandy wash. Above the rim, the land rises gently as a grand staircase of low cliff bands and taluses dotted with pine to a crown of standing pillars.

For a different perspective, from the water tank walk the road 50 yards back to a road on the right. It follows a narrow ridge northeast 0.1 mile to the remains of a winch mounted on a wooden slant. It may have been the winch installed by Keys and his son Willis to transport ore across the gulch in 1948, when the road was too damaged to use.

The Desert Queen Mine can be reached from the water tank on a rocky trail that zigzags down into the gulch. To slow down damage to the hillside, walk back instead to the ruins, a cluster of three rooms with thick stone walls. The main room was entered via a low doorway,

Stone house ruins along the trail to the Desert Queen Mine

still supported by a wooden lintel. The style of the construction suggests that it dates from around the turn of the previous century. This is the last of several buildings that once stood in this general area, including a stone cabin and three redwood cabins—treat it with respect.

From the house ruins, a foot trail descends southeast and soon joins the old access road to the mine. The rocky road then descends to the bottom of the gulch, crosses the wash, and climbs across the hillside to the main tunnel, beneath a screen of vertical monoliths. It passes by two secondary tunnels, and a fine example of an air compressor connected to a reservoir, which likely powered pneumatic drills. Minecar rails still lead into the depths of the tunnel, blocked a few steps in by a metal gate. The tunnel is the portal to a complicated three-dimensional network of crosscuts, drifts, stopes, and raises totalling more than 1,000 feet in length. On a hot day, the adit is a good shady spot to rest, if a rattlesnake has not claimed the spot first.

Past the tunnel the road continues as a trail that climbs a little to the level rim of the gulch. This area has a few grated shafts. Just north of where the trail makes a long U bend to the southeast, there is a long alignment of shafts and tunnels, some of which connected to the main tunnel 50 feet underground. They have all caved in, leaving a slight depression edged by angular bedrock. Stained with metal oxides, the rock is much darker than the surrounding White Tank Monzogranite. Like the waste rock, it is coated with the secondary minerals—the emerald-green of chrysocolla, the sky-blue of turquoise—that likely triggered Frank James' discovery, and eventually resulted in his tragic demise.

The wash below the mine is a great area to explore. The plateau above it is a patchwork of yuccas and big sagebrush, nolina and pancake prickly-pear, ratany and California juniper. In the wash the moister environment supports a greener vegetation of oak, more plentiful juniper, and occasional pinyon pine. Down canyon from the trail crossing, the sand is littered with equipment relocated by gravity—a grizzly, a huge metal air duct, an ore car that unloaded sideways, and machinery that technology abandoned long ago. A short adit is hidden under a gargantuan oblong boulder. A little further, 50 yards before the right bend in the wash, is the site of Phelps and Saunders 1935–1937 leaching operation. Set on three levels just up the east slope, it had three cyaniding tanks, a water reservoir and a pump above them, and a slurry tank below them. The water was trucked in from Barker Dam, stored in a tank on the west rim (possibly at the viewpoint), and piped down. The reservoir, pieces of equipment, low stone walls, and broken concrete foundations are still there, partly buried under fallen rocks.

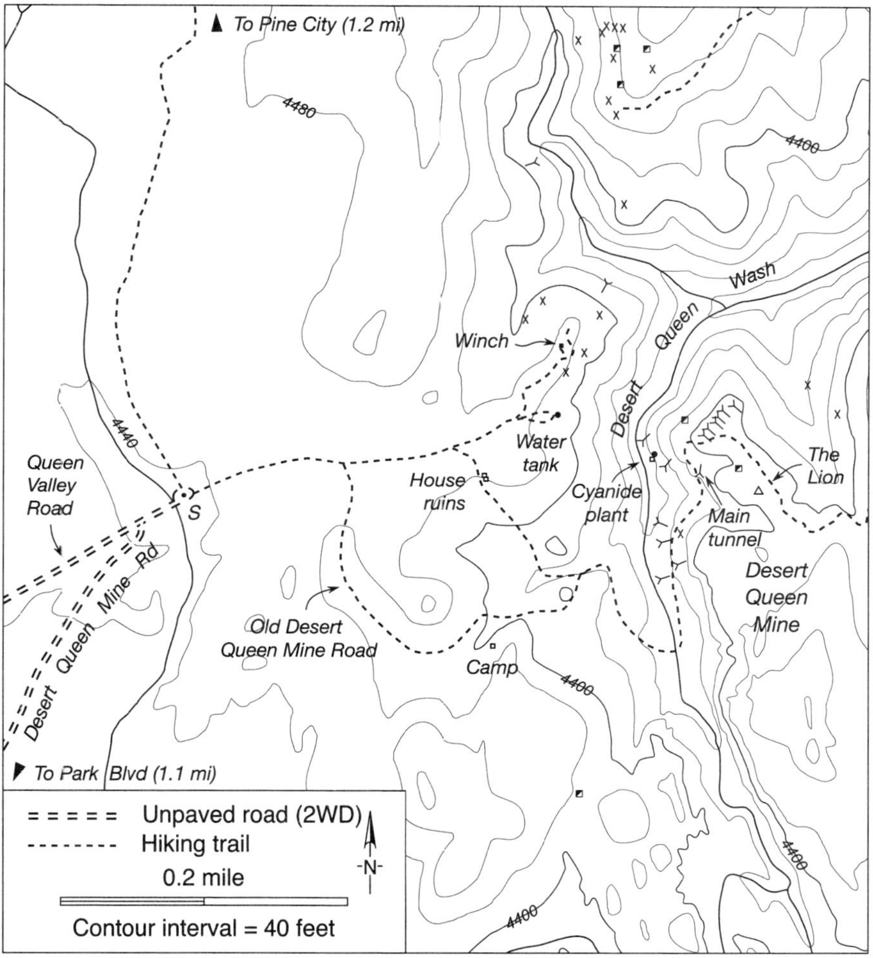

The Desert Queen Mine		
	Dist.(mi)	Elev.(ft)
Desert Queen Mine Road	0.0	4,436
Stone house ruins (junction)	0.2	~4,460
Water tank overlook	(0.05)	~4,425
Winch overlook	(0.15)	~4,445
Back to stone ruins (junction)	0.3	~4,460
Wash crossing	0.55	4,300
Desert Queen Mine tunnel	0.75	~4,365
Upper workings	0.8	~4,410
Return via west-side trail	1.6	4,436

Chicago Pneumatic Tool Company air compressor at the Desert Queen Mine

The Desert Queen Mine has so many remains hidden in different places that one can return several times and discover something overlooked on previous visits. You will have to poke around, and take side trips into unsuspected areas. There are traces of mining camps, historic dates and initials pecked on rock faces, and enough tailings to occupy a curious mind for hours. If you trudge far enough down Desert Queen Wash, you might come across the carcass of a vintage car from the model-T era. When you return, your route on the map will look like you got repeatedly lost, or gone mad under the desert sun.

The Desert Queen Mine is a little gem, and one of the few mines in this crowded park that still has much to show. Leave everything where you find it for other visitors to enjoy after you. Every bit of wood and metal scrap, however insignificant as it may seem, is part of this country's heritage, and protected by law.

■

THE EAGLE CLIFF MINE

Less than a mile beyond the Desert Queen Mine, hidden on the stony south rim of Gold Dust Gulch, there is a small gold mine from the 1890s that holds the distinction of still having one of the very few miner's cave dwellings left in the park. Reached by a primitive trail that meanders through scenic monoliths and high-desert vegetation, it is an exciting destination, and a testimony to the persistence of early miners who found ingenuous ways to adapt to the desert wilderness.

General Information

Road status: Hiking on primitive trails; excellent graded access road
Eagle Cliff Mine: 1.8 mi, 490 ft up, 370 ft down one way / easy–moder.
Main attractions: Unusual troglodytic miner's house, scenic inselbergs
USGS 7.5' topo map: Queen Mountain
Maps: pp. 155*, *65*

Location and Access

The Eagle Cliff Mine is located in the southeastern reaches of the Wonderland of Rocks, just behind the tiered cliffs east of the Desert Queen Mine. It can be reached on a short trail that branches off the Split Rock Loop to the south, or on a trail 50% longer that starts at the Desert Queen Mine. Being a logical extension of the short hike to the Desert Queen, the latter route is described here. Follow the driving directions to the Desert Queen Mine given in the previous section.

Route Description

The Eagle Cliff Mine was originally located in May 1895 by Robert Muir, a year after the turbulent beginnings of the Desert Queen Mine. We know very little about the extent of Muir's involvement in the mine development. Just a year later the main inclined shaft had already been blasted 75 feet to a wide gold ore vein. The property changed hands twice over the next four years—not usually a good sign—although a milling test on one ton of ore returned $125. Around 1916, after most of the region's gold mines had given out their best, Bill Keys held the mine under the new name of Black Eagle. Until at least the 1930s, he and his immediate family carried out assessment work and occasionally extracted ore of lower value. Then as in earlier years, the ore was packed out on a burro, and no road was ever built to

Atrium, Eagle Cliff Mine

improve access. The Eagle Cliff Mine was likely not a winner.

In spite of its less than glorious past, the Eagle Cliff Mine is a special place to visit. It is accessed by the same circuitous unimproved burro trail as 120 years ago, still unsigned and lightly visited, and its workings and improvements are not all easy to locate. From the trailhead you first work your way to the Desert Queen Mine's main tunnel, then up to the cluster of grated shafts at the gulch's rim (see *Desert Queen Mine*). The trail continues along the irregular rim, weaving around three consecutive north-draining side canyons. At the first one it passes to the left of a blocky split monument known as the Lion, crosses the shallow wash, then climbs out of it along a straight and easy grade still supported by its original low wall. The second side canyon crossing is short and fairly level. The third crossing is longer and a little more demanding. The trail cuts south-southeast in and out of the wash twice before ascending in rocky switchbacks to just below the head of the side canyon. There it meets the trail coming up from the Split Rock Loop, right by a short adit. Finally, it climbs 20 feet to a ridge, crosses over into the fourth tributary, and descends to the Eagle Cliff Mine. The scenery is beautifully landscaped with ever-changing displays of rounded outcrops and boulders, and dozens of plant species. There are spiky plantations of nolina, pockets of scraggly pine and oak, and gardens of blackbush, pygmy cedar, and California buckwheat. During the spring, many plants introduce radiant colors—the bright orange of globemallow, the deep purple of ratany, the vibrant red of mound cactus, and the bubblegum pink of cushion foxtail cactus.

The Eagle Cliff Mine is set on a grassy meadow edged by large oak and pinyon pine. On the mountain side it is enclosed by impressive giant monoliths, on the other side by an abrupt ledge overlooking the gulch and Queen Mountain. The mine's inclined tunnel is near the

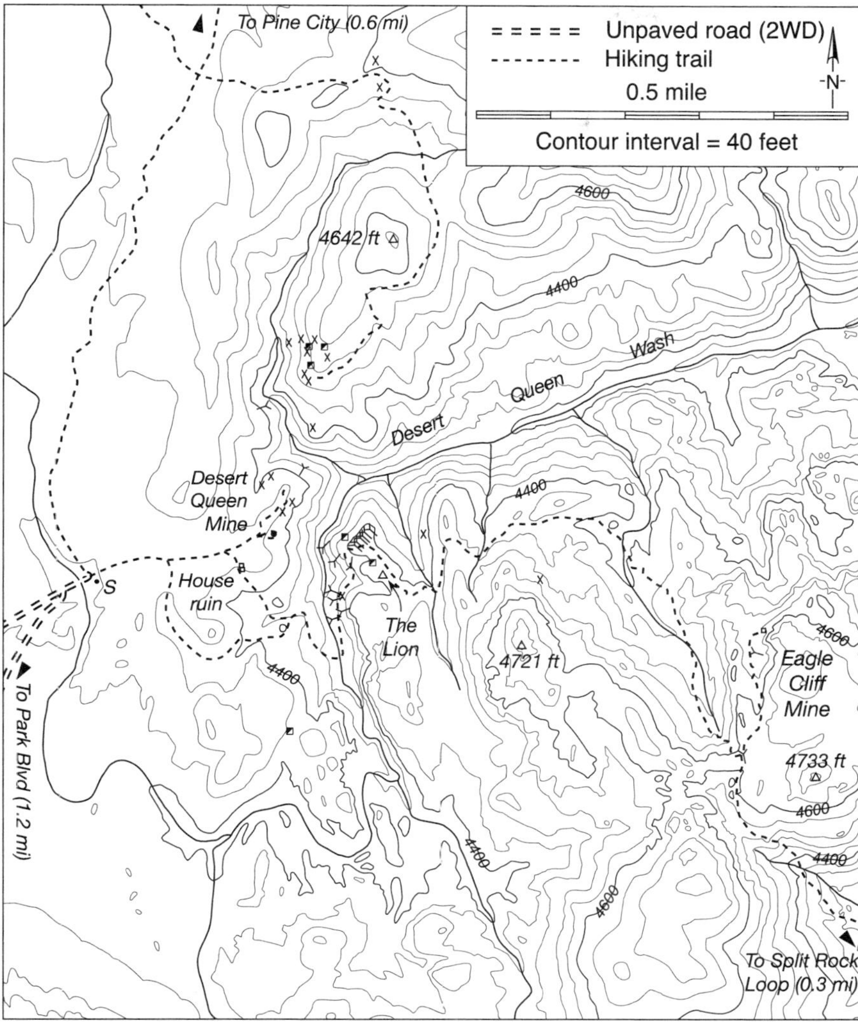

The Eagle Cliff Mine

	Dist.(mi)	Elev.(ft)
Desert Queen Mine Road	0.0	4,436
Stone house ruins (junction)	0.2	~4,460
Wash crossing	0.45	4,300
The Lion	0.75	4,420
Trail junction	1.6	4,610
Split Rock trailhead	(1.0)	4,280
Eagle Cliff Mine cave dwelling	1.8	~4,550

Cave dwelling interior, Eagle Cliff Mine

entrance to the meadow, and the cave dwelling a little further, below the largest rocks. You enter through a doorless frame of knotted logs into a small atrium with a fireplace. The main room just beyond occupies a tall cavity formed by a tepee of behemoth boulders. The thin gaps between them were sealed with masonry of carefully selected rocks that taper with rustic elegance to the 10-foot ceiling, merging function and decoration. The far wall doubles up as a chimney for a small oven. A six-pane glass window brings a little natural light into the dark room. The narrow roof was weatherproofed with a trellis of gnarled tree trunks tiled with flattened cans. The atrium once had a roof too, but it collapsed decades ago. Rusted utensils, jars, vials, and cans from another time still rest on rickety shelves and cabinets.

This modern-day cave dwelling is in several ways a fascinating piece of the American-West history, a poignant testament to early settlers' ability to modify the natural environment minimally to create a comparatively comfortable space in an inhospitable desert. It is a priceless gem. Leave all objects and natural materials undisturbed.

There are more tunnels, more cave shelters, and the ruins of an old forge, some tucked in the bouldery canyon that drains north to Gold Dust Gulch. If you make it through, from there it is a leisurely walk up the sandy wash back to the Desert Queen Mine's access road.

■

SPLIT ROCK LOOP

Of the many trails that explore the Wonderland of Rocks' fantastic landscapes of naked sculpted stone, Split Rock Loop ranks among the most enjoyable. It wanders through a checkerboard of secluded coves loosely enclosed by erratic battlements of eroded monuments, and livened up with the vivid greens of desert shrubs, cactuses, and conifers. Not to spoil the reverie that this enchanting maze is likely to trigger, do what it takes to avoid rush hour, even if it means coming here in the heat of summer.

General Information

Road status: Hiking on trail; graded access road
Split Rock Loop: 2.4 mi, 330 ft up loop / very easy
Main attractions: Scenic trail through a maze of spectacular inselbergs
USGS 7.5' topo map: Queen Mountain
Maps: pp. 159*, 65

Location and Access

The Split Rock Loop is near the Wonderland of Rocks' southeastern tip, close to the popular Jumbo Rocks. The signed graded road to it takes off Park Boulevard 2.2 miles west of Pinto Wye, or 0.6 mile east of Skull Rock, on the north side. Drive this road 0.5 mile to the parking loop at its end. Split Rock is at the end of the loop, a plump 20-foot monolith cleaved in two pieces, the bulk of it resting over a vault big enough to stand. The northern trailhead is to the left of Split Rock, and the western trailhead on the left side of the loop. For greater visual impact, start at the western trailhead and hike the loop trail clockwise.

Route Description

The Split Rock area is in the final stage of its geological life. Located at the thinner edge of the range, it has been shredded by erosion into a frayed landscape. Regions of extreme weathering, from China's Shilin Stone Forest to France's Baux de Provence and Utah's Arches National Park, hold some of the planet's most stunning and unconventional landforms. The island of worn stones surrounding Split Rock is no exception. The streets and avenues that crisscross much of the Wonderland of Rocks have been widened here to broad trenches and coves, and the city blocks between them reduced to skeletal protrusions. The trail makes an irregular, 2-mile oval loop through

Sensual rock compositions along Split Rock Loop

this fragmented topography. Wide and nearly level, it winds quietly through half a dozen coves. Each one has its own character, as do the stony divisions that encircle them, anything from long crenulated ramparts to scarified cliffs, crowns of turrets, batteries of fins, and parades of elephants. The diversity of shapes is astonishing, some massive, others whimsical. There is a lone spear hollowed like a meteoroid, an arch wedged under a gigantic suspended boulder, and a towering slab sliced at its top by a deep vertical slit, as if it had been partly split with a saw. Many formations and natural carvings bear singular resemblance to familiar figures—a wall stamped with a caricatural parrot's head, Tulip Rock, a pregnant lady, the male anatomy that induced said pregnancy, and the lifesize lower back of a woman. At its southernmost point, the trail traverses a corridor framed by collapsed boulders bigger than pick-up trucks. A spur trail on the left ends shortly at Face Rock, a 30-foot outcrop shaped like a humanoid head with a freakishly tall brow, with a second face hidden behind it. Half a mile further, past more delicate formations, the main trail exits this fairyland of sculptures and circles clockwise just outside of it. For the grand finale, along the last quarter mile the trail re-enters it and wanders through a series of sensual inselbergs before ending back at Split Rock.

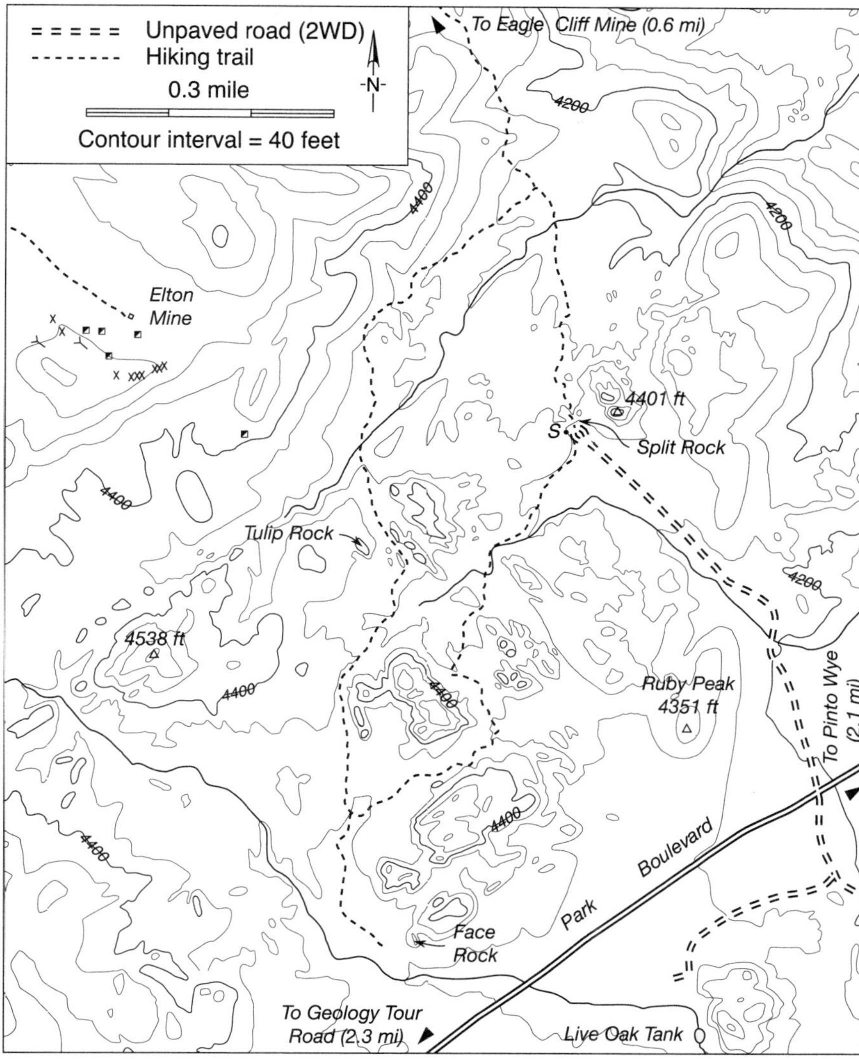

Split Rock Loop		
	Dist.(mi)	Elev.(ft)
Western trailhead	0.0	4,280
Trail junction to Face Rock	0.7	~4,320
Face Rock	(0.2)	4,290
Exit fairyland of rocks	1.1	~4,290
Re-enter fairyland of rocks	1.75	~4,230
Northern trailhead	2.0	4,280

Hollowed stone along Split Rock Loop

This area's strong charisma stems not only from its natural sculptures but also its vegetation, and the strange partnership between them. The outcrops are generally a little smaller and tighter than elsewhere, just big enough to impress without overwhelming. The vegetation matches this trend. Other than a few large pine trees, plants are comparatively small, seemingly fuller, more diverse. The coves are patches of gravel peppered with mesquite, paperbag bush, ratany, Joshua trees, nolina, cacti, and everywhere the emerald crowns of California juniper. On the edge of the inselbergs, plants are much more sparse, often in arrangements so carefully balanced that they seem staged. An outcrop will be decorated with one lone pancake prickly-pear or Mojave yucca, with a little spherical boulder resting in an alcove above it like an ornament. Wandering through these serene natural designs along the neat stone-lined trail is a meditative experience, like a stroll through a Zen garden.

The trail is at the mercy of the unpredictable geography. After crossing a rocky ridge it will change course abruptly, redirected by a new alignment of stones. Each time, the scenery changes, and looking back will reveal a scene you could swear you have never seen before. Often thrown into a different direction, you never know exactly where you are, how far you have gone, or how far you still have to go—the attribute of mazes. Time seems to be suspended. At the end of one of my visits I was shocked to realize that I had been in there two hours, on a short and clear trail just about as level as the sea. Perhaps it was the heat of June. Perhaps it was the time I took to admire a jackrabbit munching on a cholla stem without getting pricked. But it also happened at other times, in February, without the rabbit distraction. I think it is the beauty of the land. It will slow you down to a crawl.

■

JOHNS CAMP

In Joshua Tree as throughout the West, the desert mountains hide in their folds the ruins of countless small-time mines from long ago. They were often developed by lone miners hoping to strike it rich, who located a promising quartz seam, set up camp, and blasted a few holes in search of gold. More often than not the quartz was too barren, and after a few years they left empty-handed. Johns Camp, tucked at the southeastern edge of the Wonderland of Rocks, is a good example. Reached by a very easy walk on an old road through thick cactus gardens, it gives a glimpse of the frugal life of these hard-rock miners, their strenuous labor, and their tenacious dream.

General Information
Road access: Hiking mostly on old road; paved access road
Gold Hill Mine: 1.2 mi, 130 ft up, 30 ft down one way / very easy
Main attractions: Mining ruins, cactus gardens, mining history
USGS 7.5' topo map: Queen Mountain
Maps: pp. 163*, *65*

Location and Access

To get to the trailhead, drive Park Boulevard to the two facing paved pullouts on both sides of the road 1 mile west of Pinto Wye. Coming from the other direction, this is 2.4 miles east of the signed turnoff to the Jumbo Rocks Campground. Johns Camp is near the mouth of Desert Queen Wash, visible as a gap in the hills less than a mile to the northwest.

Route Description

If you are unfamiliar with hiking on unsigned trails, this is a good place to try—there is a road most of the way, you are never far from your car, and it would take a rare talent not to find the paved road on the way back. The road to Johns Camp starts in the bushes a few yards from the pavement, right across from the east end of the south-side pullout. If you miss it, just head toward the gap in the hills, and you will likely run into it. There is only one spot where the road alignment is obscured by plants, but it is easy to find the road again by continuing in the same general direction.

The road crosses the edge of the nearly level valley that bridges the gap between the Wonderland of Rocks and the Pinto Mountains. The

Outdoor oven at Johns Camp

vegetation is so unconventional that it looks like an alien vegetable garden. Silver chollas stick out like bleached broccoli, sprigs of ephedra try to pass for herbs, barrel cactus mimic upright watermelons, and Mojave yucca and Joshua trees rise above the rest like tousled scarecrows. The tangled purple spikes of diamond chollas, usually scarce to a fault, poke out like weeds.

After 0.5 mile, near the base of the range, the road descends 10 feet to a sandy wash and vanishes. Follow the wash roughly north (right) down about 125 yards, and angle left into the broad opening of Desert Queen Wash. There the road resumes, and goes a short distance west on a broad bench at the edge of the wash to Johns Camp.

Johns Camp was part of the Gold Hill Mine, whose tailings are clearly visible a quarter of a mile up canyon. It consisted of a group of six claims co-owned by Anvil B. Johns, J. A. Johns, and C. H. Wiser, all from the San Bernardino area. The camp has two small remains, the most interesting being an unusual outdoor oven. It is made of a steel casing partly sheathed in crude masonry and crowned by a canted smoke pipe. It was wisely set against the south canyon wall, away from the murderous late afternoon sun, in the wind shelter of large boulders. A little further is a thin concrete slab, cracked and frayed, the

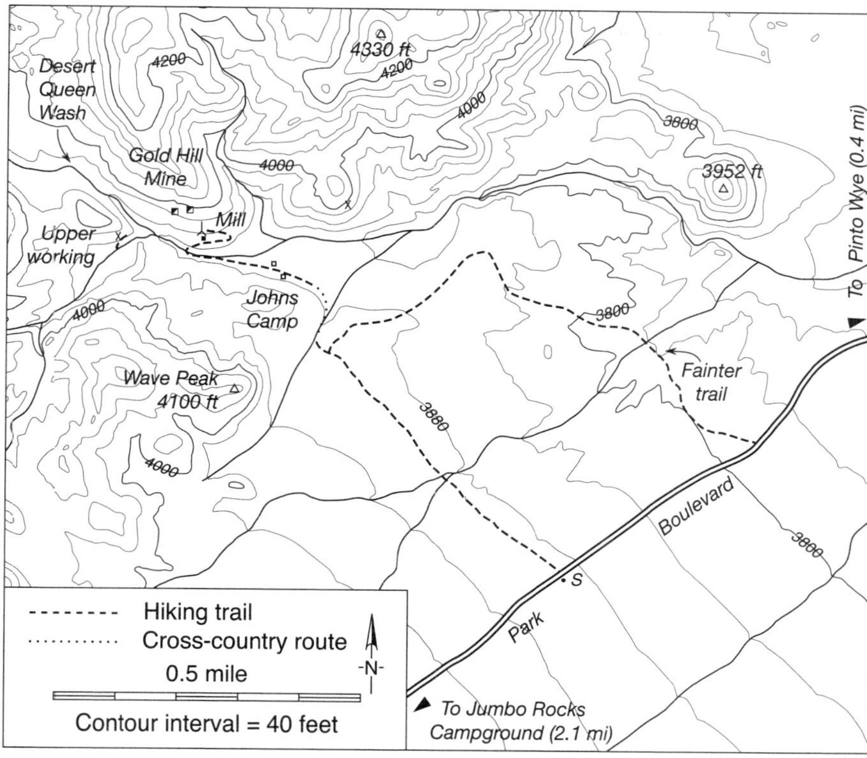

Johns Camp		
	Dist.(mi)	Elev.(ft)
Pullout on Park Boulevard	0.0	3,884
Wash at edge of mountain	0.55	3,890
Johns Camp (outdoor oven)	0.7	3,870
Foot of main tunnel's tailings	0.9	3,875
Gold Hill Mine tunnel & mill	(0.1)	3,925
Upper working	1.05	3,935

foundation of the camp's small cabin. A cellar, still lined with sheet metal, is sunk in the barren ground behind it. Other remains are scattered nearby—broken porcelain, splintered lumber, tobacco cans, a box spring collapsed into a wad of entangled coils, and two dumps of rusted cans.

The mine has its own centerpiece, the concrete foundations of a mill, located at the top of the main tunnel's tailings. From the camp it is a short walk (0.2 mile) up the wash to the tailings. Rather than scrambling up the loose tailings, which will over time undermine the mill, use the road. It starts a few steps past the base of the tailings, behind the only pancake prickly-pear around. The mill was a simple affair, two levels of concrete pilings and a top landing, now collapsed. The initials of one of the owners (A. B. J.) and the date of April 1, 1931 are inscribed in the concrete. Faded trails climb to two shafts and several prospects above the tunnel. The upper working is 0.15 mile up canyon, in the left fork. It is a very short tunnel at the base of a wall of pale granite neatly cleaved by a few precise blasts of dynamite.

Little is known about the history of the Gold Hill Mine. Yet the ruins are substantial enough that by applying logic and knowledge of the history of similar mines, some of it can be inferred. Based on the minimal tailings and infrastructure, it was undoubtedly a small operation. The Johns were likely relatives, perhaps father and son or brothers, the most common familial relationships in mining ventures. The presence of Anvil Johns' initials at the mill suggests that he was directly involved. The mine may have been run on a shoestring budget, possibly bankrolled by personal savings. Co-owner Wiser may have joined the team to provide financial support, expertise, and/or manual labor. Like others, the miners may have come to the desert to escape the hardships of city life during the Great Depression. The dumps contain only a few hundred cans. Unless they took out their trash, which would have been rather un-miner like, this represents a relatively short occupation. The mine may have been active in total a couple of years or less, likely scattered over several years. The most enigmatic piece of the puzzle is the mill. The erection of a mill was time-consuming, labor-intensive, and expensive, and it was not a decision that would have been made lightly. In 1931, the state's annual average income per capita was just shy of $1,400. Gold was worth only $17 an ounce. One would have to process tens of tons of decent gold ore to pay for a mill, then five or ten times this amount again to meet the average income. Before building their mill, it is logical that the miners would have exposed enough good ore to know that a mill was indeed warranted. Yet, curiously, there is no sign of mill tailings. The mill was either never completed, or it did only coarse work and the crushed ore was extracted with mercury. It is, after all, possible that the mine produced a few high-grade pockets. Possible, but not likely. The odds are that the Johns did not make it rich. Perhaps it was more important to them to have a place to escape, to sit by the oven under the stars, cook a meal of beans or a rabbit stew, and chill. In the end, pursuing their dream might have been a greater satisfaction than a handful of gold dust.

■

ARRASTRA CANYON

The Pinto Wye Arrastra is a restored historic mill located at the head of a scenic canyon, an easy cross-country walk from the road junction after which it was named. As interesting as it is, however, it is eclipsed by the monumental canyon that opens up below it. Scrambling down its steep corridor clogged with boulders, deep beneath high sculpted walls, is pure pleasure. Combining mining history and imposing scenery, this is a gem of a loop hike.

General Information

Road access: Hiking cross-country; paved access road
Pinto Wye Arrastra: 1.0 mi, 130 ft up, 100 ft down one way / easy
Arrastra Canyon: 2.8 mi, 320 ft up loop / moderate (Class 2)
Main attractions: Well-preserved arrastra, spectacular bouldery canyon
USGS 7.5' topo map: Queen Mountain
Maps: pp. 167*, 65

Location and Access

The Pinto Wye Arrastra is near the eastern tip of the Wonderland of Rocks, near the head of the Arrastra Canyon drainage. The starting point is a pullout on Park Boulevard 0.1 mile north of Pinto Wye, or 4.4 miles south from the park's north entrance station, on the east side. The arrastra is on the far side of the low hills to the northwest.

Route Description

In early mining, one of the highest operating costs was transportation of the ore to markets. A common practice to lower this cost was to extract the gold prior to shipping. A stamp mill did this well, but it was too expensive for small mines. A good poor man's alternative was a primitive mill called an arrastra. The ore was placed in a circular channel with a flat bottom, water was added to it, and heavy flat stones were dragged across it until the ore was ground to a slurry. Arrastras were powered by a horse or a mule, humans, or a motor. The gold was then extracted from the slurry with cyanide or mercury.

To get to the Pinto Wye Arrastra, walk north along Park Boulevard 250 yards to a wash crossing, just after the first left bend, then head left up the wash. In 0.1 mile, past a green grove of tall willow, you will enter some short narrows. Just past them, angle right and climb up the low bank out of the wash onto a plateau. Head northwest across it,

Pinto Wye Arrastra

paralleling the hills to your right, 0.4 mile to the head of Arrastra Canyon's shallow upper drainage. The arrastra becomes visible from there, to the northwest, on the canyon's eastern talus just below the tailings of a tunnel. It is an easy walk to it down the lazy wash.

This is a delightful stretch of desert. The narrows' walls rise straight out of soft sand, their low rims crowned with acrobatic catclaw. Long thin dikes slash the grainy monzonite. On hot summer days, the coves provide welcome shade to sit, back pressed against cold stone. The plateau is equally scenic, flush with nolina, small Joshua trees, and juniper. Across from it, the hill is studded with smooth standing rocks, as neatly arranged as megalithic monuments.

The Pinto Wye Arrastra sits amid this crisp landscape, on a sloped shoulder above the canyon wash. It is an exceptional piece, the finest of the park's few arrastras, albeit restored. It holds the distinction, like only one other on NPS lands, of using a wagon wheel as its axle. It still has two of its dragstones, chained to their spokes, its rock walls, most of its floor stones, and even its wood-framed drain where the slurry came out. Its builder had a keen sense of aesthetics, and embellished the edge of the spinning frame with an overlay of fine wood shingles.

The Pinto Wye Arrastra was clearly used—the floor stones are flush and scored with the parallel circular lines left by the dragstones. But it is a mystery. Where did the ore come from? The tunnel above it would be the logical source, but being all of 10 feet long it did not need a mill. Also, where did the water come from? If it was brought in, why

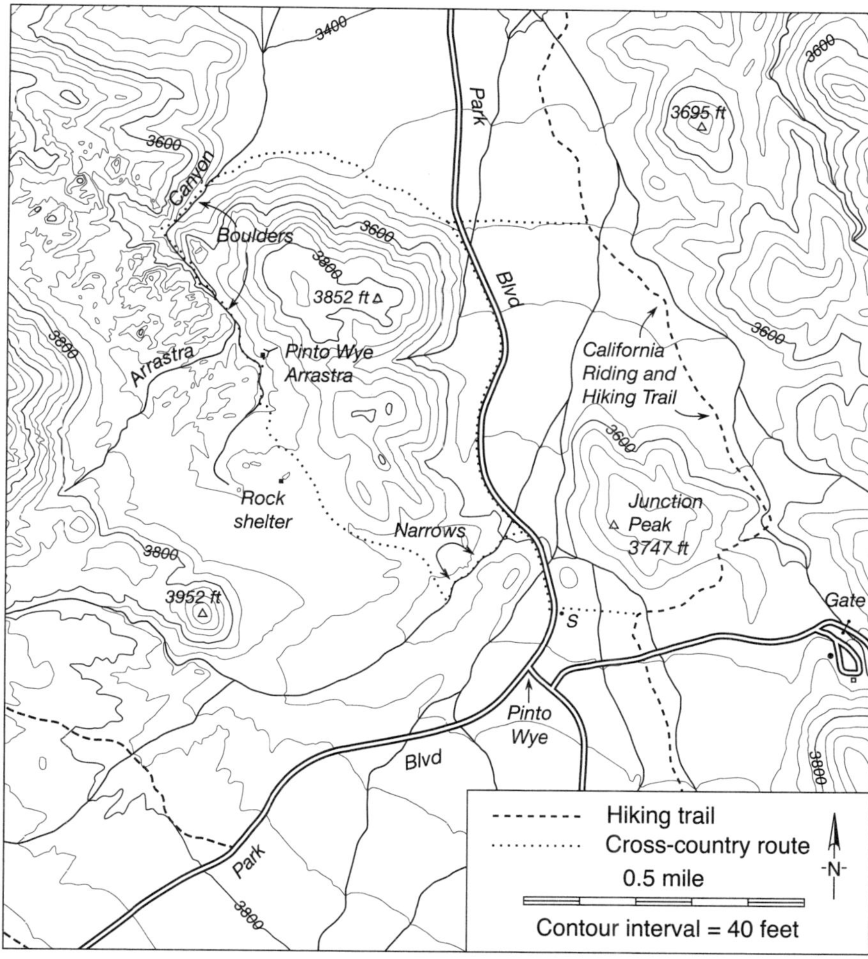

Arrastra Canyon		
	Dist.(mi)	Elev.(ft)
Pullout on Park Boulevard	0.0	3,625
Narrows	0.25	3,610
Head of Arrastra Cyn drainage	0.7	3,690
Pinto Wye Arrastra	0.8	3,640
Upper end of boulders	1.0	3,610
Lower end of boulder section	1.35	3,460
Park Boulevard	1.9	3,480
Back to pullout via CRH Trail	(1.4)	3,625
Back to pullout via Park Blvd	2.7	3,625

Arrastra Canyon from top of boulders section (route goes right at the bottom)

is there no trace of an access trail or road? It is almost as though someone put it there as a hoax to puzzle future generations...

The best is yet to come. Downstream from the arrastra the wash gradually succumbs to boulders. It soon drops down a rough ramp of giant boulders, brightened here and there with pine and the apple-green whisps of catclaw. The entire descent is in full view of an awesome amphitheater, a confluence of fault-bounded canyons where every rock aspires to verticality. At the amphitheater you stare up the towering columns of fins and spires, and precarious boulders so gigantic that surely they should fall. There Arrastra Canyon angles sharply right and tumbles down the same distance again, through equally outrageous scenery, to the open canyon mouth. This traverse is only a third of a mile long but it is a great Class-2 workout, true to the turbulent spirit of the Wonderland of Rocks. Everything in this landscape is excessive and oversized, and infused with the raw drama of chaos. You move through it as if you were inside a colossal geode, every step and hand move getting you closer to some sacred heart.

From the canyon mouth, the return is almost level and easy, east back to the road, then south either along the road or via the CRH Trail east of the road (see map), which is a bit longer but much quieter.

■

— 6 —

PINTO MOUNTAINS

Bookended by the Wonderland of Rocks to the west and the Coxcomb Mountains to the east, the Pinto Mountains are the antithesis of a desert range. They are not a single massif but an agglomerate of multiple groups of arid hills, the highest rising only 4,613 feet above sea level, laced with small valleys and strewn over some 800 square miles. Uplifted along the Blue Cut Fault on their southern boundary in Pinto Basin, they drop more abruptly into the basin and more gently into Dale Lake's shallow sink to the north. The mountains' dark austerity is tempered along their northern edge by beautiful sweeps of sand dunes blown in from the sink. Most of the range lies outside the park in "the bite," the BLM-managed rectangular section in the northern Pinto Mountains that was excluded from the national monument in 1950 to re-open this gold-rich area to mining. The rest of the range—about a third—is in Joshua Tree National Park; most of it is protected in wilderness areas. The southwestern corner of the bite, contiguous to the park, is preserved in the 24,348-acre Pinto Mountains Wilderness.

Geology

The Pinto Mountains are a complex collage of colorful Mesozoic igneous rocks and Proterozoic metamorphic rocks. Medium-gray biotite quartz monzonite dominates in the north central and eastern range. The western quarter is a mosaic of granite, diorite, gneiss, and more quartz monzonite. Pinto Mountain, the hills directly northwest of it, and the hills east of Ivanhoe Peak, contain a colorful, locally famous formation formerly known as Pinto Gneiss. Widespread in the Transverse Ranges, it is the remnant of a metamorphic complex, about

Pinto Mountains in stormy evening light, from Turkey Flat

1.68 billion years old and the size of a county, that was shattered and metamorphosed by tectonic movements along a major fault in the Mesozoic.. Three sub-units crop out in this range, including the Joshua Tree augen gneiss and two distinct meta-sedimentary suites of quartzite, schist, dolomite, and granofels. The Joshua Tree augen gneiss is one of the region's most attractive rocks, often covered with fine wavy or swirled striations, black mixed with white and pink, or bluish. Ironically, it is the colorfulness of this then-unnamed gneiss that inspired the name of these mountains long ago, and the name of the mountains that more recently inspired the name Pinto Gneiss. The only sizable exposure of volcanic origin is on Ivanhoe Peak—it is made of the fine-grained felsite that held most of the mountains' gold.

Mining History

The Pinto Mountains were the region's richest. The Gold Park Mining District, around Music Valley at the west end of the range, had mostly humbugs—deceptive properties—as the name of a nearby mountain suggests, except for the Italy Mine. But in the vast Dale and Monte Negras districts covering the rest of the mountains, over 50 mines were operated off and on until the 1980s and harvested more millions in gold than all the other ranges in the park combined.

When gold was first reported at the northern edge of the range around 1883, the area experienced a minor gold rush. One of the early miners who made a name for himself was John Burt. He dug a well at the edge of Dale Lake, near today's junction between Highway 62 and the Gold Crown Road, and milled placer gold in a burro-powered arrastra. As hundreds of prospectors and gold-placer miners joined him over the following months, a small town named Virginia Dale grew around his well. It had a pump house, a water tank, and enough tents and cabins to support a population of nearly 1,000.

As prospectors fanned out, more substantial gold deposits were discovered in the interior of the Pinto Mountains. The Virginia Dale Mine was first to open, in 1885, near a pass 4.5 miles south of Dale. By 1887, a five-stamp mill had been installed and water was piped to it from Burt's well. In response, the population moved to a second town below the mine, although it took nearly two decades for Old Dale to be fully abandoned. The Virginia Dale Mining District, organized around 1886 and later renamed Dale for short, encompassed most of the range. When the Virginia Dale Mine shut down in 1889, a few major mines to the east and south replaced it. The OK Mine and the Brooklyn Mine, both located in 1890 by John Burt again, and the Carlyle Mine some years later, became the district's new backbone. By 1899 the district was churning out a healthy $6,000 in gold a month.

Unlike in most districts, where the best lodes were almost always discovered early, here the richest mines came last. The largest producer, the Supply Mine, did not become active until around 1900. As its production was ramped up, the town was moved a third time about 3 miles further south, halfway between the Supply and the OK mines. New Dale had several buildings, a post office, a restaurant, and a saloon that served as a hotel. A weekly stage coach connected it to the budding town of Palm Springs. Until it shut down during World War I, the Supply Mine was the uncontested golden heart of the district.

The Gold Crown Mine, further out near the southeastern edge of the range, was the last rich property to open. From 1926 to 1941, it produced intermittently, eventually acquiring a 50-ton cyanide plant and piping water to it from a well at New Dale. The mill also processed ore from local mines, which significantly increased its output. For a few years it shipped gold bullion regularly to the US Mint in San Francisco.

Many mines—the Brooklyn, Carlyle, Ivanhoe, Los Angeles, Supply, and Virginia Dale—were resurrected through the 1920s and into the 1940s. The history of that era is convoluted, involving serial ownerships, intermittent production, acquisitions that ran mines in groups, and shared mills. The district was the greatest mining success

Suggested Hikes in the Pinto Mountains					
Route/Destination	Dist. (mi)	Elev. gain	Mean elev.	Difficulty	Pages
Short hikes (under 5 miles round trip)					
Arch Rock and White Tank	0.7	120'	3,860'	Very easy	201
Gold Rose Mill and Well	1.5	40'	1,400'	Very easy	213
Grand Tank	1.0	190'	3,840'	Very easy	201
Lorman Mine	1.8	800'	2,140'	Easy	179
Mission Mine	0.9	110'	1,570'	Very easy	219
Mission–Sunset–Golden Egg mines loop (1)	2.9	410'	1,620'	Easy	213
Nightingale Dunes	2.4	1,110'	2,150'	Easy-mod.	184
Old Mission Mill loop (1)	0.2	20'	1,430'	Very easy	216
Pinto Basin Dunes	1.0	90'	1,760'	Very easy	209
Snow Flake Mine	1.5	170'	1,680'	Very easy	194
Sunrise Mine	0.7	180'	1,460'	Very easy	216
Supply Mine	1.0	490'	2,150'	Easy	179
Twentynine Palms Mtn	2.4	1,740'	3,980'	Moderate	175
Vulture Arch loop (1)	3.5	~450'	3,860'	Easy	205
Intermediate hikes (5-12 miles round trip)					
Carlyle Mill	2.9	680'	1,500'	Easy	185
Carlyle Mine	3.6	1,430'	1,630'	Moderate	185
Iron Age Mine	3.5	580'	1,880'	Easy	193
Outlaw Peak	4.3	1,530'	2,220'	Moderate	197
Pinto Mountain	4.5	2,670'	2,240'	Difficult	209
Snow Flake Mine–Iron Age Mine loop (1)	8.0	730'	1,860'	Difficult	191

Key: (1) Loop; (2) HC or 4WD access road
Distances: one way for out-and-back hikes, round-trip for loops
Elev. gain: sum of all elevation gains on round-trips and on loops

in the Joshua Tree area. Hardly ever idle, it produced gold, silver, lead, iron, copper, and manganese worth altogether over 4 million dollars.

Hiking

Thanks to their relative isolation, and because they are mostly outside the park, the Pinto Mountains are little traveled. Yet the diversity of terrain and geology, the long history of productive mining, and the

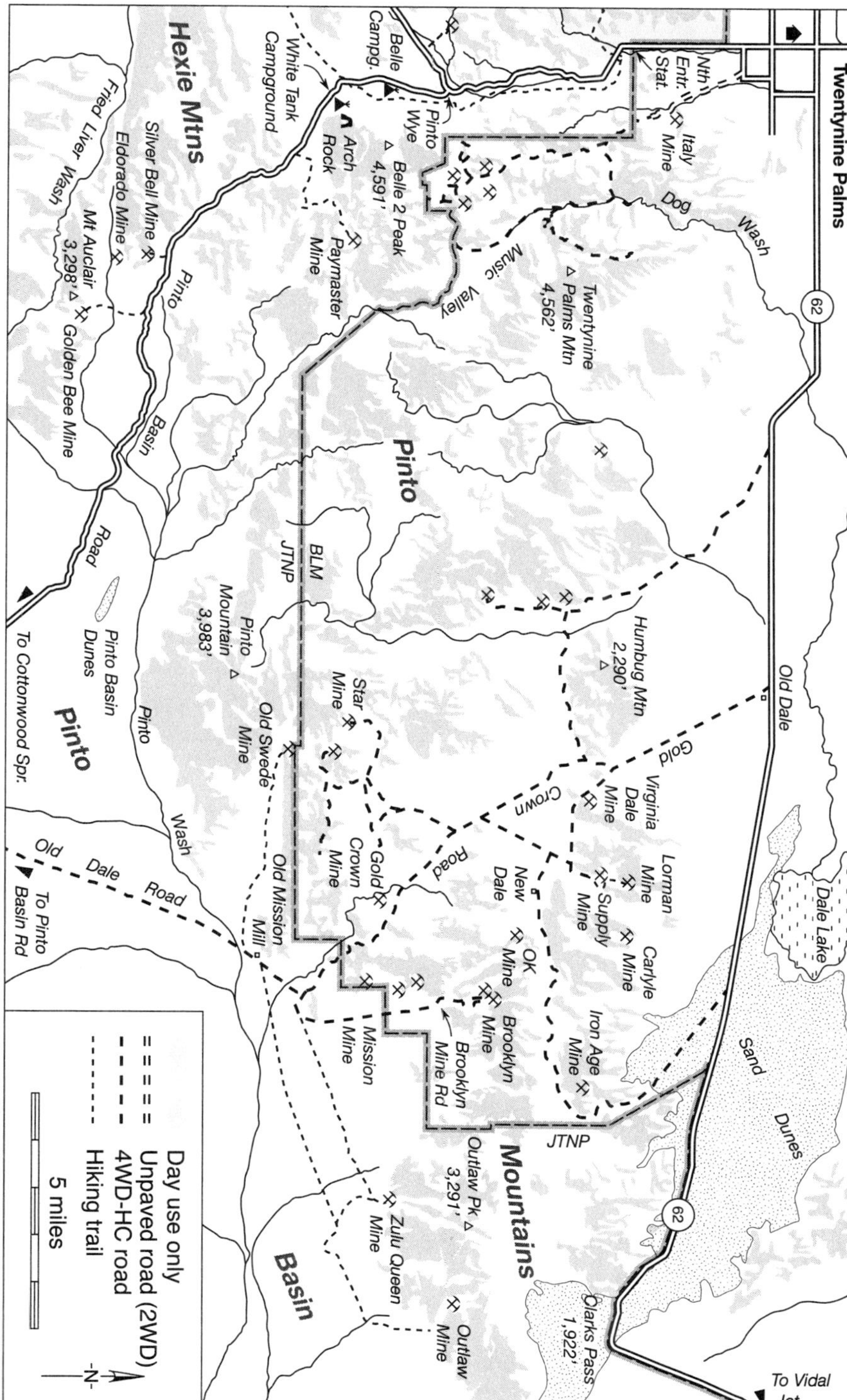
Twentynine Palms
62
Nth Entr. Stat.
Italy Mine
Dog Wash
Belle Campg.
Pinto Wye
White Tank Campground
Arch Rock
Belle 2 Peak 4,591'
Hexie Mtns
Silver Bell Mine
Eldorado Mine
Fried Liver Wash
Mt Auclair 3,298'
Golden Bee Mine
Paymaster Mine
Music Valley
Twentynine Palms Mtn 4,562'
Pinto
Pinto Basin
BLM
JTNP
Road
Pinto Mountain 3,983'
Pinto Basin Dunes
To Cottonwood Spr.
Humbug Mtn 2,290'
Old Dale
Gold Crown Road
Star Mine
Old Swede Mine
Pinto Wash
Virginia Dale Mine
Lorman Mine
Supply Mine
New Dale
Gold Crown Mine
Old Mission Mill
Old Dale Road
To Pinto Basin Rd
Carlyle Mine
OK Mine
Dale Lake
Sand Dunes
Iron Age Mine
Brooklyn Mine
Brooklyn Mine Rd
Mission Mine
JTNP
Mountains
Outlaw Pk. 3,291'
Zulu Queen Mine
Basin
Outlaw Mine
Clarks Pass 1,922'
To Vidal Jct
Day use only
Unpaved road (2WD)
4WD-HC road
Hiking trail
5 miles
N

White Tank Monzogranite pinnacles and fins near Arch Rock

sheer number of abandoned mines, mills, and camps, make them particularly interesting to explore. One can spend days wandering through this hilly range, following old foot trails just to see where they go, climbing a random peak for a different view, or wandering into a remote valley because no one has been there in a long time. Unlike in other parts of the park, here you can engage in these searches without manmade signs telling you where you should go. You might not see people, but if you do, it will be a very different subspecies of *homo sapiens* on the two sides of the range. The bite, on BLM land, is threaded with miles of mining roads and foot trails. It attracts weekend warriors dressed in camouflage, motorcyclists and ATVs hiding behind dust masks, and caravans of four-wheelers hell-bent on finding one more secret mining camp. The south side, in the park, abounds in the opposite direction: all but three roads were closed decades ago. There you will likely run into no one at all, or perhaps a lone athletic übermensch powering through his lifelong quest for the little-known, wielding GPS and trekking poles, fueled by a diet of electrolyte water and organic sugar-free granola bars. The Pinto Mountains give us a chance to experience both of these immiscible worlds.

■

TWENTYNINE PALMS MOUNTAIN

The second highest summit in the Pinto Mountains, Twentynine Palms Mountain is a prominent thumb-shaped sub-range that overlooks Morongo Basin to the north. This climb is mostly along a road that switchbacks up the mountain's abrupt base, followed by an easy cross-country stretch. Twentynine Palms Mountain stands out for its interesting plant ecology, uncommon ancient schists, ferocious wind, and expansive views of the southern Mojave Desert.

General Information
Jurisdiction: Public lands (BLM)
Road status: Hiking on road and cross-country; 4WD-HC access road
Twentynine Palms Mtn: 2.4 mi, 1,560 ft up, 180 ft down one way / mod.
Main attractions: View of Pinto Mountains and southern Mojave Desert
USGS 7.5' topo maps: Queen Mountain, Twentynine Palms Mountain*
Maps: pp. 177*, *173*

Location and Access

On Highway 62 in Twentynine Palms, about a mile east of the town center, turn south on Utah Trail, signed as the north entrance to Joshua Tree National Park. Follow it 1.6 miles to Morning Drive, on the left. Coming from the park, this street corner is 2.5 miles south of the north entrance station. Turn east on Morning Drive and go 0.7 mile to the corner of Bedouin Avenue. Twentynine Palms Mountain is the long ridge rising to the southeast.

At this corner take the primitive road on the right (south-southeast), which is the Gold Park Road (periodically signed JT 1901). After 1.8 miles, ignoring several side roads used by the locals to reach shooting ranges, JT 1901B splits off on the right. Keep left on JT 1901. After 2 miles the road enters a shallow canyon. At mile 3.0 there is a bedrock exposure that takes practice and high clearance to drive over. At mile 3.6 the road forks. Take the left fork, which climbs a little, then splits after 200 feet. This junction is easy to miss. Take the rockier road that climbs on the left (signed JT 1906). Follow it east across a low broad saddle 1.3 miles to Dog Wash. Turn right up the wash on JT 1909, paralleling Twentynine Palms Mountain to the east. After 1.25 miles (6.25 miles from pavement) an unsigned fork on the left climbs to a radio installation on the mountain's crest about 1.5 miles north of the summit. Drive it 0.45 mile up to the first switchback and park (there is nowhere to park without blocking access between here and a locked gate 0.1 mile further). The Gold Park Road is sandy, and the cutoff to Dog Wash (JT 1906) is rocky and has a few steep grades. It would be heroic to make it without high clearance and four-wheel drive.

Route Description

At 4,562 feet, Twentynine Palms Mountain is not a giant by desert-climbing standards, but most of the climb is along a rough road that makes up for it a little. To negotiate the steep, fault-bound lower flank of the mountain, sharp switchbacks were cut into it, abrupt and rocky enough to defeat a Hummer. After a 0.7-mile ascent the switchbacks end on a ridge that parallels the main crest. Twentynine Palms Mountain becomes visible to the east around this point, the highest of a string of broad open hills sprinkled with low boulders. The summit is separated from the ridge by two steep-walled canyons, making a direct east route difficult. The road offers much easier access, as it climbs north-northeast along the relatively moderate ridge another mile to a pass, circumventing the canyons in the process.

The rest of the route is cross country. The crest can be gained by heading due east from the pass, then followed to the top. A quicker and easier alternative is to stay below the crest on its west flank, aiming generally southeast and climbing just enough to skirt below the crest's rockier crown. On the south side of the 4,442-foot summit, Twentynine Palms Mountain comes into view again. It is then a short descent to the shallow wash at the northern foot of Twentynine Palms Mountain, and from there a short 200-foot climb to the summit.

Twentynine Palms Mountain has classic desert geography, in subtle ways different from most. It is part of the region's Precambrian igneous and metamorphic complex, mostly granites but also uncommon schists, their cleaved planes sparkling with gold, silver, or charcoal crystals. In all directions the hills are bare, much more rocks than plants, horizontal outcrops defined by ancient metamorphism poking through them like ribs. The plant diversity does not increase with elevation as it usually does at these mid-elevations, but *decreases*. The washes and lower slopes are covered with yucca, silver and diamond cholla, creosote, saltbush, ephedra, wishbone bush, and many other plants. Higher up the selection shrinks to a skeletal creosote-burrobush community peppered with rogue cactus—calico, beavertail, and cushion foxtail. The final slope is mostly a monoculture of dwarf blackbush growing on scratchy lawns of dry bunch grass, the vermillion heads of isolated barrel cactus the only bright notes. The wind is partly responsible for this inverted botany. When I was there it was howling up

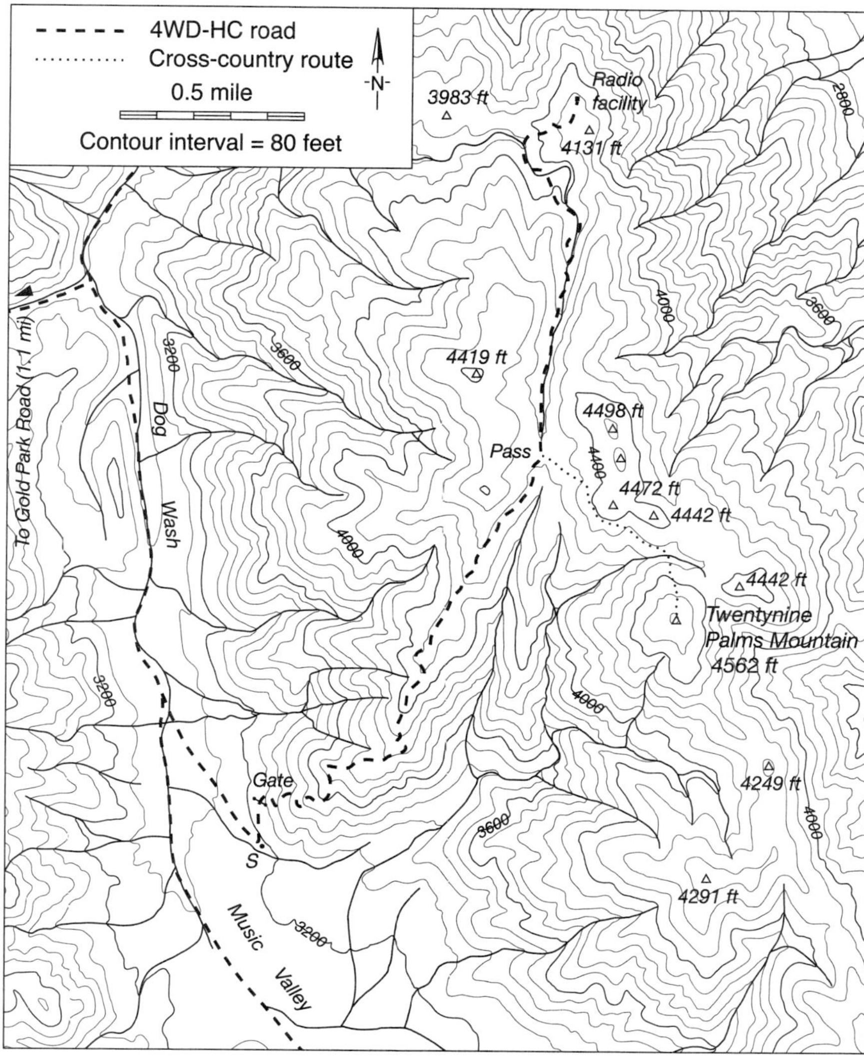

Twentynine Palms Mountain		
	Dist.(mi)	Elev.(ft)
Telecom road (1st switchback)	0.0	3,180
Main ridge	0.7	3,840
Pass	1.7	4,250
Bypass false summit	~2.0	~4,380
Wash crossing	2.2	4,280
Twentynine Palms Mountain	2.4	4,562

Pinto Mountains from the summit of Twentynine Palms Mountain

from Music Valley, triggering melodic resonances that justified its name. It was strong enough to challenge my balance and redirect my steps. During most of the day for seven months a year, only a few road cuts and low outcrops in the hills offer slivers of shade. You wished the mountain was a little true to its name and held—forget the other 28—at least one cool shady palm as a relief from the inferno.

The summit is a nice symmetric dome that rolls off in all cardinal directions to aprons of low angular boulders and sweeping views of the southern Mojave Desert. In the early morning the centerpiece is the long chain of the Little San Bernardino and Eagle mountains wrapping around nearly half of the horizon. In the late afternoon the show is stolen by the Pinto Mountains stretching out many miles eastward. There is perhaps no better place to appreciate the extent and sere beauty of this fragmented range. Its northern shores spill out in long parallel ridges into Morongo Basin and the sand-encrusted sink of Dale Lake, brilliant against the Sheep Hole Mountains. The access road, the radio antenna, and all but a wedge of Twentynine Palms are hidden by the mountain, so that in spite of its proximity to civilization this mountaintop gives a gratifying sense of remoteness.

■

THE SUPPLY MINE

> *With a production exceeding one ton of gold, the Supply Mine was the uncontested star of the rich Pinto Mountains. Its extensive ruins, easily accessible on foot, are a great example of a full-fledged 1930s mining and milling operation. The landscape is so devoid of humans and vegetation, and so raw in its design, that you would be excused if you believed you had landed on another planet. This is a must for any fan of mining history, desolate landscapes, or four-wheeling the Mesozoic.*

General Information
Jurisdiction: Bureau of Land Management
Road status: Hiking on primitive roads; 4WD-HC access road
Supply Mine: 1.0 mi, 460 ft up, 30 ft down one way / easy
Lorman Mine: 1.8 mi, 520 ft up, 280 ft down one way / easy
Nightingale Dunes: 2.4 mi, 610 ft up, 500 ft down one way / easy-moder.
Main attractions: Extensive ruins of rich gold mines, history, dunes
USGS 7.5' topo maps: Humbug Mountain, New Dale*
Maps: pp. 183*, *173*

Location and Access

The Supply Mine is in the northeastern Pinto Mountains, in the massive hills east of Humbug Mountain. Like several other rich historic gold mines in that area, it is reached by rough roads that branch off the Gold Crown Road, once the Dale Mining District's main artery. From Utah Trail in Twentynine Palms, this unsigned road is 14.3 miles east on Highway 62, on the right, which is the site of historic Old Dale. Look for a BLM board 100 yards from the highway. Drive this wide and generally good high-clearance road about 4.5 miles to a narrow passage through some hills. This area has two rough spots that require four-wheel drive. Soon after, the road bends gradually to the left until it heads due east. About 1.1 miles after it straightens out, or 6.2 miles from the highway, the main road veers to the right (south) at a fork. Continue straight instead (east) on the Doberman Mountain Road 0.1 mile to a four-way intersection. The tailings of the Supply Mine are visible in the middle of the hills to the left. The Doberman Mountain Road goes the short remaining distance to the Supply Mine, but it is very rough near the mine, and it is classified by the BLM as "undesignated" part way up. It is best to park at this last intersection and walk.

Route Description

Of the dozens of gold lodes that were exploited in the Pinto Mountains, the Supply Mine was far and away the richest. Operated off and on between the early 1900s and 1942, it was the largest gold producer in the Joshua Tree region, four times richer than the Lost Horse Mine, and it broke record after record. Its main shaft was possibly the deepest of thousands of mines in San Bernardino County, and it sprouted nearly one mile of galleries. The mine produced, literally, a ton of gold, 1.2 tons to be exact, valued then at one million dollars.

Unlike most desert gold mines, the Supply Mine had a sustained production for years at a time. In its early days it was run by the Seal of Gold Mining Company, which made enough profit to draw the attention of mining tycoon Charles Schwab. Former president of the billion-dollar U.S. Steel Corporation, Schwab had immense wealth and a flair for profitable mines. From Goldfield in Nevada to the Inyo Mine in Death Valley, he had invested wisely in gold, silver, and copper properties throughout the West. When he heard of the Supply Mine, he financed the United Greenwater Copper Company to take over, and injected large sums of money into infrastructure, machinery, and manpower. His gamble paid off. During the 1910s, several thousand tons of ore were extracted from a giant shaft that eventually reached 1,250 feet underground, then dry-crushed and cyanided in a 100-ton mill. When the company closed shop in the winter of 1915, nearly half a million dollars in gold had been harvested.

The Supply Mine was re-opened in 1927-1928 by the Arrowhead Development Company, which exploited the nearby Jean vein. But the mine did not get its second wind until 1929, when it was leased by the Gold Crown Mining Company. Besides working its Gold Crown Mine a few miles south, the company went after the northern extension of the Supply Mine's bountiful main vein. Known as the Lorman Mine, the property explored a long ore shoot that averaged 9 feet in width, and it turned out to be equally rich. The Nightingale Shaft was sunk on the vein via a tight ladder of winzes and tunnels that bottomed out 825 feet below the surface. Starting in 1935, the ore was trucked to the Gold Crown Mine for treatment in a new 60-ton ball mill and cyanide plant. Some days this ore alone kept the mill running at nearly full capacity. The Gold Crown Mine played out in 1938, after producing its own $385,000 in gold. The company moved its mill to the Supply Mine property and continued working through the Lorman Mine's large reserve. The Supply Mine died with a bang in 1942, when the government ordered mines that produced minerals not essential to the war effort to shut down. By then the Nightingale Shaft had added over

Supply Mine (right of center) from lower end of access road

$500,000 to the Supply Mine's exceptional tally. If its entire production had been melted together, it could have been fashioned into a sphere 20 inches in diameter. Today, it would be worth $65 million.

The route to the Supply Mine is simple: just continue on foot on the Doberman Mountain Road, first east briefly, then north-northeast up along the flank of a small bay. The old grade is mostly gentle, littered with ankle-twisting cobbles. It is obvious from the start that this was no ordinary mine. Up ahead, at the top of the bay, the Supply Mine's huge tailings drip down the mountain in long abrupt drapes. As you near the mine, the road overlooks a small sand dune, then the bowl below the mine where the mill tailings were impounded. Storm runoffs have sculpted them into miniature badlands of sharp pinkish ridges dissected by vertical furrows.

After 0.75 mile the road reaches a pass at the head of the bay, and the ruins of the Supply Mine. The nearly level road that cuts west from the pass leads 0.2 mile to the heart of the mine—the foundations of its 100-ton mill just past a deep open shaft. When it was active, it occupied a good portion of the space, and two large buildings stood near it. Below the mill, a long trestled structure snaked along the top of the mill tailings. Just before the shaft the road angles right and climbs the very steep hill behind the mill, past the gaping main shaft, to the ridge top. It ends at a couple of small open shafts, and a good bird's-eye view of the mine. The pass area has the older stone ruins of a dwelling and a primitive mill, and the perimeter foundations of what may have been a house and utility buildings connected by a raised concrete pathway.

From the pass it is about 1 mile to the Lorman Mine. Continue on the main road as it descends generally north into a canyon. In 0.2 mile, go left at a fork. The road passes by the low tailings of the tunnel and shafts that explored the Jean vein in 1928. It then winds down to a side canyon, and finally climbs up this side canyon to a pass, and the Lorman Mine just beyond.

Located high up at the head of a narrow canyon that drops precipitously toward Wonder Valley, the Lorman Mine is impressive as much for its sweeping view of Dale Lake as for its numerous ruins. Enough of its complex mill is left to make it a fun site to decipher. At the pass stand the stocky foundations of a mill. The main 1930s installations were 400 feet further, spilling down four levels of spur roads cut into the canyon slope. Level 4 at the top was mostly a protection from falling rocks. The Nightingale Shaft, on level 3, is an intimidating hole 20 feet across. It was serviced by a metal headframe and electric hoists. The concrete slab with heavy bolts in front of it supported a building that may have housed the compressors that blew air into the shaft. Through the little concrete arch next to the shaft, the ore pulled up from the shaft was hauled up a tilted conveyor to a cabin perched on a tall cylindrical ore tower. The tower sat in the semicircular stone wall 100 feet past the arch. In the cabin, the ore was crushed by a grinder and dropped in the tower. It proceeded to the ball mill, located right below the tower—its massive foundations still cascade down in giant steps to level 2 and level 1. The slurry from the mill was treated in a fat

The Supply Mine

	Dist.(mi)	Elev.(ft)
Jct off Gold Crown Road	0.0	1,950
Road junction at pass	0.75	2,270
Supply Mine (mill ruins)	(0.15)	2,250
Supply Mine (upper shafts)	(0.3)	~2,380
Fork in road (go left)	0.9	2,210
Lorman Mine (main shaft)	1.7	~2,250
Lorman Mine (lower shafts)	1.9	~2,170
Top of Nightingale Dunes	2.4	2,070

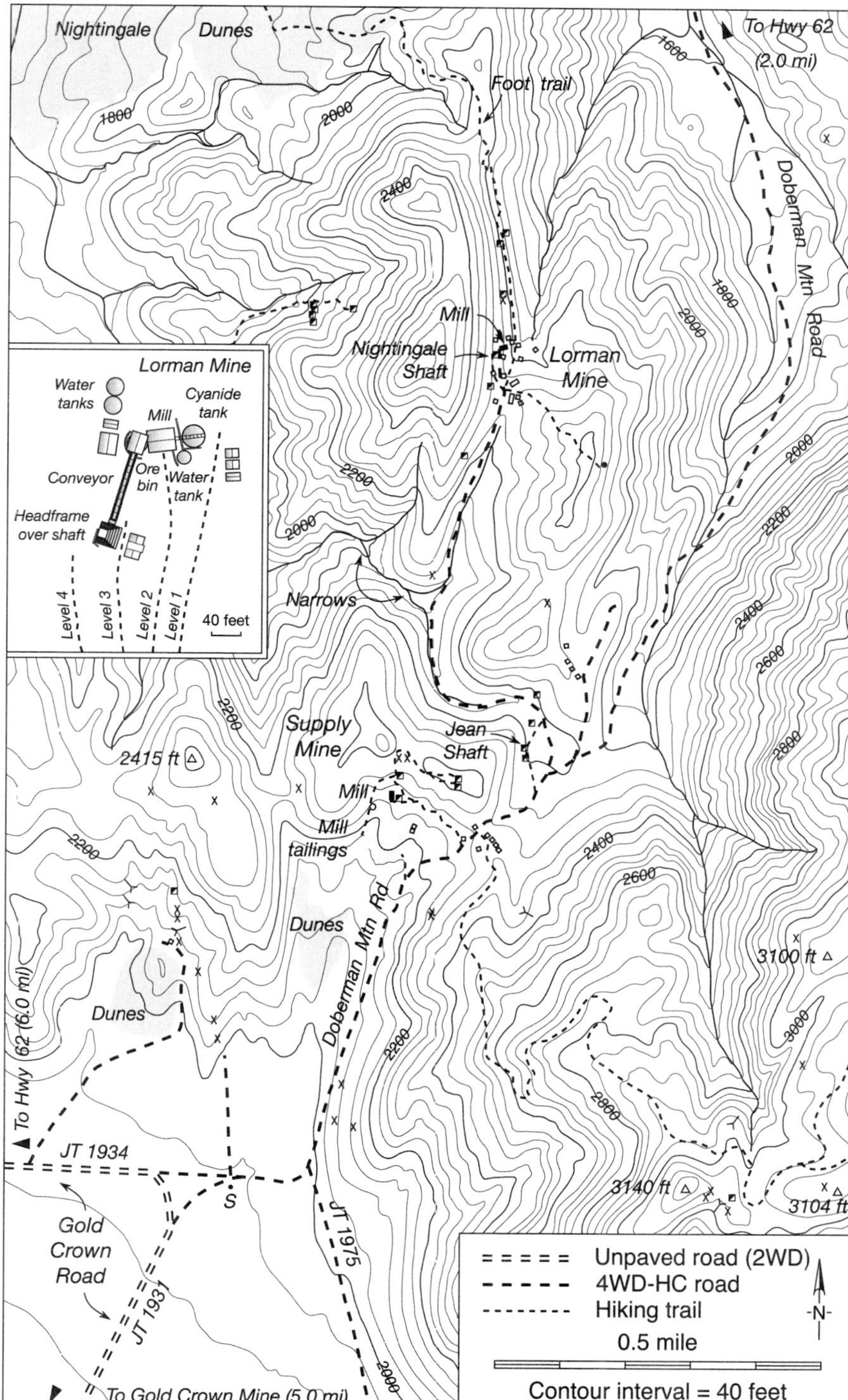
Nightingale
Dunes
To Hwy 62
(2.0 mi)
Foot trail
1600
1800
2000
2400
Doberman Mtn Road
Mill
Nightingale Shaft
Lorman Mine
Lorman Mine
Water tanks
Cyanide tank
Mill
Conveyor
Ore bin
Water tank
Headframe over shaft
Level 4
Level 3
Level 2
Level 1
40 feet
2200
Narrows
Supply Mine
Jean Shaft
2415 ft
Mill
Mill tailings
2600
2800
Dunes
Doberman Mtn Rd
3100 ft
3000
Dunes
To Hwy 62 (6.0 mi)
JT 1934
S
3140 ft
3104 ft
Gold Crown Road
JT 1975
JT 1931
To Gold Crown Mine (5.0 mi)
Unpaved road (2WD)
4WD-HC road
Hiking trail
N
0.5 mile
Contour interval = 40 feet

Concrete foundations and gas tank supports at the pass, Lorman Mine

cyaniding tank that stood beside the concrete culvert at the end of level 1. When it was fired up, it kept a crew of 80 busy and made a racket that could be heard from town...

Even without the slightest interest in mining history, it is hard not to have a good time on this hike. The mountains are beautiful, tight and steep, cloaked with darkly stained outcrops. The land is so sparsely vegetated that it feels alien. Every high point delivers a long peek into raw wilderness, and unveils more places to explore. The short miner's trail beyond the Lorman Mine is a perfect example. From the mill it cuts across the canyon slope to the mine's lower shafts, then switchbacks up to the canyon rim. Most of the way the radiant playa of Dale Lake is in full view. On the other side of the rim the trail wiggles down into another canyon, and soon emerges at the top of pristine sand dunes that I felt compelled to name Nightingale. They flow several hundred feet down the mountain to a broad wash, and spill out on its far side in a long rippling sheet. If you trudge far enough in this range, you are likely to run into secret places like this, forgotten by time.

At both mines the shafts are deep, unprotected, and dangerous. Several concrete structures have open manholes or basements. Watch your step, and stay away from the shafts' crumbly edges. If you must hike back at dark, have a good light on at all times.

■

THE CARLYLE MINE

The Carlyle Mine has more physical remains than most mines in the Joshua Tree area. Scattered over several mining sites in a colorful canyon, it has a similar appeal as Beveridge, the legendary ghost town lost in the Inyo Mountains—minus the remoteness and rough access. The sprawling Carlyle Mill, one of the region's most extensive, is an easy hour-and-a-half walk from a paved road. Following the overgrown mining trails that climb into the mountains above the giant mill in search of tunnels, tailings, and remnants of the mine's half-mile aerial tramway makes for an exciting foray into the gold-mining history of the Pinto Mountains.

General Information

Jurisdiction: Bureau of Land Management
Road status: Hiking on dirt roads and mining trails; graded access road
Carlyle Mill: 2.9 mi, 680 ft up, 20 ft down one way / easy
Upper tramway terminal: 3.6 mi, 1,340 ft up, 90 ft down one way / mod.
Main attractions: 1900–1930s mining ruins in a roadless canyon
USGS 7.5' topo map: New Dale
Maps: pp. 189*, *173*

Location and Access

The Carlyle Mine is tucked away in a nameless canyon on the north slope of the eastern Pinto Mountains, due south of Dale Lake. The road used to access it in historic times branches off Highway 62, on the south side, 19.2 miles east of Utah Trail, or 1.55 miles west of the signed Ironage Road. It is easy to miss; slow down and look carefully for a sandy track. Four-wheel drive is needed to negotiate the first half a mile of deep sand, and high clearance for the last stretch. If you do not have the right vehicle, park at the highway and hike there: it is an easy and pleasant walk. Follow the road 1.6 miles to a Y junction just inside the mountains. Take the left fork, up a narrowing canyon. After about 1 mile, where the canyon splits at a tight spot, leave the wash and take the fainter rocky road on the right. Park at the turnout 0.2 mile in, just before a washout, in sight of the Carlyle Mill up canyon.

Route Description

When approaching the mill on the steep final grade, it is clear that the Carlyle Mine meant business. Its mill was *big*. Covering 6,000

The Carlyle Mill overlooking Dale Lake and the Sheep Hole Mountains

square feet, its grand staircase of reinforced concrete housed five levels of heavy machinery. In its heyday, from June 1937 to March 1939, it processed 13,250 tons of ore and recovered $124,000 in gold, silver, and lead—and it produced some more until it shut down in 1941. From the mine up canyon, a half-mile-long aerial tramway lowered the ore 600 feet to the mill. From top to bottom, the mill had a 60-ton ore bin to stock the raw ore, a gyratory crusher to grind it to 1-inch chunks, an 80-ton bin to store the crushed ore, a ball mill to pulverize it to the size of sand, a classifier to recover the coarse gold, and a closed circuit of cells to produce the final flotation concentrate, which carried at least $800 per ton in gold. The whole thing was powered by a 225-horsepower diesel that also drove a 150-kW generator. There were conveyor belts, a 4-mile pipeline that brought water from a well on Dale Lake, a 30,000-gallon water tank, and a compressor that sent pressurized air up a pipeline to the upper tunnel to power the air drills. It cost $150,000 to set this all up, and it took 30 men to run it.

The machinery has been long gone, but the imposing foundations are still there. It is now a naked amalgam of vats, studded pilings, lumber floors, and retaining walls thicker than bunkers. Sheets of roofing, 55-gallon drums, bits of ducts and pipeline, and suntanned lumber are scattered all over. Although it is too far gone to mentally reconstruct, it still attests that the Carlyle Mine was a major player in the district.

From the mill on up, there never was a road. Today, the mine's tunnels are still accessed by the same foot trails that the miners used to go to work. The trails are narrow cuts across the canyon's rubbly slopes, now partly reclaimed by fallen rocks and opportunistic plants. The main trail follows the tramway's crooked path, passing close to three mining areas before ending at the upper tunnel. Being rare and endangered—this is the only one in the Joshua Tree area—the tramway is the center of attention. Three of the four intermediate towers are still miraculously standing. The first tower, visible from the mill, is a slender square frame looking out to Marvel Valley. The two cables that it once supported now lie on the ground—the larger cable that supported the buckets, and the thinner cable that towed them. Everywhere, the cables point the way to the next mining area.

Engine block and flywheel at the Carlyle Mine's old mill

Every mining area is different. The first one, just before the first tower, has a dislocated ore chute and sheer tailings that drop a long way into the canyon's depths. The second one has two adjacent tunnels, the longest 1,500 feet. The third one, the side tunnel, is hidden in a side canyon past the third tram tower. Below it, the trail changes character: it disappears at a rocky ravine crossing, reappears, then shoots up in tight switchbacks to a blunt ridge. The fourth tower is up there, anchored on a thick concrete base. Because the cable made a sharp angle at this point, it was a sturdier control tower. From there on up the trail is straight and easy to the fourth mining area, wedged in a tight ravine below a sheer escarpment. Its massive tailings plug the wash under a 40-foot dam of crushed granite as bright as talcum. The main producer, this last tunnel sprouted a mile of galleries. Just outside, the tramway's upper terminal was blown to pieces. What remains is the waterline, the compressed-air pipeline, an engine block, and the giant cogged wheel that looped the cables around.

What took it over the top for me was the area around the third tower. You know at first glance you have stumbled onto a hidden treasure. There is the tramway tower of course, the support cable still straddling it, and the two 1,500-pound buckets used in the past lying nearby. But there is also a second mill, much older. It has an ore bin, two banged-up zinc cylindrical cyaniding tanks, and the concrete and wood foundations of a small mill with—rarest of the rare—its engine still mounted on it. Higher up, the wooden staves and iron hoops of an old-fashioned water tank have collapsed on themselves. Small pinkish mill tailings drip down into a nearby ravine. This may be the original location of the mine, then spelled Carlisle, a property that *The Mining And Metallurgical Journal* reported in April 1900 had "a fine body of high grade ore" and was "considered one of the best properties of the district." The ore came from a tunnel further up the ravine, reached by a faint trail overrun by boulders and shrubs.

As abandoned mines go, the Carlyle Mine still has enough ruins to host a small citizenry of ghosts. The miners left their signs all over. In crude black letters they wrote their names and addresses on a tunnel wall. Deep inside a gallery, someone with a grim sense of humor left the plastic skeleton of a dog wearing a dusty rag and a canary-yellow hard hat. The mill operators impounded the mill tailings in a narrow dam, thinking they might return and tease out the leftover gold. A few employees shared a house at the edge of the wash. From the top of the mill, a path drops to it, now a flattened heap of lumber and corrugated iron. Perhaps one day, one of the residents on his way back from town

The Carlyle Mine

	Dist.(mi)	Elev.(ft)
Highway 62	0.0	1,240
Y junction (left)	1.6	1,480
Fork to Carlyle Mill (right)	2.65	1,665
End of road (washout)	2.8	1,770
Carlyle Mill	2.9	~1,860
Old mill	3.3	~2,245
Upper tramway terminal	3.6	2,495

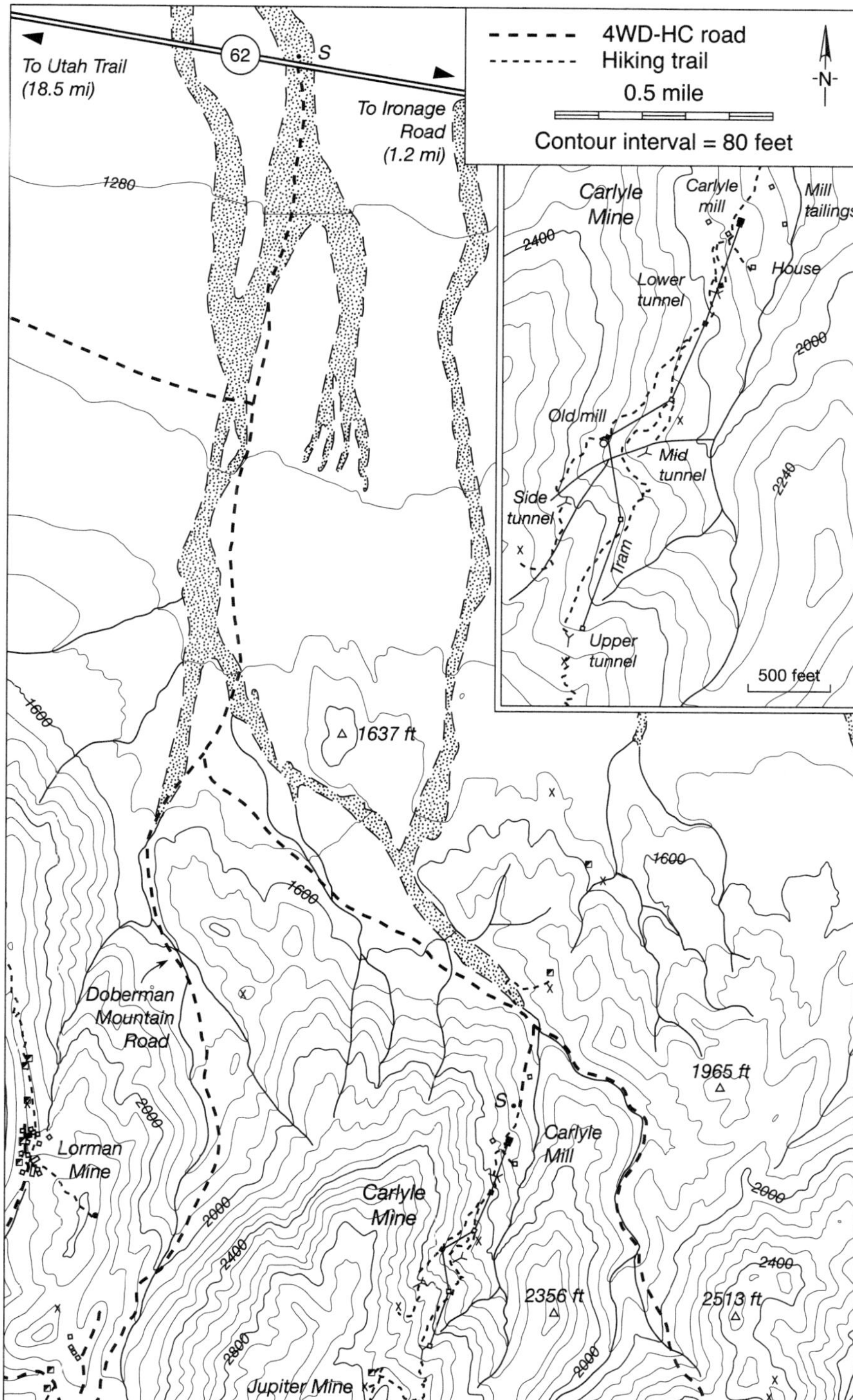
4WD-HC road
Hiking trail
0.5 mile
Contour interval = 80 feet
-N-
To Utah Trail (18.5 mi)
62
S
To Ironage Road (1.2 mi)
1280
Carlyle Mine
Carlyle mill
Mill tailings
House
Lower tunnel
Old mill
Mid tunnel
Side tunnel
Tram
Upper tunnel
500 feet
2400
2000
2240
1600
1637 ft
1965 ft
Doberman Mountain Road
Lorman Mine
Carlyle Mill
Carlyle Mine
2356 ft
2513 ft
2800
Jupiter Mine

Tramway tower at the Carlyle Mine

slipped on the steep path, dropped his bag of groceries, and ruined his breakfast of bacon and eggs. The trail was upgraded with stairs constructed with flat stones. The stairs, the salvaged tailings, the skeleton, the names on the wall—they are all there.

The Carlyle Mine is a rare survivor from a vanished culture. Its species is slowly dying. Rain rusts through its nails and crumbles its concrete. Sunlight shreds its lumber. Gravity pulls down its loose boards, and gales scatter the pieces around. Prize remains disappear. People with too little education and no respect for the sacred paint graffiti on what is left. Custodians turn a blind eye, claiming insufficient resources when what is missing is passion. Soon, all that will remain is the original land—a serene canyon, raw hills spiked with outcrops the color of dried blood, the charcoal-tipped heads of cushion foxtail cactus, the paperbag bush that sound like a rattlesnake when brushed, and the bone-dry ranges pinned on the horizon, more alien than Mars. It may be, arguably, what matters most, the way it ever was. But until it is all gone, out there in this vast desert wilderness a little gem of a mine is still hanging on, haunted by memories, waiting.

■

THE IRON AGE AND SNOW FLAKE MINES

A penchant for geology and/or historic mines is a good reason for visiting these two iron properties. They have indeed much to show—awesome pits and tailings, rusted cars, mill foundations, plenty of iron ores, and the junkyards of generations of miners. But do come here even if mines do not get your heart racing. It will give you a chance to check out an overlooked corner of the desert, to stroll in a scenic canyon, negotiate a bouldery gulch, and enjoy dunes, distant views, the beauty of rocks, and the desert's fragrances and solitude.

General Information

Jurisdiction: Public lands (BLM)
Road status: Hiking on primitive roads; 2WD access road
Iron Age Mine: 3.5 mi, 560 ft up, ~20 ft down one way / easy
Snow Flake Mine: 1.5 mi, 80 ft up, 90 ft down one way / very easy
Snow Flake Mine–Iron Age Mine *loop:* 8.0 mi, 730 ft up loop / difficult
Main attractions: Iron quarries and ore, car cemeteries, scenic canyons
USGS 7.5' topo map: New Dale
Maps: pp. 195*, *173*

Location and Access

The Iron Age and Snow Flake mines are in the northern foothills of the eastern Pinto Mountains, in the portion of the range managed by the BLM. Two roads can get you there. The first one is the signed Ironage Road. From Utah Trail in Twentynine Palms, drive Highway 62 eastbound 20.7 miles. At the wide dirt skirt on the right, two roads branch off. The one on the left (the Ironage Road, or JT 1957) cuts east-southeast 2.5 miles across the open desert to its junction with the second access road, which will be joining in from the left, near the foot of the mountains. Unless you want to drive to the mines, park in this area. This road has soft sand and requires good clearance and traction. The second road is 1.5 miles further east on Highway 62, on the right. Drive it 1.3 miles south, then south-southeast, to the same junction. This road was once paved, and although it has a small sandy dip, then rocks, it is drivable with a standard-clearance vehicle.

History

The mining history of the California desert was built on the skills and tenacity of countless prospectors, unsung heroes whose invaluable contributions are rarely acknowledged. One of them was Marcus Pluth, an emigrant from Austria with a flare for minerals. His name first appeared in the 1885 records of Calico, one of the region's richest silver mining centers. Then aged 31, he alternatively located silver lodes as a prospector and worked leased properties as a miner. When the price of silver dipped to an all-time low in 1902, Calico busted and Pluth went on to prospect far and wide. Some of the properties he discovered then were still running in the 1930s. Although he had a keen eye for silver and gold, his most lasting legacy was a huge deposit of a more prosaic rock—limestone. In 1921, he sold 1,600 acres of limestone claims that he and a friend, Tom Scofield, had astutely located near a remote siding on the Santa Fe Railroad in Ward Valley. The limestone mine was so prolific that until 1954 it supported nearly continuously a real town called Chubbuck, supplying in particular lime for the construction of the Colorado River Aqueduct in the 1930s.

The discovery of the Iron Age deposit is also credited to Marcus Pluth and Tom Scofield, around 1900. Although Scofield's name was not associated with the mine's subsequent history, Pluth and his estate were until at least the 1950s, as were the heirs of Doc Igo, a drugstore owner during Calico's glory days. Their patented claims witnessed slow beginnings. The deposit consisted of over 50 veins of solid iron ore, most of them small. The only three large ones combined covered just one acre. Assuming that they extended to a depth of 80 feet, the ore reserve was around half a million tons, which is petty cash for an iron mine. The Iron Age was exploited for a time via shallow shafts and open cuts. By 1951, less than 2,000 tons of ore had been taken out.

But the mountain was not to be left alone in the end. A few years later, steel magnate Henry Kaiser, always on the lookout for iron to feed his Fontana plant, sent mining engineers to the Iron Age, who upgraded the estimate of the ore reserve to three million tons. The heirs of the Pluth-Igo property leased it to a Twentynine Palms outfit for open-pit mining. The top of the mountain was blasted to install a crusher. The ore was trucked north around Dale Lake on a new road to the Amboy Road, and from there to Amboy, where it was loaded on Santa Fe Railroad cars and transported to Fontana. Between 1964 and 1969, the mountain was beheaded, creating a crater big enough to hold a city block. The tonnage of iron removed from it and from the nearby Snow Flake Mine pit was around 1.3 million tons, less than half what the engineers had estimated. Compared to the 120 million tons that came out of Kaiser's iron mines in the Eagle Mountains, the Iron Age and Snow Flake production was just a drop in the bucket. But Pluth had done well for himself and his descendants.

Automobile cemetery at the Iron Age Mine

Route Description

The Snow Flake Mine. The mine is not visible from the junction on the Ironage Road, but it is easy to get to it. Walk the road southeast 250 yards, and you will see the mine's raised roadway striking off to the right. It cuts a straight 0.8-mile path to the mine, across a low apron of sand sprinkled with emaciated creosote, burrobush, and cholla. To the north the land is wide open to Dale Lake's dazzling white salt flat.

The Snow Flake Mine is announced by sprawling low tailings of gray overburden. Well before reaching it, iron ore is plentiful. This road and all local roads are littered with pieces of hematite, less commonly magnetite. These inch-size metallic fragments radiate the strange beauty of iron meteorites. Pick up a piece; hold it in your hand. Its high density exerts a satisfying pressure. It holds the darkness of space, the wavy finish of fallen stars, the mystery of a distant genesis. The million-ton tailings also have ochre limonite and prismatic crystals of goethite, both oxidized forms of hematite. The pit is straight ahead, a narrow, 400-yard-long crater that drops in steep terraces 60 feet into the ground. A rough track descends into it a little, then dissolves in rubble. If you walk to the sandy bottom, where storm water pools and grasses flourish, you will find a leftover wall of massive hematite. Like the seams mined long ago, it was formed when iron solutions filled cracks in igneous rock. The contact between the ore and the light-gray granite is so sharp that it can be traced with a fingernail. When the sun is acting up and the hematite wall is in the shade, it is soothing to sit against it and let its heat-conducting surface cool you off while admiring the silver and ochre stairs of granites overhead.

The Iron Age Mine. The Iron Age Mine is located near the head of a main canyon that cuts into the mountains just south of the junction. For the easiest route to the mine, walk back to the Ironage Road and follow it 2 miles up this canyon. The road has seen much better days, but the grade is easy and the canyon colorful. Its mouth is framed by tall golden dunes. Further on its wide sand wash is punctuated with the turquoise puffs of smoke trees. The wash eventually narrows and winds below rocky walls covered with hollows, fissured outcrops, and clusters of pinnacles. About 1.5 miles in, just before the wash angles left, take the narrow side canyon on the right (the second one in the canyon). The mine's tall tailings will soon come right up to the road. After 0.6 mile, this fork opens up and the road turns sharply left and down into the wash. Instead of joining the wash, follow the edge of the tailings southwest up a deeply rutted track. It climbs to the top of the tailings along the chain-link fence that blocks access to the mine's pit.

To visit the Iron Age Mine, amble along the road that spirals clockwise to the top of the tailings; it passes by all the points of interest. The centerpiece is the open pit. A short trench on the right, past a one-of-a-kind concrete chute, leads to its abrupt edge. It is an awe-inspiring excavation, 80 feet deep and 500 feet on the side, often plunged in darkness. The road goes on to a car cemetery at the west end; it gathers models that have not turned over since JFK won the presidency. The concrete foundations and pilings further north may have supported the jaw crusher that ran here around 1951. If you push on to the top, you will stare 160 feet down the pit's grand stairway of rocky terraces. Everywhere you go you run into hematite, the pebbles and cobbles from the underworld that sparked this massive undertaking.

The Iron Age and Snow Flake Mines

	Dist.(mi)	Elev.(ft)
Road junction	0.0	1,640
Trail to connecting canyon	1.0	1,700
Snowflake Mine (pit bottom)	(0.5)	1,630
Mining camp (join wash)	1.6	1,815
Leave canyon wash	2.6	1,925
Iron Age Mine (top of tailings)	3.5	2,172
Back to jct via Ironage Road	7.0	1,640

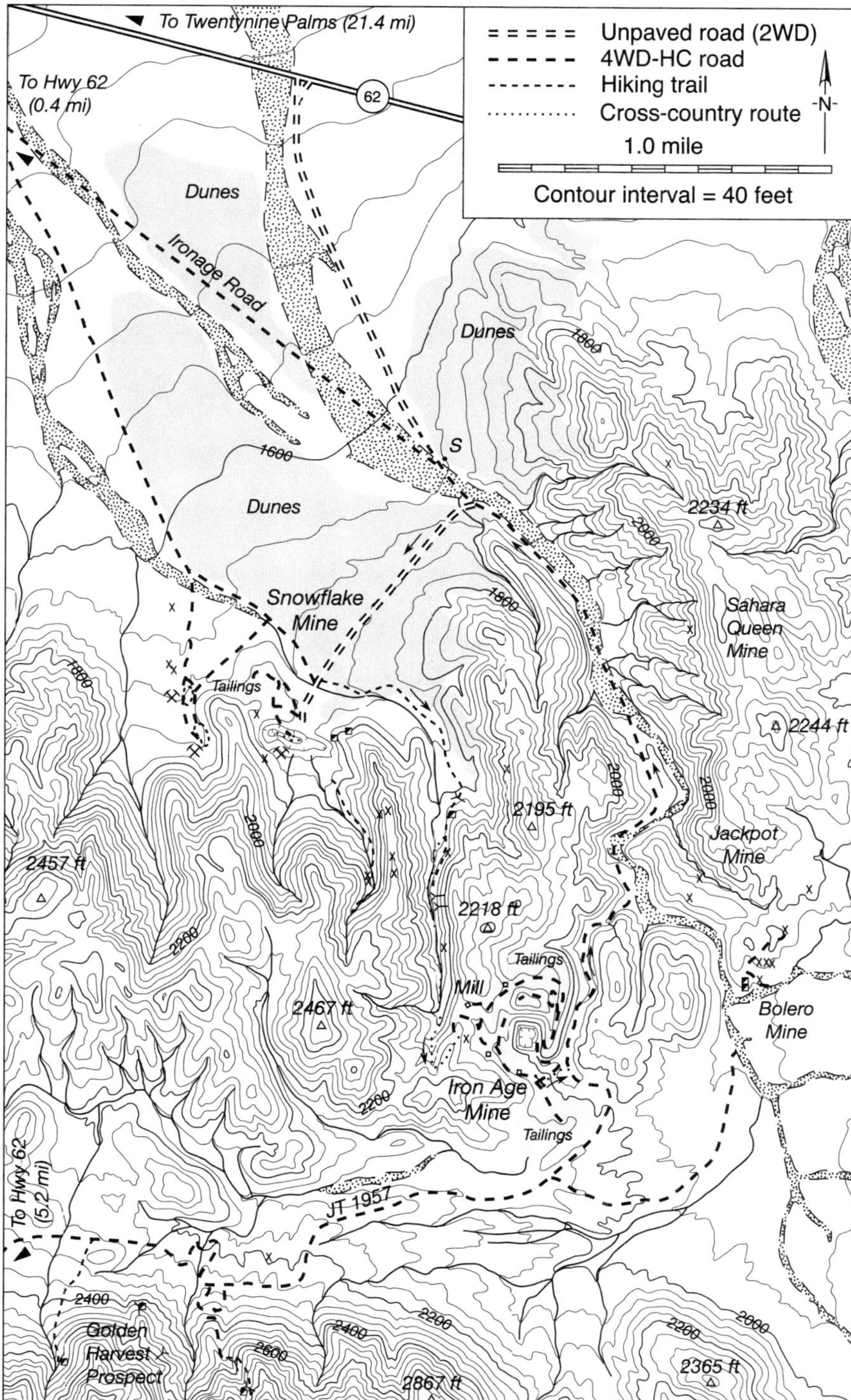
To Twentynine Palms (21.4 mi)
Unpaved road (2WD)
4WD-HC road
Hiking trail
Cross-country route
N
1.0 mile
Contour interval = 40 feet
To Hwy 62
(0.4 mi)
62
Dunes
Ironage Road
Dunes
1800
S
1600
Dunes
2234 ft
2000
Snowflake
Mine
1800
Sahara
Queen
Mine
1800
Tailings
2244 ft
2000
2000
2195 ft
Jackpot
Mine
2000
2457 ft
2218 ft
2200
Tailings
Mill
2467 ft
Bolero
Mine
Iron Age
Mine
2200
Tailings
To Hwy 62
(5.2 mi)
JT 1957
2400
Golden
Harvest
Prospect
2400
2600
2200
2200
2000
2365 ft
2867 ft

Terraced pit at the Snow Flake Mine

The canyon loop. From the Snow Flake Mine there is a second, more adventurous route to the Iron Age, up the next canyon west. From the pit, walk back to the fork just north of the tailings. Where the main road widens 25 yards further on the right, an abandoned road starts off on the right, behind a low bulldozed heap of rocks. Follow it east, then south, into a canyon lined by a long dune in its outer bend. In 0.6 mile you will reach the ruins of a camp below a tunnel. Descend west into the nearby canyon wash, and continue up the wash.

For close to a mile you will snake between arid 45-degree slopes dusted with pale bushes and darkly stained rocks. The wash quickly becomes a mess of low boulders, creosote, and desert lavender. Along the canyon's upper half, located just below the Iron Age, less organic objects show up: the miners used this canyon as their junkyard and threw into it anything from stoves to metal shelves, drums, car parts, and entire trucks. A few vintage carcasses hang high up the east slope. The most popular junk was tires—dozens are strewn all over. Some tires were rolled from the rim, and they gathered enough momentum to bounce clear across the canyon and land on the opposite slope. Near its upper end, the canyon veers left and opens up. Soon after, climb out of the wash on the east slope to the canyon rim, quite low by now, which will put you right above the Iron Age Mine's car graveyard.

The return down the Ironage Road, likely in the evening by the time you are done visiting the Iron Age, can be even more spectacular, as the rocky canyon walls fill up with crisp details in the setting light.

■

OUTLAW PEAK

Peak bagging in Joshua Tree takes all shapes. You can climb a summit like Ryan Mountain, close to paved roads, tamed by a well-groomed trail, and visited by hundreds of people on any cool-season weekend. At the other end of the spectrum the park has summits like Outlaw Peak, remote, trailless, omitted from many maps, where you can indulge in a long desert climb with no one else around, and discover the hidden sides of the park's wildest ranges.

General Information

Road status: Roadless; two-wheel-drive access road
Outlaw Peak: 4.3 mi, 1,470 ft up, 60 ft down one way / moderate
Main attractions: Isolated peak, sweeping views of eastern park
USGS 7.5′ topo map: Clarks Pass
Maps: pp. 199*, *173*

Location and Access

Located in the vast wilderness that preserves all of Pinto Basin and most of the Coxcomb Mountains, Outlaw Peak is the easternmost high summit in the Pinto Mountains. From Utah Trail in Twentynine Palms, drive Highway 62 east 27.8 miles toward the Sheep Hole Mountains, past Dale Lake, to a short spur up on the right, parallel to the highway. Coming from the other direction, it is 1.2 miles west of the pronounced right bend at Clarks Pass. Park at the upper end of the spur.

Route Description

Every peak is unique in that it has something different to offer—plants, rocks, approach, terrain, distance, difficulty, isolation, views, plus this undefinable quality that is the mood of a mountain. Outlaw Peak is a dark prominence, denuded even by desert standards. Its plant cover is widely spaced, mostly ground-hugging burrobush, tufts of dehydrated grass, and the silvery webs of creosote. Increasingly deprived of water, the vegetation grows thinner with elevation. The ground is a tight litter of cobbles. The rocks date from the Jurassic, andesite most of the way up, and quartz monzonite in the summit area. They can be hard to differentiate: the rocks have not moved, have eroded so little, and suntanned for so long, that they have acquired the uniform cocoa patina of thick desert varnish. The only bright notes are the infrequent red heads of barrel cactus, very much at home in this sunbaked heaven. In comparison, the approach along the mile-wide inner valley below the mountain seems almost verdant. The plants are bigger, more diverse, greener. This is the kingdom of creosote, cheese-bush, rabbitbrush, ephedra, and pygmy cedar. Catclaw and smoke tree are even large enough to supply a little shade.

In spite of the long approach, and thanks to the absence of obstacles on the mountain, it is a relatively easy climb. The greater distance from urbanism and from the park's main points of entry also guarantees, at least for now, blissful solitude: in the tiny notebook in the summit register, only about ten parties signed their names since 1993. The chance of running into another biped is about one in a thousand.

Route finding is also easy. From the parking area continue east along the spur road, now closed to motor vehicles, down to a broad wash, then up the wash as it angles right. As soon as the wash clears the point of the mountain and enters the inner valley, ten minutes out at most, Outlaw Peak comes into view 3.5 air miles to the south-southwest, its broad flat-topped obviously the tallest summit around. There are three legs to this climb. The first one is approximately 2.2 miles up the inner valley's main wash as it skirts the base of a mountain to the right, to where it starts bending to the west (right). For the second leg, leave the wash and cut a beeline south-southwest to the rounded promontory that projects from the peak's north base. This part of the inner valley is a low bajada of desert pavements dissected by small arroyos. The last wash is crossed just before the promotory. Its 10-foot trench of vertical fanglomerate provides the first serious shade. The final leg is up the mountain, mostly along the northern shoulder. The nose of the promontory is a little steep. Then comes a couple of small rocky outcrops and very shallow saddles. The next stretch climbs a second steep section, off to the right to avoid a rocky incline. The rest is a gradual open grade to the summit.

Outlaw Peak is an almost featureless knoll—no great rock formation to greet you at the finish line. But it makes up for this barrenness with an awesome panorama. In the morning the best direction is west,

Outlaw Peak		
	Dist.(mi)	Elev.(ft)
End of road spur	0.0	1,875
Leave wash (head SSW)	2.2	~2,045
Base of Outlaw Peak	3.3	~2,295
Outlaw Peak	4.3	3,291

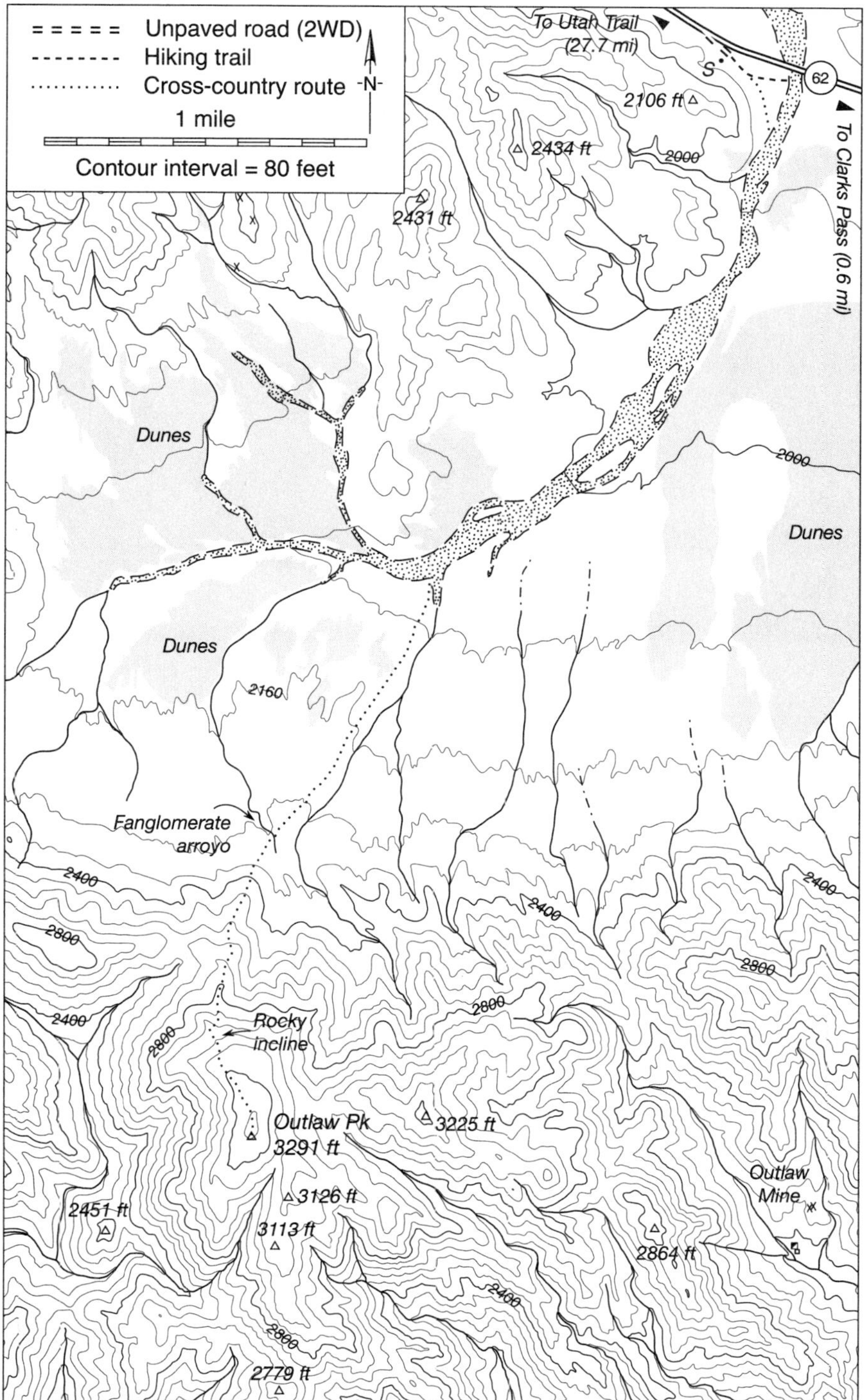

Unpaved road (2WD)
Hiking trail
Cross-country route
N
1 mile
Contour interval = 80 feet
To Utah Trail (27.7 mi)
S
62
To Clarks Pass (0.6 mi)
2106 ft
2434 ft
2431 ft
2000
Dunes
Dunes
Dunes
2160
Fanglomerate arroyo
2400
2800
Rocky incline
Outlaw Pk 3291 ft
3225 ft
3126 ft
3113 ft
2451 ft
2864 ft
2779 ft
Outlaw Mine

Looking north-northeast down at the inner valley from the ridge to Outlaw Peak

toward Pinto Basin and the fractured islands of blistered hills that make up the Pinto Mountains' long chain. In the afternoon it switches to the east and south. The Eagle Mountains sprawl across the southern horizon. The singularly straight line that clips their northern base is the Blue Cut Fault, the fault that slashes east-west across most of the park. To the east, the Coxcomb Mountains' hidden west flank and a vast arm of Pinto Basin fill the view, a hundred roadless square miles that hardly anyone ever sees. The basin floor is etched by a network of long parallel washes that all split from a master wash and curve southward, in perfect unison, to spread across Pinto Basin. Just east of the summit there is a providential outcrop just tall enough to sit in its shade and take in this life-size display of unhurried desert hydrology.

The final highlight comes during the descent, when looking down at the great sweep of sand that engulfs a good portion of the inner valley below, and the deeply creased Bullion and Sheep Hole mountains rearing up behind it. It is a magnificent landscape, raw and unspoiled. That so many wild places like this one in the West still gives us the exhilaration to immerse ourselves completely in boundless undeveloped spaces is one of America's most invaluable assets.

■

ARCH ROCK AND GRAND TANK

Located next to the White Tank Campground, this is a popular destination that gives a good opportunity to sample the large field of wild stone sculptures on the southwestern piedmont of the Pinto Mountains. Of all the areas in Joshua Tree that I have visited, it ranks close to the highest in scenic value. The local stars are Arch Rock, a beauty in itself, and Grand Tank, which holds a peaceful rock-rimmed pond after heavy winter rains, but also the arresting slots framed by narrow fins that abound all around them.

General Information
Road status: Paved access road
Arch Rock–Grand Tank: 1.0 mi, 150 ft up, 40 ft down one way / very easy
Main attractions: Trails to a natural arch, scenic tanks, and rock mazes
USGS 7.5' topo map: Malapai Hill
Maps: pp. 203*, 207, *173*

Location and Access

Arch Rock, Grand Tank, and White Tank are part of the striking area of granitic sculptures that form the backdrop of the White Tank Campground, at the extreme southwestern corner of the Pinto Mountains. If you are staying at the campground, hike from your campsite. Otherwise, parking at the campground to hike in this area is not permitted. Instead, park at the Twin Tanks parking and walk the short trail from there to Arch Rock. This parking is along the Pinto Basin Road 0.5 mile north of the White Tank Campground, on the left. Coming from the north, it is 2.2 miles south of Pinto Wye.

Route Description

From the south end of the Twin Tanks parking (furthest from the entrance), take the connector trail that heads south, parallel to the Pinto Basin Road. After 0.15 mile it ends at the California Riding and Hiking Trail. Turn left. In about 40 yards it crosses the road and splits right away. Take the Arch Rock Nature Trail, on the right. In 0.4 mile it crosses a plateau of low bushes to its junction with the Arch Rock Loop. Turn right and follow this short loop (~0.2 mile) clockwise to the interpretive sign that points to the arch, just off the trail to the right.

Arch Rock is a delicate 40-foot span of monzogranite resting on a stocky fin. Only a few feet thick at its thinnest, it seems too slender to

Arch Rock

hold a fool, which does not stop most visitors from climbing onto it to have their photograph taken. Here as at nearby Skull Rock, strong on-line and on-site advertising have downgraded it to a Disneyland attraction overrun by discourteous people who shout things like "Bobby why don't you get in the pitcher too?" as if they were in their living room. It can be too hectic to savor the arch's beauty. When the crowds are gone, however, especially when the campground is closed in summer, there are plenty of surfaces around to sit and enjoy this fine work of art, and to reflect on the time it took erosion to carve it, on the chance that it would, and on how much longer it might stand.

Arch Rock sits at the northern edge of a spectacular area of bare granite sliced north-south into long, parallel alignments of narrow fins separated by tight corridors. In the other direction, the fins are cut by swarms of more minor breaks, even tighter. This erosional pattern has created a maze of secret passages that are fun to explore. Some of them go on for a while; others pinch off into unscalable cracks that widen a little further. The easiest destination is White Tank, a small drainage that was dammed to catch rainfall and supply water for livestock. It is a short walk to the dam's low concrete wall, along the straight corridor past the arch, then down a staircase of furrows to a sandy wash. Broken at its base, the dam no longer holds water, but its name still stands prominently. The plutonic formation responsible for the park's

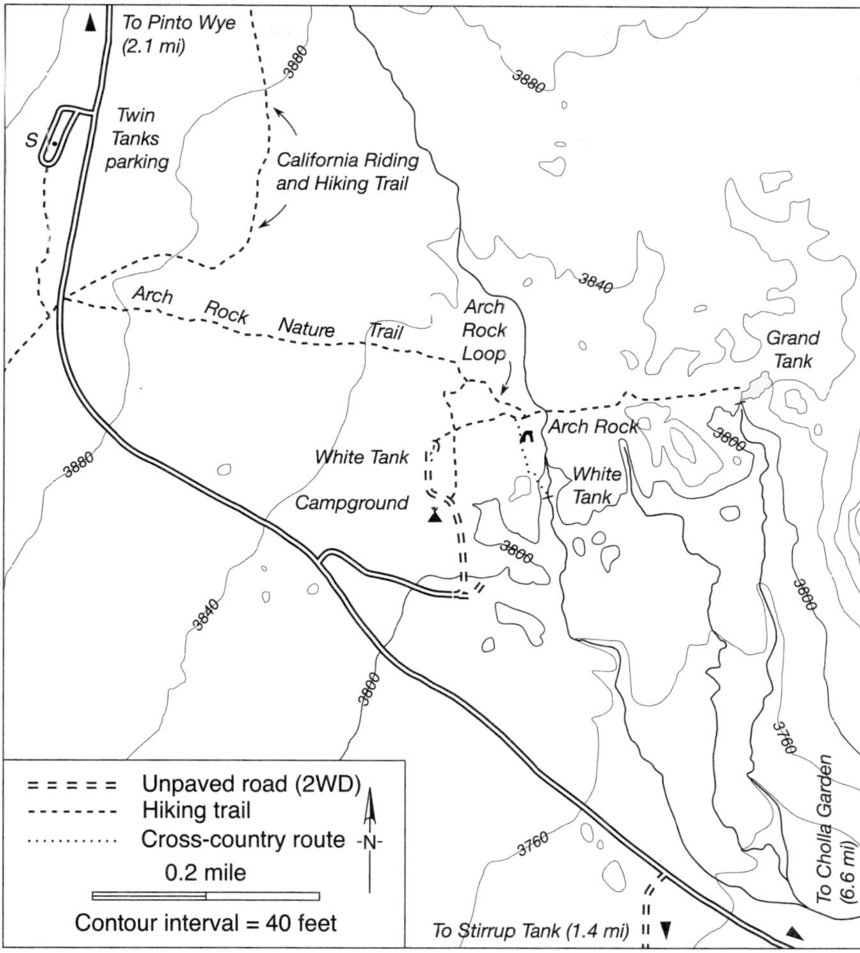

Arch Rock and Grand Tank	Dist.(mi)	Elev.(ft)
Twin Tanks parking	0.0	3,910
Cal. Riding & Hiking Tr. (left)	0.15	3,890
Arch Rock Nature Trail (right)	0.17	3,890
Arch Rock Loop (right)	0.55	3,825
Arch Rock junction (right)	0.65	3,815
Arch Rock	(0.02)	3,815
White Tank	(0.05)	~3,795
Grand Tank junction (right)	0.6	3,815
Grand Tank	0.9	~3,800

Late-winter reflections in Grand Tank (dam is at base of fin at extreme right)

most spectacular stone monuments is so well represented around White Tank that geologists designated this area as its type locality and named it White Tank Monzogranite.

Unsigned and hardly publicized, Grand Tank receives thankfully only a small fraction of the local visitation. Still, it is easy to find. Return to Arch Rock Loop, turn right, and go 50 feet to the next interpretive sign, which discusses soil erosion. The primitive trail to Grand Tank starts right in front of the sign, heading east. In 0.25 mile it goes down and up and down again a little to a tangle of vegetation, jogs left and right to go over bare outcrops, then descends gently to Grand Tank. On the final stretch the trail overlooks vast swaths of the maze of fins and rounded heads of boulders all around Arch Rock.

Most of the time Grand Tank is a bone-dry bowl of sand. But every five to ten years, a wet winter will fill it up for a season or two with a rare desert pond. The trail then ends between huge boulders at the water's edge, facing a flooded wall of stacked fins on the opposite bank. The water is surprisingly dark, its obsidian surface a perfect mirror that reflects stone and sky in stunning inversion. Reflection of land in water often creates beautiful scenery; here the beauty is even more dramatic, intensified by the rarity of so much water at one place.

■

VULTURE ARCH LOOP

In this land of superlatives where many places vie for visual supremacy, the 150-acre area of superbly carved granite in the vicinity of White Tank may well be the most exceptional. If the brief exploration of Arch Rock left you hungry for more, it has other arches, caves, fins, slots, split rocks, balanced rocks, slickrock, and quite possibly a few undiscovered gems. This mostly cross-country hike makes a wide loop around it, then a smaller loop at its heart. The goal is to locate two of the most striking sculptures, a huge heart-shaped boulder and a curious arch with a disturbing resemblance to a vulture. Even after finding them, this intriguing landscape plucked out of another planet is so addictive that you will want to return.

General Information

Road status: Roadless; paved access road
Vulture Arch loop: ~3.5 mi, ~450 ft up loop/easy
Main attractions: Cross-country loops across a fantasyland of rocks
USGS 7.5' topo map: Malapai Hill
Maps: pp. 207*, *173*

Location and Access

Like for the hike to Arch Rock and Grand Tank, the starting point of this double-loop hike is the paved Twin Tanks parking (see *Arch Rock and Grand Tank*).

Most of this hike is cross-country. To minimize your impact on the land, whenever possible walk in washes, on stone surfaces, and on wildlife tracks and human-made trails. Do not step on plants, or on cryptogam, which is common on compacted gravel. If you get disoriented, look for cars on the Pinto Basin Road, which is visible off and on less than a mile away, and walk to it.

Route Description

Like many places in Joshua Tree, this area is in the final stages of erosion. Once a tall flexure of plutonic rock, it has been leveled down by rain, wind, frost, and heat into disjointed groups of formations hardly ever higher than 40 feet, and often smaller. These same forces have also fashioned the remaining bedrock into a fairyland with a most unusual purity of forms. Erosion is so rapid that except for recent breaks, there are no sharp edges. Over an area approximately half a mile in diameter, every corner of every rock is well rounded. Desert varnish does not have time to grow; every surface glows with the smooth radiance of freshly cut granite. Green plants—juniper, yucca, catclaw, creosote—are just numerous enough to accent the beauty of the rocks without detracting from it. This convergence of circumstances has created an extraordinary landscape of meticulously crafted stonework, often in swarms, with soft shapes and an elegance bordering on grace.

The loop starts the same way as the hike to Arch Rock: down the connector trail to the California Riding and Hiking Trail, then left and across the road. Keep left on the CRHT, and go north 0.45 mile to a small outcrop just left of the trail. Leave the trail on your right and go 0.25 mile east to an extensive area of bare outcrops. Continue 0.25 mile east-northeast to a huge lone monolith looking very much like a voluptuous derrière that Rubens would have appreciated. Then cut generally south 0.7 mile, between the boulders and the mountain front, to a use trail that descends a steep slope of dirt and rubble. At the bottom, you will reach the wash that drains out of Grand Tank, the first of three north-south washes over the next 0.2 mile. Walk down this wash a few steps to a faint use trail on the right climbing the dirt bank out of the wash. It crosses west over a low rise to the second wash. Turn right (west) up this wash and go 50 yards to where it angles right into a canyon. There, a faint trail on the left goes west, over to the third wash. White Tank is 60 yards up this wash. From there, go up the wash a little and climb the staircase of narrow steps on the left to Arch Rock and the Arch Rock Loop.

To get to the inner loop, turn right on the Arch Rock Loop. After 100 yards, leave the trail to the right and cut a beeline east-northeast along a shallow, straight drainage framed by low rocks. You will soon run into a sandy wash, which is then easier to follow. After 0.2 mile there will be a wide open wavering slickrock on the right, backed by a large group of scenic outcrops, with a twice-split boulder. From this area, turn around and cut northwest 0.2 mile to a group of taller outcrops with interesting caves. To close the loop, return south to the Arch Rock Loop (the tall fins south of Arch Rock make a good landmark).

Within and between these waypoints, there are dozens of other stunning compositions and views, constantly changing as you move from place to place. The area just east of the CRHT has curious alignments of homomorphic obelisks and two small arches. The Rubens monolith has been hollowed out at its base into a deep, dark shelter. Along the mountain front rise jumbles of fins, boulders, and leaning towers interspaced with diminutive Joshua trees and gold-specked

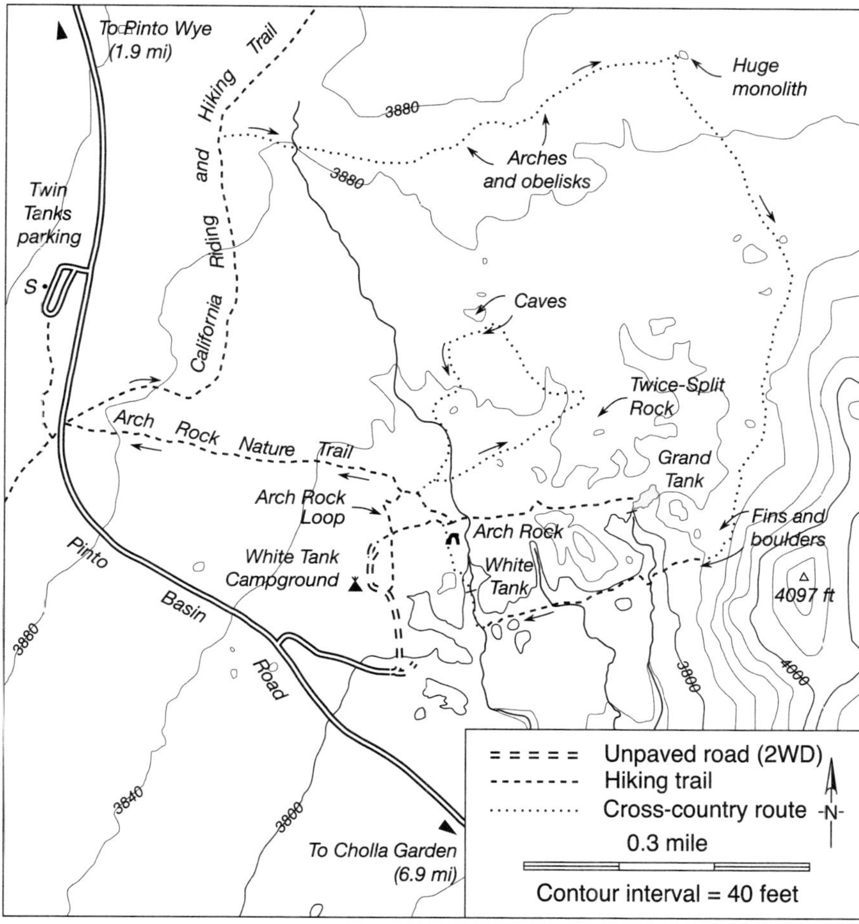

Vulture Arch Loop		
	Dist.(mi)	Elev.(ft)
Twin Tanks parking	0.0	3,910
Cal. Riding & Hiking Tr. (left)	0.15	3,890
Cluster of boulders (leave trail)	0.6	3,890
Arches and fins	~0.9	~3,890
Huge boulder	1.15	3,910
White Tank	2.1	~3,795
Twice-Split Rock	2.4	3,845
Arch Rock Nature Tr. via caves	2.85	3,825
Cal. Riding & Hiking Tr. (left)	3.25	3,890
Twin Tanks parking	3.4	3,910

Vulture Arch (photo by Alice Fermigier)

desert senna. South of Grand Tank, the bedrock is thick enough to host small canyons, anything from mere slots to delightful passages filled with scrub oaks and spherical boulders. The scenery reaches a Zen climax along the inner loop, where the formations have coalesced into a continuum united by waves of sensual slickrock. The central caves are cool overhangs blessed with perennial darkness, gentle air currents driven by thermal gradients, and cozy ledges to rest.

In this resplendent Ali Baba's cave, two jewels shine even brighter than the rest. One is Cupid's Rock, a 10-ton sculpture in the shape of a caricatural heart with nearly perfect symmetry, displayed on a broad slickrock shelf. The other is Vulture Arch, a small opening with a striking likeness to a vulture, perched high on a rib of stone. Its symmetry is even more remarkable, each side offering a mirror image of its beak, head, eye, wrinkled neck, and shoulderless body. I had heard of these formations but did not know their locations. Searching for them was so much fun that for now, I will only give out this much: they are within 100 yards of the loops. It is great if you find them, even better if you don't and have to return for a deeper look. On my second attempt, I spiced up the search with a prize: whoever in my party found the arch would get his or her photograph of it published. You know who won...

■

PINTO MOUNTAIN

> *Though not the highest named peak in this range, Pinto Mountain is impressive for its sheer mass and prominence. Its longer approach and Class-2 scrambles make it also one of the most difficult of the popular climbs in the park. The summit area provides sweeping views from half a mile up of the corrugated southern fringe of the range, of vast Pinto Basin, and of the entire eastern portion of the park. The little sand dunes on the way there add a fine bonus.*

General Information

Road status: Roadless; paved access road
Pinto Dunes: 1.0 mi, 40 ft up, 50 ft down one way / very easy
Pinto Mountain: 4.5 mi, 2,430 ft up, 240 ft down one way / difficult
Main attractions: Dunes, hard scrambles, views of eastern Joshua Tree
USGS 7.5′ topo map: Pinto Mountain
Maps: pp. 211*, *173*

Location and Access

Pinto Mountain is near the south end of the central Pinto Mountains, overlooking Pinto Basin. The starting point is the Turkey Flat backcountry board, on the Pinto Basin Road 16.1 miles south from Pinto Wye (or 13.7 miles north from the Cottonwood Visitor Center).

Route Description

From the edge of Turkey Flat, a conical peak rises 4 air miles to the northeast, looming over Pinto Basin's luminous emptiness. This is not Pinto Mountain but its eastern satellite; the true summit is just left of it, hidden by its own mass. The obvious canyon directly below the eastern satellite, past the Pinto Basin Dunes visible 1 mile away, is the shortest route, but it is full of large angular rocks, and steep at the end. The canyon's eastern ridge is a more popular route: it is steep and rocky at first, and a little easier once on high ground.

From the road, it is a very easy level walk across Turkey Flat to the canyon. In the 1920s, a misguided farmer attempted raising turkeys in this hot and sandy wasteland, where wispy creosote are the only source of shade. The turkeys are gone—they were likely dead well before Thanksgiving—but the name stuck. Better equipped animals find Turkey Flat perfectly fine. We saw lizards, sidewinder tracks, red-tailed hawk, turkey vultures, and tortoise dens. Fringe-toed lizards live here too, a rare species with webbed toes that "swims" under the sand. Kangaroo rats are so numerous that we had to constantly circle around their intricate burrows to avoid sinking ankle deep into them.

The first stop is the Pinto Basin Dunes. By desert standards, they are minimal. This plural is in fact *almost* singular: other than lazy drifts of sand, they are composed of two whaleback dunes a few tens of yards wide and tall, and about a mile long each. They are well vegetated with creosote, burrobush, saltbush, and grass. Following a wet winter, they are inundated with phacelia, pincushion, sunflowers, and other wildflowers—the improbable desert lily, the delicate birdcage evening primrose, and the sprawling pink beds of sand verbena.

From the dunes it is another 1.5 miles across the open drainage of Pinto Wash to the canyon. This area is a fierce wind tunnel. When in action it blots out the scenery behind a shroud of high-velocity particles, and every shrub shakes erratically, as if it were possessed.

Pinto Mountain is girdled with high buttressed escarpments that lift straight up from the basin, as if to guard the mountain against the savage winds. After eons of abuse, they are in a state of unstoppable erosion, their abrupt inclines surfaced with ruined daggers of stone. The least painful way up is the canyon's east ridge. It starts with a bang, ascending 940 feet over 0.8 mile, most of it along the first half. Its narrow spine is crowded with darkly varnished Mesozoic granitic spikes and large colonies of reddish barrel cactus. Small broken rocks litter the slopes. They rest just below the angle of repose and slip underfoot at the slightest provocation. Parts of this ascent border on Class 2—hands help at places, and trekking poles on the descent.

At the top of this first steep section, a broader ridge merges in from the right. Gently sloped, it angles generally north. Along the next half a mile, it crosses a more subdued terrain of smooth, closely spaced low hills. A potpourri of metamorphic rocks from the ancient Mesoproterozoic—hornfels, marble, schists, and quartzite—this

Pinto Mountain

	Dist.(mi)	Elev.(ft)
Pinto Basin Road	0.0	1,790
Top of Pinto Basin Dunes	1.0	1,780
Base of Pinto Mountain	2.5	1,800
Main ridge	3.3	~2,740
Start of steepest section	3.9	~2,960
Pinto Mountain	4.5	3,983

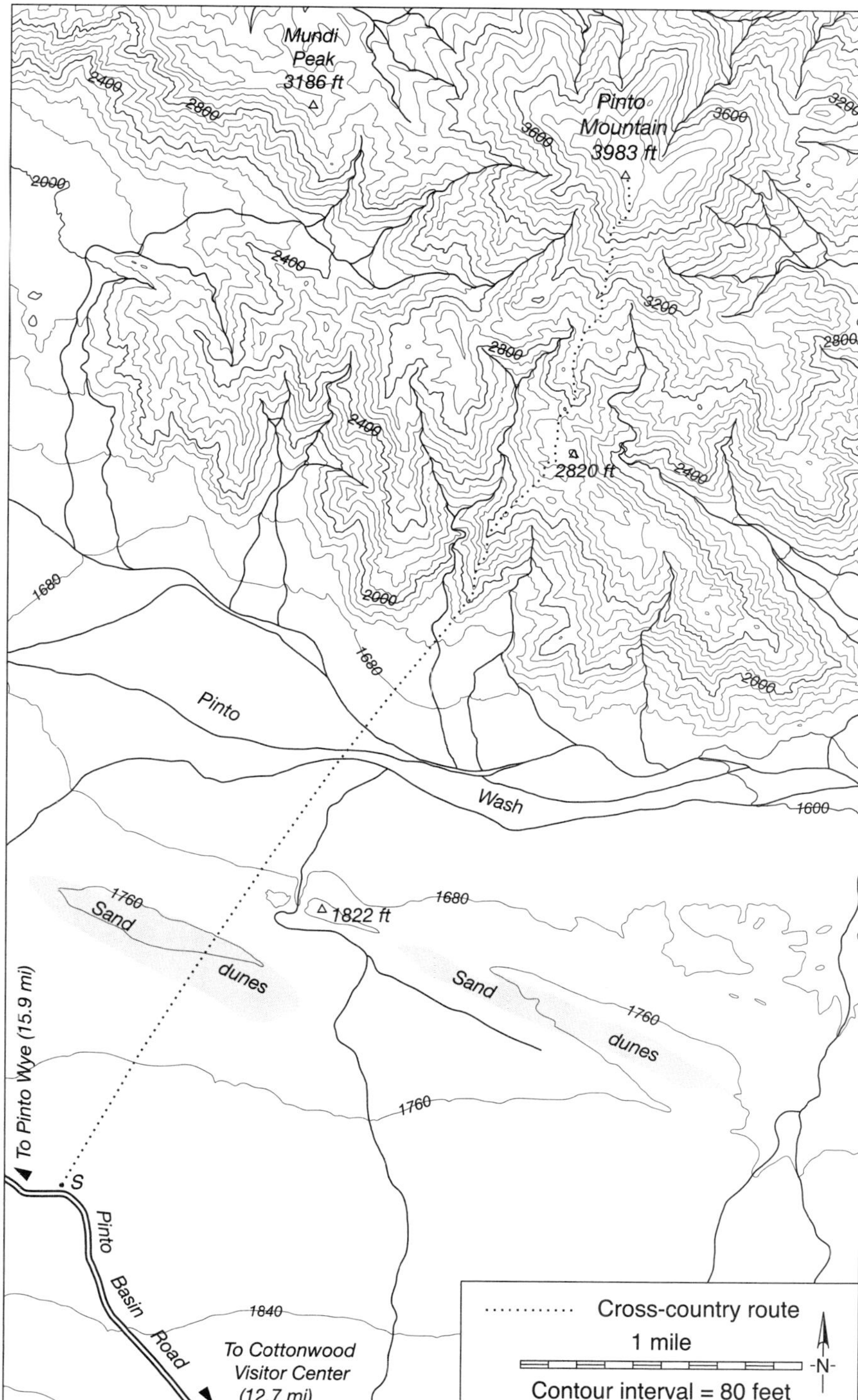
Mundi Peak 3186 ft
Pinto Mountain 3983 ft
2820 ft
1822 ft
Pinto
Wash
Sand dunes
Sand dunes
To Pinto Wye (15.9 mi)
S
Pinto Basin Road
To Cottonwood Visitor Center (12.7 mi)
Cross-country route
1 mile
N
Contour interval = 80 feet
2400
2800
2000
3600
3200
1680
1600
1760
1840

Sand storm looking at Pinto Mountain from the Pinto Basin Dunes

uncommonly variegated area alone may well have inspired Pinto Mountain's name. You meander from hill to hollow across narrow strips of land delineated by sharp boundaries, a random patchwork of rust, green, blue-gray, and blinding white. A primitive trail wiggles up through this contrasted landscape, riding along a narrow ridge toward the steep hump of Pinto Mountain. The terrain is easier, smooth and open, sparsely covered with creosote and brittlebush, barrel cactus and diamond cholla. You have just crossed into the Mojave Desert, but tufts of ocotillos linger, tokens of the Sonoran Desert you left behind.

The final pitch, up the mountain's south-southwest brow to the summit plateau, is the most arduous. The elevation gain is about the same as the lower pitch but in about half the distance. Much of it is a battlefield of small boulders, and the cluster of angular crags half way up is a good Class-2 scramble. The trail pushes on, but there is nothing solid underfoot. This is an aerial climb, with Pinto Basin filling 180 degrees of the viewshed 2,000 feet below, daunting in its immensity. The broad summit just beyond it encompasses the park's wildest geomorphic province, a striking juxtaposition of the basin's wide-open creosote plain and the stolid ranges that encircle it. The reward of this climb is discovering not only what is up on Pinto Mountain, but the awesome perspective of Pinto Basin from half a mile up.

■

PINTO BASIN'S MILLS AND WELLS

In the 1930s and 1940s, when two dozen mines were working the Pinto Mountains for gold, it was fashionable to own a mill. Even marginal mines that could not afford a mill had one, usually out of unbridled optimism, or to fool investors. The mills needed water, so mining companies sunk wells in Pinto Basin below the mines, and to reduce costs they erected their mills close to the wells. These two fun and easy hikes explore the ruins of the mills and wells scattered in this scenic valley, places layered in history and replete with ghost camps, odd mining paraphernalia, and stranded vintage cars.

General Information
Road status: Graded access road (HC recommended)
Gold Rose Mill: 1.5 mi, 10 ft up, 30 ft down one way / very easy
Sunrise Mine: 0.7 mi, 120 ft up, 60 ft down one way / very easy
Main attractions: Historic wells and mills ruins, easy valley-floor hikes
USGS 7.5' topo map: San Bernardino Wash
Maps: pp. 217*, *173*

Location and Access

Pinto Basin's mills and wells are grouped on the north side of the basin, near the foot of the Pinto Mountains. The Old Dale Road, which gave access to the Dale and Monte Negras mining districts in historic times, is still the best way to reach them. It starts 6.8 miles north of the Cottonwood Visitor Center on the Cottonwood Springs Road, on the right (or 22.9 miles from Pinto Wye on the Pinto Basin Road). Two roads split off at this junction: the Old Dale Road is the one on the left. Drive it 9.75 miles across Pinto Basin to the Mission Well pullout on the right. Park here to visit the wells. To hike to the Sunrise Mine, park at the next pullout, 0.35 mile further on the left. This is a wide graded road, free of rocks and plants, almost level (2% grade), most of it a washboard, and a little sandy at spots. If it is dry a sedan can make it, but given the distance it is safer to come here with a stronger vehicle.

History: Of Mills and Wells

Mission Well, closest to the Old Dale Road and most prominent, was dug in 1934. It provided water for the nearby Mission Mill and the Mission Mine. When it was not jealously guarded by the mine owners, this well was a popular watering hole. The Gold Rose Well, about a

Stone reservoir and settling basin at Mission Well

mile to the east, became active a few years later. Its water was originally used at the Gold Rose Mill next to it, which serviced the Gold Rose and Brooklyn mines 5 miles north. In later years, it was privately owned and also a source of water for local residents.

The mine with the largest footprint in the valley, even though it was not exactly rich, is the Sunrise Mine, about a mile north of Mission Well. San-Diego-based Sunrise Mines, Inc., acquired its claims in 1929 and proceeded to invest upward of $50,000 on the property. In 1932, the Sunshine Shaft looked promising enough that a mill was erected just below it, and a camp for the dozen workers. This mill, not the one half a mile south shown on modern maps, was the Sunrise Mill. It was an ambitious facility, with two five-stamp Straub mills, a popular brand at the time. Sunrise Well was dug that same year close to Mission Well; a 3/4-mile pipeline delivered the well water to the mill and camp. The miners lived in frame cabins and a bunk house, and enjoyed the luxury of a mess hall and a fishpond with a fountain for relaxation. As was too often the case, hopes ran high but never came true. In 1933 the company produced all of 68 ounces of gold and 28 ounces of silver from 218 tons of ore, which may have come from other properties. The mill's concrete alone cost more than that trifling return. In January 1939, the mill was bankrupt. A few miles north, the Gold Crown Mine had just relocated its own mill to the Supply Mine and quit performing custom milling. A company called Pinto Basin Mining and Milling jumped into that market, leased the Sunrise Mill, and converted it to a 25-ton cyanide mill. It processed custom ore until 1942, when it was forced to shut down by the War Production Board. During the post-war gold-mining revival, the Sunrise Mine was controlled by

W. C. O'Connor, a developer who also owned the nearby Mission Mine (a joint ownership that may be at the root of the mix-up in the name of the Old Mission Mill). One would think there were enough mills as it was, but he erected yet another, a 100-ton cyaniding plant. It was likely not a success either. By 1958, all equipment at the Sunrise Mine had been removed. The mill-and-well craze was over.

Route Description

In a park with a dearth of long primitive roads and a surfeit of visitors, the Old Dale Road is a special treat. You get to drive on dirt, mostly alone, far from asphalt, signs, and planned turnouts, as is commonplace in larger desert parks. The scenery is beautiful. You cross wide-open country, skirting for several miles the imposing scarp of Pinto Mountain. As you descend into bone-dry Pinto Basin, the idea of running into water wells, of all things, grows increasingly dubious. Plants species, abundant at the start, disappear one by one. The smoke trees are first to go, then the bladderpod and chollas, until even the resilient burrobush are turned off by the dryness, and all that is left is a monoculture of creosote. At the lowest point, where the road crosses Pinto Wash, creosote grows more densely, stimulated by storm runoffs. The difference is subtle, yet the old-timers knew that this slightly greener belt was where they would find water—and they did.

Mission Well and Gold Rose Well. Mission Well is just a few steps from the pullout. Its ruins are just extensive enough to glimpse how it worked. The concrete pilings with a Peerless water pump was the pump house. It was once sheltered in a rudimentary shack of corrugated iron. The site has a settling basin, a small reservoir of crudely mortared stones, and pieces of the pipes that transported the water. A large arrastra lies dormant in the weeds, slowly filling up with sand.

From Mission Well it is a straightforward hike to the other two wells, although a compass may help. Walk due east 300 yards to Sunrise Well at the south edge of Pinto Wash, then 100 yards north to the unknown mill just north of the wash (possibly O'Connor's 100-ton mill), and finally 1.1 miles east to Gold Rose Well and Mill. This last stretch follows the trace of the former road to the well, about 100 yards north of the wash. This remote section of Pinto Basin epitomizes the sublime austerity of the desert. The landscape is reduced to its simplest expression, square miles of bare terrain ringed by mysterious serrated mountains. On a clear winter day they look so close you could walk to them in minutes. On a stifling summer day, when every step takes a conscious effort, they seem impossibly far. In this immensity,

Gold Rose Well is fortunately announced from afar by the metal frame of its pump house and the mill ruins rising above the creosote.

The area has interesting nuggets, some of them hard to decipher. The 14-inch rusted casing sticking out of the ground at Sunrise Well is the well itself. Its disarming simplicity belies both the labor that went into it (its bore hole is 480 feet deep) and its historic importance (it delivered an impressive 65 gallons per minute). The puzzling row of five concrete ties at the mill near Sunrise Well was a cool support for a cylindrical water tank. The 7-foot metal cone at the Gold Rose Mill is a cone classifier. Gold-bearing mill slurry was dumped into the upright cone. Water was pumped into the cone through the two valves at the bottom and flushed upward through the slurry. The gold flakes floated to the surface and were collected with the overflow at the top of the cone. Gold Rose Well is littered with the remains of a camp where a caretaker named Walt Rose lived until the 1960s. Behind the camp, an eerie line of vintage cars from the mid-twentieth century is stranded along the wash, tossed sideways or upside down, as if a parade had rolled through here and been obliterated by a sudden cataclysm.

Old Mission Mill and the Sunrise Mine. From the Mission Well pullout, either drive or walk to the Old Mission Mill. Built into the side of a 20-foot hill right beside the road, this relatively large site actually had two mills, the main one at the center and a smaller one near the east end. The elegant main mill, with its slanted walls capped by a circular stone altar, suggests a modern portrayal of a Maya temple. You half expect to find a hieroglyphic stela or carvings of feathered serpents hidden among the concrete pilings. It is an interesting site, with several

Pinto Basin's Mills and Wells

	Dist.(mi)	Elev.(ft)
The Gold Rose Mill		
Old Dale Road	0.0	1,408
Mission Well	0.02	1,408
Sunrise Well	0.2	1,406
Gold Rose Mill	1.35	1,392
The Sunrise Mine		
Old Dale Road	0.0	1,420
Old Mission Mill (top)	0.1	1,440
Sunrise Mill	0.5	1,480
Sunrise Shaft	0.7	1,485

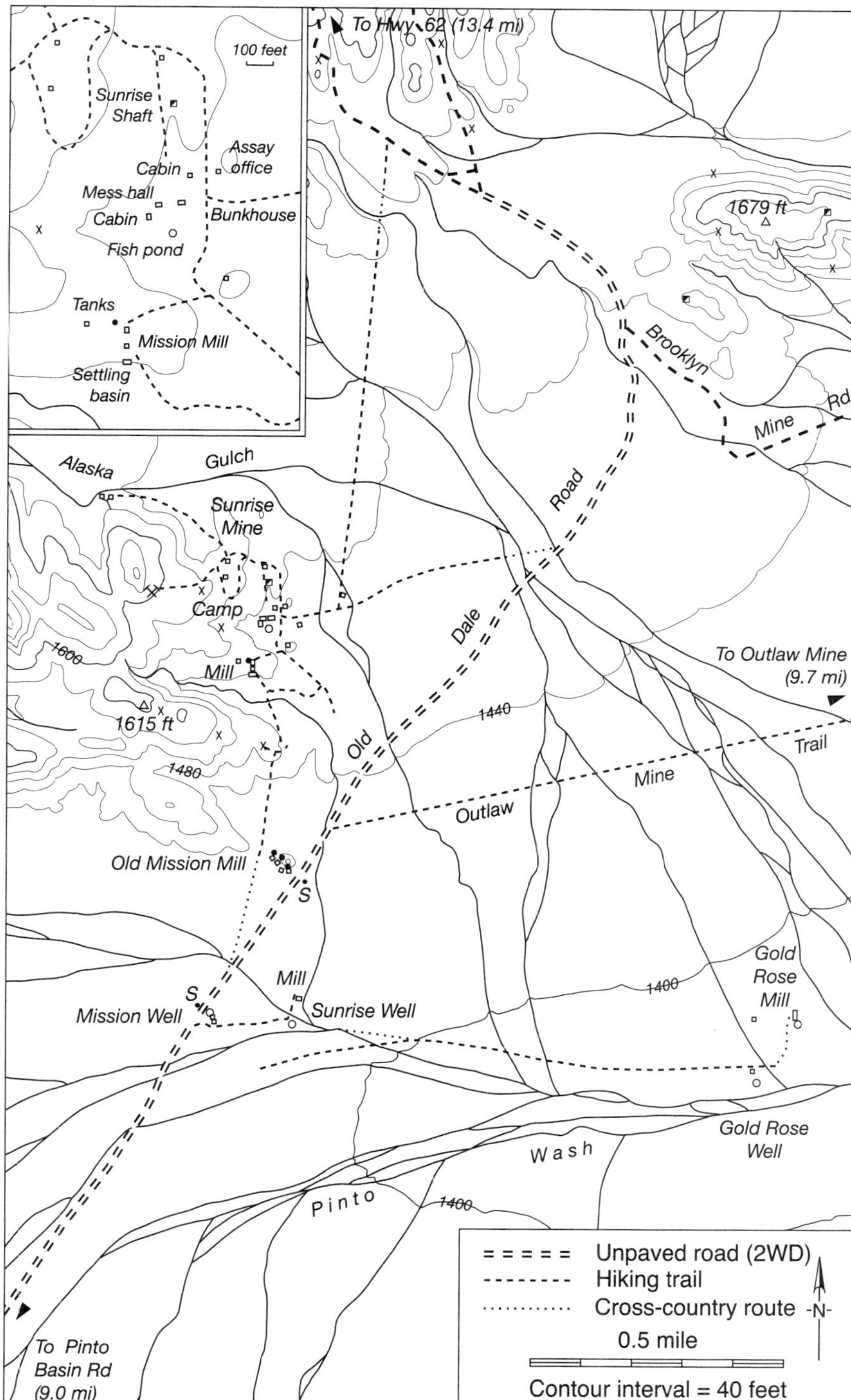
To Hwy. 62 (13.4 mi)
100 feet
Sunrise Shaft
Assay office
Cabin
Mess hall
Cabin
Bunkhouse
Fish pond
Tanks
Mission Mill
Settling basin
1679 ft
Brooklyn
Mine
Rd
Alaska
Gulch
Road
Sunrise Mine
Camp
Mill
Dale
1600
1615 ft
Old
1440
1480
To Outlaw Mine (9.7 mi)
Trail
Mine
Outlaw
Old Mission Mill
S
Gold Rose Mill
Mill
1400
S
Mission Well
Sunrise Well
Gold Rose Well
Wash
Pinto
1400
To Pinto Basin Rd (9.0 mi)
Unpaved road (2WD)
Hiking trail
Cross-country route
N
0.5 mile
Contour interval = 40 feet

Main concrete and stone foundations at the Old Mission Mill

cyanide vats, steel water tanks, a curious underground chamber, and a unique stone platform, which likely supported a large ore bin.

To get to the Sunrise Mine, walk to the shallow saddle at the west end of the Old Mission Mill. There an abandoned road cuts north across an embayment, a 50-foot ridge, then a second embayment to the foot of the next ridge, a distance of 0.5 mile. The ruins of the original Sunrise Mill are graded into a gully in the ridge. The four large concrete vats at the bottom, just above the mill tailings, were used for cyaniding. The mill proper, which used to be partly housed in a building, occupies split levels above the vats. It has massive foundations, staircases, a small fuel building, and large stone walls.

The mine camp was in the small cove just north of the mill. It is now reduced to impersonal concrete slabs. The circular fishpond is still there, as is the cabin with a front yard lined with white stones, and past it the large mess hall and bunk house across from each other. Beyond a second cabin are the mine tailings, and above them the timbered Sunshine Shaft, which reached 300 feet down to three levels of galleries. The wooden headframe and hoist were solidly anchored onto the concrete foundations beside it. For a brief moment while you visit, your knowledge of its layout and past, as imperfect as it is, will instill a little life back into this empty camp largely forgotten by history.

■

THE MISSION MINE

The Mission Mine is special. It has been around for over a century. Its gold vein was discovered in 1887, it was last worked in 1981, and geological studies for a potential revival were carried out as recently as 2011. It had at least four mills, and a well dug in 1934 to provide water to the mine. Several of these facilities are still extant, which is rare. The crown jewel of this long legacy is its 1980s mill, which is the region's most complete modern mill. The mine is reached by a long dusty drive across Pinto Basin, past its former well and mill, and a short walk into the mountains. The mill's complex assemblage of cogs, belts, bins, ladders, catwalks, and tanks is an impressive structure, fun to scrutinize. This easy hike can be extended on mining roads to include two interesting historic mines.

General Information
Jurisdiction: Joshua Tree National Park (NPS) and public lands (BLM)
Road status: Graded access road (HC recommended)
Mission–Sunset–Golden Egg mine loop: 2.9 mi, 410 ft up loop / easy
Main attractions: A well-preserved modern gold mill, historic ruins
USGS 7.5' topo map: San Bernardino Wash
Maps: pp. 221*, *173*

Location and Access

The Mission Mine is near the southern front of the Pinto Mountains, just outside the park. Directions are the same as for Mission Well (see *Pinto Basin Mills and Wells*). First, drive the Old Dale Road 10.1 miles to the Mission Well pullout, then 0.35 mile to the Old Mission Mill pullout. Both sites are well worth visiting before seeing the mine itself. Then drive 1.35 miles to the signed Brooklyn Mine Road, and go straight 0.4 mile to the unsigned road to the Mission Mine on the right (0.75 mile). The Old Dale Road is fairly smooth up to this junction, but this last road to the mine is a little rough. Unless you are driving a four-wheel-drive vehicle, park at this fork and walk it.

Route Description

For years the Mission Mine was known as the Huff and Lane Mine, after its discoverers George Lane and his partner E. C. Huff. Work was sporadic until the late 1920s, although by then the mine had a 21-ton ball mill and its two shafts had been opened. Both explored the Water Well Vein, an ore shoot exposed over two thirds of a mile and more than 600 feet deep. Its name was changed to Mission Mine in the mid-1930s, when it was leased to a venture managed by Tom Ake. Ore was then processed in an arrastra, and at the Mission Mill in Pinto Basin. After the 1940s, other owners followed, which is not usually a sign of great wealth. Records concur: the property was often idle, and it never employed more than half a dozen men. In 1941 and 1942, Ake extended the main shaft to 600 feet and made a small killing shipping 850 ounces of gold—around $30,000. Production was recorded only six other years and averaged a mere $400. No known production came out of the 1980s efforts, when the gold mill that stands at the mine today was built. It was not for lack of gold. Recent exploratory work estimated that the vein holds around 120,000 ounces of gold, about 200 million dollars at today's prices. The gold was too diluted—less than one ounce per ton—and the price of gold too low for profitable mining.

It is a quick walk on the road to the Mission Mine, first across the edge of Pinto Basin, then over low hills sprinkled with darkly stained granite. The mill is visible from the very start, painted in aggressive colors as if to clash even more violently with the natural environment. In the wash below the mine, the road passes by a storage of mining junk, then a small quarry, before reaching the mill. It is a clever piece of engineering, custom designed to fit the local terrain. The towering steel headframe stands on the high bank of the wash. Below it the two-compartment shaft drops 650 feet—60 floors—past 3,000 feet of galleries split on five levels. The headframe pulled the ore out of the shaft and dumped it in a storage bin. After enough ore had been collected, it was released onto a conveyor belt that took it up over the abrupt edge of the wash and dropped it into a series of finer and finer grinders. The pulverized ore was then lifted up inside a slender red square tower by a chain of quart-size buckets. At the top of the tower, it flowed down a slanted gutter into the three giant cylindrical tanks that loom in the wash, where it was soaked in cyanide to extract the gold. The mill is so complete that it seems that with a few trips to Home Depot one could bring it back to life and watch it turn rock into gold again.

The site still has other ruins, whatever has not yet been looted by lowly thieves—the two empty frames of trailers from the 1930s, water tanks, and concrete foundations that might have supported the 1920s ball mill. The road that goes up along the wash past the mill ends shortly at a collared shaft. This may be Huff and Lane's second shaft, now connected to the main shaft's second level 120 feet underground. Between the two shafts the hill is pockmarked with a line of prospects that trace the perfectly straight gold-bearing Water Well Vein.

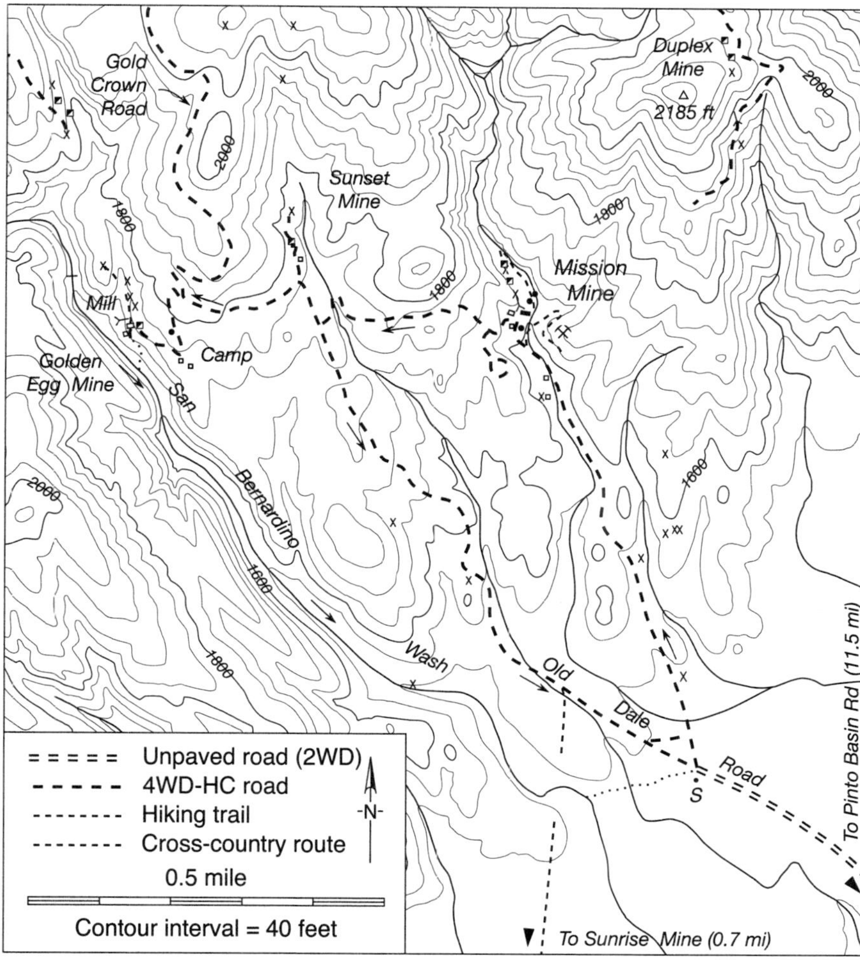

The Mission Mine

	Dist.(mi)	Elev.(ft)
Old Dale Road	0.0	1,515
Mission Mine (mill)	0.75	1,610
Junction with Old Dale Road	1.1	1,740
Sunset Mine Junction	1.15	1,765
Sunset Mine (painted bunker)	(0.05)	1,780
Golden Egg Mine Junction	1.35	1,825
Golden Egg Mine (mill)	1.6	1,700
Back to car via Old Dale Road	2.5	1,515
Back to car via S. B. Wash	2.8	1,515

Gold mill at the Mission Mine

Rather than returning the same way, there is an easy alternative return route that loops back through two nearby historic mines. From the Mission Mine walk west up the continuation of the access road 0.35 mile, up and down low hills, back to the Old Dale Road. Turn right and go up the road 120 yards to a junction, then right again to the Sunset Mine, visible from a distance. This site has a colorful concrete bunker, the slab of a house built in 1966 with a long flagstone bench, and a cemetery of mangled automobiles, mining gear, and appliances strewn in the wash below it. The bunker is a local icon (watch the unprotected shaft right next to its entrance). Two adjacent walls are painted in screaming colors with the American and California flags.

From the Sunset Mine, continue west on the Old Dale Road 0.25 mile to a junction. The road on the left winds down the same distance again to the Golden Egg Mine. This site has the foundations of a camp and several tunnels. Its centerpiece is a reasonably well-kept mill from the 1940s, a funky construction of flagstone, sheet metal, concrete, and lumber built on multiple levels, hanging precariously at the sharp rim of San Bernardino Wash. At the end of the road just below the mill a steep ravine drops to the wash, a scenic and fairly open path to return to your car (1.2 miles).

■

— 7 —

Coxcomb Mountains

Covering 58,000 acres, the Coxcomb Mountains are the easternmost range in the park, at the edge of the vast undeveloped desert stretching east to the Colorado River. Almost entirely protected as a designated wilderness, this rugged range is home to an extraordinary wealth of superb scenery. Square miles of the range's pale, fine-grained monzogranite has been carved into fanciful formations that rival with the Wonderland of Rocks. In a park where large tracts have been dewilded by over-visitation and associated developments, they are by far the least visited. What has prevented them so far from suffering the same fate is their greater distance from cities, their poor accessibility, and their rebellious topography. They are easily the most formidable range in the park. This is the Wonderland of Rocks half a century ago, with no signs, no pit toilets, no parking lots, no backcountry boards, no named natural features except for a few peaks, and nobody. Most areas see fewer visitors than space. *Terra incognita.*

Geology

Most of the Coxcomb Mountains, from their northern tip overlooking Cadiz Valley to their narrow waist a few miles from their southern tip, is made of Coxcomb Granodiorite, a pluton that intruded this area between 71 and 65 million years ago and gave this range its abrupt topography. This highly cohesive rock grading into different varieties of granite has the remarkable property of weathering into massive domes, fins, arches, and dense groves of pinnacles, just fast enough to stay a step ahead of oxidation and keep its surface the pale beige that gives this range its brilliance. It is single-handedly responsible for the

Massive monzogranite formations come a dime a dozen in the Maze

spectacular Aqua Peak massif and the fantastically sculpted hills at the north end of the range.

In contrast, the southern tip of the range is a darker 10-square-mile mountainous mass dissected on its east flank into deep canyons and spikes of long peninsulas. It is made of rocks found nowhere else in the park, a sequence of strata that tells the story of McCoy Basin, an east-west rift basin that opened up east of the present-day Coxcomb Mountains around 120 million years ago. It may have formed like Coachella Valley, along a major strike-slip fault. Earthquake by earthquake, the basin grew bigger, eventually stretching nearly 90 miles to the Dome Rock Mountains in southwestern Arizona. As it sank deeper, it collected thousands of cubic miles of alluvia brought in mostly by a river that may have originated near the Mogollon Rim. Over the course of 25 million years, as the source material and hydrology evolved, the alluvia changed many times, sometimes abruptly, from silt to sand, pebbles, and cobbles. The basin was ultimately filled to a depth of 4.5 *miles*. The pressure of so much rocks was so intense that it welded the cobbles into conglomerate, glued the sand into sandstone, and squeezed the silt into hard slate. Subsequent faulting folded the basin's edges over themselves and metamorphosed rocks into schists and quartzite. Much later, block faulting and uplifting exhumed portions of the buried basin in the Coxcomb and Dome Rock mountains, and in the four main ranges between them. This discordant sequence was named the McCoy Mountains Formation, after the mountains where it is more prominent, near the middle of the basin.

Mining History

Mining never made it big in the Coxcomb Mountains. The only known mineralized region is the short fault zone that slashes diagonally across the central part of the range, near the boundary between its two main formations. The fluids that contained the ore—gold, silver, lead, iron, manganese, and arsenic—may have been delivered toward the end of the granite intrusions. There is also uranium in the McCoy Mountains Formation. Of the dozen sites that were explored, only half graduated to the status of mine—the Last Chance, Moser, Vault, Fortuitous, and Long Hunt. Between the discovery of gold in the 1880s and the 1990s, they were active only episodically. Only the Moser Mine had a recorded production—a measly few ounces of gold.

The only mine about which we know a little history is the Long Hunt Mine. The story goes that rich gold and silver ore was discovered there in the 1880s. Some decades later, the owner sold the mine, but following a car accident he forgot its exact location. Two miners, Frank Webb and Nick Molitor, obtained from him general directions to the mine, and after a long search—which may be the origin of the mine's name—located it and its old stone cabin in April 1931. The new owners shipped some ore in December—and probably not much after that.

Flora and Fauna

Of the desert's many blooming plants, one of the rarest and most striking is the desert lily. With a lot of walking you might spot one every few years. In the lowlands at the southern tip of the Coxcomb Mountains, they are so numerous that a 2,000-acre preserve was created and named after them. March is the best month to see these elegant white flowers growing right out of the desert sands.

Perhaps thanks to the small human footprint, the fauna seems to be a little more abundant. Many areas show signs of the recent passage of bighorn sheep. The variety of reptiles is also impressive. Encounters with zebra-tailed are common, and even chuckwalla, desert horned lizard, desert iguana, and desert spiny lizard are more numerous. Tortoise dens are particularly abundant in the sandy bays surrounding the mountains. It is also not uncommon to spot a western speckled rattlesnake or sidewinder, or a (harmless) tarantula, so stay alert.

Suggested Hikes in the Coxcomb Mountains					
Route/Destination	Dist. (mi)	Elev. gain	Mean elev.	Difficulty	Page
Short hikes (under 5 miles round trip)					
Cat Eyes Arch	2.0	310'	1,850'	Very easy	237
The Grotto (The Maze)	1.5	300'	2,030'	Easy	229
Tunnel Arch (The Maze)	2.3	340'	2,130'	Easy	232
Windows Rock	1.9	310'	1,850'	Very easy	238
Intermediate hikes (5–12 miles round trip)					
Bighorn Canyon narrows	4.0	1,160'	1,740'	Moderate	253
Bighorn Canyon (the Slab)	4.9	1,630'	1,830'	Difficult	253
Coxcomb Peak	5.5	3,330'	1,820'	Strenuous	271
Inner Basin Pass	5.3	1,330'	2,270'	Moderate	249
Kawi'a Peak	4.1	2,090'	1,480'	Strenuous	271
Last Chance Mill	5.3	1,980'	2,040'	Moderate	241
Last Chance Mine	5.7	2,510'	2,060'	Difficult	241
Moser Mill	3.2	650'	1,250'	Easy	265
Moser Mine (shed)	3.9	1,020'	1,340'	Easy-mod.	265
Oxbow Canyon narrows	4.1	940'	1,410'	Moderate	259
Oxbow Canyon (the Oxbow)	5.7	1,330'	1,600'	Difficult	259
Pyramid Gulch					
Arch loop (1)	5.7	500'	1,930'	Easy	235
Windows Rock loop (1)	6.3	700'	2,010'	Easy	238
Saubel Canyon (amphith.)	2.8	950'	1,160'	Easy	271
The Maze (1)	5.2	460'	2,160'	Moderate	229
Vault Mine	2.6	540'	1,210'	Easy	265
Long hikes (over 12 miles round trip)					
Inner Basin (The Rocks)					
via Bighorn Canyon	6.6	2,060'	2,070'	Strenuous	259
via Inner Basin Trail	7.4	1,870'	2,420'	Difficult	249
via Oxbow Canyon	7.8	1,980'	1,880'	Strenuous	264
Lone Spring	8.8	2,380'	2,520'	Strenuous	249
Pinto Basin Viewpoint	8.4	2,140'	2,490'	Difficult	249
Spectre Peak	7.6	3,350'	2,590'	Strenuous	245
Tensor Peak	7.5	3,290'	2,570'	Strenuous	245

Key: (1) Loop; (2) HC and/or 4WD access road
Distances: one way for out-and-back hikes, round-trip for loops
Elev. gain: sum of all elevation gains on round-trips and on loops

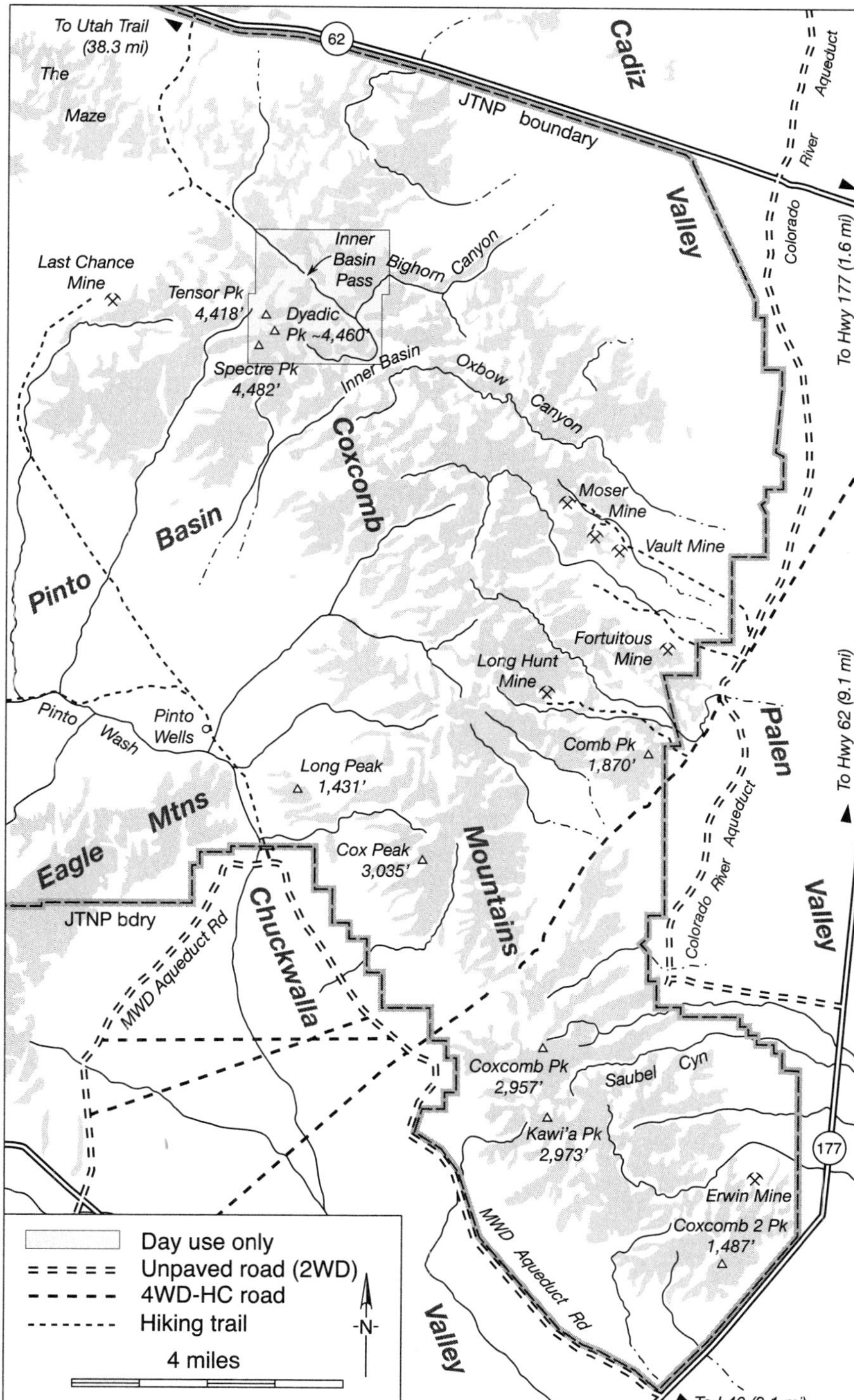
To Utah Trail (38.3 mi)
The Maze
62
Cadiz
JTNP boundary
Colorado River Aqueduct
Valley
To Hwy 177 (1.6 mi)
Inner Basin Pass
Bighorn Canyon
Last Chance Mine
Tensor Pk 4,418'
Dyadic Pk ~4,460'
Spectre Pk 4,482'
Inner Basin
Oxbow Canyon
Coxcomb
Moser Mine
Vault Mine
Basin
Pinto
Fortuitous Mine
Long Hunt Mine
Palen
To Hwy 62 (9.1 mi)
Pinto Wash
Pinto Wells
Comb Pk 1,870'
Long Peak 1,431'
Mtns
Eagle
Cox Peak 3,035'
Mountains
Colorado River Aqueduct
Valley
JTNP bdry
MWD Aqueduct Rd
Chuckwalla
Coxcomb Pk 2,957'
Saubel Cyn
Kawi'a Pk 2,973'
177
Erwin Mine
Coxcomb 2 Pk 1,487'
MWD Aqueduct Rd
Valley
To I 40 (8.1 mi)
Day use only
Unpaved road (2WD)
4WD-HC road
Hiking trail
4 miles
N

Hiking

From a recreational standpoint, the Coxcomb Mountains are special. It is the one range where hikers can still be sure to find this thrilling combination of wildness, solitude, and spectacular landscapes. The cover charge is on the high side. The only road that makes headway into the mountains is the primitive maintenance road of a power line, and it does not even cross them. It generally takes a few miles of walking just to get to the mountains. The only three access trails are abandoned roads that barely enter the range. To say that the Coxcomb Mountains are rugged would be a gross understatement. The slopes and ridges are often guarded by giant anarchic outcrops of solid stone. The best ingress is the few boulder-jammed canyons threading between them along providential faults. They put up a persistent resistance to motion. Hiking becomes an exercise in agility, upper body strength, and endurance. Hikers used to well-groomed trails and the mental comfort of frequent signs may find it daunting, and the isolation makes it a little worse. Only a small percentage of desert aficionados have the stamina, experience, and confidence to brave these defiant mountains, and enjoy doing it.

The Coxcomb Mountains also have arguably the most awesome scenery in the park. The vertically sliced landscape in the heart of the main northern block is a prime example, unique in its otherworldliness. The low foothills along its northern front boasts rock formations that may be more diverse, plentiful, and astounding than anywhere else. The trio of peaks there has the cool distinction of having the highest prominence in the park—over 2,500 feet. They are easily the park's most demanding and exciting summits to climb. Although much lower, the two highest summits in the southern part of the range are also more challenging than most peaks in the park. To compensate for the paucity of features named after the region's native tribes, I named the highest of these two summits Kawi'a Peak to acknowledge the Cahuilla, and the canyon that leads up to it in honor of Katherine Saubel, an internationally acclaimed Cahuilla tribal leader who worked tirelessly to preserve the history and culture of her people.

For all their ruggedness, the Coxcomb Mountains are fragile. If you go, keep them wild. Tread lightly. Learn to recognize cryptogamic soil, which is as common as it is precious, and do not step on it. To preserve the sense of isolation of future visitors, do not build cairns. Hikers who come here know their way around and do not need help. To reduce stress on wildlife, make sure not to camp in the four-square-mile day-use-only area centered on Inner Basin Pass.

■

THE MAZE

This is the most outstanding place in all of Joshua Tree. A low relief of polished granite lacerated by random passages, the Maze encompasses several square miles of hoodoos more packed, diverse, and extravagant than in the Wonderland of Rocks itself. Everywhere the landscape is a whirlwind of towers, domes, fins, tafoni, alcoves, overhangs, caves, balanced rocks, and jumbles of boulders, and possibly more arches than known to exist in the rest of the park. You navigate through this frenzied topography along segments of washes and gulches so erratic that most of the time you are not sure where you are, and how you will get out. After a dozen visits, you will still be discovering scenery you had completely missed.

General Information

Road status: Paved access road; cross-country hiking
Moray Rock: 1.1 mi, 170 ft up, 10 ft down one way / very easy
The Grotto: 1.5 mi, 210 ft up, 90 ft down / easy
Tunnel Arch: 2.3 mi, 310 ft up, 30 ft down one way / very easy
The Maze loop: 5.2 mi, ~460 ft up loop / moderate
Main attractions: A labyrinth of washes and canyons with wild rock formations and dozens of arches
USGS 7.5' topo map: Cadiz Valley SW
Maps: pp. 233*, 243, *227*

Location and Access

At their very north end, the Coxcomb Mountains' gargantuan mass of peaks and spires gives way to an accretion of sharp hills, then to a nondescript spread of granite. From a distance, this scatter of rock formations is so unremarkable that over the years I drove by it many times without taking a second look. Upon closer inspections, it turned out to hide in its midst more weird formations per acre than any other place in the park, scattered randomly in a wild network of crisscrossing canyons and gulches of all sizes. This is the Maze.

The Maze can be entered on foot from anywhere along a 3.5-mile stretch of Highway 62 starting from the pass into Cadiz Valley, which is 35 miles from Utah Trail. About 1.7 miles east of the pass on the right, there is a paved pull-out with an emergency call box. Park on the shoulder just before or after it. Coming from the east, this is 13.8 miles from Highway 177.

Looking through Periscope Arch at the hills in the southern section of the Maze

Route Description

The sprawling bench of granitic rock visible from the road was the perfect raw material for a maze. Covering approximately 5 square miles, it is big enough to command respect. When it was uplifted, it snapped into multiple small blocks along minor faults at odd angles to each other. Erosion has since then widened the faults into a grid of washes and gulches, and dissected the blocks into gaps ranging in size from fissures to hallways. The washes, the gulches, and the gaps, numbering in the thousands, now form collectively an intricate network of partly interconnected pathways that can be combined in endless routes along which to wander and get lost.

To preserve the mystery of this exceptional place, I have omitted from the map the routes I took through the Maze. Only the approximate locations of a few of the highlights I came across are shown as potential destinations. From the vicinity of the emergency lane the Maze can be entered at several points. For the closest approach, aim south-southwest across the open desert, toward the rightmost and lowest of the hills on the horizon. In 0.6 mile you will reach the first outcrops at the edge of the Maze. Beyond, you are on your own.

The local igneous stock was instrumental in creating the Maze's unparalleled assortment of formations. It is a monzogranite of exceptional quality, part of the Coxcomb Granodiorite formation that produced the profusion of vertical monuments unique to this range. Fine-grained, resilient, and a cheerful very pale tan in color, it has a propensity to erode into smoothly rounded forms with an amazingly wide spectrum of the outlandish shapes.

Granitic domes and Chicken Rock in Grotto Canyon

After a few thousand centuries of patient erosion, the diversity is undescribable. It starts slowly, with clusters of small monuments huddled together and low slickrock domes. Deeper in, the formations get more imposing and crowded, until eventually every direction is a source of amazement. There are checkerboards of spherical boulders of disturbingly similar sizes, ranks of parallel fins stashed as orderly as books on a shelf, and fields of exfoliating sculptures that seem to have melded and flowed like putty in the sun. Isolated towers often protrude from the landscape, some over 25 feet tall, sometimes leaning so strongly that surely they should tumble. In Grotto Canyon, one of the area's longest, stream erosion has dug the Grotto, a twisted, narrow passage that hardly ever sees direct sunlight. It is a cool place in both senses of the term, sunk beneath the desert floor and shut off by fluted walls. Inside it there is a caldron worn by eddies, large enough to bathe. A local favorite is tafoni, ellipsoidal cavities etched in the rock by chemical and physical weathering. They are all over, in sizes ranging from rows of egg-size pockets to alcoves and caves as big as a room. The Maze may have in fact more caves than any other region in the park. Some areas are so packed with caves, some tough to reach, that one could spend days visiting all of them. There are many other distinct erosional features. I came upon gatherings of whimsical goblins, a rippling field of little domes like petrified dunes, and a slickrock slant littered with collapsed monuments, as if a tornado had swept through it. Everywhere bedrock has been fractured, sliced, diced, hollowed, carved, and polished into inventive surfaces mottled with desert varnish. In this endless sculpture garden displaying every shape imaginable, it is easy to recognize familiar figures. I saw a llama, a giraffe's head, a giant moray eel, a 30-foot chicken, and Jabba the Hutt.

And then there are the arches. In a day of hiking it would be hard not to spot at least a dozen. The Maze hides several times this many. Most arches were formed after weathering deepened a tafone until it perforated a fin. The smallest are mere inches across, the largest tall enough to stand. ET Arch is a 10-foot horizontal slit too slim to crawl under, backed by a dome lined with porthole-shaped tafoni like a flying saucer. Tunnel Arch, thicker than it is tall, is punched at the center of a heart of stone. Perched on a low cliff, it is a fun arch to climb to, up a sloped crack or a staircase of boulders. In the tall alcove next to it, you can slither up into a sunless recess and stare through the narrow window of Periscope Arch at the brilliant world outside, like in a one-man submersible. The search for these geological treasures, rare elsewhere yet miraculously abundant here, becomes an irresistible spell that lures you over and over, along unpredictable paths, deeper into the Maze.

Labyrinths are, by design, confusing places. Their unsettling attributes are plentiful in the Maze. At all times you know approximately where you are, but you do not know your exact position, whether the wash you are on goes through, or what challenges lie ahead. You are sometimes railroaded by vertical bluffs, with no other option but going forward or back. Occasionally a route will end at an unsurmountable obstacle and force you to turn around and try elsewhere. The Maze is also a superb master of illusion. Some areas look alike, as if to intentionally get us turned around. A canyon will widen into an encouraging open wash, only to collapse moments later in a stack of boulders,

The Maze		
	Dist.(mi)	Elev.(ft)
Highway 62 to	0.0	1,985
Buttress Arch	0.9	2,110
Moray Rock	1.1	2,130
The Grotto	1.5	~2,100
Butting Heads Arch	1.8	2,270
Tunnel Arch	2.3	2,280

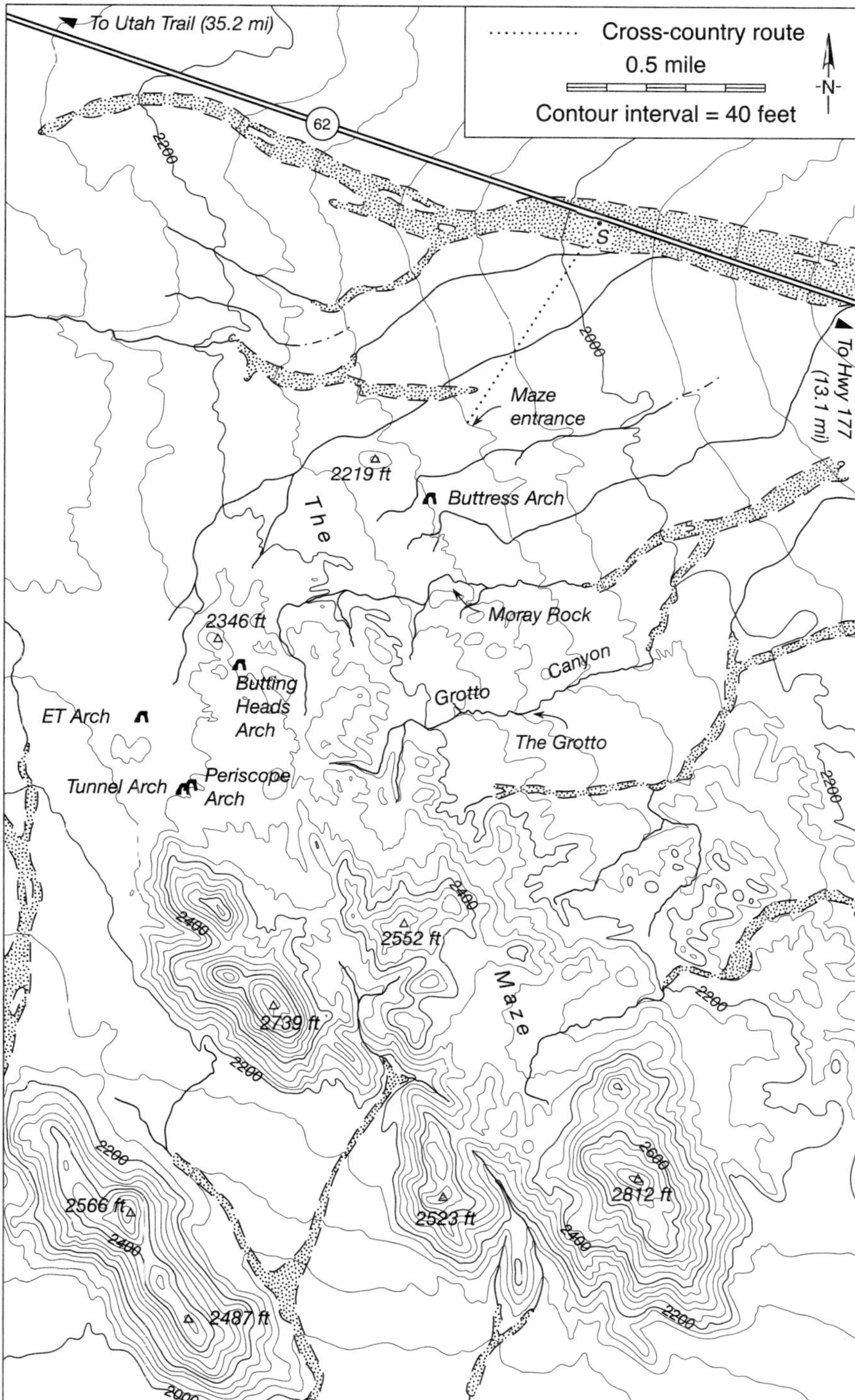
To Utah Trail (35.2 mi)
Cross-country route
0.5 mile
Contour interval = 40 feet
N
62
S
To Hwy 177 (13.1 mi)
Maze entrance
2219 ft
Buttress Arch
The
Moray Rock
2346 ft
Butting Heads Arch
Canyon
Grotto
ET Arch
The Grotto
Tunnel Arch
Periscope Arch
2552 ft
2739 ft
Maze
2566 ft
2487 ft
2523 ft
2812 ft
2200
2000
2400
2600

Standing fins at the lonely heart of the Maze

or slip though a slit barely wide enough to get by. Often a scene so attractive will pop up on the side that you must go and check it out, and from there something else will trick you in yet another direction, until you lose track of your whereabouts. You find yourself wandering on capricious paths, like along the cloned corridors of a cunning haunted house. The biggest danger, and the most distinctive feature of the Maze, is coming to a dead end, only to discover that you cannot figure out how to get back...

This is confounding country, not a place for novice or GPS addicts. A GPS will tell you how to retrace your steps, but it cannot find a way through for you. Heavy GPS users are also conditioned to focus their attention away from the land, which puts them at greater risk. Of course a route could be downloaded from the Internet, should one be posted in the future. But following it would make as much sense as filling in a crossword puzzle by looking up the solution. It would rob the Maze of its very spirit. At the end of the day, the exhilaration comes from having used your native skills—sense of direction, memory, knowledge, even sensations and intuition—to get in and out of the Maze.

■

PYRAMID GULCH

I came upon this enchanted place by accident, as some discoveries are made, while driving the lonesome stretch of highway toward the Coxcomb Mountains. On the long descent into remote Cadiz Valley, the notched high crest of Aqua Peak rising up ahead usually eclipses everything else. But that day it was the cluster of sharply pointed hills at the peak's base that caught my attention. In the diffused light of morning, their edges had lost their crispness as if they were engulfed in a fog, and they had the aura of ancient pyramids. The narrow gulch that runs through them turned out to hold a surfeit of surprises—arches, narrows, odd rock formations, a dozen pyramidal hills, and divine solitude.

General Information

Road status: Paved access road; cross-country hiking
Cat Eyes Arch: 2.0 mi, 310 ft up, 0 ft down one way / very easy
Arch loop: 5.7 mi, 500 ft up loop / easy
Windows Rock: 1.9 mi, 310 ft up, 0 ft down / very easy
Windows Rock loop: 6.3 mi, 700 ft up loop / easy
Main attractions: Arches, pyramidal hills, rock formations, solitude
USGS 7.5′ topo map: Cadiz Valley SW
Maps: pp. 243*, 227

Location and Access

From Utah Trail in Twentynine Palms drive Highway 62 35 miles to the broad pass into Cadiz Valley, then 3.5 miles to the unsigned trailhead to Inner Basin on the right. This spot can be easy to miss: it is at the first low point in the road in several miles. Continue 0.6 mile to a long wash crossing (the shoulder on the left is paved) and park. The wash is the distributary of Pyramid Gulch. The gulch is 0.7 mile up the wash, in the pyramidal hills visible to the south-southwest. Coming from the east, this wash crossing is 11.4 miles from Highway 177.

Route Description

Arch loop. I have to admit at the outset to a certain bias: I fell in love with this place. Ambling among the everchanging sculptures of weathered stone that line Pyramid Gulch felt like being in Alice's wonderland. Unexpected things pop out of nowhere, each encounter more astonishing than the previous one, as if the world had gone mad. The

Looking down the west fork of Pyramid Gulch

magic begins minutes up the wash: you enter a diminutive forest of desert willow and smoke tree showcased in virgin spreads of sand, a scene so green that it surely got misplaced. Quickly the forest vanishes, the wash narrows, sinks into the fan, and morphs into a miniature gulch. Rows of small caves roofed by protruding caps of fanglomerate pierce the low granitic banks like troglodytic dwellings. You imagine a timeless village of unknown spirits, patiently waiting for the next generation of believers. The first set of pyramids get closer and more ominous. Then comes a surge of boulders in a brief tightening, a intimation of impending change. Soon after, past a right-angle left bend, the wash splits, demanding a choice. Which rabbit hole to take?

The main fork is the least conspicuous of the two, a narrow side draw that shoots at 90° to the right. It does not look like much, but it's actually packed. It slowly skirts the pyramids, stately edifices decorated with the darkest desert varnish. Each one is kludged from boxcar boulders tipped on edge and grafted to each other, yet they mimic remarkably well the geometry of ancient Egypt's royal tombs. Every minute the rock formations grow imperceptibly taller, bigger, more present. There are bulging domes, walls of stacked fins, and hillsides of tossed boulders. As the first set of pyramids recedes, another one rises on the opposite side, an alignment of progressively taller pyramids, supernatural in its precise symmetry. The last monument tapers to a giant black arrowhead firmly wedged into the sky.

Across from it there is a mangled outcrop of welded rock, and peering over it a slanted arch shaped like an eye. If you don't look at just the right moment, it is gone. Walking towards it you realize that there are actually two arches, mirror image of each other, side-by-side like 1950s cat-eyes spectacles. Closer still, a tiny third arch opens up right between them. A very rare triple arch—curiouser and curiouser.

Cat Eyes Arch, west fork of Pyramid Gulch

Deeper in the gulch, everything changes again, abruptly and often. Intriguing caves are suspended tens of feet up. A procession of tall pinnacles parades on a high crest like a cemetery of skyscrapers, rounded as if they had melted in the sun. One of the towers, tipped with a sheep's head, stares down as you walk by. Turn around a few minutes later, and it is still looking at you. Then the land bunches up in a rogue wave of compressed bedrock, and the gulch briefly turns into a canyon as it cuts deeply through it. A first 7-foot fall clips the wash, followed by a second one, then a slick 12-foot parabola of pale monzonite that curves gracefully to verticality. Ten thousand years ago, when the planet was wetter and greener, water glided over its surface and collected in the shallow pothole at its base. As the Ice Age stepped back, large mammals may have taken turns gathering around this providential watering hole. Today the fall's face is as dry and smooth as glass. It has just the right curvature to curl up into it, and, at the right time, just the right temperature—pleasantly cool in summer evenings, gratifyingly warm in the sunny mornings of winter.

Above this fall, bypassed up a ramp of boulders, the west fork emerges on an open plateau sprinkled with worn formations. There is one more fall up ahead, where the wash tries to squeeze between buttresses. A little before it, a shallow fork splits off on the right. It cuts east to the edge of bedrock and the Inner Basin Trail, which loops back to the highway along the backside of the pyramids. Here the landscape is different again. You descend along a lazy wash of sand toward a sloping valley and the eminently harmonious peaks of the Calumet Mountains. In the evening, the pyramids are faced with a full cloak of coppery boulders, and they radiate from within the deepest red glow.

Windows Rock Loop. In this strange land that delivers doses after doses of pure excitement, it is hard to stay on track. At any moment you may be drawn off to the side by a sight that you must go check out from up close. And you may find something perplexing—like Windows Rock. While exploring the east fork for an encore, I ran into a fantastically shaped creature. It was a fabulous petrified snake-like beast of darkly stained monzonite, 200 feet long and grotesquely deformed. Its mouth was a suspended alcove frozen in a blood-curdling roar, its dorsal fin a monstrous sugarloaf, and its tail a stinger-shaped pinnacle. It rippled atop a low rise like Nessie floats out on

Pyramid Gulch

	Dist.(mi)	Elev.(ft)
Highway 62	0.0	1,705
Caves	0.7	~1,820
Constriction (go right)	1.35	1,915
Junction with east fork	1.45	1,930
Windows Rock	(0.4)	~2,010
Head of east fork	(2.1)	2,405
Back to Highway 62 via wash	(4.8)	1,705
Cat Eyes Arch	1.95	2,010
Pinnacles	2.15	2,030
12-foot fall	2.35	2,105
Fork in wash (go right)	2.60	2,160
Inner Basin Trail (go right)	2.80	2,205
Old track (go right)	5.00	1,835
Highway 62	5.65	1,705

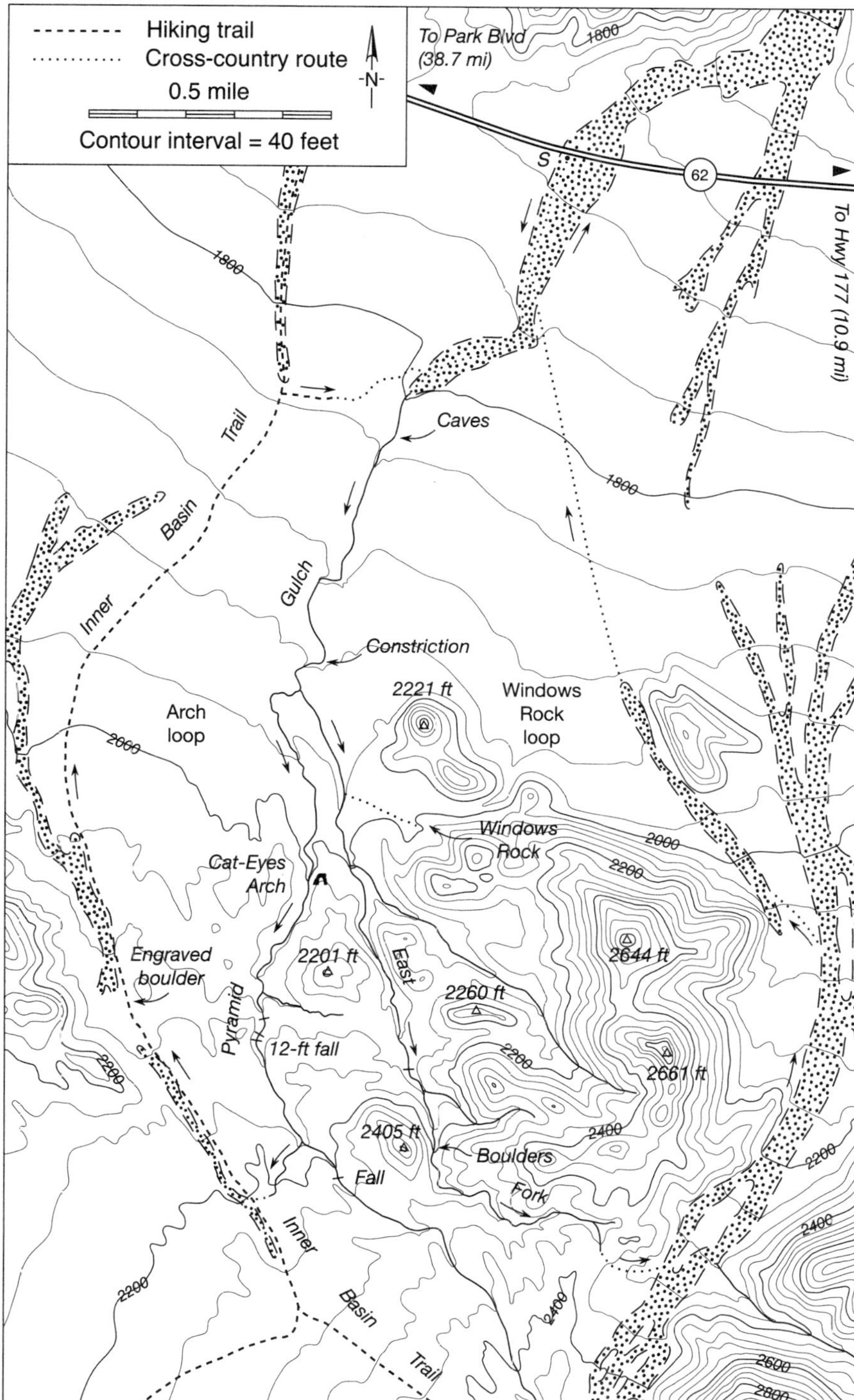

Hiking trail
Cross-country route
0.5 mile
Contour interval = 40 feet
N
To Park Blvd (38.7 mi)
To Hwy 177 (10.9 mi)
62
S
1800
Caves
Inner Basin Trail
Gulch
Constriction
2221 ft
Windows Rock loop
Arch loop
2000
Windows Rock
2200
Cat-Eyes Arch
2201 ft
East
2644 ft
Engraved boulder
2260 ft
Pyramid
12-ft fall
2661 ft
2405 ft
2400
Boulders
Fall
Fork
Inner Basin Trail
2600
2800

Windows Rock, east fork of Pyramid Gulch

Loch Ness on a perfectly foggy day—a Nessie totally into body piercing. Even more than its comical shape, what was remarkable is that it was decorated with no fewer than ten windows—likely the most little arches in one spot in hundreds of square miles.

That day, time itself was also oddly altered, languishing in some hidden fold of consciousness. When I reached the twisted end of the east fork and topped a low ridge overlooking Aqua Peak, beyond stocky towers and a wall covered with the cryptic scribbles of tafoni, it was inexplicably already evening. As I hiked back to the road down the broad wash that spills out of Inner Basin Pass, the magic spell lingered. Shadowy fingers crept out of the hoodoos and spread across the wash. The canary-yellow blossoms of a million dandelions carpeted the wash. A smoke tree trembled in a sudden gust. Was it a coyote that just slipped out of the bushes and suddenly disappeared? Far away, the headlights of a car rushing silently through the thickening twilight now seemed less real than the world I was about to leave. This is the amazing power of this little gulch. Like Alice's mirror, it is a portal into a parallel world where reality is naturally augmented. Long after you return, you will not be quite sure that it fully let go of your mind.

▪

THE LAST CHANCE MINE

On the remote west side of the Coxcomb Mountains, near the geometric center of the park's vast roadless eastern region, are the ruins of the Last Chance Mine, a small gold mine whose name does not appear on any map. It is just far enough—a little over 11 miles round trip—to border on a minor trek. Enough is left at the site to recount a forgotten piece of the American West history, and to elicit our admiration for the unknown man who endeavored to mine and mill a little gold. The appeals lie in searching for these hidden ruins, in the surge of elation upon finding them, and in getting immersed in the solitude of a vast wilderness engulfed in beauty.

General Information

Road status: Cross-country hiking; graded access road
Last Chance Mine: 5.7 mi, 2,120 ft up, 390 ft down one way / easy
Main attractions: Remote gold mine and mill
USGS 7.5' topo map: Cadiz Valley SW
Maps: pp. 243*, 227

Location and Access

The starting point for the hike to the Last Chance Mine is the Inner Basin Trail. Refer to *Aqua Peak* for directions to the trailhead.

Route Description

Next to nothing is known about the history of the Last Chance Mine, not even its owner's name. All we have to go by is its ruins, which are just extensive enough to speculate on its story. The mine was developed after the 1910s, possibly during the Great Depression, when automobiles were making it easier to explore deeper into the desert. The miner built his own access road by driving the eight miles of smooth bajada from Pinto Wells to the south. He trucked all the supplies needed for a self-sustained mining operation—concrete, dynamite, lumber, pipes, power tools, sheet metal—and lots of water. He likely did this on a budget, with no heavy equipment except perhaps a blade to clear the steep final grade to the mine. He erected a crude custom mill and set up a temporary camp. For a time he blasted a shaft to his quartz vein, crushed the ore at the mill, soaked it in cyanide tanks, and trucked the solution away. The end of the story is still written in the mine tailings. Decades later, geologists analysed tailings samples and found mere traces of gold. The tiny mill tailings, just a few cubic yards, confirm their conclusion. The miner found out the hard way how little gold there was and he quit, his last chance shattered.

The Inner Basin Trail heads up a long sandy fan before tightening into a wash framed by scenic hills of boulders. To the right is the Maze, to the left Pyramid Gulch, landscapes that demand contemplation. Once a four-wheel-drive road, the trail has long been closed to motor vehicles. Most of it is now distinguishable only by the footprints of the rare hikers on their way to Aqua Peak. After 3 miles the rock formations on the right, which have been gradually getting lower, end completely. At this point, angle at 2 o'clock over an open pass into Pinto Basin, and look for a faint road that descends west-southwest along the Coxcomb Mountains. Finding it is not essential: it ends in half a mile anyway. The rest of the route is southwest down a miles-wide bajada, aiming for the southernmost visible point of the mountains. The descent is gradual, in and out of countless gullies carved by rainstorms. Desert tortoise dens are everywhere, under diamond cholla or creosote, and out in the open. A little before reaching the mine, a wash parallels the base of the mountains. A sand river dotted with desert lavender and smoke tree, it provides the first decent shade since the pass. Soon after, a short road on the left cuts up into a low bench toward the mountains. This is the upper end of the old Last Chance Mine Road. The mill is on the bench, 125 yards up this road.

The mill was a simple affair. The grinder was housed in a shack on a concrete slab. A small water tank sat next to it, secured in a circular concrete trough. Two interconnected metal cyaniding tanks are 20 feet down the slope, sunk below ground to reduce evaporation. The shack's sheet-metal walls have been torn off and twisted by the wind, and its heavy lumber partly burnt by ignorance. Half of the trough is gone, and the tank has slipped off. This is still a satisfying site to inspect, to attempt reconstructing its operation, to glimpse the hopes of a forgotten dreamer, and pay hommage to his determination.

The Last Chance Mine

	Dist.(mi)	Elev.(ft)
Highway 62	0.0	1,700
Trail junction at pass (right)	3.0	2,290
End of trail	3.5	2,210
Last Chance Mine (mill)	5.3	2,020
Last Chance Mine (quarry)	5.7	2,530

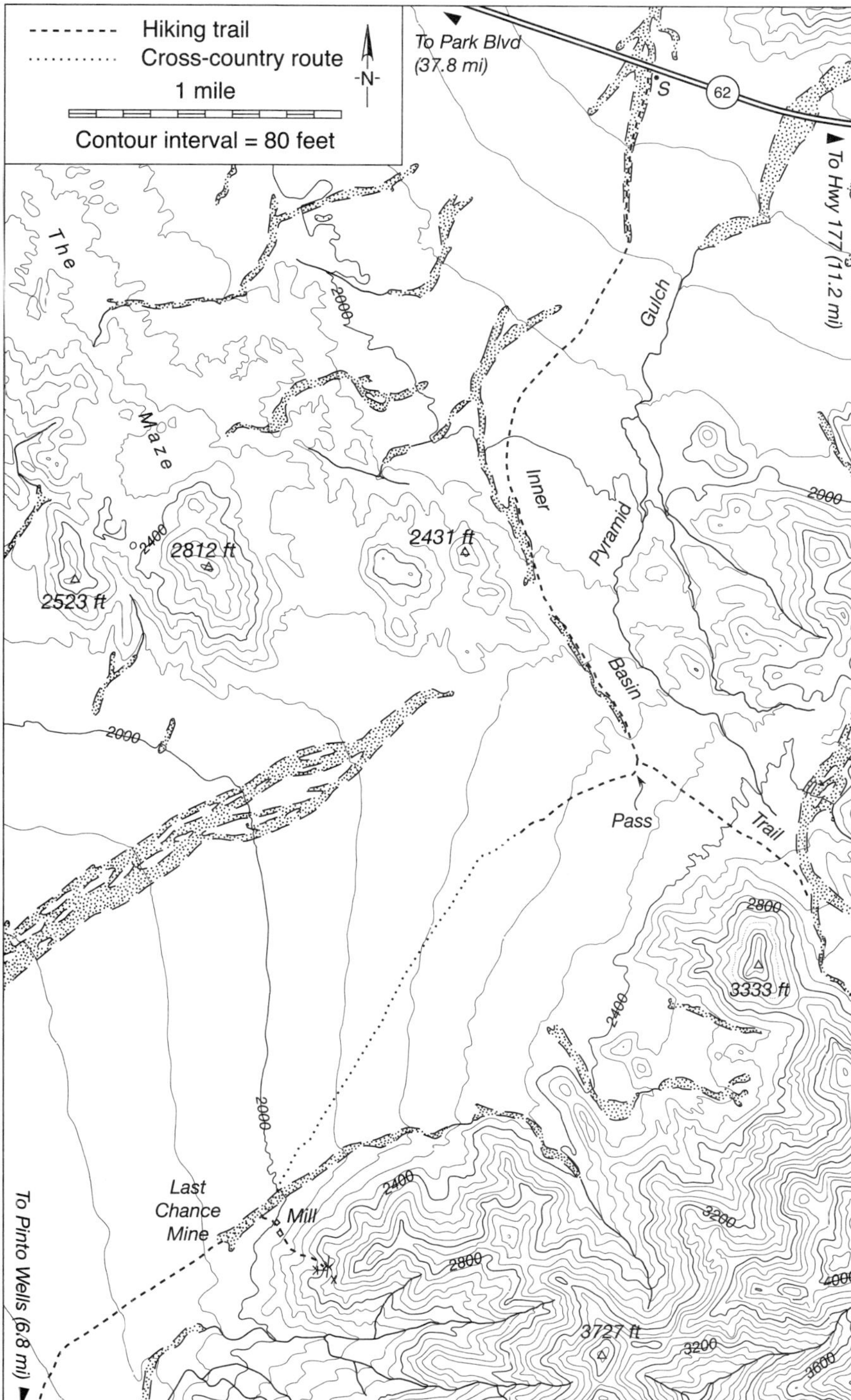

Hiking trail
Cross-country route
1 mile
Contour interval = 80 feet
N
To Park Blvd (37.8 mi)
62
S
To Hwy 177 (11.2 mi)
The Maze
Gulch
Inner Pyramid Basin
2812 ft
2523 ft
2431 ft
2000
2400
Pass
Trail
2800
3333 ft
Last Chance Mine
Mill
3200
4000
3727 ft
3600
To Pinto Wells (6.8 mi)

Mill ruins at the Last Chance Mine

Behind the mill, the mountain is pried open by a steep open ravine flanked by Mesozoic rock spurs in mottled shades of buffs, browns, and dark grays. The mine is near the top of the ravine. Just uphill from the mill there is a 20-foot-long loading ramp, a rectangular rock-wall perimeter backfilled with stones. The road to the mine starts right behind it. It was quite a road: it climbed 500 feet in a third of a mile. Up in the ravine, storm runoffs have churned it into an avalanche of rocks. The grade was so steep that ore and/or equipment were ferried on a metal sled attached to a cable and winched over the roadway. The steepness explains the electrical poles that parallel the road: it was easier to power tools at the mine with electricity than gasoline.

The mine workings are clustered along the upper end of the road—an inclined tunnel now partly caved, twin tunnels facing each other inside a common slot blasted in a vertical rock face, then a small quarry. The quarry's 20-foot-wide wall is stained with red hematite veined with black tendrils, and capped by sparkling dark-gray mica-schist. The miner may not have recovered his money's worth in gold, but if he was half a poet he will have enjoyed the magnificent view from his mine, which overlooks the vast desolation of Pinto Basin and the Pinto Mountains broken up into dark archipelagos. At sunset, the entire Coxcomb Mountains glow the deepest shade of red, the incandescent amber of coals just before they die off.

■

AQUA PEAK

Tensor Peak is the lowest of the three close-by summits that crown the northern Coxcomb Mountains. Along with its two neighbors Spectre Peak, the high point of the range, and Dyadic Peak, the second highest, they are collectively known as Aqua Peak, after the benchmark on Tensor Peak. These ascents are the most strenuous in the park. They call for a long approach, followed by a taxing Class-2 scramble up a steep corridor of large boulders, and finally Class-3 climbs on rough ridges. To make matters worse, Aqua Peak is in a day-use area, so you must climb back down the mountain the same day. The scrambling is fun, the achievement is memorable, and the views rank among the most otherworldly in the California desert.

General Information
Road status: Roadless; paved access road
Tensor Peak: 7.5 mi, 3,010 ft up, 280 ft down one way / strenuous
Spectre Peak: 7.6 mi, 3,070 ft up, 280 ft down one way / strenuous
Main attractions: A long taxing ascent over boulders, awesome views
USGS 7.5' topo map: Cadiz Valley SW
Maps: pp. 247*, 227

Location and Access

When you take the long drive east from town on Highway 62 across the finally empty desert, the first good look of the Coxcomb Mountains you get is where the road tops the wide-open pass into Cadiz Valley. The sight of Aqua Peak's spiky summits stabbing the sky up ahead is memorable. This favorite among diehard peak baggers is reached via the Inner Basin Trail. From Utah Trail in Twentynine Palms, drive Highway 62 up to this pass (35 miles), then 3.5 miles down to the unsigned Inner Basin trailhead, at a sandy hollow on the right. It is easy to miss: it is at a shallow low point in the road, the first one since the pass. Coming from Highway 177, it is 11.4 miles.

Route Description

The standard route to the three summits is via the eastern base of Aqua Peak. The approach is the same longish but pleasant and uncomplicated route to Inner Basin. From the trailhead, hike up to Inner Basin Pass (5.3 miles), then down toward the basin (see *Inner Basin*). Past the pass 0.7 mile, where the canyon widens noticeably, a side canyon opens up on the right, flanked by a battery of short cliffs and pinnacles. This side canyon is the standard route to Aqua Peak.

From there to the crest, the side canyon is a steeply inclined trench chock-full of boulders. Steep it is: in 1.3 miles it gains 1,350 feet. It is a hell of a workout. Stretches of open gravel are rare; you walk mostly on the backs of boulders. There are woody shrubs waiting in ambush, ankle-twisting cobbles, and several falls, the tallest one a slanted recess of grooved monzonite 16 feet tall hacked in convenient steps. The scrambling is fun, although after your thousandth boulder it wears a little thin. Consciously or unconsciously, you are always scanning the terrain up ahead for the easiest way to go. It is slow going. If you are not used to extended scrambling, you might need to build up a tolerance for pain before coming here. Focusing constantly on where your next footstep should go can be so absorbing that you may well miss the beauty of your surroundings. The canyon is pure rock. The walls, tilted at a persistent 45-degree angle, are littered with a chaos of massive boulders and solid outcrops all tilted inward. Every rock seems to be stretched upward. Even the boulders along the bottom are a source of wonder, neatly cleaved or smoothly rounded, slashed by pink dikes, blistered with protuding megacrysts.

The canyon eventually emerges in a small bowl at the base of the three peaks. After the canyon's confinement, it is a refreshingly open space sprinkled with yucca, nolina, and a few shaggy pines, not all still alive. The final push to Tensor Peak is up Class-2 jumbles of boulders on either the shallow gully on the south slope or the northwest shoulder, which are the easiest of several possible approaches.

The view from the summit is astounding. For a change it is not the far distance that is most breathtaking—although it too contributes to the euphoria—but the immediate geography. In almost all directions the nearby mountains are bare monzogranite sheared off vertically on

Aqua Peak

	Dist.(mi)	Elev.(ft)
Highway 62	0.0	1,700
End of trail inside canyon	3.7	2,530
Inner Basin Pass	5.3	2,980
Side canyon junction (right)	6.0	2,725
Bowl at base of peaks	7.35	4,080
to Tensor Peak	(0.2)	4,418
to Spectre Peak	(0.25)	4,482

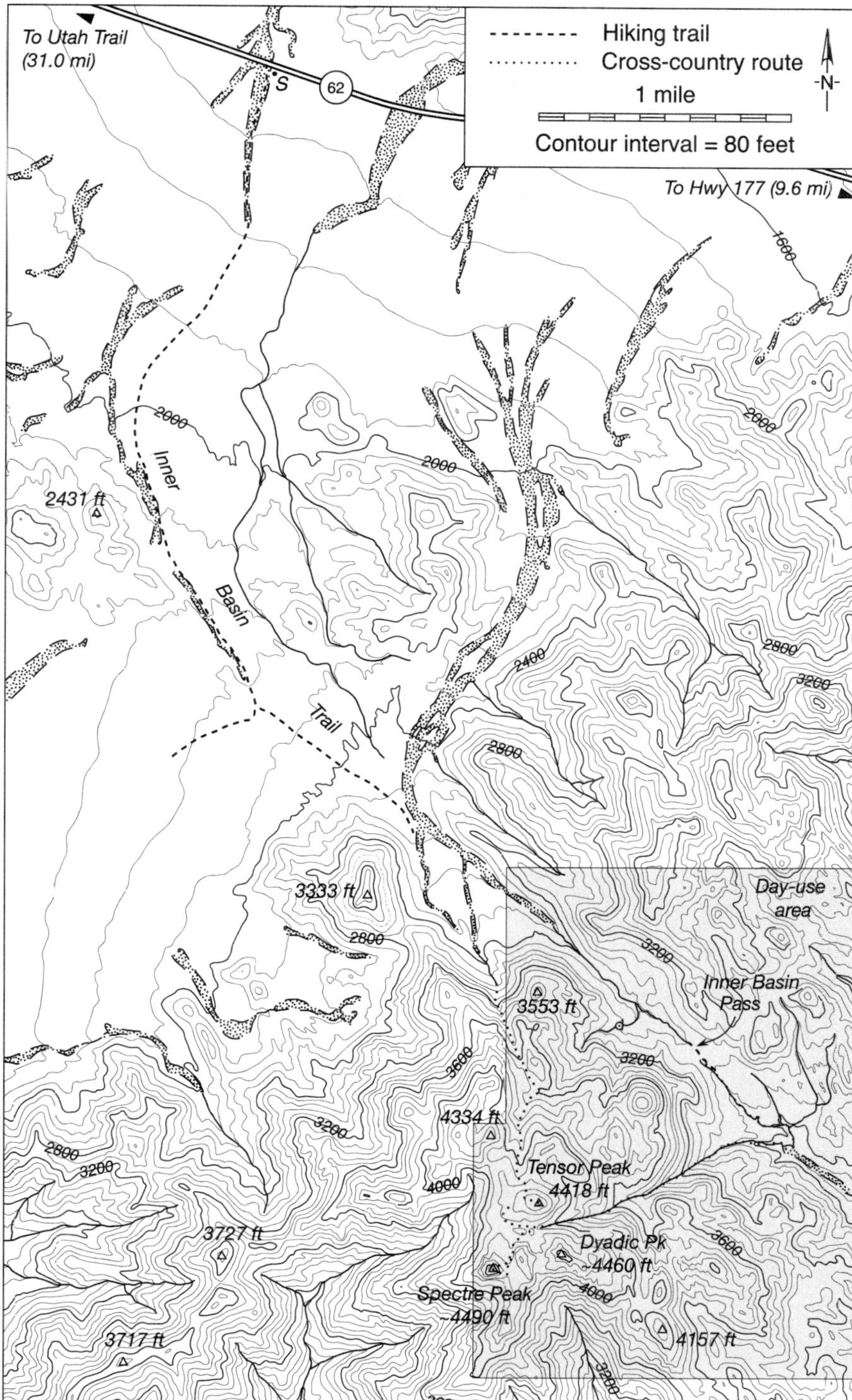

Hiking trail
Cross-country route
1 mile
Contour interval = 80 feet
N
To Utah Trail (31.0 mi)
To Hwy 177 (9.6 mi)
S
62
Inner Basin Trail
2431 ft
3333 ft
3553 ft
4334 ft
Tensor Peak 4418 ft
Dyadic Pk ~4460 ft
Spectre Peak ~4490 ft
3727 ft
3717 ft
4157 ft
Day-use area
Inner Basin Pass
1600
2000
2400
2800
3200
3600
4000

The main route to Aqua Peak (steep couloir at center)

a surprisingly small and regular spatial scale. Less than a quarter of an air mile to the south, the sheer flanks of Dyadic Peak seem to have been sliced by a giant machine. Spectre Peak right behind it, the range's highest summit, is a soaring sail fringed with standing rocks. Beyond them, the middle ground is a sea of surreally sharp hills with the same unsettling, artificial-looking symmetry. You feel as though you have stepped into a freakish alternate reality where mountains are assembled from upright slabs pressed together.

Between Tensor Peak and Spectre Peak, there is hardly a square yard that qualifies in almost anyone's book as walkable terrain. The route to Spectre Peak is seriously arduous. From the bowl, first scramble south up to the saddle east of the summit (Class 2). The last 200 feet of elevation gain on the precipitous eastern arete is the crux. You need to plot an ever-changing course to minimize Class-3 moves up a staircase of perpendicular blocks. Traversing below the arete across the north slope is also a go—you trade some blocks for boulders. Expect loose rocks, exposure, slow progress, and cursing. Make sure you are not over your head: this is a serious undertaking, and by far the hardest climb in this book. From the summit, the view south down the long tapering spine of the Coxcomb Mountains is superb. The summit overlooks a vast territory spanning from most of the park on one side to as far back as the Turtle Mountains halfway to Arizona on the other.

■

INNER BASIN

Inner Basin is a small high-desert valley at the center of the Coxcomb Mountains' rugged northern section, and one of the park's most remote locations. Enclosed by spectacular spiky mountains, it is a hauntingly wild place that embodies the outlandish rockscapes of this unique range. All access routes to it are long and require both stamina and time. The one described here is the classic approach via the Inner Basin Trail. Hiking to Inner Basin is just the beginning: the many canyons that drain in and out of the basin are challenging avenues to explore the basin's stunning ring of craggy mountains.

General Information

Road status: Hiking partly on trail; paved access road
Inner Basin Pass: 5.3 mi, 1,310 ft up, 20 ft down one way / moderate
Inner Basin (the Rocks): 7.4 mi, 1,530 ft up, 340 ft down one way / diff.
Lone Spring: 8.8 mi, 2,030 ft up, 350 ft down one way / strenuous
Pinto Basin Viewpoint: 8.4 mi, 1,800 ft up, 340 ft down one way / diff.
Main attractions: A remote inner valley, spectacular spiky mountains
USGS 7.5' topo maps: Cadiz Valley SW, Cadiz Valley SE
Maps: pp. 251*, *227*

Location and Access

The starting point is the Inner Basin trailhead. Refer to *Aqua Peak* for driving directions.

Route Description

Inner Basin Pass. Of the three routes to Inner Basin described in this book, this is the easiest because it has far fewer boulders. The first segment, on the Inner Basin Trail, is leisurely and enjoyable (see *The Last Chance Mine*). After 3 miles the trail, by then better defined as a twin track, crosses a high fan toward Aqua Peak, rising majestically up ahead. It heads into the broad V of a canyon to the left of the peak, and ends shortly after entering the canyon. This is the first of an alignment of three canyons eroded along a fault that shoots straight to the heart of the Coxcomb Mountains. It climbs 1.6 miles to Inner Basin Pass. Except for a 400-foot-long ramp of boulders that requires a little scrambling, most of it is clear sand. The landscape slowly morphs into the epitome of Inner Basin's vertical terrain. The slopes are increasingly studded with hoodoos eerily stretched upward, as if they were pulled skyward by an invisible force field. A little before the pass, the canyon forks. The right fork leads to a 14-foot fall, and two neat little stone catchment basins erected for wildlife. The main wash continues straight, squeezes by three tall spherical boulders, then narrows and fades. A use trail picks up and climbs a very short distance to the pass.

Inner Basin Pass is a long saddle of ruined granitic knobs slowly disintegrating into gravel. When you look down its far side toward Inner Basin, you realize that the vertical distortions you passed were just a sample. To the south, the mountain is a procession of unnaturally pointed hills plated with tight ranks of razor-sharp slabs. You peer down into an avenue of fanciful castles out of a fairy tale. It is impossible not to feel as if you are about to trespass into some other world.

Inner Basin. The remaining 1.8 miles to Inner Basin are the most scenic, as they cross this vertically exaggerated landscape. From the pass, walk down the trail 200 yards to where it is easy to drop into the ravine on the right, follow its rocky course to the wash of the canyon visible below. Its easy wash of immaculate sand descends gently to its confluence with Bighorn Canyon. This third canyon's equally smooth and gradual wash then climbs to the basin's northern rim.

Inner Basin is beautiful, in an otherworldly sort of way. About a mile long by half a mile wide at its widest, it is a gently sloped valley cocooned by fantastical mountains. The mountains are naked rock, almost devoid of vegetation. They rise in long rows of successively higher hills reaching 1,000 feet above the valley. Long ago the bedrock was fractured underground into an extensive matrix of thin vertical slices. This pattern is now exposed all over, in the two dozen boulder islands strewn across the basin, in the towering groves of parallel fins that stagger up the hills, and in the spears that pierce the skyline like fence posts. The landscape is so directional that it seems to have been conceived not by nature but by an artificial intelligence that did not quite know how to incorporate randomness in its design.

The boulder stack labeled "The Rocks" on the map is a good spot to camp while exploring Inner Basin. The walk up to the basin's western rim is a nice introduction. The basin floor is made of stream sediments deposited during the Pleistocene's pluvial era. The boulder islands are high points in the bedrock spared by the floods. They all rival for audacity in shape, and they quickly become the main focus. The basin peters out at the Pinto Basin Viewpoint, a scenic gap that peers down a steep canyon into Pinto Basin and the Eagle Mountains.

The local topography can be disconcerting. Inner Basin is drained in not one but two directions: Bighorn Canyon flows out of it northeast

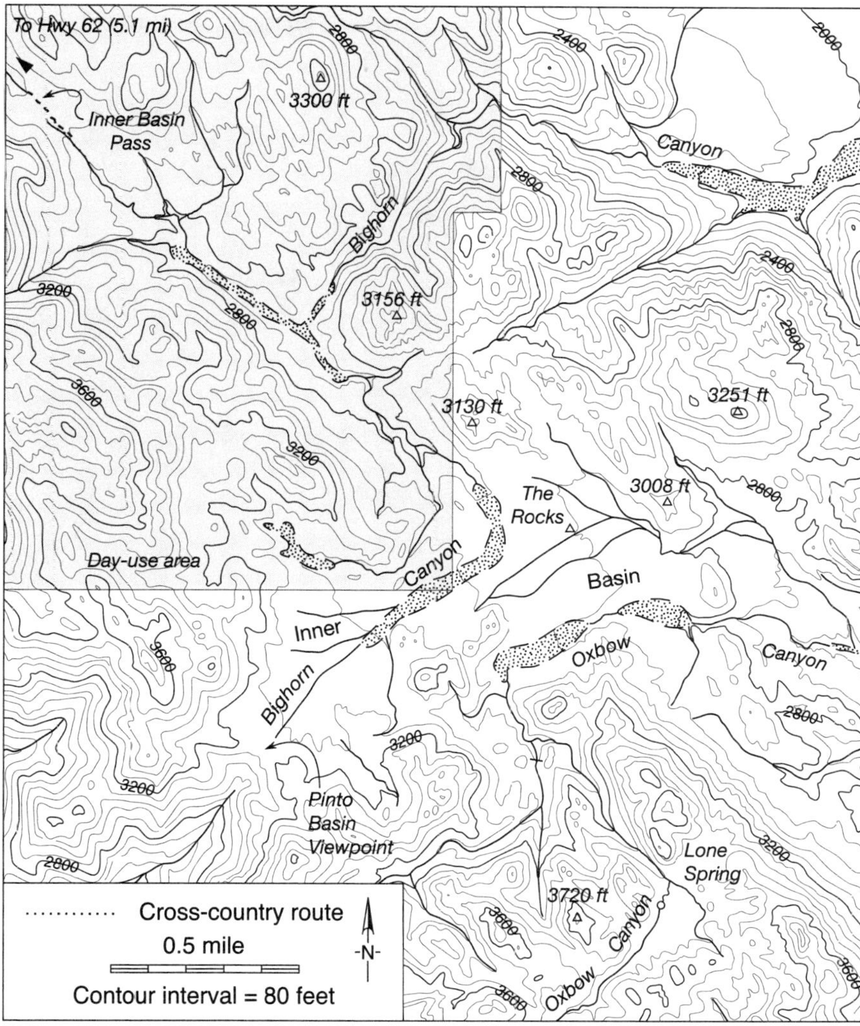

Inner Basin	Dist.(mi)	Elev.(ft)
Inner Basin Trail on Hwy 62	0.0	1,700
End of trail inside canyon	3.7	2,530
Inner Basin Pass	5.3	2,980
Inner Basin (edge)	7.1	2,860
The Rocks	7.4	~2,885
to Pinto Basin Viewpoint	(1.0)	3,140
to Lone Spring	(1.5)	3,370

View southeast from Inner Basin Pass

into Cadiz Valley, and Oxbow Canyon southeast into Palen Valley. The Slab in Bighorn Canyon and the Oxbow are great targets for a day hike. Yet the most interesting destination is the spring hidden in upper Oxbow Canyon. From the Rocks, cut due south a quarter of a mile to the sunken wash of Oxbow Canyon. The wash has sculpted into the basin's soft deposits a long bank of badlands fringed with humanoid hoodoos. Just uphill the wash angles south into the mountains and splits shortly after. The main canyon is the inconspicuous left fork, an impressive trench filled with four staircases of enormous boulders and swollen slickrock. Physically and psychologically, this place is bursting with free energy. The boulders are in concerningly precarious equilibrium; some of them seem to be ready to roll. The largest ones are 20 to 40 feet across, with gaps between them big enough to be swallowed alive. The workout is good, challenged by obstinate catclaw—a good warm-up if you are planning to climb Aqua Peak the next day. Lone Spring, in the right fork just past the top of the boulders, is an unusually dense grove dwarfed by towering monoliths. In this supremacy of stone refractory to life, this rare spring is a miracle to revere.

There is much more to see: the limitation is not the land but the amount of water you can carry in with you. Inner Basin is far from civilization. Plan your trip carefully to maximize your time there.

■

BIGHORN CANYON

> *On the return hike from Bighorn Canyon, tired and elated, I sat down by the rock island and entered in my notebook a single word: monumental. Even in a park acclaimed worldwide for its incredible formations, Bighorn Canyon easily rivals the best. From its mouth to its head below Aqua Peak, it is literally covered with temples of stone. It has narrows, giant boulder dams, bedrock intricately carved and polished by water, slopes crawling with sculpted formations, and razor-sharp crests crowded with spires. The price is steep: the canyon is 3 miles from the closest road, and overrun with boulders. It may still become one of the best outdoors day in your life.*

General Information
Road status: Roadless; paved access road
The narrows: 4.0 mi, 960 ft up, 200 ft down one way / moderate
The Slab: 4.9 mi, 1,410 ft up, 220 ft down one way / difficult
Inner Basin: 6.6 mi, 1,830 ft up, 230 ft down one way / strenuous
Main attractions: Spectacular canyon with high sculpted walls
USGS 7.5' topo maps: Cadiz Valley SE*, Cadiz Valley SW
Maps: pp. 257*, *227*

Location and Access

From the heart of the rugged northern section of the Coxcomb Mountains, Bighorn Canyon drains generally northeast into the very southern tip of Cadiz Valley. The starting point is easy to find. From Utah Trail in Twentynine Palms drive Highway 62 42.6 miles to the road to the Cadiz Lake salt evaporators on the left, at this point a very large turnout for mining trucks. Coming from the east, this junction is 8.0 miles from Highway 177. Park on the turnout. The mouth of Bighorn Canyon is approximately 3 miles south as the crow flies.

Route Description

The approach is long, up a spacious alluvial fan that epitomizes the vastness of the Great Basin. From the road it is 1.7 miles south along the base of the mountains to the edge of a mile-deep embayment. From there, a cluster of three small rock islands become visible on the fan a little west of south. The next target is the furthest and largest island—1 more mile. It is then 0.6 mile, in the same direction, to the canyon rim. The fan offers scant entertainment. It is thinly vegetated with creosote and catclaw, wispy and dark from dehydration, brightened only by an occasional cholla. At an average height of 3 feet, they are the tallest plants. The main rock island, a misshapen castle of plump blocks melded together, has the only shade the whole way. Cryptogam, that unique collage of cyanobacteria, mosses, and lichens, is abundant on the fan, where it grows in crusts of black florets on the ground. It is very slow growing and inconspicuous, yet important in slowing down erosion. Avoid stepping on it by walking as often as practicable in the innumerable water channels that crisscross the fan's surface.

Narrows in Bighorn Canyon

The long walk pays off as soon as you reach the edge of Bighorn Canyon, which should be, if things went as planned, just below its mouth. The canyon rim is soft mounds of badlands eroded into the thick delta of fine sediments deposited by the river that scoured the canyon long ago. In recent millennia, sediment-starved flashfloods exiting the canyon have excavated a deep channel into the sand-colored consolidated sediments. The wash, pure sand punctuated by the emerald pools of well-watered plants, is stranded at the bottom of it, 160 feet below the fan. Across from it, the mountain is mantled with fantastically shaped formations.

The shallow ravines eroded in the channel's bank are the easiest ways down into the canyon. At the bottom, the wash is open for less than half a mile, until it squeezes through the tightest of Bighorn Canyon's several narrow passages. The narrows are good, 150 yards long and trapped between short vertical walls, tight enough to be in darkness much of the day. The shallow slot at their center is too narrow to walk. You squeeze through it by either stemming or creeping up sideways, your back and your feet pushing against opposite walls.

Towering latticed wall along the gorge in central Bighorn Canyon

Along its 3-mile course, Bighorn Canyon has cut some of the grandest sculpted rockscapes in the California desert. The sheer number, density, variety, and boldness of formations are simply staggering. The canyon slopes rise hundreds of feet straight from the wash at a persistent 45-degree tilt. From base to rim, they are overrun by squadrons of pinnacles, banks of fins, shards of rocks, and screes made not of dirt and cobbles but of Humvee-size boulders casually tossed by gravity. Bare rock lays open everywhere, carved by millennia of rain, wind, sun, and frost, often without a single plant to challenge its monopoly. A short distance in, the south wall is crawling with parallel fingers all pointing skyward in silent admonition, oddly similar in shape and dimensions. Bryce Canyon may not be so well stocked. The central gorge is deep and narrow enough that in mid afternoon direct sunlight is blocked off and the air glows a surreal orange. In the middle of it, a magnificent wall of monzogranite hundreds of feet high presides over the wash. Its polished surface is latticed with vertical joints that break it up into a giant jigsaw. Boulders rest precariously on the tips of its pinnacles. All along the canyon, the crests are tipped by rows of steeples, the proud cockscombs that may have inspired this range's name. Almost everywhere, it would take serious skills and stamina to make headway up into this neck-craning topography; lunacy might be a pre-requisite.

As it is, the canyon bottom offers ample opportunities for immersion in this exceptional landscape. For nearly a mile and a half, the narrow wash is littered with the thousands of boulders that lost the battle against gravity. Open strips of sand are a luxury. More often than not, you walk around or on top of boulders. In narrower passages the force of flood water has stripped off the sand to bedrock and carved into it facets, chutes, sharp lips, caldrons, and long slits several feet deep. Their smooth surfaces still relate the story of the river, where it shimmered on slickrock, washed over an angular edge, and spun in foaming eddies inside potholes. The monzogranite is encrusted with striking twinned crystals of feldspar the size of dominoes. Where polished, it displays the random geometric patterns of ancient mosaics.

In this geologic chaos, progress is challenged at a dozen places by oversized boulders resting several layers deep on top of each other. The first blockage is a pair of awkwardly shaped facing walls 8 feet tall that push you away no matter how you approach them. The last and most impressive obstruction is a high dam capped by the Slab, a phenomenal block 6 feet thick and 50 feet wide that spans most of the wash. Beneath this matrix of overlapping stone, the wash survives in patches of sand thrown in perpetual darkness. There is a way around all obstacles, and it can take time. It did not seem to matter. In this outdoor festival of shapes where excitement is implicit in every little discovery, the perception of time is dislocated, its dictatorship banished.

Bighorn Canyon is anything but straight. Redirected often by orthogonal faults, it jogs half a dozen times in abrupt 90-degree zags, covering most cardinal directions. The sun moves around a lot, quickly resetting patterns of light and shadows. The most visually striking

Bighorn Canyon

	Dist.(mi)	Elev.(ft)
Highway 62 at Cadiz Valley Rd	0.0	1,280
Rock island	2.7	1,940
Canyon rim	3.3	2,110
Narrows	3.9	2,010
Start boulders	4.05	2,050
The Slab	4.85	2,470
90° fork (left)	5.5	2,675
Fork (left)	6.0	2,770
Edge of Inner Basin	6.35	2,880
Inner Basin (the Rocks)	6.6	2,875

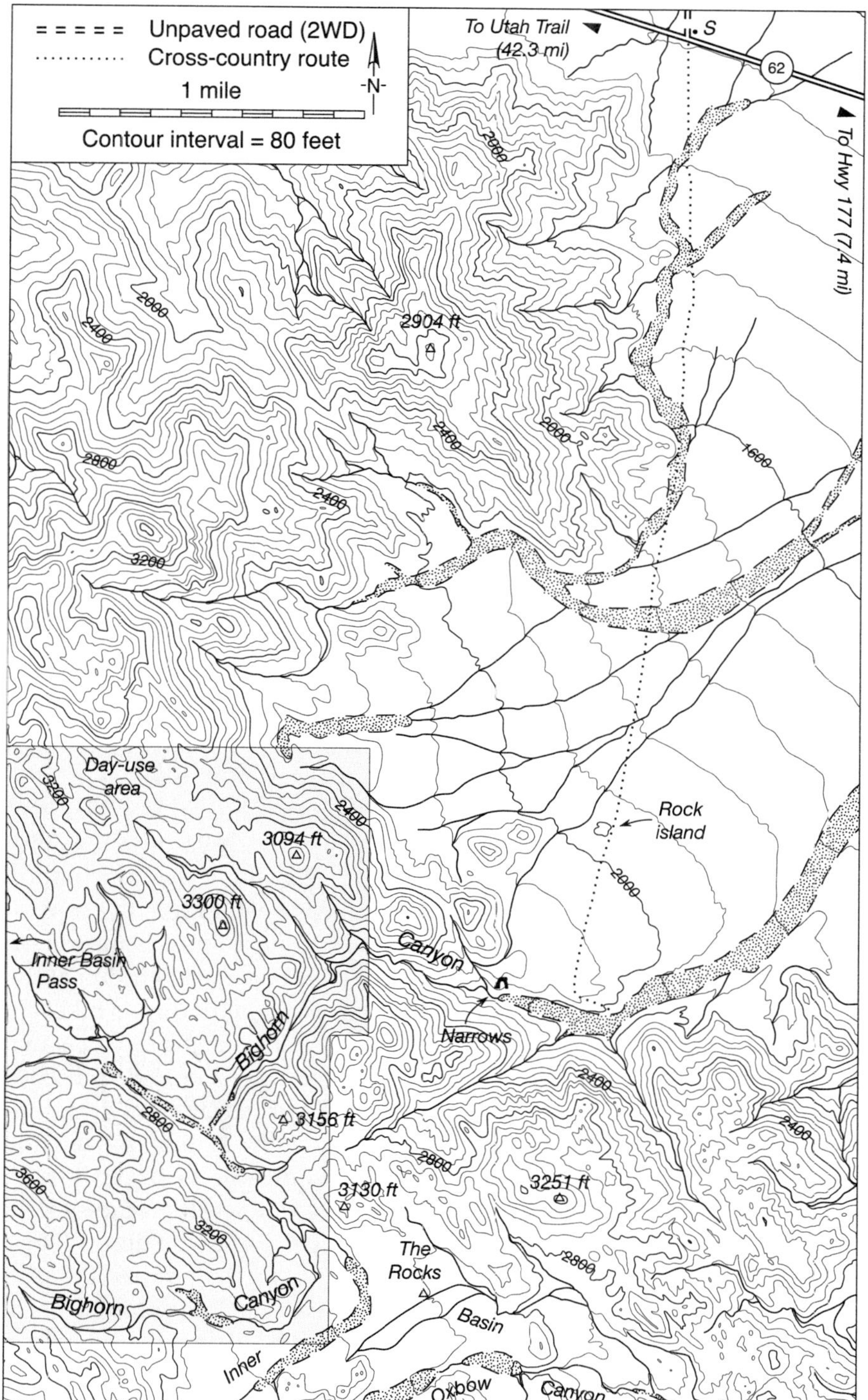
Unpaved road (2WD)
Cross-country route
1 mile
N
Contour interval = 80 feet
To Utah Trail (42.3 mi)
S
62
To Hwy 177 (7.4 mi)
2904 ft
2000
2400
2800
3200
1600
Day-use area
3094 ft
3300 ft
Inner Basin Pass
Rock island
Canyon
Narrows
Bighorn
3156 ft
3600
3130 ft
3251 ft
The Rocks
Bighorn
Canyon
Basin
Inner
Oxbow
Canyon

Looking down Bighorn Canyon's monumental central gorge

fault is shortly past the last boulders, where the wash rams at 90° into the mountain and splits at 180°. The side canyon on the right, coming down from Inner Basin Pass, and the main canyon climbing on the left, are perfectly aligned with each other and with the fault line.

From this junction to Inner Basin, Bighorn Canyon is wider and free of boulders, and still framed by spectacular hills bristling with impossibly sharp formations. As the basin gets closer, the anticipation grows, and so does the elation of an imminent goal. Where the canyon finally opens up it does so abruptly, and the basin bursts into view, encircled by surreally pointed hills. This secret place well hidden at the heart of a rebellious range is a befitting end to an adventurous hike.

Almost all of Bighorn Canyon has been set aside as a day-use area to protect wildlife, in particular bighorn sheep. Signs of their presence are ubiquitous. They have churned the sand, grazed part way through softer plants, stripped the bark of desert lavender, and pawed the gravel to lie down more comfortably. Droppings are generously scattered all over. Occasional bleached bones litter the wash. In pre-settlers time, bighorn had a much broader distribution. Today the desert fabric is fraying, stretched thin by human activity. It is a long day to the central gorge and back, much longer to Inner Basin. Turn around early enough to be out of the day-use zone before nightfall.

■

OXBOW CANYON

Of the hundreds of canyons that slice through the rocky ranges of Joshua Tree, Oxbow Canyon is on the short list of most outstanding. A deep gorge carved through the granitic core of the Coxcomb Mountains, it hosts a wealth of fantastic formations, narrows, walls of spires, banks of tall fins, streams of easy boulders, the Oxbow where the canyon nearly folds upon itself, and ultimately the carved badlands of remote Inner Basin. The cover charge is steep: it is the longest canyon in the Coxcomb Mountains, and it takes a long shadeless hike up its vast alluvial fan just to get to it. The price is right: Oxbow Canyon epitomizes the greatest attributes of this exceptional range—raw wildness, sheer isolation, and a mysterious territory that may not have been fully explored.

General Information

Road status: Roadless; paved access road
The narrows: 4.1 mi, ~910 ft up, ~30 ft down one way / moderate
The Oxbow: 5.7 mi, 1,290 ft up, 20 ft down one way / difficult
Inner Basin: 7.8 mi, 1,930 ft up, 50 ft down one way / strenuous
Main attractions: A remote canyon, stunning rock formations, isolation
USGS 7.5' topo maps: Coxcomb Mountains, Cadiz Valley SE
Maps: pp. 263*, 227

Location and Access

Starting from the abrupt western rim of the Coxcomb Mountains 2.5 miles southeast of Aqua Peak, Oxbow Canyon cuts a long meandering path clear across the mountains to their east side before emerging at the edge of remote Palen Valley. The shortest access to it is from Highway 177, at the eastern boundary of the park. From Utah Trail in Twentynine Palms drive Highway 62 east to its end at Highway 177, a distance of 50.5 miles. Turn right (south) on Highway 177 and follow it 3.5 miles down Palen Valley, which is 0.9 mile past a power line crossing. At this point there will be a wide graded road on the right. Drive it 1.3 miles down to an open bulldozed area with a few piles of rocks on the left, just before the Colorado River Aqueduct, and park.

Route Description

The approach. Even if this is not your first time, a close look at the Colorado River Aqueduct is likely to be a memorable moment. A

The Oxbow (photo courtesy of Pierre-Baptiste Vigneron)

remarkable feat of engineering, it carries across the desert a whole river of cool, swiftly moving water, 20 feet wide and deep enough to drown. The sight of this incongruous turquoise river in a place that sees so little rain invariably triggers a mixture of admiration and incredulity, even if tempered by the awareness of the ecological disruption it has caused. From the car park you cross the aqueduct at one of the aqueduct's many inverted syphons, a buried U-shaped channel the size of a subway that forces the river to briefly flow underground. The syphons provide a passage where infrequent storm waters can cross the aqueduct without flooding and fouling it.

On the west side of the aqueduct, you will be at the confluence of two long 10-foot-tall levees that funnel storm waters coming down the fan to the opening at the inverted syphon (see map). The mouth of Oxbow Canyon is due west, approximately in the direction that bisects the levees, about 3 miles up the alluvial fan that comes down from the Coxcomb Mountains. Shortly into the approach, two small rocky islands jutting from the fan come into view 2 miles ahead. The mouth of Oxbow Canyon is not far behind them in the same direction, so they make a convenient beacon. Being the only source of deep shade on the fan, they are also a good rest stop in hot weather. It is a bit of a walk, although the slope is gentle and plants are squat, their growth thwarted by the extremes of this exposed valley. You fall into a rhythm

Standing rocks in the Oxbow's outer bend

cadenced by the familiar symphony of poles poking the ground, shoes crunching gravel. The Coxcomb Mountains rising up ahead are a powerful incentive: as their rugged rockscape gets gradually closer, you become acutely aware that you are closing in on a special place.

Lower Oxbow Canyon. The beauty of Oxbow Canyon is that unlike most canyons in the park, which are glorified gulches embedded in low hills, it is a genuine canyon. Deep and relatively narrow, it snakes wildly between imposing walls often crowded with rock formations. It also happens to be one of the longest canyons in the park: there is a lot of it to see. Past a long sandy curve above its mouth, it narrows into a passage a third of a mile long hemmed by rough cliffs tinted a beautiful rust color by desert varnish. A 15-foot pillar of granite that recently broke off the north wall rests upright in the sand, its sheared face still largely pristine. At the head of the narrows, a 7-foot fall of cleaved blocks obstruct the wash—it can be climbed in one dynamic move, or bypassed. A third of a mile further, Mesquite Spring graces a straight passage with a long row of low mesquite and baccharis. This may be the only place for miles where wildlife can be seen in greater numbers than one. Small birds, lizards, ground squirrel, and coyote all take advantage of its greater shade and humidity. Further up, the formations grow in size and audacity. At the sharp 90° left bend 1.8 miles into the canyon, the outer wall is sliced vertically into a colony of tall parallel fins that stopped me dead in my tracks.

In the canyon the walking is comparatively easy. The grade is moderate, and the wash is mostly open sand. Boulders are plentiful, but most of them are easy to walk around. Catclaw and desert lavender abound, yet most of the time they stay out of the way.

Many interesting geological features are scattered along the canyon. Just above the canyon entrance on the west side there is a wall of tan silt in which large boulders are entombed, the result of catastrophic floods that scoured the canyon during the Pleistocene's torrential rains. Up in the canyon, flowing water has left its marks at numerous places, in small chutes, on faceted boulders, and as smooth waves imprinted on bedrock. Although most of the canyon is made of pale-gray granitic rocks from the Late Cretaceous, entire walls expose older rocks filled with biotite and hornblende as black as jade. Many eye-catching boulders of a dark bluish gneiss also rest in the wash. They are slashed by thin veins of clear feldspar and pink pegmatite, freckled with crystals, or laced with olive-green chlorite.

The most unusual feature is the Oxbow, after which I named this canyon. About 2 miles in, the wash makes a nearly complete loop on itself, like the Greek letter Ω. Oxbow bends are common in modern rivers flowing in flood plains and deltas, but there are rare in igneous mountains. As you walk the Oxbow from end to end you cover about a quarter of a mile, yet you end up only 90 yards from your starting point. Besides being a geological curiosity, it is also an impressive sight. The long curved wall in the oxbow's outer bend has been dissected into a battery of tall fins that climb in giant leaps all the way to the canyon's serrated rim.

Oxbow Canyon		
	Dist.(mi)	Elev.(ft)
Aqueduct/Park boundary	0.0	1,000
Oxbow Canyon (mouth)	3.3	1,700
Top of narrows (fall)	4.1	1,880
Mesquite Spring	4.4	2,020
The Oxbow (upper end)	5.7	2,270
Boulders	6.2	2,420
End of boulders	6.5	2,560
Leave wash (right)	7.5	2,850
Inner Basin (The Rocks)	7.8	2,880

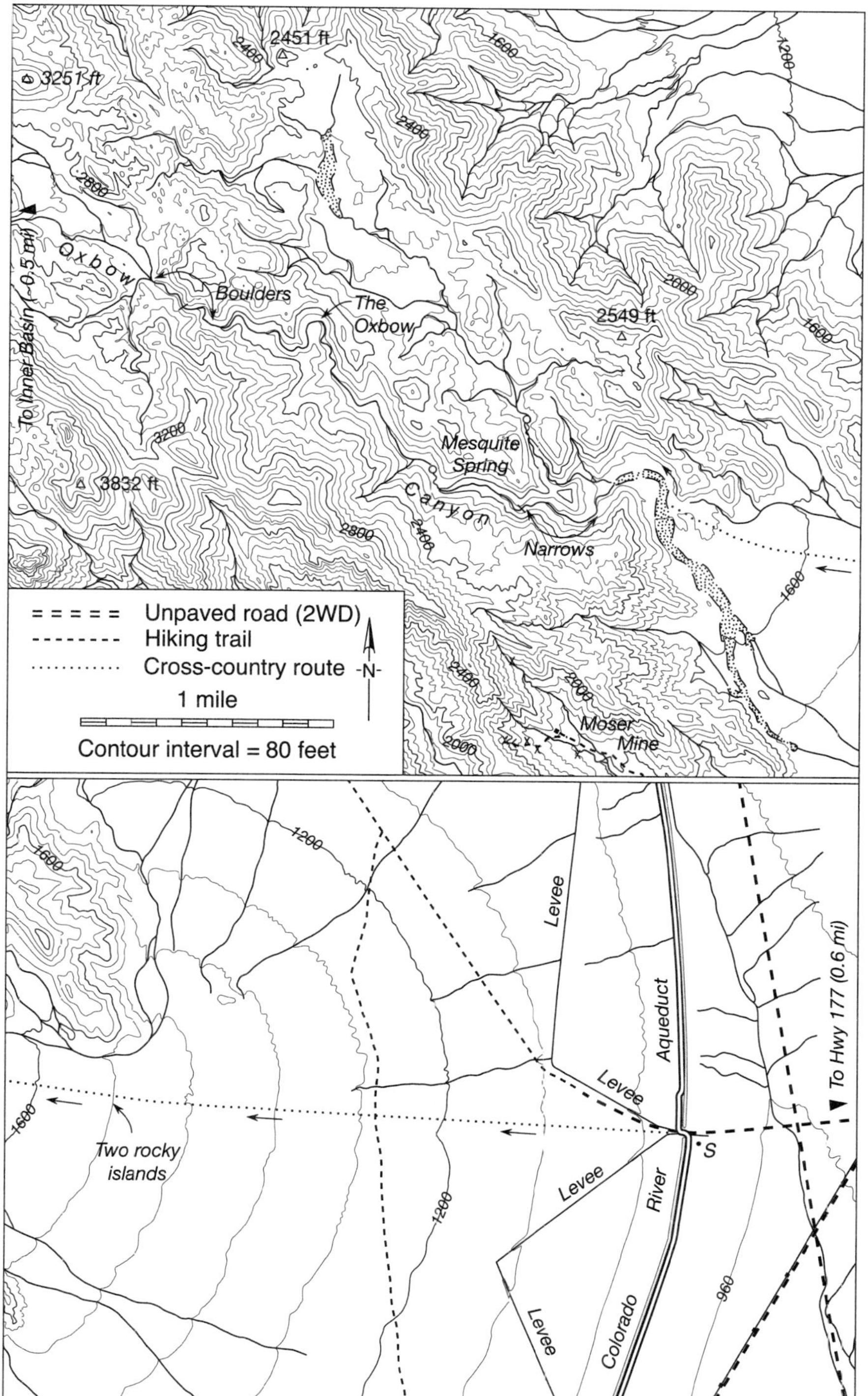

2451 ft
3251 ft
To Inner Basin (~0.5 mi)
Oxbow
Boulders
The Oxbow
2549 ft
Mesquite Spring
3832 ft
Canyon
Narrows
Moser Mine
Unpaved road (2WD)
Hiking trail
Cross-country route
N
1 mile
Contour interval = 80 feet
Levee
Aqueduct
To Hwy 177 (0.6 mi)
Two rocky islands
S
River
Colorado

In a park overrun with people and hemmed in by developments, Oxbow Canyon's main asset is its remoteness. You start this hike after a one-hour drive from town, in the middle of nowhere. You walk more than three miles just to reach the canyon, then nearly as much again to reach the Oxbow. By then you *are* far from everything. Isolation in wilderness is as essential as it is priceless. Here it defines the very mood of the canyon, and permeates every moment of the day.

Mid-canyon to Inner Basin. Still, there is more to this canyon—and the hardest is yet to come. Shortly past the Oxbow, the scenery intensifies, as does the difficulty. The canyon becomes more intimate as it twists and turns more tightly. The wash narrows to a thin strip of sand locally packed with boulders, with a little fall in the middle of it. The rock formations become increasingly taller and denser, and large bare-rock faces bigger and more numerous. The mountain slowly morphs into Inner Basin's quintessential spiky landscapes.

At the top of the boulder section, everything changes instantly. The wash opens up as it enters the Inner Basin's wide open space. Over the next 1.6 miles, it describes a slow counterclockwise arc along the basin's southern perimeter. A fantastical crest of mountains crowded with sharp crags rises on the south side. On the north side the wash is edged by a 40-foot wall of wrinkled badlands. It squeezes through a tighter channel between two hills of bare granite, opens up again, then approaches a second constriction, much lower. If you leave the wash just before it, a mile past the end of the boulders, and climb up one of the shallow ravines to the nearby north rim, you will see a quarter of a mile to the north-northwest a lonesome outcrop lost in the middle of a dissected plain. This is the Rocks, the heart of Inner Basin.

There is still more to Oxbow Canyon (see *Inner Basin*). The upper canyon is rough, and by the time you reach its base you will have covered nearly 8 miles—just about as far as even a desert rat will dare go. If you have not already, this is a good place to turn around and tackle the long hike back. It is also an ideal spot to camp, recharge your batteries, and explore the next day the last of this exceptional canyon.

■

THE MOSER MINE

The eastern Coxcomb Mountains are deeply gouged by short canyons that dead-end abruptly, like fjords that never felt the grinding weight of glaciers. In one of them, long ago prospectors found a small gold lode and developed it under the name of Moser Mine into a bone fide operation with a mill, rails, pipes, workshops, and small, cozy camps. Thanks to its remoteness, this site has the most extensive mining-related physical structures within the park boundaries. In a place where most mines have been allowed to decay or stripped of their mystery by on-site interpretation, the survival of this moving window into the past is a small miracle.

General Information

Road status: Graded access road
Moser Mill: 3.2 mi, 640 ft up, 10 ft down one way / easy
Moser Mine (shed): 3.9 mi, 990 ft up, 30 ft down one way / easy–moder.
Main attractions: Mining camps, mining equipment, scenic mountains
USGS 7.5' topo map: Coxcomb Mountains
Maps: pp. 269*, 227

Location and Access

The Moser Mine is in a short canyon on the eastern flank of the Coxcomb Mountains, a little north of the middle of the range. It can be accessed on foot only, starting from the service road that parallels the Colorado River Aqueduct. Take Highway 62 to Highway 177, 50.5 miles east of Utah Trail. Turn right (south) on Highway 177 and follow it 3.5 miles down Palen Valley to a wide graded road on the right, 0.9 mile past a power-line crossing. Drive it 1.3 miles down to a bulldozed depression with piles of rocks on the left, just before the aqueduct (the starting point to Oxbow Canyon). Turn left on the graded aqueduct road, go 2.65 miles to the second syphon (#86), and park well off to the side. If you are not comfortable parking on this road, drive another 0.4 mile to just before the next syphon, turn left on a primitive road, and park after 100 yards under the power line. Other than this last sandy stretch, two-wheel drive vehicles can make it easily.

Route Description

When it comes to either gold or beauty, not all granites were created equal. In the Pinto Mountains, they are loaded with gold but they produced subdued landscapes. In the Coxcomb Mountains, the granites have eroded into the most amazing landforms, but they are nearly devoid of mineral wealth. The Moser Mine, the richest in the range, has an inferred reserve of a measly 9,000 ounces of gold. Even at today's soaring gold prices, it would be worth $20 million, pocket money for the gold-extraction industry. Yet in the post-war years, two miners invested a great deal of time and energy trying to monetize it. A man from Gardena named Carl Moser owned the mine's five claims. His business partner Edward Severson held a half interest in two of the claims, and leased the other halves. Between 1944 and at least the early 1960s, they explored the fractured deposit at a few locations. Roads were bladed. Small infrastructures and camps were erected. Over 1,000 feet of galleries were blasted, and ore was milled locally. But after 20 years of hard work, no sustained production had been recorded. Only 18 tons of ore are known to have been shipped, in 1947 and 1948. After smelting, the return was all of $2,000 in gold and silver. Later, others gave it a try. Around 1980, when the price of gold spiked, every so often a few ounces of gold were produced. The Moser Mine was not the bonanza its original owners had dreamed of. In these stunning but mineral-challenged mountains, even the richest mine was a dud. Yet, ironically, this unremarkable mine left a priceless legacy—the largest mine-related ruins in the park.

When you step out of your car and set eyes on the mountains, the excitement of exploring a mine may actually be instantly eclipsed by the scenery. Your destination, the Coxcomb Mountains a few miles across the fan, are crowned by a high crest so spiky and bright that it seems too extreme to be natural. Forget the mine—you want to be there below the peaks, engulfed in this superb landscape. The old Moser Mine Road gets you there fairly easily. From the aqueduct road, cross the syphon, and the old mining track will be on the right, following the levee's straight base. After 0.4 mile the road angles sharply left, leaves the levee, and cuts a beeline 2 miles west-northwest across the gentle fan to the mountains. Most of it is deep sand, and not the most comfortable of paths. It has also been erased by flashfloods at a few spots, although it is so straight that it is hard to lose it. Unless the weather is miserably cold or miserably hot, it is a satisfying walk, far from crowds, constantly graced by the majestic peaks up ahead.

Where it reaches the wide entrance of a canyon at the base of the mountains, the road splits. The left fork winds up a quarter of a mile to the Vault Mine. All that remains of this marginal property is its shaft, the metal pipeline that brought air up to it, and its collapsed cabin. The Moser Mine's camp is half a mile up the main fork. The closest of its

Moser Mine Camp

two cabins parades surreally in the middle of the broad canyon floor. It is a handsome construction, in a funky sort of way. The plywood walls are sheathed in sheet metal streaked with dark-red rust, and patched up with shiny corrugated iron. It had a veranda, now falling apart, and mosquito nettings on its picture windows. A midden of rusted cans and glass bottles spills down its back side. Just up the main road, the carcass of a vintage sedan rests in the wash, forever stranded.

At this first cabin, the road splits again. The left fork climbs to the Moser Mine's lower installations. On its way there, it soon passes by the second cabin. As mining accommodations go, it was surprisingly well appointed. It had twin kitchen sinks, an oven, a Whirlpool refrigerator, and a gas range from O'Keefe and Merritt, a brand popular around the 1950s. A cast-iron stove made the cold winter nights more bearable. One wall is covered with yellowed newspapers packed with old-fashioned ads and grainy photographs. A metal-frame bed lie outside in the open amid discarded household items from another era.

This little forgotten cabin left another legacy, unique because it is so rare and personal. A miner kept a diary on a wall. It is a list of dates followed by a dollar value or a few words. A gold weight of 209 grams is listed on Christmas eve 1980, then 149 grams on January 17, 1981. January 21 was marked as a "bad day," February 10 as "sick." A week later, the entry was "No fire needed over 90°." The event noted on February 19 was "1st snake." Interestingly, most entries are not gold-production figures but the daily market price of gold. In 1979–1980 the price of gold had quadrupled. Now it was plummeting, and the miner was worried. Almost every day he anxiously listened to his transistor radio, jotted down a price, and tried to time the market. If he sold his gold on February 12, the date flagged as "Decision day," he would have pocketed $6,000. The last entry is "Fr 414.40." It was March 18, 1983. Decades later, through these terse scribblings, we can reconnect with a long-gone miner, his concerns and fortunes. This is priceless.

The tunnel and mill at the end of the side road have more mining remains than any other site in the park. From the tunnel, a narrow-gauge rail curves to the top of the mill. Unlike at some richer mines, its mill was not ordered from equipment catalogues but kludged from scavenged parts. Below its basic ore bin are the concrete pilings of its ball mill, now gone. A metal ladder is propped against it. A circuit breaker is still nailed to a joist. The ball mill was powered by the engine and drive train of a pick-up truck welded to a metal frame and bolted to its own pilings. It is an incongruous contraption, the exhaust and air filter sticking out, the gas tank oddly relocated, as in a school project gone awry. At the next level down, there is a small sink, like dentists used to have. Below it, the crushed ore was cyanided in two vats made of a steel tank sliced in half with a cutting torch. Above the mill, a shabby lean-to houses a large engine stained with grease. The compressor that powered the drills is parked nearby, a bright-yellow machine the size of a tractor. From the shed, an overgrown trail swings up to a shaft, where a cableway lowered ore from a higher working.

From the junction at the first cabin, the Moser Mine Road wanders another mile up canyon to the upper workings. Along the way, the canyon narrows, the high-rising slopes are increasingly covered

The Moser Mine

	Dist.(mi)	Elev.(ft)
Power-line road	0.0	1,010
Moser Mine Road (leave levee)	0.4	1,050
Junction near base of mountain	2.4	1,380
Vault Mine (shaft)	(0.25)	1,530
Moser Mine Camp (junction)	2.9	1,490
Moser Mill	(0.3)	1,640
Junction	3.65	1,710
Cabin	(0.05)	1,730
Moser Mine (workshop)	3.9	1,960

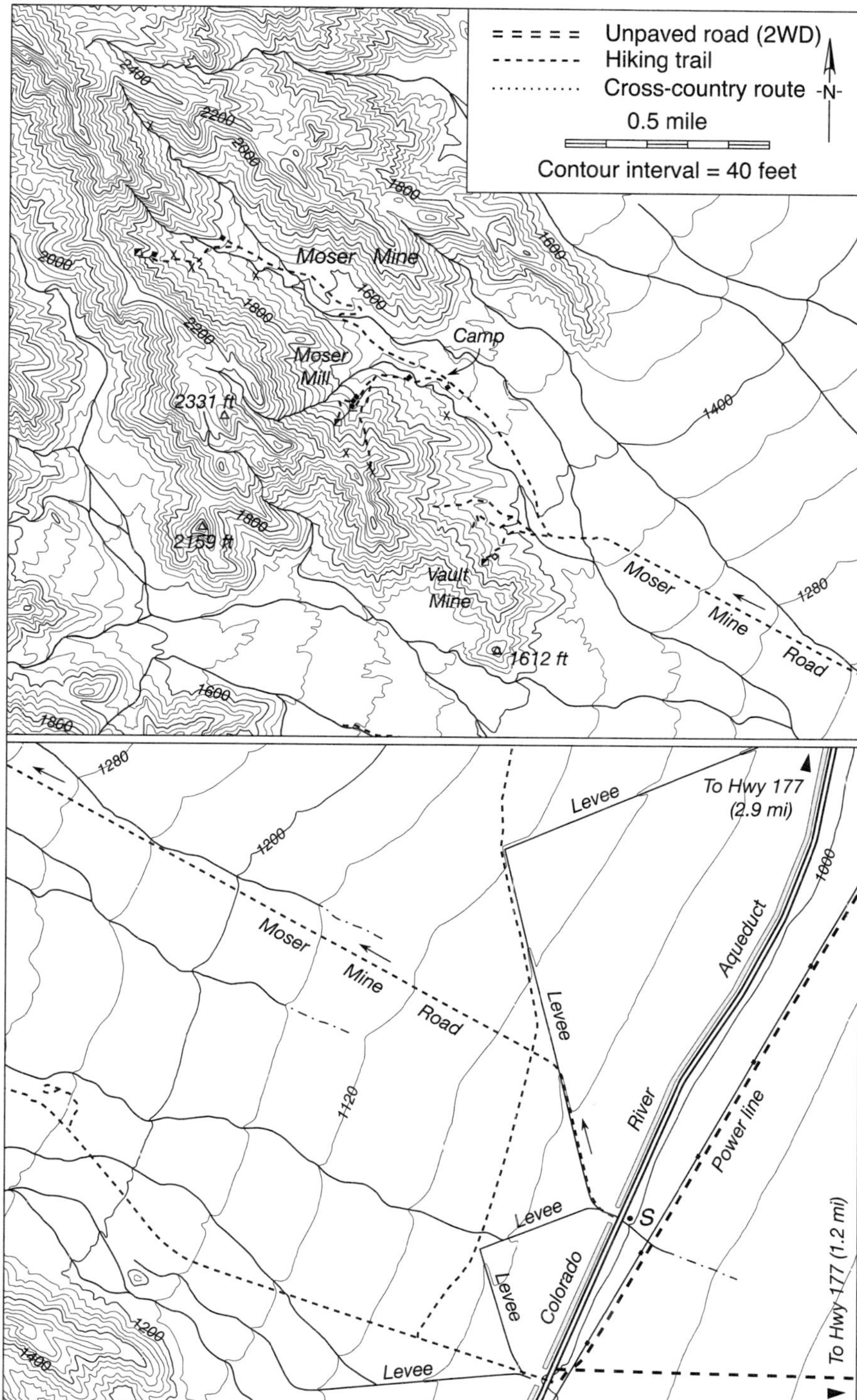
Unpaved road (2WD)
Hiking trail
Cross-country route
N
0.5 mile
Contour interval = 40 feet
Moser Mine
Camp
Moser Mill
2331 ft
2159 ft
Vault Mine
1612 ft
Moser Mine Road
To Hwy 177 (2.9 mi)
Levee
Aqueduct
River
Colorado
Power line
S
To Hwy 177 (1.2 mi)
2400
2200
2000
1800
1600
1400
1280
1200
1120
1000

Car carcass at the Moser Mine camp

with sherds of cinnamon granite. At the end of the box canyon, there is a third cabin, older, built in the sober style of mining shacks of the first half of the twentieth century. Erected on a sturdy concrete slab and protected by a recently repaired roof, it is a humble two-room shell of wood planks, now cracked, warped, and patined by decades of relentless sunlight. It was strictly functional, with netting on the windows, but no ornaments or shelves, and a single doorway, now doorless.

Past the cabin, the road angles up sharply to climb to the upper workings. The final grade is so steep that a cable had to be rigged to assist heavy trucks. A steel eyelet was anchored in bedrock to guide the cable, spooled nearby. At the top of the grade, a large tin workshop is propped against the mountain. A rail squeezes between it and a bubblegum-pink rocky outcrop, and sneaks into a tunnel guarded by a steel door. A bulbless lantern hangs from a rafter. Sections of rail and pipeline, water heaters, and rusted parts are scattered around. It is, here too, a place that makes you ponder over the motivations of these miners. Gold was surely a major one. As were roughing it, being self-sufficient, nonconformist, and successful at it. One would think that they also treasured the wild, the peace, the remoteness, and the grand cockscomb summits. At the end of a hard-day's work, they too may have sat at the tip of the rail overlooking the canyon, and savored the view of Palen Valley and the desert ranges while listening to eternity.

■

SAUBEL CANYON

The desert's boundless landscapes of naked rocks would not be as meaningful without knowledge of their history. In Saubel Canyon, they recount the story of the enormous rift basin that split open southeastern California in the reign of the dinosaurs, and died buried under miles of alluvia. Hiking this scenic canyon framed by sharp spurs gives us a chance to glimpse into a vanished world, to sample its history in its unusual rocks, to ponder over the ageless cycle or erosion—and to gauge, from its high rim, how rapidly the desert is being destroyed under the pretense of green energy.

General Information
Road status: Cross-country hiking; graded access road
Saubel Canyon: 2.8 mi, 6,50 ft up, 100 ft down one way/easy
Kawi'a Peak: 4.1 mi, 2,090 ft up, 100 ft down one way/strenuous
Coxcomb Peak: 5.5 mi, 2,660 ft up, 670 ft down one way/strenuous
Main attractions: Deep canyon, striking sedimentary rocks, peak climb
USGS 7.5' topo maps: Coxcomb Mountains, East of Victory Pass
Maps: pp. 273*, 227

Location and Access

Saubel Canyon is near the southern tip of the Coxcomb Mountains, just south of where the Colorado River Aqueduct tunnels into the mountains. From the westbound exit on Interstate 10, take Highway 177 north 15.2 miles to a wide, well-maintained graded road on the left, marked by too low shacks, each with a thin antenna. Coming from the north, this junction is 11.7 miles from Highway 62. Drive the graded road 2.6 miles west to the road that follows the Colorado River Aqueduct, at the foot of the mountains. Make a left, go counterclockwise 0.2 mile around the loop, and park on the bench on the right.

Route Description

The sprawling bench at the end of the road is the repository of the six million cubic feet of rock that were blasted out of the mountain to create the aqueduct tunnel. It stands at the boundary between two worlds. To the west rise craggy peaks of the vibrant Late-Cretaceous igneous rocks that form most of the range. To the south, the dark low ridge that transects the middle ground is the exhumed cap of the 4.5-mile stack of sediments that collected in the giant McCoy Basin in the

Jurassic. Saubel Canyon, just behind the ridge, slices through this singular hodgepodge of rift deposits. You are about to enter another time.

From the tailings, cut east-southeast across the flat bottom of the canyon that comes down from the right, aiming for the eastern tip of the low ridge, and in 15 minutes Saubel Canyon will open up on the right. It is right away an imposing place. Escarpments dissected in sharp ridges rise more than 1,000 feet up at breakneck angle. Parallel waves of warped strata protrude from the slopes in stark relief, the neatly laid-down beddings of ancient McCoy Basin now bent by tectonic compression. This is one of the region's rare canyons that is not igneous, and its a gem. The rocks in the wash are almost all sedimentary, often metamorphosed to delicate textures. There are glass-sharp blades of dark-blue slate, schists of alternating dark-gray and cream layers, deformed fossils, and a pale boulder emblazoned with black tree-like dendrites. The conglomerates are the most striking. These lake beds cemented by pressure gather collections of random cobbles transplanted from as far away as Grand Canyon country. The cobbles are well rounded, polished by the rivers that brought them down here eons ago. They still carry in them the ancient patience of running water. Some conglomerates were buried so many miles down that they were squashed them like pancakes. The inclusions locked in them were stretched several times their original thickness, and they are now displayed in tiled mosaics of elongated stones.

Even without a fondness for geology, it is hard not to enjoy this raw canyon. The walls run high and deep, a front brow rising straight from the wash, backed by further rows staggering higher. Alignments of ruddy spurs protrude from rubbly slopes. Side canyons scream up steep ravines to seemingly unreachable crests. A thousand honey mesquite grow all over the wash, some over 12 feet high, still green in the dead of winter. The air is pungent with desert lavender. The whole place exudes the aura of unvisited places. There are rabbit and coyote prints, but no footprints, no cairns, no disturbed rocks, no snapped branches. Even the silence seems deeper.

About 2 miles into Saubel Canyon, the wash is boxed in at a 200° cirque dominated by the two highest summits in the southern Coxcomb Mountains. You stand in a monumental amphitheater, dwarfed by a towering rim of toothed peaks, a grand scenery that seems almost too steep, too fractured, too outrageous to be real.

Both summits can be reached from this canyon, with a lot of hard scrambling. After the amphitheater, the main fork (left) squeezes between low vertical cobbly walls. Soon the wash is clipped by two falls back to back. The lower fall, 12 feet tall, has good holds (Class

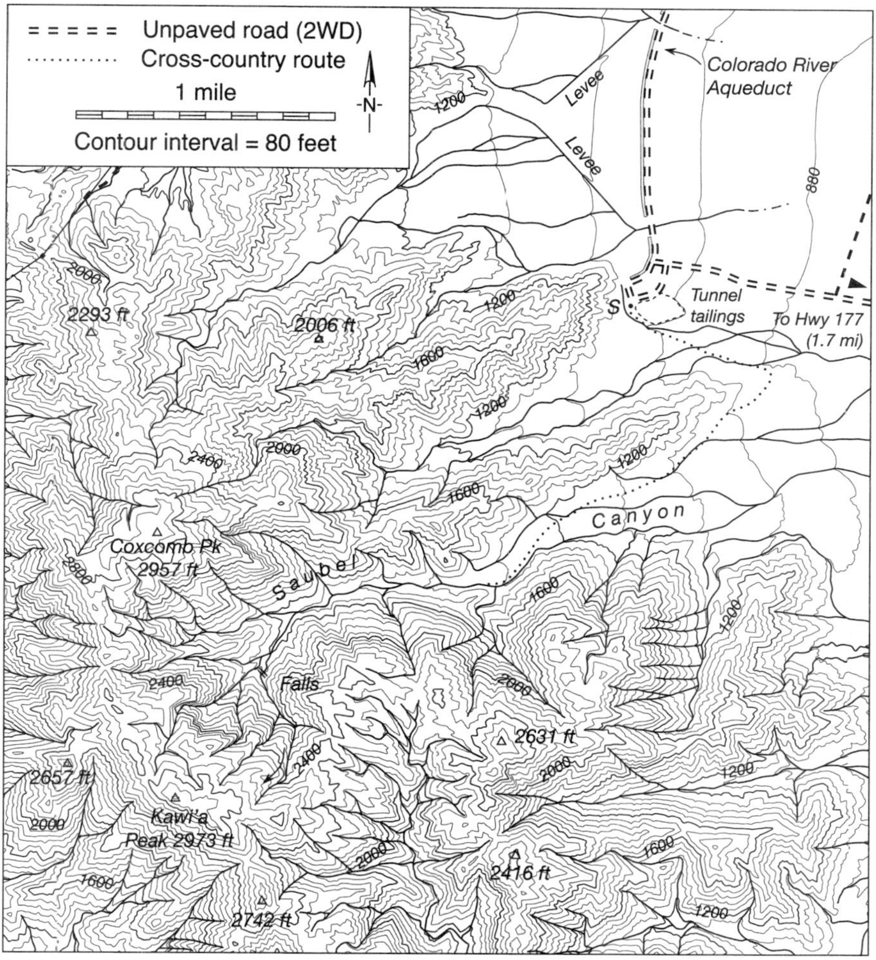

Saubel Canyon

	Dist.(mi)	Elev.(ft)
Aqueduct tailings	0.0	985
Saubel Canyon mouth	0.6	~910
Fork at amphitheater (left)	2.8	1,530
Twin falls	3.1	1,680
Fork (left)	3.3	1,990
Crest	3.9	2,780
Kawi'a Peak	4.1	2,973
Main saddle	4.7	2,620
Coxcomb Peak	5.5	2,957

Ring of summits at the end of Saubel Canyon

3–4); the second fall, 10 feet tall, is tougher (about 5.8). They can be bypassed on the left a little before the lower fall, on slippery 45° taluses with nothing much to grab onto. Past the falls, the wash is as punishing as it is complacent in the canyon. It is a sheer ravine clogged with large boulders that ascends 1,200 feet in under a mile. Some areas border on Class 3. Once on the crest, it is a short walk west to Kawi'a Peak. Coxcomb Peak is reached by an aerial hike in and out of half a dozen saddles, and around multiple rocky spurs along the crest.

The crest hands out a bittersweet reward. To the east it overlooks heartwarming rows of pristine ranges stretching out to eternity. To the west the land is disfigured by the monstrous power plant rapidly swallowing Chuckwalla Valley down below. These little-known summits are a strong reminder of the finite size and extreme vulnerability of our desert. They also carry a powerful message: on a large enough scale, no source of energy is green. The desert is forever damaged.

As I hiked back down the canyon, nature gave me a measure of comfort. The wind picked up and whipped long plumes of sand down canyon. Somewhere I heard the clatter of rocks set free by gravity. The same agents of erosion and transportation that created these rocks 100 million years ago are still at work. They are now tearing them apart and hauling them into Palen Valley, another rift basin, endlessly recycling the planet's 4.65-billion-year-old crust—and anything on it.

■

— 8 —

Little San Bernardino Mountains

About 43 miles long by 13 miles wide at their widest, and capped by 5,813-foot Quail Mountain, the Little San Bernardino Mountains are Joshua Tree National Park's huge southwestern backbone, its tallest range, and its largest mountain mass. To the north, they rise barely 2,000 feet above the park's central high plateau. To the south, they drop nearly one vertical mile into Coachella Valley's parched below-sea-level trench. When you drive the long grade on Highway 62 from Palm Springs to the park's north side, you trace this blatant asymmetry and climb from low to high desert. When the road crests Yucca Valley, the Little San Bernardino Mountains look completely different, a long creased crest dotted with the green orbs of oaks, pine, and junipers that beams a spare and sensuous beauty.

The majority of the range is in the park, and most of that is a designated wilderness. Its western tip is part of Sand to Snow National Monument. Only its southern foothills along Coachella Valley are mostly unprotected. The scenic Indio Hills, a narrow sub-range in northern Coachella Valley separated from the main range by a strand of the San Andreas Fault, are partially protected by the 14,000-acre Coachella Valley Preserve and a few smaller parcels, owned and managed by a coalition of government agencies and private organizations.

Geology. Part of the Transverse Ranges, the Little San Bernardino Mountains were shaped by extreme tectonism. Compressive forces along the San Andreas Fault, which cuts along the entire base of the mountains in Coachella Valley, lifted them out of the Earth while the valley was sinking. In the past 1,200 years, this fault segment has seen five titanic earthquakes powerful enough to rupture the earth's surface. The average time between them is 215 years. The last one was around 1680. This part of California is overdue for a major rearrangement. Because the zone of deformation extends miles on both sides of the fault, the next Big One could well happen in the mountains. It would be good news for Coachella Valley's crowded cities, but possibly devastating for the tunnel that bores through the mountains and carries Colorado River water to Los Angeles.

This range is made of a similar assemblage of crystallized rocks as its neighbors. The eastern half of the crest to Covington Flat is a broad swath of Mesozoic rocks grading from granite to granodiorite to quartz monzonite. The crest's western half, Lost Horse Mountain, and Ryan Mountain expose a complex suite of Proterozoic gneiss. These pretty metamorphosed sedimentary and volcanic rocks are among the most unusual in the region. They are often strongly migmatized, their metamorphic components mixed over short distances—often inches—with granitic intrusions to form complex structures as captivating as art. All these rocks have eroded into muted landforms, yet their composition and texture often vary greatly over short distances, sometimes mere steps. The White Tank Monzogranite exposed along the mountains' northern edge makes up for this generally subdued topography with a profusion of abrupt outcrops and elegant boulders.

Botany. Thanks to a broad range of elevations spanning over a mile, the Little San Bernardino Mountains rank high in botanical diversity. Their southern foothills, along Coachella Valley, support a low-desert creosote community and lush palm groves. The mid-elevations along their central axis, especially Juniper Flats, Lower Covington Flat, and Upper Covington Flat, are extensive high-desert woodlands of Joshua trees locally mixed with California juniper. The western crest is covered with emerald pelts of oaks and conifers unusually mature at this modest altitude. This complex mosaic of plant zones hosts a remarkable number of species, some rare and endangered. In recent decades, several major wildfires have scorched large areas to the ground, notably around Lower Covington Flat to the west, Quail Mountain and Lost Horse Mountain near the center, and north of Little Berdoo Peak to the east. Hiking through these areas, still largely barren after several decades, is unavoidably tainted with the sad realization that they are greatly impoverished and will continue to be on the scale of a human lifetime.

The Indio Hills have nine palm groves, including Thousand Palms Oasis, one of the state's largest. Like other oases in the region, they

California fan palms at Thousand Palms Oasis

have the same origin: movements along major fault lines, in this case the two main strands of the San Andreas that bracket the hills, opened deep cracks in the crust that allow subterranean water to rise to the surface. Exploring these rare tropical islands is one of the most unusual outdoor experiences in the desert.

Mining History. Considering its size, this range saw comparatively little mining, but it did have two important sites, both in its eastern section near Pleasant Valley. One was the Lost Horse Mine, the park's largest gold producer. Operated between 1894 and 1936, it returned an estimated $260,000, most of it in the first two and a half years. Its milling complex, including its restored ten-stamp mill, is one of the finest examples of a small ore-processing plant in the California desert.

The other site was Pinyon Spring, located just inside a canyon in the central part of the range, and the only source of water for miles. A well was sunk around 1890, and a two-stamp mill shortly after. The availability of water was so critical that the mining district was named after it. Created in 1892, the Pinyon Mining District encompassed a huge region covering the eastern part of the range, the Hexie Mountains, and the southern Wonderland of Rocks. Until the 1910s, the mill served a vital role by treating the ore of several mines in the district, including the Lost Horse and the Desert Queen. A few gold mines were active in the mountains above Pinyon Well, including the

Suggested Hikes in the Little San Bernardino Mountains					
Route/Destination	Dist. (mi)	Elev. gain	Mean elev.	Difficulty	Page
Short hikes (under 5 miles round trip)					
Black Rock Spring	1.6	430'	4,140'	Easy	295
Covington Flat (1)	4.2	450'	4,710'	Easy-mod.	281
Eureka Peak (from road)	0.15	60'	5,490'	Easy	299
Hansen Well	2.4	1,000'	4,070'	Easy-mod.	331
High View Point (1)	1.4	350'	4,270'	Easy	291
Inspiration Peak	1.0	830'	5,430'	Easy-mod.	317
Lost Horse Mine	2.1	700'	4,860'	Easy	325
Lost Horse Mountain	2.2	900'	4,880'	Easy	325
McCallum Grove	1.0	100'	600'	Easy	338
Pine Knot Deposit	0.75	430'	4,690'	Easy	286
Pinyon Well	0.8	270'	3,750'	Very easy	331
Pushawalla Palms	2.4	500'	440'	Easy	346
Ryan Mountain	1.4	1,070'	4,960'	Easy-mod.	321
Samuelson's Rock	2.3	500'	3,900'	Easy	303
Smith Water Cyn narrows	2.4	620'	4,420'	Easy	285
South Park Peak (1)	0.7	260'	4,240'	Easy	294
Thousand Palms Oasis (1)	0.35	10'	540'	Very easy	337
Willis Palms Loop (1)	4.2	540'	500'	Easy	341
Intermediate hikes (5–12 miles round trip)					
Eureka Peak	4.7	1,800'	4,480'	Moderate	299
Herman's Hike (1)	7.7	1,040'	660'	Moderate	344
Johnny Lang Canyon	5.6	1,020'	4,040'	Moderate	309
Lang Copper Mine	4.6	1,300'	4,010'	Moderate	311
Lost Horse Loop Trail (1)	7.3	1,320'	4,870'	Moderate	325
Moon Country Canyon	3.2	630'	790'	Easy	340
Mount Minerva Hoyt	4.3	2,520'	4,350'	Difficult	313
Pinyon Mine	3.3	1,510'	4,270'	Moderate	331
Pinyon Mountain	3.7	1,690'	4,360'	Moderate	331
Quail Mountain	5.5	3,490'	4,600'	Very diff.	313
Quail Springs Historic Trail	3.9	400'	3,820'	Easy	309
Samuelson's homestead	2.9	550'	3,870'	Easy	303
Wilhem Peak (1)	6.0	1,040'	670'	Easy-mod.	341

Key: (1) Loop; (2) HC or 4WD access road
Distance: one way for out-and-back hikes, round-trip for loops
Elev. gain: sum of all elevation gains on round-trips and on loops

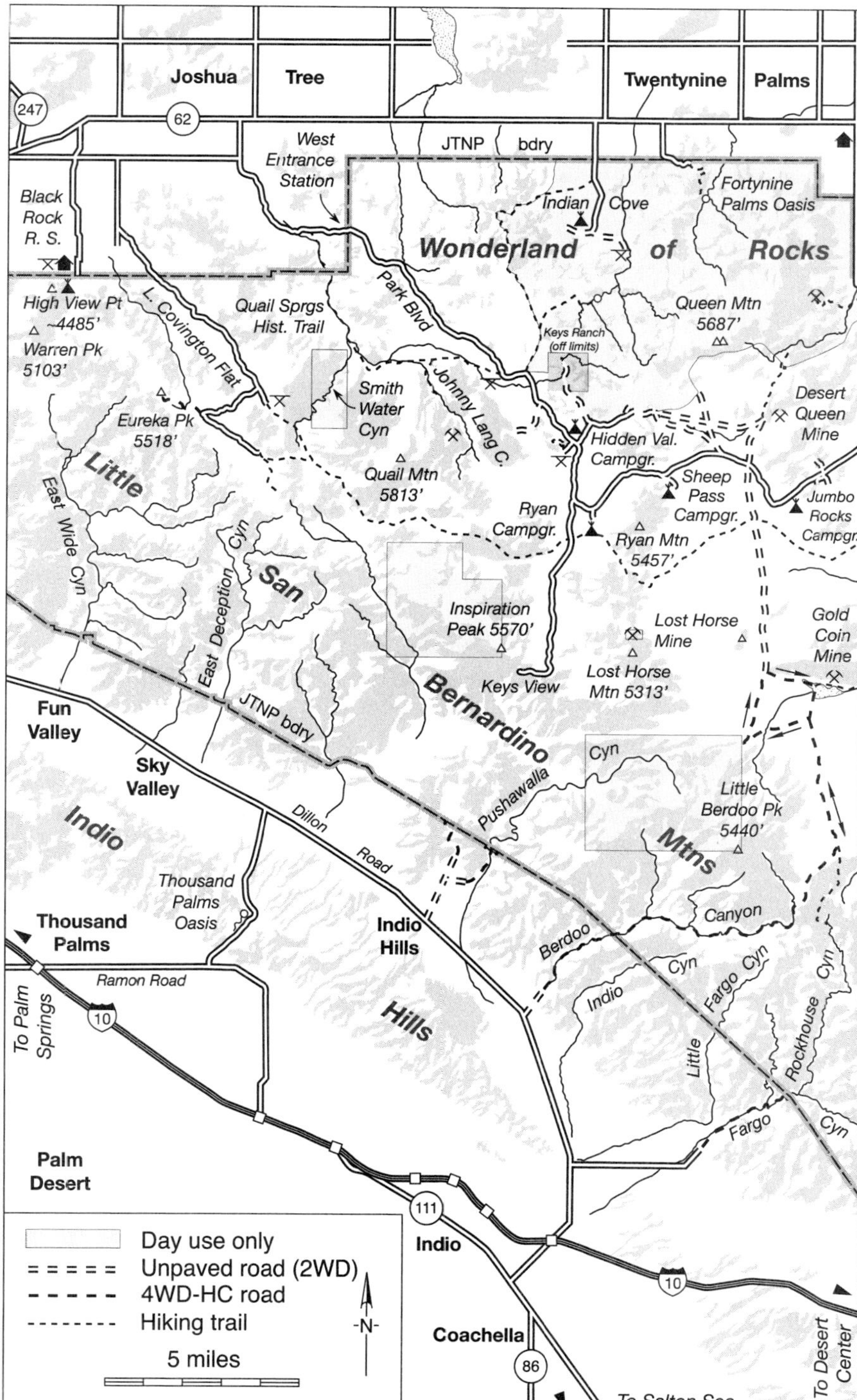
Joshua
Tree
Twentynine
Palms
247
62
West Entrance Station
JTNP bdry
Black Rock R. S.
Indian Cove
Fortynine Palms Oasis
Wonderland of Rocks
High View Pt ~4485'
Warren Pk 5103'
L. Covington Flat
Quail Sprgs Hist. Trail
Park Blvd
Queen Mtn 5687'
Keys Ranch (off limits)
Smith Water Cyn
Johnny Lang C.
Eureka Pk 5518'
Desert Queen Mine
Hidden Val. Campgr.
Little
Quail Mtn 5813'
Sheep Pass Campgr.
Jumbo Rocks Campgr.
East Wide Cyn
Ryan Campgr.
Ryan Mtn 5457'
San
East Deception Cyn
Inspiration Peak 5570'
Lost Horse Mine
Gold Coin Mine
Lost Horse Mtn 5313'
Keys View
JTNP bdry
Bernardino
Fun Valley
Sky Valley
Pushawalla Cyn
Little Berdoo Pk 5440'
Indio
Dillon Road
Mtns
Thousand Palms Oasis
Thousand Palms
Indio Hills
Berdoo Canyon
Indio Cyn
Little Fargo Cyn
Rockhouse Cyn
Ramon Road
To Palm Springs
10
Hills
Fargo Cyn
Palm Desert
111
Indio
10
Coachella
86
To Salton Sea
To Desert Center
Day use only
Unpaved road (2WD)
4WD-HC road
Hiking trail
N
5 miles

Suggested Hikes in the Little San Bernardino Mountains (Ctn'd)					
Route/Destination	Dist. (mi)	Elev. gain	Mean elev.	Difficulty	Page
Intermediate hikes (5–12 miles round trip)					
Smith Water Canyon					
to lower spring	3.1	880'	4,320'	Moderate	285
to Quail Springs	4.8	1,200'	4,110'	Moderate	285
Warren Peak	3.0	1,160'	4,380'	Easy-mod.	295
Warren View	2.7	950'	4,320'	Easy-mod.	295
Long hikes (over 12 miles round trip)					
Smith Water Canyon					
to Quail Spr. picnic area	8.2	1,440'	4,000'	Difficult	285
Key: (1) Loop; (2) HC or 4WD access road Distances: one way for out-and-back hikes, round-trip for loops Elev. gain: sum of all elevation gains on round-trips and on loops					

Pinyon Mine, one of the oldest in the park, although none produced very much. From 1918 until the late 1930s, the water from Pinyon Well was piped across Pleasant Valley to the mill at the rich Eldorado Mine.

Hiking. The size of the range translates into a generous number of particularly diverse hiking destinations. There are a total of 28 named canyons, scores of unnamed canyons, and more named peaks (42!) than any other range in California's share of the Mojave Desert. This unusual abundance gives a broad range of options for novices and seasoned desert rats alike, from short and easy trails to multiple-day treks. On the long southern slopes, many seldom-visited canyons offer memorable wilderness experiences. Choices run from the long trails in Thermal Canyon and Pushawalla Canyon to trailless places like Fan Canyon and Rockhouse Canyon. The central and eastern mountains are largely undeveloped and seldom visited. The west end has a network of popular trails that see dozens of hikers on weekends. The best times for peace and quiet are summer and weekdays in the colder months—temperature extremes are still an effective deterrent. In the summertime, being the highest in the park this range's forested crest is also the coolest—although still too hot for most visitors.

■

COVINGTON FLAT

Lower and Upper Covington Flats are narrow, parallel, fault-bounded valleys in the high Little San Bernardino Mountains. With the exception of springs, one would be hard pressed to find, in all of Joshua Tree, places that are more beautiful because they are so green. They are home to some of the park's thickest woodlands and largest conifers and Joshua trees. Partly destroyed by wildfires in the 1990s, Lower Covington Flat is also a prime outdoor laboratory to observe nature's healing process. This hike, mostly on trails, loops between the two flats and samples these two extreme ecosystems, one filled with exuberant vegetation, the other struggling to recover.

General Information

Road status: Hiking on trails and cross country; graded access road
Covington Flat loop: 4.2 mi, 450 ft up/easy-moderate
Main attractions: Lush high-desert vegetation, wildfire aftermath
USGS 7.5' topo map: Joshua Tree South
Maps: pp. 283*, *279*

Location and Access

Lower Covington Flat is the upper reaches of the long high-desert valley that starts at the western base of Quail Mountain and knifes southeast down across the Little San Bernardino Mountains into Yucca Valley. Upper Covington Flat, shorter and about 200 feet higher, parallels it to the south. To get to Upper Covington Flat, take Highway 62 to the signed La Contenta Road, 2.7 miles east of Highway 247. Turn south on La Contenta Road and go 1 mile to the crossing with Yucca Trail. La Contenta Road makes a slight jog to the right and continues south as a graded road. Drive it 1.8 miles to a Y junction, and take the Vermiculate Mine Road at 10 o'clock. After 1.7 miles, the road enters the park as the Lower Covington Flat Road, and continues 4.2 miles to a signed junction. The Lower Covington Flat Road (straight) ends in 0.55 mile at a picnic area. Make a right instead, go 1.8 miles to a T junction, and turn left on the Upper Covington Flat Road. The trailhead is at the end of this road, 1.9 miles further. This beautifully secluded ride foreshadows Upper Covington Flat's exceptional flora as it passes through unusually dense communities of Joshua trees, juniper, pine, and high-desert shrubs. These roads are graded, and except after heavy rains they are driveable with a standard-clearance vehicle.

Route Description

There are three highly contrasted segments on this loop hike. The first one follows a portion of the California Riding and Hiking Trail (CRHT) east over the low divide separating Upper Covington Flat and Lower Covington Flat. The second segment goes down Lower Covington Flat on a trail that connects to the picnic area at the end of the Lower Covington Flat Road. The final segment links back to the starting point up the roadless middle fork of Smith Water Canyon.

The CRHT starts with a bang. A tenth of a mile out, it passes by the largest known Joshua tree in the park, a stately giant with multiple trunks 3 feet across and a good 28 feet in height. When you stand under it and stare up at its crown, you see much more tree than sky. The trail wanders east through the open woodland of respectably large Joshua trees that spreads all around it. The vegetation is impressive not only for its size but also its diversity and obvious segregation. It is first dominated by California juniper, rabbitbrush, desert almond, ephedra, and silver cholla. Then as the trail climbs slowly to the hilly divide, meandering, rising and falling a few feet at a time, one species drops out to be replaced by another, and this assemblage changes rapidly. The Joshua trees thin out as oak, pine, and cliffrose move in. Desert almond are supplanted by manzanita, buckwheat, and big sagebrush. Near the divide, more cacti make an appearance—Mojave yucca, mound cactus, and grizzly bear cactus. Along the switchbacks down from the divide to Lower Covington Flat, nolina and beavertail cactus show up briefly, then vanish. By the time you reach Lower Covington Flat, the flora has undergone a thorough makeover.

After 1.65 miles the CRHT crosses the main wash that drains Lower Covington Flat, climbs out of it 100 yards onto the eastern bench, and forks. Take the trail on the left, which follows the open bench north-northeast toward the picnic area. All along this connecting trail, the landscape is drastically different. This is the edge of a large area that was burnt to the ground by lightning fires in the 1990s. Desert plant communities recover exceedingly slowly. A quarter of a century later, this area is still a manifestly diminished grassland sparsely populated by mostly small specimens of a limited selection of species. The steep hillsides to the east are even more bare. What is most visibly missing is the pinyon pine, the juniper, the Joshua trees, and the oak that gave the original plant cover its green fullness. For them to return and reach maturity, it will take several centuries. Interestingly, some species are doing very well, especially desert almond, Mojave yucca, and the uncommon yucca buckwheat, an odd plant that looks like the tail end of a witch's broom. Here and there,

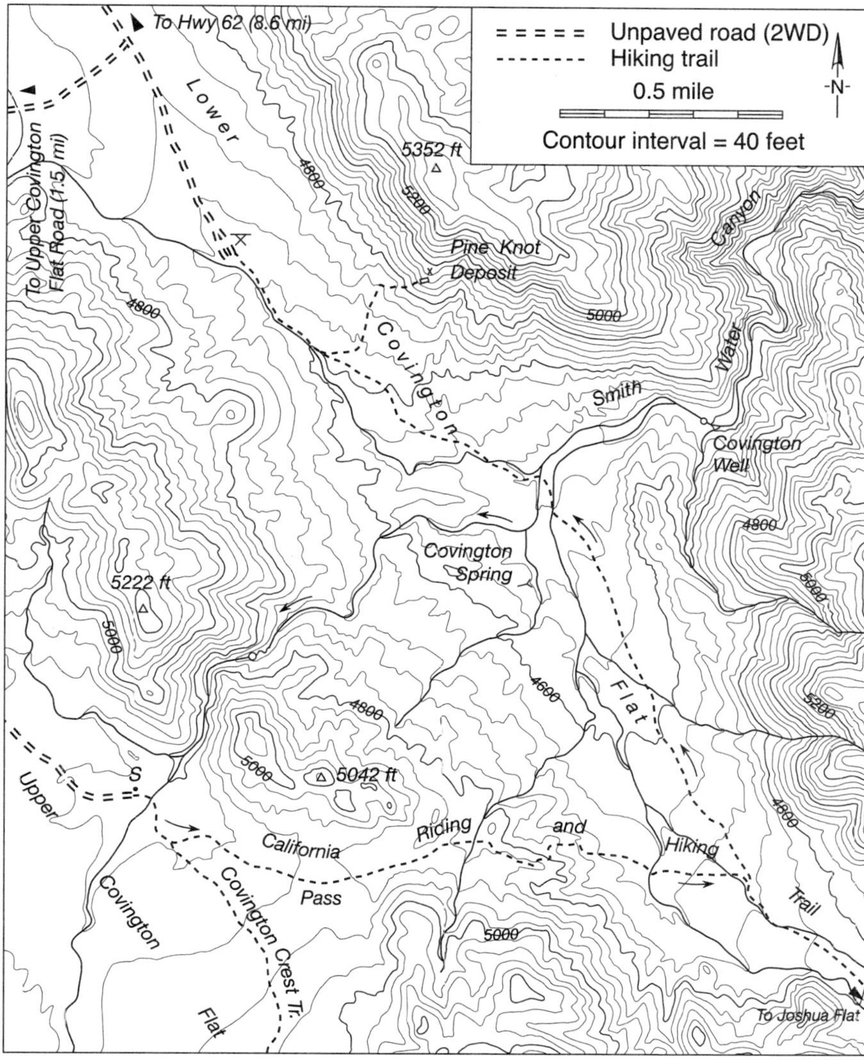

Covington Flat

	Dist.(mi)	Elev.(ft)
Upper Covington Flat Road	0.0	4,815
Pass into Lower Covington Flat	0.55	4,895
Junction with lower trail (left)	1.65	4,710
Smith Water Canyon wash (left)	2.7	4,480
Spring/boulders	3.7	4,710
Upper Covington Flat Road	4.2	4,815

The park's tallest known Joshua tree; a distinguished Antwerp physician for scale

the charred skeletons of the trees that perished long ago still stand. Taking an up-close look at this crippled ecosystem triggers conflicting emotions, a mix of sadness, curiosity, and hope.

About 1.0 mile past the trail junction, the trail reaches the main wash of Smith Water Canyon and crosses it. Where the trail enters the wash, hike up the wash to the canyon opening in the hills to the left (west). Gently sloped and mostly easy to walk, this shallow canyon winds tightly up through the ridge that divides the lower and upper flats. Most of the canyon bottom is a narrow ribbon of sand sunk between low banks sprinkled with small outcrops. Part way up there is a first set of boulders, then a spring marked by denser vegetation and small trees, and finally a bouldery passage between bulging rock walls. About 1.4 miles up canyon from the trail, the wash emerges on the edge of Upper Covington Flat and soon reaches the CRHT in sight of the trailhead. This is a perfect place to contrast the old with the new—along its entire length the wash courses the exact boundary of the burn, its north side largely barren, its south side fully clothed with pinyon pine, juniper, and Joshua trees.

■

SMITH WATER CANYON

In all of Joshua Tree, there might be no canyon like Smith Water Canyon. The reason is embedded in its very name: signs of water, past and present, are everywhere. Plentiful subsurface water irrigates open groves of desert willow, three lush springs, and rich botanical gardens. In the tortuous central gorge, departed rivers have carved enticing narrows through a striking cross-section of plutonic rocks. There is much more—historic ruins, a rock shelter, and abundant wildlife—but also, and mostly, plenty of solitude.

General Information

Road status: Mostly roadless; graded access road
Pine Knot Deposit: 0.75 mi, 370 ft up, 60 ft down one way / easy
Smith Water Cyn narrows: 2.4 mi, 30 ft up, 590 ft down one way / easy
Lower spring: 3.1 mi, 40 ft up, 840 ft down one way / moderate
Quail Springs: 4.8 mi, 170 ft up, 1,030 ft down one way / difficult
Main attractions: A rugged canyon with springs, narrows, and falls
USGS 7.5' topo map: Joshua Tree South
Maps: pp. 289*, *279*, 65*

Location and Access

Smith Water Canyon is a northeast-trending drainage on the northern slopes of the central Little San Bernardino Mountains, just west of Quail Mountain. Its upper half runs from Upper Covington Flat down across a low ridge to Lower Covington Flat. From there the more major lower canyon winds down through the mountains to Quail Wash. For most of its length, this lower portion has been designated a day-use area to ensure that its many springs are available to wildlife at night. It is a long canyon, so given this restriction, get an early start to see it all.

The starting point of this hike is the picnic area in Lower Covington Flat, where a trail connects to the midpoint between the lower and upper canyon. To get there, in Yucca Valley drive Highway 62 2.7 miles east of Highway 247 to the signed La Contenta Road and turn right (south). Drive 1 mile to the crossing with Yucca Trail. La Contenta Road makes a slight jog to the right and continues south as a graded road. Go 1.8 miles to a fork, and take the Vermiculate Mine Road at 10 o'clock. After 1.7 miles, the road enters the park as the Lower Covington Flat Road. Continue 4.2 miles to a signed junction, then straight 0.55 mile to the picnic area at the end of the road.

Route Description

This canyon is named after Oliver Smith, the first person to graze livestock in what became Joshua Tree National Park. He raised Texas longhorns in this area as early as 1870, using Quail Springs below the canyon, and likely the springs in the canyon, to water his stock. Years after he left in 1876, other locally famous ranchers followed his lead—Jim McHaney, C. O. Barker, and William Covington, whose name is immortalized on a nearby spring and well.

The Pine Knot Deposit. It is an easy walk from the picnic area to the canyon. The trail follows a narrow wash in a broad gradual valley that descends into Smith Water Canyon. It starts in the 1990s burns, a depleted cover of grasses, yucca, and desert almond, and reaches into a cheery old-growth woodland. Between these two extremes lies a rare transition zone where several dominant plants wiped out by the fires have already grown back, species like oak and juniper that normally take much longer to re-establish themselves, or never return.

Part way down this trail, up the steep hillside that borders it to the north, there is an unusual mine that attempted to exploit a black to green mica known as biotite. Mica has little commercial value, and the deposit was not of the highest quality. Yet the mine developer went through the trouble of erecting a long track to lower an ore car from the mine with a winch line. The road to the mine starts on the left side of the trail (at 11 o'clock), 0.3 mile in, where the wash below the trail makes an abrupt short jog to the right. You have to know that it is there to spot it, a barely discernible twin-track sneaking between the brush. It climbs gently east at first, then veers north and goes up a shallow ravine. In 0.25 mile and 120 feet up, the road ends. Angle due east and climb on a steep, faint trail 0.1 mile to the lower end of the track, just below the crest, an 80-foot ladder of weathered, parallel ties spared by the blaze. On the way up, two charred posts mark what may have been the track's lower terminus. Thin plates of mica are still exposed at the mine's half a dozen shallow holes above the track.

Smith Water Canyon. After returning down to the wash and continuing down the trail, in just under 1 mile the trail crosses the sandy wash of Smith Water Canyon. Leave it and head north down the canyon. From this point down to its mouth, a distance of 3 miles, the canyon cuts a meandering path in three sections of comparable lengths. The first one is a relatively sedate wash with occasional pockets of scattered boulders. The second section, more challenging and the most scenic, is the central gorge, a rugged narrow corridor with two

12-foot fall midway down Smith Water Canyon

thick springs separated by short narrows with falls, and a smaller third spring. The third section is a mirror image of the first one.

The signs of water start as soon as you head down the wash. The sand is peppered with full-grown desert willow, small trees that need subsurface water to survive. Well into summer they brighten the canyon with their graceful crowns covered with sultry lavender flowers. Further down, the wash is a sea of green baccharis, another water indicator. The rest of the canyon is a botanical haven where low-desert and high-desert species cohabit—thirsty and drought-resistant plants, stern cactuses and fluid riparian vegetation. Over very short distances grow saltbush and oaks, cliffrose and Mojave yucca, juniper and locally rare sacred sage, a stately shrub with broad star-shaped leaves. Drawn by the higher humidity, pinyon pine come right down to the wash's edges. This unusual profusion lends the canyon a surprisingly lush look, almost cheery in its walled fortress of stone.

And then there are the springs, the most surprising of all. The first one is a long wall-to-wall tangle of willows. Its spindly trees are packed so densely that even with the use trail that traverses it, it is hard not to get snagged. The narrows start at the bottom of this spring, a crooked passage punctuated with low falls and terminated by a Class-2 12-foot fall that takes a little care to descend. The middle spring, past a pronounced S-shaped meander, is a continuous ribbon of willow and old cottonwoods that completely fills the canyon floor, too thick to ford. The third spring, just a couple of bends past it, is a smaller plug of willows in a stretch of wash filled with boulders. These two springs are bypassed on the right side by uneven use trails.

On its descent to Quail Wash, Smith Water Canyon has dug a thousand feet into the mountains' granitic core. Fallen rocks the size of a dinner table are on display in the middle of the wash like prized specimens in a mineralogy museum. There are sparkling slabs of black mica-schist, angular chunks of contorted gneiss, and boulders freckled with pink feldspar crystals. Shattered cliffs of cleaved diorite rise above the wash, lone pines silhouetted on their rims.

The story of flowing water is written all over the rocks. At the start of the gorge, fluvial abrasion has polished a long sweep of gray slickrock crisscrossed with straight white veins of feldspar. In the main fall it has gouged an architectural cascade of caldrons several feet deep. The pressure of sand and running water has worn sharp cusps at the lips of falls, smooth domes on the tops of boulders, slick channels, and rhythmic waves on bedrock. It has buffed fallen trees into driftwood. After a heavy storm, the canyon comes alive for a few days with the alluring sound of water, which gathers in hollows, pools deep in the springs, and trickles down algae-covered falls. Wildlife make good use of these occasional wetlands, anything from deer to coyote, desert iguana, quails, turkey vultures, chipmunks, and bees.

Smith Water Canyon

	Dist.(mi)	Elev.(ft)
Covington Flat picnic area	0.0	4,660
Trail to mica mine	0.3	4,600
Pine Knot Deposit	(0.4)	~4,960
Smith Water Canyon wash	0.95	4,470
Upper spring	2.2	4,200
Narrows	2.3	4,150
12-foot fall	2.35	4,100
Middle spring	2.65	4,000
Lower spring	3.05	3,870
Mouth/Cutoff trail (right bank)	3.9	3,710
Quail Springs Historic Trail	4.35	3,655
Side trail to Quail Spr. (right)	4.55	3,689
Quail Springs	(0.25)	~3,750
Quail Springs picnic area	8.2	3,979

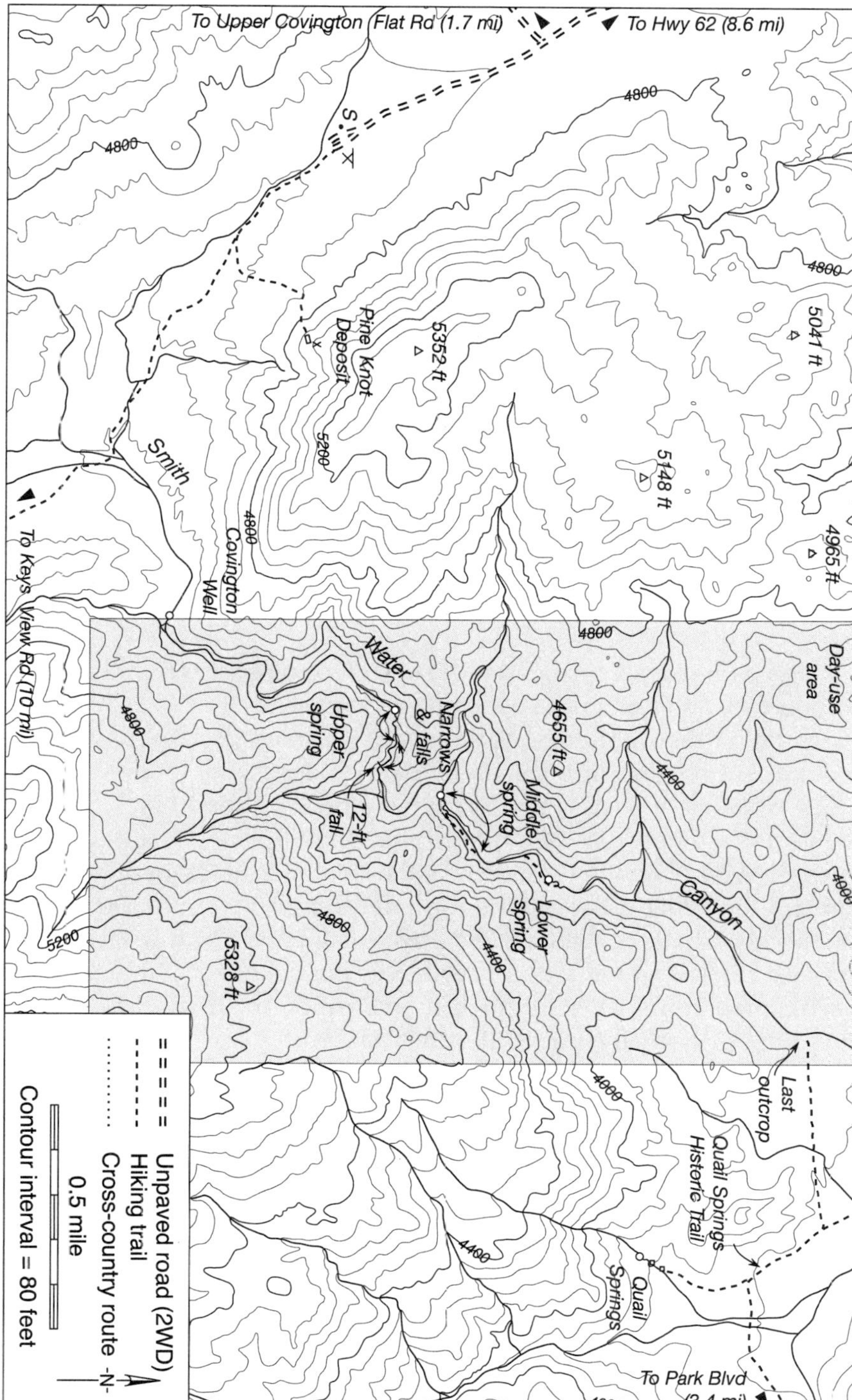
To Upper Covington Flat Rd (1.7 mi)
To Hwy 62 (8.6 mi)
4800
Pine Knot Deposit
5352 ft
5200
5041 ft
5148 ft
4965 ft
Smith
Covington Well
Water
Canyon
Narrows & falls
Upper spring
12-ft fall
4655 ft
Middle spring
Lower spring
Day-use area
4400
4000
5328 ft
5200
To Keys View Rd (10 mi)
Last outcrop
Quail Springs Historic Trail
Quail Springs
To Park Blvd (3.4 mi)
Unpaved road (2WD)
Hiking trail
Cross-country route
0.5 mile
Contour interval = 80 feet
N

Lower spring in Smith Water Canyon

Below the lower spring, the last stretch of canyon gradually sheds its boulders and becomes a widening river of sand. It ends at low twin outcrops on the right edge of the wash. This is a good place to turn around, but having come this far, it would be a shame to miss nearby Quail Springs. Just past the outcrops, a beat-up road takes off east across the canyon fan 0.45 mile to the Quail Springs Historic Trail. Turn right on it, and in 0.2 mile take the side trail on the right to Quail Springs (0.25 mile). The site has an interesting square cistern, with a smaller tank built in a corner and a watering trough at its base. In the springs' catclaw grove 200 feet further, water collected in a long compartmented trough, from which it was piped to the cistern. These structures of carefully mortared stones date back to the area's ranching days. A frequent user was John Samuelson, who drove from his nearby homestead (see *Samuelson's Rock*) to fill up on clear spring water.

From Quail Springs you can return to civilization along the historic trail, which cuts east to the Quail Springs picnic area along Park Boulevard. It is about a mile shorter and a third as much elevation gain as returning to Covington Flat. The cons are that the trail crosses a long and unsightly burn, and that you will need to arrange a shuttle. The best reason for returning the way you came is Smith Water Canyon: it is so beautiful that it is well worth seeing it twice.

■

HIGH VIEW POINT AND SOUTH PARK PEAK

These two adjacent hills in the quiet western section of the park are a tale of two orthogonal worlds. Both are reached by an easy loop trail, and both deliver panoramic views of San Gorgonio Mountain and the nicely forested Little San Bernardino Mountains. But one is surrounded by untouched wilderness, while the other is burnt and overlooks Morongo Basin's urban sprawl. Hiking them one after the other is a vivid reminder of the value of conservation.

General Information
Jurisdiction: NPS and Town of Yucca Valley
Road status: Trails to summits; graded access road
High View Point: 1.4 mi, 350 ft up loop/easy
South Park Peak: 0.7 mi, 260 ft up loop/easy
Main attractions: Trail climbs, botany, views of San Gorgonio Mountain
USGS 7.5' topo map: Yucca Valley South
Maps: pp. 293*, 279

Location and Access

To get to the common starting point of these two loop trails, in Yucca Valley take Highway 62 to Avalon Avenue, 1.7 miles east of Highway 247. Drive 0.95 mile south to Yucca Trail, where Avalon Avenue becomes Palomar Avenue. Continue south on Palomar Avenue 2.0 miles and turn left on Joshua Lane. At the T junction 0.9 mile further, turn right on San Marino Drive. This road soon veers 90° left and turns into Black Rock Canyon Road, then in 0.3 mile it divides. Drive the good graded road on the right, along the park boundary, 0.65 mile to the large dirt parking area at its end and park. High View Point is on the ridge to the south; the signed High View Nature Trail starts on the south side of the lot. Before heading out, stop at the ranger station to pick up an interpretive guide that provides information tied to the numbered markers along the trail. South Park Peak is at the top of the hill to the north, in the town of Yucca Valley.

Route Description

High View Point. From the parking area the trail heads southwest and splits almost right away. To follow the markers in increasing order, and to minimize views of the towns, go left and hike the loop clockwise. For a slightly more gradual ascent, and for a fuller enjoyment of the west-side canyon, go right (counterclockwise), the direction described here. Soon after, the trail crosses the signed West Side Loop, then circles across gentle terrain to the west side of the ridge. There it angles roughly southeast and follows a short open canyon. Near the end of the canyon, the trail climbs northeast to a saddle, and finally swings to below the summit to a vista point with a register. From there a spur climbs the last 50 yards to High View Point. To return, go back to the register, take the trail down the ridge line, then down the ridge's northern foothill, and back to the parking area.

This is a nice well-built trail, partly urban, partly wild. It has switchbacks and a dozen flights of natural-stone stairs to ease the climb, benches to take in the scenery and rest, and the numbered signs periodically confirm, if you are new at this, that you are not lost yet.

What is special about this loop is the vegetation. The hillsides are radiant with the lushness of trees, and the harsh desert light is tempered by a cheery continuum of plants. The trail traverses ever-changing botanical gardens that host many species, crowned by the exotic spikes of nolina and yuccas. The four largest plants—the Joshua trees, scrub oaks, juniper, and pinyon pine—most strongly shape the scenery. Their solid-green foliages lend the countryside a charm and serenity that the lower desert often lacks, and a visual appeal that makes up for the subdued landforms. Even over this minor elevation change—350 feet—the vegetation evolves conspicuously. Paperbag bush are much more numerous near the bottom, and nolinas near the top, where specimens are balanced on rough trunks over 7 feet tall. Joshua trees and juniper are more plentiful on the west side, and oaks and pine on the east side. One of the most scenic areas is the short west-side canyon, where clusters of Joshua trees loom over the trail. Rocky outcrops are few, but being composed of intriguing Pinto Gneiss, they engage us with jagged, eye-pleasing shapes coursed by wavy veins of sparkling black mica. Even at midday in three-digit heat, hare, cottontail, white-tailed antelope squirrels, and lizards often go at their daily business, under the watchful eyes of turkey vultures. In the spring and fall, it is not uncommon to spot a desert tortoise.

On an absolute scale, the low-angle views are no match to the grand vistas of greater summits, but to a novice they are enchanting. The southern horizon is a long canvas of wrinkled hills dark with conifers, while to the north the views of the urbanized valley are fortunately partly shielded by South Park Peak. The centerpiece is the San Bernardinos to the west. Their high point, San Gorgognio Mountain, at 11,499 feet southern California's titan, is 25 miles away, yet it is so monumental that it seems much closer.

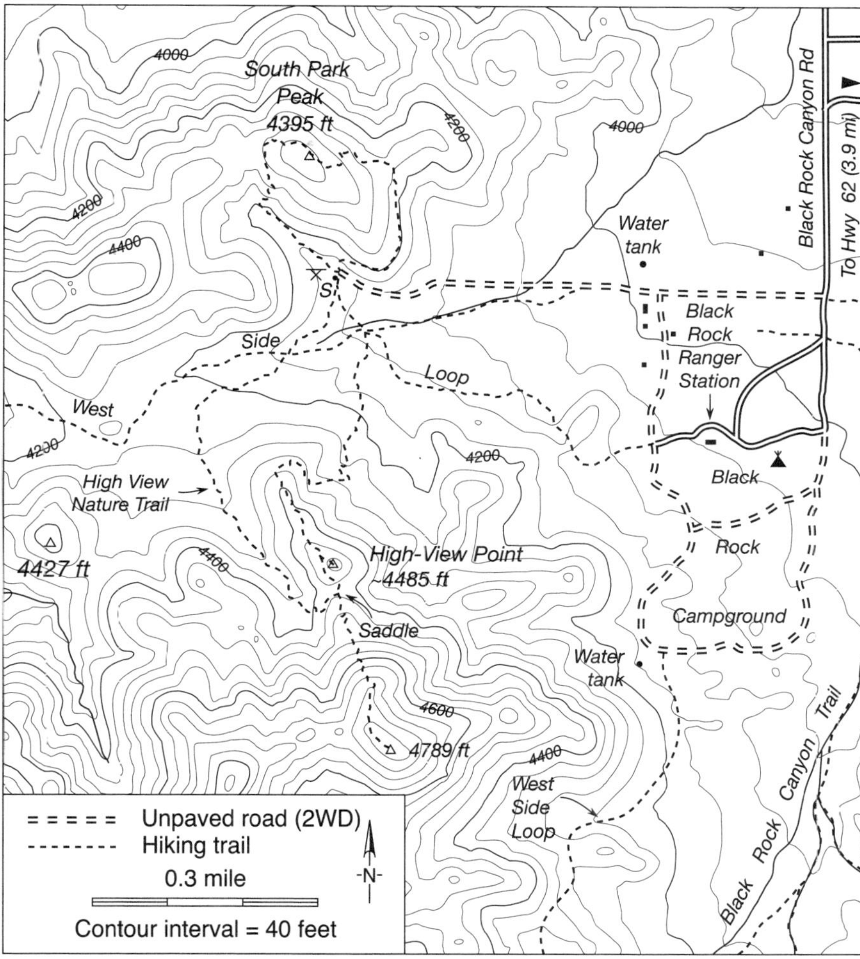

High View Nature Trail and South Park Peak		
	Dist.(mi)	Elev.(ft)
High View Nature Trail		
Trailhead	0.0	4,140
Trail jct at register via west fork	0.75	4,470
High View Point	(0.05)	~4,485
Trailhead via east fork	1.3	4,140
South Park Peak		
Trailhead	0.0	4,140
South Park Peak via east fork	0.4	4,395
Trailhead via west fork	0.7	4,140

Joshua trees along trail west of High View Point

South Park Peak. One would be hard pressed to find two neighboring trails that are so different. While the park's nature trail is surrounded by pristine lands, the trail to South Park Peak climbs through an area ravaged by fire that overlooks tentacular suburban sprawl. The trail starts on the north side of the parking lot, 50 feet west of the only large Joshua tree. Take the right fork, counterclockwise up the hill, for better views of the park on the way back down. For the first quarter of a mile the hillside is lush with California juniper. When the trail reaches the bench on the hill's northeastern shoulder, everything changes. The towns burst into view, and you enter the burn. The scraggly cover of grasses, Mojave yucca, and desert almond does not even begin to cover the barren ground. The rest of the way to the summit, the views embrace the towns of Yucca Valley and Joshua Tree. This vibrant human hive arranged in neat rectilinear streets in the middle of a desert may elicit admiration for the adaptability of humankind. More often, however, this stark dichotomy triggers among hikers praises for the National Park Service's long-standing success at holding back urban development. Without Minerva Hoyt's and Teddy Roosevelt's visionary creation of Joshua Tree National Monument nearly a century ago, the world would be a lesser place.

■

WARREN PEAK

This is an easy climb, along a popular trail that wanders up almost imperceptibly along a rock-free sandy wash to the crest of the Little San Bernardino Mountains. The scenery is a peaceful landscape of sharp hills generously forested with an incongruous medley of oak, pinyon pine, juniper, and Joshua trees. The views from the summit encompass the Morongo Basin and Bullion Mountains to the north, the towering San Jacinto Mountains to the south, and the long, finely sculpted flanks of the San Bernardino Mountains to the west.

General Information

Road status: Trails to summit; paved access road
Black Rock Spring: 1.6 mi, 410 ft up, 20 ft down one way / easy
Warren Peak: 3.0 mi, 1,140 ft up, 20 ft down one way / easy
Main attractions: Trail climb, botany, views of San Bernardino Mtns
USGS 7.5' topo map: Yucca Valley South
Maps: pp. 297*, *279*

Location and Access

Warren Peak is the highest of the named summits near the west end of the Little San Bernardino Mountains, about two miles southwest of the Black Rock Canyon Ranger Station. It was named in honor of Mark Warren, a settler who came to Morongo Basin around 1880 and dug a well there in 1881. His ranch grew to be a stop on the stage coach from Dale to Banning starting in 1898, then a social center for local ranchers, and it seeded the settlement that became Yucca Valley.

To get to the ranger station, in Yucca Valley take Highway 62 to Avalon Avenue, 1.7 miles east of Highway 247. Drive 0.95 mile south to Yucca Trail, where Avalon Avenue becomes Palomar Avenue. Continue south on Palomar Avenue 2.0 miles and turn left on Joshua Lane. At the T junction 0.9 mile further, turn right on San Marino Drive. Follow this road, which soon veers 90° left and turns into Black Rock Canyon Road, 0.35 mile to the backcountry board on the left side, 100 yards after the road divides. There is a one-lane parking area along the east side of the road. If it is full, park at the ranger station 0.2 mile further. The trail to the summit starts at the backcountry board. Alternatively, park at the ranger station and walk uphill through the campground. A foot trail at campsite #30 connects via a water tank through scenic hills to the Black Rock Canyon Trail (0.6 mile, see map).

Sunset over stormy Morongo Valley from Warren Peak

Route Description

At their slender west end the Little San Bernardino Mountains are about as little as they get, their crest a thin rim of hills pegged to a low horizon. South from the campground the desert is an irregular undulating valley that rises gently to the flank of the mountains. Warren Peak is the local highest summit, hidden from view by nearby hills. Like other parts of the high desert that have been spared the indignity of fire since prehistory, this area is surprisingly lush. The understory is an unruly sagebrush rebellion of plump blackbush, thorny ephedras, bushy rabbitbrush, frazzled yucca and cactus, and a smattering of squawbush. From it rises an eclectic mix of trees that seem to have been plucked from the state's four corners, canyon live oak, juniper, Joshua trees, and pinyon pine. Against the burnt hills to the south, shiny in their nakedness, the desert looks all dressed up.

The climb is about as easy as it gets. From the backcountry board, first take the unsigned California Riding and Hiking Trail 300 yards down, then up, to a fork. The trail on the right follows the wash of a minor drainage grandly named Black Rock Canyon, a swath of sand that lazily traces shallow creases in the terrain. Most of the walking is in this soft gradual wash churned daily by dozens of boots. Cold metal signs religiously signal the few trail junctions. In the summer the hills

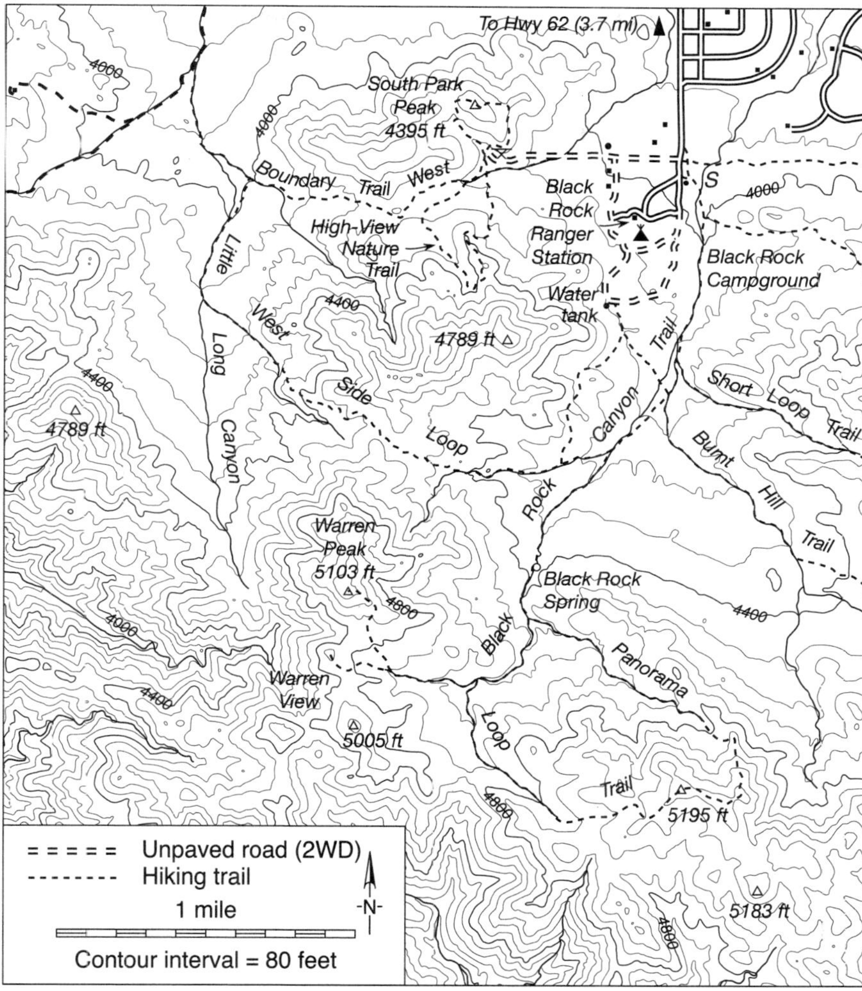

Warren Peak

	Dist.(mi)	Elev.(ft)
Black Rock Canyon Trail	0.0	3,980
Burnt Hill Trail	0.8	4,130
Black Rock Spring	1.6	4,365
Panorama Loop Tr. (north end)	1.8	4,435
Panorama Loop Tr. (south end)	2.15	4,560
Viewpoint Trail	2.45	~4,715
Warren View	(0.25)	4,890
Warren Peak	3.0	5,103

dissolved in shadeless torpor, and canteen water was hot enough to brew Darjeeling. Now, in late November, the pallid sun barely rose on its low arc and filled every wrinkle with crisp violet shadows. Water was a few degrees warmer than ice. Halfway to the crest, the wash enters the only part of Black Rock Canyon that passes for a canyon, a shallow defile between broken perpendicular outcrops. Black Rock Spring is tucked just inside the defile. On wet years it spawns a frail creek. After a few rainless seasons it shrivels to a hole of murky water at the base of a blocky wall, barely big enough for a coyote's thirst. Hairy hedges of dark-green baccharis frame the spring, betraying underground water even during protracted droughts. The curvy forested passage beyond it has beautiful exposures of intensely metamorphosed gneiss. Heat and pressure folded the ancient rock upon itself in black twirls embroidered with rose felspar and silvery mica.

Above the canyon the trail cuts up through more open hilly country. Up there the trail markers are still old-fashioned organic wooden posts, signed with the hand-painted initials of the trail—PL for Panorama Loop, WP for Warren Peak, WV for Warren View. They will likely not survive long, to be replaced by sturdier metal signs as romantic as steel. Only then, at the very end, just past the last junction to a fine viewpoint on the crest, does the grade steepen as the trail wiggles up the last half a mile along the peak's rock-strewn western spine.

At the crest the thin rim reveals with unexpected suddenness what it had been hiding all along. To the west the land rolls off nearly one vertical mile into the bowels of Coachella Valley, only to scream up the corrugated wall of the San Jacinto Mountains on the opposite side. As we approached the crest the dispersed clouds coalesced and shut off the sun, compromising the views. Brilliance turned instantly into gloom. A hardening chill seeped into every surface, magnified by the slightest air current. Way down below, Palm Springs' untidy suburban sprawl was lost in perpetual haze. But just as we reached the summit everything changed. Somewhere over San Jacinto Peak the sun broke through holes in the stormy clouds and beamed across the valley long spokes of light solidified by veils of smog. It was, ironically, a most dramatic sunset, the sunbeams spotlighting a fairyland of furrowed hills out of the penumbra below us. The popular summit was deserted, drained of humans early that day by the call of turkey dinner. My wife and I sat on the cramped summit on our own for a long time, huddled against a rock spur and each other for warmth, mesmerized by a scene so surreal and color-saturated that it could have been computer generated. The desert had once again managed to surprise us.

■

EUREKA PEAK

> *Eureka Peak tests our laziness. It can be climbed with little effort by driving a long primitive road to very near the summit, or by taking a moderate but long hike using any number of combinations of a dozen hiking trails. The road and the trails cross particularly scenic valleys in the vicinity of Covington Flat, an area resplendent in its profuse high-desert vegetation. The summit encompasses expansive views of upper Coachella Valley and several 10,000-foot summits.*

General Information
Road status: Trails to summit; paved or primitive access road (2WD)
Eureka Peak via road: 0.15 mi, 60 ft up one way / very easy
Eureka Peak via trail: 4.7 mi, 1,670 ft up, 130 ft down one way / moder.
Main attractions: Green desert hills, views of Coachella Valley area
USGS 7.5' topo maps: Yucca Valley South, Joshua Tree South
Maps: pp. 301*, 279

Location and Access

To climb Eureka Peak the easy way, work your way to La Contenta Road, a signed city street that crosses Highway 62 2.7 miles east of Highway 247, at the east end of Yucca Valley. Drive La Contenta Road 1 mile south to its crossing with Alta Loma Drive. Continue south (from this crossing La Contenta Road is graded) 1.8 miles to a fork. Turn left onto the Vermiculate Mine Road, which leads in 1.7 miles to the entrance sign into Joshua Tree National Park. For the next 4.2 miles the road follows Lower Covington Flat to a junction. Turn right, and climb over some low hills 1.8 miles to a T junction in Upper Covington Flat. Turn right again. The road ends in 1.3 miles, in sight of Eureka Peak to the north. This road is hard-packed dirt, and in dry weather it is drivable with a standard-clearance vehicle. A very short trail (0.15 mile, 60 feet of elevation gain) connects the end of the road to the peak.

To climb Eureka Peak on one of the trails from the Black Rock Canyon Ranger Station, follow the directions to the backcountry board near the ranger station (see *Warren Peak*).

Route Description

The mountain leading up to Eureka Peak does not have the hard edge of desert mountains or the flourish of Joshua Tree's signature landscapes. No outrageous castles of boulders, no defying ridges inclined at gravity-busting tilts. The countryside is a more gentle topography of narrow valleys and canyons confined between low billowy ridges. Mostly untouched by fire in recent decades, it is flush with oak, juniper, bitterbrush, desert almond, and pinyon pine linked in a puzzle of jade, moss, bottle green, and emerald. Joshua trees are ubiquitous, their lime-colored rosettes saturated with sunlight. It is a striking place, crisp and intimate, so bursting with potential that it instantly ignites our craving for beauty.

This exceptional landscape did not go unnoticed—between Black Rock Canyon and the summit, the mountain is crisscrossed with some 25 miles of foot and hoof trails. Four main trails converge toward Eureka Peak, generally following canyon bottoms, and five shorter trails hop over ridges to interconnect them. One could climb this summit a dozen times and never take the exact same route. Most junctions are duly signed; even a GPS addict on withdrawal should not go missing.

The most direct route, and the backbone to which the other main trails eventually hook up, is the Eureka Peak Trail. From the trailhead at the backcountry board it is reached by following the California Riding and Hiking Trail (CRHT) 300 yards south to the Black Rock Canyon Trail on the right. Stay on the CRHT (left) 1.15 miles, over scenic hilly terrain, to the Fault Trail branching off on the right. The Fault Trail cuts south 0.45 mile across the side of a low hill to the Eureka Peak Trail. The latter follows the sandy wash of a canyon and the remaining 2.9 miles to the summit. The canyon changes character several times. It starts as a twisted passage, goes through a straight corridor between steep facing hillsides, twists some more, then opens up before finally worming up a steepening ravine to the crest just below Eureka Peak. This is the shortest route, and it is the most scenic. The landscape is enchanting, in a spiny sort of way, generously dotted with large shrubs and trees. The proximity of the hills traps the canyon wash in a seclusion that breeds a deep sense of closeness. The Bigfoot Trail is a close second best when it comes to windiness. So is the Canyon View Trail. More open and occasionally up on higher ground, it offers low-angle perspectives of the surrounding desert country.

When all is said and done, the choice of trail is secondary. The trails are all delightful primitive tracks, sandy and unruly, often wandering off around intervening trees, adapting to rather than altering nature. Each trail gives us contentment in an economy of motion that reveals the value of details. I found myself stopping often to check out the tiny lobes of a bitterbrush, the silky veins on a slab of gneiss, the mistletoe on a juniper, or the ossified remains of a hapless cholla. Like

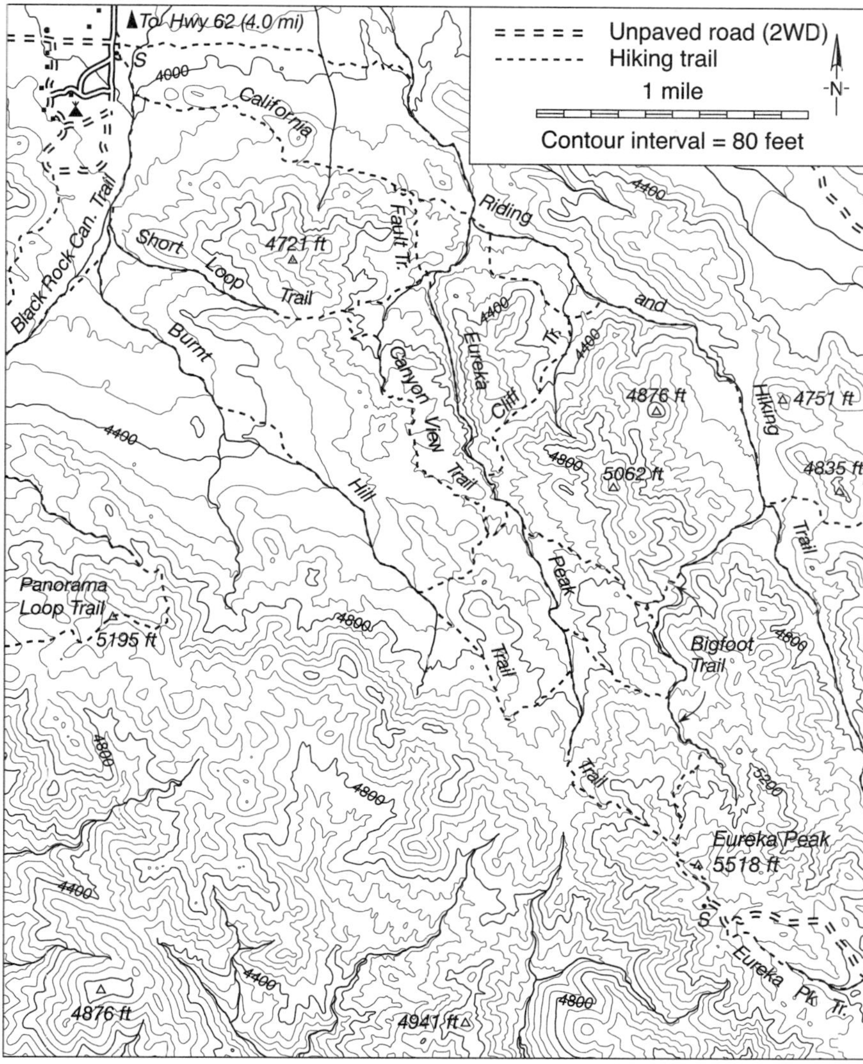

Eureka Peak	Dist.(mi)	Elev.(ft)
Backcountry board	0.0	3,980
Fault Trail (right)	1.35	4,150
Eureka Peak Trail (left)	1.8	4,200
Canyon View Trail junction	2.9	4,500
Burnt Hill Trail junction	3.5	4,720
Eureka Peak	4.7	5,518

Coachella Valley and San Jacinto Mountains from Eureka Peak

people-watching, the Joshua trees are an endless source of amusement—they are all there, the infants shaped like fuzzy bottlebrushes, the gawky teenagers, the ascetic marathon runners, the alpha males on steroids, and the saggy elders struggling to stay upright. Many trees with impressively thick crowns loom tall above the trails.

All approaches, be it the road or any of the trails, are entrenched below hilltops and offer limited distant views until the very last moment, when you crest the final ridge and Coachella Valley bursts open way down below. It is a sight to remember—the chiseled foothills freckled with oak and juniper rolling down into the valley, the spacious valley sloping gently to the distant shores of the Salton Sea, and the two-mile-high San Jacinto Mountains leaping out of the valley floor. The western horizon is closed off by the stately San Bernardino Mountains, their long ridge of ten-thousand-foot peaks crowned by the silvery dome of San Gorgonio Mountain. Another quarter of a turn and you are staring out at the sprawling Bullion Mountains and the bright Mojave Desert. The sudden encounter with this sumptuous panorama is Eureka Peak's greatest gift.

■

SAMUELSON'S ROCK

In a secluded valley of sand and Joshua trees framed by the Wonderland of Rocks' spiky skyline, there is a small island of boulders that was the heart of a lonesome homestead run by Swedish emigrant John Samuelson and his wife Margaret in the late 1920s. Bitter, scornful, and mentally unstable, John chiseled on the rocks passionate messages that reflect his social views on politics, nature, and religion, and encapsulate the dispirited climate of the Great Depression era. The scenic trail hike to this historic site and the search for the ruins of the Samuelsons' homestead are a moving excursion into the past of a troubled misfit with a strange life story, who worked hard as a miner, and died a murderer.

General Information

Road status: Trail hike; paved access road
Samuelson's inscriptions: 2.3 mi, 110 ft up, 390 ft down one way/easy
Samuelson's homestead: 2.9 mi, 160 ft up, 390 ft down one way/easy
Main attractions: Historic messages in stone, history, Joshua trees
USGS 7.5' topo map: Indian Cove
Maps: pp. 307

Location and Access

Samuelson's Rock is in the crooked nameless valley, sometimes referred to as Quail Valley, drained by Quail Wash along the northern base of the central Little San Bernardino Mountains. From the park's west entrance station, drive 2.3 miles to a paved parking lane on the right, just about where the road tops the park's western plateau, and park. Coming from inside the park, this is 6.4 miles from the Hidden Valley turnoff. Samuelson's Rock is approximately 2 miles due south.

History: Samuelson's Bizarre Love Story with Princess Kk-Kk

Perhaps even more than his curious writings in stone, it is John Samuelson's tumultuous life story that is most intriguing. After working as a miner near Salt Lake City in the 1910s and in the oil field in Compton, California in the 1920s, he and his wife Margaret moved to the Queen Valley area in 1926. In these difficult post-war years, many people relocated to the country to escape the hardships of city life. In February 1928, during a chance encounter with American pulp writer Erle Stanley Gartner near Quail Springs, Samuelson recounted his strange personal reason for moving to the desert. It was rooted in an event so fantastic that after hearing it, Gardner published it in the fantasy magazine *Argosy* as a short novel titled *Rain Magic*. As Gartner wrote decades later, he took some liberties with Samuelson's bizarre tale, but he was faithful to its highlights, convinced after some research "that his story was, at least, founded on fact."

When he was a young man, Samuelson was enrolled by force on a merchant vessel. During a violent storm off the coast of Ghana, he escaped on a raft in shark-infested waters and landed ashore barely alive, only to be captured by a cannibal tribe. Princess Kk-Kk, daughter of the king, bought him as a slave to save him from a much worse fate. His job was to help her feed a colony of 2-inch carnivorous ants guarding a quartz vein filled with gold. Samuelson and Kk-Kk fell in love, which pit him against a hairy knuckle-dragger, half monkey and half human, who also had his eyes on the princess. In retaliation for stealing gold to beat his rival and buy his beloved from the king, the lovers were given a drug that erased their memories. He woke up in a colonial outpost, unable to remember his name. After returning to civilization, every time it rained the smell of wet vegetation made him black out for days. Doctors diagnosed auto-hypnosis, and short of a cure suggested moving to a dry climate. This is the reason Samuelson came to the desert—to get away from the sleeping curse. After an infrequent desert rain, the jungle smells came back and he still fell into a long slumber. But every time he woke up, his memories of Africa returned a little more, and with them his longing for his lost love.

When he arrived in Queen Valley Samuelson met local tycoon Bill Keys, who hired him as a ranch hand and a helper at his Hidden Gold Mine. A year later, the Samuelsons started a homestead near Quail Springs. It is then that John Samuelson, enraged at the country's politics and other *bêtes noires*, set out to inscribe his prophetic words on the boulders above their home. Although he was denied title to his homestead because he was not a US citizen, the couple continued to live in the area through the 1930s. He worked mainly at the Hidden Gold, which he ultimately acquired from Keys, packing his ore by mules up to a point on the crest that would be known, years later, as Keys View.

In 1942, the couple was back in Compton, where he worked as a night watchman, and their lives took a tragic turn. Tempestuous John got into a bar brawl and shot a man dead. He was spared from the death penalty by pleading not guilty on grounds of insanity. In April 1943, at age 69, he was committed to the Mendocino State Hospital.

After three years of good conduct, on July 1946 Samuelson got tired of confinement and flew the coop. No one knows what happened

One of the seven boulders on which John Samuelson inscribed his "verities"

to him afterwards. Some say he ended up in a logging camp in Washington and died in 1954 from complications following a logging accident. Other evidence suggests that he was caught in 1955 and transferred to another state hospital. Either way, Samuelson never returned to the desert nor saw again what he referred to as his "eternal verities of existence." Today he might be pleased to hear that anyone on the planet can, almost instantly, access his old-fashioned tweets.

Route Description

Lucky are the few who get to discover Samuelson's heartfelt messages in their original setting, with sand in their shoes, sun in their eyes, and sweat on their back. The trails make finding the site easy, although the excess of signs along the first part take away the seclusion and wildness. From the trailhead walk down Creosote Trail, through colorful botanical gardens in a gap of bouldery hills. After 0.65 mile this trail ends at the Bighorn Trail. Turn left and follow this trail south about 1.5 miles down into Quail Valley, along a shallow wash, then a second, broader wash, to Samuelson's Rock. In the valley the biodiversity shrinks to a luminous prairie of golden grasses and catclaw packed with Joshua trees. The spiky trees are gathered in an ever-changing parade, one every few steps, all misshapen, each one fiercely different. Up ahead, the Little San Bernardino Mountains rise 2,000 feet across the near horizon, dotted with conifers.

Samuelson's Rock is a 50-foot hill of boulders standing alone on the valley's edge. Concealed by the trees and the slight curvature of the land, his Rock of Faith and Truth remains largely hidden until the last few hundred yards. Yet when you reach it, it instantly commands your full attention, a tall upright slab shouting to the world in crisp block letters this enigmatic message:

> THE ROCK OF FAIHT AND TRUHT
> NATURE IS GOD
> THE KEY TO LIFE IS CONTACT
> EVOLUTION IS THE MOTHER AND FATHER OF MANKIND
> WITHOUT THEM WE BE NOTHING
> JOHN SAMUELSON
> 1927

Read in the silence of the desert, out of the way, these words from a distant time carry the power of a scroll. You want to know what they mean, where are the other inscriptions, what they say—and this nondescript hill suddenly becomes priceless.

Samuelson wrote eight proclamations on seven boulders, all but one scattered near the hilltop. To minimize impact on this historic site, use existing paths, and do not touch the stones. From the Rock of Faith and Truth walk around the left side of the hill 25 yards to an overgrown grade that climbs to the summit. Although Samuelson was embarrassed by his poor English, he took pride in his writings and eagerly showed them to his rare visitors. Most of them are arcane, and to decipher them it helps to know a little about the era's political figures, and that he was a fervent populist. The "Mr Mellon" he addresses in one of his rantings was Secretary of the Treasury. As a wealthy

Samuelson's Rock

	Dist.(mi)	Elev.(ft)
Creosote Trail at Park Blvd	0.0	4,030
Jct with Bigfoot Trail (go left)	0.65	4,020
The Rock of Faith and Truth	2.1	3,730
Samuelson's Rock summit	2.5	3,782
Corral	2.25	~3,727
Samuelson's Homestead	2.8	3,765
Well	2.9	3,768

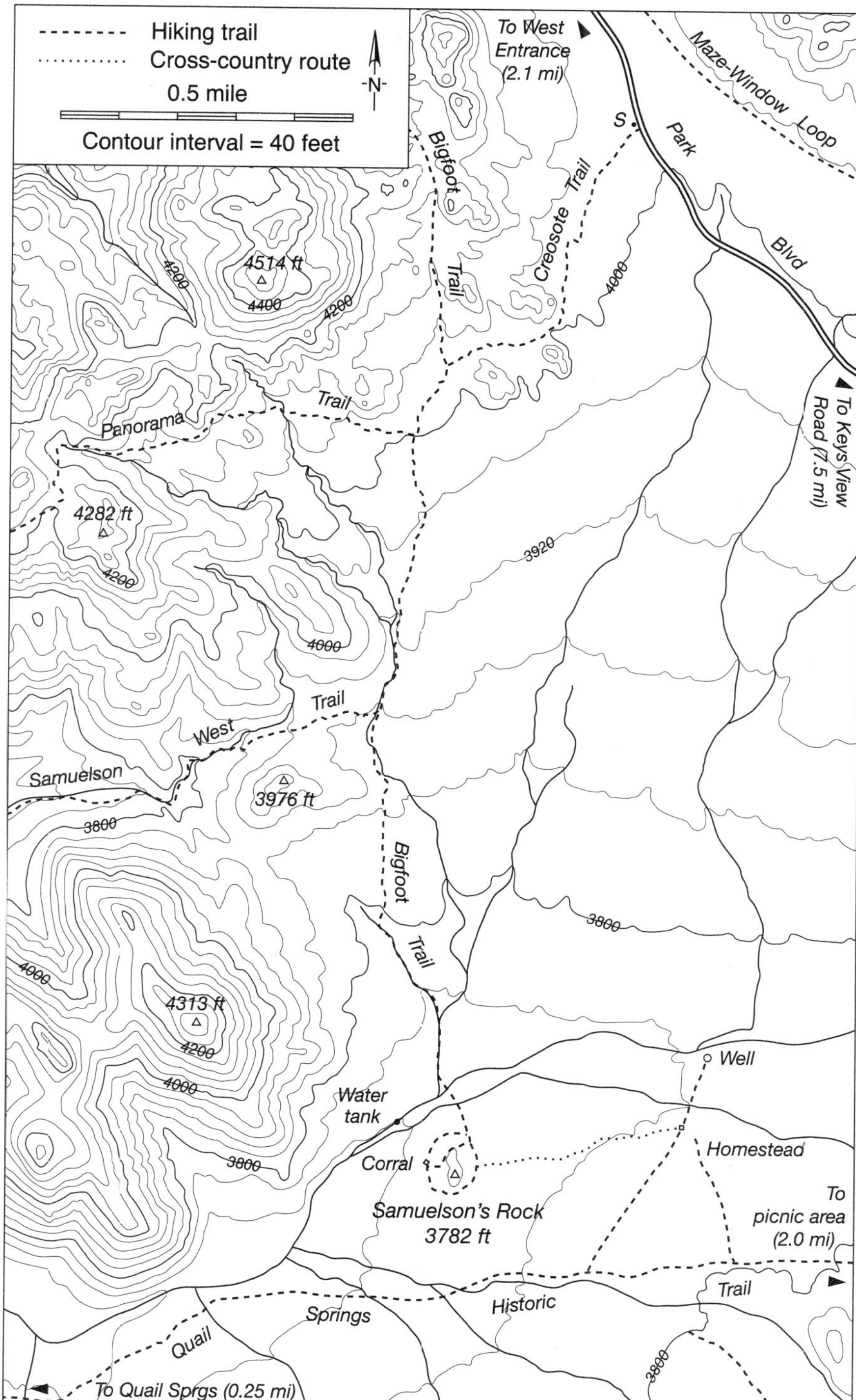
Hiking trail
Cross-country route
0.5 mile
N
Contour interval = 40 feet
To West Entrance (2.1 mi)
Maze-Window Loop
S
Park Blvd
Bigfoot Trail
Creosote Trail
4514 ft
4400
4200
4000
Panorama Trail
4282 ft
4200
3920
To Keys View Road (7.5 mi)
4000
West Trail
Samuelson
3976 ft
3800
Bigfoot Trail
3800
4000
4313 ft
4200
4000
Well
Water tank
Homestead
Corral
3800
Samuelson's Rock 3782 ft
To picnic area (2.0 mi)
Trail
Historic
Springs
Quail
3800
To Quail Sprgs (0.25 mi)

Corral at John and Margaret Samuelson's 1920s homestead

industrialist, Andrew Mellon had reformed federal tax laws to offer large tax cuts to the rich and boost the economy, a policy that prompted Samuelson to call for rebellion. On the other hand Samuelson praised Judge Ben Lindsen for his liberal views on abortion, birth control, suffrage for women, and economic justice. The aphorism in which he addresses Herbert Hoover is less clear. Samuelson may have been touched by Hoover's humanitarianism during World War One, or infuriated by his economic policies as president.

There are other poignant remains of the Samuelsons' passage a century ago—a barbed-wire fence, a galvanized water tank, and a scenic corral at the base of the hill. A metal bed parades at the summit, in full view of Quail Mountain. If you walk due east 0.3 mile from the eastern base of the hill you will run into the trace of a road. About 150 yards north-northeast up this road are the ruins of what may have been the Samuelsons' cabin, which burned down in the 1930s. Next to well-designed stone foundations, a staircase descends into a cellar, a clever addition to take shelter from the winter and summer extremes. There is a curious outdoor fireplace nearby, the carcass of a 1920s truck, and the rusted casing of a well. This site, far more isolated in the 1920s than it is today, might have inspired Samuelson to extoll in his chiseled messages the importance of living close to nature.

■

JOHNNY LANG CANYON

This canyon was named after an outcast who was banished for stealing gold and lived here around 1900 while mining a small bismuth deposit. When the Memorial Fire roared through this area in 1999, it spared the canyon's upper half, now an island of high-desert forest surrounded by devastated hills. In spite of the long approach trail to the canyon mouth across a valley still very thinly vegetated, this is a good place to visit. The wash in the lower canyon has witnessed significant recovery, the mine in the mid-canyon is fun to look for, the gneiss exposures are as contorted as anywhere, and the seldom-visited upper canyon is lush with oaks and conifers.

General Information

Road status: Roadless, hiking partly on trails; paved access road
Lang Copper Mine: 4.6 mi, 1,050 ft up, 250 ft down one way / moderate
Johnny Lang Cyn (head): 5.6 mi, 740 ft up, 280 ft down one way / moder.
Main attractions: A forested canyon, a historic bismuth mine
USGS 7.5' topo map: Indian Cove
Maps: pp. 315*, *279*

Location and Access

Johnny Lang Canyon drains the east flank of Quail Mountain, in the central Little San Bernardino Mountains. It can be reached via one of two trails. Both trails start at the Quail Springs picnic area, which is off Park Boulevard 5.8 miles from the west entrance station, on the right. Coming from the other direction, it is 2.9 miles from the Hidden Valley turnoff. The Quail Springs Historic Trail starts at the west end of the parking loop and heads roughly west to the canyon mouth. The Ryan Johnny Connector Trail (see *Quail Mountain*) starts a few steps to the left of it, and cuts southwest across low hills to the mid canyon.

Route Description

The access trails. On its way to Johnny Lang Canyon, a distance of 1.85 miles, the Quail Springs Historic Trail crosses the barren plain of scrawny shrubs and bleached fallen Joshua trees left behind by the 1999 Memorial Fire. The main attraction is just before the canyon mouth, a scenic hillside coated with spheroidal boulders. The Johnny Lang Canyon Trail branches off to the left just past it, and cuts southwest over a low bank to the wide entrance into Johnny Lang Canyon.

Granite domes, midsection of Johnny Lang Canyon

The lower canyon. Johnny Lang was a miner who co-owned and worked at the Lost Horse Mine in the 1890s. After he was caught high-grading ore from his partners (see *Lost Horse Loop Trail*), Lang moved to a derelict cabin in this canyon, and filed claims to the Lang Copper Mine in the mid canyon around 1900. In subsequent years, he developed this small magnetite deposit, and reportedly produced 20 tons of bismuth in 1904. Oddly enough, historic records disagree as to whether the ore came from Lang's Mine or from the Lost Horse Mine. To deepen the mystery, neither mine shows traces of bismuth...

Johnny Lang Canyon begins as a broad valley framed by low hills. The Johnny Lang Canyon Trail weaves through it, starting as the twin-track that once serviced the Lang Copper Mine. Combined with the negligible incline, it makes for quick progress. Most of the larger shrubs and full-grown trees that once flushed the lower canyon with pleasing greens have been killed by the fire. But unlike in the valley below, smaller plants are steadily returning, stimulated by greater runoffs in the wash. In the spring, grasses and annuals coat the canyon floor with a green five o'clock shadow. Beavertail and calico cactus scream for attention with arresting bright-red blossoms. Daisy-like white tidy-tips grow like weeds. The few burnt Joshua trees that are still standing now provide shade and nutrients to new shoots.

The Lang Copper Mine. A little less than a mile in, the scenery changes radically. The transition occurs at a small spring in the wash, dry but announced loudly most of the year by two bright-green cottonwoods. On a hot day, their leaves vibrating in the breeze will fool your mind with the illusion of rain. A few rocks by the trail just south of the spring mark the site of the Lang Cabin and an assay office. By then the hills have grown taller and moved in. The more protected wash is lined with thickets of saltbush and desert almond, ephedra and rabbitbrush, nolinas and Mojave yucca. Oaks and California juniper make an appearance higher up, then pinyon pine. Less common species find refuge here—rock pea, live forever, and sacred sage. The taller hills up canyon are capped by bright monzonite boulders and clipped bedrock. The gneiss exposures along the trail are wild, coursed by fine wavering veins, crossed by dikes, sparkling with golden mica.

Past the camp, the road turns into a single track. It avoids the rocky wash by staying mostly on its west side, occasionally splitting into two trails, one on each side. The road used to start its mile-long climb to the mine half a mile past the spring, at an elevation of 4,070 feet. This turnoff is now gone. Before reaching its former location, the trail crosses a low hump with a small granitic outcrop between it and the wash to the left, then descends 200 yards to the wash. It then follows a left bend in the wash 70 yards, and leaves the wash on the west side. At this point a shallow ravine comes in from the south, and a second one 100 yards further. Strike south up on the low swell between

Johnny Lang Canyon		
	Dist.(mi)	Elev.(ft)
Quail Springs picnic area	0.0	3,979
Johnny Lang Canyon Trail (jct)	1.85	3,812
Spring/Lang Cabin	3.15	3,960
Leave wash toward mine	3.65	4,070
Join mining road	(0.15)	~4,155
Lang Copper Mine	(0.9)	4,780
Ryan Johnny Connector Trail	4.0	4,160
Quail Springs picnic area	(2.1)	3,979
Fork	4.9	4,360
Lost Horse Valley Overlook	5.6	4,440

them, and after 250 yards drop left into the second ravine. The road is then visible across the wash, climbing southeast up a hillside. It ascends 160 feet to a ridge, and angles right up this ridge to a 4,549-foot point. The mine tailings become visible in this vicinity, up the hillside to the southeast. The road then veers left and descends to a wash, crosses it, and finishes the ascent as a single track.

Not much of Lang's operation is left today—a 200-foot crosscut adit, a short tunnel above it, and a 100-foot shaft at the end of the trail. Lang did not make a mint on bismuth. He made a scant living, occasionally bagging a vagrant cow to put meat on his plate, and selling to Bill Keys himself over the years nearly $18,000 of the gold he had pilfered. After 1926 he lived off and on in the old bunkhouse at the Lost Horse Mine. On January 25, 1926, at the age of 72, he set off to town for supplies, but never made it back. About two months later Bill Keys and some friends found his desiccated body, still wrapped in his bedroll. A carved tombstone marks the spot where he was found and buried, ironically right by the road to the Lost Horse Mine.

The upper canyon. Over the next few wiggles in the canyon, the trail bypasses rocky stretches of wash, first on the right side, then on the left. Beyond, there is no more trail. The slopes become much more rocky and capped by tall granitic domes. This rugged terrain also effectively blocked the wildfire; from there onward the narrow wash winds through high-desert country brightened by conifers and old-growth vegetation. A few occlusions, short falls, and a generous allotment of small boulders add a little challenge to what would otherwise be an easy walk. The lower canyon sees little visitation, the upper canyon even less. This is a fun walk, in perfect solitude, beneath steep slopes peppered with naked angular blocks. After 1.3 miles, the wash splits. The west fork cuts 0.6 miles through rocky hills, then reaches the burn and proceeds another twisted mile to its head on a barren ridge. The shorter east fork is much more scenic. Untouched by the blaze, it wanders through a long passage rimmed with bright boulder piles, before emerging on a broad upland overlooking Lost Horse Valley.

The Ryan Johnny Connector Trail is a good alternative return route, more forested than the lower canyon, and 2 miles shorter. To locate it, return to the main fork in the canyon, then go 0.9 mile to the side canyon on the right at an elevation of 4,160 feet. This is 50 yards past where the trail climbs onto the west bank, and where the canyon direction changes to the west-northwest (left). Refer to *Quail Mountain* for details on this route, which requires good orienteering skills.

■

QUAIL MOUNTAIN

At 5,813 feet, Quail Mountain is the highest point in Joshua Tree National Park. By Mojave Desert standards it is not very high, and it stands only 2,000 feet above its surroundings. But the classic route to it is fairly long and circuitous, across a small valley, through a winding open canyon, and finally up the mountain's tortuous eastern shoulder. The payoffs are interesting geology, scattered woodlands, a small historic mine, and far-reaching views from the summit. Quail Mountain's neighbor Mount Minerva Hoyt is a good alternative, being a little closer yet offering similar views.

General Information

Road status: Climbing on trail and cross-country; paved access road
Mt Minerva Hoyt: 4.2 mi, 1,970 ft up, 550 ft down one way / difficult
Quail Mountain: 5.5 mi, 2,660 ft up, 830 ft down one way / difficult
Main attractions: Outstanding views, mining history, geology, botany
USGS 7.5' topo map: Indian Cove
Maps: pp. 315*, *279*

Location and Access

Quail Mountain is the high point of an 11-mile northwest-trending ridge on the western flank of the Little San Bernardino Mountains. Mount Minerva Hoyt, a subsidiary summit on the same route, is about one air mile northeast of Quail Mountain. Start from the Quail Springs picnic area (see *Johnny Lang Canyon* for directions). From the parking loop, Quail Mountain is the bulky dome to the southwest, and Mount Minerva Hoyt the pointed summit in front of it.

Route Description

Much of Quail Mountain was ravaged by the Memorial Fire in May 1999. The largest historic wildfire in the park, it burned for four days, consumed 14,000 acres, and stripped the vegetation off many miles of mountain front. All routes to Quail Mountain cross terrain that is still greatly impaired. The route suggested here is the shortest, and it maximizes the time spent in areas that the fire did not touch.

First you will have to get to the Lang Copper Mine. The route described under *Johnny Lang Canyon* will get you there, but the Ryan Johnny Connector Trail is a better alternative. It is shorter by 1.1 miles with only 280 feet of extra elevation change, and it is more scenic. The trail starts at the west end of the picnic area, about 15 steps to the left of the signed Quail Springs Historic Trail. It first cuts southwest across the western edge of Lost Horse Valley. After 0.45 mile, leave the trail and go west (right) 0.1 mile to a wide wash. Cross it and look for an old twin track 0.15 mile to the west, climbing between two boulder piles. In 0.4 mile it circles up around a hill and down into a canyon wash. Past this point, there are only short segments of trail. Turn left down the wash and go 90 yards to a fork. Turn right, and right again at the next fork in 0.15 mile. Continue south, up this fork to a pass, then down a ravine that soon curves west-southwest and joins Johnny Lang Canyon. Make sure to take the book map with you, although there are several variances to this route. Going directly up the short canyon that the twin track bypasses is a shorter approach with fun boulder jams.

Once in the canyon, go up the wash 50 yards to a trail on the west (right) bank, and follow it down canyon 0.4 mile until it runs into the wash again. In this vicinity, leave the wash to the south to climb to the Lang Copper Mine (refer to *Johnny Lang Canyon* for details).

From the mine, climb south toward the false summit (5,041 feet), and skirt it on its west side. From there a plump ridge curves gracefully as it descends southwest to a saddle, then ascends steeply northwest to Mount Minerva Hoyt. This peak was named recently in honor of a determined lady from South Pasadena who developed a passion for the desert in the 1910s and was instrumental in convincing President Franklin D. Roosevelt to create Joshua Tree National Monument.

Navigation on the rest of the ascent, about 1.3 miles and 700 feet up, is easier, with Quail Mountain a constant beacon. Mount Minerva Hoyt's broad southwestern shoulder drops down in slow waves to a

Quail Mountain		
	Dist.(mi)	Elev.(ft)
Quail Springs picnic area	0.0	3,979
Pass into Johnny Lang Canyon	1.6	4,290
Johnny Lang Canyon wash	2.1	4,160
Leave wash toward mine	2.5	4,070
Join mining road	2.65	~4,155
Lang Copper Mine (shaft)	3.4	4,780
Bypassing 5,041-ft summit	3.5	~5,000
Mount Minerva Hoyt	4.2	5,405
Low point on ridge	4.75	5,190
Quail Mountain	5.5	5,813

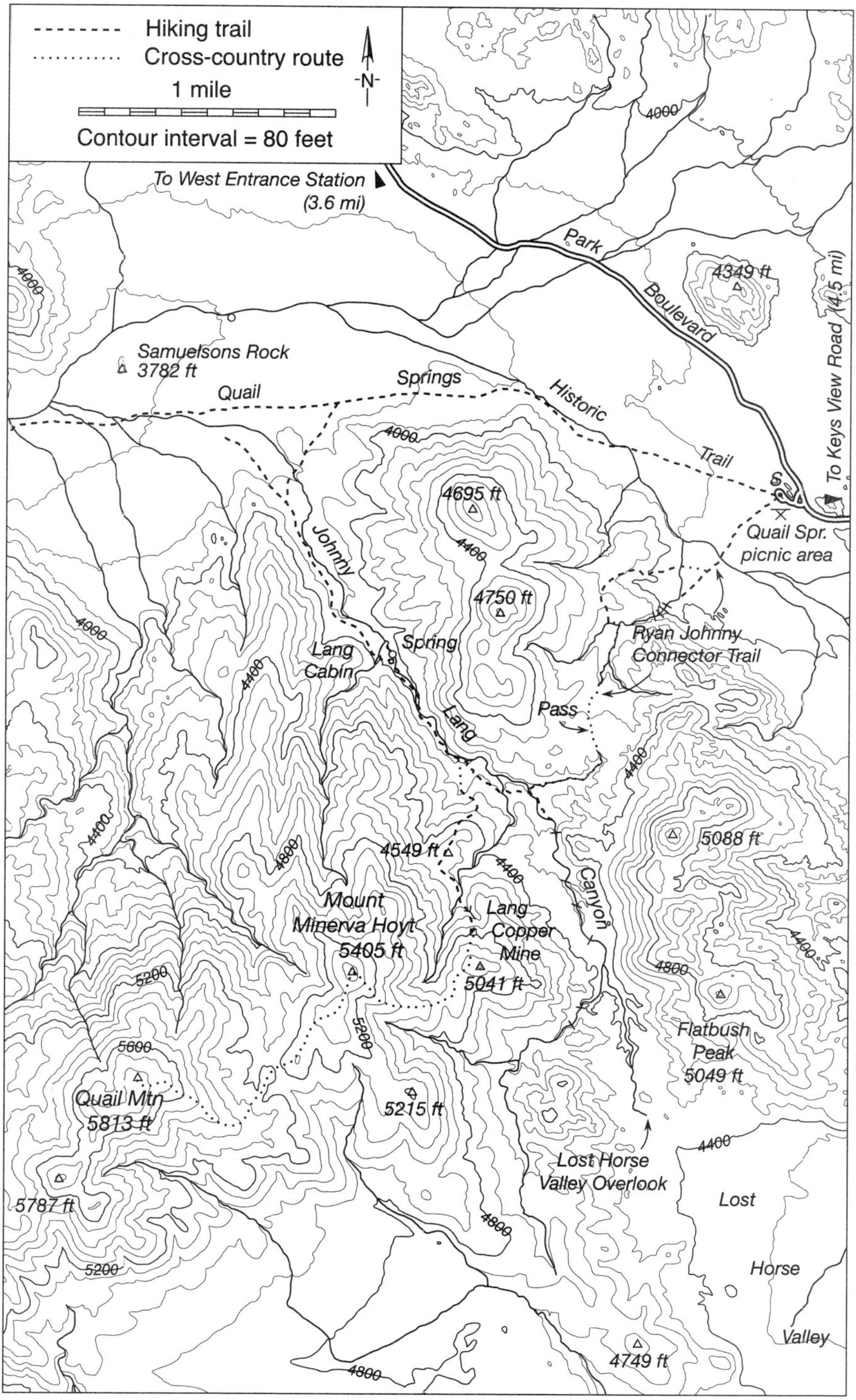
Hiking trail
Cross-country route
1 mile
N
Contour interval = 80 feet
To West Entrance Station
(3.6 mi)
Park
Boulevard
To Keys View Road (4.5 mi)
4349 ft
4000
Samuelsons Rock
3782 ft
Quail
Springs
Historic
Trail
Quail Spr.
picnic area
4695 ft
4750 ft
4400
Johnny
Lang
Cabin
Spring
Lang
Ryan Johnny
Connector Trail
Pass
Canyon
5088 ft
4549 ft
4800
Mount
Minerva Hoyt
5405 ft
Lang
Copper
Mine
5041 ft
5200
5600
Quail Mtn
5813 ft
5215 ft
Flatbush
Peak
5049 ft
Lost Horse
Valley Overlook
5787 ft
Lost
Horse
Valley
4749 ft

Mount Minerva Hoyt from below mouth of Johnny Lang Canyon

pass at the head of two facing drainages. Spared by the blaze, this area has kept its original woodland and offers the only good tree shade since the mine area. The final stretch is up Quail Mountain's southeastern shoulder, steep only briefly near its upper end. This is a long route, but the ridges are open and rocky outcrops are few and easy to avoid.

The two summits are very different. Quail Mountain is a spacious and exposed plateau, too degraded by fire to hold but a smattering of bleached, wind-combed shrubs and aberrantly green ephedra. Mount Minerva Hoyt is a high nipple encrusted with angular fragments of beautifully lustrous, dark-gray igneous schists. They share similar views, luminous and breathtaking. To the west the land is a rough sea of rounded ridges, crossed in the distance by the daunting sails of San Gorgonio Mountain and San Jacinto Peak. To the east Quail Mountain bounces down languidly to a fragmented landscape of interconnected valleys and isolated stands of peaks. The Wonderland of Rocks takes center stage, boiling out of the Earth in a 10-mile strip of fantastic hoodoos. After a rainstorm has wiped the air clean, this is a sumptuous theater, filled with the random performance of clouds and light.

■

INSPIRATION PEAK

This is a delightful short climb, up and down a steep primitive trail that closely follows the abrupt rim of the Little San Bernardino Mountains. It offers remarkable views of the mountains' rumpled southern scarp, of all of Coachella Valley from the Salton Sea to Palm Springs, and of the San Jacinto Mountains soaring like a wall out of the valley floor. With its intact pocket of vegetation spared by the wildfire that ravaged the area, the summit is a refreshing island of clean air and greenery.

General Information

Road status: Climbing mostly on use trail; paved access road
Inspiration Peak: 1.0 mi, 620 ft up, 210 ft down one way / easy–moder.
Main attractions: Gorgeous views of the southern Joshua Tree region
USGS 7.5' topo map: Keys View
Maps: pp. 319*, *279*

Location and Access

Inspiration Peak is approximately in the middle of the Little San Bernardino Mountains, near the popular observation point at Keys View. To get to Keys View, from Highway 62 in the business district of the town of Joshua Tree take Park Boulevard 5.1 miles south, then east, to the park's west entrance station. In the park, drive generally southeast 10.5 miles to Keys View Road and turn right (south). This scenic byway crosses Lost Horse Valley and one of the park's thickest and most impressive forests of Joshua trees, many of them taller than 15 feet. It ends at Keys View after 5.5 miles. Inspiration Peak is less than 1 air mile up the ridge to the northwest, hidden by a false summit. The faint trail to it starts on the north side of the parking area, near two adjacent curbside boulders.

Route Description

The views are awesome the whole way. From start to finish the sharp-edged ridge leading up to Inspiration Peak overlooks the expansive southern slopes of the Little San Bernardino Mountains, a dissected scarp that drops 5,000 feet into the sprawling lowlands of Coachella Valley. The unbroken chain of the Santa Rosa and San Jacinto mountains loom in the distance, draped with snow in winter. There is a little trail most of the way to the top, fortunately not much of one, and not

Joshua tree and pinyon pine along crest to Inspiration Peak

yet spoiled by signs or cairns. It winds its way, often straight up the rock-strewn slope, occasionally looping around a couple of loose switchbacks, gaining 325 feet to a first false summit. It then drops to a saddle overlooking Lost Horse Valley and its army of pointed inselbergs to the north.

A wildfire raged through this area in recent years. The barren ground is still littered with blackened wood debris and Joshua tree bark. Many plants have started to grow back, especially yucca and ephedra. One of the annuals that has recovered most quickly is chia, a handsome herb with erect leafless stems that bear pale-blue flowers arranged on spiky spheres. Long after the flowers have withered the spheres continue to decorate the dried plant. The Cahuilla were fond of chia seeds, which they harvested with a seed beater and prepared into a drink or a cake. They periodically applied prescribed burns to stimulate the growth of the plant. The proliferation of chia on these burnt slopes shows that they knew what they were doing.

Past the saddle the ridge climbs again to a second false summit (5,558′) crowned by an interesting outcrop of gnarled and layered gneiss. A little further the ridge is capped by a mound of close-packed monzogranite boulders deformed by erosion. For the shortest route,

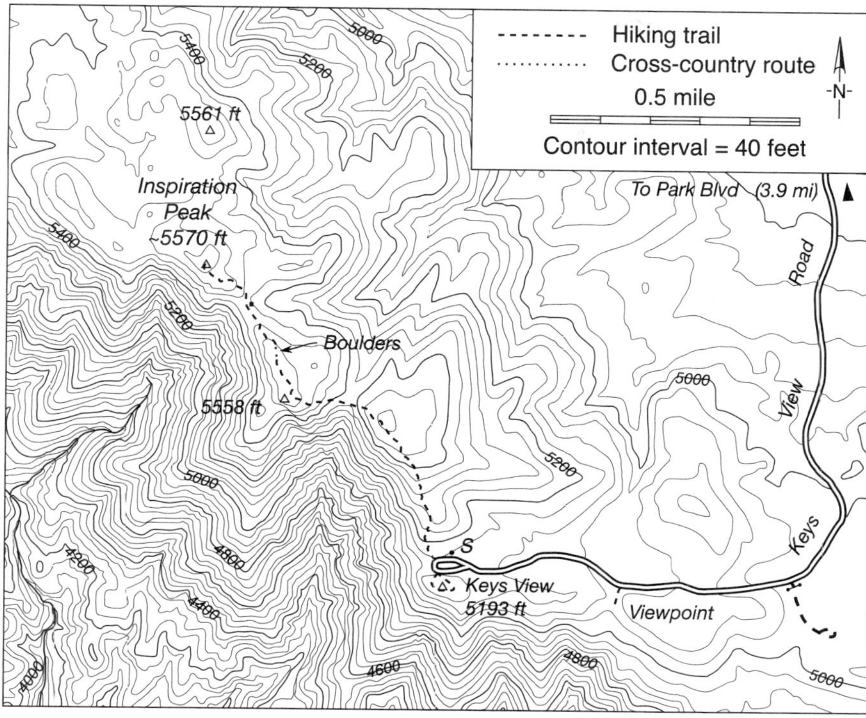

Inspiration Peak		
	Dist.(mi)	Elev.(ft)
Keys View	0.0	5,160
False summit	0.35	~5,485
5,558T point	0.65	5,558
Boulders area	0.7	~5,550
Inspiration Peak	1.0	~5,570

clamber over and between the boulders. Large scrub oak live among them, spared from the blaze by their shield of boulders. The trail resumes just beyond, drops into a second saddle, then ascends one last pitch to Inspiration Peak.

The summit area is a scenic billowing plateau sprinkled with boulders and high-desert vegetation. Spiny plants like Mojave yucca, nolina, Joshua trees, silver cholla, and scattered cactuses grow intermixed with softer species like oak and juniper. Isolated pinyon pine stand on the rim of the mountain like lone sentinels guarding the high desert from the encroaching cities below. All around lies dry hot desert, but

Nolina near Inspiration Peak

up here everything is suddenly greener, cooler, and more fragrant, a secret world stolen from the desert.

The panorama from the summit is spectacular. It is not vastly different from Keys View, but it will be all yours, and the serenity won't be disturbed by cars beeping every minute. To the south the mountain falls in long wrinkled waves to the distant floor of Coachella Valley. On a clear day, usually after a rainstorm has scrubbed the atmosphere, one can clearly see the main agent responsible for this great upthrust of land—the San Andreas Fault, marked by the long sliver of Indio Hills at the base of the mountains. The views then extend from the Salton Sea and the Santa Rosa Mountains to the southeast, to Palm Springs and 11,499-foot San Gorgonio Mountain to the west. Much like Death Valley and Owens Valley, Coachella Valley is a place of staggering proportions, a huge tectonic sink much deeper than most, surrounded by mountains much taller than most. Its low point, the Salton Sea, lies some 288 ft below sea level, while San Jacinto Peak soars 10,804 ft above sea level. From base to summit San Jacinto's elevation differential is about 10,000 feet in 9 air miles, one of the steepest mountain fronts this tall in the conterminal United States.

Inspiration Peak was named decades ago, when Coachella Valley was still relatively unspoiled. Things have changed. When climbing down in the evening, the lights of the cities piercing through the smog reveal the disturbing extent of the suburban sprawl down in the valley, now home to several hundred thousand people. The inspiration that once came from marveling at so much wilderness is now tempered by sorrow over what we have lost. The bittersweet mixture of emotions reinforces our appreciation for the dedicated organizations that have been toiling to preserve what has not yet been paved over.

■

RYAN MOUNTAIN

This popular summit is a great perch to admire Lost Horse Valley and its outlandish piles of boulders—Joshua Tree's most distinctive signature. It is reached on a gradual trail with artful stairways built of beautiful local gneiss. The route offers close-up views of several imposing outcrops of polished monzogranite, especially Saddle Rocks, a superb cluster of towering sugarloaves. The desert flora is equally striking, green desert gardens that combine Joshua trees and juniper, yucca and nolina, and cactus of all sizes and shapes.

General Information

Road status: Trail to summit; paved access road
Ryan Mountain: 1.4 mi, 1,070 ft up, 0 ft down one way / easy–moderate
Main attractions: Striking formations, views of Wonderland of Rocks
USGS 7.5' topo maps: Indian Cove, Keys View*
Maps: pp. 323*, 279

Location and Access

Ryan Mountain is at the center of the park's popular western section, between Lost Horse Valley to the west and Queen Valley to the east. In the business section of the town of Joshua Tree on Highway 62, take Park Boulevard, which is well signed from either direction. Drive it south, then east, 5.1 miles to the park's west entrance station. In the park, drive generally southeast 10.5 miles to the junction with Keys View Road. Continue straight on Park Boulevard 2 miles to the signed parking area for the Ryan Mountain Trail on the right, and park. The trailhead is near the east end of the parking area. Ryan Mountain rises directly to the south.

Route Description

This is a Joshua Tree classic climb, true to the National Park Service's dedication to developing well-built trails to particularly scenic areas. The path to Ryan Mountain is indeed perfectly groomed, hard dirt where the terrain is nearly level, and elegant staircases of granitic slabs where the slope exceeds a few percent, which is often. It makes for unusually easy walking, and greater ease to observe the surroundings. It also draws a cohort of hikers and joggers year round, so expect company.

Saddle Rocks (left) and Ryan Mountain (right of center) from Park Boulevard (photo courtesy of Cathy Cho)

The trail starts with a bang. It squeezes by a group of stunning formations, monumental humps of jointed White Tank Monzogranite polished into fantastic shapes. The westernmost outcrop is the site of Indian Cave, a series of natural chambers among boulders that local bands of Native Americans—Cahuilla, Serrano, and Chemehuevi—used as seasonal shelters. Past these outcrops the trail ascends the open western flank of Ryan Mountain at a leisurely angle. The steep slope above and below it are covered with gardens of low juniper, blackbush, ephedra, young Joshua trees, and Mojave yucca, some of them boasting plump trunks the size of small trees. Dehydrated calico cactus, flaming-red cottontop cactus, and blue-green beavertail cactus grow between the rock litters, as do full-grown pancake prickly-pear. This luxuriant community is all the more valuable since several nearby areas have been decimated by wildfires.

Because of the views it commands, this portion of the route is the most scenic. Lost Horse Valley sprawls below, pinpricked with an impressive density of Joshua trees right up to the Wonderland of Rocks to the north. The scenery's most exceptional element is Saddle Rocks, the stately outcrop of sculpted monzogranite that bulges out of the

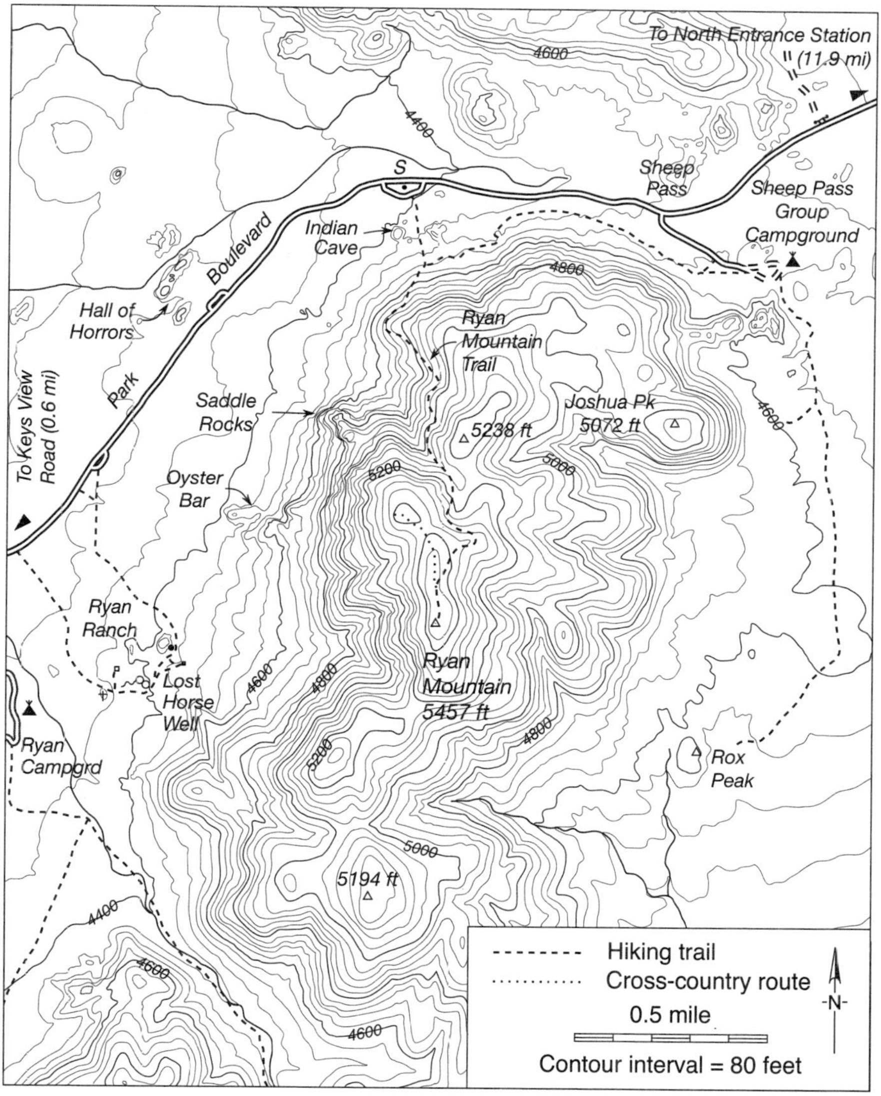

Ryan Mountain	Dist.(mi)	Elev.(ft)
Park Boulevard	0.0	4,390
Trail junction	0.2	4,520
Sheep Pass Group Campgr.	(1.0)	4,530
Saddle on ridge	0.9	5,150
Ryan Mountain	1.4	5,457

Stairs along the Ryan Mountain Trail

side of the mountain. Its four piggybacked sugarloaf summits rise proudly from a scree of boulders peppered with pinyon pine. This is one of the tallest formations in the park—and the only one that requires four pitches to be climbed. It is highly prized among rock climbers, who scale it along routes with funky names like Right On and Walk on The Wild Side.

After 0.75 mile the trail reaches a shallow ravine and climbs along it a short distance to the ridge. A tall pinyon pine lives right below the ridge. In the middle of the day in the summertime, it provides the only deep shade around. Soon after, the trail enters a scenic hollow at the crest, sprinkled with similar but greener and denser vegetation. From there it is a short meandering climb across the west side of this small hanging valley to the top of Ryan Mountain.

The summit itself is unfortunately disappointing. Stripped bare by some climbers' meaningless practice of harvesting local rocks and piling them up at the summit, it has all the charm of a vacant lot under construction. To add insult to injury, a bureaucrat who missed Wilderness 101 further defaced the site by erecting a sign that announces the summit, should anyone think they inadvertently climbed Everest. But the views of the park are good, north into the Wonderland of Rocks' surreal boulder piles, west to the rocky Little San Bernardino Mountains, and south to the Santa Rosa and San Jacinto mountains. This hike is short enough that it is not too hard to be here around the two best times of the day, shortly after daybreak when the sun slowly chases shadows from the mountains, and in the evening when light and shadows switch roles. The pristine, slightly lower summit 0.3 mile to the north-northwest offers even better, unobstructed panoramic views of Lost Horse Valley and the Wonderland of Rocks.

■

LOST HORSE LOOP TRAIL

Most hikers come here to visit the Lost Horse Mine, a rich gold property that has spawned more than its fair share of lore. It is an easy ascent on the popular historic mining road to the well-preserved ruins of its 1890s mill. From near there a faint trail climbs to the summit of Lost Horse Mountain, which commands great views of Pleasant Valley, the Hexie Mountains, and the Wonderland of Rocks. An enjoyable trail loops back to the starting point though the hilly southern end of the mountain and one of the park's greatest Joshua-tree forest.

General Information

Road status: Climbing on trail and cross-country; graded access road
Lost Horse Mine: 2.1 mi, 610 ft up, 90 ft down one way/easy
Lost Horse Mountain: 2.2 mi, 810 ft up, 90 ft down one way/easy
Lost Horse Loop Trail and Mountain: 7.3 mi, 1,320 ft up loop/moderate
Main attractions: Restored mill, history, gold mines, views, Joshua trees
USGS 7.5' topo map: Keys View
Maps: pp. 329*, *279*

Location and Access

Lost Horse Mountain is a small sub-range on the northern flank of the eastern Little San Bernardino Mountains, sandwiched between Ryan Mountain to the north and the bulk of the range to the south. The Lost Horse Loop Trail is a 6.3-mile trail that circles around most of it. To get to the trailhead, drive Park Boulevard to Keys View Road (see *Ryan Mountain*). Turn south on Keys View Road and drive 2.4 miles to the signed Lost Horse Mine Road. Turn left on this good graded road and park at the end of it (1 mile), just inside a gulch in the foothills.

History: Joshua Tree's Richest Gold Mine

The character most central to the history of the Lost Horse Mine is a lanky cattleman by the name of Johnny Lang. In the 1880s, he and his father George gradually moved cattle west to satisfy growing markets, eventually establishing headquarters around Indio. The story goes that in 1893, while grazing their animals near Witch Springs (now Lost Horse Well), they met a prospector named Frank Diebold, who told them about a gold strike he had made on a nearby mountain. For some years the area had been under the control of cattle rustlers headed by

Jim McHaney, who had driven Diebold off his land. Johnny Lang himself had had a run-in with the McHaney gang. One of his horses had wandered off into their camp, never to be seen again. Inspired to invest in mining after a chance encounter with local mine investors, George Lang purchased Diebold's find for $1,000. In December 1893 the Langs took three partners as protection against the gang and filed some 34 claims, naming the best one Lost Horse.

Under the management of Johnny Lang and his partners, the Lost Horse Mine rapidly became the region's best gold producer. Throughout most of 1894, ore containing up to 25 ounces of gold per ton was hauled several miles to the Pinyon Well Mill for processing. Some hand-sorted ore was so rich that it was sold directly to dealers as jewelry gold. One museum-quality piece was a chunk of quartz as big as an apple and laced with gold. By November, to improve production and profits a two-stamp mill had been erected at Witch Springs.

What precipitated the end of this first era is Johnny Lang's propensity to steal. By 1895, his partners became suspicious that when he was transporting the amalgamated gold to Los Angeles for refining, he was skimming. George Lang came to the rescue and bought them out. But when Johnny continued to steal, his father sold the mine to the Ryan family, long-time friends of the Langs. In spite of his wrongdoing, Johnny Lang was allowed to retain an interest in and work at the mine.

The Ryans ushered the Lost Horse Mine into its golden years. They developed a small ranch at Witch Springs to host the miners. Deeper in the main shaft, they hit the main gold vein that would make their mine the park's richest. With so much ore exposed, in April 1897 the Ryans purchased a second-hand 10-stamp mill and rebuilt it at the mine. Water was brought in by a 3.3-mile pipeline from the springs. For a time, two wagons made the five-day, 65-mile journey every week to deliver tens of tons of ore to Banning. Incorrigible Johnny continued to steal—his partners noticed that he produced much less gold during his night shifts than they did during the day—but this time he did not get away with a slap on the fingers. They gave him the option to sell his share or to be turned to the authorities. Lang was bought out for a generous $12,000, and he disappeared from the scene.

By the end of 1900 the Lost Horse Mine had given out its best. It operated continuously until 1908, then it was leased off and on for years, but returns were much smaller. The Ryan family teased out what little gold was left, in 1931 by mining the underground pillars, and in 1936 by cyaniding the tailings. When it closed down that year, the Lost Horse had yielded a remarkable output, some 16,400 ounces of silver and 11,700 ounces of gold—a cube 10 inches on the side.

The 10-stamp mill at the Lost Horse Mine

Route Description

The Lost Horse Mine. After over a century of erosion, the aging road to the mine has become one with the landscape—rocky, ravined, dusted with gravel. Long stretches are lined with wavy exposures of 1.7-billion-year-old gneiss smoothed by a million boots. Dazzling outcrops dot the slopes, coursed by sinuous veins of dark-gray biotite that sparkle in the sunlight. The road winds slowly up and down into the mountain, past a scraggly cover of juniper, Mojave yucca, nolina, ephedra, and small Joshua trees. One better appreciates how green the high desert is when reaching the burn part way up, a stripped open space of sienna soil pinpricked with bare rocks and charred trees.

One of the few miners at the Lost Horse Mine who left his mark is Frank James. In early 1894, he was up on his luck and discovered the rich Desert Queen Mine, only to be murdered for it shortly after (see *The Desert Queen Mine*). About 0.2 mile into the burn, where the road briefly heads east and reaches a low point at a wash crossing, a stone ruin is visible 25 yards on the right. This was James' house, and, according to some accounts, the site where he was killed.

The Lost Horse Mine pops into view suddenly, at a bend in the road, hanging on the side of a hill. At the junction below it, a side road on the left makes a long switchback up to the mill, past flat-topped tailings and the eroding cyanide heaps from the 1930s. Refurbished by the NPS, the mill is a mammoth construction of tanned lumber and rusted steel that still houses its stamp battery and the camshafts that lifted the stamps. It was, like most mills from that era, designed for efficiency, which demanded compactness. At its base, the two antiquated engines that powered it are still anchored to their foundations. The amalgamation plates would have been next to them, in front of the stamps. Three cyaniding troughs from the 1930s lie just below the road. The shaft is on the split level up behind the mill. Farther above the shaft is the winch that hoisted the ore out of it. It is a complex mechanical gem, with multiple cogs, wheels, and flywheels, and a handbrake that still works after 125 years. Just above the winch are the two stone cisterns where water from the spring was stored. A long trestle bridge once connected the winch to a low headframe that stood over the shaft. The bridge also likely conveyed the water from the cisterns to the mill. The 2-inch pipe that hangs over the largest cistern is the pipeline terminus. From this point the pipeline track can still be traced most of the 3.3 miles to Lost Horse Well, punctuated with remnants of the pipe. The imprints of the camp's cookhouse and of the bunkhouse that Johnny Lang used as temporary quarters in the last years of his life are on the low rise across the road from the mill.

Lost Horse Mountain. Shortly past the mine the road reaches its high point at a pass. Just before it a vague path on the right climbs 300 yards, straight up, to the top of Lost Horse Mountain. It is not exactly an epic climb, but the view is good. To the east the rock-strewn summit

Lost Horse Loop Trail

	Dist.(mi)	Elev.(ft)
Lost Horse Mine Road (end)	0.0	4,590
Junction to Lost Horse Mine	1.8	5,000
Lost Horse Mine (cistern)	(0.3)	5,090
Trail junction below pass	2.0	5,110
Lost Horse Mountain	(0.2)	5,313
Lang Mine	2.4	4,805
Optimist Mine	2.8	4,785
Wash crossing	4.1	4,830
Gold Standard Mine	(0.55)	4,880
Back to starting point	6.3	4,590

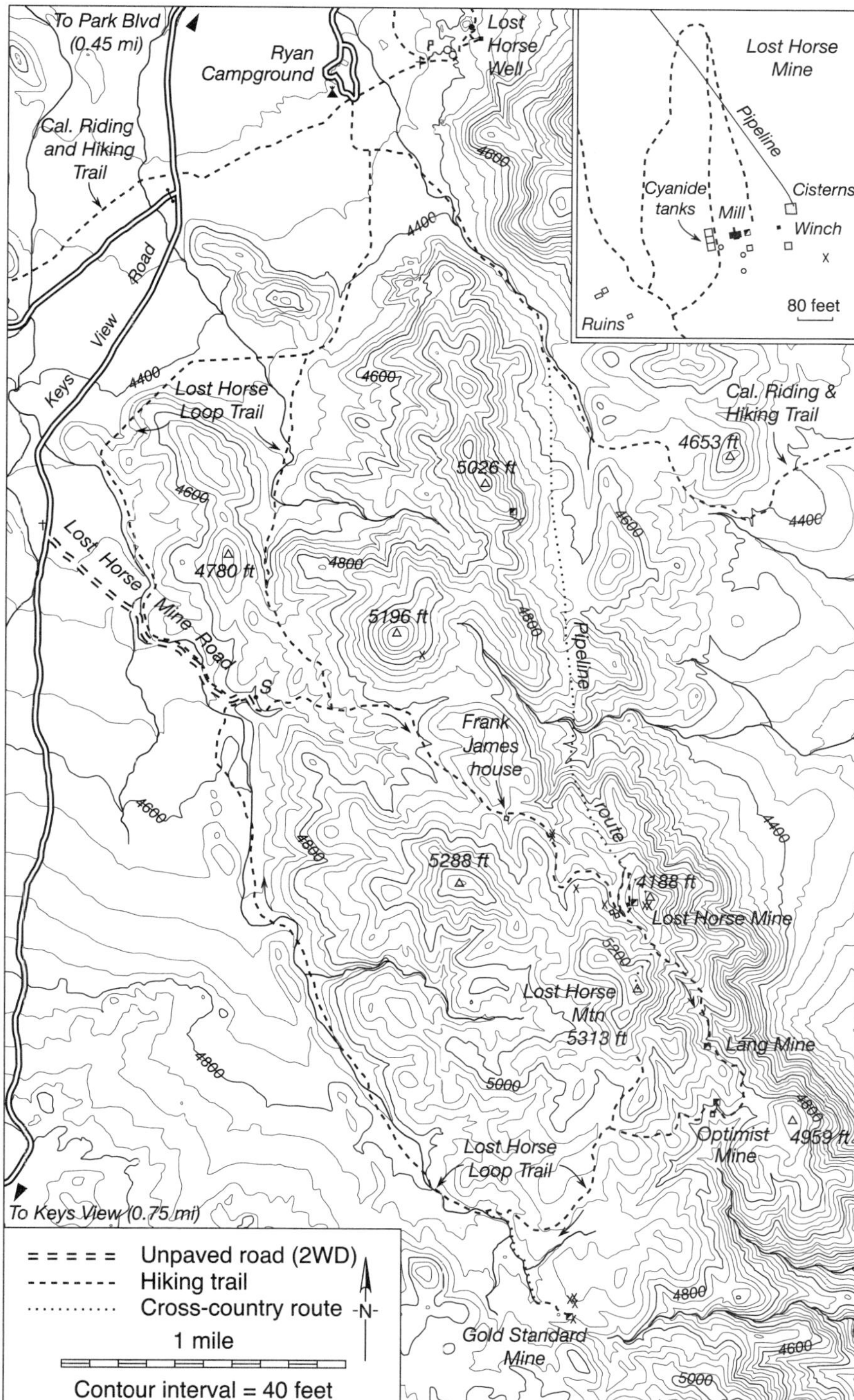
To Park Blvd (0.45 mi)
Ryan Campground
Lost Horse Well
Cal. Riding and Hiking Trail
Keys View Road
Lost Horse Loop Trail
Lost Horse Mine Road
Lost Horse Mine
Pipeline
Cyanide tanks
Mill
Cisterns
Winch
Ruins
80 feet
Cal. Riding & Hiking Trail
4653 ft
5026 ft
4780 ft
5196 ft
Pipeline
S
Frank James house
route
5288 ft
4188 ft
Lost Horse Mine
Lost Horse Mtn 5313 ft
Lang Mine
Optimist Mine
4959 ft
Lost Horse Loop Trail
Gold Standard Mine
To Keys View (0.75 mi)
4400
4600
4800
5000
5200
Unpaved road (2WD)
Hiking trail
Cross-country route
N
1 mile
Contour interval = 40 feet

Winch at the Lost Horse Mine

overlooks secluded Pleasant Valley, Malapai Hill's chocolate domes, and the Hexie Mountains. Quail Mountain and the Wonderland of Rocks' saw-toothed skyline dominate the northern horizon.

The Lost Horse Loop. From the pass, the road descends steeply along the south side of Lost Horse Mountain, snaking in and out of shallow folds in the hilly terrain. This part of the loop is much less crowded, and the vegetation is back in full force. It passes by three more gold mines, all at the other end of the business spectrum—small, little known, and unsuccessful. The first one is the Lang Mine, 0.4 mile below the pass. Possibly claimed by Johnny Lang, all it has to show today is a caved tunnel and a shaft. The next one, overlooking a steep drainage, is the Optimist Mine. When his optimism ran out, the miner packed out his cabin's lumber and left the chimney. It now stands incongruously by itself, a neat monument of carefully selected slabs of local gneiss. From there the road climbs a little, crosses a pass, and drops to a wash crossing. The third mine, the Gold Standard, is up this wash on the left, then up its left fork and a short segment of road (0.55 mile). It had a shaft and several pits and trenches, although it is best known for the ruin of its Joshua tree log cabin.

Soon after, the trail reaches the foot of the mountain and proceeds north along the edge of Lost Horse Valley. The last 2 miles is a peaceful conclusion to this scenic roller coaster around Lost Horse Mountain, mostly in a wash and all slightly downhill, through prime high-desert flora dominated by juniper and a dazzling collection of Joshua trees.

■

PINYON MOUNTAIN

Pinyon Mountain is the name given by miners to the forested high plateau at the crest of the central Little San Bernardino Mountains where they searched for gold in the late 1800s. The mines and the summit are reached by hiking up the nameless and now roadless canyon that once gave access to this area from Pleasant Valley. The canyon has a rich vegetation and granitic formations, finding the mines and mill ruins is a fun challenge, and it is a pleasure to scramble on the boulder stacks at the summit, in a setting of juniper and pinyon pine. The views from the summit of the Salton Sea, Coachella Valley, and the park are particularly enjoyable.

General Information

Road status: Trail and cross-country hiking; primitive access road
Hansen Mill: 2.4 mi, 1,000 ft up, 0 ft down one way / easy–moderate
Pinyon Mine: 3.3 mi, 1,490 ft up, 20 ft down one way / moderate
Pinyon Mountain: 3.7 mi, 1,650 ft up, 40 ft down one way / moderate
Pinyon Well: 0.8 mi, 270 ft up, 0 ft down one way / very easy
Main attractions: Forested summit, history, gold mills and mines
USGS 7.5' topo map: Malapai Hill
Maps: pp. 335*, *279*

Location and Access

The hike starts at the southern tip of the Geology Tour Road. Refer to *The Gold Coin Mine* for driving directions. At the rusted tanks of the Gold Coin Mill, the road angles right, crosses Pleasant Valley's small dry lake, then climbs toward the Little San Bernardino Mountains. At the fork 3.95 miles from the mill, turn right and drive up 1.8 miles to a sharp right bend at the foot of the mountains. Park at the pullout on the right just past the bend. The Geology Tour Road's southern loop has some rough spots with rocks. An experienced driver can make it in dry weather with a standard-clearance vehicle, but high clearance will minimize the risk of something going wrong. The mouth of the canyon that climbs to Pinyon Mountain is across the road, to the southwest.

Mining History: Tingman and Holland's Legacy

Early on in the mining history of the region, Pinyon Mountain attracted more than its fair share of gold seekers, to the point where a whole mining district was named after it. The two main historic sites,

Pinyon Well and the Pinyon Mine, were the brainchild of Alfred Tingman and Ed Holland, both prominent Indio citizens with a weakness for gold mining. Tingman had come to Coachella Valley in 1875 as a telegraph operator and construction manager for the Southern Pacific. After the railroad's completion, he stayed in Indio as a company agent. Versed in geology, he often explored the desert for gold and silver in his spare time, and made valuable strikes. He eventually built the first store in Indio, where he traded with homesteaders, miners, and railroad workers, and became known as the "grand-daddy" of Indio. Ed Holland, much younger, was a merchant too, and he had a formal education in mine engineering. Starting in the 1880s, the two men invested in several mines in the Pinyon Mining District, for which Holland eventually acted as the recorder. Around 1890, they teamed up to develop a gold seam near the head of a nameless canyon high on Pinyon Mountain. From Indio they built a road that wound 3,300 feet up Pushawalla Canyon and crossed the crest to their Pinyon Mine. Then they extended the road down canyon to a spring, where they erected a mill to process their ore. The spring had a small underflow, which they tapped with shallow wells to supply water to the mill.

Over the next few years, as they worked the Pinyon Mine, they were involved in some of the more visible local mines. In December 1893, Holland (and possibly Tingman as an associate) and three partners filed a historic notice of location on the Lost Horse Mine, which soon became the region's richest gold mine. As word of Pinyon Well's mill was passed around, it saw increasing use for custom jobs. Among its prized runs were a few rich shipments from the Desert Queen Mine in 1895, which yielded over $10,000 in gold. Their road up Pushawalla Canyon was for a time the main access to the district from Indio, and their well a precious source of water for the mining community.

In 1896 Tingman and Holland sold the Pinyon Mine, which was by then fairly extensively developed. The rest of the mine's history was fragmented. Until 1907, it changed hands three more times. Each owner planned to develop some of the claims or mill the existing tailings, but we do not know whether these plans came through. We do know that it produced 484 ounces of gold in 1896 and 8 ounces in 1907. With a grand total of $10,000, it was not a bad little mine. In the 1920s, the inactive property ended up in the Keys' extensive mine collection, although they likely never exploited it. Pinyon Well started a more successful second life in 1918, when the New Eldorado Mine, in the Hexie Mountains, acquired water rights to it. An 8.5-mile pipeline was installed from the well across Pleasant Valley to the mine, where for 20 years the water quenched the thirst of the mill, miners, and travelers.

Tingman's passion eventually caused his demise. He died in 1900 while prospecting in the Chocolate Mountains. Yet by establishing early on the existence of valuable gold deposits in the region, providing early mill services, access roads, and investments, that same passion that consumed him and Holland also turned out to be instrumental to the welfare of the local mining industry.

Route Description

Tingman and Holland's road, once so vital a connection between Pleasant Valley and Indio, is gone. Now the canyon wash is the trail. A quiet ribbon of sand, the wash is as sedate as it gets, without the drama of boulders or brush. A few decades ago, the area was ravaged by wildfires. The headless trunks of charred Joshua trees still stand against empty hills of yellow grasses and scattered rocks. Being the ultimate recipient of local rains, the wash has recovered faster than the hills. Bladderpod, ephedra, catclaw, desert willow, Joshua trees, and Mojave yucca thrive along its edges. Their seeds, dispersed by the wind, are slowly repopulating the lower hills. Life always finds a way.

Pinyon Well, 0.7 mile up canyon, is announced by a bushy growth of water-loving baccharis, then a metal trough sunk in the wash, and finally the three large concrete cisterns where the well water was stored. Their capacity underscores the historic importance of this site. With its mill and its rare and abundant water supply, Pinyon Well was a lifeline to many people and enterprises. In the 1900s a few families, including women and children, lived here in small cabins. The steam-powered two-stamp mill, a tall wooden structure that stood below the cisterns, served local mines for over 40 years, until it was moved to the Wall Street Mill building in 1933. The New Eldorado Mine would not have succeeded without the water from Pinyon Well.

Beyond Pinyon Well the wash continues its unhurried course, meandering between largely naked hills. Rocky outcrops are few but particularly impressive. A stately cliff of Cretaceous granodiorite rises in a sharp bend, fractured and lacerated by offset dikes, beautiful in its complexity. The mountain's granitic backbone is also exposed as house-size chunks high on towering hillsides, and in the wash as slick ramps cleanly washed by flood scour. The rock is steel gray, veined with interlocked crystals of white and pink felspars. The most striking ramp is a 100-foot-long slant incised with a deep water-worn channel. The arc of road on its north side, built for ore wagons to bypass it, is the sole remaining segment of the historic road.

After 1.7 miles, the wash reaches the end of the burn and the open forest of juniper and pinyon pine returns. Soon after, the canyon splits:

the wider left fork, the main canyon, is the way to Hansen Mill. Follow it 0.1 mile, then head up the narrow fork on the right. In 0.2 mile there will be a tailing on the left. The obstruction above it can be bypassed on a trail that starts on the right 25 yards before the tailing. In 200 yards the trail returns to the wash at Hansen Mill. This is the most interesting site in this drainage. Along the narrow, brush-invaded wash are the ruins of four dry-wall stone cabins and a stone chimney, the largest cabin 20x15 feet and 3 feet tall with a nice little doorway. They may have been a blacksmith shop or an assay office, and/or living quarters for men working the Pinyon Mine and later on the mill. The mill stood in the more level space past the cabins. Operated in the mid-1910s, and possibly much earlier, it served local mines. It was a roller mill: it worked on the same principle as pre-motorization arrastras, except that the dragstones were replaced by heavy rollers that each spun around a horizontal axle. The arrastra's circular track is gone, but the rollers are still there, two steel drums filled with rocks and concrete. At the upper end of the site, amid a spring of baccharis, there is a partly subterranean trough of carefully fitted stones cemented together. This was likely Hansen Well. It also played a vital role in the local history, as its water supported this mill and was piped later on to the New Eldorado Mine.

Fractured wall above Pinyon Well

To get to the Pinyon Mine, from the fork in the main canyon 2.1 miles in hike west up the smaller side canyon on the right. Its sandy wash, only 10 feet wide and mostly free of boulders and brush, climbs steadily the remaining 0.4 mile to Pushawalla Pass. Fifty yards before the pass, a foot trail on the left climbs out of the wash. From there to the mine, it wanders 0.8 mile south up a series of low shoulders, most of it discernible twin tracks. At two spots the grade is quite steep: in historic times the rear wheels of wagons heading downhill had to ride on heavy steel plates that skidded on the road! It is a pleasant climb, across a refreshing landscape of mature oak, pine, juniper, and Joshua

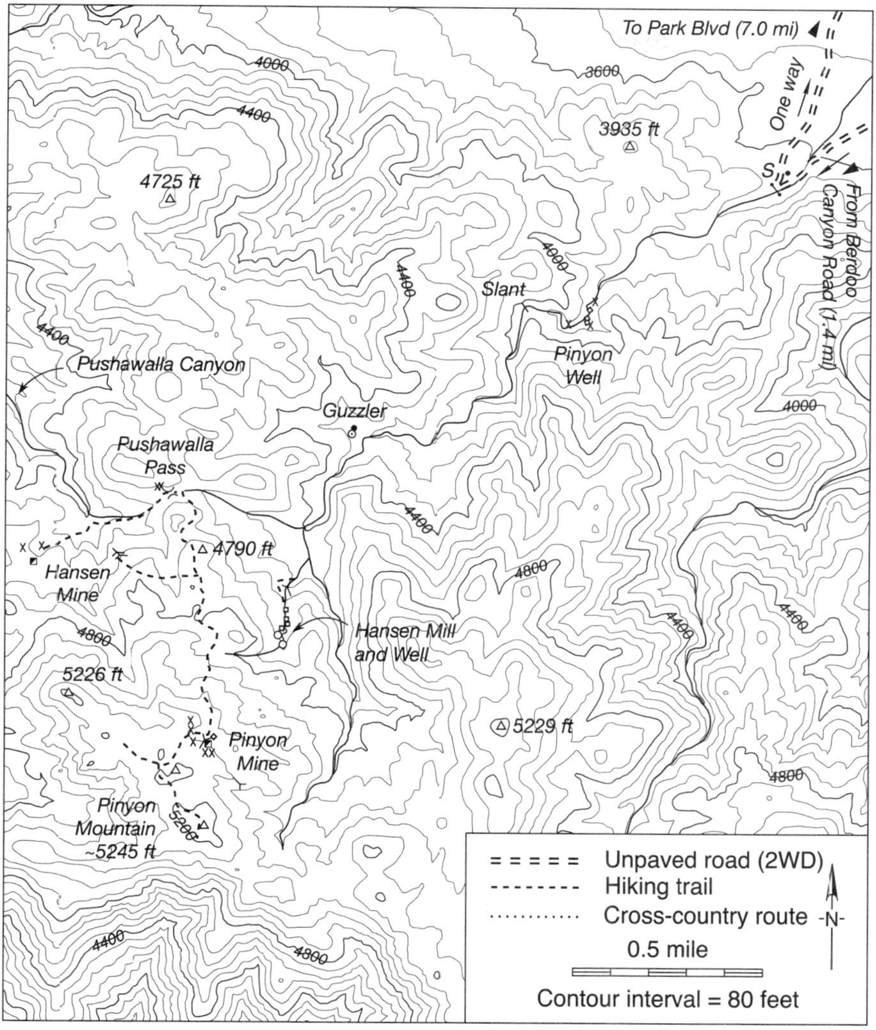

Pinyon Mountain		
	Dist.(mi)	Elev.(ft)
Geology Tour Road	0.0	3,630
Pinyon Well	0.7	~3,880
Fork to Hansen Mill and Well	2.1	4,400
Hansen Well	(0.35)	4,630
Pushawalla Pass	2.5	4,625
Pinyon Mine (stone cabin)	3.3	5,100
Pinyon Mountain	~3.7	~5,240

San Gorgonio Mountain and Coachella Valley from Pinyon Mountain

trees growing among boulder heaps. The road commands aerial views of Pleasant Valley and its surreal eruptions of isolated boulder stacks.

The Pinyon Mine is betrayed by its large tailings, which constitute most of its physical remains. There is a rock-walled cabin at the base of the tailings, a few metallic odds and ends, and not much more. It is still an interesting site for the size and placement of its waste dumps. There are a dozen of them, at different elevations on a steep hillside. The largest one, at the base, came out of the main shaft. Collectively, they emphasize the heroic efforts that Tingman and Holland invested, more than 130 years ago, to tease gold out of the desert.

As always, even if mines leave you cold, there are other rewards. Here it is the pleasure of locating well-hidden historic sites, the serenity of a sky island's green belt, and climbing its inviting wide-open summit. Pinyon Mountain actually has two summits, of sensibly the same elevation, about 0.4 mile further up the trail. The trail is locally very faint, but they are trivial to locate: two 15-foot piles of boulders protruding from a broad forested plateau, fun to scramble. The views are awesome, encompassing the Salton Sea, the San Jacinto Mountains, Coachella Valley, San Gorgonio Mountain, and all of Pleasant Valley.

That said, if mines *are* your thing, do not miss the Hansen Mine, in an amphitheater in the upper drainage of Pushawalla Canyon (see map). A well-built trail still climbs up to its shaft and the large retaining stone wall and concrete pilings of its dismantled mill.

■

THOUSAND PALMS CANYON

Part of the Coachella Valley Preserve in the central Indio Hills, Thousand Palms Canyon is home to some of the state's largest fan-palm groves. You can stroll on a shaded boardwalk through magnificent Thousand Palms Oasis, take the easy hike to the McCallum Grove, where palms are reflected in a peaceful pond alive with prehistoric fish, or indulge in the longer hike to Moon Country Canyon and follow its wild meanders through spectacular badlands.

General Information

Jurisdiction: Coachella Valley Preserve
Road status: Hiking on trails; paved access road
McCallum Grove: 1.0 mi, 90 ft up, 10 ft down one way / easy
Moon Country Canyon: 3.2 mi, 620 ft up, 10 ft down one way / easy
Main attractions: Extensive palm groves, wetlands, badlands canyon
USGS 7.5' topo map: Myoma
Maps: pp. 339*, 345, *279*

Location and Access

To get to the Coachella Valley Preserve Visitor Center, in Indio take the Washington Street exit on Interstate 10. From the westbound exit, drive north on Washington Street 4.3 miles to the signed Thousand Palms Road. Turn right and drive up to Thousand Palms Canyon, then up this broad canyon through the Indio Hills. After 2.1 miles, turn left to the signed visitor center just off the road, and park.

Route Description

Thousand Palms Oasis. Long before reaching the visitor center you will see the oasis up ahead spread across the canyon, a solid band of vegetation so large and impossibly green against the pale and barren landscape that it looks like a plantation. One reason is that it was, for a time, well, a plantation. First homesteaded in 1902, the original 80 acres of Thousand Palms Oasis were sold to Louis Wilhelm in 1905 for the ridiculous sum of a wagon and two mules. The Wilhelms used it for decades, first for camping, then to rent rustic cabins to visitors. In 1949, Louis' son Paul planted a 15,000-palm nursery. Later threatened by development, the property was purchased in 1983 by the Nature Conservancy for $2 million as part of an effort to preserve the endangered fringe-toed lizard that lives in sand swales just to the south.

McCallum Grove from lower end of Moon Country Trail

Thousand Palms Oasis is a remarkable ecosystem that was well worth its price tag. As soon as you step into it, the desert is gone. You enter a dim, slightly humid tropical forest of six-story fan palms, their trunks clad from ground to crown in thick dry fronds. The Palm Log Visitor Center is just inside, in a small dark clearing. Smoketree Ranch Trail, the 0.3-mile loop that circles around the heart of the oasis, starts in front of it. It descends to a boardwalk that snakes leisurely along tall corridors of palms. Their fronds were shaved 8 feet off the ground to make room to walk under the trees. The sunlight reflecting off the palms casts an apricot glow. Thin sheets of clear, slowly moving water flood the ground. The water rises from the bowels of the San Andreas Fault, and it fills the air with the metallic smell of sulfur. You might spot dragonflies, pupfish, water-loving reeds and rush, or colorful birds that do not seem to belong to the desert. The trail weaves in and out of the grove, occasionally crossing pockets of willow, mesquite, inkweed, and arrowweed. Everything is so lush that you would think you had been transported to a jungle in the Philippines.

McCallum Grove. The signed trail to the McCallum Grove starts at the north end of the oasis loop. Groundwater is so close that riparian vegetation extends almost continuously between the two palm

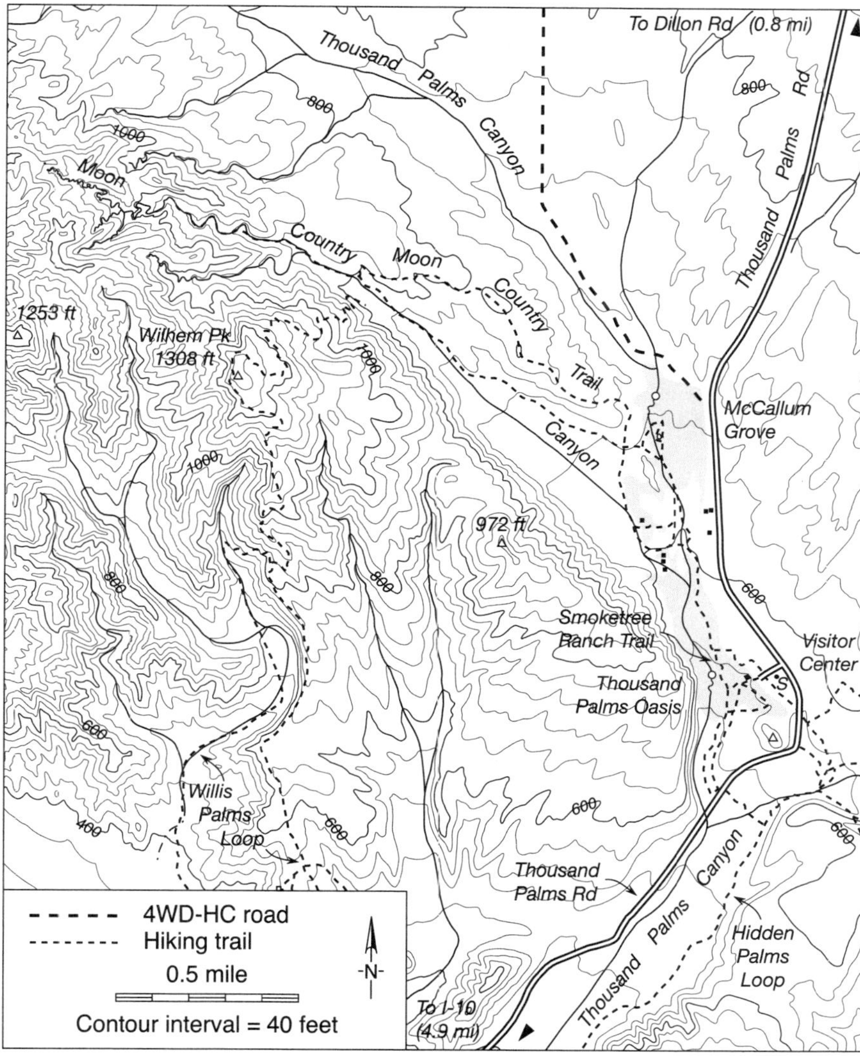

Thousand Palms Canyon		
	Dist.(mi)	Elev.(ft)
Parking area	0.0	560
Thousand Palms Oasis (loop)	(0.35)	~540
McCallum Trail (fork)	0.8	620
McCallum Grove loop	(0.35)	~630
Moon Country Cyn (mouth)	2.0	830
Moon Country Cyn (ridge)	3.2	~1,160

groves. At first the trail is hemmed in by 7-foot hedges of arrowweed, then comes a short stretch of open desert with a few ocotillo on the hillsides, and finally a sea of tall goldenbush. Just before reaching the McCallum Grove, the trail forks. To walk the loop around the grove back to this point (0.35 mile), take the right fork. Here too the vegetation is simply amazing, a luxuriant mix of cottonwood, screwbean mesquite, willow, aquatic plants, and ranks upon ranks of stately fan palms. What makes it even more scenic is Simone Pond, the largest of a few small reservoirs in the preserve. The reflections of the palms in the pond's tranquil water are a sight to be remembered. Desert pupfish live in the shallow pool. Unlikely survivors from the Pleistocene, they are among the rarest wildlife in the California desert, and one of the *raisons d'être* of the preserve.

Moon Country Canyon. The oases notwithstanding, badlands are easily the most striking natural feature in the Indio Hills, and Moon Country Canyon is a perfect place to get immersed in this exceptional landform. From the fork below the McCallum Grove, make a left, go 250 yards northwest to a crossing, and continue straight. The signed trail goes up a broad tributary of Thousand Palms Canyon locally known as Moon Country Canyon. It supports a dense community of beautiful low-desert plants, including species uncommon in this range such as the handsome turtleback and the ghostly desert holly. It is a pleasant walk, up an almost imperceptible grade, in gentle terrain that belies its hazards. The San Andreas Fault cuts a straight line a stone's throw away, right along the canyon's south side. Not often do we get to walk practically *on* such a major, world-famous fault.

The canyon gradually narrows, until after about a mile it splits into two forks that veer sharply left into the Indio Hills. Moon Country Canyon is the right fork. You are, once again, thrown abruptly into another world. For the next mile, the narrow sandy wash meanders through a brilliant landscape of tightly wrinkled hills. The topography changes quickly, pointed buttes alternating with fluted cliffs, slick mudstones with layered fanglomerates, open spaces with steep banks and undercuts. The wash snakes in increasingly tight oxbows that bend its course almost completely back on itself. This intriguing land is revealed one piece at a time, in sudden bursts around each bend. At the end of all this, the wash finally peters out at the foot of an amphitheater. A quick scramble and you top a ridge at the head of the canyon, a spectacular viewpoint looking out over the badlands and the imposing 2-mile-high mountains that surround Coachella Valley.

■

WILLIS PALMS LOOP AND HERMAN'S HIKE

For a more natural hike in the preserve, with fewer people and signs, try the Willis Palms Loop. It passes by a handsome palm grove, then climbs through a canyon and up onto the scenic Indio Hills, before looping back along the canyon rim. This loop can be extended to include the easy ascent of Wilhem Peak, the preserve's high point. For an even longer loop, continue from the summit on Herman's Hike, which goes by the McCallum Grove and Thousand Palms Oasis. In the hills, the views of the badlands and the surrounding high ranges rank among the most spectacular in the region.

General Information

Jurisdiction: Coachella Valley Preserve
Road status: Hiking on trails; paved access road
Willis Palms Loop: 4.2 mi, 540 ft up loop / easy
Wilhem Peak: 6.0 mi, 1,040 ft up loop / moderate
Herman's Hike: 7.7 mi, 1,040 ft up, 1,040 ft down loop / mod.
Main attractions: Palm groves, wetlands, easy summit, scenic badlands
USGS 7.5' topo map: Myoma
Maps: pp. 345*, 339, 279

Location and Access

To get to the Willis Palms trailhead, follow the directions to the Thousand Palms Road (see *Thousand Palms Canyon*). Drive north on the Thousand Palms Road 0.45 mile to a small dirt parking area on the left, at the mouth of the canyon, and park. The Coachella Valley Preserve is open Wednesday through Sunday 8 am to 4 pm. Entering the preserve on foot after 4 pm is prohibited, but hiking out of it after 4 pm is permitted. You can start Herman's Hike from the signed visitor center instead, 1.6 miles further up the road. However, parking at the visitor center after 4 pm is prohibited. So if you anticipate returning to your car after 4 pm, start from the Willis Palms Loop trailhead.

Route Description

Willis Palms Loop. From the trailhead it is a short walk to this elegant grove, visible down a gentle, brush-covered fan on the edge of permanently sunny Coachella Valley. Its tightly clustered palms grow at a spring oozing out of the Banning Fault, the strand of the San Andreas Fault that traces the southern base of the Indio Hills. All aligned along the fault, the trees seem to be stitched to the landscape. Sharply offset against the grayish hills, their long dark-green canopy tapers off gracefully toward the massive San Bernardino Mountains, bigger than life like a fantasy computer-generated landscape. The trail follows the 0.4-mile length of the grove. Short paths sneak into its cool shade, beneath high fronds whispering in the breeze. The grove suffered heavy fire damage in 1953, then again on November 26, 2010. Few trees died that day. Most of them still have blackened trunks but have grown back a full crown. Many seedlings were born, which now grace the oasis with lush ground-level fronds.

Past Willis Palms the trail follows the edge of the Indio Hills, then after half a mile turns right into an open canyon. The scattered town buildings visible from the trail disappear instantly. You wander up a wide wash livened by surprisingly mature vegetation—the blue-green puffs of smoke trees, the apple green of cheesebush and desert lavender, the yellow-green of creosote. The canyon is framed by bluffs of bare fanglomerate fluted by rain. At a major fork in the wash, the trail cuts straight, into the east fork. It pushes on a short distance to an old dirt road on the right that climbs steeply out of the wash.

The trail tops the canyon rim at a junction. To complete the Willis Palms Loop, take the broader trail on the right. It describes a long arc as it descends along the abrupt rim of the canyon you just climbed. There are good views over the Indio Hills and the surrounding mountains. At the junction 1 mile down, go straight on a foot trail that continues down a long ridge. It soon drops along the side of the ridge, passes right over Willis Palms, then switchbacks down into it. This is one of the best places to take a closer look at Willis Palms. After crossing the oases down a short ravine, the trail emerges on the edge of the valley and joins the access trail about half a mile from the parking area.

Before completing this loop, at the rim junction it is well worth taking the trail on the left, which climbs Wilhem Peak, the high point of the preserve. Its switchback crawl lazely up the hump of the Indio Hills, so sun-baked and wind-swept that they support mostly creosote and scruffy grasses. Here too, you are in suspect terrain. The Indio Hills are sandwiched between the parallel Banning and Mission Creek faults, both very much active. The ground underfoot is valley fill, a hodgepodge of silt, sand, gravel, pebbles, and cobbles washed down from the Little San Bernardino Mountains by Pleistocene floods. The Indio Hills were uplifted when the strip of land between the two faults was squeezed by compressive forces, like toothpaste out of a tube. The trail overlooks this long and prominent bulge, a graphic example of the massive forces at play within the mighty San Andreas Fault.

Willis Palms

What makes this climb special is the magnificent perspectives over the Indio Hills, desolate and furrowed to the east, eroded into vast badlands to the west. On the way up, the trail flirts with the sharp edge of a deep ravine that plummets into the badlands. Its mud walls are sliced into a web of pinnacles and razor-sharp ridges. The views are best around Wilhem Peak, a domed prominence perched over hundreds of acres of creased badlands. The day before my visit, a heavy snow storm had raged all over the mountains surrounding Coachella Valley. Under the immaculate blue sky, the San Bernardino Mountains shined like the French Alps. Above a straight horizon at 3,500 feet, the national park was blinding white for 25 miles to the Cottonwood Mountains. As if to add drama to this serene scene, the San Jacinto and Santa Rosa mountains were obscured by towering black clouds.

Herman's Hike. To complete this 7.7-mile loop, from the summit continue down the trail into Moon Country Canyon. Then follow the canyon downhill, past the McCallum Grove, to Thousand Palms Oasis (see previous section). Finally, take the short trail that heads generally south, crosses the Thousand Palms Road, and connects to the Hidden Palms Loop, and follow this last trail southwest down the canyon back to the Willis Palms parking area.

As the longest loop in the preserve, Herman's Hike crosses a greater range of topographies and plant communities, and its difficulty being moderate, it is quite satisfying. The trail that switchbacks down into Moon Country Canyon commands expansive views of the Little San Bernardino Mountains and the still nearly virgin narrow valley that separates them from the Indio Hills. The trail along Thousand Palms Canyon is also quite scenic, a stone's throw from a little stream that gurgles happily, so it seems, across the open gravel wash.

Willis Palms Loop and Herman's Hike

	Dist.(mi)	Elev.(ft)
Willis Palms Loop		
Parking area	0.0	375
Willis Palms (trail junction)	0.5	340
Trail angles right into canyon	1.0	380
Trail climbs out of wash	2.0	700
Jct at top of Willis Palms Loop	2.15	825
Wilhem Peak	(0.9)	1,308
Trail junction (go straight)	3.1	545
Willis Palms (trail junction)	3.7	340
Back to parking area	4.2	375
Herman's Hike		
Parking area	0.0	375
Trail angles up into canyon	1.0	380
Jct at top of Willis Palms Loop	2.15	825
Wilhem Peak	3.05	1,308
Moon Country Canyon wash	4.1	775
McCallum Grove (fork)	5.05	620
Thousand Palms Oasis	5.8	~540
Hidden Palms Loop (right)	6.35	510
Trail junction (right)	7.4	380
Back to parking area	7.7	375

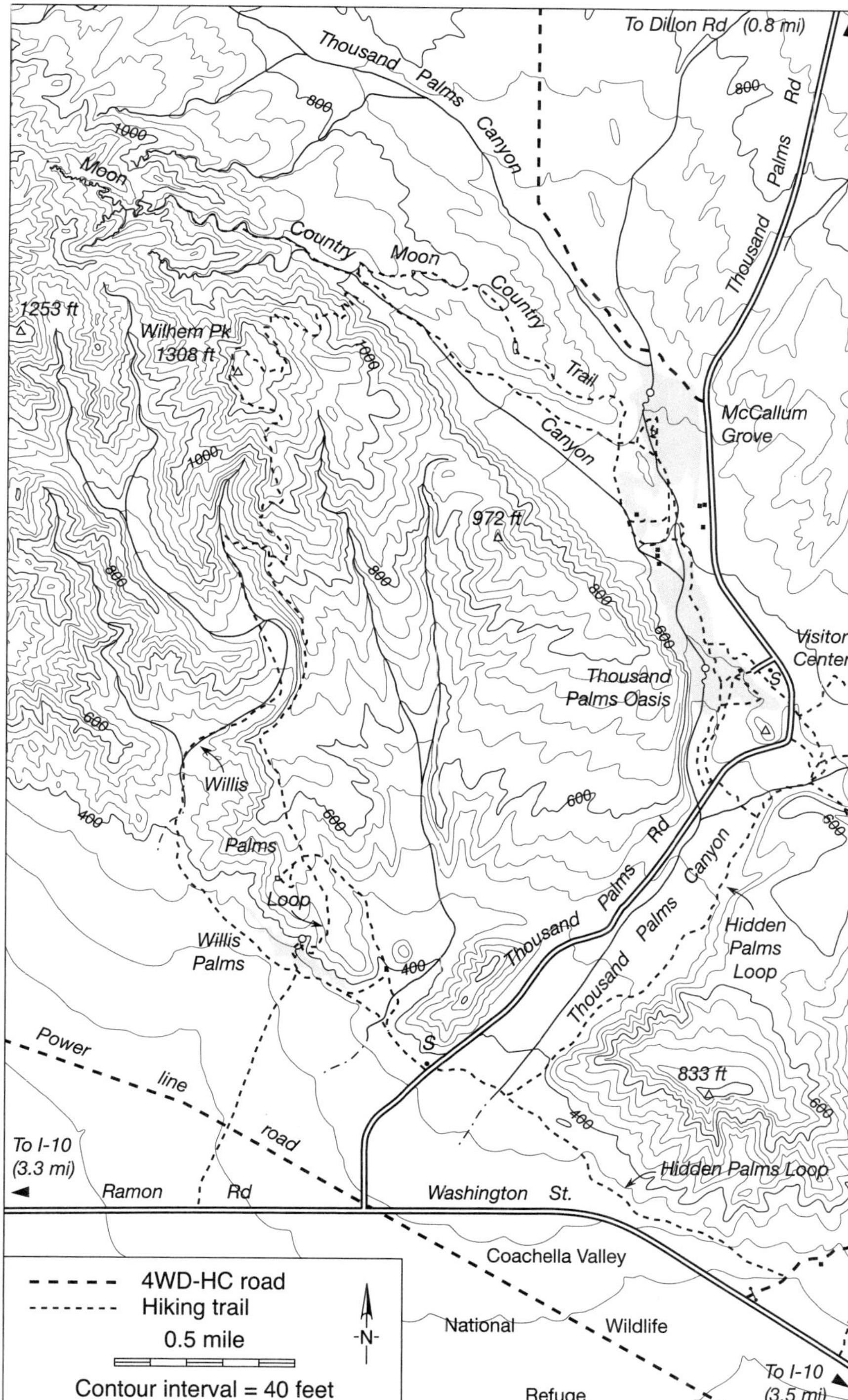
To Dillon Rd (0.8 mi)
Thousand Palms Canyon
Thousand Palms Rd
Moon Country
Moon Country Trail
Canyon
1253 ft
Wilhem Pk 1308 ft
McCallum Grove
972 ft
Visitor Center
Thousand Palms Oasis
Willis Palms Loop
Willis Palms
Thousand Palms Rd
Thousand Palms Canyon
Hidden Palms Loop
Power line road
833 ft
Hidden Palms Loop
To I-10 (3.3 mi)
Ramon Rd
Washington St.
Coachella Valley National Wildlife Refuge
To I-10 (3.5 mi)
4WD-HC road
Hiking trail
0.5 mile
N
Contour interval = 40 feet

Badlands and San Bernardino Mountains in fresh snow from near the summit

That said, there are two downsides to this loop. On the valley floor (about half of it) it is far too heavily signed (think one sign every 100 steps). It takes away what little wildness is left in this small natural gem unfortunately trapped in an expanding metropolis. The trail in Thousand Palms Canyon is also within earshot of the noisy road, and the last 2-mile stretch is anything but a relaxing ending. For a quieter hike, take the loop up to the summit and down to Moon Country Canyon, optionally exploring the upper canyon (see previous section), and return the same way. The silence is well worth the extra climbing.

Pushawalla Palms (no map). Hiking to this beautiful oasis, quite possibly the most scenic of all, is also a quieter experience. Start from Washington Street (the trail at the bottom right corner of the map). This route is easy (2.4 miles and 500 feet of total elevation change), partly on old dirt roads, and it goes by Hidden Palms and Horseshoe Palms. The longest in the preserve, Horseshoe Palms stretches half a mile at the foot of a long crinkled ridge. Pushawalla Palms is just beyond it, sunk below Pushawalla Canyon's abrupt rim. Almost as long, its lush belt twists and turns along the sheltering, narrow trench, until it ends abruptly at the edge of the parched wash. Sheer delight.

■

— 9 —

HEXIE MOUNTAINS

The Hexie Mountains are the central piece in the jigsaw of mountain ranges that tiles Joshua Tree National Park's high-desert plateau. Relatively compact, they are sandwiched between the Pinto Mountains to the north and the Little San Bernardino Mountains and Cottonwood Mountains to the south. It is a little bit of an odd range, slashed by faults that slip the wrong way, the home of Bingo Peak, Fried Liver Wash, and Porcupine Wash, of a mine once run by a clergyman who converted to gold, and blessed with just one spring so tiny that it couldn't quench a desert rat's thirst. Most of the range is a stark desolation of unadorned burnt-sienna ridges too low to hold a single juniper, occasionally heightened by eruptions of small darkly stained angular blocks and granitic shards the color of rust. Preserved in a designated wilderness, roadless for decades, it is a good place to seek solace and silence, away from the crowds that invade with clockwork regularity the more charismatic areas of the park.

Geology

The geology of the Hexie Mountains is complex in its details but simple in its overview. Gneiss makes up 90% of the range, rocks occasionally similar to Pinto Gneiss, often beautifully migmatized at a time when they were deeply buried and as malleable as butter, mixed with schists or much younger intrusive rocks. The rest is granitoids from the Mesozoic, confined to the range's extreme eastern end, on both sides of Porcupine Wash's long estuary. Together with a fringe of White Tank Monzogranite along the northwestern front of the mountains, these eroded hills of pale granodiorite and quartz diorite, sometimes lightly

Teddy-bear cholla in storm,
Pinto Basin below Hexie Mountains

metamorphosed, rank easily among the most scenic in the Hexie Mountains.

Like all other ranges in the region, the Hexie Mountains were extensively eroded in the Tertiary and Quaternary. Two fault zones slice east-west across them, the Blue Cut Fault and the Porcupine Wash Fault south of it. A third one, the Smoke Tree Wash Fault, is slowly severing this range from the Cottonwood Mountains. Most faults in California, like the San Andreas, are right-lateral—if you stand on one side of the fault, the opposite side is displaced to the right. All three faults in the Hexie Mountains shift in the opposite direction. Each side has been displaced by one to two miles to the *west* of its southern neighbor. These parallel tectonic motions have given the Hexie Mountains their characteristic outline of a fragmented range sheared into three offset pieces separated by long straight washes.

Botany

The Hexie Mountains straddle two deserts—their body lies in the Mojave Desert while their eastern toes dip into the Sonoran Desert. On the west side, the plant communities are typical Mojave Desert fare, including scattered Joshua trees and the full array of cacti. The main common species that are obviously missing are conifers, which find it too dry and hot. If you hike through the mountains eastward, you slip from one desert into the other along an invisible boundary drawn by vegetation. The differences are subtle, much of the landscape being dominated by creosote, brittlebush, grasses, and low gray shrubs that look dead most of the year. But then at some point you will run into a plant so different that it surely has no business in the Mojave. It could be a palo verde, so fond of chlorophyll that its trunk and branches are green. Or a grove of smoke trees, an attractive puff of turquoise cloud weaved out of thorns that can skewer a small bird. There are other distinctive plants—the rare ironwood, the chuparosa in bloom, its thick mane of vermillion flowers screaming for hummingbirds' attention, and the ocotillo, a plumed seaweed plucked out of *Twenty Thousand Leagues Under the Sea*. The most curious Sonoran plant may well be the deceptively cute teddy-bear cholla. Pinto Basin just north of the central Hexie Mountains is home to the park's largest known colony. Over an area of some 200 acres, they dominate the local biomass. The Cholla Garden Nature Trail, the quarter-mile trail that loops through a particular dense grove, is the most popular roadside attraction in the eastern part of the park. Be alert for the countless fallen stem-joints littering the ground. They are as eager to hook up with you as the plant itself.

Mining History

The Hexie Mountains had about 15 mines, more than any other range in the park—the Pinto and Eagle mountains had more, but most of them were outside the park. The first one to open may have been the Captain Jinks Mine. If its start date of 1874 is correct, it is the oldest mine in the region, and one of the oldest in the California desert. Oddly enough, it is located at the geometric center of the range, one of the most difficult areas to reach. The Hexahedron Mine, after which this range was likely named, came next, in 1893 or earlier. The Gold Coin and the Eldorado opened around 1900, and most others in the 1930s. By 1942 all mines had closed down, although sporadic exploratory work continued on a few properties until the 1960s.

Almost all of these mines were exploring gold veins; a few were after lead, tungsten, vanadium, molybdenum, and manganese. The total reported gold production was around 3,000 ounces. Two thirds of

Route/Destination	Dist. (mi)	Elev. gain	Mean elev.	Difficulty	Pages
Suggested Hikes in the Hexie Mountains					
Short hikes (under 5 miles round trip)					
Cholla Garden Nat. Trail (1)	0.25	0'	2,190'	Very easy	349
Eldorado Mine	2.1	560'	2,450'	Easy	359
Gold Coin Mine (1)	1.5	460'	3,380'	Easy	381
Golden Bee Mine	1.75	890'	2,380'	Easy-mod.	363
Golden Bell Mine	1.1	690'	2,720'	Easy	356
Lela Peak (southern route)	2.3	1,000'	4,110'	Easy	377
Malapai Hill	0.8	520'	3,910'	Easy-mod.	373
Mount Auclair	2.0	1,210'	2,480'	Moderate	366
Paymaster Mine loop (1)	4.0	1,090'	2,410'	Moderate	368
Silver Bell Mine					
Lower gold tunnel	1.0	620'	2,690'	Easy	353
Quarry (summit)	0.8	470'	2,710'	Easy	353
Silver–Golden Bell mines (1)	3.3	600'	2,550'	Easy-mod.	353
Towers of Uncertainty					
North	1.2	120'	4,450'	Easy	369
South	1.8	300'	4,420'	Easy-mod.	369
Intermediate hikes (5-12 miles round trip)					
Hexahedron Mill	3.4	220'	3,200'	Easy	390
Hexahedron Mine	4.5	1,070'	3,370'	Moderate	385
Lela Peak (northern route)	2.5	920'	4,060'	Moderate	377
Monument Mountain (2)	2.9	1,850'	4,030'	Moderate	391
Key: (1) Loop; (2) HC or 4WD access road Distance: one way for out-and-back hikes, round-trip for loops Elev. gain: sum of all elevation gains on round-trips and on loops					

it came from the local hero, the Eldorado Mine, which was owned for a time by the aforementioned clergyman. The rest of the gold came from seven properties, anywhere from 522 ounces for the Golden Bee Mine to a dismal 23 ounces for the Gold Point Mine. All other mines were marginal and produced either a few tons of ore, or nothing at all. Surprisingly, four properties had mills, which in the end cost more than the mines ever returned. Some of these underused mills still performed a valuable service for the mining community by treating the ore of neighboring miners who could not afford a mill.

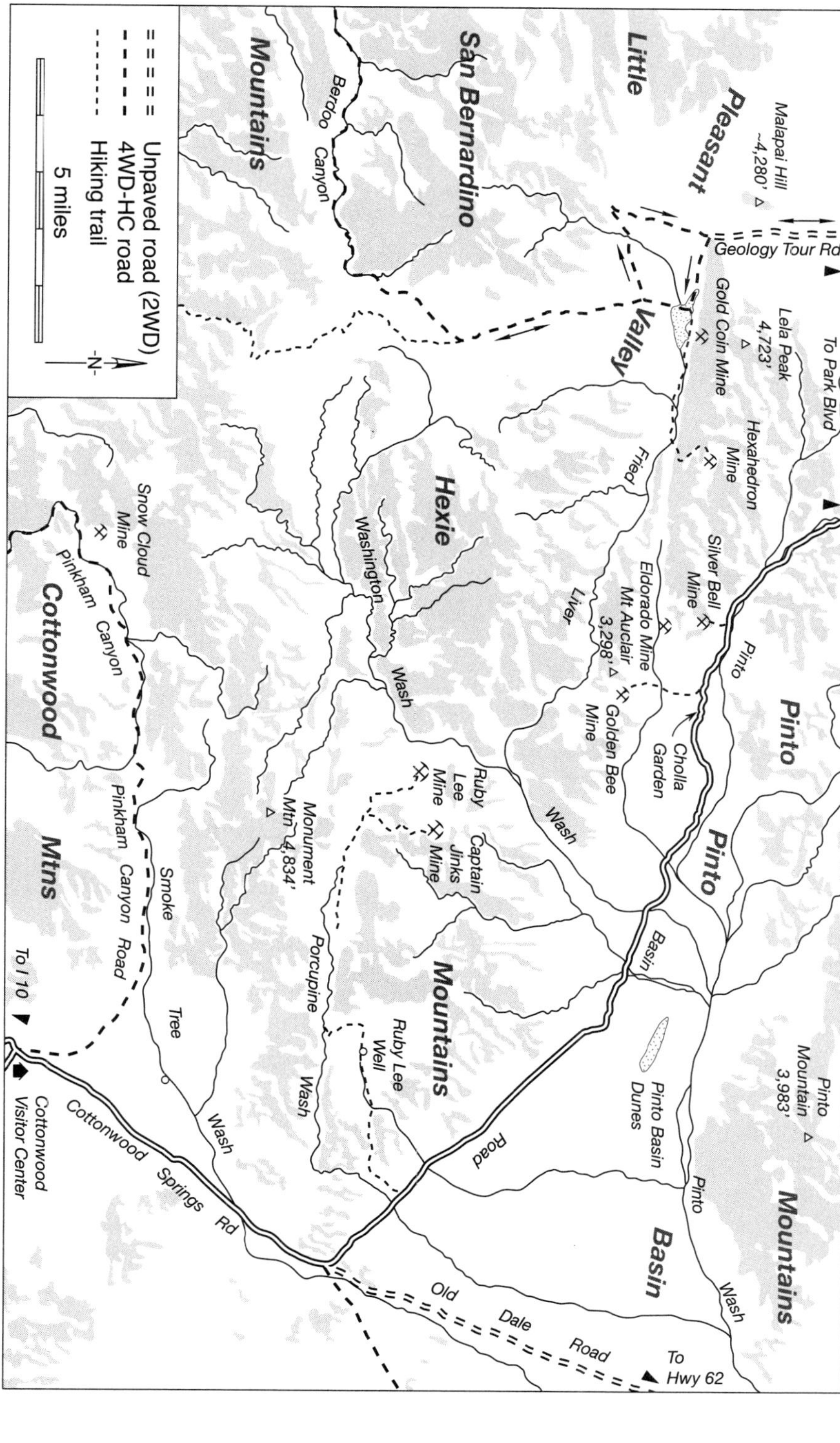

Unpaved road (2WD)
4WD-HC road
Hiking trail
5 miles
N
Little
Pleasant
Valley
Malapai Hill
~4,280'
Geology Tour Rd
To Park Blvd
Lela Peak
4,723'
Gold Coin Mine
Hexahedron
Mine
San Bernardino
Mountains
Berdoo
Canyon
Hexie
Fried
Liver
Washington
Wash
Silver Bell
Mine
Eldorado Mine
Mt Auclair
3,298'
Golden Bee
Mine
Cholla
Garden
Pinto
Pinto
Basin
Pinto Basin
Dunes
Pinto
Mountain
3,983'
Pinto
Wash
Mountains
Basin
Ruby
Lee
Mine
Captain
Jinks
Mine
Monument
Mtn 4,834'
Porcupine
Wash
Ruby Lee
Well
Mountains
Road
Snow Cloud
Mine
Pinkham
Canyon
Cottonwood
Mtns
Pinkham
Canyon
Road
Smoke
Tree
Wash
To I 10
Cottonwood
Visitor Center
Cottonwood
Springs
Rd
Old
Dale
Road
To
Hwy 62

Hiking

In a range so steeped in mining history, it is not surprising that many common hiking destinations revolve around mines. Several of the Hexie Mountains' mines have interesting remains. The Hexahedron Mine has two stone cabins and a mill site, the Silver Bell Mine two well-preserved ore bins and colorful ore, the Golden Bell Mine a funky cyaniding tub, and the Eldorado Mine a large milling complex and the ruins of a camp. Most of them are relatively easily accessible on foot. Unlike in more scenic parts of the park where a network of hiking trails has been created for visitors, in this range the trails are limited to the roads and paths that the miners built to move around. Even if you are not hiking to a mine, chances are that you will be following in their footsteps, like on the Fried Liver Wash Trail, which was once used by miners at the Eldorado Mine to access the mill at Pinyon Well, or the old four-wheel-drive track in Porcupine Wash, which serviced the Ruby Lee Mine and Captain Jinks Mine in the middle of the range.

Ore bin detail, Silver Bell Mine

The Hexie Mountains have much more to offer. They have awesome boulder stacks on their periphery, beautiful outcrops of twisted, banded gneiss, rows upon rows of rippling hills, and a complex web of canyons. Their greatest asset may well be isolation. Although the range is surrounded on all sides by roads, it is roadless, and it is large. Getting to and exploring its remote heart can only be done with a backpack and a few days. The three major canyons that cut deep into the range—Washington Wash, Porcupine Wash, and Fried Liver Wash—are the main thoroughfares. Alternating between broad rivers of gravel and delightfully tortuous passages, these long corridors are perfect for extended solitary walks into this seldom-explored area of the park.

■

THE SILVER BELL AND GOLDEN BELL MINES

The Hexie Mountains' northern hills hum with history. They were home to the Silver Bell Mine, which produced no silver but a bit of copper. Miners at the nearby Golden Bell did find gold, although not enough to make it worthwhile. The Rich Gold Mine likely had nothing at all to show. The ruins they left behind are a monument to both man's folly and a past we never lived. Some of them are easy to get to, like the Silver Bell's massive ore bins and colorful copper ores. It takes some orienteering skills to outwit the quirky network of abandoned trails that crisscross the hills and find the other ruins, among them a cabin floor tiled with natural stones, a partly buried car, a lonesome hopper, and impressive mine openings.

General Information

Road status: Roadless; paved access road
Silver Bell Mine (quarry): 0.8 mi, 420 ft up, 50 ft down one way/easy
Golden Bell Mine: 1.1 mi, 360 ft up, 330 ft down one way/easy
Silver Bell Mine–Golden Bell Mine loop: 3.3 mi, 600 ft up/easy-moderate
Main attractions: Gold-copper mines, mining structures, mining trails
USGS 7.5' topo map: Fried Liver Wash
Maps: pp. 357*, 361, *351*

Location and Access

The Silver Bell Mine is perched at the top of a secondary ridge along the northern front of the Hexie Mountains, at the mouth of Wilson Canyon. The Golden Bell Mine is part way down the southern slope of the same ridge. They are both accessed from the Pinto Basin Road to the north. From Pinto Wye, drive this road 7.9 miles, down through Wilson Canyon, to the paved interpretive pullout for the Silver Bell Mine on the right, and park. Coming from the east, this is 2.0 miles past the Cholla Garden. The twin ore bins of the Silver Bell Mine are visible just below the crest half a mile almost due south.

Route Description

The Silver Bell Mine. It is almost a straight shot to the mine. From the pullout a nearly level trail wanders south halfway there, across the uneven valley, to the lower end of the old mining road. The trail is a little faint at places, but even if you lose it, it would be hard not to find the road, in plain view up ahead. The road will take you the rest of the way, up the flank of a steep ravine. Severely damaged by storm runoffs, it is just a memory of the roadway that once took ore trucks to the mine. It spices up the short ascent with foot-deep trenches, crumbling edges, and bristly bushes sprouting through stripped bedrock.

The Silver Bell Mine was operated off and on between 1934 and 1962. Initially owned by local mining magnate Bill Keys, it was prospected for gold in the 1930s. After 1942, when the government issued an executive order that stopped all non-war-related mineral production, it was explored for lead. In the 1950s, a new owner ran it as a copper mine, and had the ore milled in Twentynine Palms, near today's golf course. In spite of this wealth of minerals, the Silver Bell was almost certainly a dead loss. Its only known production is a few tons of copper ore, which were not even sold...

The twin ore bins looming against the mountain near the top of the road are a beauty. About 10 feet high and anchored on two levels of sturdy stone walls and concrete pads, they are huge constructions of heavy lumber and foot-long bolts designed to hold some 70 to 80 tons of ore each. They were loaded with a skid, a conveyor of small buckets that each lifted a bit of ore and dumped it onto a grizzly placed on top of the bin. The grizzly blocked larger rocks and only let small rocks drop into the bin. The ladders and parts of the catwalks used to service this equipment are still in place. The site did not have a mill. The bins simply stored the ore until there was enough of it to be trucked to a custom mill. Their design was unusual: the ore came out of them not in a side chute but through their tapered bottom. The ore was loaded in a truck that parked in a trench on a third level just below the lower bin. In light of the mine's idle past, one wonders why an ore bin was needed at all, let alone two. In their wishful thinking, the mine developers vastly overestimated the mine's wealth. Decades later, we should be grateful for their *folie des grandeurs*, which gives us a chance to admire an obsolete piece of technology in its original setting.

The ore was extracted from the one-acre quarry on the crest just above the bins. It was worked on several split levels connected by short roads. The lower terrace is the largest. One hundred yards long, it is backed by rock walls slashed with thick multicolored bands. A road switchbacks up past the equally colorful upper terraces to the top of the quarry. The dominant reds are oxidized pyrite and hematite, and the bright ochres limonite, all iron ores. The greens and blues are malachite, chrysocolla, and azurite, the copper ores extracted in the 1950s. This is one of the park's most colorful mineralized zones. The ground is littered with small rocks coated with sky-blue chrysocolla, limonite, iridescent purple smears of bornite, and gun-metal lead ore.

The two ore bins at the Silver Bell Mine

Past the top of the quarry, a trail winds up the remaining 50 yards to a nameless summit. If mines are not your thing, the view will likely be the highlight of the hike. The summit, like the ore bins area, overlooks deep swaths of undeveloped Pinto Basin, its vast creosote empire framed by austere mountains.

The tunnels prospected for gold in the 1930s are a third of a mile down the hill southeast of the quarry. If you follow the lower terrace to its south end, then scramble down to the base of the tailings, you will see the old access road that climbs up to the tunnels from the wash way down below. Proceed down the slope below the tailings; it is steep and slippery with small rocks. Look for the faint miner's trail that crosses the slope down to the top of the road; it makes the descent easier. The trail switchbacks down to the apron of the 160-foot upper tunnel, where it meets the old road. The road descends to the twin lower tunnels, located right under the roadway. The longest was 280 feet. The three tunnels explored a fractured zone filled with intrusions. They are bare today, and the rock that was pulled out of them was also likely worthless. Here as throughout these hills, it is fun to explore the variety of ancient plutonic rocks, a mix of banded gneiss, black granite, and sparkling schists. The road ends at the broad wash a short distance below the lower tunnels.

The Golden Bell Mine. Located about a third of a mile east of the Silver Bell, the Golden Bell Mine has more interesting workings. From the saddle at the quarry, an obvious road heads east to a partly collapsed dugout on the left, then narrows down to a foot trail. This old path is the quickest route to the Golden Bell. It cuts east at a constant elevation, then climbs northeast to the crest, crosses over it and back, then descends in a long clockwise arc to the Golden Bell Mine's upper shaft.

The Golden Bell had only marginally better luck than its neighbor. Located in July 1931, it produced every year but one between 1934 and 1941. Its known production, however, was not exactly fabulous: 219

Cyanide tub and hopper at the Golden Bell Mine

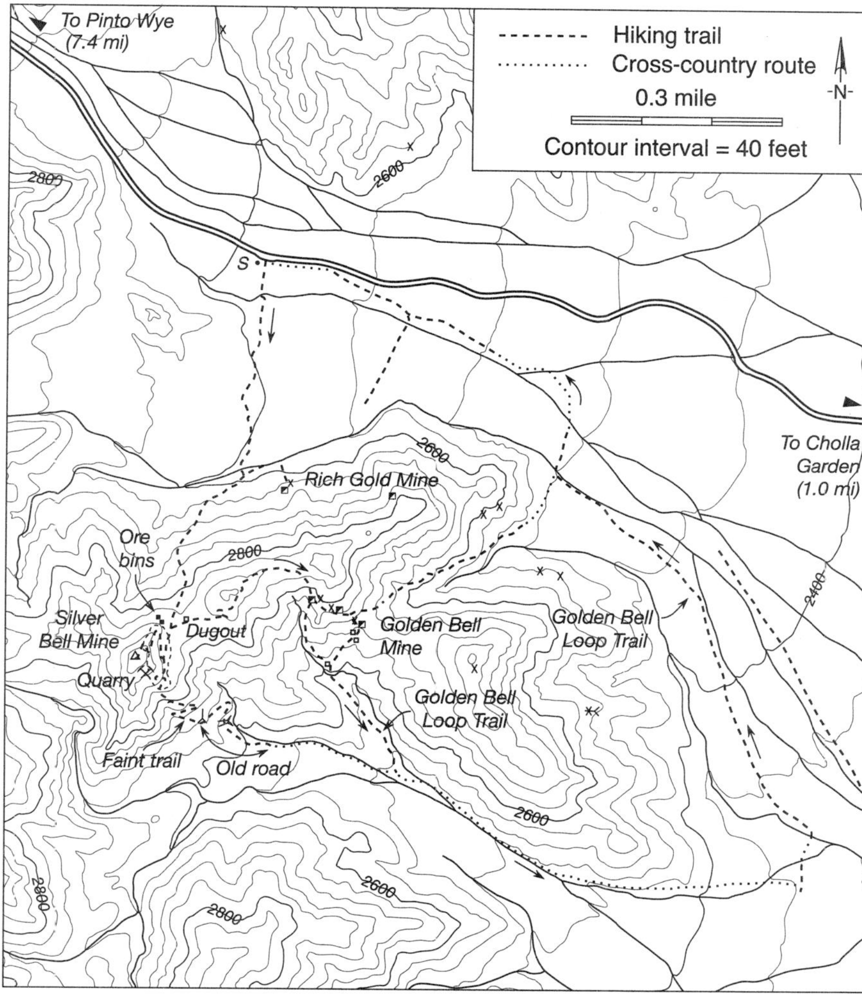

The Silver Bell and Golden Bell Mines

	Dist.(mi)	Elev.(ft)
Pinto Basin Road	0.0	2,590
Silver Bell Mine ore bins	0.6	2,840
Summit above quarry	(0.15)	~2,980
Lower gold tunnels (from bins)	(0.35)	2,620
Golden Bell Mine (lower shaft)	0.95	~2,690
Golden Bell Loop Trail ends	1.25	2,515
Golden Bell Loop Trail resumes	1.9	2,360
Pinto Basin Road	3.3	2,590

ounces of gold and 53 ounces of silver, more than half of it the first year. At 1930s prices, this represents only a few thousand dollars in gold, and not even enough silver to cover the miners' beer.

Its minimal output notwithstanding, the Golden Bell Mine was thoroughly developed. As the trail descends from the upper shaft to the lower shaft at the bottom of the mine, a distance of 0.1 mile, it comes close to the abrupt edge of several interconnected workings. For a small mine, they are impressive, deep angular trenches cut into solid bedrock. They were all sunk into the same nearly vertical vein of fractured gneiss, up to 4 feet wide, filled with auriferous quartz stringers. About 80 feet underground, right beneath the trail, the length of the vein was explored along a 435-foot inclined tunnel via multiple drifts, stopes, and winzes. The ore was pulled out at the lower shaft and treated at various times either in a small on-site mill near it or at the nearby Eldorado Mine's mill. Below the lower shaft, where the trail meets the old Golden Bell Loop Trail, there is still a wooden hopper lined with sheet metal, and a curious galvanized tub that served as a cyaniding tank. Both may date from clean-up work done in the mid-1950s—which recovered all of one ounce each of silver and gold... The road continues down to a collapsed cabin, now furnished only with the box springs on which miners dreamt of riches that never came.

There are several options to return. You can go back the same way; or from the lower shaft northeast down the Golden Bell Loop Trail, then around the tip of the mountain counter-clockwise to the paved road; or down the Golden Bell Loop Trail the other way, past the collapsed cabin to the wash, then up the wash to the road to the Silver Bell tunnels, and from there up the trail to the quarry. I liked the fourth and longest way best, the one traced with arrows on the map, past the collapsed cabin to the wash, then southeast down the wash. About 250 yards past the point where the wash enters Pinto Basin, on the low left bank, there is still a segment of the Golden Bell Loop Trail. From there it cuts north-northwest almost continuously to within earshot of the Pinto Basin Road. Taking the long tour around these timeless hills filled with ghosts, hopping from segment of road to segment of road in the footsteps of forgotten miners, is a befitting way to pay homage to these small mines out on their luck.

■

THE ELDORADO MINE

The Eldorado Mine was one of the three most important mines in the park's history. From its opening in 1901 until its final days around 1939, it had over at least half a dozen lessees and owners, but it was well developed and produced a decent amount of gold. Reached by an easy cross-country hike, this is a colorful site to visit, with enough remains to figure out how it worked, and just isolated enough to get a deeply satisfying sense of discovery.

General Information

Road status: Hiking cross-country; paved access road
Eldorado Mine: 2.1 mi, 420 ft up, 140 ft down one way/easy
Main attractions: Ruins of camp and mills of a rich historic gold mine
USGS 7.5' topo map: Fried Liver Wash
Maps: pp. 361*, *351*

Location and Access

The Eldorado Mine is just inside a nameless east-west canyon along the Blue Cut Fault in the northwestern Hexie Mountains. From Pinto Wye, drive the Pinto Basin Road 8.6 miles, down Wilson Canyon, to a paved pullout on the right, and park. This is 0.75 mile past the interpretive pullout for the Silver Bell Mine. Coming from the east, this is 1.25 miles past the Cholla Garden.

Route Description

The discovery of the Eldorado Mine deposit is credited to James "Chuckawalla Jim" Wilson, one of a motley crew of lanky prospectors who lived then at the Twentynine Palms oasis. In 1901, while on a random trip searching for gold and for his favorite dish—chuckwallas—out in the Hexie Mountains he spotted a boulder laced with the yellow metal. He was so thrilled by his find, which quickly made him $500 (enough to buy a house in Indio) that he named it Eldorado, after the fabled city of gold. Around 1903 he sold the property to former clergyman John White, who carried out the first serious development work, before running out of funds. In 1907 the mine was re-organized as the New Eldorado Mine and a shaft sunk to 300 feet, with three levels of crosscuts. It closed again in 1910, only to re-open in 1912, under the superintendence of Fred Vaile. The next period was the most productive. Until 1916 the recorded production was 1,550 ounces of gold and

Mill ruins at the Eldorado Mine

375 ounces of silver. In 1918 an 8.5-mile pipeline was deployed from Pinyon Well to bring water and run a small mill. Through the 1920s, Vaile and White remained key players, Vaile as the owner and White as a periodic lessee. By 1929 the shaft had reached 500 feet. The ore was pulled out with a gas hoist, and processed in the mill. The second most prolific era was 1930 to 1938, when the mill size was increased to ten stamps and an optimistic 1,000-ton capacity to process the old tailings. It squeezed out another 360 ounces of gold, and a little silver.

The Eldorado Mine shut down soon after; its pipeline was dismantled in 1940, and the mill in 1941–1942. By then it had recovered more metals than most mines in the park, including lead, tungsten, vanadium, and molybdenum, and generated over $100,000. Until its final years, it also played a vital role by offering custom milling services. The Golden Bell, Hexahedron, and other local mines would not have survived as long without the support of the Eldorado Mill.

The Eldorado Mine is not visible from the Pinto Basin Road, but its general location is easy to spot. Due south from the road, Pinto Basin rolls off gently about a mile to the base of the Hexie Mountains. To the right of this line of sight, two low ridges taper down eastward into the valley. The furthest one is crowned at its east end by a small pointed cap of rusty rock. The Eldorado Mine is just behind that ridge. Before heading in, look back due north and identify a prominent peak in the

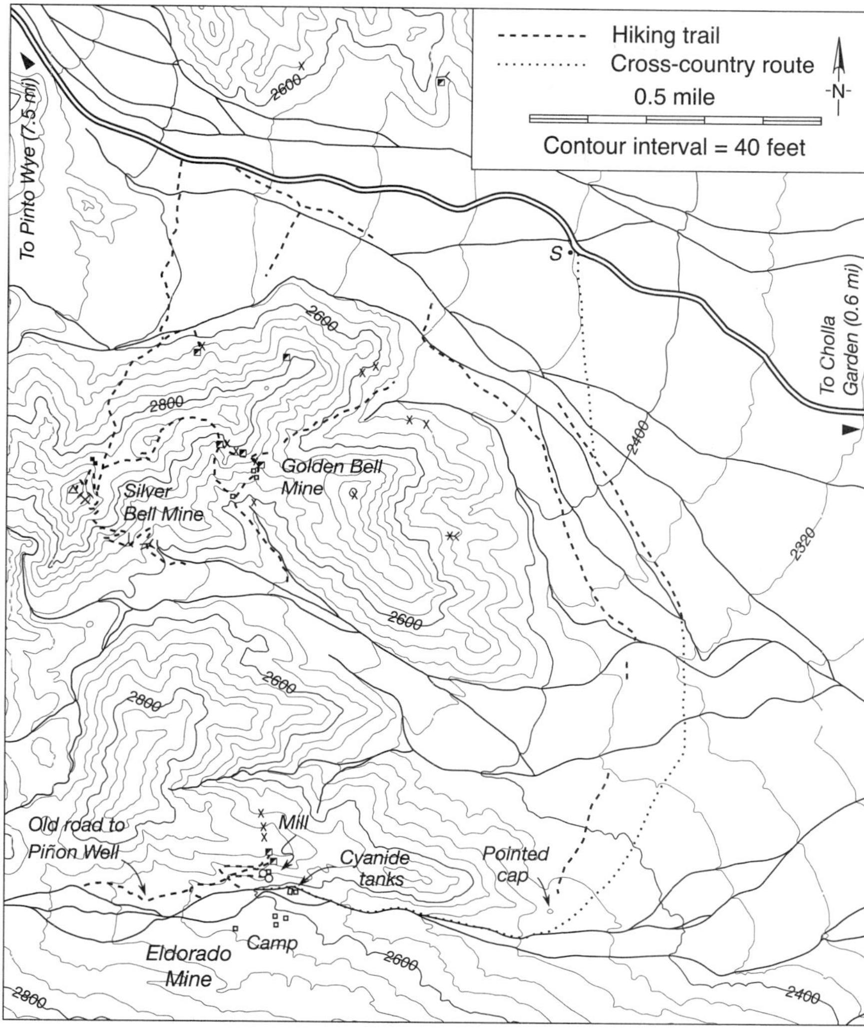

The Eldorado Mine

	Dist.(mi)	Elev.(ft)
Pinto Basin Road	0.0	2,440
Crossing two main washes	~0.8	~2,325
Main wash to mine (right)	1.3	2,470
Cyanide tanks in wash	1.75	2,585
Foot of upper road to shaft	1.85	2,610
Mining camp	(0.05)	2,640
Eldorado Mine (shaft)	2.0	2,690

Pinto Mountains to guide you back to your car when you return. Even if you do not spot the pointed cap, head due south across the valley. In 0.35 mile you will run into an old road that goes south-southeast. Follow it the same distance again (or keep going south if you miss it), until it ends at a wash, and resume a southerly course. It is a pleasant hike, on nearly level terrain slashed by shallow washes. Between 0.75 and 1 mile you will cross two main washes coming out of a canyon on the right. Past the second wash, angle southwest up a gentle fan spiked with ocotillo. In 0.3 mile it leads to a large wash that drains eastward along the base of the Hexie Mountains, just past the pointed cap. The Eldorado Mine is about 0.5 mile west up this wash.

The Eldorado Mine is an imposing sight. Hanging on a steep hillside 80 feet above the wash, it dominates the landscape. The mill's two metal tanks are balanced at the edge of massive gray tailings that drip down the hill at a 45-degree angle. The first ruins are the largest, two cyaniding tanks erected on a low bank in the wash below the mine. Each one has two rectangular compartments made out of steel and concrete walls and linked by steel pipes. The tall heap of mill tailings next to them attests to the large volume of ore they processed. The camp was on a low bench just south of the wash. Over time it had several white canvas tents and wood cabins, and a house. What remains is three collapsed cabins, stone foundations, and a dump of food cans. The largest cabin lies splayed open as if it had exploded, its roof blown away, its zinc counter blinking in the sunlight. From the camp the three roads that climb up to the mine are clearly visible, their retaining stone walls slashing the hillside. To get to them, from the tanks follow the wash up canyon 150 yards to a ravine on the right. The washed-out road in the ravine climbs in 60 yards to the junction between the three roads, which are also connected at the mine. The lower road climbs to the mill. The mill's top level had an ore bin, now long gone, which fit in a square niche blasted in bedrock. The stocky concrete pillars below it supported the stamps. On the same level are the rare remains of a concentration table, its rifles betrayed only by lines of nails. Each of the two lowest levels still has its corrugated-iron cyanide tank.

The main shaft, just above the mill, has been filled in. It commands a great panorama of the whole mine, the canyon spread out below, and the mountains. It is a fine platform to linger, not only to take in the view, but also to imagine the hustle and bustle of the mine a century ago, and to reflect on the lives of the men and women who passed through here to tease a little gold out of the desert.

■

THE GOLDEN BEE MINE

Of the park's many small mines, the Golden Bee is one of the most engaging. Its history is better known than most, it did produce some gold, it still has interesting physical remains, and it commands spacious views of Pinto Basin and the Pinto Mountains. Although there is a trail to the mine, visitation is light. This short hike can be extended, on a faint miners' trail, to return down a parallel canyon with another gold mine, and to climb a small prominence for great views of the undulating Hexie Mountains.

General Information

Road status: Hiking on old trails and cross-country; paved access road
Golden Bee Mine: 1.75 mi, 790 ft up, 100 ft down one way/easy-moder.
Mount Auclair: 2.0 mi, 1,110 ft up, 100 ft down one way/moderate
Paymaster Mine loop: 4.0 mi, 1,090 ft up/moderate
Main attractions: Gold mines, peak climb, views of Pinto Basin, botany
USGS 7.5' topo map: Fried Liver Wash
Maps: pp. 367*, *351*

Location and Access

Like a medieval fortress, the Golden Bee Mine secured a privileged spot for itself. It is perched high up a shallow canyon in the northern front of the Hexie Mountains, overlooking a vast territory. The old mining road (now a foot trail) that climbs to it starts right off the Pinto Basin Road, 9.4 miles south from Pinto Wye. As you approach this spot along the curvy road below Wilson Canyon, there will be two adjacent low conical hills along the right side of the road. The mining road starts between them, close to the first hill and just before a left bend. Park on the shoulder. Coming from the other direction, this is 0.45 mile past the Cholla Garden Nature Trail.

Route Description

The Golden Bee Mine. From the starting point the mining road is visible a mile to the south, across the valley, curling up into a steep canyon to its end at the Golden Bee Mine. Around 1940, when mining was in full swing, the road was smooth enough for a sedan to make it all the way up there. In just 80 years, the sparse local rains have done considerable damage to it. On the valley floor, water rarely collects into sizable flows and the road is well preserved. Half a mile in, the road crosses a wash. Since mining stopped, flashfloods have seriously re-arranged its rocky bed. On this 0.3-mile crossing, the road is spotty at first, then gone. You just walk among rocks, aiming for the next segment of road visible up ahead on the canyon fan. There the terrain is broad and the slope modest, and the road is mostly fine again. Higher up, runoffs on the steep canyon slope have reduced it to a rock-strewn path. At the final wash crossing just below the upper workings, the road has been wiped out again. Unbeknownst to miners, their roads are today unwitting subjects in long-term experiments that help geologists measure how fast desert erosion reshapes the landscape.

On the way up, you will get to enjoy your own personal gardens of teddy-bear cholla and ocotillo. A few teddy-bear cholla grow beside the trail about 0.5 mile in. There is a cholla garden about 200 yards west of the road—not as large as at the popular site along the Pinto Basin Road, but large enough, and free of people. The ocotillos are at the mouth of the canyon, on the right slope just above the road.

The Golden Bee Mine was a late bloomer. One of its two claims was filed in 1934, well after most mines had closed shop. It produced gold every year from 1935 until it shut down in 1942. The early work was done by the original owner, Eloge "Frenchy" Auclair. The property was later sold and leased, but Auclair eventually retained an interest in it as manager. During its eight active years, the 812 tons of ore that the mine shipped were treated at the Gold Crown Mine in the Pinto Mountains and at a mill near Soledad Mountain south of Mojave. 522 ounces of gold and 66 ounces of silver were recovered, two thirds of it in 1936, worth around $18,000. Early on, honey bees attracted by water stored at the mine nearly drove Auclair and a coworker out. This being long before ecological concerns were part of our mind set, they took care of the bees by poisoning the water with cyanide. This incident was likely the origin of the mine's name.

The Golden Bee Mine was unusual in several ways. Although the lode it exploited was small, it employed at one time a sizable crew. The mining camp alone, located just up the fan, had at least five cabins, enough to house five to ten miners. What remains today is the splintered frames of two large collapsed cabins, the stone platforms and imprints of other cabins, and sheets of roofing. The camp's midden is a healthy litter of cans, broken glass, and refuse, evidence of a significant cumulated occupation. The mine was diligently explored, in two main areas and at scattered tunnels and prospects. The lower workings are accessed by a spur road on the right, 0.25 mile past the camp. The ore was stored in a curious bin kludged together with a cylindrical corrugated-steel tank. It serviced three shafts, all protected by steel nets. The

Ore bin at upper workings of the Golden Bee Mine

main shaft's headframe toppled onto its net; it now rests sideways suspended over the shaft like a fallen trapeze artist.

The upper workings are 0.2 mile further up the road, past a forgotten cemetery of spooled cable, lumber, roofing, pipes, and drums. Its centerpiece is a well-preserved ore bin, a sturdy construction of dark lumber with an inner lining of sheet metal. The spacious, L-shaped apron above it was the heart of the mine, with the ore bin at the tip of its short branch and a small mill at its corner. The main workings, a 180-foot inclined shaft and 100-foot tunnel, gape behind the ore bin. The hillside behind them, once honeycombed with shafts and drifts, caved in. The tops of their buried ladders and wood frames protrude from a landslide of clay. A photograph from 1941 reveals an infrastructure long gone. A skinny headframe then straddled the shaft. A prefabricated cabin stood on the stone platform next to it. An ore car was parked on a rail that curved along the apron, and a small power line paralleled the rail. Open shelters lined the sides of the apron. Today, what is left is the foundations, boiler, and underground plumbing of the mill. "Frenchy Mine Nov. 30, 1937" is inscribed on the mill's concrete pillar. That year, the ore grade plummeted from a respectable 1.7 ounces per ton to a measly 0.1 ounce. Little did Auclair know that the golden days were over, and that there was no need for a mill...

At the northern tip of the apron's L, overlooking Pinto Basin, there used to be a good-size cabin. By the 1980s it had collapsed onto itself. It is still there, broken in hundreds of pieces, capped by its tin roof. It may have been the mine's office, or a bunkhouse. Given the spectacular panorama of Pinto Basin that it commands, one would hope, for the miners' sake, that it had a room with a view.

Mount Auclair. Even if mine ruins are not your cup of tea, it is well worth coming up here to climb the summit that rears up behind the mine, and get both a little exercise and even better views. For convenience, and to honor an unsung historic figure, I refer to it as Mount Auclair. From the mine a trail climbs about halfway to it. It starts a few steps in front of the mill, on the 15-foot ridge to the right of the mill. It is old and teetering on the brink of extinction, but still traceable. It follows the rocky ridge straight up 0.2 mile and 230 feet up to a saddle on the crest. The rest is 200 feet cross-country up the peak's open northeastern shoulder.

Mount Auclair overlooks a good portion of the park's north-central region. Somehow, when seen from this particular crest of the Hexie Mountains in the late afternoon, the Pinto Basin and the long and colorful Pinto Mountains rising behind it always seem to glow a deeper sheen of gold than other ranges in the park. With binoculars, dozens of sites near and far come into sharp focus—Queen Mountain, Queen Valley's Jumbo Rocks, the Arch Rock area, and the aligned trenches of the Golden Bell Mine. The Hexie Mountains themselves are easily the most striking, their hills and ridges as deeply sculpted as dunes.

The Golden Bee Mine

	Dist.(mi)	Elev.(ft)
Pinto Basin Road	0.0	2,280
Golden Bee Mine camp	1.2	2,380
Junction	1.45	2,620
Golden Bee Mine lower level	(0.05)	2,640
Golden Bee Mine upper level	1.65	2,870
Saddle on crest	1.85	~3,100
Mount Auclair	(0.15)	3,298
Leave trail	2.05	3,040
Paymaster Mine	2.25	~2,610
Road jct at canyon mouth	2.8	2,250
Back to Pinto Basin Road	4.0	2,280

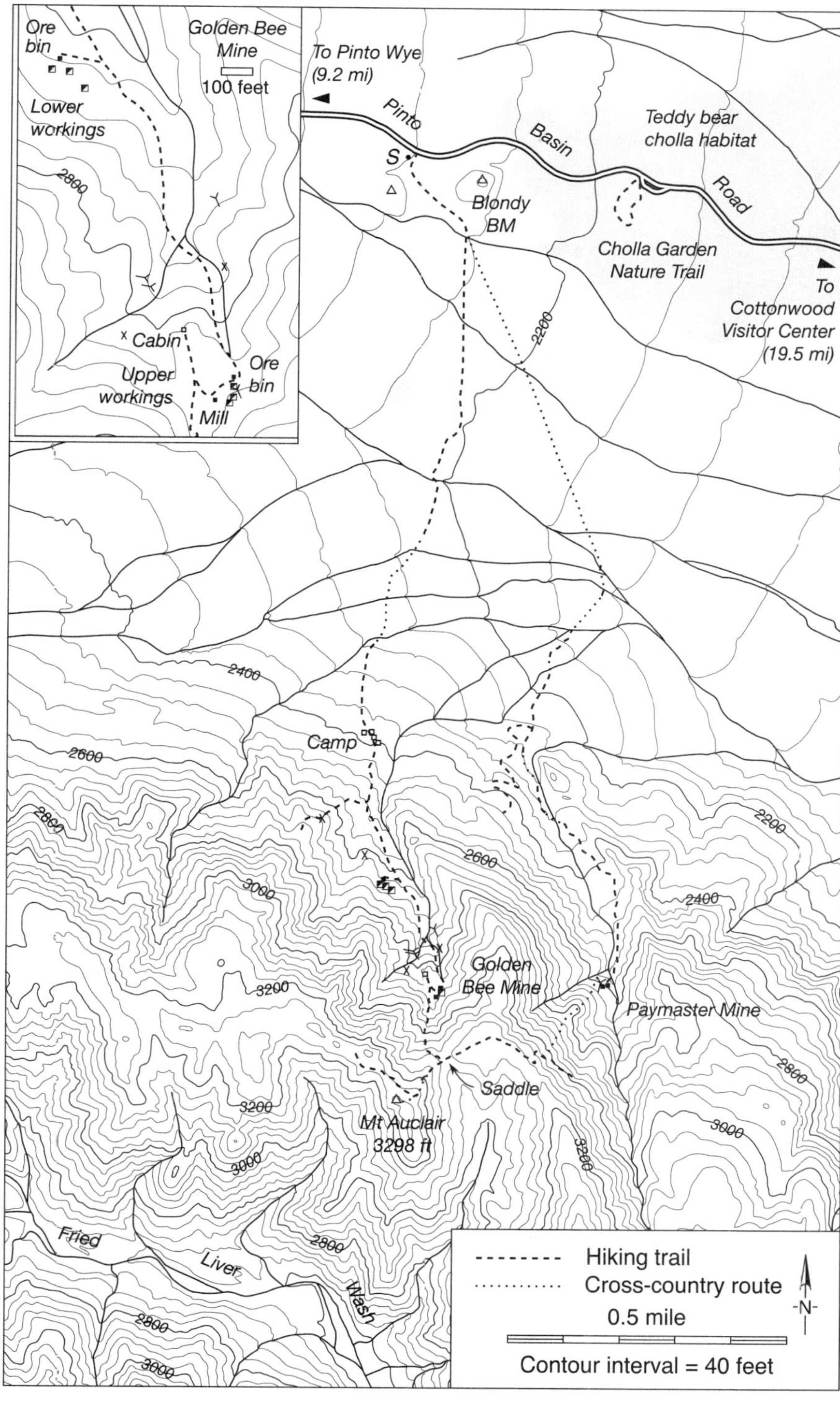
Ore bin
Golden Bee Mine
100 feet
Lower workings
2800
Cabin
Upper workings
Ore bin
Mill
To Pinto Wye (9.2 mi)
Pinto Basin Road
Teddy bear cholla habitat
S
Blondy BM
Cholla Garden Nature Trail
To Cottonwood Visitor Center (19.5 mi)
2200
2400
2600
2800
Camp
3000
3200
Golden Bee Mine
Paymaster Mine
Saddle
Mt Auclair 3298 ft
Fried Liver Wash
Hiking trail
Cross-country route
0.5 mile
N
Contour interval = 40 feet

Looking northwest across the Hexie Mountains from summit of Mount Auclair

The Paymaster Mine. The trail that climbs from the Golden Bee Mine to the crest actually continues into the next canyon east. It gains a little elevation eastward just below the crest, then descends a little into that canyon. In it there was a mine named Paymaster. Contemporary with the Golden Bee Mine, it shipped only in 1935, 1936, and 1940, and produced only 20% as much gold. Old mining trails like this one can be deeply satisfying. It was not used much when the mines were active, and even less since they shut down. You never know exactly what you will find. After two sharp switchbacks, the trail fades away at the top of a steep ravine. You will have to find your way down 300 feet to the mine, located on the west side just above a major fork in the canyon. Going down the ridge just after the second switchback is easier than the ravine. From the mine, an old road once ran down the length of the canyon and connected with the main road in Pinto Basin. Here too, two sections of road are gone at wash crossings, but it still leads down to the canyon mouth and the foot of the fan a third of a mile below it. From there it is almost all washed out; it is easiest to cut a beeline across the valley floor back to the two hills. If you are familiar with cross-country hiking, this is a great way to complete this hike without retracing your steps.

■

THE TOWERS OF UNCERTAINTY

At the northern edge of Pleasant Valley lies a group of strange and beautiful inselbergs known as the Towers of Uncertainty. The very name makes you ache to go. And you should. Divided into two groups separated by a rocky hill, it is an exceptional place, the north end a playground of whimsical fins and pinnacles that holds at its heart a mysterious tank, the south end a carousel of imposing pillars. The myriad intriguing formations, the confounding topography, the Joshua trees—will reinforce the unsettling feeling that you have been transported to an improbable world.

General Information

Road status: Hiking partly on maintained trail; graded access road
North Towers: 1.2 mi, 40 ft up, 80 ft down one way / easy
South Towers: 1.8 mi, 50 ft up, 250 ft down one way / moderate
Main attractions: Spectacular fins and spires, little-known tank
USGS 7.5' topo map: Malapai Hill
Maps: pp. 371

Location and Access

To get to the North Towers, take Park Boulevard to the signed Geology Tour Road, 9.6 miles from the north entrance. Drive south on this well-graded road 1.5 miles to a backcountry board on the left, and park. The Towers Hills are just visible about 1 mile to the south-southwest, poking over a bulge in Pleasant Valley. For the most direct route to the South Towers, park 1.3 miles further south at stop #3, on the right. The primitive trail at the pullout leads 0.5 mile west-northwest to the towers, visible from the road. The South Towers are occasionally closed, usually from late March through June, to allow nesting red-tailed hawks to mature. Inquire at a visitor center before coming here.

Route Description

From the backcountry board, head southwest on the California Riding and Hiking Trail across the slightly downhill valley floor. At this relatively high elevation, average temperatures are lower and the ground humidity is higher, and Pleasant Valley is just about as lush as it gets. After 0.35 mile, the trail crosses a small sandy wash just before a slight left bend. The pale outcrops of the North Towers of Uncertainty are then visible due south. Leave the trail and head down

Fins in the North Towers of Uncertainty

the wash toward them. The wash does not go all the way there: where it peters out, continue south cross country.

As you approach and enter the North Towers, you know instantly that you are in for some exceptional scenery. All around rise breathtaking clusters of standing rocks, tight ranks of parallel fins, split domes, leaning turrets, and sliced bedrock. The formations are comparatively small, hardly ever taller than 25 feet, but they are slender, vertical, and tightly packed. Some fins are implausibly sharp, as on a child's drawing. Others are as finely chiseled as three-dimensional lace. Just inside the North Towers there is a low dam known as Surprise Tank. It is a bit of a mystery, forgotten by history books, as hermetic as an unmarked grave. Its thin concrete wall, anchored in misshapen slickrock, is shaped like a caricatural lightning and crowned by decorative cobbles. Only three feet at its highest point, it is still embossed with the ripples of the corrugated iron that molded it. When the rains have filled up the tiny flood plain behind it, Surprise Tank covers only a fraction of an acre. Yet it is then a memorable sight, its dark-blue waters a perfect mirror that duplicates the surrounding stonework. More often than not it is waterless, a patch of parched mud invaded by grass. Long after the rains, coyotes and bighorn sheep dig deep holes in it to drink the groundwater.

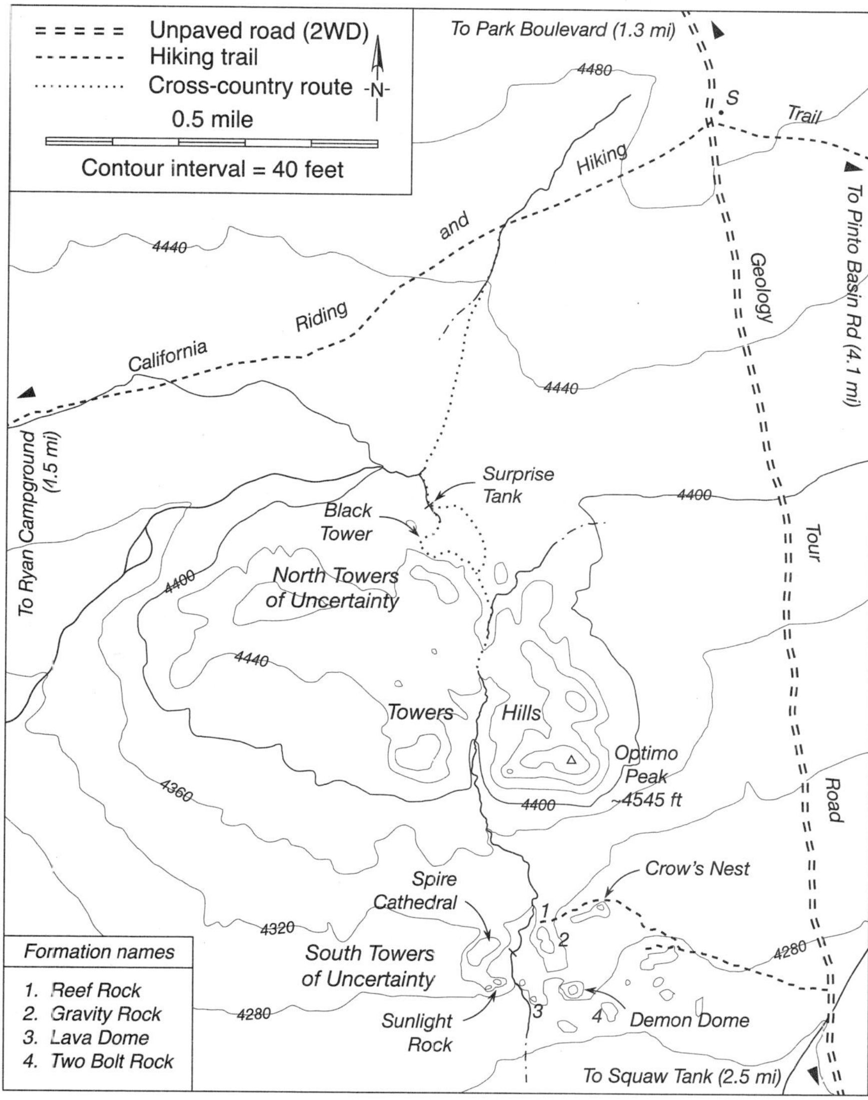

The Towers of Uncertainty

	Dist.(mi)	Elev.(ft)
CRHT at Geology Tour Road	0.0	4,493
Leave CRHT Trail	0.35	4,460
Surprise Tank	0.8	4,420
Pass	1.35	~4,445
South Towers of Uncertainty	1.8	~4,270

For an easy loop into this remarkable rock gallery, from the tank walk up the flood plain to a blockade of boulders, then let the passages between hard rocks guide you generally west up the hillside. When you have had your fill, return east across mostly slickrock, then south along the North Towers' east side. The work of erosion is different here, as if it had been powered by the crushing gravity of a giant planet. The dislocated remains of defunct monuments lie everywhere, gigantic blocks crashed into fins, screes of boulders, broken columns waiting for the next 8.0 earthquake to tip them over. A black pinnacle known as the Dark Tower looms over this devastation. Yet fate has spared a collection of standing structures with symmetric shapes, incongruous in this upheaval. Even the plants conspire to add strangeness. Live forever grow all over, far more than I have ever seen, their fleshy pink stems poking out of cracks like an alien invasion.

Although the South Towers of Uncertainty are a short walking distance from the Geology Tour Road, it is more satisfying to hike to them from the North Towers over the Towers Hills. From the tank, head southeast across the flood plain, making short jogs left or right to avoid outcrops, to the south end of the North Towers (0.2 mile). Then veer south just far enough to enter the shallow drainage down to the left. Follow it south 0.3 mile to a pass west of Optimo Peak. Then continue south down a narrow, twisted wash 0.5 mile to the far end of the South Towers. This is a fun traverse, with only 50 feet of elevation gain and a little scrambling, peaceful and just adventurous enough to make it exciting. Much of it crosses scenic, boulder-strewn hills, along open drainages livened by quite a few juniper. After exploring the South Towers, return along the east side of the Towers Hills, or on the road.

The South Towers of Uncertainty are composed of about a dozen distinct inselbergs shooting right out of the valley floor. In contrast to the North Towers, here almost everything is big, tall, massive, a landscape that makes you crane your neck. All the pieces are different, like on an oversized chess board at the end of a game. Reef Rock, the first one on the left, is an imposing stack of irregular walls sliced by fine cracks. The monument across the wash is Spire Cathedral, an impossibly complex assemblage of pinnacles of all sizes. At the south end, Sunlight Rock is a magnificent twin pillars, and Demon Dome an 80-foot cone of boulders. Or are they? When viewed from a different side, they look entirely different. After wandering through them for a while, you are no longer sure where you are, as if someone had moved the pieces around. The name Towers of Uncertainty, even though it was likely coined by a climber high on adrenaline, is devilishly accurate.

■

MALAPAI HILL

Rising steeply 500 feet at the muted divide between Queen Valley and Pleasant Valley, Malapai Hill is an old stock of magma that intruded a mountain of granite but fell short of erupting as flowing lava. Climbing it is short and sweet—a peaceful stroll through an open desert garden, a brief vigorous climb, and you are there. The cooling magma formed intriguing columnar joints exposed among cliffs near the summit. The broad volcano overlooks the two spacious valleys and their alien plantations of Joshua trees and inselbergs.

General Information
Road status: Roadless; graded access road (2WD)
Malapai Hill: 0.8 mi, 480 ft up, 40 ft down one way / easy–moderate
Main attractions: Volcanic hill, balanced boulder, columnar joints
USGS 7.5' topo map: Malapai Hill
Maps: pp. 375*, *351*

Location and Access

From Park Boulevard inside the park drive to the signed Geology Tour Road, which is 9.6 miles from the north entrance station, or 21.3 miles from the west entrance station. Drive south on the graded Geology Tour Road 4.65 miles to a slanted sandy pullout on the west (right) side, across from a low pile of boulders to the west, and park. Malapai Hill is the isolated mountain about half a mile west of the road—it is clearly visible along the last 3 miles. Standard-clearance vehicles routinely make it down this well-graded road.

Route Description

Malapai Hill is a peculiar mountain. Its dark twin domes seem to have been plopped down onto Queen Valley's bajada like two discarded scoops of partly melted chocolate ice cream. The hill is made of congealed magma that rose in at least two pulses of volcanism starting 16 million years ago when the crust was thinned by extensional tectonic forces, possibly along the San Andreas Fault. The magma may have brought along with it the hydrothermal solutions that mineralized the rich deposits at the nearby Lost Horse Mine.

Being unusually symmetrical, Malapai Hill can be climbed via many routes of comparable difficulty. The most direct route is up to the saddle visible on the crest following a course north of the crease

Balanced boulder below Malapai Hill

between the two humps, then along the gentle crest to either of the two summits. From the pullout on the Geology Tour Road it is a pleasant stroll southwest toward the base of the hill, skirting south of the boulder pile that stands half way there. The approach is inviting, across a peaceful desert garden on an open bajada of compacted coarse sand peppered with boulders. Every plant seems to have its place, as carefully positioned as in a manicured garden. Small Joshua trees, Mojave yucca, silver cholla, ephedra, manzanita, honey mesquite, and even tufts of grass, all grow a respectful distance from each other, unwilling to share too little rain with too many. The area is home to healthy diamond cholla, armed to the teeth with golden rosettes of two-inch spines. A local landmark not to miss is the impressive balanced boulder 150 yards south of the boulder pile's west end. About 16 feet tall and up to 20 feet across, shaped like a hot-air balloon, it stands on a base much narrower than its girth.

From the balanced boulder, the elevation drops a little to the wash that runs along the eastern base of Malapai Hill. Originally buried under White Tank Monzogranite, the hill's lower slopes were subsequently exhumed by erosion. A small field of white boulders was left behind up ahead. Just south of this field, a long talus of darker basalt spills down the flank of Malapai Hill. The talus is free of vegetation

Malapai Hill

	Dist.(mi)	Elev.(ft)
Geology Tour Road	0.0	3,840
Balanced boulder	0.25	3,835
Wash at foot of eastern slope	0.4	3,810
Saddle at crest	0.7	4,000
Malapai Hill	0.8	~4,280

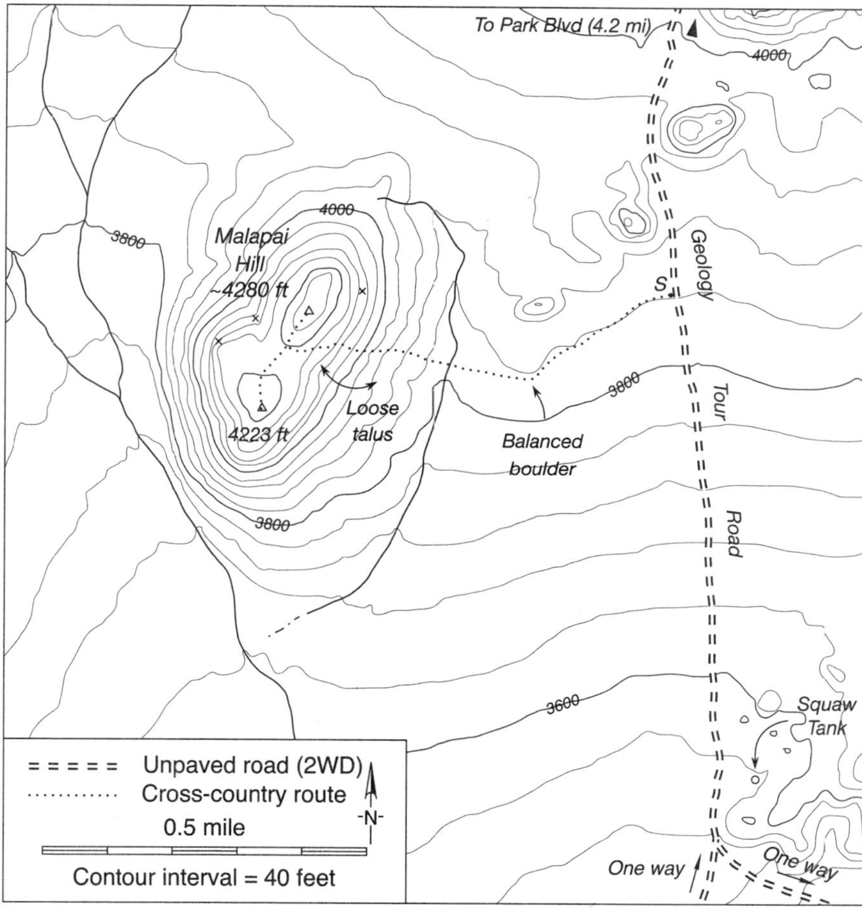

and slightly more gradual, but it is made of loose rocks of precisely the wrong size, too small to step on and too large to ignore. The best route starts below the boulder field. Cut a beeline up across the boulders toward the saddle, then continue in the same direction, avoiding the talus by staying north of it. The hillside is an iconic wasteland of steel-gray basalt cobbles sun-baked to burnt sienna. The vegetation quickly thins down to a meager cover of tousled grasses, desiccated shrubs, and scrawny yucca. Even the calico cactus seem to have a hard time, although occasionally a red-spined cottontop cactus radiating with life illuminates the dark rocks. For a diminutive mountain, Malapai Hill manages to put up a good fight shortly above the boulders, where the pitch steepens to a healthy 40%, but the crest is not far away.

When magma cools, especially in contact with groundwater, it contracts and fractures in hexagonal cracks that propagate through the

Malapai Hill seen from Squaw Tank

solidifying rock and form tall stacks of parallel prismatic columns. There are many world-famous examples of imposing columnar joints, Wyoming's Devils Tower being one of the most striking in the U.S. Malapai Hill has basalt columnar joints of its own, albeit on a small scale. The largest exposure is west of the saddle. In a steep cleft below the rim, the wall is coated with inclined geometric facets, like the inside of a giant geode. There is another outcrop, more accessible but more eroded, on the open slope northeast of the summit.

The views from the summit embrace two valleys of very different origin, cupped in a ring of desolate mountains. Pleasant Valley to the south is a structural basin formed by the sinking of two mountain blocks. Long ago, when the rains were generous, it held a small pluvial lake at the tip of the Hexie Mountains. Queen Valley to the north is the tilted pediment left behind by the erosion of a mountain. Whimsical boulder piles knife out of its bulging bajada. When the sun slips over the Little San Bernardino Mountains, every single boulder glows like amber, and for a few minutes the valley radiates a thousand points of light. Malapai Hill is close and easy enough that it gives us the luxury to attend a glorious sunset and return before full darkness.

■

LELA PEAK

Lela Peak is a nice little mountain that can be climbed via two very different routes, one a fairly quick ramble up a short rock-strewn canyon, the other a tougher scramble up through an exciting ravine clogged with boulders. It is a delightful stroll through a scenic cove to the foot of the range where the two routes diverge, the mountain has plenty of interesting cacti and rocks, and the summit commands tremendous views over Queen Valley and the southern Mojave Desert.

General Information

Road status: Roadless; graded access road (2WD)
Lela Peak (southern route): 2.3 mi, 940 ft up, 60 ft down one way / easy
Lela Peak (northern route): 2.5 mi, 900 ft up, 20 ft down one way / moder.
Main attractions: Views of Queen Valley's boulder piles, bouldering
USGS 7.5' topo map: Malapai Hill
Maps: pp. 379*, *351*

Location and Access

Lela Peak is the highest summit in the western Hexie Mountains, overlooking both Queen Valley and Pleasant Valley. The starting point for this climb is the same as for Malapai Hill. Lela Peak is about 2 air miles due east, hidden by the false summit capped with dark rocks at the east end of the pronounced cove in the mountain.

Route Description

The only difficulty in this climb—difficulty being a big word—is circumventing the false summit (~4,525 ft) to get to its east side. This can be done either on its south side or on its north side. Both routes share a common start, across the open cove east of the road. Aim west-southwest, towards the green valley on the false summit's south side. About a mile deep by a mile wide, the cove is a scenic bajada enclosed to the south by a rising ridge of pale granitic lumps, and to the north by a crest of pointed inselbergs. The vegetation is typical Joshua Tree fare, a green garden of creosote, manzanita, and desert almond spiked with silver and diamond chollas, Mojave yucca, and small Joshua trees. From late February to May the hard-packed gravel is bedecked with a congregation of wildflowers covering the alphabet, from aster to desert gold poppies, globemallow, nama, and wooly daisies.

After 0.9 mile you will cross a wash coming down from the northeast. This is where the two routes diverge. For the easier route, continue in the same direction (west-southwest), past a thin obelisk—the only shade since the road—up the boulder-strewn wash that scoots around the southern flank of the false summit. The wash soon splits. Take the left fork, a stony drainage on the cusp between a large ravine and a small canyon. Its wash, cluttered with rocks, can be bypassed close by on the tilted north side, where a use trail is starting to emerge. This area is striking when the cacti are blooming, especially the calico cactus and their fluorescent purplish-magenta flowers. At its upper end the canyon opens out to a small playa in full view of Lela Peak. The area up ahead is a billowing plateau, sparsely vegetated, with ground as smooth as sifted gravel. The rest is straightforward, first across the plateau to the foot of the peak, then up to the saddle southwest of it, and finally northeast along the open ridge to the summit.

Thanks to its central position and relatively high elevation, Lela Peak commands fine views of the park in every direction. The unusual viewing angles mystify the landscape and obscure familiar features, but all of the local mountains are showcased, in a complex kaleidoscope of colors and shapes. The most striking element in this vast panorama is the many pyramids of boulders that dot Queen Valley to the west, as mysterious as a township of ancient Maya temples.

For the second route, at the wash 0.9 mile from the start angle left (northeast) along its open strip of sand. Over the next 0.4 mile the

Lela Peak

	Dist.(mi)	Elev.(ft)
Southern route		
Geology Tour Road	0.0	3,840
Wash crossing	0.9	3,835
Playa at head of south-side cyn	1.5	4,340
Saddle	1.9	~4,580
Lela Peak	2.3	4,723
Northern route		
Geology Tour Road	0.0	3,840
Wash crossing	0.9	3,835
Start of boulder jam bypass	1.45	3,955
Top of boulder jam	1.65	~4,200
Leave wash (NW shoulder)	2.15	~4,430
Lela Peak	2.5	4,723

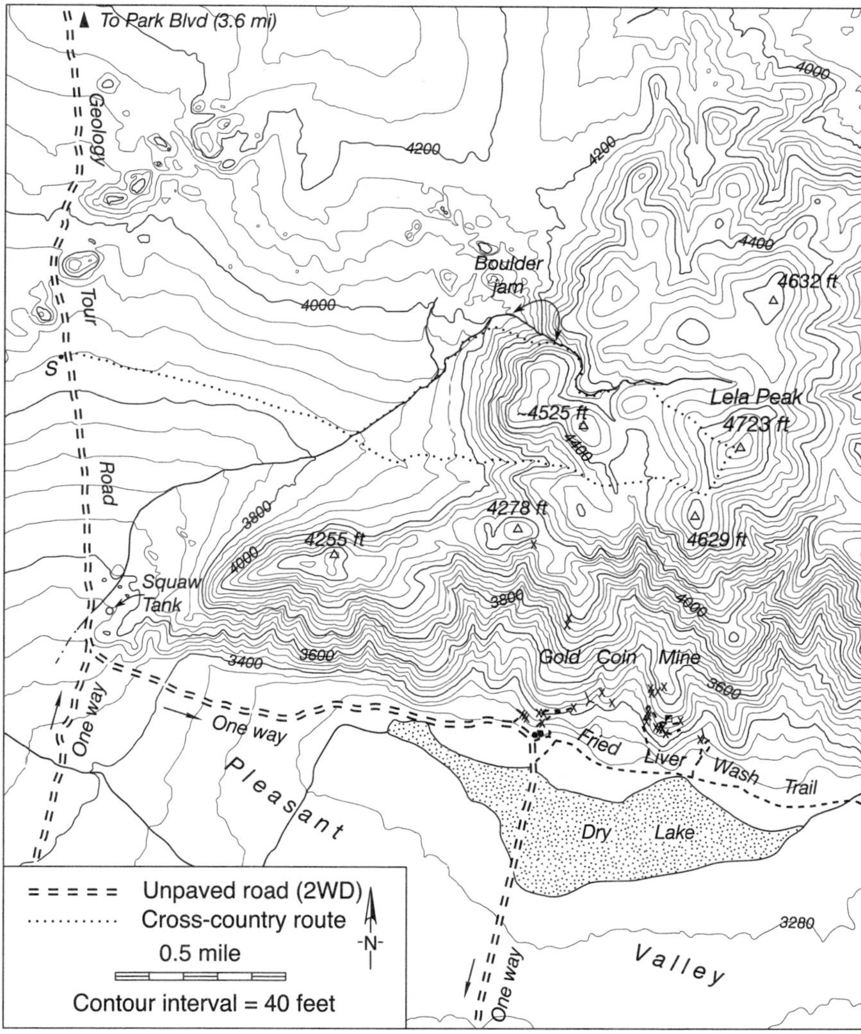

wash forks twice; take the right fork each time. Near the mountain, shallow banks rise steeply on both sides. The wash then makes a sharp 90° right bend around a huge boulder, and soon after disappears into a steep ravine choked under a monumental jumble of giant boulders. Slithering, crawling, and clawing up this column of smooth rounded rocks is the most fun on this climb, even though every boulder seems to have a wish to fall. One of them did, near the top of the jam, a bolt of granite that came to rest to fashion a delicate window. If this looks too daunting, leave the wash at the bottom, 50 yards before the sharp right bend (see map), when you are abreast with a tall conical boulder

Queen Valley's boulder pyramids from boulder jam on north route to Lela Peak

smeared with a patch of chalk on the west bench. Exit the wash and climb the steep, relatively open slope east-southeast, aiming for the canyon at the top of the boulder jam, where it gives way to darker rocks above. There are several ways to enter the canyon in this vicinity.

From there on up, the canyon is less steep and still has boulders for about 250 yards, but they are angular, easier to negotiate (Class 2 at most), and they progressively thin down. This canyon is greener than the rest of the mountain, its boulders capturing moisture that attracts catclaw, ephedra, wishbone bush, and manzanita the size of small trees. At the fork, keep left. About half a mile past the boulder jam, leave the wash on the right, and follow Lela Peak's northwestern shoulder up to the summit.

Returning down the jam's pillowy boulders is Lela Peak's greatest offering. The views over Queen Valley's pyramids are even more spectacular than from the summit. In the golden hours of evening, every boulder is sharply highlighted against its own shadow. Down in the cove, the backlit cholla glow in golden fluorescent light. In April, when the paperbag bush are blooming, their countless translucent pods capture the setting sun's rays and light up like Christmas bulbs.

■

THE GOLD COIN MINE

At the eastern point of the Hexie Mountains, where they knife into the cramped tectonic sink of Pleasant Valley, a sprawling mine named Gold Coin struggled for a few decades in the early twentieth century. Most of the countless visitors who drive by its abandoned cyanide tanks every year barely stop, and they miss the best. Take the time to explore and become acquainted with this forgotten gold mine down on its luck. The hills are honeycombed with workings, and navigating the miner's trails that loop through them while enjoying the views of the valley's dry lake is a lot of fun.

General Information
Road status: Primitive access road (HC); hiking on old mining trails
The Gold Coin Mine loop: 1.5 mi, 460 ft up loop/easy
Main attractions: Gold mine, mining trails, views of dry lake and valley
USGS 7.5' topo map: Malapai Hill
Maps: pp. 383*, 389, *351*

Location and Access

The Gold Coin Mine is a popular stop along the Geology Tour Road, mostly for its conspicuous historic twin tanks. Refer to *Malapai Hill* for directions to this signed road. Drive it south 5.5 miles to the junction where it becomes one way. Turn left and go 1.4 miles to a pullout on the left, next to the tanks. This road is drivable with a standard-clearance vehicle to the junction. It is one way beyond, and the loop returning to the junction has some rough spots, so although a standard sedan can make it, a high-clearance vehicle is preferable.

Route Description

The Gold Coin Mine is one of these singular mines that were worked extensively yet had nothing to show in the end. Between its opening around 1900 and its final throes in the 1930s, a total of ten shafts, several tunnels, and at least two dozen exploratory workings were sunk in three areas scattered across nine claims on a steep mountain slope. Two companies worked on it intermittently, the German-American Mining and Milling Company from its earliest years to 1916, then the Gold Galena Company until the 1930s. A brave couple gave it a try too around 1911, then Bill Keys himself in 1920 and subsequent years. One of the directors of the first company, F. C. Longnecker, saw enough value in the property to be president of the second company, then to own it until the 1950s. In all those years, miners built roads into the mountain to access the workings, a cableway to lower the ore to the valley, a mill to extract the gold, and a camp to retire at night. But no production was ever recorded. We can only speculate that like most gold mines, if it produced at all it was in its earliest years. It is possible that sizable earnings were realized then, and not declared for tax evasion. But it is improbable: had the Gold Coin Mine been prolific, it would have been noticed. In all likelihood, this aspiring mine with a catchy name never generated more than a few sacks of gold coins...

From the pullout it is a short scramble to the mine's rusted twin tanks. The mill's concrete foundations are on a narrow bench just above them, a small affair that might have consisted only of a crusher. The tanks and the mill were installed around 1929, at the start of the Great Depression's mining revival. In early years, the water needed at the mine was hauled over the rough road from Pinyon Well, which was providentially just a few miles away. The mill likely used the same source. The lack of tailings hints that it did not treat very much ore.

The mine had three groups of workings strung along half a mile of mountain front past the mill. The mine's backbone was a road known today as the Fried Liver Wash Trail, which starts at the parking area and strikes east along the base of the mountains. Three spur roads split off from it and climb to each group. The first one is just uphill from the mill and ascends to the west group's main shaft (0.2 mile). The second road is 0.3 mile down the trail. It is washed out at its lower end, but it is visible from the trail and easy to walk to. It is approximately 0.3 mile to the middle group's extensive workings. The third spur is 0.3 mile further along the trail. It ends shortly in an elongated loop, visible from the trail, with its apex at the east group.

The workings seem to be strewn randomly across the hills, as if the miners were searching for a lost lode without a clue. But there was a reason to their apparent madness. The workings are actually locally aligned. The gold was brought up in the Mesozoic when magma rose through faults and formed granite dikes. Metal-rich molten silica wicked into cracks in the sheared host. The silica solidified into quartz, the lead and gold into auriferous galena, and the iron into neat cubes of pyrite. Knowing their geology, the miners looked for these elusive gold-bearing quartz stringers along the straight edges of the dikes.

The most interesting way to visit the Gold Coin Mine is to seek out the miners' old foot trails. They link the workings in a wavering daisy chain that contours the hills almost continuously from the mill to the east group, a distance of 0.7 mile. From the mill, hike up the road

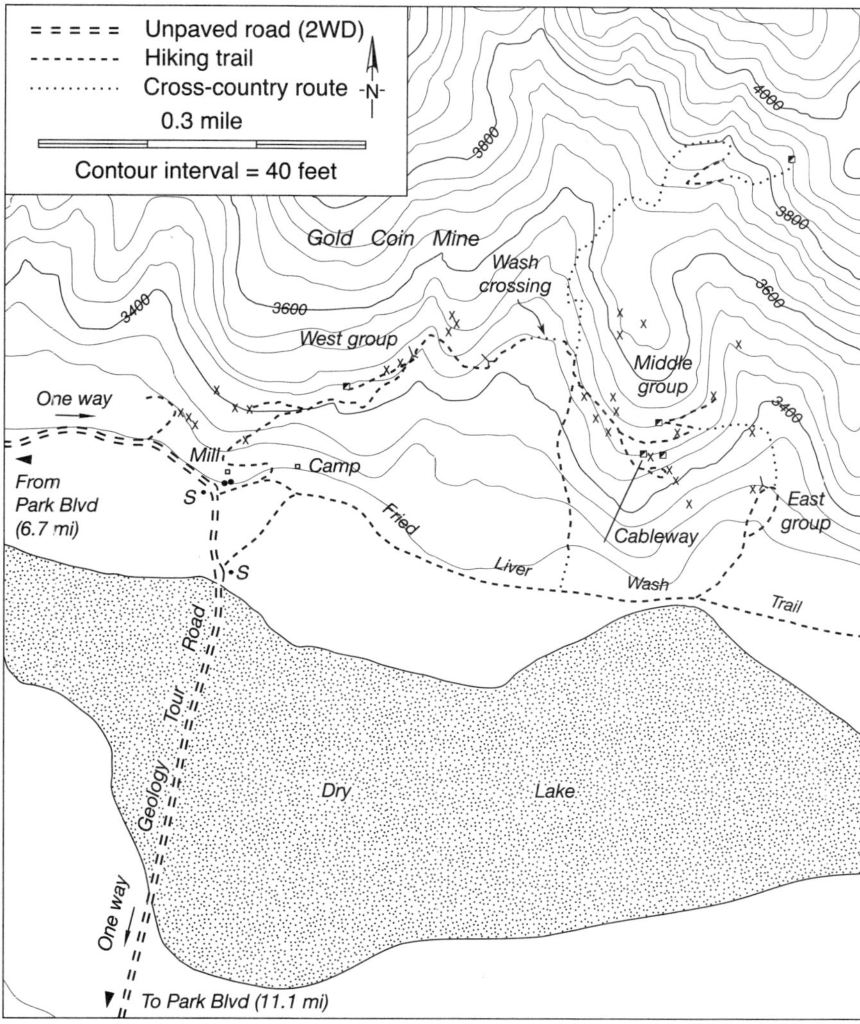

The Gold Coin Mine		
	Dist.(mi)	Elev.(ft)
Geology Tour Road	0.0	3,275
West group (shaft)	0.2	3,435
Wash crossing	0.4	3,435
Middle group (switchback)	0.6	3,500
East group (top of loop road)	0.7	3,500
Fried Liver Wash Trail	0.8	3,250
Back to Geology Tour Rd	1.25	3,275

Twin cyanide tanks and mill foundations at the Gold Coin Mine

northeast to the first shaft, then past it in the same direction on a foot trail to the next working. A fainter path continues across a ravine, then around a ridge to a steep wash, where it ends. Cross the wash eastward to another trail on its far side. It climbs southeast 200 feet to the switchback along the middle spur road. Take this road up to a fork. Both forks lead to shafts with large tailings. To close the loop, from the left switchback in the upper road descend cross-country, east then south, to the east group, then return along the Fried Liver Wash Trail.

Devoid of signs, slowly succumbing to the encroaching hand of nature, these forgotten trails are a lot of fun. The hills are packed with angular gneiss black with desert varnish, sunbleached grasses, and the red heads of barrel cactus. The site takes in fine views of Pleasant Valley and its small dry lake, and the staggered ridges of the Little San Bernardino Mountains beyond. The tailings are stained with the blood and ochre hues of iron ores, the greens of copper minerals, and the gray smears of galena. The workings are all different, from small craters to twin tunnels and inclined shafts that stare from the depths of the Earth. Strangely, a couple of them have been carefully sealed with mortared stone, as if to bottle in a prodigious treasure. Perhaps, after all, the Gold Coin was not as destitute as history leads us to believe...

■

THE HEXAHEDRON MINE AND MILL

The Hexahedron Mine's greatest asset is its isolation. Tucked in the folds of the Hexie Mountains, it is far enough to be lightly visited and to give a satisfying sense of remoteness. Not that it is a hard hike: a mining trail climbs all the way to it, a very easy path along Pleasant Valley at first, then a rocky, aerobic wagon road up to and over the crest. The highlights of this small gold mine out on its luck are its picturesque stone cabin, interesting ore, and spacious views of the central region of the park. The site of its lost mill, which had five stamps, a well, and a stone cabin, can be reached for a fraction of the effort, along a scenic wash lined with willow.

General Information

Road status: Graded access road (HC)
Hexahedron Mine (tunnel): 4.5 mi, 840 ft up, 230 ft down one way / mod.
Hexahedron Mill: 3.4 mi, 50 ft up, 170 ft down one way / easy
Main attractions: An old trail to a remote gold mine, mill, and cabins
USGS 7.5' topo map: Malapai Hill
Maps: pp. 389*, *351*

Location and Access

The Hexahedron Mine is located just below the crest of the northern block of the Hexie Mountains, north of the eastern edge of Pleasant Valley. The starting point is the same as for the Gold Coin Mine.

Route Description

The Hexahedron Mine. This is one of the region's oldest mines. It started around 1893–1894, within a few months of the Lost Horse and the Desert Queen, although it was not anywhere near as rich. It was then owned by Ed Holland and Alfred Tingman, local mine developers who also co-owned the nearby Pinyon and Lost Horse mines. The Hexie Mine, as it became affectionately known, was fairly busy for a time. It was said to have a well, a five-stamp mill, and in 1907 it employed as many as a dozen workers. It was company-owned and still running in 1914, but four years later the site was abandoned and the mill hauled away. In the 1930s, John and Margaret Samuelson, of Samuelson's Rock fame, reclaimed the property. But like others before them, they likely came home empty-handed. The Hexie Mine's only recorded production is a little shy of 120 ounces of gold in 1893, then

Looking west at Pleasant Valley from lower end of the Hexahedron Mine Trail

valued at a pitiful $2,413... It is once again a puzzle that none of the usually savvy early miners involved here realized sooner—before the investments, the costly mill, the 500 feet of diggings, the long hours of back-breaking work—that the Hexie was a dud.

The Hexahedron was unremarkable, but its access road makes up for it. From the Geology Tour Road the aging twin tracks of the Fried Liver Wash Trail closely follows the straight scarp of the Hexie Mountains at the edge of Pleasant Valley's dry lake. On the far side the valley unfolds several miles to the Little San Bernardino Mountains. On the other, the mountain rises sharply from a fault in scalloped hills mantled with darkly stained blocks of gneiss. Here at the valley's lowest point, the lake's alkaline soil is poisoning most plants. All it can support is a stubby grassland studded with widely spaced creosote. Only after a mile do other plants join in—small Joshua trees, then yucca, burrobush, big sagebrush—until the desert is flushed with vegetation. The foothills are blanketed with dwarf forests of Mojave yucca and an invasion of barrel cactus, flaming-red among the dark rocks.

For a long time, the trail is so gentle that it is hard to tell whether it is level or going down. Only where the vegetation picks up does it begin to perceptibly descend alongside Fried Liver Wash. After 2.6 miles, it splits: the main trail continues alongside the wash, while the

Stone cabin at the Hexahedron Mine

Hexahedron Mine Trail takes off on the left. This junction is gone and thankfully not signed, and searching for it adds a little fun. To find it easily without electronic assistance, about half a mile before getting to it look up ahead for a pointed 150-foot hill that protrudes from the range front. It is the west end of a half-mile linear ridge parallel and connected to the range front by a low saddle. About 0.2 mile before this hill, the trail reaches a low hump of pale-gray gravel on the right side of the wash. Leave the trail and cut a beeline at 11 o'clock (east), across the wash, toward the saddle. The Hexahedron Mine Trail soon becomes visible where it starts its short climb to the saddle, between two metal posts. When you reach the saddle, the long ramp of the mining road will be in full view, climbing across the mountain front.

Supported by well-built sturdy walls, this trail has stood the test of time. It is extant the whole 1.8 miles to the mine, first as the rocky ramp that climbs the mountain diagonally, then as a grade stripped to bedrock that shoots up a steep ridge, and finally as a leisurely path across the broad crest and down the far side to the mine. The rewards of this puffing ascent are expansive views of the valley and surrounding mountains, and a close look at the mountain flora, a hardy mix of calico, beavertail, and cushion foxtail cactus, diamond and silver cholla, manzanita and brittlebush, and literally thousands of barrel cactus.

The Hexahedron Mine must have taken pride in its stone cabin, set on a narrow promontory against a scenic backdrop of slanted outcrops. It commands a grand view of northern Pleasant Valley, Queen Valley, and their rings of mountains, impressive for its spaciousness and isolation. Its six-foot walls are made of small blocks of granite and gneiss carefully selected to minimize gaps and keep the weather out. Its picture window frames a peaceful view of the hilly canyon below.

At the cabin, the road forks into two short spurs. The upper road curves up to four trenches. The lower road drops to the main tunnel, which was 300 feet long and serviced by rail tracks. The Hexahedron Mine is different from all other gold mines in this range: here the gold was not found in milky quartz but in a volcanic dike. The host is felsite, a matrix of quartz and feldspar so fine-grained that it looks like a sedimentary rock and breaks in conchoidal surfaces like porcelain. The gold was dispersed in it in very fine specks barely visible to the naked eye. Many of the rocks exposed around the mine are felsite. Some bear the black dendritic markings of manganese ore, especially on the rock walls at the workings. Many have a reddish coating of oxidized pyrite. None look like they belong in a gold mine...

The sheltered terrace on the cabin's east side would have been a great place to watch the sunrise; to stay cool on blazing summer afternoons; and to cook and sleep after a hard day's work playing with power tools, repairing equipment, and loading ore in dark tunnels. Most of us have to wait for the weekend to have this much fun, and we do not get to blow up rocks. When staring at the immensity of the surrounding desert, it is hard not to ponder... Back in the early 1890s, before automobiles and satellite images, in a desert so vast that in a lifetime of wandering a person on foot cannot humanly cover but a fraction of it, how did Holland and Tingman discover this place?

The Hexahedron Mine and Mill

	Dist.(mi)	Elev.(ft)
Geology Tour Road	0.0	3,275
Hexahedron Mine Trail (jct)	2.6	3,168
Hexahedron Mill	(0.75)	3,155
Saddle	2.9	3,210
Pass at crest	4.2	3,970
Hexahedron Mine cabin	4.5	3,900
Upper trenches	(0.05)	3,920
Main tunnel	4.55	3,880

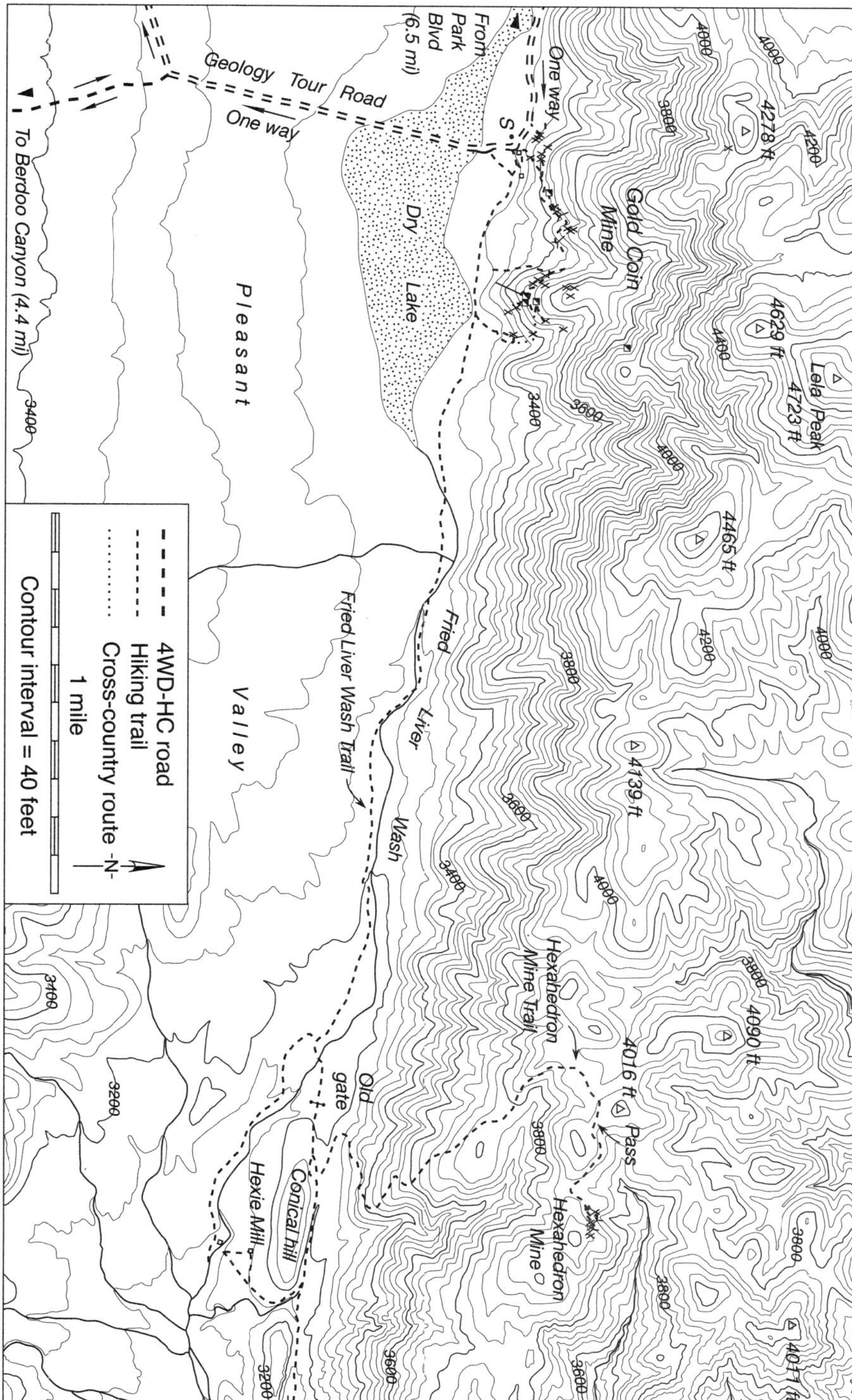
Geology Tour Road
One way
From Park Blvd (6.5 mi)
To Berdoo Canyon (4.4 mi)
S
Dry Lake
Pleasant Valley
Gold Coin Mine
4278 ft
4629 ft
Lela Peak 4723 ft
4465 ft
4139 ft
Fried Liver Wash
Fried Liver Wash Trail
Hexahedron Mine Trail
4090 ft
4016 ft
Pass
Hexahedron Mine
Old gate
Conical hill
Hexie Mill
4011 ft
4WD-HC road
Hiking trail
Cross-country route
1 mile
Contour interval = 40 feet
N

The Hexahedron Mill. The Hexie Mill is an enduring mystery. We do not know who built it or when, how much of the Hexie ore it processed, whether it treated custom ore, and what became of it after it was dismantled. For decades its exact location, in fact its very existence, were speculative. But it did exist, at a logical location, up a small slope at the southeast end of the linear ridge. It is easy to get to it. After returning to the bottom of the Hexahedron Mine Trail, continue east along the Fried Liver Wash Trail, or down the wash itself if the trail gets too faint to follow. It is a pleasant walk, infused with solitude and the quiet euphoria of vast open spaces. The braided wash of clear sand is soon sprinkled with the apple-green of large willows. Small Joshua trees grow on the open banks. Here as all along this drainage, the banks are pockmarked with the dens of desert tortoise.

After 0.6 mile, the wash makes an abrupt 90° elbow to the right. From that point down, the left bank is a 250-foot-long wall excavated by flashfloods into the valley's brilliant sediments. The millsite was in this area. Across from the eastern end of the wall, on the right bank, is the crumbling ruin of a stone cabin that may have housed the mill workers—hopefully not too many of them, as it is sensibly the same size as the mine cabin. It was built more crudely, of rough stones mortared with local mudstone. The capped well is in this area too. Just across the wash, climb onto the bank and you will see an old road that climbs a tenth of a mile to the "lost" mill. It is marked by debris, a web of fading road spurs, and what looks like a few thousand cubic feet of eroding mill tailings. If the ore that was processed here carried the average gold value of local mines, and if it all came out of this property, the Hexahedron Mine produced indeed very little.

■

MONUMENT MOUNTAIN

Located at the edge of the Sonoran Desert, this remote summit commands far-reaching views into two different deserts, long empty bajadas on one side, and saw-toothed mountains on the other. The incline is modest, up a long series of steps capped with boulders and low outcrops. The area is replete with igneous and metamorphic rocks of all kinds, and host to an interesting combination of plants brought together by the convergence of two worlds.

General Information
Road status: Roadless; primitive access road (HC)
Monument Mountain: 2.9 mi, 1,720 ft up, 130 ft down one way / moder.
Main attraction: Isolated summit overlooking two deserts
USGS 7.5' topo map: Washington Wash
Maps: pp. 393*, *351*

Location and Access

The highest point in the Hexie Mountains, Monument Mountain dominates the southeastern tip of the range, its distant pointed summit girdled by a broad shield of sinuous ridges. If it weren't for the primitive road in Smoke Tree Wash, the wide east-west drainage south of the summit that divides the Hexie Mountains from the Cottonwood Mountains, it would be a long hike to it. To get to this road, take Interstate 10 to the Cottonwood Springs Road exit. This is prime undeveloped country, some 22 miles east of the last busy exit back in Indio, and further still from the next busy exit in Blythe, near the Arizona border. Follow the Cottonwood Springs Road north, up through Cottonwood Canyon along the boundary between the Cottonwood Mountains to the west and the Eagle Mountains to the east. In early spring the lower desert is brilliant with palo verde and ocotillos in bloom. After 6.8 miles you will reach the Cottonwood Visitor Center—the last chance to fill up on water. Just before it, a good graded road on the left side heads north. Follow it 1 mile to a locked gate. The dirt road on the left at the gate is the Pinkham Canyon Road. It curls slowly west by northwest around the Cottonwood Mountains, then skims the edge of Smoke Tree Wash. It is a slow road, hemmed in by healthy creosote, slashed by countless erosion channels that turn the ride into a choppy flight. Even with high clearance it is hard not to scratch bottom at the deepest trenches. Park after 4.2 miles at a two-car turnout on the left, across from metal stakes lining the road. Monument Mountain is a little west of north, hidden by its own massive foothills.

Route Description

At the road you are in the Sonoran Desert. Monument Mountain, less than 3 air miles away, is in the Mojave Desert. As you cross Smoke Tree Wash north from the road toward the mountain you slip from one desert into the other. This stretch of Smoke Tree Wash has no smoke trees, a denizen of the Sonoran Desert, although there are plenty a few miles downhill. It supports instead a scatter of bright-green desert willow that subsist on the moisture buried beneath its sand. On the north side of the wash, where the plain swells into foothills, you are standing at the edge of the Sonoran Desert. As in celebration of this invisible division, one ultimate grove of ocotillo graces the hillside, their long skinny arms tipped with bright vermillion flames in the spring.

Plated with large rocks, dark and bulky, Monument Mountain looks a little tough from a distance. The ascent follows the ridge that climbs behind the ocotillo grove, which is the mountain's south shoulder. It is a long series of steps capped with rocky outcrops. Somehow there is always a convenient way around the obstacles. The first section is the steepest. It crosses the first two local summits, best bypassed on the west side along sloped causeways of monzonite. These paler exposures are generally relatively clear of large rocks and easier to navigate than the darker outcrops. Above the second summit the main ridge is gained across more open ground. It offers the first views into the desolate northeastern section of the park. The next false summit is very rocky and rougher, but there are a few good routes to circumvent it on the east side. The rest is generally easier, over broader and gentler ridges that offer plenty of options to avoid the hard-rock caps

This mountain is not spectacular in the classical sense. It is dry, hot, and remote. At midday in the summer the only solid shade is the spiky shadows of Mojave yucca. Shrubs grow a respectable distance from each other. Even in the spring there is no tufts of grass, only diminutive specimens of annuals that bloom for a few weeks and die. We still climb it to satisfy our hunger for unexpected discoveries, because it is wild, secret, and immersed in a hundred square miles of no man's land. There is indeed plenty to enjoy on this unrevered mountain. The igneous rocks are beautiful. Their composition changes from one extreme to the next in just a few steps. There are twisted gneiss, sparkling schists, bright monzonite, and diorite as dark as coal. The flower show is minimalist but delightfully eclectic. At different times chia, lupine, and phacelia cover the purple spectrum; evening

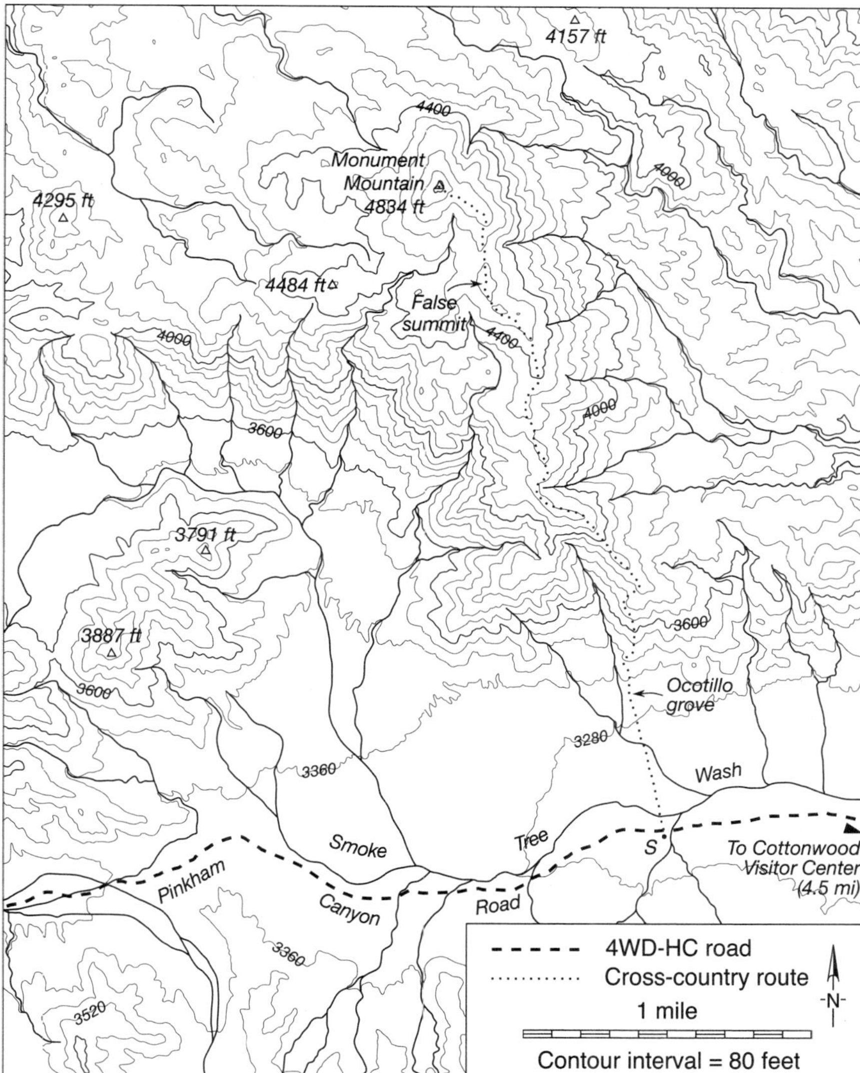

Monument Mountain	Dist.(mi)	Elev.(ft)
Smoke Tree Wash Road	0.0	3,250
Foot of mountain	0.5	3,320
Main ridge	1.0	3,930
False summit	2.6	~4,600
Monument Mountain	2.9	4,834

Smoke Tree Wash and Eagle Mountains on the way to Monument Mountain

primrose, brittlebush, and desert gold poppies supply the complementary yellows; beavertail and calico cactus dazzle with shocking reds; windmills, wishbone bush, and cushion foxtail cactus fill the gap with cotton-candy pinks.

The views are good from the moment you step onto the mountain. The ridge provides fine vistas of the Eagle Mountains and Cottonwood Mountains at first, then of the Hexie Mountains in one direction and the mysterious Coxcomb Mountains in the other. The summit illustrates the sharp contrast between the two provinces it straddles. From the west clockwise to the northeast the Mojave Desert is rippling with rugged crests, from the imposing alignment of the Little San Bernardino Mountains to the Providence Mountains. From the east to the south the Sonoran Desert is far more open, a land of lower mountains, immense bajadas, and shimmering seas of dark-green creosote. On a clear winter day, you may peer clear across to the Algodones Dunes, past the dark hump of the Chocolate Mountains. You might even catch a glimpse of Mexico. One desert tells a story of thrusting, upheaval, and creation; the other epitomizes the ravages of endless erosion.

■

—10—

EAGLE MOUNTAINS

Covering 250 square miles in the park's remote southeast quadrant, the Eagle Mountains are the second largest in the park. They are framed to the north by the vast gulf of Pinto Basin, to the west by the Hexie and Cottonwood mountains, and to the south and east by Chuckwalla Valley. A good portion of this range, including its southern margin, is a spectacular region of sculpted rockscapes that rival for majesty with the Wonderland of Rocks. This is hard-to-reach country, a reassuring distance from urban sprawl, most of it protected in two large designated wilderness areas. The Black Eagle Mine Road, on the northwestern fringe, is the only road that makes ingress into the range, and it does not go through. To get almost anywhere, you have to walk, often great distances. Other than the extreme southwestern corner near the Cottonwood Visitor Center, easily accessible on the park's south entrance road and popular for its stately palm groves, visitation is one of the lowest. The Eagle Mountains are one of the few areas in the park that still provides the solitude so prevalent in California's other large desert preserves. This little-known range is a perfect place to discover springs, palm oases, boulder-choked canyons, lost mines, volcanic hills, and isolated summits with no one around.

Geology

Being located at the east end of the Transverse Ranges, the Eagle Mountains have been rotated at an odd angle by peripheral tectonic forces. Caught between two worlds, they point to the northeast, partway between the east-trending Transverse Ranges to the west and the north-trending ranges to the east. They are shaped roughly like a

Chuckwalla Mountains from the top of Boulder Canyon

square pie sliced into nine irregular squares, along two north-south and two east-west faults. Erosion has widened the gaps between squares and carved out a central block surrounded by eight disjuncted blocks. There are actually only seven: the northwest block is missing, its space occupied by a portion of Pinto Basin. The largest fault, along the southern edge of the central block, has opened a half-mile-wide trench that transects the range from east to west. This long valley is coursed by two major washes, one appropriately named Big Wash that flows east into Chuckwalla Valley, the other a nameless drainage that wanders in the opposite direction into Pinto Basin.

The Eagle Mountains are made almost exclusively of many different igneous rocks emplaced over hundreds of millions of years. The fairylands of hoodoos covering the three southern blocks are carved out of light-colored quartz monzonite and quartz diorite. The middle three blocks are granodiorite, volcanic dikes, and igneous gneiss as artfully convoluted as locally famous Pinto Gneiss. The northern two blocks are laced with mica-schists, quartzite, and marble bookended between volcanic rocks, all rare to nonexistent elsewhere in the park. The volcanic rocks are basalt and andesite flows that erupted only 8 to 10 million years ago. The marble and quartzite are the metamorphosed remnants of a thick sequence of sandstone and limestone beds that accumulated in a Neoproterozoic and Paleozoic ocean. Later still, tongues of magma infiltrated the old sedimentary beds and deposited the wealth of metals that were mined here in the past.

Mining History

Without fail, desert mines fell into two groups: winners and losers; there was hardly ever anything in between. The Eagle Mountains were no exception. They had at least 91 mines. Of these, 84 never rose above the rank of prospect. Of the remaining seven, four had a dismal recorded production between 1 and 32 ounces of gold. The last three were among the richest in the region. The best was the richest ever.

The oldest of these three stars is the Iron Chief Mine. Possibly located as early as 1890, it was exploited by two parties between 1897 and 1902, and generated $200,000 during this short time. At 1900 prices, this is a hefty 9,700 ounces of gold, which comes close to the park's record held by the Lost Horse Mine.

The second star was the Black Eagle Mine. Operated off and on between the 1920s and 1940, it differed from most rich mines: it produced little gold but record quantities of lead (at least 1.5 million pounds) and copper (at least 128,000 pounds). Its main output was silver, a total of over 32,400 ounces, far more than any mine in the park. It generated over $280,000, enough to support over time a small camp, two mills and a smelter, and up to 20 miners. Like its neighbor the Iron Chief before it, its operation was supported by a pipeline that brought in water many miles from Cottonwood Spring.

The brightest star was the Eagle Mountain Mine. In the 1900s, the Southern Pacific was anxious to acquire iron mines to become less dependent on east-coast businesses for the manufacture of its rails. As part of this plan, it purchased a total of 187 iron claims in the northern Eagle Mountains, including the Iron Chief and the Black Eagle, for $300,000. Somehow, it never followed through. The sprawling property remained idle until 1944, when industrialist Henry Kaiser, of Kaiser Permanente fame, purchased it and turned it into the largest iron mine in the West. Until 1983, the mine's three giant pits yielded 120 million tons of ore valued at around two billion dollars. It had its own 52-mile railroad, which carried a steady stream of 100-car trains to the Kaiser Steel Corporation's mill in Fontana, where the iron went into ship and car manufacturing. At its peak, it supported 1,500 employees and the bustling town of Eagle Mountain. All three mines and the town were located in the gun-shaped northeastern section of the range that was excluded from the park when it was created in 1994, should we ever need to recover the remaining 335 million tons of iron ore.

Suggested Hikes in the Eagle Mountains					
Route/Destination	Dist. (mi)	Elev. gain	Mean elev.	Difficulty	Page
Short hikes (under 5 miles round trip)					
Cotton Spring	0.5	70'	3,040'	Very easy	416
Cottonwood Spring	0.1	50'	2,980'	Very easy	415
Difficult Canyon				Class 2	
to California Arch	0.85	340'	1,520'	Strenuous	437
to top of central gorge	1.2	520'	1,590'	Strenuous	437
Dragon Wash				Class 2	
to amphitheater	2.0	520'	1,530'	Moderate	443
to Boulder Cyn Overlook	2.2	720'	1,580'	Moderate	443
Iron Chief Mine (2)	1.5	560'	2,380'	Easy	405
Mastodon Mine (1)	2.4	410'	3,140'	Easy	421
Mastodon Peak (1)	2.6	520'	3,160'	Easy-mod.	421
Moorten's Mill	1.0	280'	2,910'	Easy	418
Storm Jade Mine (2)	1.0	190'	2,050'	Very easy	401
Winona Mill	0.5	70'	3,040'	Very easy	416
Wood Spring	0.8	210'	2,960'	Very easy	418
Intermediate hikes (5–12 miles round trip)					
Anschutz Peak	2.7	2,030'	1,820'	Strenuous	443
Difficult Cyn–Dragon W. (1)	5.4	1,460'	1,560'	Strenuous	437
Eagle Mountain				Class 2	
via Conejo Well Trail	5.0	2,610'	3,890'	Very diff.	409
Lost Palms Oasis	3.6	1,440'	3,230'	Moderate	425
Munsen Canyon				Class 2	
to Arch Oasis	5.6	1,950'	2,580'	Very diff.	436
to Munsen Oasis	4.5	1,340'	2,390'	Moderate	431
to Summit Springs	3.8	1,060'	2,300'	Moderate	431
The Gallery	2.5	480'	3,370'	Easy	411
Victory Palms	4.6	1,850'	3,170'	Difficult	428
Long hikes (over 12 miles round trip)					
Eagle Mountain via Munsen Canyon	7.2	3,680'	2,990'	Strenuous	431

Key: (1) Loop; (2) HC and/or 4WD access road
Distance: one way for out-and-back hikes, round-trip for loops
Elev. gain: sum of all elevation gains on round-trips and on loops

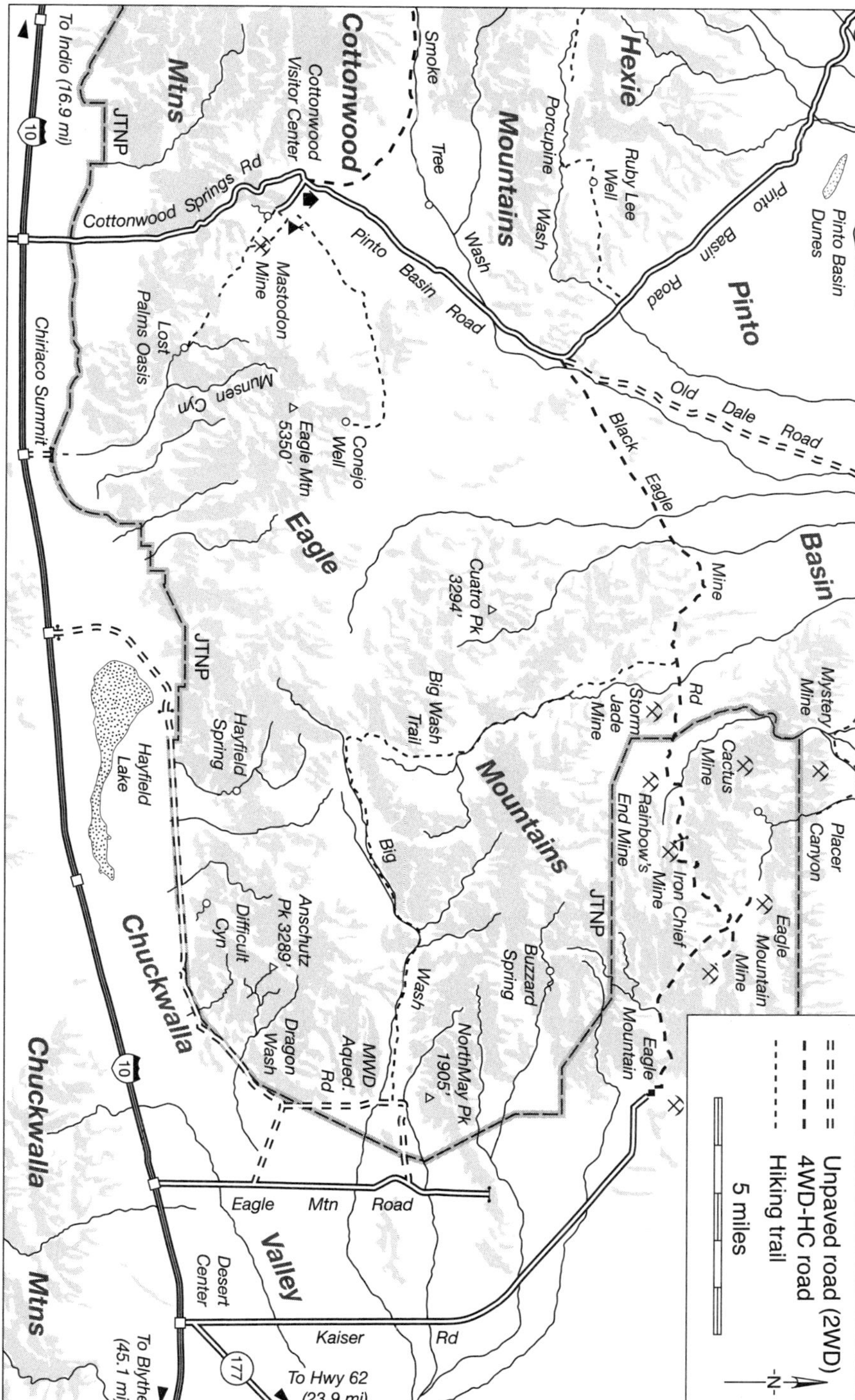

Unpaved road (2WD)
4WD-HC road
Hiking trail
5 miles
N
Pinto Basin Dunes
Pinto
Basin
Hexie
Mountains
Ruby Lee Well
Porcupine Wash
Smoke Tree Wash
Pinto Basin Road
Old Dale Road
Black Eagle Mine Rd
Cottonwood
Cottonwood Visitor Center
Cottonwood Springs Rd
Mtns
JTNP
To Indio (16.9 mi)
10
Mastodon Mine
Lost Palms Oasis
Munsen Cyn
Conejo Well
Eagle Mtn 5350'
Chiriaco Summit
Eagle
Cuatro Pk 3294'
Big Wash Trail
Mountains
Mystery Mine
Storm Jade Mine
Cactus Mine
Placer Canyon
Rainbow's End Mine
Iron Chief Mine
Eagle Mountain Mine
Buzzard Spring
Eagle Mountain
Hayfield Spring
Hayfield Lake
Big Wash
Anschutz Pk 3289'
Difficult Cyn
Dragon Wash
MWD Aqued. Rd
NorthMay Pk 1905'
Chuckwalla
Chuckwalla Mtns
Eagle Mtn Road
Valley
Desert Center
Kaiser Rd
177
To Hwy 62 (23.9 mi)
To Blythe (45.1 mi)

Botany

The Eagle Mountains is part of the Sonoran Desert. They have no Joshua trees, but many plants characteristic of this generally lower and hotter desert. Ironwood and palo verde are found in sizable dispersed stands on alluvial fans and in lower canyons on the southern edges of the range, as are smoke trees and occasionally olive trees. Ocotillo and teddy-bear cholla often grace open slopes. In the spring and summer the fragrance of desert lavender permeates many canyons. A few summits are high enough to support woodlands of juniper and pinyon pine. Their biodiversity ranks among the park's greatest, and it is a true pleasure of climbing here. Yet this range is better known for its elegant groves of California fan palms, scattered along at least three major canyons—Cottonwood, Lost Palms Oasis, and Munsen—where they thrive in greater numbers than anywhere else in the park.

Hiking and Camping

In a park that is being loved to death, the Eagle Mountains' greatest asset is isolation. Access is generally difficult. The northern and central parts can only be reached with long walks from either the Old Dale Road, the Black Eagle Mine Road, or the Eagle Mountain area. The southern part is hemmed in by the Colorado River Aqueduct, which either follows the foot of the mountains or tunnels under them. The aqueduct is understandably heavily protected by the Metropolitan Water District. The Hayfield Road and Red Cloud Road off Interstate 10, which get close to the mountains, are closed to the public, posted as such, and the MWD means business. The next two exits east, Eagle Mountain Road and Desert Center, are open and give access to the southeast corner of the range, and to quiet dirt roads to camp. So does the upper end of the Black Eagle Mine Road outside the park.

The Cottonwood Visitor Center area has several easy to moderate trails to delightful palm groves, a historic gold mine, and the ruins of two gold mills. Almost all other hikes are harder and explore remote and rarely visited areas. Nearby Eagle Mountain is one of the park's more demanding climbs. The rough Black Eagle Mountain Road leads to the vicinity of several remote historic mines. At the north end of the mountains, the Placer Canyon area has the ruins of gold placers from the 1930s. Eagle Mountain, at the east end, is possibly the largest ghost town in the country, with many blocks of abandoned homes. The ore at the mine above it is strangely beautiful, white marble laced with black magnetite and greenish minerals. For anyone willing to put in serious mileage, there is considerably more.

■

THE STORM JADE MINE

The Storm Jade Mine stands out not for its illustrious past but for its owner Barry Storm, a gun-toting treasure hunter who spent his life searching for lost gold mines. He never found much gold, but he wrote books on the lore of lost lodes, one of which was made into a Hollywood movie in the black-and-white era. The jade mine was his last hurrah, a low-grade seam that he claimed was the lost source of jade of the ancient Maya. If you can drive the long access road, it is an easy stroll to this isolated gemstone mine with no gems but unusual green minerals and an engaging history.

General Information

Road status: Hiking on old road; primitive access road (HC-4WD)
Storm Jade Mine: 1.0 mi, 180 ft up, 10 ft down one way / very easy
Main attractions: History of Barry Storm, jade mine, minerals
USGS 7.5' topo map: Conejo Well
Maps: pp. 403*, *399*

Location and Access

The Storm Jade Mine is the first of several small historic mines along the long road to the Black Eagle Mine. From Pinto Wye, drive the Pinto Basin Road 22.9 miles to two major primitive roads on the left. Coming from the south, this is 6.8 miles from the Cottonwood Visitor Center. The signed Black Eagle Mine Road is on the right. Drive it 8.4 miles to a line of green metal stakes and a gate on the right, and park. The Storm Jade Mine is a mile up the track beyond the gate. This road is a little rocky and requires high clearance.

Route Description

Born John Griffith Climenson in 1910 in Seattle, Barry Storm developed early on a fascination for fabled gold mines. Around 1937, he moved to Phoenix and started a long, nearly obsessive quest for the derelict gold mines scattered in the Superstition Mountains east of town. He made a few dollars by working as a guide into this mysterious range. Storm befriended Barry Goldwater, who would later become Arizona Senator and presidential candidate. They first met by chance in Goldwater's family-owned upscale department store in Phoenix. Storm, occasionally accompanied by Goldwater, combed the Superstitions with a diligence driven by passion.

Although he was surprisingly successful, none of his rediscoveries had much gold. For want of making it rich, he settled for chronicling his expeditions under the pen name of Barry Storm, inspired by Goldwater's first name. His greatest success, *Thunder God's Gold*, came out in 1945. It disclosed new maps, photographs, rock inscriptions, and historical data about a dozen lost gold mines, and scores of little secrets. His prose was rambling and convoluted. Speculations were mixed with well-known facts and technical jargon to lend them credence. But in two years he printed 10,000 copies, and they captivated the small but passionate subculture of fortune seekers of the time.

Thunder God's Gold also drew the attention of Hollywood. Perhaps to compete with Republic Pictures' 1948 release of *The Treasure of the Sierra Madre*, Columbia Pictures adapted it into a motion picture. *Lust for Gold*, starring Glenn Ford, used the generic plot of black-and-white westerns—a rich gold mine, villains, betrayals, shoot-outs, and a love triangle—but it did not hold a candle to Humphrey Bogart's classic. Storm filed a lawsuit against Columbia for misrepresenting his character in the movie and damaging his reputation, and settled out of court.

Around 1956, disgruntled Storm moved to the Joshua Tree area. While poking around the Eagle Mountains, he made what turned out to be his greatest discovery. It was not gold but green jade. Even though government records show that jade had been located in the area a decade earlier, Storm pretended that his mine was the elusive source of jade of the Maya cultures of 3,500 years ago. In interviews, he claimed to have discovered a scepter, a ceremonial figurine, burial grounds, and stone tools from these ancient civilizations. The truth? The tools were likely made by local Native Americans. We know today that the Maya jade came from Guatemala. Most of Storm's jade did not have gem quality anyway: it was a lower grade variety called nephrite. He did dig up "nuggets" that weighed tens of pounds, but very little approached the translucent purity that would have pleased a Mayan ruler. The adjacent Green Giant Mine, exploited in the 1960s by a Palm Springs resident, was crushed and sold as ordinary roofing granule...

Storm lived his final years in a shack at his mine, a radical switch from the time he mingled with politicians and Hollywood stars. He scraped a living by selling nephrite to shops and visitors. He died in the Veterans Hospital in Long Beach, two weeks shy of 61. Like many desert miners, he had become an eccentric hermit, prone to tall tales, yet he left a rare legacy. His books' infectious optimism have been a source of inspiration for generations of treasure hunters of all ages.

The fading track to Storm's last home skirts the base of a low hill into a small valley that juts into the Eagle Mountains. It is a lazy

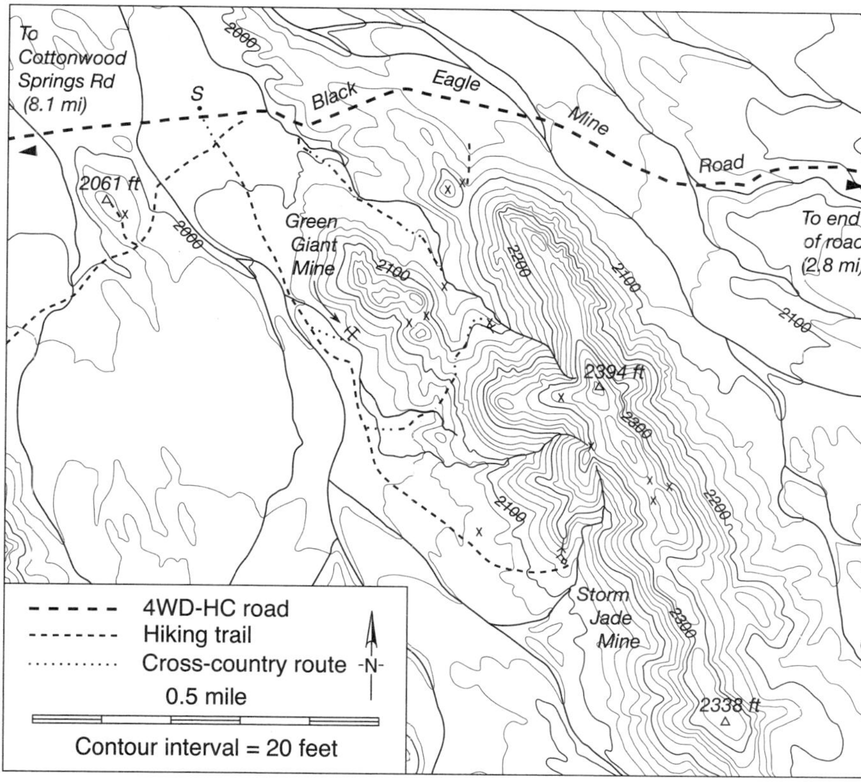

The Storm Jade Mine		
	Dist.(mi)	Elev.(ft)
Black Eagle Mine Road	0.0	1,995
Green Giant Mine turnoff	0.3	2,025
Green Giant Mine	(0.05)	2,035
Storm Jade Mine	0.95	2,160

landscape of desert foothills, Zen in its minimalism and timelessness, its dwarf vegetation waiting languishly for the day to end. The first mineralized zone is a few minutes up the trail. The Green Giant Mine's shallow quarry, dug into the base of the hill, exposes a 20-foot wall of pistachio-green rock. A mixture of epidote and vesuvianite sprinkled with ruby-red garnet crystallites, it was formed, like the jade, when quartz monzonite intruded and metamorphosed dolomite. The area is littered with pieces that fell off trucks in the 1960s. There is nephrite too, although it is a little difficult to distinguish because it is often

Contact plane and iron door to dynamite storage at the Storm Jade Mine

covered with a light-tan coating. Only broken samples reveal on their exposed conchoidal breaks the dull, milky green of nephrite.

Storm's camp was a secluded retreat, a mile out from the road, overlooking the little valley and the Pinto Mountains brooding on the horizon. The camp was spartan. Three concrete slabs mark the former structures—the plywood house Storm built, a bathroom, and a small shed. Discarded appliances and Storm's burned-out trailer, in which he lived his final years, are slowly returning to rust.

The mine is a two-minute walking commute up the hill. The lower adit goes 50 feet into the pay zone. The upper adit, guarded by a padlocked steel door with a horseshoe as a handle, was used to store dynamite. Storm knew his geology. The crushed rock around the door is quartz monzonite. Four feet to the right, the monzonite ends abruptly at its nearly vertical contact with thick slanted slabs of bluish dolomite. The jade was located right there along the contact plane.

Gemstone mines are the stuff of dreams. Remembering childhood books, we conjure up images of caves mantled with giant crystals, and still feel the enchantment. It may be why we enter tunnels, hoping for something valuable, hidden and forgotten. We might see nothing at first, and feel cheated. If we look again differently, we might find what we have missed. The hill is pitted with nephrite and vesuvianite workings. In the beam of a headlamp, deep inside a granite tunnel, the million sparkles of quartz and muscovite can be magical. In Barry's books as in his dusty tunnels, wonder is in the eye of the beholder.

■

THE IRON CHIEF MINE

The Iron Chief Mine is a gold property developed extensively around 1900 in the remote northeastern Eagle Mountains. It is reached by an adventurous ride on one of the park's longest primitive roads, followed by an easy walk. Set in dormant naked hills imbued with the serenity of seldom-visited places, the architectural stone foundations of the Iron Chief Mill rank among the largest and most interesting in the region. Together with smaller structures, multiple workings, and unusual tailings curiously sculpted by erosion, they give a gratifying glimpse of the significant efforts that were spent in just a few years to recover a record amount of gold.

General Information
Jurisdiction: Public lands (BLM), mining property (private)
Road status: Hiking on dirt roads; primitive access road (HC-4WD)
Iron Chief Mill: 1.5 mi, 390 ft up, 170 ft down one way / easy
Main attractions: Stone ruins of 1900 gold mills, history, iron ore
USGS 7.5' topo map: Buzzard Spring
Maps: pp. 407*, *399*

Location and Access

The Iron Chief Mine is just outside the park along the Black Eagle Mine Road. Follow the directions to this road off the Cottonwood Springs Road (see *The Storm Jade Mine*). Drive it 8.4 miles to the jade mine gate, then another 3.9 miles. You will know when you get there: a gorgeous two-ton white boulder of mineral-rich skarn, rare for its size, sits squarely in the middle of the road. Park and walk the remaining 0.2 mile to the Iron Chief Mill. The Black Eagle Mine Road is alternatively rocky and sandy, and it has a crown. A high-clearance four-wheel-drive vehicle is mandatory. There is a persistent rough spot 9.9 miles in, where the road drops steeply into a wash, then crosses it. The road is soft and deeply gouged, and driving it back up takes power. The second challenge, 1.4 miles further, is a descent over a crop of sharp rocks. If your vehicle has street tires, it is safest to park at the top of the rise before it and walk from there, which will add about a mile.

The Iron Chief Mine is on private mining claims owned by Santa-Monica-based Eagle Crest. There were no *No Trespassing* signs when I visited, but if you do not feel comfortable, request permission. If no trespassing warnings are posted in the future, turn around.

Retaining walls and tailings of the 1900 gold mill at the Iron Chief Mine

Route Description

The Iron Chief Mine was true to its namesake: its main ore was iron—hematite—but the ore was speckled with more valuable free gold, and it was actually a gold mine. Its discovery, credited to San Bernardino residents William Stevens and Thomas Dofflemeyer, may have occurred as early as 1890. In 1897 they sold their claims to a man from San Francisco named Charles Lane, who installed a small mill and worked the mine. Although his mill recovered only about half of the gold, he quickly made $50,000. When Lane failed to make payments, the property reverted to its original owners. They installed a 50-ton mill and mined and processed ore worth up to $100 a ton, recovering $150,000. When their shaft encountered low-grade iron sulfides in 1902, they quit. Seven years later, together with two partners, Stevens and Dofflemeyer made good again by selling their joint properties, a total of 187 iron claims, for $300,000 to the Southern Pacific. In 1944, the sprawling property was acquired by the Kaiser Steel Corporation, who developed it on a massive scale. The Iron Chief Mine had much less iron than other claims, and it was left untouched. It had served its purpose anyway: by 1902 it had become the largest gold producer in the range, and generated almost as much gold as the Lost Horse Mine.

After driving over ruts and rocks for an hour, walking the remaining mile to the mine is a relief. The aging road weaves in and out of a canyon wash that winds up between low hills of crushed rocks. Plant

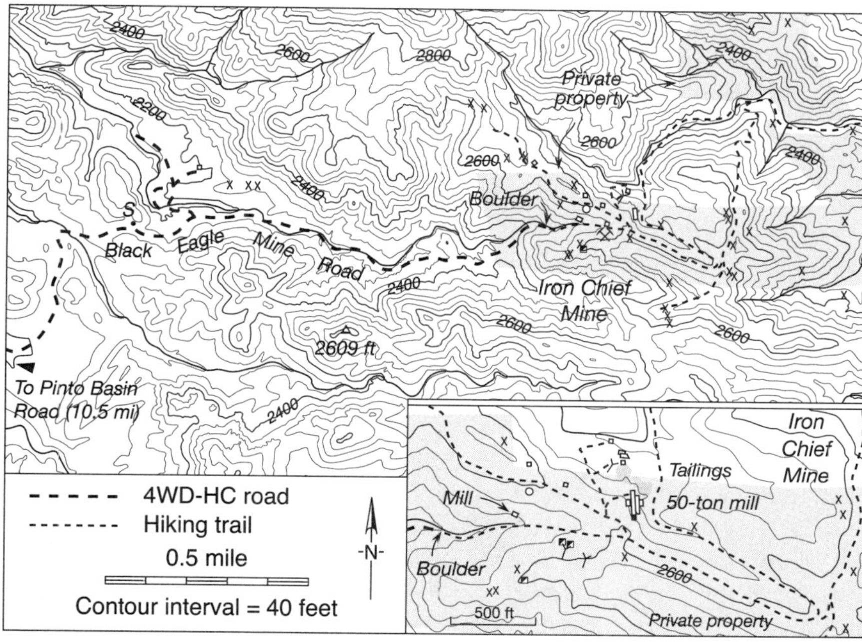

The Iron Chief Mine		
	Dist.(mi)	Elev.(ft)
Top of rise on road	0.0	2,270
Boulder on road	1.15	2,440
Iron Chief Mine's twin pits	1.3	2,560
Pass	1.35	2,600
Iron Chief Mill	1.4	~2,540
Tunnel ruins	1.5	~2,490

life is reduced to the bare minimum. Squat clusters of dark rocks are their only ornaments. In the winter months, the slanted sunrays brightens this stark landscape by painting on the hills countless shades of earth tones, and clouds constantly touch up the canvas. In the summer, heat haze melts this contrasted palette into washed-out browns.

Just before the pass, the road reaches the Iron Chief Mine's gold workings, two connected pits probed by two short adits and two shafts. The walls are encrusted with iron oxides—ochre limonite and blood-red oxidized hematite. The largest shaft, 140 feet deep, was the main producer. Just a little further, the road caps a broad flat at a pass. In this muted landscape, the ruins of the Iron Chief Mill cascading down the far side of the pass and its neatly furrowed tailings beg for attention, like a work of art in an empty room. It is bigger and more elaborate than most. Its three long terraced levels, shored by sturdy stone walls, were carved out of a long hillside. The terraces were shaped with nooks, an elegant curved wall, and a protruding platform to accommodate the mill machinery. When active, the mill was covered by a rippling wooden structure that housed two jaw crushers and rolls. Its eight 18-foot steel cyanide tanks were likely set on the large wooden deck that extended below the lowest terrace. At the top terrace, the mill's leftovers were hauled onto the tailings on short rails. The camp was at the pass. It had a sizable wood cabin, a blacksmith shop, and a huge ore bin. It took back-breaking work to bring water to this remote site: a 17-mile pipeline was laid down all the way from Cottonwood Spring. During hot spells and cold snaps, someone with a high tolerance for pain rode a burro to check the pipe for leaks.

Little of this equipment is left—an ore bin, the top and bottom of a steel tank, a hook driven into solid rock, sun-bleached lumber, cannisters—and the walls. Made of carefully interlocked local rocks, they were built with longevity in mind. They are still intact after 125 years. Some blocks are dolomite and quartzite, rocks common in the Mojave Desert but rare in the region: they outcrop almost exclusively here. The two 30-foot mill tailings below the terraces store the 10,000 tons of crushed hematite regurgitated by the mill. The ground is littered with the mill's jade-black pellets. Remnants of the rails' trestles still protrude from the top of the tailings. A century of desert rain has shaped the tailings into curious beehives, oxidized them to a rich cocoa, and carved into their flanks braided pleats as delicate as badlands.

At the pass, a narrow foot trail drops north into a ravine. Rocky and faint, it has not seen much use; it is easy to discount it as not going anywhere. But it does. It ends at a tunnel hidden behind the largest tailing. Just below the tunnel, another set of tiered terraces tumbles down the hill. They are smaller, yet pleasantly symmetric and as finely crafted. The tunnel turns out to be a wonder of early mining: it was bored 500 straight feet right under the main mill to connect with the gold-bearing zone at the 140-foot shaft. Was this second installation an attempt to harvest the gold more easily than via the shaft? Is it the site of Lane's 1897 mill? Or was Lane's mill the small roadside stone platform just before the pass? Smaller ruins are scattered throughout the area. Like the rocks to which they are anchored, they can be coaxed into recounting the events that took place a long time ago. In some sense, we seek these forgotten mines to listen to their stories.

■

EAGLE MOUNTAIN

The ascent of Eagle Mountain, the highest summit in the eastern half of the park, is one of the most entertaining. To get there you cross a bajada sprinkled with beautiful formations, climb a steep canyon filled with small boulders, and traverse a plateau dissected into scenic fins, in the company of almost every plant mentioned in this book. The summit commands far-reaching views into the park, most of the way to Arizona, and as far south as Mexico. That said, it is a long and demanding climb. If this is not for you, consider going only as far as the Gallery, near the base of the canyon. This exquisite sculpture garden is an extensive array of miniature domes, towers, and wavy bedrock displayed in the casual disarray of an artist's studio. This is a destination of its own that begs for aimless ambling to simply enjoy the quiet beauty of the stone.

General Information

Road status: Mostly cross-country hiking; paved access road
The Gallery: 2.5 mi, 450 ft up, 30 ft down one way / easy
Eagle Mountain: 5.0 mi, 2,410 ft up, 200 ft down one way / very diff.
Main attractions: Spectacular rock formations, a great peak climb
USGS 7.5' topo maps: Cottonwood Spr.,* Porcupine Wash, Conejo Well*
Maps: pp. 413*, *399*

Location and Access

Eagle Mountain is near the southwestern end of the Eagle Mountains, about 5 air miles east of the Cottonwood Visitor Center. The climb starts on the Conejo Well Trail at the top of the Cottonwood Campground. Drive to the visitor center (refer to *Cottonwood Spring Walkabout* for directions), and turn off on the paved Cottonwood Oasis Road. Go 0.7 mile and turn left toward the campground. You will soon drive by a long row of parking spaces on the left. Most of them are reserved for group camping. The last few spaces, just before the campground entrance, are marked "picnic" and OK for day hikers. If they are full, park at the visitor center. From either location, walk to campsite B17. The Conejo Well Trail is marked by a no-camping sign.

Route Description

Upon perusing the map, it is tempting to cut a beeline to the base of Eagle Mountain. It is indeed the shortest path, but it also calls for

Petrified domes at the Gallery, on the way to Eagle Mountain

more ups and downs across low hills and washes, which takes longer than the slightly longer way around on the Conejo Well Trail. This trail bypasses these hills and climbs a little to an open bajada and a clear shot at the mountain. The trail is straight, wide, and easy, hedged by tall vegetation, with lots of boot prints to confirm that you are on the right track. After 0.8 mile the trail goes over a patch of caliche, nearly white, grainy stream deposits exposed on the right side in a low vertical bank with rows of small cavities. In this area, leave the trail and head off at 1 o'clock into a narrow wash. The scenery improves almost right away. You walk across bright fields of low grasses sprinkled with a riot of desert plants—the large crowns of creosote and bladderpod, the spiny heads of silver cholla, diamond cholla, and Mojave yucca, the cheery blossoms of blue bell, and the first emerald clumps of California juniper. The wash gradually angles to the right, toward Eagle Mountain rising to the south. The obvious canyon that slashes down the middle of the mountain is the route to the summit. After 0.3 mile, take the left fork and follow it 0.4 mile to the first of several monzogranite-boulder stacks stained with desert varnish that dot the bajada up ahead. At this point the wash veers south, away from the mountain; leave it and cut a beeline toward the canyon. From there to the canyon the highlight is the boulder stacks. First comes a bulge of bedrock quartered by deep linear cracks, then a swell of granite with a long spine of 100-ton boulders. You soon pass between two parallel alignments of more complex stacks. The last one is Tortoise Rock, 1.3 miles from the trail. There is what looks like an arch at its west end. Upon close examination, it is not a true arch but the gap under a 12-foot slab that leans against the stack. When viewed from the north side, the whole outcrop bears a striking resemblance to a tortoise, its neck outstretched, its head to the ground, as tortoises do to munch on ground-hugging plants.

Hoodoos at the Gallery, on the way to Eagle Mountain

The best is yet to come. From Tortoise Rock, angle northeast to the horizon of paler rocks about 200 yards away. Covering 20 acres, the Gallery is an expanse of solid bedrock eroded into countless hoodoos with the simplest and most elegant of shapes. The stone is brilliant, pale-beige monzogranite, with the cohesion that gives the Wonderland of Rocks its rare quality. The southern edge is a sea of rolls and hemispheres a few feet tall, with barely enough space between them to walk. Beyond, the bedrock morphs into small pointed domes, turrets, and odd-shape knolls. You wander between them along alleys of immaculate sand and over smooth humps of stone, oohing and aahing as new sculptures pop up. There is a hanging slot wedged between bulging walls, an anvil-shaped rock balanced on a narrow spine, a flat-topped tower standing guard over petrified dunes, and lone spherical boulders posing like hermetic modern art. At the heart of this whimsical playground is Cat Face Rock, an eerily symmetric caricature of a feline's face etched in a tall rock face. It is hard to shake the feeling that an anonymous sculptor has playfully indulged in some personal fantasy. Even the sparseness of the vegetation—a manzanita here, a pancake cactus there—seems deliberate, as if each plant had been carefully positioned to accent the nakedness of the sculptures.

The canyon, less than a mile away from the Gallery, is reached by crossing a rocky fan, then following a narrow wiggly wash. The canyon floor is right away overrun by rocks. It is a messy place where yucca, blood-thirsty shrubs, and sizable trees vie for space with small boulders. From mouth to head it is consistently steep, gaining 1400 feet in about 1.3 miles. Combined with the obstacles, it makes for slow going. Fortunately, the rocks in the wash are often naturally arranged in convenient steps that make climbing a little easier, and very large boulders are few. There is also only one fall, a nearly vertical 12-foot polished funnel in very short narrows just inside the canyon, which is easily circumvented on a slickrock bench on the right side. This ascent is definitely not as difficult as some other canyons, like Bighorn or Gunsight. As cluttered as it is, the canyon has a charm of its own. The slopes are crowded with a contrasted blend of tan angular outcrops and green oak, juniper, and pinyon pine. At one spot the wash squeezes through a curiously skewed passage between parallel walls leaning at 45 degrees. The views are increasingly spacious, embracing both San Jacinto Peak and San Gorgonio Mountain.

Once at the top of the canyon, the physical difficulties are over. The remaining 0.8 mile to the summit is over a much easier and enjoyable rolling plateau. At 5,000+ feet the air is purer, and the light holds this distinct brilliance that induces a little giddiness. The route follows an east-southeast course, first up a little to a knoll from which the false summit just before the true summit becomes visible. It then descends into a tiny hidden valley, and finally climbs to the right of dense rows of tall fins to an open dome and the summit. This approach crosses a

Eagle Mountain

	Dist.(mi)	Elev.(ft)
Conejo Well Trail (site B17)	0.0	3,135
Leave trail	0.85	3,310
Tortoise Rock	2.15	3,540
Cat Face Rock	2.45	3,550
Canyon mouth	~2.9	~3,680
Top of canyon	4.2	5,080
Valley	4.6	4,950
Eagle Mountain	5.0	5,350

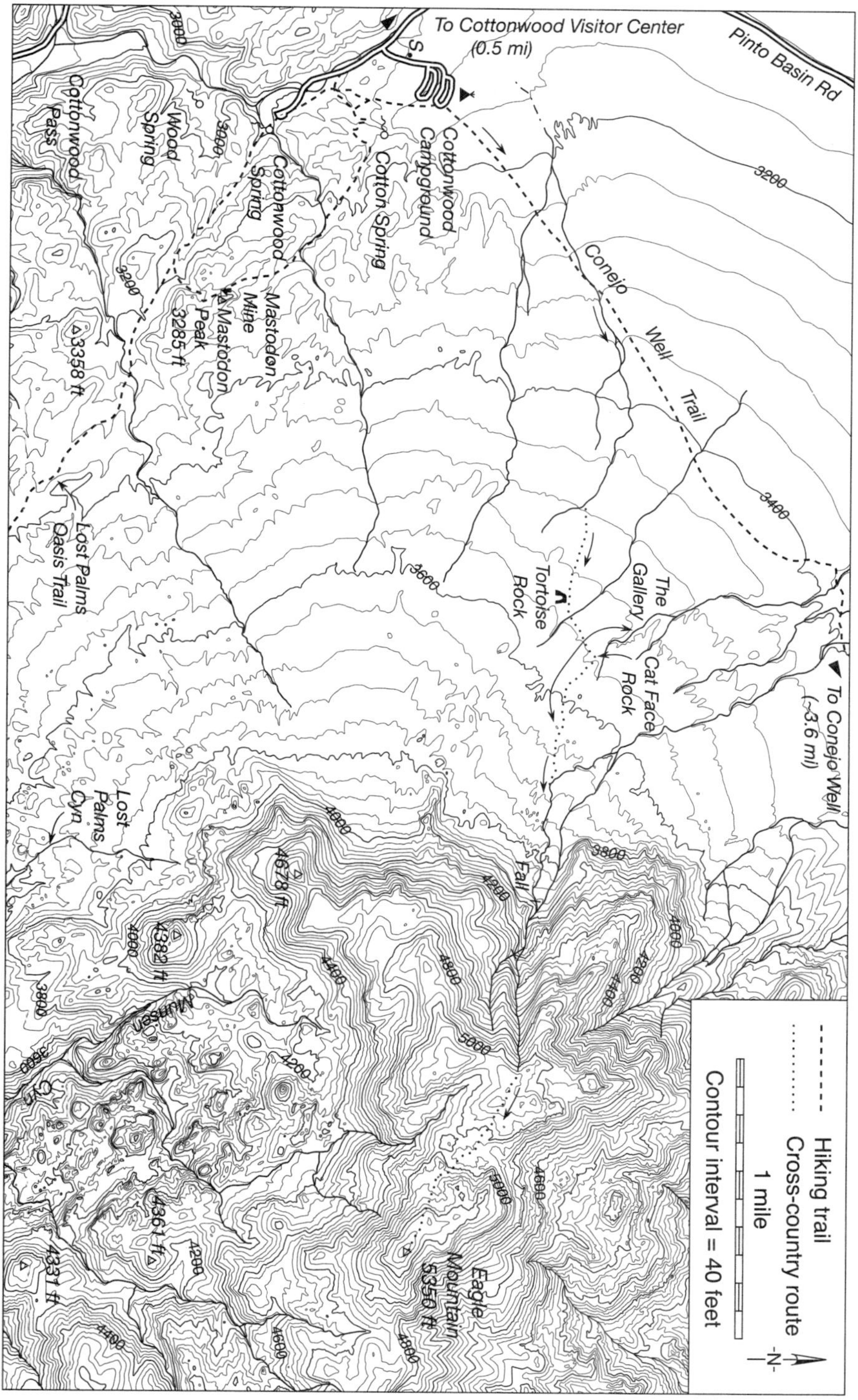
To Cottonwood Visitor Center
(0.5 mi)
Pinto Basin Rd
Cottonwood Campground
Cotton Spring
Cottonwood Spring
Wood Spring
Cottonwood Pass
Mastodon Mine
Mastodon Peak
3285 ft
3358 ft
Conejo Well Trail
Lost Palms Oasis Trail
Tortoise Rock
The Gallery
Cat Face Rock
To Conejo Well
(~3.6 mi)
Fall
Lost Palms Cyn
4678 ft
4382 ft
Munsen Cyn
4361 ft
4331 ft
Eagle Mountain
5350 ft
Hiking trail
Cross-country route
1 mile
Contour interval = 40 feet
N

Pinnacles in lower half of canyon leading up to Eagle Mountain

surfeit of peculiar formations—diced parapets, slender boulder stacks, shattered pinnacles, groves of sharp fins all tilted at the same angle. They rise out of the most delightful of desert gardens, a dense mixture of nolina, yucca, chollas, and pancake cactus sprinkled with oak, pine, and juniper. Finding a path that minimizes obstacles may not be trivial, but the plateau is only about a quarter of a mile wide, and it is hard to get lost. Wandering off the optimum course a little could be in fact a blessing in disguise. You may stumble upon a particularly pleasing view or rock formation that you would have otherwise missed.

Thanks to its prominence, Eagle Mountain is a perfect observatory to discover from a different angle places you might have visited before—the Pinto, Sheep Hole, and Coxcomb mountains, and the Eagle Mountains themselves, sprawling for miles to the northeast in diminishing waves of furrowed ridges. The highlight is the armada of bare-stone vertical formations that rise from Munsen Canyon and Lost Palms Canyon on the south flank of the mountain. This dramatic perspective gives us an even better appreciation of the complexity and majesty of one of the park's greatest canyon systems. Deeper south, partly concealed behind the Orocopia Mountains, the Salton Sea adds a touch of incongruity to this pure desert scene. In the winter the paradox is even more striking—you are immersed in exotic cactus, gazing out at an horizon of snow-capped summits. After a wet cold snap, the elevation is high enough that there might even be snow on the ground.

■

COTTONWOOD SPRING WALKABOUT

In a land notorious for its widespread lack of water, the Cottonwood Spring area stands out for being the home to three springs wet enough to support sizable groves of fan palms and cottonwoods. In historic times, they attracted Native Americans, then homesteaders, teamsters, miners, and travelers, who left behind grinding holes, arrastras, gold mills, wells, old cars, and wagon roads. Reached by short and easy hikes, mostly on trails, these delightfully scenic springs make for interesting destinations filled with history.

General Information
Road status: Hiking on trails and cross-country; paved access road
Cottonwood Spring: 0.1 mi, 10 ft up, 40 ft down one way / very easy
Cotton Spring: 0.5 mi, 70 ft up, 0 ft down one way / very easy
Moorten's Mill: 1.0 mi, 50 ft up, 230 ft down one way / easy
Main attractions: Scenic fan-palm groves, history, gold mills
USGS 7.5' topo map: Cottonwood Spring
Maps: pp. 419*, 423, *399*

Location and Access

Cottonwood Spring is in the middle of a tributary of Cottonwood Canyon, at the very western tip of the Eagle Mountains. To get to it from the north, from Pinto Wye on Park Boulevard drive the long and desolate Pinto Basin Road 29.7 miles to the Cottonwood Visitor Center. Coming from Interstate 10 to the south, this is 6.8 miles north on the Cottonwood Springs Road. At the visitor center, turn southeast on the paved Cottonwood Oasis Road. Park at the end of the road 1.2 miles further, at the parking overlooking Cottonwood Spring.

This area can also be accessed by walking down the short Cottonwood Spring Nature Trail from the Cottonwood Campground (see map). Pick it up at the east end of either loop A or loop B. Parking at the campground is allowed only if you have a campsite, so most visitors hike from the Cottonwood Spring parking.

Route Description

Cottonwood Spring. Cottonwood Spring is a stately grove of old fan palms and cottonwoods rising improbably out of bone-dry sand. At the bottom of the paved access ramp, a boardwalk wanders through it, right by its soaring trees. Everything about the palms is big—their heights, their untrimmed manes of dried fronds, their feathery crowns—and some of the cottonwoods are even taller. The trees are so tightly packed that the grove's interior is in perpetual darkness. On a hot summer day, it is a soothing place to sit and relax, while the wind rustling through the leaves brings up the nostalgia of rain. The trail leaves the grove abruptly, too soon it seems, throwing you from a pleasing penumbra into the harsh desert light in seconds. From the far side the spring's kaleidoscope of greens is even more impressive—the oaks on the rocky slopes right behind it, the understory of arrowweed, and the skirts of mesquite and big sagebrush all around.

Humans have relied on Cottonwood Spring for centuries. The Cahuilla cherished its abundant water. They harvested the uncommon arrowweed for dwellings, mesquite beans for food, and big sagebrush for stomach aches. To the right of the trail 100 feet past the spring, low granite outcrops still bear the narrow mortars in which they ground food and medicine. Starting in 1870, prospectors, miners, cattlemen, as well as freighters and travelers crossing between Morongo Basin and Coachella Valley, all depended heavily on the spring's water. The arrastra that rests by the trail, like a mosaic floor from Ancient Rome, is an early mill from that era. Matt Riley was an unlucky traveler who did not make the hazardous trip. On July 4, 1905, after a very long journey on foot from the Dale Mining District in three-digit heat, he died of dehydration minutes from the spring. His grave marker stands near the visitor center. For several years around 1900, the water was piped to the Iron Chief Mine, clear across the Eagle Mountains. After the pump house was abandoned, squatters used it as a residence and kept a fruit and vegetable garden. Today, even though no surface water is visible from the trail, bighorn sheep and other mammals sneak in early morning for a quick drink.

Cotton Spring and the Winona Mill. Although Cottonwood Spring is the local star, Cotton Spring half a mile to the north is just as interesting, and much more peaceful. From the parking, walk back 125 yards to the signed Cottonwood Spring Nature Trail, on the right. Follow it to, then up a sandy wash, 0.25 mile to a trail crossing marked by multiple signs. The nature trail continues on the left up to the campground (0.3 mile)—the way you will be coming if you hike from the campground. The wash straight ahead ends in 0.15 mile at the base of Cotton Spring.

Encased in a shallow ravine, Cotton Spring has three very different groves spread over 500 feet of twisted wash. The lowest one is a disheveled mix of fan palms and cottonwoods of all ages. The second one is a row of handsome eucalyptus, all white trunks and peeling red bark. The third grove is a long thicket of willow. Cotton Spring is a cool place, in both senses of the word, funky in its look and its fusion of native and exotic species. The four turkey vultures that were hanging out high in the eucalyptus seemed to rather enjoy it, checking out every one of my moves, should I suddenly collapse.

Over time, miners and homesteaders also lived at Cotton Spring. The wash is still lined with the stone foundations of their cabins. The largest was probably the living quarters of the Hulsey family in the 1930s, who was running the nearby Mastodon Mine.

The ruins of the Winona Mill hang on the low canyon rim south of Cotton Spring. At the low end of the spring a beat-up trail climbs to

Cottonwood Spring

them in 100 yards. The mill was probably built in the 1920s to perform custom jobs for small mines in the Hexie Mountains, although we can only speculate how much work it did then. It was active in the second half of the 1930s under George Hulsey's ownership, and possibly into the 1940s after it changed hands.

In its heyday the Winona Mill was a proud multi-story edifice that housed a jaw crusher and a ball mill powered by a Buick engine, a classifier, and amalgamation plates. A few concrete structures connected by battered roads still bear witness to its former size, including the mill pilings, the foundations of a residence or office, and a 7-foot roofless room possibly used for water storage. The now-capped well that likely supplied water to the mill is still in place down in the spring.

Wood Spring and Moorten's Mill. From the Cottonwood Spring parking, walk back alongside the road (northwest) 0.15 mile to a wide wash crossing. Turn left into the wash, and follow its windy course 0.8 mile down to Moorten's Mill. It is an easy walk in soft sand, along low dry hills and clumps of boulders. The vegetation is a typical Sonoran Desert medley of creosote, willow, ocotillo, mesquite, and palo verde, a tree so fond of chlorophyll that its trunk and branches are green. Halfway down, a narrow side canyon on the left leads in a few minutes to Wood Spring. Infrequently visited, it is the most enjoyable of the three springs. It is an open garden of mesquite, willows, scattered palms and cottonwood in a long swath of sand below bouldery ridges. In the warm season it is fringed with shade, a little cooler, and calm. Just past this side canyon, the main wash is clipped by an abrupt bedrock fall once known as Little Chilcoot Pass. Before automobiles, wagons came up this wash as a shortcut to the rest stop at Cottonwood Spring. The short cobbled road used then to bypass the fall is still there, overgrown with palo verde.

Cottonwood Spring Walkabout

	Dist.(mi)	Elev.(ft)
End of Cottonwood Oasis Rd	0.0	3,010
to Cottonwood Spring mortars	0.1	2,980
to Cotton Spring	0.5	3,080
to Winona Mill	0.5	3,080
to Cottonwood Campground	0.65	3,135
to Wood Spring	0.8	3,000
to Moorten's Mill	1.0	2,830

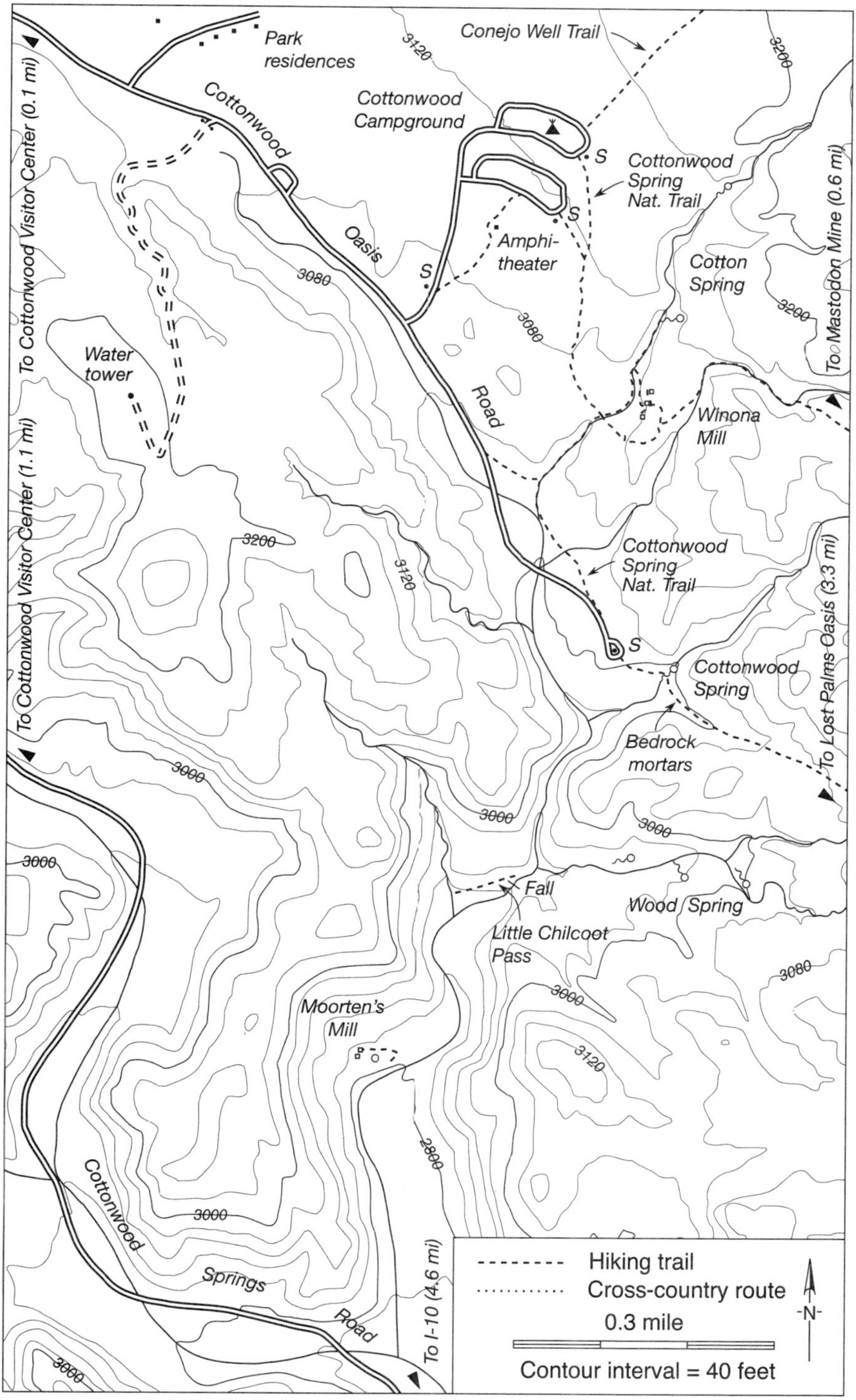

Park residences
Conejo Well Trail
Cottonwood Campground
Cottonwood Oasis Road
Cottonwood Spring Nat. Trail
Amphitheater
Cotton Spring
To Mastodon Mine (0.6 mi)
To Cottonwood Visitor Center (0.1 mi)
To Cottonwood Visitor Center (1.1 mi)
Water tower
Winona Mill
Cottonwood Spring
Bedrock mortars
To Lost Palms Oasis (3.3 mi)
Fall
Little Chilcoot Pass
Wood Spring
Moorten's Mill
Cottonwood Springs Road
To I-10 (4.6 mi)
3000
3080
3120
3200
2800
Hiking trail
Cross-country route
0.3 mile
Contour interval = 40 feet
N

The ruins of Moorten's Mill are just before the third major bend below the fall (a left bend), on the right bank. The five-stamp mill was erected around 1934 by Chester Moorten and Edith Hopper, one of the rare women in mining history. Moorten was a lumberjack and a railroad worker in Washington before he moved to California to mine gold in Kern County and the Little San Bernardino Mountains. While in the desert, he grew a passion for cacti that, combined with his slender build, earned him the nickname of "Cactus Slim." While selling cacti in Los Angeles, he landed a job in the movie industry, and ultimately appeared in films with famous actors like W. C. Fields and Buster Keaton. He was involved in particular in the 1910s Keystone Cops, a popular silent-film slapstick comedy. Diagnosed with tuberculosis in the early 1930s, he moved to Palm Springs to recover, and returned to gold mining. His mill processed ore from several mines he and Hopper owned, including the nearby Coyote Mine in the Cottonwood Mountains. It also served as a custom mill for local miners. By the fall of 1939 he had treated only a few tons worth next to nothing, and abandoned the mill. By then he had already opened his first cactus museum in Palm Springs. After he married a USC botany student in 1940, the couple expanded his business to a five-acre cactus arboretum that showcased worldwide botanical treasures. It still thrives today as the Moorten Botanical Gardens, a popular Palm Springs attraction. Talented horticulturalists, they landscaped the homes of Frank Sinatra and Bing Crosby, and Walt Disney's Frontierland, one of Disneyland Park's original theme parks. In spite of Little Chilcoot Pass's hopeful name, likely inspired by the gold rush at Klondike's Chilkoot Pass, there was much more glamor and money in cactus than gold.

Considering how small and short-lived Cactus Slim's operation was, it is a pleasant surprise that as much of it is left as there is—the mill's concrete slab, a cluster of vats, a platform of neatly stacked rocks, a galvanized tank, and misshapen relics. Was the carcass of the vintage car where he reportedly lived while working his mill? What makes this place special is that for a change, we know something about its owner. His story alone makes us want to check it out, if only to reflect on this great land of opportunity where a manual laborer can end up socializing with Hollywood celebrities, and being honored for his lifetime achievements on Palm Springs' prestigious Walk of Stars.

■

MASTODON PEAK

This is the most popular trail in this area of the park, for good reasons. It passes by a shaded palm oasis, a gold mill from the 1930s, stony landscapes, cool Sonoran Desert plants, fine views of the Salton Sea, and Mastodon Peak's mammoth dome diced into slabs the size of up-ended trucks. It does not hurt that the trail is short and easy, with barely 400 feet of elevation gain, and a loop to boot. Throw in a quick extra scramble up Mastodon Peak's backside for cinematic views worthy of the Wonderland of Rocks itself.

General Information

Road status: Paved access road; hiking mostly on trails
Mastodon Mine: 2.4 mi, 410 ft up loop/easy
Mastodon Peak: 2.6 mi, 520 ft up loop/easy–moderate
Main attractions: Scenic boulder fields, gold mine and mill, peak climb
USGS 7.5' topo map: Cottonwood Spring
Maps: pp. 423*, 413, 399

Location and Access

Mastodon Peak is a low eminence in the western Eagle Mountains, less than a mile east of Cottonwood Spring. The Mastodon Mine is perched on the peak's southwestern shoulder. They are both reached via the Mastodon Mine Loop Trail, which starts at the east end of the Cottonwood Oasis Road (see *Cottonwood Spring Walkabout* for driving directions). Alternatively, if you are staying at the campground, from the east end of loop A or loop B you can walk down the Cottonwood Spring Nature Trail 0.3 mile to its signed junction with the loop trail.

Route Description

The Mastodon Mine Loop Trail is a 2.4-mile oblong loop that straddles the western flank of the Mastodon Peak ridge. From the parking, a short ramp will first take you down to Cottonwood Spring, a resplendent stand of mature palms and cottonwoods that charms many park visitors every day (see *Cottonwood Spring Walkabout*). The trail then climbs up a little as it follows a shallow gulch 0.6 mile to the base of the peak. At first the focus is the vegetation, a vibrant botanical garden with open patches of ocotillo, plantations of Mojave yucca, and a dense cover of catclaw, manzanita, blackbush, desert almond, and paperbag bush. Near the head of the gulch, the signed trail to the

Rock formations along the loop trail, Mastodon Peak in the distance

Mastodon Mine splits off to the left and ascends Mastodon Peak's rocky pedestal. The trail winds up among intricate outcrops, assisted by occasional stone stairs. You climb past typical White Tank Monzogranite extravaganza, jointed bluffs, cleaved rocks, and exfoliating ledges decorated with ocotillo, juniper, and plumed nolina. Mastodon Peak grandstands up ahead at the ridge top. Its resemblance to a Pleistocene elephant is not obvious, but there are definite hints of a formidable beast in its hulking carapace armored with giant pointed blocks. From close-up, it is quite a sight.

At the top of this quarter-mile ascent the trail levels off at the broad base of Mastodon Peak, a great viewpoint of the formations you just crossed and the surrounding ranges. To get to the summit, take the use trail that branches off to the right (northeast). It soon fades away; just cross the sloped slickrock bench 200 feet to past the ridge line, and look to the left for a ledge a few feet wide that climbs across the summit block's northeast slope. It is a surprisingly easy ascent up this uneven ramp of dirt and stones to the boulder-clogged summit.

Mastodon Peaks' three summit rocks command spectacular views of this austere corner of the California desert. To the east the long fan sloping down from the Eagle Mountains is lacerated with parallel

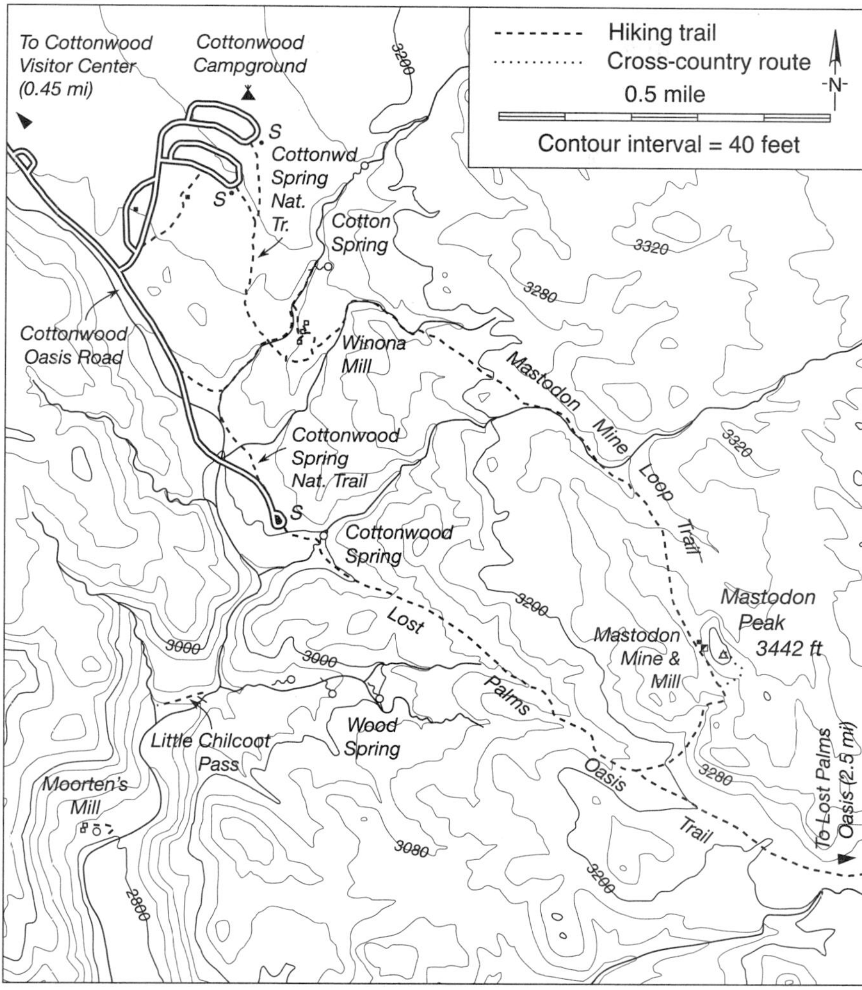

Mastodon Peak Loop

	Dist.(mi)	Elev.(ft)
End of Cottonwood Oasis Rd	0.0	3,010
Cottonwood Spring	0.05	2,970
Trail junction (go left)	0.7	3,170
Overlook	0.95	3,335
Mastodon Peak	(0.1)	3,442
Mastodon Mine and Mill	1.05	3,330
Trail crossing in wash	2.05	3,045
Back to starting point	2.4	3,010

alignments of carved granite, an ethereal fairyland of balanced spherical boulders of all sizes competing for audacity. From the slightly higher northernmost summit rock, pierced by a tiny arch, the ridge cascades down over more sculptures to badland hills and arroyos green with juniper and manzanita, all cradled in distant mountains. Turn around and you will see a mirage—the Salton Sea in the far distance, impossibly blue against the mile-high Santa Rosa Mountains.

Upon returning from the summit, turn right (northeast) on the Mastodon Mine Loop Trail and walk 100 yards to the Mastodon Mine's shafts and renovated mill. The Mastodon Mine was a latecomer. It was first recorded in 1934, during the Great Depression, a time when many jobless people moved to the desert hoping for a better life. Owners George W. Hulsey and his family worked the small one-claim operation mostly in the 1930s, then infrequently until 1971. Their mill was a simple affair that crushed the ore by rolling a heavy cylinder over it. It might have also used a ball mill, in which heavy steel balls and ore were placed in a rotating enclosure, and the balls did the crushing. An office building stood on the ledge right above the mill. The ore was quite rich at first, valued at $740 per ton. George Hulsey also owned the larger Winona Mill a mile away near Cotton Spring, perhaps as a backup should much more rich ore be exposed. Unfortunately, the gold vein ended too soon, which was not uncommon in faulted bedrock. The inclined shaft was extended to 75 feet, and a 20-foot shaft was sunk near it, but the rest of the vein was never found. The Hulseys likely recovered at most 30 tons of quartz averaging $40 per ton. The Mastodon Mine was far from the bounty they had dreamed of.

The return is easy, down the old road that once serviced the mine, on high ground with a view at first, then along two sandy washes. After 1 mile the trail winds down a flight of stairs to a broad wash and meets the Cottonwood Spring Nature Trail. To complete the loop, take this trail either straight, across the wash and uphill to the campground, or left, down the wash to the Cottonwood Spring parking (0.35 mile either way). The high country west from the mine is quite scenic, peppered with pale bubbly boulders and almost bucolic for its variety of low desert plants. Even in summer all kinds of lizards—whiptail, side-blotched, and desert horned—have a predilection for this area. Zebra-tailed lizards curled their tails over their bodies, scorpion-like, and moved them sideways to warn me off. I ran into an old chuckwalla, wrinkled and richly colored, his claws audibly scratching at the granite as he lumbered away. Some species blended in so remarkably well with the gravel that when they stopped moving, they became invisible.

■

LOST PALMS CANYON

This is another Joshua Tree classic, a longer hike that will take you to three beautiful palm oases, all very different. The first one, Cottonwood Spring, is right past the trailhead. The second one, Lost Palms Oasis, is a few trail miles out, tucked in a narrow canyon framed by towering monuments. The last one, Victory Palms, is further down canyon, beyond an obstacle course of boulders. Sullied by too many manmade contraptions, the trail has lost its wildness, but it is a fine area to explore, and the trailless finale is still wild.

General Information

Road status: Paved access road; hiking mostly on trail
Lost Palms Oasis: 3.6 mi, 760 ft up, 680 ft down one way/moderate
Victory Palms: 4.6 mi, 770 ft up, 1,080 ft down one way/difficult
Main attractions: Longer trail to three palm oases and stunning canyon
USGS 7.5' topo map: Cottonwood Spring
Maps: pp. 429*, 423, 413, *399*

Location and Access

Lost Palms Canyon is a 5-mile drainage that clips the southwesternmost tip of the Eagle Mountains and emerges at Chiriaco Summit, the broad pass between Shavers Valley and Chuckwalla Valley along the southern edge of the park. It is best known for the large fan-palm oasis by the same name located near its center, about 4 air miles southeast of the Cottonwood Visitor Center area. The canyon and the oasis are reached on the popular Lost Palms Oasis Trail, which starts at the east end of the Cottonwood Oasis Road (see *Cottonwood Spring Walkabout* for driving directions).

Route Description

The Lost Palms Oasis Trail. The first part of this hike is the same as the loop to the Mastodon Mine—down the short concrete ramp to and through Cottonwood Spring, then up to the Mastodon Mine junction 0.7 mile in. At that junction, continue straight instead of turning left to the mine. For the next 2.3 miles, the trail gradually climbs the long and broad western shoulder of Eagle Mountain to two low divides of sensibly the same elevation (~3,450'). At the first one the trail descends into a small canyon that drains into Shavers Valley. It then follows and climbs out of it to the divide with Lost Palms

Canyon. From there it is an easy 0.5-mile descent along a tributary of Lost Palms Canyon to a lookout above the oasis at the canyon's abrupt rim. Although the grades are quite modest, the trail dips in and out of many small washes that radiate down from the mountain, and you accumulate more elevation gain than expected.

The trail crosses a wide open, gentle slope of pale sediments furrowed by erosion and sprinkled with beautiful core-stones. Early on, at the foot of Mastodon Peak, they have been sculpted into long parallel rows of spires. They erupt from the ground in random clusters, their white bases grading into rusty tops, so alien-looking that we seek resemblances. Some look like the protruding spine of a fossilized antediluvian beast. Others rise in orderly ranks like the skyscrapers of a futuristic city, only too oddly pointed, slender, and finely chiseled to belong to this earth. Further on, the mountain crest recedes to the north, leaving only the low crinkled hills dotted with giant bubbles of granite. The plant cover seems to strive to intensify the strangeness of the landscape. All things sharp and spiny grow on these denuded heights, spidery ocotillos, armored barrel cactus, Mojave yucca like derisory scarecrows, nolinas tipped with tall daggers, the small blades of manzanita, and treacherous teddy-bear cholla.

Here as on other trails that have become too popular for their own good, trail signage has become epidemic. Central Park may have fewer trail signs. If you find it occasionally challenging to navigate on unsigned trails, you will likely feel comfortable here. If you prefer your nature natural, you may find the signs invasive—they tell you when to turn, when to go straight, and how far you have gone, even when it would be obvious to a ten-year old. Human tinkering has robbed this special oasis of its spirit. Now it is lost only in name.

Lost Palms Oasis. If all the trail signs are not justified, the popularity of the oasis certainly is. Of all of the park's canyons, Lost Palms ranks among the most imposing, at least around the oasis. The canyon is a temple of stone, a 400-foot-deep gorge with steep sides buttressed by massive fins that rise all the way to the rim. Every rock, outcrop, and fallen monolith is freshly polished to a pale smoothness lightly touched by desert varnish. The main palm grove is tucked at the bottom of this trench, aberrantly lush in this barren rockscape. Behind and above it, suspended in the tight gash of a steep side canyon, two smaller groves poke out of a river of boulders. Even without the palms it would be a scene of exceptional beauty. The palms add majesty, delightful incongruity, and an acute sense of scale—the trees are over 25 feet tall, yet they are lost in this monumental landscape.

Lost Palms Oasis from the trail that winds down into Lost Palms Canyon

From the lookout a short trail drops to the canyon floor—narrow, uneven, a little steep, and the only stretch that may bump up the difficulty of this hike from easy to moderate. At the bottom of it you are in a different world. The air is cooler, the harsh desert light softened by dappled shadows and lively shades of green. The straight trunks of mature fan palms soar above you, dwarfed by the columnar monoliths behind them. Unlike in other palm oases, here you are free to walk around. Up canyon, the oasis ends shortly in a tumble of angular boulders. Down canyon it unfolds for quite some distance along a narrow, twisted wash peppered with occasional boulders, so that you often do not see what lies ahead. If you walk all of it, you will pass by several dozen palms, inviting sand beaches, tufts of tule, thickets of squawbush, mesquite, and baccharis, and a few puddles of spring water, some quasi-permanent and clogged with green algae. The grand prize goes to the side canyon near the lower end of the access trail. There the forest of palms is thickest, darkest, most impressive. The two small groves higher up take a little scrambling to be reached, but they are rare treasures. When the day is not too hot, these alluring enclaves of greenery are great spots to sit and rest, back against cold rock, engulfed in their cocoon of stone.

Victory Palms. The second part of the hike, down Lost Palms Canyon to Victory Palms, could not be any more different than the first: there are no more trails, no signs, no distant views, very few people if any, and the hiking is more serious. The oasis thins down to small isolated stands of palms, until the last tree finally cedes the stage back to the sunbaked desert. Soon comes the first difficulty, a wall-to-wall plug of large boulders that blocks the way. It can be crossed on the left, around the back of an overhanging behemoth. The next boulder jam is easy. The sandy wash manages to wiggle through the third jam interrupted, slipping by the two halves of a neatly cleaved giant rock. In this area, the canyon floor is punctuated with segments of a pipeline installed long ago to divert the spring water, probably for mining activities, which must have been quite an endeavor. The fourth and last obstacle is the largest, tallest, and hardest. It is a 300-yard-long ramp of helter-skelter boulders that can take a half hour to negotiate. You will likely have to duck under a massive pile of boulders, slip down tilted rock faces, scramble down an abrupt edge or two, get snagged on incorrigible catclaws, and try a few routes here and there.

Lost Palms Canyon

	Dist.(mi)	Elev.(ft)
End of Cottonwood Oasis Rd	0.0	3,010
Cottonwood Spring	0.05	2,970
Trail junction (go straight)	0.7	3,170
Divide into Lost Palms Cyn	3.0	3,450
Trail junction	3.45	3,300
Lost Palms Oasis lookout	(0.05)	3,290
Lost Palms Oasis (end of trail)	3.6	3,180
Lost Palms Oasis (lower end)	3.9	3,060
First boulder jam	4.0	3,030
Fourth boulder jam	4.4	2,870
Victory Palms	4.6	2,720

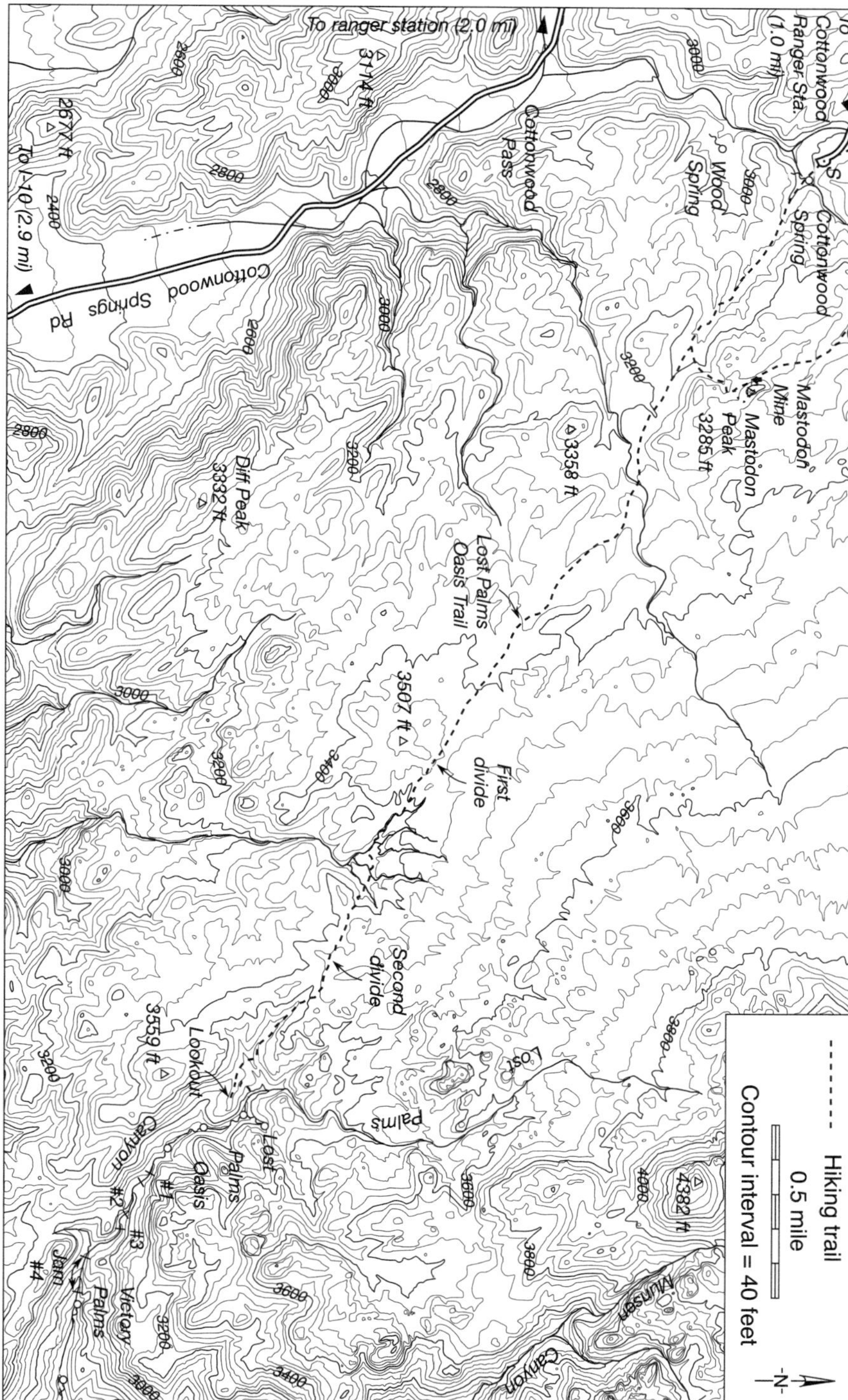
To ranger station (2.0 mi)
To Cottonwood Ranger Sta. (1.0 mi)
To I-10 (2.9 mi)
Cottonwood Springs Rd
Cottonwood Pass
Cottonwood Spring
Wood Spring
Mastodon Mine
Mastodon Peak 3285 ft
3114 ft
2677 ft
3358 ft
Lost Palms Oasis Trail
Dike Peak 3332 ft
3507 ft
First divide
Second divide
3559 ft
Lookout
Lost Palms
Lost Palms Oasis
Canyon
#1
#2
#3
Jam
#4
Victory Palms
Munsen Canyon
4382 ft
Hiking trail
0.5 mile
Contour interval = 40 feet
N

Down in the oasis

Keep this place wild: do not stack rocks to help you find your way back; memorize or photograph your route instead.

Victory Palms is at the bottom of this final occlusion, a row of half a dozen lonesome fan palms growing alongside the rocky wash. Below it the canyon straightens out and levels off, as if exhausted from its struggle against the boulders. Its wash is lined with feathery thickets of blue palo verde. Although not nearly as lush and charming as Lost Palms Oasis, Victory Palms is much wilder, more secret, quieter too, and seemingly far more remote, protected from human intrusions by this natural barrier of boulders. The flat boulders surrounding it offer just enough comfort to lay back and admire the rocky canyon walls.

If you return late in the evening as I once did, you will likely be treated to a colorful sunset beyond the Santa Rosa Mountains, which dominate the southern horizon, and a small surprise. During the day you may not see the Salton Sea from the trail, occulted as it is by the fierce daylight scattering off air-borne dust. But at dusk it often shines through, right after the last of the direct sunrays have gone, and the pale reflection of the sky turns it into liquid silver.

■

MUNSEN CANYON

Palms are extremely rare: only approximately 450 grow in the park. A third are found in Munsen Canyon, which makes it easily the best palm oasis hike. It beats the competition on all metrics—its grand stone monuments, the fun boulder climbs, the record number of palm groves, the absence of trail, and the palpable isolation. Thanks to their remoteness, the canyon's seven groves are also by far the least visited in the park. Each one is a cool haven of peace, filled with exotic plants and welcoming shade, more remote and mysterious than the previous one. Diehard hikers can push on and ascend Eagle Mountain at the head of the canyon, an offbeat route to a beautiful summit surrounded by elegant cactus gardens.

General Information

Road status: Graded access road; hiking on old road and cross-country
Summit Springs: 3.8 mi, 1,050 ft up, 10 ft down one way / moderate
Munsen Oasis: 4.5 mi, 1,320 ft up, 20 ft down one way / moderate
Arch Oasis: 5.6 mi, 1,920 ft up, 30 ft down one way / very difficult
Eagle Mountain: 7.2 mi, 3,610 ft up, 70 ft down one way / strenuous
Main attractions: A sculptural canyon with multiple palm oases
USGS 7.5' topo maps: Hayfield,* Cottonwood Spring
Maps: pp. 435*, *399*

Location and Access

From the lofty heights of Eagle Mountain, Munsen Canyon slices a convoluted path south down through the Eagle Mountains before merging with Lost Palms Canyon near the foot of the range. It is possible to approach it via Lost Palms Oasis and Victory Palms (see *Lost Palms Canyon*), then continuing down canyon to the confluence with Munsen Canyon. This longer route does not leave much time to explore Munsen Canyon and its many oases. For a shorter and much more private route, it is best to approach it from the other direction, hiking up into Lost Palms Canyon from the park's southern boundary. Drive to the Chiriaco Summit exit on Interstate 10. At the stop sign at the end of the eastbound-exit ramp, turn left and go over the freeway 250 yards to a T junction. Make a right, and after 225 yards, just before the commercial area, turn left on a graded road. Follow it 0.65 mile north, past the General Patton Museum and a repository of vintage tanks on the left, to the wide loop at the end of the road, and park.

Summit Springs

Route Description

The fence at the end of the road marks the national park boundary. Beyond it, the road continues as a foot trail toward the wide gap of Lost Palms Canyon 1 mile north. It is not the most glamorous starting point for a hike into a remote wilderness, within sight of fast-food joints and earshot of eighteen-wheelers rumbling down the interstate. The old twin track fortunately makes for a quick escape. By the time the road ends beside the rock island at the entrance into Lost Palms Canyon, the noise has subsided to a hum. Beyond it, the broad wash makes a very wide curve left and narrows ever so slowly, until it takes more intimate dimensions at the mouth of Munsen Canyon 3.3 miles out. This is the Sonoran Desert.The wash is sprinkled with teddy-bear chollas, shaggy ironwood, and isolated palo verde. Past the rock island the dominance switches. You walk through an open forest of palo verde, and the ironwood become the underdog. Further on, smoke trees join in. Every species eventually finds its own niche, segregated by chemical affinities. The desert willows occupy the wash. The ironwood and palo verde favor the edges. The 40-foot banks of compacted alluvia that border the wash are lined by ghostly ocotillos on one side, and thousands of teddy-bear chollas in impressively tight ranks on the other.

Munsen Canyon does not give away its secrets easily. Almost immediately, its wash is subsumed by boulders. Large gray blocks are packed on bedrock scooped long ago by ancient water. At places, 8-foot monoliths have piled up in intricate dams, and it takes a little searching to find a way through. It is good Class-2 fun, although all too short: in 300 yards the boulders thin down, some of the sand returns, and the walking gets easier.

Dried fronds, Munsen Oasis

The first palm grove, Summit Springs, is just a few more minutes up canyon. The largest in Munsen Canyon, it is a striking spot. Two dozen palms are clustered in the narrow wash, their tousled manes a vibrant lime-green against the canyon's pale monzonite. A second grove is visible just up a side canyon, sprouting out of an apron of boulders. High slopes of fractured outcrops rise all around, capped by slick monuments carved in bare stone. In the sanctuary of the groves the mood changes radically. There is deep shade, a pleasantly higher humidity, and cooler air. The fronds rustle in the slightest breeze, filling space with the joyous sound of rushing water. It is a relaxing environment to take in the beauty of this secluded canyon, and the variety of plants that thrive in and around the oasis—cattail, baccharis, coyote tobacco, ocotillo, barrel cactus, and delicate clumps of deer grass.

The next stretch to Munsen Oasis is easier. Boulders still rule, but often a narrow strip of sand will open up at the last second and guide you through easily to what looked like a hard scramble. Unlike the first grove, Munsen Oasis shows up gradually, first a single isolated palm, then two, and finally the main grove up in the V of the canyon. Set in a narrow bend, its tall palms rise majestically against high walls patterned with bare cliffs. This oasis is wilder, slightly more open, more inviting. In its midst, you wobble awkwardly on springy mats of fallen fronds that crack underfoot like kindling. Sunlight reflecting off the dry fronds hanging down the trunks casts a cheery orange glow that permeates the air. In a bathtub-size hollow in the wash, the sand was a little wet. The foot-tall chute that sometimes feeds creek water into it is plated with white carbonates. A thicket of arrowweed just downstream is patiently waiting for the creek to return. After the long shadeless walk up from the valley, it is hard to resist the temptation to lay down on a sun-warmed rock and surrender to this serene refuge.

Past Munsen Oasis, all hell gradually breaks loose. There are five more main groves, ranging from four to over a dozen palms, and half a dozen occurrences of one or two palms interspersed between them. The anticipation is a powerful incentive to go on. The disincentive is equally strong: the canyon is fiercely guarding these hidden jewels. Entire sections are clogged with boulders or dense brush. You are either scrambling or bushwhacking. At the worst spots, you do both, and climb over boulders ensnared in thorny bramble. Every so often another oasis pops up in the distance like a mirage, and you push on with renewed energy.

Little by little, the canyon takes on monumental proportions. The walls angle steeper; exposures of solid rock become more prominent. On one side sharp high ridges have been chiseled into ladders of pinnacles. On the other, lone towers lean over staggered layers of sheared stone. The scenery displays an ever-changing mix of isomorphic blocks, slanted cliffs, sugarloaves and domes. Blue sky blazes behind it all. Soon the first clumps of juniper grace the wash, then pinyon pine, oak, mesquite, nolina, and pancake cactus, a canvas of greens and shapes that rivals the exuberance of the rocks.

Munsen Canyon

	Dist.(mi)	Elev.(ft)
Park boundary	0.0	1,760
End of road at rock island	1.0	2,090
Munsen Canyon mouth	3.35	2,630
Summit Springs	3.8	2,830
Munsen Oasis	4.45	3,090
Twin Oases (upper)	5.25	3,470
Fork (go right)	5.3	3,460
Arch Oasis	5.6	3,670
Narrows (Class 3)	6.2	3,950
Eagle Mountain	7.2	5,350

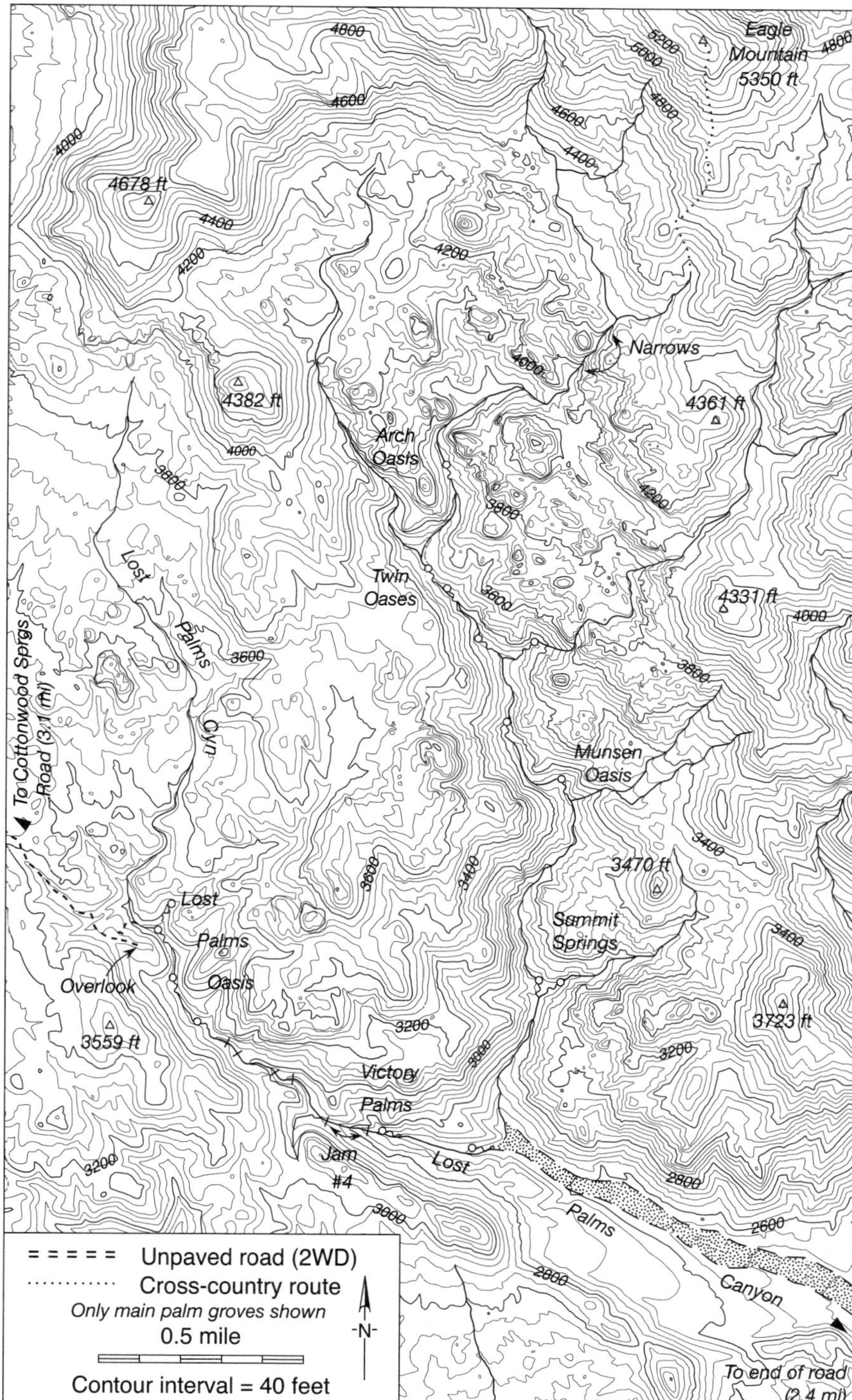
Eagle Mountain 5350 ft
4678 ft
Narrows
4382 ft
4361 ft
Arch Oasis
Twin Oases
4331 ft
Lost Palms Cyn
To Cottonwood Sprgs Road (3.1 mi)
Munsen Oasis
3470 ft
Lost Palms Oasis
Overlook
Summit Springs
3723 ft
3559 ft
Victory Palms
Jam #4
Lost Palms Canyon
To end of road (2.4 mi)
= = = = = Unpaved road (2WD)
.... Cross-country route
Only main palm groves shown
0.5 mile
N
Contour interval = 40 feet

Munsen Canyon below Munsen Oasis

The last large grove in Munsen Canyon itself is Twin Oases, two groves of towering trees, the upper one wedged in a tight passage just before a main side canyon on the right. The final grove, Arch Oasis, is in the side canyon, past a resilient patch of shrubs. This is where the canyon's architectural splendor reaches its climax. The walls have solidified into sweeps of massive monzonite that rise straight from the wash. In the winter months, when the sun describes a low arc in the sky, chimneys, ledges, and recesses are all cast in shadows of different depths and stand out with crisp prominence. For its setting, remoteness, and small pool of turbid water where red spotted toads frolick, Arch Oasis may be the most special. Its stately palms cast long straight shadows that intensify their presence. Up on the east wall past the grove, a small arch rests on the back of a slanted fin. Shaped like a squinting eye, it has been watching over the oasis for millennia, and witnessed the lives and deaths of untold generations of palms.

If you are ambitious and want to go on to the summit of Eagle Mountain, this fork will take you there. Follow it through two stocky portals into a beautiful open desert garden, then scramble up steep narrows filled with high stacks of boulders. At the top, the canyon splits. Angle into the right fork and follow it east and north to a ridge, then climb the ridge north to the summit. It is strenuous, especially the Class-3 scramble, but it is a memorable route to an eye-filling summit. Even seasoned hikers will be content with hanging around some of the palm groves on the way back, and enjoying a little longer the distinct aura of places that are rare, remote, and a little secret.

■

DIFFICULT CANYON

It would be challenging to find a canyon with a name less inspiring and romantic than Difficult. It would also be hard to find, in all of Joshua Tree, a canyon as exceptional in most metrics—accessibility, scenery, solitude, and physical challenge. Difficult Canyon's central gorge is a grand rockscape of looming monuments and balanced boulders with a wash filled with gigantic boulders, so strenuous that it is little traveled, so little traveled that in its sublime chaos I discovered a beautiful 12-foot arch. There are likely other unreported wonders if you are game to explore this strenuous landscape.

General Information
Road status: Graded access road (2WD); cross-country hiking
California Arch: 0.85 mi, 310 ft up, ~30 ft down one way / strenuous
Dragon Wash pass: 1.6 mi, 630 ft up, ~40 ft down one way / strenuous
Main attractions: A beautiful rugged canyon filled with boulders
USGS 7.5' topo map: Desert Center, Hayfield Spring*
Maps: pp. 441*, 445, *399*

Location and Access

Difficult Canyon and its close neighbors Boulder Canyon and Dragon Wash to the east are short gorges that drain the very rugged southeastern front of the Eagle Mountains into Chuckwalla Valley. Work your way to the Eagle Mountain Road exit on Interstate 10, which is 20.3 miles east of the Cottonwood Springs Road exit. Drive the Eagle Mountain Road north 2.1 miles (measured from the westbound exit) to the MWD Aqueduct Road at 10 o'clock. Drive this excellent graded road 1.8 miles to a fork, and make a left (southwest). This next road follows the front of the Eagle Mountains on the right and crosses a power line once (1.2 miles), then a second time across from low hills on the left (2.0 miles), then makes a sharp right (2.5 miles) and a small left (2.8 miles) before reaching Difficult Canyon (2.9 miles). Its entrance is marked by a narrow gateway 200 yards to the right.

Route Description

It all starts unexpectedly easily, like a bucolic stroll in the park. Just beyond the short gateway at its mouth, Difficult Canyon is a playa of pure sand free of rocks, smoothed by the wind to a flawless finish. Large palo verde, ironwood, desert lavender, and creosote grow in isolated islands in the wash, too green for the low desert. Little by little the canyon shows its true colors. You pass by pointed piles of boulders, then gradually enter a narrowing gorge with bare-granite walls dissected from base to summit into organ pipes. Every rock aspires to verticality. Tight ranks of tall pinnacles rise up ahead, random in size yet in patterns and shapes strikingly repetitive. The symmetry is a little unsettling, as if you were contemplating the work of some greater intelligence. This feeling of being elsewhere is, more than anything else, the hallmark of this exceptional canyon. And it gets grander, stranger, and more beautiful...

In a place so sheer and crowded with vertical monuments, smooth sailing is short-lived. What makes matters worse is that the local granite is extremely strong. When it breaks, it does not shatter but splits into gigantic chunks that erosion polishes to smooth spheroids. When thrown off balance by earthquakes, these rounded boulders become unstoppable and roll down all the way to the wash. This is what happened in Difficult Canyon. Half a mile up, at the entrance into the narrower central gorge, the sandy wash disappears abruptly under a landslide of gargantuan rocks.

For the next 0.6 mile, with the exception of a few brief open stretches, the canyon floor is crammed with boulders. It is an impressive obstruction: the boulders average 5 or 6 feet across, many reach up to 20 feet in their largest dimension, and they are often stacked in multiple layers. Polished and bulging, they offer little purchase for climbing. The sides of the canyon are rough, and workable bypasses are few. To cross this three-dimensional maze, you hop from stone to stone when possible, scramble over the boulders that are manageable, squeeze between the ones that are too big, and hope that the route you chose does not dead-end. Many routes do. At the largest boulders, when all else fails there is sometimes a way through *under* the boulder. You down-climb into dim caves beneath 100-ton behemoths, slither over coarse sand with a few inches of clearance over your head, dragging your pack along, and on the far side you wiggle back up to the surface through an opening shaped like a coat hanger.

As often with challenging places, the payoffs are exceptional. Difficult Canyon holds some of the California desert's most awesome sculpted rockscapes. Early on the steep walls are covered with towering columns suntanned to an auburn veneer. Further up, the canyon opens a little onto a staircase of polished granite littered with fallen boulders that seem to be holding by a thread. Several hundred feet up, the rims are bristling with turrets. Everywhere you turn there are balanced rocks, elegant tafoni and windows hollowed out in rock faces,

California Arch

enormous split boulders, long smooth drops of stone, and intriguing hoodoos. In the middle of this mineral monopoly, a palo verde will occasionally erupt like a miracle and pose gracefully against barren stone.

And then there is the arch. Halfway through the boulder jam, the canyon angles sharply west and the boulder jam gets particularly gnarly. I was so intently looking at the ground for a passage that I walked right below the arch a few times, until I finally found a way through, looked up, and saw it staring down at me. Eroded in a vertical buttress of granite pigmented with desert varnish, its opening is about 12 feet tall and shaped like the Golden State. It is an elegant geological work of art, intensified by the remoteness and the magnificence of its surroundings. Last time I discovered an arch, in Arches National

Side arm of Difficult Canyon

Park, someone else took the liberty to name it. This one became, that day, California Arch.

About 150 yards past the arch the boulder madness stops temporarily and the sandy wash resumes. Where it makes a left turn to the west, it passes by a particularly finely sculpted side canyon on the right filled with a nightmarish jury of hooded figures. Soon after, the wash angles north and enters the Slot, a 100-yard, slanted corridor of low vertical walls where boulders challenge passage. Getting through this second crux is a little tricky, but it can be done. Once over it, the gorge and its river of boulders end in 150 yards.

Difficult Canyon goes on about twice as far again, generally west through more open terrain, not quite as dramatic but still festooned with imposing sugarloafs and standing rocks. There are a few boulder jams to cross, much shorter, though one of them is challenging. By the time you are through with them you might not be in the mood to descend through the boulders again. Fortunately, there is another way to return, down Dragon Wash. It is three times longer but much easier, and you will get to see two canyons in one day.

To cross into Dragon Wash, from the top of the Slot hike up the wash a quarter of a mile, past a short boulder jam, to a lone boulder just before a fork. Take the smaller right fork, and after just 20 yards,

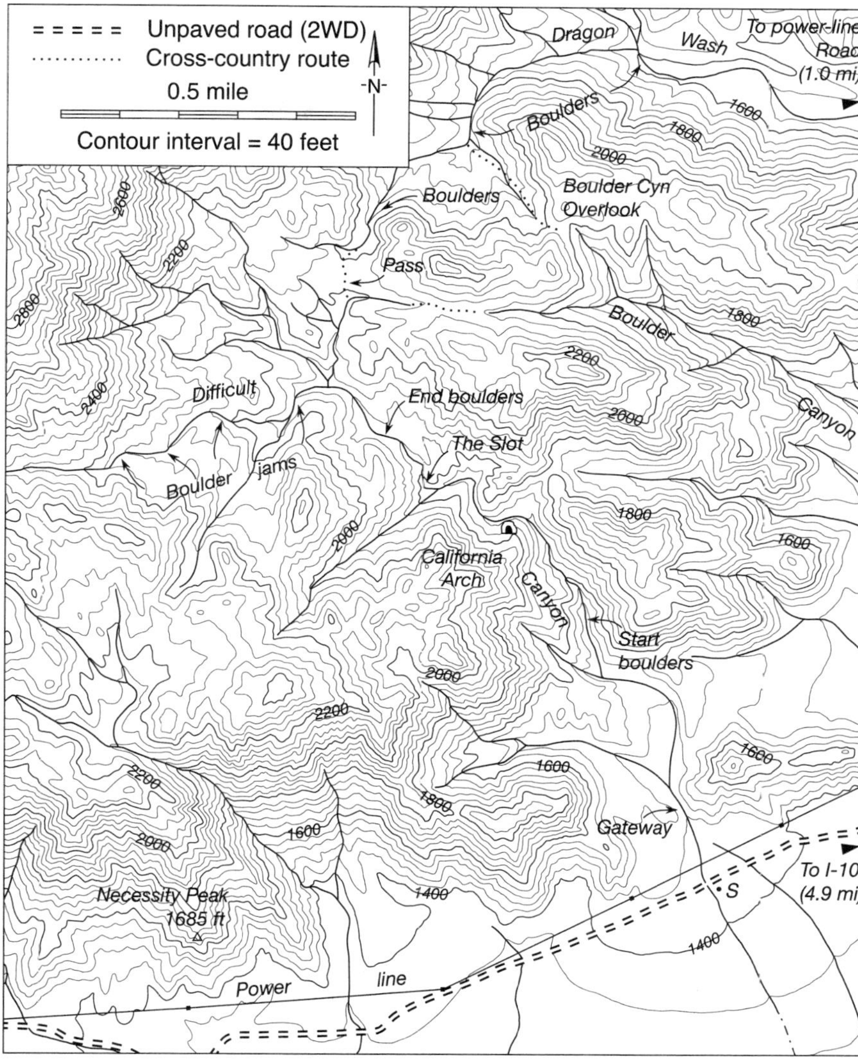

	Dist.(mi)	Elev.(ft)
Power-line road	0.0	1,420
Start of boulders	0.55	1,515
California Arch	0.85	1,740
The Slot	1.05	1,780
Fork at lone boulder	1.35	1,900
Pass into Dragon Wash	1.6	2,010

Difficult Canyon

Boulder cave in Difficult Canyon's central gorge

turn right into an even smaller fork. Follow this twisted ravine north 0.2 mile and about 100 feet up to where it angles sharply right (east). Continue north instead a very short distance to the open pass into Dragon Wash, then drop north down into this drainage. There is soon a run of large boulders, only a tenth of a mile long; its lower section can be circumvented on the right side. At the end of the descent (0.4 mile), you will be at the center of the amphitheater in upper Dragon Wash. Hike down this rocky canyon to the MWD Aqueduct Road (see *Dragon Wash*), then follow this level road 1.5 miles southwest back to your car.

One of this canyon's most precious assets is that it is infrequently visited. Please keep it pristine. If you must put up a cairn for yourself, make it look natural, like a small stone wedged between rocks instead of on a boulder. Remove it on your way back. If you accidentally leave it there, it will not be noticed or bother other visitors.

"Difficult" is not an exaggeration. Hiking in this canyon is strenuous if you are physically fit, punishing otherwise. It will put to the test your physical strength, mental resolve, and patience on the way up, and your memory when looking for your way back down. If scrambling is not for you, do take the short stroll up to the edge of the central gorge. Try it during the golden hour, when every one of the thousands of monuments that blanket the canyon's flanks is outlined by a thin shadow. It gives an impressive glimpse of Difficult Canyon's raw spirit.

■

DRAGON WASH

The dragon is there, in plain view on the map of the twisted canyon. The long snaking lower canyon is the tail, the two side canyons flapping above its spine the wings, the lineup of tributaries above its head the spiky crest, and the two side canyons below it the fire-breathing snout. Unlike its neighbors, Dragon Wash is a fairly easy path into this rough section of the Eagle Mountains, with an open forest of ironwood and ocotillo, striking rock gardens, and a scenic amphitheater at its end. The exception is Anschutz Peak, at the very head of the canyon: it will let you know in no uncertain terms that like the chaos that it symbolizes, the dragon can get rough.

General Information

Road status: Graded access road; cross-country hiking
Amphitheater: 2.0 mi, 520 ft up, ~20 ft down one way / easy–moderate
Anschutz Peak: 2.7 mi, 1,980 ft up, 50 ft down one way / strenuous
Main attractions: A scenic canyon, rock formations, ironwood, and a peak climb
USGS 7.5' topo maps: Desert Center, Hayfield Spring*
Maps: pp. 445*, 441, *399*

Location and Access

Dragon Wash is about a mile northeast of Difficult Canyon, at the very southeastern corner of the Eagle Mountains. Directions from the Eagle Mountain Road exit on Interstate 10 are the same as for Difficult Canyon, except that after angling left on the power-line road, go only 1.25 miles to where the power line crosses the road, and park 0.2 mile further. Dragon Wash is the broad wash on the right.

Route Description

Most of this canyon is indeed particularly tame, and made up of a long river of sand flushed with a verdant open forest. The visual effect is striking: here you are, in a desert just 1,400 feet above sea level that receives mere inches of rain annually, and you are surrounded by *trees*. The wash is dotted with tall ironwood and palo verde, desert lavender, smoke tree, and desert olive. Overlapping generations of ironwood thrive in the parched sand, all imprinted with the same genetic shagginess—the fuzzy youngsters, the full-grown adults rising 20 feet in the air, the elderly trees burdened with broken limbs that drag onto the

Anschutz Peak (right) from amphitheater; the couloir route is above the ocotillo

ground, and the ancient snags burnished to a mahogany glaze. The adjoining hills display astonishing galleries of rounded granite sculptures that locally seem to be a replica of each other. The hillsides are crammed with hoodoos, the ridges crested with pinnacles. There are battlements of turrets, bookshelves of upright slabs, and fields of giant balls that bulge right out of the earth. Every surface is richly colored with the burnt sienna of very old desert varnish. Where the canyon opens up onto its two major tributaries and makes a wide left, a row of classic desert peaks comes into view up ahead and steals the show. The canyon heads west towards the highest one—Anschutz Peak, the dragon's crest. Eons ago, when the climate was much wetter, the perennial stream that ran through here gouged a channel 40 feet deep into the alluvia that filled the canyon floor. Its legacy is a narrowing passage, serene and more intimate, sprinkled with shady trees. Skeletal ocotillo stand guard stoically up on the leftover alluvial banks.

After 1.5 miles the tail joins the dragon's body, a half-mile section of boulders. Compared to neighboring canyons, the boulders are relatively small and sparse, the slope is modest, and so is the challenge. Ironically, wherever the going gets a little harder a thick plant will

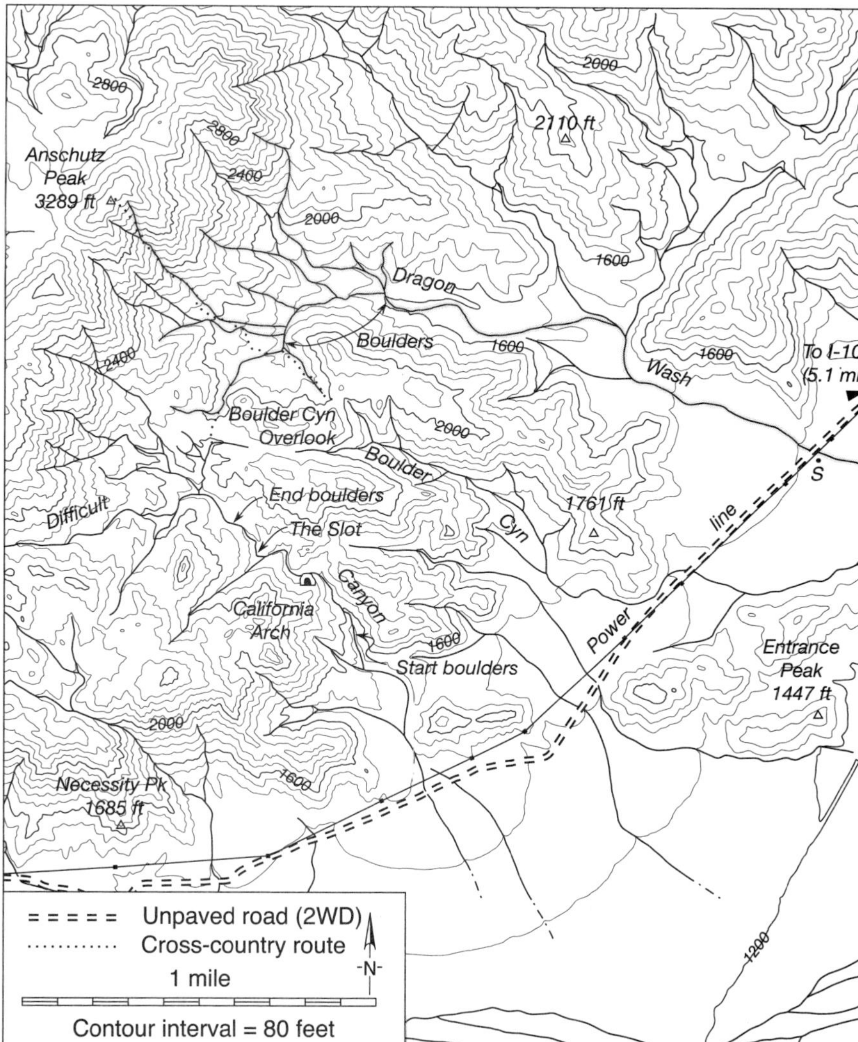

Dragon Wash		
	Dist.(mi)	Elev.(ft)
Power-line road	0.0	1,350
Main fork in canyon	0.7	1,470
Start of boulders	1.5	1,600
Fork at amphitheater	1.95	1,830
Boulder Canyon Overlook	(0.25)	2,010
Anschutz Peak	2.7	3,289

invariably be in the way, usually not a soft brittlebush but some resilient and eminently prickly shrub...

The boulders end just past a small stream-polished slant of granite. The canyon's grand terminus is just beyond, a spacious amphitheater ringed with escarpments hundreds of feet high. Its open floor is sprinkled with palo verde and low weathered ribs of coarse granite. Wild formations hang all around—fins, bluffs, exfoliating prongs, fallen towers leaning across each other, and high up on a rim a truck-size boulder that appears to be exempt from gravity. A 50-foot dome shattered into interlocked boulders parades in the middle of all this like a tortoise carapace, dwarfed by Anschutz Peak soaring behind it.

There are plenty of nooks and crannies to explore in the area. You can hike up the canyon's southeastern arm—the dragon's jaw—on a gravelly ramp, past ocotillo and a small arch, to the pass into Boulder Canyon for a peek into Chuckwalla Valley. You can clamber up the bouldery southwestern arm instead and drop into Difficult Canyon. It is tempting to loop back down one of these rougher canyons, but before you do make sure you know what you are getting into, and that you have the stamina to turn around if you cannot make it through.

Yet the most thrilling goal is the dragon's rough crest. The route to it is the couloir cluttered with slabs and boulders, clearly visible from the amphitheater, that screams down Anschutz Peak's southeastern face. Skirt the east side of the tortoise shell to the base of the couloir, and climb it straight up. Conquering this landslide of angular rocks resting at precarious angles is a minor epic. From wash to summit the elevation gain is 1,460 feet over 0.8 mile. From up close the perspective of this sheer couloir flanked by darkly stained crags is vertiginous. Two thirds of the way up, at a leaning square tower on the left, take the right fork. The inflection point is up in there; at 55%, the grade is so steep that you have to clutch at rocks to stay upright.

The view is, as almost always, captivating, although it may feel secondary to the elation of success. On one side the desert unfolds many miles to the dark crenulated flanks of the little-known Palen Mountains and Chuckwalla Mountains. On the other, the narrow summit drops precipitously into the long valley that slices through the heart of the Eagle Mountains. This wild scenery epitomizes graphically the paradox of our desert wilderness, its immeasurable value, and its remarkable success as an instrument of conservation. You are standing on a summit that does not see a human footprint for years, within sight of a four-lane transcontinental freeway that moves 60,000 vehicles a day. This is the beauty of the American West.

■

BIBLIOGRAPHY

Aubury, L. E. "The copper resources of California." *Cal. St. Mining Bureau Bull.* 50 (1908): 19–23, 325–340.

Barth, A. P., J. L. Wooden, C. E. Jacobson, and K. Probst. "U-Pb geochronology and geochemistry of the McCoy Mountains Formation, southeastern California: A Cretaceous retroarc foreland basin." *Geol. Soc. Am. Bull.* 116, No. 1–2 (2004): 142–153.

Bean, L. J., and K. S. Saubel. *Temalpakh: Cahuilla Indian knowledge and usage of plants.* Morongo Indian Reservation, Ca.: Malki Museum Press, 1972.

Belden, L. B. "Lizard hunter uncovers rich hoard of gold." *San Bernardino Sun Telegram* (Jan. 15, 1961): 57.

Benedict, R. F. "A brief sketch of Serrano culture." *Am. Anthrop.* 26, No. 3 (1924): 366–392.

Brown, J. S. "The Salton Sea region, California." *USGS Water-Supply Paper* 497, 1923.

Calzia, J. P., *et al.* "Mineral resource potential map of the Coxcomb Mountains Wilderness Study Area (CDCA-328), San Bernardino and Riverside Counties, California." *U.S. Geological Survey* MF-1603-A, scale 1:62,500, 1983.

Cloudman, H. C., *et al.* "San Bernardino County, Tulare County." *Rept. of the State Mineralogist* 15 (1915–1916): 773–852.

Crawford, J. J. "Mines and mining products of California." *Annual Rept. of the State Mineralogist* 12 (1894): 21–141, 223, 224.

Crawford, J. J. "Mines and mining products of California." *Annual Rept. of the State Mineralogist* 13 (1896): 32–185, 230, 311, 313, 315, 319–330, 606–609.

d'Autremont, H. *West of Dawn.* New York, NY: Exposition Press, 1971.

DeLisle, H. F. *Amphibians and Reptiles of Joshua Tree National Park California.* (online) 2003.

Dibblee, T.W., Jr. "Geologic map of the Joshua Tree quadrangle, San Bernardino and Riverside Counties, California." *USGS Miscellaneous Geologic Investigation Map* I-516, scale 1:62,500, 1967.

Dibblee, T.W., Jr. "Geologic map of the Twentynine Palms quadrangle, San Bernardino and Riverside Counties, California." *USGS Miscellaneous Geologic Investigation Map* I-581, scale 1:62,500, 1968.

Dibblee, T. W., Jr., and J. A. Milch. "Geologic map of the Thousand Palms & Lost Horse Mountain 15 minute quadrangles, Riverside County, California." Santa Barbara, Ca.: Santa Barbara Museum of Natural History, Dibblee Geology Center Map No. DF-372, scale 1:62,500, 2008.

Earle, D. D. "The Mojave River and the central Mojave Desert: Native settlement, travel, and exchange in the eighteenth and nineteenth centuries." *J. Cal. and Great Basin Anthr.* 25, No. 1 (2005): 1–38.

Fiero, B. *Geology of the Great Basin*. Reno, Nev.: Univ. of Nevada Press, 1986.

Force, E. R. "Eagle Mountain Mine—geology of the former Kaiser Steel operation in Riverside County, California." *USGS*, Open-File Rept 01-237, 2001.

Frizzell, V. A., Jr., J. M. Mattinson, and J. C. Matti. "Distinctive Triassic megaporphyritic monzogranite: Evidence for only 160 km offset along the San Andreas Fault, southern California." *J. Geophys. Res.* 91 (1986): 14080–14088.

Fumal, T. E., *et al.* "Timing of large earthquakes since A.D. 800 on the Mission Creek strand of the San Andreas Fault Zone at Thousand Palms Oasis, near Palm Springs, California." *Bull. Seism. Soc. Am.* 92, No. 7 (2002): 2841–2860.

Gardner, E. S. "Rain Magic." *Argosy* 198, No. 5 (1928): 580 *et seq.*; *Fantastic* 12, No. 4 (1963): 82–119.

Gardner, E. S. *The Court of Last Resort*. William Sloane Associates, New York (1952).

Goodwin, J. G. "Lead and zinc in California." *Cal. J. Mines and Geol.* 53 (1957): 351– 724.

Gray, C. H., Jr., J. R. Evans, and R. B. Saul. "Mines and mineral resources of Riverside County, California." *Cal. Div. of Mines and Geol.*, 1961.

Greene, L. W. *Historic Resource Study: A History of Land Use in Joshua Tree National Monument*. Denver Service Center, 1983.

Harding, L. E. *Tectonic Significance of the McCoy Mountains Formation, Southeastern California and Southwestern Arizona*. Doctoral dissertation. Tucson, Az.: The University of Arizona, 1982.

Harrington, E. *Summary Report on the Mission Property, Dale Mining District, Riverside and San Bernardino Counties, California, USA*. Prepared for Bullion River Gold Corp, Reno, Nev., 2007.

Heizer, R. F., and A. B. Elsasser. *The Natural World of the California Indians*. Berkeley, Ca.: Univ. of California Press, 1980.

Henderson, R. *Wild Palms of the California Desert*. Desert Magazine, Palm Desert, Ca., 1951.

Ingram, S. *Cacti, Agaves, and Yuccas of California and Nevada*. Los Olivos, Ca.: Cachuma Press, 2008.

Jaeger, E. C. *Desert Wildlife*. Stanford, Ca.: Stanford Univ. Press, 1950.

Jenkens, O. P. *Cal. J. Mines and Geol.* 47, No. 2 (1951): 352–353.

Jette, C., A. Blotkamp, Y. Le, and S. J. Hollenhorst. "Joshua Tree National Park: Visitor Study Winter 2010." National Park Service, Fort Collins, Colorado, 2011.

Kaiser, J. *Joshua Tree: The Complete Guide*. Destination Press, 2023.

Karlstrom, K. E. "Refining Rodinia: Geologic evidence for the Australia–Western U.S. connection in the Proterozoic." *GSA Today* 9, No. 10 (1999): 1–7.

Kidwell, A. *Ambush: The Story of Bill Keys.* Twentynine Palms, Ca.: Desert Moon Press, 1995.

Knowles, P. H. "Report on the validity of the Sunrise Group of Claims, Joshua Tree National Monument, Riverside County, California." File L3023, Office of Mining and Minerals, WRO, NPS, San Francisco, Ca., 1974.

Knute, A. *Plants of the East Mojave: Mojave National Preserve*. Barstow, Ca.: Mojave River Valley Association, 2002.

Kohler-Antablin, S. "Mineral land classification of the eastern half of Riverside County, California." *California Department of Conservation, Division of Mines and Geology,* Open-File Rept 94-11, 1994.

Kroeber, A. L. *Handbook of the Indians of California*. Bureau of American Ethnology Bulletin No. 78. Washington, D.C., 1925.

La Doux, T., L. Chris, and E. Babich. "A summary of the Joshua Tree National Park vegetation mapping project." *NPS Vegetation Inventory Program Natural Resource Technical Report* NPS/JOTR/NRTR—2013/723, 2013.

Laird, C. *The Chemehuevis*. Banning, Ca.: Malki Museum Press, 1976.

Lightfoot, K. G., and O. Parrish. *California Indians and their Environment: An Introduction*. Berkeley, Ca.: Univ. of California Press, 2009.

MacKay, P. *Mojave Desert Wildflowers*. Guilford, Conn.: The Globe Pequot Press, 2013.

MacMahon, J. A. *Deserts*. National Audubon Society Nature Guides, New York: Alfred A. Knopf, Inc., 1997.

Merrill, F. J., and C. A. Waring. "Mines and mineral resources of Riverside County: California." *Min. Bur. Rept*. 15 (1917): 522–589.

Munz, P. A. *Introduction to California Desert Wildflowers*. Revised edition. California Natural History Guides, 2004.

Nadeau, R. *The Silver Seekers*. Santa Barbara, Ca.: Crest Publishers (1999): 119–132.

Sampson, R. J. *Rept. of the State Mineralogist* 41 (1945): 130–147.

Stewart, K. M. "A brief history of the Chemehuevi Indians." *Kiva* 34, No. 1 (1968): 9–27.

Swope, K. K., and C. J. Gregory. "Mining in the southern California deserts: A historic context statement and research design." *Statistical Research, Inc.* Prepared for the Bureau of Land Management, Tech. Rept. 17-42 (1993).

Taylor, R. J. *Desert Wildflowers of North America*. Missoula, Mt.: Mountain Press Publishing Company, 1998.

Thomas, K., T. Keeler-Wolf, J. Franklin, and P. Stine. "Mojave Desert ecosystem program: Central Mojave vegetation database." Final report, *USGS Science for a Changing World,* Sacramento, California, 2004.

Thompson, D., K. Longshore, and C. Lowrey. "The impact of human disturbance on desert bighorn sheep (Ovis canadensis nelsoni) in the Wonderland of Rocks/Queen Mountain region of Joshua Tree National Park, California." Final report prepared for Joshua Tree National Park, Ca., 2007.

Trent, D. D. "Geology of Joshua Tree National Park, San Bernardino and Riverside Counties." *Cal. Geol.* 51, No. 5 (1998): 1–16.

Trent, D. D. "Mines in Joshua Tree National Park." *Cal. Geol.* 51, No. 5 (1998): 17.

Trent, D. D., and R. W. Hazlett. *Joshua Tree National Park Geology.* Twentynine Palms, Ca.: Joshua Tree Nat. Park Assoc., 2002.

Tucker, W. B. *Rept. of the State Mineralogist* 17 (1920): 333–374; 18 (1921): 273–305; 20 (1924): 45, 92–95, 196–200; 22 (1926): 453–539; 25 (1929): 479, 485–486; and 26 (1930): 202–325.

Tucker, W. B., and R. J. Sampson. *Rept. of the State Mineralogist* 27 (1931): 262–401; 30 (1934): 321; 34 (1938): 13–15; 36 (1940): 47–68.

Vidutis, R., D. Hardesty, and L. Ross. "Lost Horse Gold Mill, Joshua Tree National Monument." *Historic American Engineering Record,* HAER No. CA-128, National Park Service, 1992.

Von Bernewitz, M. W. *Handbook for Prospectors and Operators of Small Mines.* New York, N. Y.: McGraw-Hill Book Company, 1926.

Vredenburgh, L. M., G. L. Shumway, and R. D. Hartill. *Desert Fever.* Canoga Park, Ca.: Living West Press, 1981.

Warren, C. N., and J. S. Schneider. "Out where the living is good: Subsistence activities on the lands of Joshua Tree National Monument." *J. Cal. and Great Basin Anthr.* 32, No. 1 (2012): 9–26.

Weight, H. A. "Legends of the Lost Horse Mine." Desert Magazine of the Southwest 42, No. 1 (1979): 8–11.

Wiseman, J. *SAS Survival Guide.* 3rd ed. New York, NY: HarperCollins Publishers, 2014.

Wright, L. A., *et al.* "Mines and mineral deposits of San Bernardino County, California." *Cal. J. Mines and Geol.* 49, Nos. 1 and 2 (1953): 49–257.

Zarki, J. W. *Images of America: Joshua Tree National Park.* Charleston, S. C., Arcadia Publishing, 2015.

Zdon, A. *Desert Summits.* 2nd ed. Bishop, Ca.: Spotted Dog Press, Inc., 2006.

■

SUMMARY TABLE OF HIKES

Destination/Trail/Route	One-way distance	Elev. change	Pages
ARCHES			
Arch Oasis	5.6 mi	1,950'	436
Arch Rock	0.7 mi	120'	201
California Arch	0.9 mi	340'	439
Cat Eyes Arch	2.0 mi	310'	237
Garrett's Arch	1.9 mi	290'	126
Piano Valley (loop)	1.4 mi	60'	118
The Maze (loop)	5.2 mi	460'	230
Tortoise Rock	2.3 mi	480'	411
Tunnel Arch	2.3 mi	340'	232
Vulture Arch Loop	3.5 mi	450'	205
Windows Rock	1.9 mi	310'	238
BACKPACKING			
Bighorn Canyon	6.6 mi	2,060'	253
Boy Scout Trail	8.1 mi	1,900'	99
Coxcomb Peak (2,957')	5.5 mi	3,330'	271
Eagle Mountain via Munsen Canyon	7.2 mi	3,680'	431
Eagle Mountain (west route) (5,350')	5.0 mi	2,610'	409
Eureka Peak (5,518')	4.7 mi	1,800'	299
Hexahedron Mine	4.5 mi	1,070'	385
Inner Basin (via Oxbow Canyon)	7.8 mi	1,980'	259
Inner Basin (via trail)	7.4 mi	1,870'	249
Johnny Lang Canyon	5.6 mi	1,020'	309
Kawi'a Peak (2,973')	4.1 mi	2,190'	271
Last Chance Mine	5.7 mi	2,510'	241
Lone Spring	8.8 mi	2,380'	249
Lost Horse Loop Trail	7.3 mi	1,320'	325
Lost Palms Canyon	4.6 mi	1,850'	425
Moser Mine	3.9 mi	1,020'	265
Munsen Canyon (Arch Oasis)	5.6 mi	1,950'	436
Outlaw Peak (3,291')	4.3 mi	1,530'	197
Pine City Canyon	5.6 mi	1,840'	141
Pinyon Mountain (~5,240')	3.7 mi	1,690'	331
Pyramid Gulch (Windows Rock loop)	6.3 mi	700'	238
Quail Mountain (5,813')	5.5 mi	3,490'	313

Destination/Trail/Route	One-way distance	Elev. change	Pages
Quail Springs (via Smith Water Canyon)	4.8 mi	170'	285
Rattlesnake Canyon to Willow Hole	2.4 mi	1,060'	82
Smith Water Cyn to Quail Spr. Picnic	8.2 mi	1,440'	285
BADLANDS			
Inner Basin (via Oxbow Canyon)	7.8 mi	1,980'	259
Moon Country Canyon	3.2 mi	630'	340
BOULDERS/SCRAMBLING			
Arrastra Canyon (loop)	2.8 mi	320'	165
Bighorn Canyon	6.6 mi	2,060'	253
Canyon to Eagle Mountain	4.2 mi	2,000'	409
Difficult Canyon	1.2 mi	520'	437
Dragon Wash	2.0 mi	520'	443
Gunsight Canyon	0.8 mi	560'	67
Hidden Valley (north entrance)	0.8 mi	120'	111
Joshua Mountain (3,682')	1.4 mi	1,190'	87
Kawi'a Peak (2,973')	4.1 mi	2,190'	271
Keys Peak (4,483')	3.6 mi	640'	105
Lela Peak (4,723') (northern route)	2.5 mi	920'	377
Munsen Canyon (Arch Oasis)	5.6 mi	1,950'	436
Pine City Canyon	5.6 mi	1,840'	141
Rattlesnake Canyon to Willow Hole	2.4 mi	1,060'	82
Sneakeye Spring Canyon	0.8 mi	680'	71
Spectre Peak (4,482')	7.6 mi	3,350'	245
Tensor Peak (4,418')	7.5 mi	3,290'	245
CANYONS			
Arrastra Canyon (loop)	2.8 mi	320'	165
Bighorn Canyon	6.6 mi	2,060'	253
Black Rock Canyon	2.5 mi	780'	295
Canyon to Eagle Mountain	4.2 mi	2,000'	409
Canyon to Pushawalla Pass	2.5 mi	990'	331
Difficult Canyon	1.6 mi	640'	437
Dragon Wash	2.2 mi	720'	443
Fortynine Palms Canyon	1.6 mi	630'	83
Gunsight Canyon	0.8 mi	560'	67
Hidden Valley (north entrance)	0.8 mi	120'	111
Inner Basin Pass	5.3 mi	1,330'	249
Johnny Lang Canyon	5.6 mi	1,020'	309

Destination/Trail/Route	One-way distance	Elev. change	Pages
Lost Palms Canyon	4.6 mi	1,850'	425
Moon Country Canyon	3.2 mi	630'	340
Munsen Canyon (Arch Oasis)	5.6 mi	1,950'	436
North Canyon	2.5 mi	900'	95
Oxbow Canyon (the Oxbow)	5.7 mi	1,330'	259
Pine City Canyon	5.6 mi	1,840'	141
Pyramid Gulch (Arch loop)	5.7 mi	500'	235
Pyramid Gulch (Windows Rock loop)	6.3 mi	700'	238
Rattlesnake Canyon (upper canyon)	2.1 mi	850'	80
Saubel Canyon (amphitheater)	2.8 mi	950'	271
Smith Water Canyon	3.9 mi	1,030'	285
Sneakeye Spring Canyon	1.0 mi	780'	71
CAVES AND BOULDER CAVES			
Difficult Canyon	1.2 mi	520'	437
Gunsight Canyon	0.8 mi	560'	67
Indian Cave	0.1 mi	10'	232
Rattlesnake Canyon (upper canyon)	1.3 mi	560'	80
Sneakeye Spring Canyon	0.5 mi	320'	71
The Grotto	1.5 mi	300'	229
DUNES			
Nightingale Dunes	2.4 mi	1,110'	184
Pinto Basin Dunes	1.0 mi	90'	209
HIKING TRAILS (LONG)			
Boy Scout Trail	8.1 mi	1,900'	99
Covington Flat (loop)	4.2 mi	450'	281
Eureka Peak (5,518')	4.7 mi	1,800'	299
Herman's Hike (loop)	7.7 mi	1,040'	344
Hexahedron Mine	4.5 mi	1,070'	385
Inner Basin Pass	5.3 mi	1,330'	249
Lost Horse Loop Trail	7.3 mi	1,320'	325
Lost Palms Oasis	3.6 mi	1,440'	426
Quail Springs Historic Trail	3.9 mi	400'	309
Warren Peak	3.0 mi	1,160'	295
Willis Palms Loop	4.2 mi	540'	341
Willow Hole	3.7 mi	340'	107

Destination/Trail/Route	One-way distance	Elev. change	Pages
Hiking trails (short) and nature trails			
Arch Rock Nature Trail	0.7 mi	120'	201
Bagley's Ranch (loop)	0.7 mi	40'	119
Barker Dam (loop)	1.4 mi	60'	115
Cholla Garden Nature Trail (loop)	0.3 mi	0'	349
Cottonwood Spring Nature Trail (loop)	1.6 mi	180'	415
Fortynine Palms Oasis Trail	1.6 mi	720'	83
Grand Tank	1.0 mi	190'	204
Hidden Valley Nature Trail (loop)	1.1 mi	130'	111
High View Nature Trail	1.4 mi	350'	291
Indian Cove Nature Trail	0.7 mi	70'	75
Mastodon Mine Loop Trail	2.4 mi	410'	421
Pine City	1.6 mi	200'	137
Samuelson's Rock	2.3 mi	500'	303
Split Rock Loop	2.4 mi	330'	157
Towers of Uncertainty (south)	0.5 mi	80'	369
Wall Street Mill	0.8 mi	70'	129
Homesteads			
Bagley's Ranch (loop)	0.7 mi	40'	119
Keys Ranch (reservation only)	1.1 mi	130'	66
Samuelson's homestead	2.9 mi	550'	303
Joshua tree forests			
Bagley's Ranch (loop)	0.7 mi	40'	119
Covington Flat (loop)	4.2 mi	450'	281
Eureka Peak	4.7 mi	1,800'	299
High View Point (~4,485') (loop)	1.4 mi	350'	291
Lost Horse Loop Trail	7.3 mi	1,320'	325
Samuelson's homestead	2.9 mi	550'	303
Wall Street Mill	0.8 mi	70'	129
Warren Peak (5,103')	3.0 mi	1,160'	295
Loop hikes			
Barker Dam	1.4 mi	60'	115
Covington Flat	4.2 mi	450'	281
Difficult Canyon–Dragon Wash	5.4 mi	1,460'	437
Gold Coin Mine	1.5 mi	460'	381
Golden Bee–Paymaster Mine	4.0 mi	1,090'	363
Herman's Hike	7.7 mi	1,040'	344

Destination/Trail/Route	One-way distance	Elev. change	Pages
High View Point (~4,485')	1.4 mi	350'	291
Lela Peak (4,723')	4.8 mi	1,000'	377
Lost Horse Loop Trail	7.3 mi	1,320'	325
Mastodon Mine Loop Trail	2.4 mi	410'	421
Mission–Sunset–Golden Egg mines	2.9 mi	410'	219
Pyramid Gulch (Arch loop)	5.7 mi	500'	235
Pyramid Gulch (Windows Rock loop)	6.3 mi	700'	238
Silver Bell–Golden Bell Mine	3.3 mi	600'	353
Snow Flake Mine–Iron Age Mine	8.0 mi	730'	191
South Park Peak (4,395')	0.7 mi	260'	294
Split Rock Loop	2.4 mi	330'	157
Vulture Arch Loop	3.5 mi	450'	205
Willis Palms Loop	4.2 mi	540'	341
MILLS			
Carlyle Mill	2.9 mi	680'	185
Eldorado Mine	2.1 mi	560'	359
Gold Coin Mill	0.1 mi	20'	381
Golden Bee Mine	1.8 mi	890'	363
Golden Bell Mine	1.1 mi	690'	356
Golden Egg Mine	1.6 mi	580'	222
Gold Hill Mill	1.0 mi	100'	161
Gold Rose Mill	1.5 mi	40'	215
Hansen Mill	2.4 mi	1,000'	331
Hexahedron Mill	3.4 mi	220'	390
Iron Age Mine	3.5 mi	580'	191
Iron Chief Mill	1.5 mi	560'	405
Last Chance Mill	5.3 mi	1,980'	241
Lorman Mine	1.8 mi	800'	179
Lost Horse Mill	2.1 mi	700'	325
Mastodon Mine (loop)	2.4 mi	410'	421
Mission Mine (mill)	0.9 mi	110'	219
Moorten's Mill	1.0 mi	280'	418
Moser Mill	3.2 mi	650'	265
Old Mission Mill	0.2 mi	20'	216
Pinto Wye Arrastra	1.0 mi	230'	165
Sunrise Mine	0.7 mi	180'	216
Supply Mine	1.0 mi	490'	179
Wall Street Mill	0.8 mi	70'	129
Winona Mill	0.5 mi	70'	416

Destination/Trail/Route	One-way distance	Elev. change	Pages
Mines			
Carlyle Mine	3.6 mi	1,430'	185
Contact Mine	2.0 mi	770'	91
Desert Queen Mine (loop)	1.8 mi	350'	147
Eagle Cliff Mine	1.8 mi	860'	153
Eldorado Mine	2.1 mi	560'	359
Gold Coin Mine (loop)	1.5 mi	460'	381
Golden Bee Mine	1.8 mi	890'	363
Golden Bell Mine	1.1 mi	690'	356
Golden Egg Mine	1.6 mi	580'	222
Gold Hill Mine	1.2 mi	160'	161
Hexahedron Mine	4.5 mi	1,070'	385
Iron Age Mine	3.5 mi	580'	191
Iron Chief Mine	1.5 mi	560'	405
Lang Copper Mine	4.6 mi	1,300'	311
Last Chance Mine	5.7 mi	2,510'	241
Lorman Mine	1.8 mi	800'	179
Lost Horse Mine	2.1 mi	700'	325
Mastodon Mine (loop)	2.4 mi	410'	421
Mission Mine	0.9 mi	110'	219
Moser Mine	3.9 mi	1,020'	265
Paymaster Mine	1.8 mi	630'	368
Pine Knot Deposit	0.8 mi	430'	286
Pinyon Mine	3.3 mi	1,510'	331
Silver Bell Mine (quarry)	0.8 mi	470'	353
Snow Flake Mine	1.5 mi	170'	193
Storm Jade Mine	1.0 mi	190'	401
Sunrise Mine	0.7 mi	180'	216
Supply Mine	1.0 mi	490'	179
Vault Mine	2.6 mi	540'	265
Mining camps			
Eagle Cliff Mine	1.8 mi	860'	153
Golden Bee Mine	1.8 mi	890'	363
Gold Standard Mine	2.8 mi	310'	330
Hansen Mill	2.4 mi	1,000'	331
Hexahedron Mill	3.4 mi	220'	390
Hexahedron Mine	4.5 mi	1,070'	385
Johns Camp	0.7 mi	40'	161
Last Chance Mill	5.3 mi	1,980'	241

Destination/Trail/Route	One-way distance	Elev. change	Pages
Lorman Mine	1.8 mi	800'	179
Moser Mine Camp	2.9 mi	540'	265
Optimist Mine	2.8 mi	1,320'	330
Pinyon Mine	3.3 mi	1,510'	331
Sunset Mine	1.3 mi	410'	222
Supply Mine	1.0 mi	490'	179
Vault Mine	2.6 mi	510'	265
NARROWS			
Bighorn Canyon	4.0 mi	1,160'	253
Gunsight Canyon (The Slit)	0.4 mi	220'	67
North Canyon	2.1 mi	790'	95
Oxbow Canyon	4.1 mi	940'	259
Smith Water Canyon	2.4 mi	620'	285
The Grotto	1.5 mi	300'	229
PALM OASES			
Arch Oasis	5.6 mi	1,950'	436
Cotton Spring	0.5 mi	70'	416
Cottonwood Spring	0.1 mi	50'	415
Fortynine Palms Oasis	1.6 mi	720'	83
Hidden Palms	0.7 mi	130'	346
Horseshoe Palms	1.6 mi	300'	346
Lost Palms Oasis	3.6 mi	1,440'	426
McCallum Grove	1.0 mi	100'	338
Munsen Oasis	4.5 mi	1,340'	431
Pushawalla Palms	2.4 mi	500'	346
Summit Springs	3.8 mi	1,060'	431
Thousand Palms Oasis (loop)	0.4 mi	10'	337
Twin Oases	5.3 mi	1,770'	431
Victory Palms	4.6 mi	1,850'	428
Willis Palms	0.6 mi	30'	341
Wood Spring	0.8 mi	210'	418
PEAKS (*SEE ALSO* VISTA POINTS)			
Anschutz Peak (3,289')	2.7 mi	2,030'	443
Coxcomb Peak (2,957')	5.5 mi	3,330'	271
Eagle Mtn (via Munsen Cyn) (5,350')	7.2 mi	3,680'	431
Eagle Mtn (west route) (5,350')	5.0 mi	2,610'	409
East Queen Mountain (5,677')	2.0 mi	1,260'	133

Destination/Trail/Route	One-way distance	Elev. change	Pages
Eureka Peak (5,518')	4.7 mi	1,800'	299
High View Point (~4,485') (loop)	1.4 mi	350'	291
Inspiration Peak (5,570')	1.0 mi	830'	317
Joshua Mountain (3,682')	1.4 mi	1,190'	87
Kawi'a Peak (2,973')	4.1 mi	2,190'	271
Keys Peak (4,483')	3.6 mi	640'	105
Lela Peak (northern route) (4,723')	2.5 mi	920'	377
Lela Peak (southern route) (4,723')	2.3 mi	1,000'	377
Lost Horse Mountain (5,313')	2.2 mi	900'	325
Malapai Hill (4,280')	0.8 mi	520'	373
Mastodon Peak (3,442') (loop)	2.6 mi	520'	421
Monument Mountain (4,834')	2.9 mi	1,850'	391
Mount Auclair (3,298')	2.0 mi	1,210'	366
Mount Minerva Hoyt (5,405')	4.2 mi	2,520'	313
Outlaw Peak (3,291')	4.3 mi	1,530'	197
Pinto Mountain (3,983')	4.5 mi	2,670'	209
Pinyon Mountain (~5,240')	3.7 mi	1,690'	331
Quail Mountain (5,813')	5.5 mi	3,490'	313
Queen Mountain (5,687')	2.0 mi	1,260'	133
Ryan Mountain (5,457')	1.4 mi	1,070'	321
South Park Peak (4,395') (loop)	0.7 mi	260'	294
Spectre Peak (4,482')	7.6 mi	3,350'	245
Tensor Peak (4,418')	7.5 mi	3,290'	245
Twentynine Palms Mountain (4,562')	2.4 mi	1,740'	175
Warren Peak (5,103')	3.0 mi	1,160'	295
Wilhem Peak (1,308') (loop)	6.0 mi	1,040'	341
ROCK ART AND HISTORIC INSCRIPTIONS			
Barker Dam (loop)	1.4 mi	60'	115
Carlyle Mine	3.6 mi	1,430'	185
Samuelson's Rock	2.3 mi	500'	303
SPECIAL FORMATIONS (*SEE ALSO* ARCHES)			
Cupid's Rock	0.8 mi	130'	208
Face Rock	0.9 mi	330'	158
Moray Rock	1.1 mi	170'	232
Red Obelisk	1.5 mi	190'	125
South Astro Dome	1.1 mi	160'	124
Split Rock	0.1 mi	10'	157
The Creature	0.7 mi	50'	123

Destination/Trail/Route	One-way distance	Elev. change	Pages
The Gallery (Cat Face Rock)	2.5 mi	480'	411
The Slit	0.4 mi	220'	70
Tortoise Rock	2.2 mi	430'	411
Towers of Uncertainty (south)	0.5 mi	80'	369
SPRINGS (*SEE ALSO* PALM OASES, TANKS, WELLS)			
Black Rock Spring	1.6 mi	430'	295
Johnny Lang Canyon Spring	3.2 mi	340'	309
Lone Spring	8.8 mi	2,380'	249
Pine Spring	2.1 mi	400'	138
Quail Springs	3.9 mi	400'	290
Rattlesnake Canyon spring	1.3 mi	560'	82
Smith Water Canyon lower spring	3.1 mi	880'	285
Willow Hole	3.7 mi	340'	107
TANKS			
Barker Dam (loop)	1.4 mi	60'	115
Grand Tank	1.0 mi	190'	204
Surprise Tank	0.8 mi	80'	369
White Tank	0.7 mi	120'	201
VALLEY-FLOOR HIKES (*SEE ALSO* NATURE TRAILS)			
Bagley's Ranch (loop)	0.7 mi	40'	119
Covington Flat (loop)	4.2 mi	450'	281
Gold Rose Mill	1.5 mi	40'	215
Hexahedron Mill	3.4 mi	220'	390
Hidden Valley	1.1 mi	130'	111
Johns Camp	0.7 mi	40'	161
Last Chance Mill	5.3 mi	1,980'	241
Moser Mine Camp	2.9 mi	540'	265
Pine City	1.6 mi	200'	137
Quail Springs (from picnic area)	3.9 mi	400'	290
Samuelson's Rock and homestead	2.9 mi	550'	303
Storm Jade Mine	1.0 mi	190'	401
Surprise Tank	0.8 mi	80'	369
Towers of Uncertainty (south)	0.5 mi	80'	369
Wall Street Mill	0.8 mi	70'	129
Willow Hole	3.7 mi	340'	107

Destination/Trail/Route	One-way distance	Elev. change	Pages
VISTA POINTS (*SEE ALSO* PEAKS)			
Boulder Canyon Overlook	2.2 mi	720'	443
Inner Basin Pass	5.3 mi	1,330'	249
Lost Horse Valley Overlook	5.6 mi	1,020'	309
Pine City Viewpoint	2.0 mi	290'	138
Pinto Basin Viewpoint	8.4 mi	2,140'	250
Warren View	2.7 mi	950'	295
WELLS			
Desert Queen Well	0.3 mi	40'	119
Gold Rose Well	1.5 mi	40'	215
Hansen Well	2.4 mi	1,000'	331
Mission Well	0.1 mi	0'	215
Pinyon Well	0.8 mi	270'	333
WOODLANDS (CONIFER)			
Covington Flat (loop)	4.2 mi	450'	281
Eagle Mtn (west route) (5,350')	5.0 mi	2,610'	409
High View Point (~4,485') (loop)	1.4 mi	350'	291
Inspiration Peak (5,570')	1.0 mi	830'	317
Pine City	1.6 mi	200'	137
Pinyon Mountain (~5,240')	3.7 mi	1,690'	331
Queen Mountain (5,687')	2.0 mi	1,260'	133
Wall Street Mill	0.8 mi	70'	129
Warren Peak (5,103')	3.0 mi	1,160'	295

INDEX

Italic numbers indicate material in a map; regular numbers indicate material in the text; in case of multiple entries, boldface numbers indicate the main pages.